BMW R1200 dohc Twins
Service and Repair Manual

by Phil Mather

Models covered

(4925-304)

R1200 GS. 1170cc. 2010 to 2012
R1200 GS Adventure. 1170cc. 2010 to 2012
R1200 RT. 1170cc. 2010 to 2012
R1200 R. 1170cc. 2011 to 2012

Covers models with dohc air-cooled engines

© Haynes Publishing 2012

A book in the **Haynes Service and Repair Manual Series**

ISBN 978 1 78521 347 2

British Library Cataloguing in Publication Data
A catalogue record for this book is available from the British Library

Library of Congress Control Number 2011944400

ABCDE
FGHIJ
KLMNO
PQ

Printed in Malaysia

Haynes Publishing
Sparkford, Yeovil, Somerset BA22 7JJ, England

Haynes North America, Inc
859 Lawrence Drive, Newbury Park, California 91320, USA

Printed using NORBRITE BOOK 48.8gsm (CODE: 40N6533) from NORPAC; procurement system certified under Sustainable Forestry Initiative standard. Paper produced is certified to the SFI Certified Fiber Sourcing Standard (CERT - 0094271)

Contents

LIVING WITH YOUR BMW R1200

Introduction

BMW – They did it their way	Page	**0•4**
Acknowledgements	Page	**0•8**
About this manual	Page	**0•8**
Identification numbers	Page	**0•9**
Safety first!	Page	**0•10**

Pre-ride checks

Engine oil level	Page	**0•11**
Brake fluid levels	Page	**0•12**
Clutch fluid level	Page	**0•14**
Suspension, steering and final drive	Page	**0•14**
Tyres	Page	**0•15**
Legal and safety	Page	**0•15**
Bike spec	Page	**0•16**
Model development	Page	**0•17**

MAINTENANCE

Routine maintenance and servicing

Specifications	Page	**1•2**
Lubricants and fluids	Page	**1•2**
Maintenance schedule	Page	**1•3**
Component locations	Page	**1•4**
Maintenance procedures	Page	**1•7**

Contents

REPAIRS AND OVERHAUL

Engine, transmission and associated systems
Engine, clutch and transmission   Page   **2•1**

Engine management systems   Page   **3•1**

Chassis components
Frame, suspension and final drive   Page   **4•1**

Brakes, wheels and tyres   Page   **5•1**

Bodywork   Page   **6•1**

Electrical system   Page   **7•1**

Wiring diagrams   Page   **7•27**

REFERENCE
Tools and Workshop Tips   Page   **REF•2**

Security   Page   **REF•20**

Lubricants and fluids   Page   **REF•23**

Conversion factors   Page   **REF•26**

MOT Test Checks   Page   **REF•27**

Storage   Page   **REF•32**

Fault Finding   Page   **REF•35**

Technical Terms Explained   Page   **REF•43**

Index   Page   **REF•47**

BMW – They did it their way

by Julian Ryder

BMW - Bayerische Motoren Werke

If you were looking for a theme tune for BMW's engineering philosophy you'd have to look no further than Francis Albert Sinatra's best known ditty: 'I did it my way.' The Bayerische Motoren Werke, like their countrymen at Porsche, takes precious little notice of the way anyone else does it, point this out to a factory representative and you will get a reply starting: 'We at BMW... '. The implication is clear.

It was always like that. The first BMW motorcycle, the R32, was, according to motoring sage L J K Setright: 'the first really outstanding post-War design, argued from first principles and uncorrupted by established practice. It founded a new German school of design, it established a BMW tradition destined to survive unbroken from 1923 to the present day.' That tradition was, of course, the boxer twin. The nickname 'boxer' for an opposed twin is thought to derive from the fact that the pistons travel horizontally towards and away from each other like the fists of boxers.

Before this first complete motorcycle, BMW had built a horizontally-opposed fore-and-aft boxer engine for the Victoria company of Nuremburg. It was a close copy of the

The roots of the GS range go back to the 2-valve Boxer engine, seen here fitted to the second generation R80GS

British Douglas motor which the company's chief engineer Max Friz admired, a fact the company's official history confirms despite

With the introduction of the 4-valve engine, the R1100GS and R1150GS models followed . . .

what some current devotees of the marque will claim. In fact BMW didn't really want to make motorcycles at all, originally it was an aero-engine company - a fact celebrated in the blue-and-white tank badge that is symbolic of a propeller. But in Germany after the Treaty of Versailles such potentially warlike work was forbidden to domestic companies and BMW had to diversify, albeit reluctantly.

Friz was known to have a very low opinion of motorcycles and chose the Douglas to copy simply because he saw it as fundamentally a good solution to the engineering problem of powering a two-wheeler. In the R32 the engine was arranged with the crankshaft in-line with the axis of the bike and the cylinders sticking out into the cooling airflow, giving a very low centre-of-gravity and perfect vibration-free primary balance. It wasn't just the motor's layout that departed from normal practice, the clutch was a single-plate type as used in cars, final drive was by shaft and the rear wheel could be removed quickly. The frame and suspension were equally sophisticated, but the bike was quite heavy. Most of that description could be equally well applied to any of the boxer-engined bikes BMW made in the next 70-plus years.

Development within the surprisingly flexible confines of the boxer concept was quick. The second BMW, the R37 of 1925, retained the 68 x 68 mm Douglas bore and stroke but had overhead valves in place of the side valves. In 1928 two major milestones were passed. First, BMW acquired the car manufacturer Dixi and started manufacturing a left-hand-drive version of the Austin 7 under license. Secondly, the larger engined R62 and R63 appeared, the latter being an OHV sportster that would be the basis of BMW's sporting and record-breaking exploits before the Second World War.

The 1930s was the era of speed records on land, on sea and in the air, and the name of Ernst Henne is in the record books no fewer than ten times: eight for two-wheeled exploits, twice for wheel-on-a-stick 'sidecar' world records. At first he was on the R63 with supercharging, but in 1936 he switched to the 500 cc R5, high-pushrod design reminiscent of the latest generation of BMW twins. Chain-driven camshafts operated short pushrods which opened valves with hairpin - not coil - springs. A pure racing version of this motor also appeared, this time with shaft and bevel-gear driven overhead camshafts, but with short rockers operating the valves so the engine can't be called a true DOHC design. Again with the aid of a blower, this was the motor that powered the GP 500s of the late '30s to many wins including the 1939 Senior TT. After the War, this layout would re-emerge in the immortal Rennsport.

From 1939 to 1945 BMW were fully occupied making military machinery, notably the R75 sidecar for the army. The factory didn't restart production until 1948, and then

. . . and were superseded by the R1200GS in 2004 . . .

only with a lightweight single. There was a false start in 1950 and a slump in sales in 1953 that endangered the whole company, before the situation was rescued by one of the truly classic boxers. Their first post-War twin had been the R51/2, and naturally it was very close to the pre-War model although simplified to a single-camshaft layout. Nevertheless, it was still a relatively advanced OHV design not a sidevalve sidecar tug which enabled a face-lift for the 1955 models to do the marketing trick.

The 1955 models got a swinging arm - at both ends. The old plunger rear suspension was replaced by a swinging arm while leading-link Earles forks adorned the front. Thus were born the R50, the R60 and the R69. The European market found these new bikes far too expensive compared to British twins but America saved the day, buying most of the company's output. The car side of the company also found a product the market wanted, a small sports-car powered by a modified bike engine, thus BMW's last crisis was averted

In 1960 the Earles fork models were updated and the R69S was launched with more power, closer transmission ratios and those funny little indicators on the ends of the handlebars. Very little changed during the '60s, apart from US export models getting telescopic forks, but in 1970 everything changed...

The move to Spandau and a new line of Boxers

BMW's bike side had outgrown its site in Munich at the company's head-quarters, so, taking advantage of government subsidies for enterprises that located to what was then West Berlin, surrounded by the still Communist DDR, BMW built a new motorcycle assembly plant at Spandau in Berlin. It opened in 1969, producing a completely new range of boxers, the 5-series, which begat the 6-series, which begat the 7-series.

In 1976, at the same time as the launch of the 7-series the first RS boxer appeared. It's hard to believe now, but it was the only fully faired motorcycle, and it set the pattern for all BMWs, not just boxers, to come. The RS suffix came to mean a wonderfully efficient fairing that didn't spoil a sporty riding position. More sedate types could buy the RT version with a massive but no less efficient fairing that

. . . and then by the twin cam R1200GS in 2010

protected a more upright rider. Both bikes could carry luggage in a civilised fashion, too, thanks to purpose-built Krauser panniers. Both the RT and RS were uncommonly civilised motorcycles for their time.

When the boxer got its next major makeover in late 1980 BMW did something no-one thought possible, they made a boxer trail bike, the R80G/S. This wasn't without precedent as various supermen had wrestled 750 cc boxers to honours in the ISDT and in '81 Hubert Auriol won the Paris-Dakar on a factory boxer. Some heretics even dared to suggest the roadgoing G/S was the best boxer ever.

The K-series

By the end of the '70s the boxer was looking more and more dated alongside the opposition, and when the motorcycle division's management was shaken up at the beginning of 1979 the team working on the boxer replacement was doubled in size. The first new bike wasn't launched until late '83, but when it was it was clear that BMW had got as far away from the boxer concept as possible.

The powerplant was an in-line water-cooled DOHC four just like all the Japanese opposition, but typically BMW did it their way by aligning the motor so its crank was parallel to the axis of the bike and lying the motor on it side. In line with their normal practice, there was a car-type clutch, shaft drive and a single-sided swinging arm. It was totally novel yet oddly familiar. And when RT and RS version were introduced to supplement the basic naked bike, the new K-series 'flying bricks' felt even more familiar.

It was clear that BMW wanted the new four, and the three-cylinder 750 that followed it, to

The R1200GS Adventure is established as one of the best long distance enduro bikes

be the mainstay of the company's production - but in a further analogy with Porsche the customers simply wouldn't let go of the old boxer. Just as Porsche were forced to keep the 911 in production so BMW had to keep the old air-cooled boxer going by pressure from their customers. It kept going until 1995, during which time the K-bikes had debuted four-valve heads and ABS. And when the latest generation of BMWs appeared in 1993 what were they? Boxers. Granted they were four-valve, air/oil-cooled and equipped with non-telescopic fork front ends, but they were still boxers. And that high camshaft, short pushrod layout

looked remarkably similar to something that had gone before...

The New 4-valve Boxers

Even by BMW's standards, the new-generation Boxers were a shock. Maybe we shouldn't have been surprised after the lateral thinking that gave us the K-series, but the way in which the men from Munich took the old opposed-twin Boxer concept that launched the company and projected it into the 21st-Century was nothing short of breath-taking in its audacity. About the only design features the old and new Boxers had in common was that they both had two wheels and two cylinders. The 4-valve engine was produced in 850 and 1100 cc version, with the later eventually being upgraded to 1150 cc for GS, R, RS and RT versions, and stretched further to 1200 cc for the C model made famous in the 007 film Golden Eye.

The new bikes mixed old and new technology in a very clever way. Fuel injection and four-valve heads were very cutting edge, high camshafts operating pushrods (for ground clearance) and air cooling (albeit with some substantial help from oil) was not. The really revolutionary stuff was in the chassis department: Telelever at the front and Paralever at the rear bolted to the motor via tubular steel sub-frames and nothing in the way of a conventional frame in the middle. The Telelever front fork is carried on a couple of wishbones with anti-dive built into the linkage. Rear Paralever suspension uses a single-sided swingingarm with a shaft drive running inside it which forms not quite a parallelogram shaped system with a tie-arm running from just below to the swinging arm pivot to the rear hub. It ensures the rear axle moves in an (almost) straight line and suppresses the old BMW

Overall luxury is provided by the fully loaded R1200RT

The R1200 R naked roadster

habit of the rear end rising when the throttle is opened. The styling was also anything but safe; the old cliché of the boring BMW was blown out of the water.

The R1200 Models

When the 1200cc version of BMW's GS on/off-road model appeared in 2004 it wasn't just an upgrade of the old 1150, it was a new generation of the Munich company's fabled Boxer twins. Thirty kilograms of weight was shed despite the engine gaining a balance shaft, and the chassis was completely revised, with the Paralever rear suspension's linkage arm moved from below the swinging arm to above it. Among a host of improvements, perhaps the most revolutionary is the Single Wire System using technology borrowed from the car world. This is basically a CAN-bus wiring circuit rather than a wiring loom connecting all control units and power-consuming components. No fuses, no relays (except for the starter motor) and built-in diagnostics make this a contender for the first motorcycle electrical system that looks like it was actually designed in the 21st-Century.

As had become usual, the GS model was the first to be launched, it had become BMW's most popular model. BMW define the GS as an 'Adventure Sports' motorcycle, which sums it up nicely. A GS is a bike that will take you just about anywhere and is equally at home on motorways, mountain hairpins and dusty tracks in the middle of nowhere.

No other manufacturer has had anywhere near this sort of success for a model that can trace its origins back to the Paris-Dakar bikes of the late 1970s and before that semi-official specials used in the International Six days Trial in the days when that event carried a lot of prestige and competitors had to ride bikes built in their own countries. Of course you'd have to be one of those Paris-Dakar heroes to contemplate taking one of today's GSs off road, but they have become favourites of riders who want to do big distances in comfort without riding a full-on tourer. Perhaps the best publicity a motorcycle has ever had came from Ewan McGregor and Charlie Boorman's TV programme 'The Long Way Round' in which the film star and his friend rode two 1150GS BMWs on their long-distance odyssey. The result was waiting lists at BMW dealers and GS-models also have the benefit of strong residual value.

For the really serious off-road hero, BMW also sold a limited-edition version of the GS, the HP2, in which HP stands for high performance. That model used a DOHC engine first seen in the HP2 Sport road bike. This is the engine that has now been put into full production for the R1200 series not confined to the comparatively expensive HP models, so it's not another generational step, more a quantum jump. The only significant changes are the cylinder heads, which have the chain-driven twin camshafts positioned horizontally operating one exhaust and one inlet valve each. The motor is of course 're-tuned' from the sports bike to give a better spread of torque.

A year after the first 1200GS was launched the range was extended with the R1200 ST and RT, These models carried on BMW's tradition of cleverly differentiated sports tourer and full-house tourer, two motorcycles that look quite similar on paper but exhibit very different characters on the road. In another indication that this was an evolution, not a revolution, most of the R1200 range got the upgrade immediately. The GS and the RT tourer plus the GS Adventure all got the new twin-cam heads in 2010. The R1200R roadster, that didn't appear until 2006, didn't get the new heads until 2011.

Most companies trying to sell large-capacity motorcycles since the financial upheavals of 2009 have not had a good time. The market for big sports bikes in particular has shrunk severely. One company that doesn't seem to have noticed the shrinking market is BMW. The mass sales of the GS, in Continental Europe particularly, has given the company the courage to field everything from singles and twins to race winning superbikes with across-the-frame four-cylinder motors. It would be impossible, though, to envisage BMW abandoning their roots. At regular intervals over many years, the death of the Boxer twin has been predicted, but it would appear that reports of its death are exaggerated.

The R1200R Classic with wire-spoked wheels

Acknowledgements

Our thanks are due to CW Motorcycles of Dorchester who supplied the machines featured in the illustrations throughout this manual. We would also like to thank NGK Spark Plugs (UK) Ltd for supplying the colour spark plug condition photographs, the Avon Rubber Company for supplying information on tyre fitting and Draper Tools Ltd for some of the workshop tools shown.

Thanks are also due to Julian Ryder who wrote the introduction 'BMW – They did it their way' and to BMW (GB) Ltd. who supplied model photographs.

About this Manual

The aim of this manual is to help you get the best value from your motorcycle. It can do so in several ways. It can help you decide what work must be done, even if you choose to have it done by a dealer; it provides information and procedures for routine maintenance and servicing; and it offers diagnostic and repair procedures to follow when trouble occurs.

We hope you use the manual to tackle the work yourself. For many simpler jobs, doing it yourself may be quicker than arranging an appointment to get the motorcycle into a dealer and making the trips to leave it and pick it up. More importantly, a lot of money can be saved by avoiding the expense the shop must pass on to you to cover its labour and overhead costs. An added benefit is the sense of satisfaction and accomplishment that you feel after doing the job yourself.

References to the left or right side of the motorcycle assume you are sitting on the seat, facing forward.

We take great pride in the accuracy of information given in this manual, but motorcycle manufacturers make alterations and design changes during the production run of a particular motorcycle of which they do not inform us. No liability can be accepted by the authors or publishers for loss, damage or injury caused by any errors in, or omissions from, the information given.

Illegal Copying

It is the policy of Haynes Publishing to actively protect its Copyrights and Trade Marks. Legal action will be taken against anyone who unlawfully copies the cover or contents of this Manual. This includes all forms of unauthorised copying including digital, mechanical, and electronic in any form. Authorisation from Haynes Publishing will only be provided expressly and in writing. Illegal copying will also be reported to the appropriate statutory authorities.

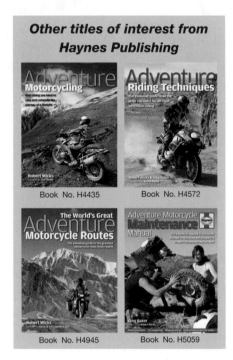

Other titles of interest from Haynes Publishing

Book No. H4435

Book No. H4572

Book No. H4945

Book No. H5059

Buying spare parts

When ordering replacement parts, it is essential to identify exactly the machine for which the parts are required. While in some cases it is sufficient to identify the machine by its title e.g. 'R1200 GS', any modifications made to components mean that it is usually essential to identify the machine by its BMW **production** or model year e.g. '2010 R1200 GS', and sometimes by its engine and/ or frame number as well (see above). The BMW production year starts in September of the previous calendar year, after the annual holiday, and continues until the following August. Therefore a 2010 R1200 GS was **produced** at some time between September 2009 and August 2010; it may have been **sold** (to its first owner) at any time from September 2009 onwards.

To identify your own machine, record its full engine and frame numbers and take them to any BMW dealer who should have the necessary information to identify it exactly. Finally, in some cases modifications can be identified only by reference to the machine's engine or frame number; these should be noted and taken with you whenever replacement parts are required.

To be absolutely certain of receiving the correct part, not only is it essential to have the machine's identifying title and engine and frame numbers, but it is also useful to take the old part for comparison (where possible). Note that where a modified component has superseded the original, a careful check must be made that there are no related parts which have also been modified and must be used to enable the replacement to be correctly refitted; where such a situation is found, purchase all the necessary parts and fit them, even if this means replacing apparently unworn items.

Always purchase replacement parts from an authorised BMW dealer who will either have the parts in stock or can order them quickly from the importer, and always use genuine parts to ensure the machine's performance and reliability. Pattern parts are available for certain components (i.e. brake pads and filters); if used, ensure these are of recognised quality brands which will perform as well as the original.

Expendable items such as lubricants, spark plugs, some electrical components, bearings, bulbs and tyres can usually be obtained at lower prices from accessory shops, motor factors or from specialists advertising in the national motorcycle press.

Frame and engine numbers

The frame serial number is stamped into the frame behind the steering head. The engine number is stamped into the crankcase below the right-hand cylinder. Both of these numbers should be recorded and kept in a safe place so they can be furnished to law enforcement officials in the event of a theft.

The manufacturer's vehicle identification plate is located on the left-hand side of the rear sub-frame, the gearbox number is stamped into the case on the left-hand side below the gearchange shaft and the colour code label is on the rear sub-frame under the rider's seat.

The frame serial number, engine and gearbox serial numbers and colour code should also be kept in a handy place (such as with your driving licence) so they are always available when purchasing or ordering parts for your machine. The procedures in this manual identify the bikes by model code and, if necessary, also by production year. The model code (e.g. R1200 GS) is used by itself if the information applies to all bikes produced over the life of the model. The production year is added where the information applies only to bikes produced in certain years of the model's life, usually when a component has been changed or upgraded.

The frame number is stamped into the frame behind the steering head

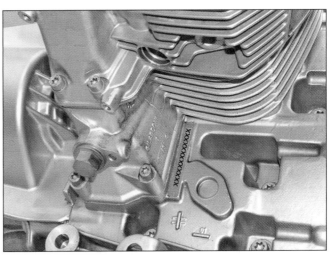

The engine number is stamped into the crankcase below the right-hand cylinder

The gearbox number is stamped into the case below the gearchange shaft

The manufacturer's VIN plate is located on the rear sub-frame

Professional mechanics are trained in safe working procedures. However enthusiastic you may be about getting on with the job at hand, take the time to ensure that your safety is not put at risk. A moment's lack of attention can result in an accident, as can failure to observe simple precautions.

There will always be new ways of having accidents, and the following is not a comprehensive list of all dangers; it is intended rather to make you aware of the risks and to encourage a safe approach to all work you carry out on your bike.

Asbestos

● Certain friction, insulating, sealing and other products - such as brake pads, clutch linings, gaskets, etc. - contain asbestos. Extreme care must be taken to avoid inhalation of dust from such products since it is hazardous to health. If in doubt, assume that they do contain asbestos.

Fire

● Remember at all times that petrol is highly flammable. Never smoke or have any kind of naked flame around, when working on the vehicle. But the risk does not end there - a spark caused by an electrical short-circuit, by two metal surfaces contacting each other, by careless use of tools, or even by static electricity built up in your body under certain conditions, can ignite petrol vapour, which in a confined space is highly explosive. Never use petrol as a cleaning solvent. Use an approved safety solvent.

● Always disconnect the battery earth terminal before working on any part of the fuel or electrical system, and never risk spilling fuel on to a hot engine or exhaust.

● It is recommended that a fire extinguisher of a type suitable for fuel and electrical fires is kept handy in the garage or workplace at all times. Never try to extinguish a fuel or electrical fire with water.

Fumes

● Certain fumes are highly toxic and can quickly cause unconsciousness and even death if inhaled to any extent. Petrol vapour comes into this category, as do the vapours from certain solvents such as trichloroethylene. Any draining or pouring of such volatile fluids should be done in a well ventilated area.

● When using cleaning fluids and solvents, read the instructions carefully. Never use materials from unmarked containers - they may give off poisonous vapours.

● Never run the engine of a motor vehicle in an enclosed space such as a garage. Exhaust fumes contain carbon monoxide which is extremely poisonous; if you need to run the engine, always do so in the open air or at least have the rear of the vehicle outside the workplace.

The battery

● Never cause a spark, or allow a naked light near the vehicle's battery. It will normally be giving off a certain amount of hydrogen gas, which is highly explosive.

● Always disconnect the battery ground (earth) terminal before working on the fuel or electrical systems (except where noted).

● If possible, loosen the filler plugs or cover when charging the battery from an external source. Do not charge at an excessive rate or the battery may burst.

● Take care when topping up, cleaning or carrying the battery. The acid electrolyte, evenwhen diluted, is very corrosive and should not be allowed to contact the eyes or skin. Always wear rubber gloves and goggles or a face shield. If you ever need to prepare electrolyte yourself, always add the acid slowly to the water; never add the water to the acid.

Electricity

● When using an electric power tool, inspection light etc., always ensure that the appliance is correctly connected to its plug and that, where necessary, it is properly grounded (earthed). Do not use such appliances in damp conditions and, again, beware of creating a spark or applying excessive heat in the vicinity of fuel or fuel vapour. Also ensure that the appliances meet national safety standards.

● A severe electric shock can result from touching certain parts of the electrical system, such as the spark plug wires (HT leads), when the engine is running or being cranked, particularly if components are damp or the insulation is defective. Where an electronic ignition system is used, the secondary (HT) voltage is much higher and could prove fatal.

Remember...

● **Don't** start the engine without first ascer-taining that the transmission is in neutral.

● **Don't** suddenly remove the pressure cap from a hot cooling system - cover it with a cloth and release the pressure gradually first, or you may get scalded by escaping coolant.

● **Don't** attempt to drain oil until you are sure it has cooled sufficiently to avoid scalding you.

● **Don't** grasp any part of the engine or exhaust system without first ascertaining that it is cool enough not to burn you.

● **Don't** allow brake fluid or antifreeze to contact the machine's paintwork or plastic components.

● **Don't** siphon toxic liquids such as fuel, hydraulic fluid or antifreeze by mouth, or allow them to remain on your skin.

● **Don't** inhale dust - it may be injurious to health (see Asbestos heading).

● **Don't** allow any spilled oil or grease to remain on the floor - wipe it up right away, before someone slips on it.

● **Don't** use ill-fitting spanners or other tools which may slip and cause injury.

● **Don't** lift a heavy component which may be beyond your capability - get assistance.

● **Don't** rush to finish a job or take unverified short cuts.

● **Don't** allow children or animals in or around an unattended vehicle.

● **Don't** inflate a tyre above the recommended pressure. Apart from overstressing the carcass, in extreme cases the tyre may blow off forcibly.

● **Do** ensure that the machine is supported securely at all times. This is especially important when the machine is blocked up to aid wheel or fork removal.

● **Do** take care when attempting to loosen a stubborn nut or bolt. It is generally better to pull on a spanner, rather than push, so that if you slip, you fall away from the machine rather than onto it.

● **Do** wear eye protection when using power tools such as drill, sander, bench grinder etc.

● **Do** use a barrier cream on your hands prior to undertaking dirty jobs - it will protect your skin from infection as well as making the dirt easier to remove afterwards; but make sure your hands aren't left slippery. Note that long-term contact with used engine oil can be a health hazard.

● **Do** keep loose clothing (cuffs, ties etc. and long hair) well out of the way of moving mechanical parts.

● **Do** remove rings, wristwatch etc., before working on the vehicle - especially the electrical system.

● **Do** keep your work area tidy - it is only too easy to fall over articles left lying around.

● **Do** exercise caution when compressing springs for removal or installation. Ensure that the tension is applied and released in a controlled manner, using suitable tools which preclude the possibility of the spring escaping violently.

● **Do** ensure that any lifting tackle used has a safe working load rating adequate for the job.

● **Do** get someone to check periodically that all is well, when working alone on the vehicle.

● **Do** carry out work in a logical sequence and check that everything is correctly assembled and tightened afterwards.

● **Do** remember that your vehicle's safety affects that of yourself and others. If in doubt on any point, get professional advice.

● If in spite of following these precautions, you are unfortunate enough to injure yourself, seek medical attention as soon as possible.

Note: *The Pre-ride checks outlined in your rider's manual covers those items which should be inspected before each journey. These checks should be made with the ignition off.*

Engine oil level

Note: BMW specify the engine oil level check be carried out at every fuel tank refill.

Before you start:

● The oil level is viewed through the window in the left-hand side of the engine. Wipe the window clean to make the check easier.

● Note that the oil level varies with engine temperature – BMW stress that an accurate reading will only be obtained after the motorcycle has been ridden to allow it to reach normal operating temperature.

● If, when the engine is cold, the level is low, topping-up will almost certainly be required – follow the details below.

Caution: Do not run the engine in an enclosed space such as a garage or workshop.

● Once the engine has reached normal operating temperature, turn it OFF and support the motorcycle on its centre stand, making sure it is in an upright position on level ground. Allow it to stand for at least five minutes to allow the oil level to stabilise.

Bike care:

● Some oil usage is normal, but if you have to add oil frequently, you should check whether there are any oil leaks. Note that oil on the underside of the engine/gearbox joint is a sign that either the engine crankshaft seal or gearbox input shaft seal has failed. If there is no sign of oil leakage from the joints and gaskets the engine could be burning oil (see *Fault Finding*).

● Never run the engine with the oil level below the bottom of the window, and do not fill it above the top of the window.

● Note that on models equipped with an oil level sensor, this doesn't obviate the need to check the oil level via the inspection window.

The correct oil

● Always top up with a good quality oil of the specified type and viscosity and do not overfill the engine. **Note:** *BMW recommends Castrol Power 1 4T motorcycle oil with the viscosity range 15W-50.*

● To fill the engine from the bottom to the top of the oil level window requires 0.5 litre of oil.

Oil type	SAE 15W/50, API SJ, JASO MA2

1 Check the oil level through the inspection window in the left-hand side of the engine. With the motorcycle upright, the oil level should be between the top and bottom of the window.

2 If the level is below the bottom of the window, use the special tool from the bike's toolkit to remove the filler cap from the right-hand valve cover.

3 Top the engine up with the recommended type and grade of oil. The level should be just below the top of the window. Take care not to over-fill the engine.

4 On completion, fit the filler cap, making sure it is secure. If there are any signs of oil leakage from around the cap, renew the sealing O-ring.

Brake fluid levels

Before you start:

● When checking the front brake fluid level, position the handlebars so that the top of the master cylinder is as level as possible.

● On RT and R models, remove the seat to view the fluid level in the rear brake master cylinder reservoir.

● Make sure you have the correct brake fluid, DOT 4 is recommended. Wrap a rag around the reservoir being worked on to ensure that any spillage does not come into contact with painted surfaces.

Bike care:

● The fluid level in the front and rear brake master cylinder reservoirs will drop slightly as the brake pads wear down. If either reservoir requires repeated topping-up this is an indication of a fluid leak somewhere in the system, which should be investigated immediately.

● Check for signs of fluid leakage from the brake hoses and components – if found, rectify immediately.

● Check the operation of both brakes before taking the machine on the road. If there is evidence of air in the system (spongy feel to lever or pedal), the system must be bled – follow the procedure as described in Chapter 5.

> ⚠ **Warning: Brake fluid can harm your eyes and damage painted surfaces, so use extreme caution when handling and pouring it and cover surrounding surfaces with rag. Do not use fluid that has been standing open for some time, as it absorbs moisture from the air which can cause a dangerous loss of braking effectiveness.**

REAR BRAKE FLUID LEVEL

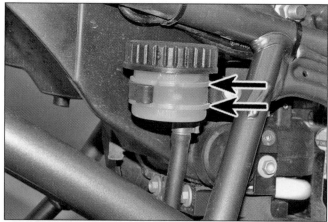

1 The fluid level is visible through the reservoir body – it must be between the MIN and MAX level lines. Do not allow it to drop below the MIN line.

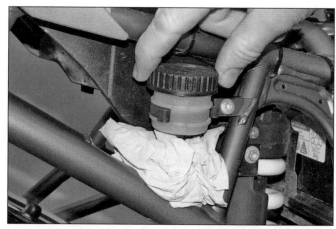

2 To top up, support the reservoir and unscrew the cap, then lift out the diaphragm.

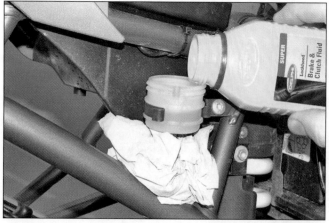

3 Top up with new, clean DOT 4 hydraulic fluid to the MAX level line. Do not overfill and take care to avoid spills (see **Warning** above).

4 Ensure that the diaphragm is correctly seated. Install the cap and tighten it securely. Ensure the reservoir is securely clipped into its holder.

FRONT BRAKE FLUID LEVEL

1 On R1200 GS/Adv and R models, the fluid level is visible through the reservoir body – it must be between the MIN and MAX level lines. Do not allow it to drop below the MIN line.

2 To top up, press the locking tabs in and unscrew the cap.

3 Remove the locking ring . . .

4 . . . and diaphragm. Do not remove the reservoir insert, where fitted.

5 On R1200 RT models, the fluid level is visible through the reservoir body – it must be between the MIN and MAX level lines. Do not allow it to drop below the MIN line.

6 To top-up, undo the cover screws and lift off the cover and the diaphragm.

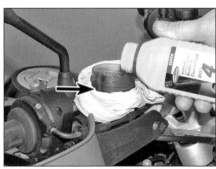

7 Top up with new, clean DOT 4 brake fluid to the MAX level line (MAX line on R1200 GS/Adv and R reservoir arrowed). Do not overfill and take care to avoid spills (see **Warning** on page 0•12).

8 On R1200 GS/Adv and R models, ensure that the diaphragm is correctly seated. Install the locking ring and tighten the cap securely.

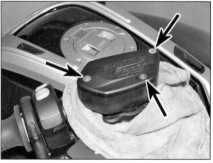

9 On R1200 RT models, ensure that the diaphragm is correctly seated and tighten the cover screws securely.

Clutch fluid level

Before you start:
● When checking the fluid level, position the handlebars so that the top of the master cylinder reservoir is as level as possible.
● Make sure you have the correct clutch fluid – Vitamol V10, available from BMW dealers. **Do not** use conventional brake and clutch hydraulic fluid. Wrap a rag around the reservoir to ensure that any spillage does not come into contact with painted surfaces.

Bike care:
● Clutch wear will cause the fluid level to rise gradually. Take care not to overfill the reservoir.
● If the reservoir requires repeated topping-up this is an indication of a fluid leak somewhere in the system, which should be investigated immediately.
● Check for signs of fluid leakage from the clutch hose and components – if found, rectify immediately.

1 The fluid level is visible through the reservoir body on R1200 GS/Adv and R models – it must not fall below the MIN level line.

2 If the level is below the MIN level line, press the locking tabs in and unscrew the cap.

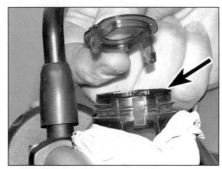

3 Remove the locking ring and diaphragm (arrowed).

4 On R1200 RT models, the fluid level is visible through the reservoir body – it must be between the MIN and MAX level lines. Do not allow it to drop below the MIN line. To top-up, undo the cover screws and lift off the cover and the diaphragm.

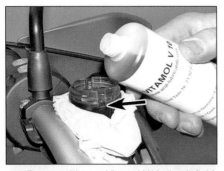

5 Top up with new Vitamol V10 clutch fluid. Do not overfill – MAX line on R1200 GS/ Adv and R reservoir arrowed.

6 Ensure that the diaphragm is correctly seated. Install the locking ring and tighten the cap securely.

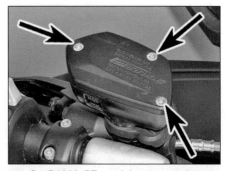

7 On R1200 RT models, ensure that the diaphragm is correctly seated and tighten the cover screws securely.

Suspension, steering and final drive

Suspension and Steering:
● Check that the front and rear suspension operate smoothly without binding.
● Check that the suspension is adjusted as required (where applicable).
● Check that the steering moves smoothly from lock-to-lock.

Gearbox and final drive:
● Check for signs of oil leakage around the gearbox and final drive housings. If there are any signs of leakage from the gearbox, check the oil level (Chapter 1, Section 8). If the final drive housing is leaking, have it checked by a BMW dealer.

Tyres

The correct pressures:

● The tyres must be checked when **cold**, not immediately after riding. Note that low tyre pressures may cause the tyre to slip on the rim or come off. High tyre pressures will cause abnormal tread wear and unsafe handling.

● Use an accurate pressure gauge.

● Proper air pressure will increase tyre life and provide maximum stability and ride comfort. Ensure that the pressures are suited to the load the machine is carrying.

● On machines fitted with integrated tyre pressure monitoring, the pressure sensors are activated by centrifugal force once the machine has reached a road speed of approximately 20 mph (30 kph). The pressures are displayed for approximately 15 minutes after the machine has come to a halt. Pressure readings are temperature compensated to indicate the pressure at 20°C irrespective of actual tyre or air temperature. If the tyre pressure drops close to the permitted limit the warning symbol on the multi-function display illuminates yellow and the tyre symbol is displayed. If the pressure falls to a critical level the warning symbol flashes red.

Tyre care:

● The need for frequent inflation indicates an air leak, which should be investigated immediately.

● Check the tyres carefully for cuts, tears, embedded nails or other sharp objects and excessive wear. Operation of the motorcycle with excessively worn tyres is extremely hazardous, as traction and handling are directly affected.

● Check the condition of the tyre valve and ensure the dust cap is in place.

● Pick out any stones or nails which may have become embedded in the tyre tread. If left, they will eventually penetrate through the casing and cause a puncture.

● If tyre damage is apparent, or unexplained loss of pressure is experienced, seek the advice of a motorcycle tyre fitting specialist without delay.

Tyre tread depth:

● At the time of writing UK law requires that tread depth must be at least 1 mm over 3/4 of the tread breadth all the way around the tyre, with no bald patches. Many riders, however, consider 2 mm tread depth minimum to be a safer limit.

● Many tyres now incorporate wear indicators in the tread. Identify the arrow, triangular pointer, TI or TWI marking on the tyre sidewall to locate the indicator bars and replace the tyre if the tread has worn down level with the bars.

Loading	Front	Rear
R1200 GS, GS Adventure and RT – rider only	32 psi (2.2 Bar)	36 psi (2.5 Bar)
R1200 GS, GS Adventure and RT – with passenger and/or luggage	36 psi (2.5 Bar)	42 psi (2.9 Bar)
R1200 R and R Classic	36 psi (2.5 Bar)	42 psi (2.9 Bar)

1 Check the tyre pressures when the tyres are cold and keep them properly inflated.

2 Measure tread depth at the centre of the tyre using a tread depth gauge.

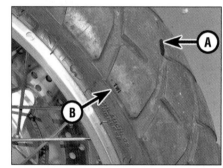

3 Tyre tread wear indicator bar (A) and its location marking (B) – usually an arrow, a triangle or the letters TI or TWI on the sidewall.

Legal and safety

Lighting and signalling:

● Take a minute to check that the headlight, tail light, brake light, instrument lights and turn signals all work correctly.

● Check that the horn sounds when the switch is operated.

● A working speedometer is a statutory requirement in the UK.

Safety:

● Check that the throttle grip rotates smoothly and snaps shut when released, in all steering positions.

● Check that the engine shuts off when the kill switch is operated.

● Check that the side stand and centre stand return springs hold the stands securely up when retracted.

Fuel:

● This may seem obvious, but check that you have enough fuel to complete your journey. Misfiring due to a low fuel level can damage the catalytic converter in the exhaust system.

● If you notice signs of fuel leakage – rectify the cause immediately.

● Ensure you use the correct grade unleaded fuel (see Chapter 3).

Weights and dimensions

R1200 GS

Wheelbase . . . . .1507 mm
Overall length . . . . .2210 mm
Overall width. . . . . .940 mm
Overall height . . . . .1420 mm
Seat height (rider's)
    Standard . . . . 850 to 870 mm
    Low rider's seat . . . . .820 mm
    Lowered suspension . . . . .790 mm
Weight (with oil and full fuel tank) . . . . .229 kg
Maximum payload . . . . .211 kg

R1200 GS Adventure

Wheelbase . . . . .1510 mm
Overall length . . . . .2240 mm
Overall width. . . . . .980 mm
Overall height . . . . .1525 mm
Seat height (rider's). . . . . 890 to 910 mm
Weight (with oil and full fuel tank) . . . . .256 kg
Maximum payload. . . . . .219 kg

R1200 RT

Wheelbase . . . . 1484.6 mm
Overall length . . . . .2230 mm
Overall width. . . . . .905 mm
Overall height (windshield lowered) . . . . .1430 mm
Seat height
    Standard. . . . . 820 to 840 mm
    Optional . . . . 780 to 800 mm
    Comfort seat. . . . . .785 mm
    Extra low seat . . . . .765 mm
    Lowered suspension . . . . .750 mm
Weight (with oil and full fuel tank). . . . . .259 kg
Maximum payload . . . . .236 kg

R1200 R

Wheelbase . . . . .1495 mm
Overall length . . . . .2145 mm
Overall width. . . . . .906 mm
Overall height . . . . .1317 mm
Seat height
    Standard. . . . . .800 mm
    Comfort seat. . . . . .830 mm
    Low seat . . . . .760 mm
    Extra low seat or lowered suspension . . . . .750 mm
Weight (with oil and full fuel tank). . . . . .223 kg
Maximum payload. . . . . .227 kg

Engine – all models

Type	Four-stroke air/oil-cooled horizontal twin
Capacity	1170 cc
Bore and stroke	101 x 73 mm
Compression ratio	12.0:1
Camshafts	DOHC, chain-driven
Valves	4 valves per cylinder
Fuel system	BMS-K electronic injectors
Clutch	Dry, single-plate, hydraulically-operated
Transmission	6-speed constant mesh
Final drive	Shaft

Chassis – all models

Type	Tubular frame, load-bearing engine
Rake and trail	
R1200 GS	64.3°, 101 mm
R1200 GS Adventure	65.2°, 88.7 mm
R1200 RT	63.4°, 109.9 mm
R1200 R	62.9°, 119.1 mm
Front suspension	
Type	BMW Telelever
Travel	
R1200 GS	
Standard suspension	190 mm
Lowered suspension	158 mm
R1200 GS Adventure	210 mm
R1200 RT	
Standard suspension	120 mm
Lowered suspension	94 mm
R1200 R	
Standard suspension	120 mm
Lowered suspension	100 mm
Adjustment	
Standard	Spring preload
Electronic Suspension Adjustment	Spring preload and rebound damping
Rear suspension	
Type	BMW Paralever
Travel	
R1200 GS	
Standard suspension	200 mm
Lowered suspension	171 mm
R1200 GS Adventure	220 mm
R1200 RT	
Standard suspension	135 mm
Lowered suspension	109 mm
R1200 R	
Standard suspension	140 mm
Lowered suspension	121 mm
Adjustment	Spring preload and rebound damping

Tyre sizes	Front	Rear
R1200 GS and Adventure	110/80 H19	150/70 H17
R1200 RT and R	120/70 ZR 17	180/55 ZR 17

Front brake	Twin discs with twin opposed-piston calipers
Rear brake	Single disc with two-piston sliding caliper

Model development

All models covered in this manual are powered by the same 1170 cc horizontally opposed, twin-cylinder engine derived from the previous generation R1200 series, but with certain major design changes. The most notable of these is the adoption of a DOHC layout on the top of the cylinder heads, the camshafts aligned horizontally and thereby operating an intake and exhaust valve each. The camshafts are still chain driven by an auxiliary shaft located below the crankshaft, but valve clearances are adjusted by hemispherical shims held in the underside of the cam followers. The radial arrangement of the valves allows for an increase in valve head diameter and requires a conical ground cam for operation.

Larger bearings have been fitted in the gearbox and the layout of the transmission shaft pinions has been revised together with repositioned gearchange selector forks and the addition of an oil deflector to improve lubrication.

Increased throttle body diameter, a less restrictive air filter element and the introduction of an electronically operated exhaust flow control valve have contributed towards an overall increase in upper rev limit, power and torque.

Specifications differ according to the state of tune of individual models, however fundamentally, all R1200 engines (known as the K2x series) feature air/oil-cooling, four valves per cylinder and a balancer shaft. The balancer shaft turns inside the auxiliary shaft and is gear driven off the crankshaft. The shaft has a one balance weight at the rear end, below the clutch, and a second weight incorporated in the drive gear at the front.

The cylinder heads, cylinders and crankcase are constructed from aluminium alloy, and the crankcase is divided vertically. The gearbox is a separate unit bolted to the rear of the crankcase. An alternator is mounted externally on the top of the crankcases and is belt driven off the front of the crankshaft.

Engine oil is contained within the crankcase and is pressure-fed for both lubrication and engine cooling by a dual-rotor pump driven by the auxiliary shaft. Oil pressure, oil temperature and, in some cases oil level are monitored by the engine control unit (ECU). An oil cooler is mounted at the front of all machines.

Power from the crankshaft is routed to the transmission input shaft in the gearbox via the clutch. The clutch is operated hydraulically and is of the dry, single-plate type, bolted directly to the rear of the crankshaft.

The transmission is a six-speed, constant-mesh unit, and drive to the rear wheel is by shaft, via a final drive unit.

BMW's own digital engine management system (BMS-K) monitors, controls and co-ordinates both the fuel and ignition system functions. The system is operated by the ECU. A second unit, the central electronics unit, is responsible for monitoring and control of all other electrical systems such as lighting, switches and accessories. The two units are linked for such functions as starting and engine immobilisation.

The ECU uses engine speed and throttle valve position as the basis for determining optimum engine operation. Additional data, supplied by temperature sensors, oil pressure, gear position and knock sensors, and exhaust gas analysers, when combined with control maps and correction values embedded within the ECU, fine tune injection volume and ignition timing to meet the engine's requirements in any given circumstance. In addition, the engine management system has in-built diagnostic functions which record and store all data should a fault occur.

All models utilise Controlled Area Network (CAN)-bus technology to create an electronic information network between the control units, sensors and power-consuming components. This allows rapid and reliable data transfer around the network. It also allows comprehensive diagnosis of the entire system from one central point.

There is no frame in the traditional sense – the front suspension and its sub-frame, and rear suspension and its sub-frame mount directly to the engine/transmission unit.

Front suspension and steering are managed separately by a BMW's Telelever system. Telelever uses an arrangement of telescopic fork legs to support the front wheel and provide steering, together with a swingarm and shock absorber to provide suspension control. At the top of the Telelever system, the fork tubes are held in a yoke, which is mounted to the front sub-frame via the steering head bearing. Midway down the assembly, the fork sliders are linked by a bridge which is attached to the front of the Telelever swingarm via a ball joint. The swingarm pivots around a shaft which passes through the front of the engine crankcases, with the shock absorber located between the swingarm and the front sub-frame.

Rear suspension is provided by a single-sided swingarm and centrally mounted shock absorber. The drive shaft to the rear wheel is housed inside the swingarm. The joint between the swingarm and the final drive unit is pivoted, with a link arm, BMW's Paralever system, controlling movement between the two. The Paralever system counteracts the adverse effect of the shaft drive on suspension movement.

Both front and rear brakes are hydraulically operated disc brakes with optional ABS. The front calipers have two pairs of opposed pistons each and the rear brake has two pistons in a sliding caliper.

R1200 GS (K25 31)

Launched in December 2009. Available with either light alloy cast wheels for road and moderate off-road riding, or wire spoked wheels for high speed, rough terrain use. ABS, electronic suspension adjustment, automatic stability control, remote tyre pressure monitoring and an anti-theft warning system were available as options, as were lowered suspension and a lowered rider's seat height.

A limited edition model, the Triple Black, was introduced for the 2011 model year. It featured wire spoked wheels with black rims, black engine unit and black fuel tank and front forks.

A second limited edition model, the R1200 GS Rallye was introduced in 2012. It too featured wire spoked wheels and a black engine unit. The white, blue and red colour scheme of the frame and bodywork was based on the R80 GS Dakar models produced to commemorate the company's success in the Paris-Dakar Rally. A number of optional extra components were fitted as standard such as electronic suspension adjustment, heated handlebar grips and hand protectors.

R1200 GS Adventure (K25 32)

The Adventure was launched in December 2009, designed and equipped for serious high speed, rough terrain use. Standard equipment included a large capacity (33 litre) fuel tank, large windshield, adjustable seat height, hand protectors, a sump guard and engine protection bars. Dual purpose tyres were fitted to wire spoked wheels and upgraded front and rear suspension offered longer travel.

ABS, electronic suspension adjustment, automatic stability control, remote tyre pressure monitoring and an anti-theft warning system were available as options, as were twin auxiliary halogen headlights and a dedicated enduro gear cluster for the transmission.

R1200 RT (K26)

Launched in December 2009, the R1200 RT shared the basic engine, transmission, suspension and chassis components of the GS, but was styled as a dedicated long distance touring machine with a package of luggage options to suit.

ABS and an electronically controlled windshield were fitted as standard and a large number of optional extras included electronic suspension adjustment, automatic stability control, heated seats, an on-board audio system and cruise control.

The design of the instrument cluster was changed from previous RT models to reduce reflection and optimise legibility of the central multi-function display, and fine headlight adjustment could be made using a knob on the cockpit trim panel. The design of the handlebar switch units and the front brake and clutch master cylinders was revised.

A special edition (SE) model was introduced for 2011 which had electronic suspension adjustment, heated handlebar grips and heated seats fitted as standard.

R1200 R (K27)

A naked style roadster, the R1200 R replaced the previous SOHC-engined model in November 2010. Most notable for its lack of bodywork and retro design, the R featured a one-piece dual seat, single round headlight, traditional looking analogue speedometer and tachometer housed in a fork top binnacle and a short, low level exhaust silencer.

The R1200 R was fitted with cast alloy wheels as standard whereas the black-painted R Classic variant featured wire spoked wheels and a chrome plated silencer.

Optional extras included ABS, electronic suspension adjustment and automatic stability control, as well as three seat height options and a range of luggage options.

Chapter 1
Routine maintenance and Servicing

Contents

Section number

Air filter 6
Alternator drive belt 9
Battery . . . . see Chapter 7
Brake system 11
Clutch system. 10
Engine oil and filter. 1
Final drive oil change 7
Gearbox oil. 8

Section number

Headlight adjustment . . . . see Chapter 7
Nuts and bolts 12
Spark plugs 5
Stand pivots. 4
Suspension. 14
Throttle cables 3
Valve clearances. 2
Wheels and wheel bearings 13

Degrees of difficulty

| Easy, suitable for novice with little experience | Fairly easy, suitable for beginner with some experience | Fairly difficult, suitable for competent DIY mechanic | Difficult, suitable for experienced DIY mechanic | Very difficult, suitable for expert DIY or professional |

Engine

Spark plugs
  Type . . . .   NGK MAR8B-JDS
  Electrode gap
    Standard. . . . .   0.7 to 0.9 mm
    Service limit . . . .   1.0 mm
Valve clearances (COLD engine)
  Intake valves. . . . .   0.13 to 0.23 mm
  Exhaust valves . . . .   0.30 to 0.40 mm

Cycle parts

Brake pad friction material minimum thickness. . . . .   1.0 mm
Brake disc minimum thickness
  Front. . . . .   4.0 mm
  Rear . . . .   4.5 mm
Throttle cable freeplay . . . .   see text

Lubricants and fluids

Engine oil . . . .   Castrol Power 1 4T SAE 15W/50, API SJ, JASO MA2
Engine oil capacity . . . .   4.0 litres
Gearbox oil type and viscosity. . . . .   Castrol SAF-XO
Gearbox oil capacity . . . .   700 cc
Final drive oil type . . . .   Castrol SAF-XO
Final drive oil capacity . . . .   180 cc
Brake fluid . . . .   DOT 4
Clutch fluid. . . . .   Vitamol V10
Miscellaneous
  Front wheel bearings . . . .   High melting point lithium grease
  Suspension bearings . . . .   High melting point lithium grease
  Lever and stand pivot points . . . .   Dry film lubricant
  Throttle twistgrip. . . . .   Dry film lubricant
  Cables . . . .   Aerosol cable lubricant

Torque settings

Centre stand pivot bolts. . . . .   40 Nm
Crash bar 8 mm mounting bolts. . . . .   19 Nm
Engine oil drain plug. . . . .   32 Nm
Engine oil filter . . . .   11 Nm
Engine sump guard
  Bracket 10 mm bolt . . . .   40 Nm
  Guard to bracket 8 mm rear bolts . . . .   19 Nm
  Guard to bracket 6 mm rear bolts . . . .   10 Nm
Final drive oil drain plug . . . .   20 Nm
Final drive oil filler plug
  R1200 GS, GS Adventure and R1200 R. . . . .   25 Nm
  R1200 RT . . . .   20 Nm
Front brake caliper mounting bolts
  R1200 GS, GS Adventure and R1200 RT. . . . .   30 Nm
  R1200 R . . . .   28 Nm
Fuel tank mounting bolts
  R1200 GS and GS Adventure. . . . .   19 Nm
  R1200 RT . . . .   16 Nm
  R1200 R . . . .   22 Nm
Gearbox oil filler cap . . . .   30 Nm
Gearbox oil drain plug . . . .   30 Nm
Rear brake caliper mounting bolts . . . .   24 Nm
Rear wheel mounting bolts. . . . .   60 Nm
Spark plugs . . . .   12 Nm
Side stand pivot bolt . . . .   40 Nm
Valve cover bolts . . . .   10 Nm
Valve cover guard bolts . . . .   10 Nm

Note: *All models covered in this manual are fitted with a 'service due' indicator in the instrument display. When the next service is due in less than one month, the service date is displayed momentarily on the multi-function display following the pre-ride check after the ignition has been turned on. If the distance to the odometer reading at which the next service will be due is less than 600 miles (1000 km) the distance is counted down in steps of 60 miles (100 km) and is displayed momentarily on the multi-function display following the pre-ride check. If the service is overdue the word SERVICE will be permanently shown. The service indicator requires resetting by a BMW dealer.*

Pre-ride
☐ Perform the Pre-ride checks listed at the beginning of this manual before carrying out any of the following procedures.

After the initial 600 miles (1000 km)
Note: *This check is usually performed by a BMW dealer after the first 600 miles (1000 km) from new. Thereafter, maintenance is carried out according to the following intervals of the schedule.*

Every 6000 miles (10,000 km) or annually
☐ Change the engine oil and fit a new filter (Section 1).
☐ Check throttle cable operation (Section 3).
☐ Check the operation of the brake system, pad and disc wear (Section 11).
☐ Check spoke tension – wire spoked wheels (see Chapter 5).
☐ Check and lubricate the stand and lever pivots (Section 4).
☐ Check the lights and turn signals (see Chapter 7).

Every 6000 miles (10,000 km)
☐ Check and adjust the valve clearances (Section 2).

Every 12,000 miles (20,000 km)
☐ Fit new spark plugs (Section 5).
☐ Fit a new air filter element (Section 6).

Every 12,000 miles (20,000 km) or two years
☐ Change the final drive oil (Section 7).

Every 24,000 miles (40,000 km) or two years
☐ Change the gearbox oil (Section 8).

Every 24,000 miles (40,000 km) or six years
☐ Fit a new alternator drive belt (Section 9).

Every two years
☐ Check the operation of the clutch system (Section 10).
☐ Change the brake fluid (see Chapter 5).

Non-scheduled maintenance
☐ Check the tightness of all nuts and bolts (Section 12).
☐ Check battery condition (see Chapter 7).
☐ Check the condition of the wheels and wheel bearings (Section 13).
☐ Check the front and rear suspension (Section 14).

Component locations on right side – R1200 GS (inc. Adventure)

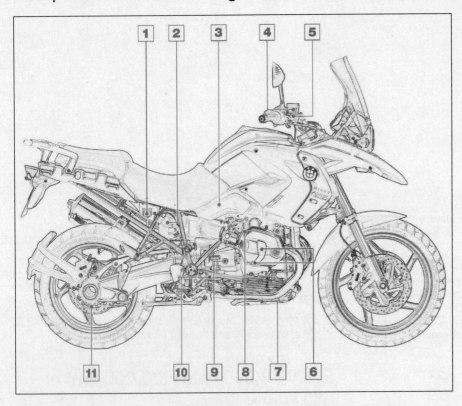

1 Rear brake fluid reservoir
2 Rear shock pre-load adjuster*
3 Air filter
4 Front brake fluid reservoir
5 Thottle cable adjuster
6 Spark plugs
7 Engine oil drain plug
8 Engine oil filler cap
9 Gearbox oil filler plug
10 Gearbox oil drain plug
11 Final drive oil drain plug
*Models without ESA

Component locations on left side – R1200 GS (inc. Adventure)

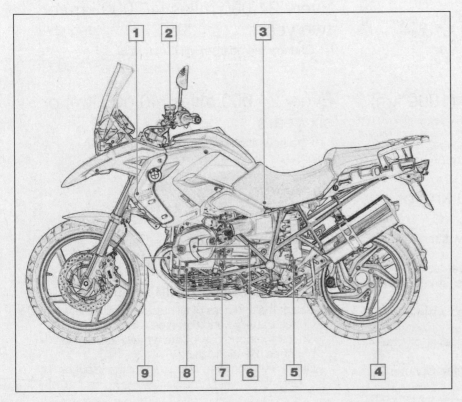

1 Front shock pre-load adjuster*
2 Clutch fluid reservoir
3 Battery
4 Final drive oil filler plug
5 Rear shock damping adjuster*
6 Spark plugs
7 Engine oil filter
8 Engine oil level inspection window
9 Alternator drive belt
*Models without ESA

Component locations on right side – R1200 RT

1 Rear shock pre-load adjuster*
2 Rear brake fluid reservoir
3 Air filter
4 Front brake fluid reservoir
5 Thottle cable adjusters
6 Spark plugs
7 Engine oil drain plug
8 Engine oil filler cap
9 Gearbox oil filler plug
10 Gearbox oil drain plug
11 Final drive oil drain plug
*Models without ESA

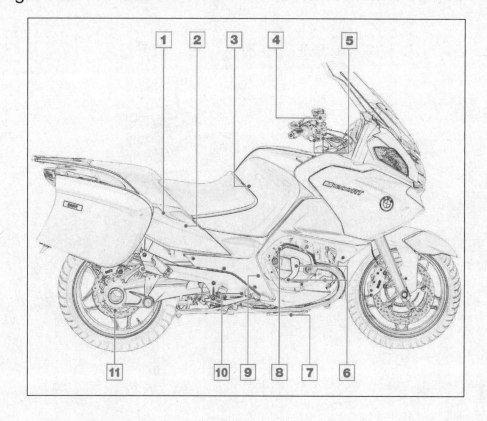

Component locations on left side – R1200 RT

1 Clutch fluid reservoir
2 Battery
3 Final drive oil filler plug
4 Rear shock damping adjuster*
5 Spark plugs
6 Engine oil filter
7 Engine oil level inspection window
8 Alternator drive belt
*Models without ESA

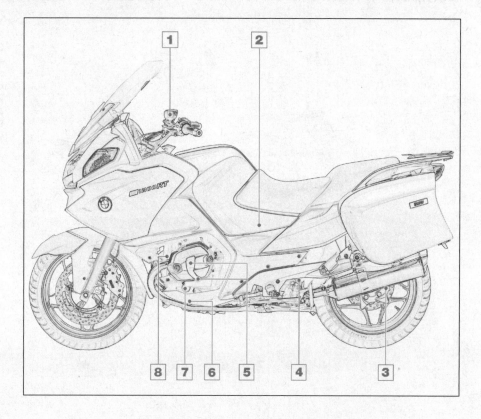

Component locations on right side – R1200 R

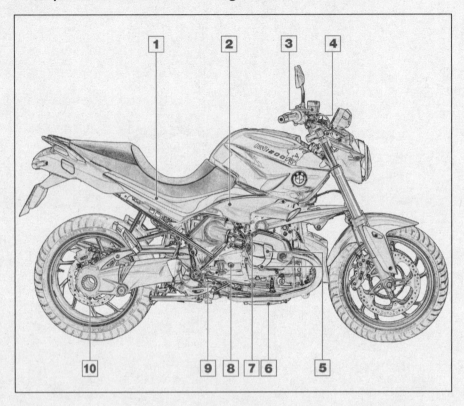

1 Rear brake fluid reservoir
2 Air filter
3 Front brake fluid reservoir
4 Thottle cable adjuster
5 Spark plugs
6 Engine oil drain plug
7 Engine oil filler cap
8 Gearbox oil filler plug
9 Gearbox oil drain plug
10 Final drive oil drain plug

Component locations on left side – R1200 R

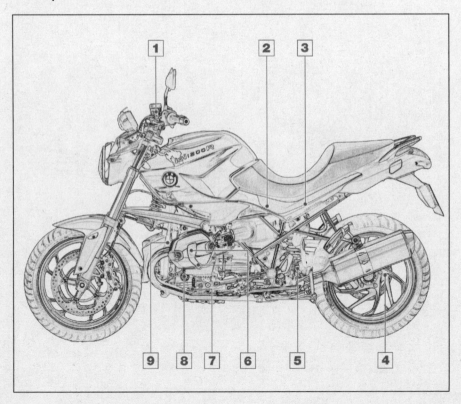

1 Clutch fluid reservoir
2 Battery
3 Rear shock pre-load adjuster*
4 Final drive oil filler plug
5 Rear shock damping adjuster*
6 Spark plugs
7 Engine oil filter
8 Engine oil level inspection window
9 Alternator drive belt
*Models without ESA

Introduction

1 This Chapter is designed to help the home mechanic maintain his/her motorcycle for safety, economy, long life and peak performance.

2 Deciding where to start or plug into the maintenance schedule depends on several factors. If the warranty period on your motorcycle has just expired, and if it has been maintained according to the warranty standards, you may want to pick up routine maintenance as it coincides with the next mileage or calendar interval. If you have owned the machine for some time but have never performed any maintenance on it, then you may want to start at the nearest interval and include some additional procedures to ensure that nothing important is overlooked.

If you have just had a major engine overhaul, then you may want to start the maintenance routine from the beginning. If you have a used machine and have no knowledge of its history or maintenance record, you may desire to combine all the checks into one large service initially and then settle into the maintenance schedule prescribed. Note that connection of the bike to the BMW MOSS diagnostic tester will show if any recall work is outstanding.

3 Before beginning any maintenance or repair, the machine should be cleaned thoroughly, especially around the oil filter, spark plug covers, valve covers, gearbox level plug etc. Cleaning will help ensure that dirt does not contaminate the engine and will allow you to

detect wear and damage that could otherwise easily go unnoticed.

4 Certain maintenance information is sometimes printed on labels attached to the motorcycle. If the information on the labels differs from that included here, use the information on the label.

5 Many of the bolts used on R1200 series BMW motorcycles are of the Torx type. Unless you are already equipped with a good range of Torx bits, you are advised to obtain a set – BMW produces a tools service set for owners wishing to carry out extended service work. Make sure you get bits that can be used in conjunction with a socket set so that a torque wrench can be applied.

Read the Safety first! *section of this manual carefully before starting work.*

---

1 Engine oil and filter

Special tool: *A filter wrench is necessary for this procedure (see illustration 1.7).*

 Warning: Be careful when draining the oil, as the exhaust pipes, the engine, and the oil itself can cause severe burns.

1 Regular oil and filter changes are the single most important maintenance procedure you can perform. The oil not only lubricates the internal parts of the engine, but it also acts as a coolant, a cleaner, a sealant, and a protector. Because of these demands, the oil takes a terrific amount of abuse and should always be changed at the specified interval together with the oil filter.

2 Before changing the oil, warm up the engine so the oil will drain easily. Make sure the bike is on level ground and support it on its centre stand.

3 If applicable, remove the engine sump guard **(see illustrations)**.

4 Position a clean drain tray below the engine. Using the special tool in the bike's tool

kit, unscrew the oil filler cap on the right-hand valve cover to vent the crankcase and to act as a reminder that there is no oil in the engine (see *Pre-ride checks*).

 An oil drain tray can be easily made by cutting away the front or back of an old five litre oil container.

5 Unscrew the oil drain plug from the bottom of the engine and allow the oil to flow into the drain tray **(see illustrations)**. Discard the sealing washer on the drain plug as a new one should be used.

6 When the oil has completely drained, install the plug using a new sealing washer and tighten it to the torque setting specified at the beginning of this Chapter **(see illustration)**. Do not overtighten the plug as the threads in the sump could be damaged.

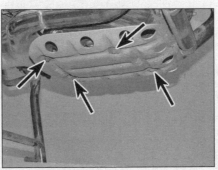

1.3a Undo the front screws and rear nuts . . .

1.3b . . . and remove the sump guard

1.5a Unscrew the drain plug . . .

1.5b . . . and drain the engine oil

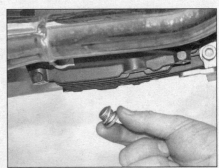

1.6 Fit a new sealing washer

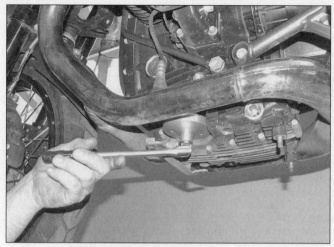

1.7 Use an end-cap type oil filter wrench

1.8 First install the filter finger-tight

7 Now place the drain tray below the oil filter. Unscrew the oil filter using an end-cap type oil filter wrench **(see illustration)**. BMW produces a service tool to do this (Part No. 114661). Once the filter has been unscrewed, tip any residual oil into the drain tray.

8 Smear clean engine oil onto the seal of the new filter, then screw the filter onto the engine until it is finger-tight **(see illustration)**. Now tighten the filter to the specified torque setting using the filter wrench. Take care not to over-tighten the filter as this may damage the seal.

9 Refill the engine using the specified type and amount of oil (see *Specifications*). Install the filler cap and tighten it securely.

10 Start the engine and ensure that the oil pressure warning light extinguishes after a few seconds.

11 To ensure an accurate check of the oil level, take the machine for a test ride so that the engine reaches operating temperature, then put it onto the centre stand and allow the oil level to stabilise for five minutes with the engine OFF.

12 Check the level again – it should be just below the top of the window. If necessary, add more oil to bring it up to the correct level, but take care not to over-fill the engine.

13 Check that there are no oil leaks from around the drain plug and the oil filter.

14 If applicable, install the engine sump guard.

15 The old oil drained from the engine cannot be re-used and should be disposed of properly. Check with your local refuse disposal company, disposal facility or environmental agency to see whether they will accept the used oil for recycling. Don't pour used oil into drains or onto the ground.

| 2 | Valve clearances | |

Special tool: *A set of feeler gauges is necessary for this job.*

Check

1 The engine must be cold for this maintenance procedure, so let the machine sit overnight before beginning.

2 Place the motorcycle on its centre stand. If applicable, undo the screws securing the upper cylinder head covers and remove them **(see illustrations)**. If optional equipment (OE)

 Check the old oil carefully – if it is very metallic coloured, then the engine is experiencing wear from running-in (new engine) or from insufficient lubrication. If there are flakes or chips of metal in the oil, then something is drastically wrong internally and the engine will have to be disassembled for inspection and repair.

2.2a Undo the screws . . .

2.2b . . . and remove the upper cylinder head covers

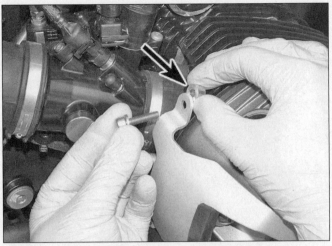

2.2c Note the location of the spacers . . .

2.2d . . . behind aluminium head covers

2.5 Ensure timing marks are correctly aligned

2.6 Check for freeplay in the cam followers

aluminium covers are fitted, note the location of the spacers between the head covers and the valve covers **(see illustrations)**.

3 Remove the primary spark plugs (see Section 5).

4 Place a drain tray underneath the side of the engine being worked on to catch any residual oil, then remove both valve covers (see Chapter 2).

5 Work on one side of the engine at a time. To check the valve clearances, the piston must be at top dead centre (TDC) on the compression stroke. To turn the engine to this position, select a high gear and have an assistant turn the rear wheel slowly by hand in the normal direction of rotation (forwards). Alternatively, remove the alternator belt cover (see Section 9) and turn the crankshaft clockwise with a spanner on the pulley nut. The piston is at TDC (compression) when the timing marks on the camshafts face each other **(see illustration)**. **Note:** *When one piston is at TDC compression, the other is at TDC exhaust and*

the marks on the camshafts on that side of the engine face away from each other.

Caution: Be sure to turn the engine in its normal direction of rotation only.

6 With the piston at TDC on the compression stroke, all the valves will be closed and there should be discernible freeplay in the cam followers **(see illustration)**.

7 Make a chart or sketch of all valve positions so that a note of each clearance can be made against the relevant valve.

8 Check the clearance on each valve by inserting a feeler gauge of the correct thickness (see *Specifications*) between the cam and the cam follower – the gauge should be a firm sliding fit **(see illustration)**. If not, use the feeler gauges to obtain the exact clearance. Record the measured clearances on your chart. **Note:** *The intake and exhaust valve clearances are different.*

Adjustment

9 When all clearances have been measured and recorded, identify whether the clearance

on any valve falls outside that specified. If it does, the shim between the follower and the valve must be replaced with one of a thickness which will restore the correct clearance.

10 Changing a shim requires removal of the appropriate cam follower. Note the location of the E-clip securing the follower, then ease off

2.8 Check valve clearance with a feeler gauge

2.10a Ease off the E-clip . . .

2.10b . . . and remove the cam follower

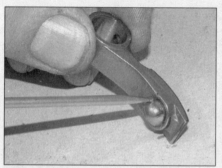

2.10c Note location of the shim

2.11 Measuring the shim with a micrometer

the clip and slide the follower off its shaft **(see illustrations)**. The shim will be stuck inside the recess in the follower – take care not to drop it when the follower is removed **(see illustration)**. Discard the E-clip as new ones must be used.

11 The shim size should be marked on its outer edge – a shim marked 5.300X is 5.30 mm thick – but the shim should be measured with a micrometer to check that it has not worn **(see illustration)**. If the shim has worn undersize, this must be taken into account when calculating the size of the new shim.

12 Compare the measured valve clearance with the specified clearance to determine the amount by which the shim size should be increased or decreased. If the measured clearance is too large, add the difference to the thickness of the existing shim to determine the size of the new shim. If the measured clearance is too small, subtract the difference from the thickness of the existing shim to determine the size of the new shim.

13 New shims are available in 0.05 mm increments from 4.60 to 5.70 mm and can be obtained from a BMW dealer. **Note:** *If an exact match to the required shim thickness cannot be found, use the nearest size to it, e.g. required thickness 5.33, nearest available thickness 5.35. If the required replacement shim is greater than 5.70 mm (the largest available), the valve is probably not seating correctly due to a build-up of carbon deposits or valve damage. Remove the valve for checking (see Chapter 2).*

14 When replacing a shim, lubricate it with engine oil and fit it into its recess in the cam follower **(see illustration 2.10c)**. Check that the shim is correctly seated, then lubricate the follower with engine oil, slide it into position and ensure the shim locates correctly on top of the valve stem.

15 Secure the follower with a new E-clip **(see illustration)**. Ensure that the open end of the E-clip securing the upper exhaust cam follower faces the cylinder head **(see illustration)**.

2.15a Always fit a new E-clip

2.15b Position the open end of the clip as shown

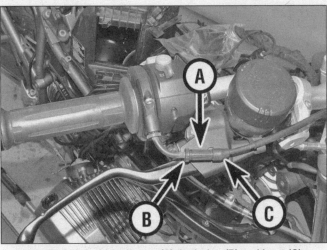

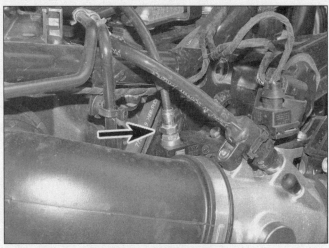

3.2 Throttle cable adjuster (A), lock ring (B) and boot (C)

3.5 Cable adjuster at the throttle body end

16 Rotate the crankshaft several turns to seat the new shim(s), then check the clearances again (Steps 5 to 8).

17 Follow the same procedure to check and adjust the valve clearances on the other cylinder. Don't forget to turn the engine until the piston is at TDC (compression) and the timing marks on the camshafts face each other **(see illustration 2.5)**.

18 On completion, lubricate the valve assemblies, cam followers and camshafts with clean engine oil, then install the covers (see Chapter 2)

19 Install the remaining components in the reverse order of removal.

3 Throttle cables

Adjustment

Note: *BMW only give a specification for throttle cable freeplay for R1200 RT models (see Step 2). An accurate assessment of cable adjustment can only be made using the BMW diagnostic testing equipment to confirm accurate synchronisation of the throttle valves.*

1 Make sure the throttle twistgrip rotates easily from fully closed to fully open with the front wheel turned at various angles. The twistgrip should return automatically from fully open to fully closed when released. If not, check and lubricate the cables (see Steps 7 to 14).

R1200 GS, GS Adventure and R models

2 Check for a small amount of freeplay in the cable between the outer cable and its seat in the cable adjuster at the twistgrip end. Pull back the boot on the cable before making the check **(see illustration)**. The handlebars should be in the straight-ahead position.

3 To adjust the cable, loosen the adjuster lock ring and turn the adjuster in or out as required. First set the adjuster with zero freeplay in the cable, then loosen the adjuster by 5 to 6 turns. Operate the twistgrip several times to settle the cable, then tighten the lock ring. Don't forget to refit the boot on the adjuster. If the adjuster has reached its limit of adjustment, fit a new cable (see Chapter 3).

4 When the twistgrip is closed, both throttle pulleys should rest on the throttle stops and there should be a small and equal amount of freeplay in the cables between the cable splitter and the throttle pulleys. If required, remove any bodywork for access (see Chapter 6).

5 If cable adjustment is necessary, pull back the boot on the throttle body end of the cable to access the adjuster **(see illustration)**. Loosen the adjuster locknut and adjust the cable as necessary **Note:** *It is essential that freeplay is the same in both cables, otherwise the operation of the throttle valves will not be synchronised.*

6 Ensure that the blanking caps on the BMW throttle body Synchro tester unions are tight **(see illustration)**. Loose or missing caps will impair engine performance and cause a fault to be registered by the engine management system (see Chapter 3).

R1200 RT models

7 Machines not fitted with cruise control have a single cable between the throttle twistgrip and the cable splitter. Check for 2 to 3 mm of freeplay measured in terms of twistgrip rotation **(see illustration)**. The

3.6 Ensure blanking caps are in good condition

3.7 Check freeplay in throttle rearward rotation

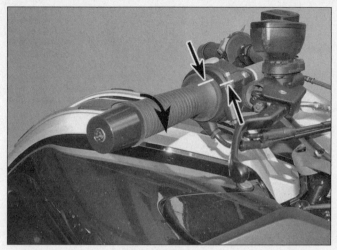

3.10 Check closing cable freeplay in throttle forward rotation

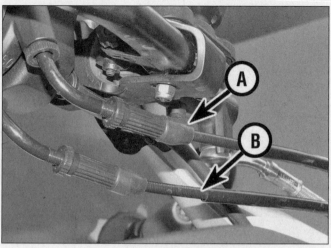

3.11 Opening cable (A) and closing cable (B)

handlebars should be in the straight-ahead position.

8 To adjust the cable, pull back the boot on the lower end of the adjuster, then loosen the adjuster lock ring and turn the adjuster in or out as required **(see illustration 3.2)**. Operate the twistgrip several times to settle the cable, then tighten the lock ring. Don't forget to refit the boot on the adjuster. If the adjuster has reached its limit of adjustment, fit a new cable (see Chapter 3).

9 Machines fitted with cruise control have two cables, an opening and a closing cable, between the throttle twistgrip and the cable splitter **(see illustration 3.11)**.

10 With the handlebars in the straight-ahead position, first check the closing cable adjustment by turning the twistgrip forwards from the idle position. There should be 2 to 3 mm of freeplay measured in terms of twistgrip forward rotation and the micro-switch inside the cable splitter housing should click within 1 to 1.5 mm of twistgrip rotation **(see illustration)**.

11 To adjust the closing cable, loosen the lock rings and adjusters on both cables, and pull back the boots on the lower ends of the adjusters **(see illustration)**. Adjust the closing cable until there is the correct amount of freeplay. Tighten the lock ring.

12 Check for 2 to 3 mm of freeplay in the opening cable measured in terms of twistgrip rearward rotation **(see illustration 3.7)**. Adjust the cable as necessary, then tighten the lock ring.

13 Operate the twistgrip several times to settle the cables and check their settings. Ensure the boots are correctly fitted on the adjusters.

14 If either adjuster has reached its limit of adjustment, fit a new cable (see Chapter 3).

15 Follow Steps 4 and 5 to check the adjustment of the cables between the cable splitter and the throttle pulleys.

16 Ensure that the blanking caps on the BMW throttle body Synchro tester unions are tight **(see illustration 3.6)**.

Check and lubrication

Special tool: *A cable lubricating adapter is necessary for this procedure (see illustration 3.18).*

17 If the throttle sticks, this is probably due to a cable fault. Remove the cables (see Chapter 3) and lubricate them as follows.

18 Note which way round the pressure adapter fits onto the inner and outer cables, then slide it over the inner cable **(see illustration)**.

19 Push the outer cable into the recess in the adapter, then tighten the screw so that the cable is gripped firmly **(see illustration)**. **Note:** *If the screw is not tightened sufficiently, lubricant will leak out of the adapter.*

20 Connect the lubricant can to the adapter and depress the button – lubricant should penetrate between the inner and outer cables along their full length **(see illustration)**. Use an aerosol cable lubricant.

21 Disconnect the adapter and check that the inner cable slides freely in the

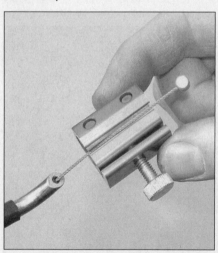

3.18 Fitting the adapter onto the inner cable

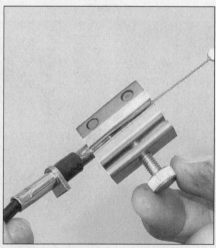

3.19 Ensure the adapter grips the inner and outer cables firmly

3.20 Connect the can of cable lubricant to the adapter

4.1 Keep stand pivots clean and lubricated

4.3 Check the condition of the stand springs

outer cable. If not, replace the cable with a new one.

22 With the cables removed, check the operation of the cable splitter (see Chapter 3).

23 Make sure the throttle twistgrip rotates freely on the handlebar – dirt, combined with a lack of lubrication, can cause the action to be stiff. Unscrew the handlebar end-weight and slide the twistgrip off. Clean the bar and inside the twistgrip, then lubricate the components with dry film lubricant. Install the twistgrip in the reverse order of removal.

24 Install the cables, making sure they are correctly routed (see Chapter 3). If this fails to improve the operation of the throttle, check for a sticking valve in the throttle bodies (see Chapter 3).

⚠️ **Warning: Turn the handlebars all the way through their travel with the engine idling. Idle speed should not change. If it does, the cable may be routed incorrectly. Correct this condition before riding the bike.**

4 Stand pivots 🔧

1 Since the stands on a motorcycle are exposed to the elements, the pivots should be lubricated periodically to ensure safe and trouble-free operation **(see illustration)**.

2 In order for the lubricant to be applied where it will do the most good, the component should be disassembled (see Chapter 4). However, if chain or dry film lubricant is being used, it can be applied to the pivot joint gaps and will usually work its way into the areas where friction occurs. If engine oil or light grease is being used, apply it sparingly as it may attract dirt (which could cause the pivots to bind or wear at an accelerated rate).

3 Check the stand springs for damage and distortion **(see illustration)**. The springs must be capable of retracting the stand fully and holding it retracted when the motorcycle is in use. If a spring has sagged or is broken, it must be replaced with a new one (see Chapter 4).

5 Spark plugs 🔧

Special tools: *An ignition coil extractor (Part No. 123561) and a wire gauge are necessary for this job* **(see illustrations 5.4a and 5.9).**

Note 1: *The spark plug caps are integral with the ignition coils. To avoid damaging the wiring, always disconnect the wiring connectors before removing the coils. Do not attempt to lever the coils off the spark plugs – use the special tool. Do not drop the coils.*

Note 2: *Make sure your spark plug socket is the correct size before attempting to remove the plugs.*

Removal

1 Place the motorcycle on its centre stand. If applicable, refer to Section 2 and remove the upper and lower cylinder head covers **(see illustrations)**.

5.1a Remove the upper . . .

5.1b . . . and lower cylinder head covers

5.2 Ease plug cover out in the direction shown

5.3 Disconnect primary ignition coil wiring connector

5.4a Install the special tool . . .

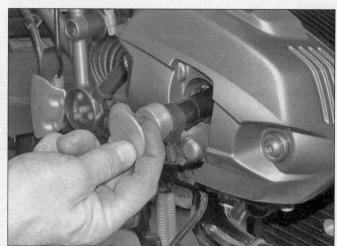

5.4b . . . and pull out the ignition coil

5.5 Unclip the primary coil wiring

5.6a Disconnect the secondary ignition coil wiring connector

5.6b Pull off the ignition coil

5.7 Use a deep socket to unscrew the spark plugs

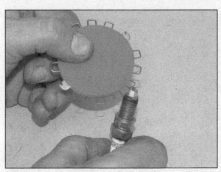

5.9 Using a wire type gauge to measure the spark plug gap

2 Ease out the plug cover in the direction shown to avoid breaking it **(see illustration).**
3 Carefully release the primary ignition coil wiring connector from the securing tab, then disconnect the connector **(see illustration).**
4 Using the special tool, pull the coil off the primary spark plug **(see illustrations).**
5 Release the primary coil wiring from the guide on the secondary ignition coil **(see illustration).**
6 Disconnect the wiring connector from the secondary ignition coil (see Step 3), then pull the coil off the secondary spark plug **(see illustrations). Note:** *The secondary spark plug coils are left and right-handed – if necessary,*

mark them to ensure they are fitted the correct way round.
7 Using either the BMW plug socket (Part No. 123611) or a 14 mm thin-walled, deep socket type wrench, unscrew the plugs from the cylinder head **(see illustration).**
8 Inspect the old spark plugs and compare them with the colour spark plug reading chart at the end of this manual. The condition of the plugs can give an indication of the general condition of the engine. Do not attempt to clean and re-use the old plugs, new ones must be fitted.

Installation

9 Before installing the new plugs, make sure they are the correct type and heat range and check the gap between the electrodes – see *Specifications* at the beginning of this Chapter. Measure the gap with a wire gauge **(see illustration)**. New plugs are pre-set to the correct gap – if the plug gap is outside the specified measurement it is likely the plug has been damaged. Never attempt to bend the plug electrodes, fit another new plug.
10 Make sure the washer is in place before installing each plug.
11 Since the cylinder head is made of aluminium, which is soft and easily damaged, thread the plugs into the heads turning the

plug socket by hand. Once the plugs are finger-tight, tighten them to the torque setting specified at the beginning of this Chapter – do not over-tighten them.

> **HAYNES HiNT** *Slip a short length of hose over the end of the plug to use as a tool to thread it into place. The hose will grip the plug well enough to turn it, but will start to slip if the plug is cross-threaded in the hole – this will prevent damaged threads.*

12 Install the ignition coils, making sure they locate correctly onto the plugs. Ensure that the terminals inside the wiring connectors are clean, then connect them securely. Secure the primary coil wiring in the guides.
13 Install the primary spark plug covers ensuring they clip into place securely **(see illustrations)**. Install the cylinder head covers and tighten the retaining screws securely.

> **HAYNES HiNT** *Stripped plug threads in the cylinder head can be repaired with a thread insert – see 'Tools and Workshop Tips' in the Reference section.*

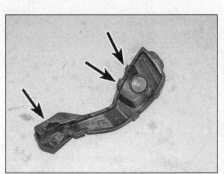

5.13a Note tabs on the inside of the spark plug covers

5.13b Ensure the covers are correctly positioned . . .

5.13c . . . and press them firmly into place

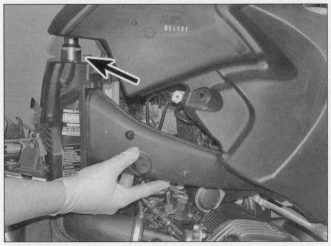

6.3 Raise the rear of the fuel tank on R1200 GS Adventure models

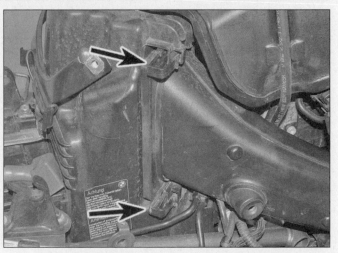

6.4 Release the clips securing the intake duct

6.5 Release the peg on the back of the duct

6.6 Remove the intake duct

6 Air filter

Caution: If the machine is continually ridden in wet or dusty conditions, the filter should be renewed more frequently.

6.7 Remove the air filter element

1 Remove the seat(s) (see Chapter 6).
2 The air filter is located in its housing at the rear of the fuel tank. On R1200 GS, RT and R models, remove the right-hand side panel, fairing side panel and tank panels applicable to gain access (see Chapter 6).
3 On R1200 GS Adventure models, the rear of the fuel tank must be raised to facilitate removal of the air intake duct. Follow the procedure in Chapter 3, Section 2, to remove the bodywork prior to removing the tank, but do not disconnect any of the fuel or breather hoses or the pump and level sensor wiring connectors. Undo the tank mounting bolts and place a suitable support between the top of the air filter housing and the underside of the tank **(see illustration)**.
4 Release the upper and lower clips securing the air intake duct to the filter housing **(see illustration)**.
5 On R1200 GS, GS Adventure and R models, release the peg on the back of the duct **(see illustration)**.

6 Prise the duct off the opening on the air filter housing **(see illustration)**.
7 Prise out the air filter element and discard it **(see illustration)**.
8 Install the new filter, ensuring it is properly seated, then install the air intake duct.
9 On R1200 GS, GS Adventure and R models, press the peg on the back of the duct into the grommet on the frame.
10 Secure the duct to the filter housing with the clips.
11 Install the remaining components in the reverse order of removal.

7 Final drive oil change

Warning: Be careful when draining the oil, as the exhaust pipes, the engine, and the oil itself can cause severe burns.

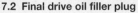

7.2 Final drive oil filler plug

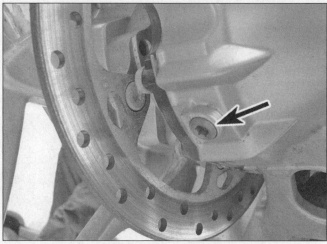

7.3 Final drive oil drain plug

1 Before changing the oil, ride the machine for a few miles so that it reaches normal operating temperature and the oil will drain easily. Make sure the bike is on level ground and support it on its centre stand. Remove the rear wheel (see Chapter 5).

2 Unscrew the oil filler plug, located on the left-hand side of the final drive housing, to act as a vent **(see illustration)**. Discard the sealing washer as a new one must be used. Clean any metal particles off the magnetic tip of the plug.

3 Position a clean drain tray below the housing, then unscrew the drain plug and allow the oil to drain – leave it several minutes to drain fully **(see illustration)**. Discard the sealing washer as a new one must be used.

4 When the oil has completely drained, fit the drain plug using a new sealing washer and tighten it to the torque setting specified at the beginning of this Chapter. Do not overtighten the plug as the threads in the casing could be damaged.

5 Inject fresh oil into the housing via the filler hole. Inject the exact amount specified with a clean syringe – do not use a syringe which has been in contact with any other fluids. BMW

produces a service tool for this purpose (Part No. 342551).

6 On completion, refit the filler plug, using a new sealing washer, and tighten it to the specified torque setting. Do not over-tighten the plug as the threads in the housing could be damaged.

7 Install the rear wheel (see Chapter 5).

8 Gearbox oil

⚠️ *Warning: Be careful when draining the oil, as the exhaust pipes, the engine/gearbox and the oil itself can cause severe burns.*

1 Before changing the oil, ride the machine for a few miles so that it reaches normal operating temperature and the oil will drain easily. Make sure the bike is on level ground and support it on its centre stand.

2 The gearbox oil filler and drain plugs are located on the right-hand side of the engine unit **(see illustrations 8.4a and b)**. If applicable, remove the fairing right-hand side panel to gain access (see Chapter 6).

3 Position a clean drain tray below the gearbox. To avoid the oil running over the hot exhaust system, use a piece of card to channel the oil from the drain plug into the tray.

HAYNES HiNT *An oil drain tray can be easily made by cutting away the front or back of an old oil container – it only needs to hold 1 litre.*

4 Unscrew the oil filler plug to act as a vent, then unscrew the drain plug and allow the oil to flow into the drain tray **(see illustrations)**. Discard the sealing washers on the filler plug and drain plug as a new ones should be used. Clean any metal particles off the magnetic drain plug **(see illustration)**.

5 When the oil has completely drained, fit the drain plug using a new sealing washer and tighten it to the torque setting specified at the beginning of this Chapter. Do not overtighten the plug as the threads in the casing could be damaged.

6 Refill the gearbox to the lower edge of the

8.4a Gearbox oil filler plug

8.4b Gearbox oil drain plug

8.4c Clean off any metal particles

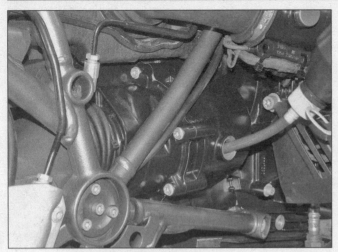

8.6a Refill the gearbox . . .

8.6b . . . to the lower edge of the filler hole

filler hole using the type and amount of oil specified at the beginning of this Chapter **(see illustrations)**.

7 Install the filler plug, using a new sealing washer, and tighten it to the specified torque setting **(see illustration)**. Do not over-tighten the plug as the threads in the casing could be damaged.

8.7 Fit a new sealing washer

9 Alternator drive belt

Special tool: *A drive belt installation tool is necessary for this job (see Step 7).*

1 The alternator belt is located behind

9.2a Undo the upper screws on both sides

the cover on the front of the engine unit. If applicable, remove the fairing left and right-hand side panels for access (see Chapter 6). On R1200 R models, follow the procedure in Chapter 2, Section 6, to remove the oil cooler.

2 Undo the screws securing the drive belt cover and remove the cover **(see illustrations)**.

3 To remove the drive belt, insert a large screwdriver or tyre lever behind the belt on the left-hand side, just before it engages with the crankshaft pulley, then lever the belt off the edge of the pulley. Turn the pulley clockwise (direction of normal engine rotation) with a spanner on the pulley nut, and carefully guide the belt all the way off with the lever **(see illustration)**.

4 Alternatively, to avoid damaging the belt, cut a section out of an old plastic oil bottle, approximately 150 mm x 60 mm. Position the plastic between the pulley and the drive belt, then turn the pulley clockwise and carefully

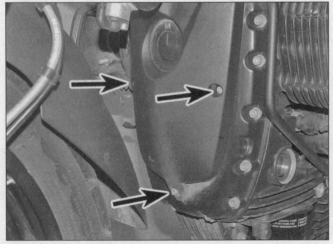

9.2b Undo the lower screws

9.2c Lift off the drive belt cover

9.3 Turn the pulley and guide the belt off

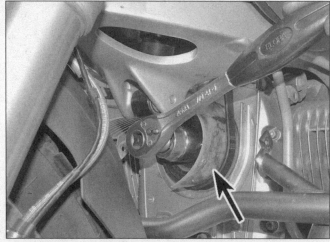

9.4 Trap the plastic (arrowed) between the belt and the pulley

9.7a Locate the belt on the service tool

9.7b Wind the belt onto the pulley . . .

9.7c . . . and remove the service tool

guide the plastic around the pulley underneath the belt **(see illustration)**. When the plastic is trapped around the lower half of the pulley, carefully lever the belt off at its lowest point.

5 Lift the belt off the alternator pulley.

6 To install the new belt you will require BMW service tool Part No. 123591.

7 Position the new belt over the alternator pulley, then fit the service tool over the crankshaft pulley nut and locate the lower end of the belt on the service tool **(see illustration)**. Turn the crankshaft clockwise and wind the new belt onto the crankshaft pulley until it is fully installed, then remove the service tool **(see illustrations)**. Turn the engine over with a spanner on the pulley nut to settle the belt.

Caution: Do not attempt to lever the new belt onto the crankshaft pulley. The belt and/or the surface of the pulley are likely to be damaged resulting in reduced service life of the belt.

8 Install the drive belt cover – take care not to over-tighten the cover screws.

9 On R1200 R models, install the oil cooler and check the engine oil level (see Chapter 2 and *Pre-ride checks*).

10 Install the remaining components in the reverse order of removal.

10 Clutch system

1 All models are fitted with an hydraulically operated clutch, for which there is no requirement for adjustment.

2 Check the fluid level in the reservoir (see *Pre-ride checks*). **Note:** *Clutch wear will cause the fluid level to rise gradually.*

3 Remove the body panels as applicable (see Chapter 6), then inspect the clutch hose, its connections, the master cylinder on the handlebars and the release cylinder at the rear of the gearbox for signs of fluid leakage, deterioration and wear.

4 If any leaks or damage are found they must be rectified immediately. Refer to Chapter 2 for details of the clutch release mechanism components.

5 Check the operation of the clutch. If there is evidence of air in the system (spongy feel to the lever, difficulty in engaging gear), bleed

the system (see Chapter 2). If the lever feels stiff or sticky, check the operation of the master cylinder and the release cylinder (see Chapter 2).

6 The clutch lever has a span adjuster that alters the distance of the lever from the handlebar. The setting is altered by turning the adjuster screw **(see illustration)**. Push the lever forwards, then turn the adjuster clockwise to increase the span and anti-clockwise to decrease it.

10.6 Location of the clutch lever span adjuster

11.7 Location of the brake lever span adjuster

11.10 Location of the wear indicator grooves on front brake pads

11 Brake system

Brake system check

1 Make sure all brake fasteners are tight.

2 Make sure the fluid level in the front and rear brake reservoirs is correct (see *Pre-ride checks*).

3 Check the brake pads and discs for wear (see Steps 10 to 16).

4 Remove the body panels as applicable (see Chapter 6), then look for leaks at the hose and pipe connections and check for damage to the hoses.

5 If the brake lever or pedal feels spongy, it is likely that there is air in the brake system and it will need bleeding – follow the procedure in Chapter 5.

Front brake lever

6 Check the brake lever for loose fittings, improper or rough action, excessive play, bends, and other damage. Replace any damaged parts with new ones (see Chapter 5).

7 The front brake lever has a span adjuster that alters the distance of the lever from the handlebar. The setting is altered by turning the adjuster screw **(see illustration)**. Push the lever forwards, then turn the adjuster clockwise to increase the span and anti-clockwise to decrease it.

Rear brake pedal

8 Check the brake pedal for loose fittings, improper or rough action, excessive play, bends, and other damage. Replace any damaged parts with new ones. Check the brake pedal freeplay (see Chapter 4, Section 3).

Brake light

9 Make sure the brake light operates when the front brake lever is pulled in and also when the rear brake pedal is depressed. On machines equipped with ABS, the brake light switches are incorporated in the ABS modulator assembly and are maintenance-free. On machines not fitted with ABS, the switches are located on the underside of the front brake lever assembly and on the inside of the brake pedal bracket. The switches are not adjustable – if they fail to work, check their operation (see Chapter 7).

Brake pad wear check

Note: *Uneven pad wear in any one caliper indicates sticking piston(s) – refer to Chapter 5 to displace and clean the calipers.*

10 Pad wear can be determined without removing them from the caliper. On the front brakes, the friction material has wear indicator grooves which are visible on the bottom edge of each pad – the grooves are visible from the front of the machine **(see illustration)**. If the friction material has worn down to the bottom of the grooves, the pads must be renewed (see Chapter 5).

11 On the rear brake, a counter-bored hole in the back of the innermost pad denotes the wear limit when viewed through a hole in the caliper from the left-hand side **(see illustration)**. If the surface of the brake disc is visible through the hole, the pads must be renewed (see Chapter 5). In addition, the rear brake caliper pad pin is marked with wear indicator grooves **(see illustration)**. When 3 grooves are visible 75%

11.11a Check rear brake pad wear through hole in backing plate

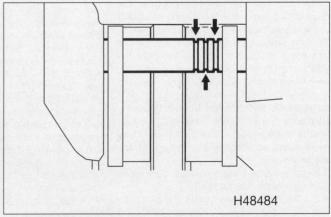

H48484

11.11b Wear indicator grooves on rear caliper pad pin

11.14 Inspect the surface of the brake discs

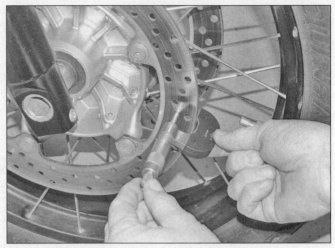

11.15 Measure disc thickness with a micrometer

of pad thickness remains; 2 grooves indicates 50% of pad thickness remains and 1 groove indicates only 25% remains.

12 If required, removing the pads on the front brakes and displacing the caliper on the rear brake will allow closer inspection (see Chapter 5). If the pads have no wear indicators, measure the thickness of the friction material and compare the result with the specification at the beginning of this Chapter.

13 Always renew both pads in the caliper at the same time, and, in the case of the front brake, renew both sets of pads at the same time (see Chapter 5).

Brake discs

14 Inspect the front and rear brake discs for wear and damage – light scratches are normal after use and won't affect brake operation, but deep grooves and heavy score marks will reduce braking efficiency and accelerate pad wear **(see illustration)**. If the disc is badly grooved, have it machined by a brake specialist, or fit a new disc (see Chapter 5).

15 Measure the thickness of the brake discs and compare the results with the specifications at the beginning of this Chapter **(see illustration)**. If any disc is worn down to the minimum thickness it should be renewed.

16 Follow the procedure in Chapter 5 to check disc runout.

Brake fluid change

17 The brake fluid should be changed at the prescribed service interval – follow the procedure in Chapter 5.

Brake hoses

18 The flexible hoses will deteriorate in time – regular checks should be made for damage and leaks, particularly where the hose joins the banjo union and where it passes through hose guides **(see illustrations)**. Damaged or leaking hoses must be renewed (see Chapter 5).

19 If a brake hose is disconnected, air will enter the brake system and the system will need bleeding – follow the procedure in

Chapter 5 to renew a brake hose. Always fit new sealing washers on both sides of a brake hose banjo union.

Brake caliper and master cylinder seals

20 Hydraulic seals will deteriorate over a period of time, particularly if the bike has been in long-term storage, and lose their

11.18a Inspect the front brake hose . . .

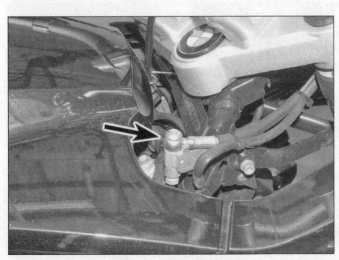

11.18b . . . and hose unions

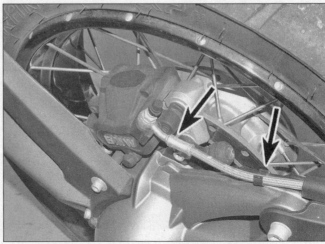

11.18c Inspect rear brake hose union and guide

effectiveness, leading to sticking operation or fluid loss, or allowing the ingress of air and dirt.

21 If the brake caliper shows signs of sticking, remove the brake pads from the caliper (see Chapter 5). Carefully ease up the dust seals around the caliper pistons and check for fluid behind the seals. If brake fluid is leaking from the caliper, the piston seals have failed and the caliper must be overhauled – this procedure must be undertaken by a BMW dealer.

22 If brake fluid is leaking from the front or rear master cylinder a new master cylinder must be fitted – seal kits are not available. Follow the procedure in Chapter 5 to renew the master cylinder.

12 Nuts and bolts

1 Since vibration of the machine tends to loosen fasteners, all nuts, bolts, screws, etc. should be periodically checked for proper tightness.

2 Pay particular attention to the following:
Spark plugs
Engine and gearbox oil filler and drain plugs
Gearchange lever, front brake lever and rear brake pedal bolts
Footrest and stand bolts
Engine mounting bolts
Shock absorber mounting bolts and Telelever/swingarm pivot bolts
Handlebar clamp bolts
Front axle and axle clamp bolt
Front fork yoke bolts
Rear wheel bolts
Brake caliper mounting bolts
Brake hose banjo bolts and caliper bleed valves
Brake disc bolts
Exhaust system bolts/nuts

3 If a torque wrench is available, use it together with the torque specifications at the beginning of this and other Chapters.

13 Wheels and wheel bearings

General

1 Make sure the valve stem cap is in place and tight **(see illustration)**. Check the valve stem for signs of damage and have it renewed if necessary. Note that on machines fitted with tyre pressure sensors, the sensor is integral with the valve assembly as indicated by the decal on the wheel rim.

2 Check that the wheel balance weights are fixed firmly to the wheel rim **(see illustration)**. If there are signs that a weight has fallen off, have the wheel rebalanced by a motorcycle tyre specialist.

3 Check the wheel runout and front/rear wheel alignment as described in Chapter 5.

Cast wheels

4 Cast wheels are virtually maintenance free, but they should be kept clean and checked periodically for cracks and other damage. Never attempt to repair damaged cast wheels; they must be replaced with new ones.

Wire spoked wheels

5 Inspect the spokes for damage, breakage or corrosion. A single loose spoke can be tightened carefully (see Chapter 5), but if a number of spokes are loose, follow the procedure in Chapter 5 to check the radial and axial runout of the wheel and, if necessary, take it to a wheel building expert for correction. A broken or bent spoke must be renewed immediately because the load taken by it will be transferred to adjacent spokes which may in turn fail.

13.1 Check condition of valve stem cap

Front wheel bearings

6 The bearings in the front wheel will wear over a period of time and result in handling problems.

7 Support the motorcycle upright on its centre stand or an auxiliary stand, and take the weight off the front wheel. Check for any play in the bearings by pushing and pulling the wheel against the hub **(see illustration)**. Also spin the wheel and check that it rotates smoothly.

8 If any play is detected in the hub, or if the wheel does not rotate smoothly (and this is not due to brake drag), remove the wheel and inspect the bearings for wear or damage (see Chapter 5).

Final drive bearings

9 The rear wheel and brake disc are bolted to the final drive unit and pivot on the bearings contained within the drive unit – there are no bearings in the rear wheel. Before checking for play, first check that the rear wheel bolts are tight – refer to the torque setting in the Specifications section of this Chapter.

10 Support the motorcycle upright on its centre stand or an auxiliary stand, and take the weight off the rear wheel. Grasp the wheel and check for any play between the rear wheel and final

13.2 Balance weights must be firmly attached to the wheel rim

13.7 Checking for play in the front wheel bearings

13.10 Checking for play in the final drive bearings

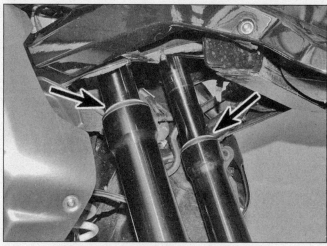

14.3 Check around the dust seals for oil leakage

drive unit **(see illustration)**. If play is evident the final drive bearings may need attention – have the machine checked by a BMW dealer. **Note:** *Play felt at the rear wheel may be due to worn pivot bearings between the swingarm and the final drive unit (see Section 14).*

14 Suspension

1 The suspension components must be maintained in top operating condition to ensure rider safety. Loose, worn or damaged suspension parts decrease the motorcycle's stability and control and are potentially dangerous.

Front suspension

2 Check that the front suspension operates smoothly and without binding. Note that due to its unconventional design, the front suspension cannot be checked by pushing and pulling on the handlebars. If problems have been noted whilst riding the bike, the front fork mountings and Telelever pivots should be dismantled and checked thoroughly (see Chapter 4).

3 Inspect the area above the dust seal on the fork tubes for signs of oil leakage, then carefully lever up the dust seal using a flat-bladed screwdriver and inspect the area around the fork seal **(see illustration)**. If leakage is evident, the seals must be renewed (see Chapter 4).

4 Inspect the shock absorber for pitting on the damper rod and fluid leakage **(see illustration)**. If leakage is found, the shock should be renewed (see Chapter 4). Ensure that the upper and lower mountings are tight.

Rear suspension

5 Remove the bodywork as necessary to access the rear suspension (see Chapter 6).

Inspect the shock absorber for pitting on the damper rod and fluid leakage. If leakage is found, the shock should be renewed (see Chapter 4). Ensure that the upper and lower mountings are tight.

6 With the aid of an assistant to support the bike, compress the rear suspension several times by pressing down on the passenger grab-rail. It should move up and down freely without binding. If any binding is felt, the worn or faulty component must be identified and replaced. The problem could be due to either the shock absorber or the swingarm components.

7 Grasp the top of the rear wheel and pull it upwards – there should be no discernible freeplay before the shock absorber begins to compress **(see illustration)**. If freeplay is felt, check that the shock absorber mountings are tight, then check for wear in the shock absorber mountings.

8 Support the motorcycle upright on its centre stand so that the rear wheel is off the

14.4 Inspect the shock for leakage and corrosion

14.7 Checking for play in the shock absorber mountings

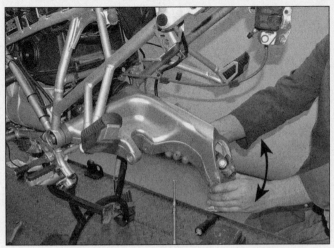

14.10a Checking for free movement of the swingarm

14.10b Checking for freeplay in the final drive unit pivot bearings

ground. Grab the swingarm and rock it from side to side to check for freeplay. If freeplay is detected, this could be due to worn swingarm bearings or loose pivots.

9 First check that the pivots are tightened correctly (see Chapter 4). Then remove the rear wheel (see Chapter 5) and shock absorber (see Chapter 4) to make an accurate assessment of the swingarm components.

10 The swingarm should move smoothly about its pivots, without any binding or rough spots **(see illustration)**. There should be no discernible freeplay felt front-to-back or side-to-side. Next, check for freeplay in the bearings between the swingarm and the final drive unit **(see illustration)**.

11 If bearing damage or freeplay is evident, the swingarm should be removed and the swingarm and final drive unit bearings and pivots inspected (see Chapter 4).

Chapter 2
Engine, clutch and transmission

Contents

Section number

Alternator . . . . see Chapter 7
Alternator drive pulley and engine timing cover. 16
Auxiliary shaft, camchains and tensioner/guide blades. 25
Auxiliary shaft drive chain, tensioner and sprockets 18
Balancer shaft gears and balancer shaft 17
Camchain tensioners 8
Cam followers and camshafts 9
Clutch. 20
Clutch release mechanism. 21
Clutch fluid level check . . . . see Pre-ride checks
Clutch system check . . . . see Chapter 1
Component access 2
Connecting rods. 15
Crankcase 22
Crankshaft bearings and connecting rod big-end bearings
– general information 23
Crankshaft main and guide bearings 24
Cylinders 12
Cylinder heads removal and installation. 10
Cylinder head and valve overhaul 11
Engine overhaul – general information. 5
Engine oil filter and oil change . . . . see Chapter 1
Engine oil level check. . . . . see Pre-ride checks

Section number

Engine removal and installation 4
Engine wear assessment 3
Gearbox oil level check and oil change . . . . see Chapter 1
Gearbox oil seals 27
Gearbox removal and installation. 26
Gearchange mechanism 29
Gear position sensor . . . . see Chapter 3
General information 1
Oil cooler and hoses. 6
Oil pressure switch and level indicator . . . . see Chapter 7
Oil pump, pressure relief valve and thermostat 19
Oil temperature sensor . . . . see Chapter 3
Pistons 13
Piston rings. 14
Running-in procedure. 31
Selector drum and forks. 28
Spark plugs . . . . see Chapter 1
Starter motor . . . . 4 (also see Chapter 7)
Transmission shafts 30
Valve clearances. . . . . see Chapter 1
Valve covers 7
Valve/valve seat/valve guide servicing 11

Degrees of difficulty

| **Easy,** suitable for novice with little experience | 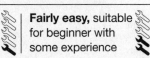 | **Fairly easy,** suitable for beginner with some experience | | **Fairly difficult,** suitable for competent DIY mechanic | | **Difficult,** suitable for experienced DIY mechanic | | **Very difficult,** suitable for expert DIY or professional | |

Specifications

General

Cylinder compression

Good	203 psi (14 Bar)
Normal	174 psi (12 Bar)
Poor	145 psi (10 Bar)
Engine oil pressure (at 80°C operating temperature).	80 to 109 psi (5.5 to 7.5 Bar)
Cylinder identification.	No. 1 cylinder (left), No. 2 cylinder (right)

Valves and valve guides

Valve clearances.	see Chapter 1

Valve radial clearance

Intake

Standard.	0.023 to 0.043 mm
Service limit	0.15 mm

Exhaust

Standard.	0.040 to 0.066 mm
Service limit	0.17 mm

Valve guides

Inside diameter.	5.5 to 5.512 mm

Cylinders

Bore diameter	
Group A	
Standard...	100.992 to 101.000 mm
Service limit	101.050 mm
Group B	
Standard...	101.000 to 101.008 mm
Service limit	101.058 mm
Group A/B	
Standard...	100.992 to 101.008 mm
Service limit	101.058 mm
Ovality (out-of-round) service limit	
20 mm from top	0.010 mm
100 mm from top	0.015 mm
Cylinder stud installed height...............................	159.5 to 161.5 mm

Pistons

Piston diameter – measured 6 mm up from bottom edge at 90° to piston pin axis	
Group A/B	
Standard...	100.953 to 100.977 mm
Service limit	100.90 mm
Piston-to-bore clearance	
Standard...	0.055 to 0.075 mm
Service limit	0.120 mm
Piston pin diameter	
Standard...	21.995 to 22.000 mm
Service limit	21.960 mm

Piston rings

Ring installation	'TOP' mark facing up
Top and second rings	
Ring end gap (installed)	
Standard...	0.10 to 0.30 mm
Service limit	0.80 mm
Oil ring	
Ring end gap (installed)	
Standard...	0.30 to 0.60 mm
Service limit	1.20 mm

Connecting rods

Small-end internal diameter................................	24.0 to 24.021 mm
Radial play of small-end bearing bore	
Standard...	0.015 to 0.030 mm
Service limit	0.06 mm
Big-end bearing shell identification – colour mark on edge of shells	
Connecting rod side....................................	blue
Rod cap side	red
Big-end bore diameter without bearing shells	51.000 to 51.013 mm
Crankpin diameter – paint mark on front crank web	
Stage 0	no paint mark
Stage 1 undersize (-0.25 mm)	paint mark
Stage 0	47.975 to 47.991 mm
Stage 1 (-0.25 mm)....................................	47.725 to 47.741 mm
Crankpin bearing width	24.665 to 24.795 mm
Big-end radial clearance	
Standard...	0.025 to 0.075 mm
Service limit	0.13 mm
Big-end side clearance	
Standard...	0.130 to 0.312 mm
Service limit	0.5 mm
Weight class identification	
2 white dots (class 0).................................	559.0 to 564.9 g
2 blue dots (class1)...................................	565.0 to 570.9 g
3 white dots (class 2).................................	571.0 to 576.9 g
3 yellow dots (class 3)................................	577.0 to 582.9 g
1 blue dot (class 4)..................................	583.0 to 588.9 g

Oil pump

Pump rotor thickness
  Pump 1 (cooling circuit) . . . . 10.965 mm
  Pump 2 (lubricating circuit). . . . . 9.965 mm
Clearance (end-float)
  Service limit . . . . 0.25 mm

Crankshaft and bearings

Crankshaft identification – paint mark on front crank web
  Stage 0 . . . . no paint mark
  Stage 1 undersize (-0.25 mm) . . . . paint mark
Crankshaft end-float
  Standard. . . . . 0.125 to 0.208 mm
  Service limit . . . . 0.24 mm
Main bearing oil clearance
  Standard. . . . . 0.023 to 0.07 mm
  Service limit . . . . 0.095 mm
Main bearing bore diameter in crankcase . . . . 64.960 to 64.979 mm
Main bearing shell identification – colour mark on edge of shells
  Stage 0
    Main bearing shell inside diameter
      Green . . . . 59.971 to 60.005 mm
      Yellow . . . . 59.718 to 59.968 mm
    Crankshaft journal diameter
      Green . . . . 59.939 to 59.948 mm
      Yellow . . . . 59.949 to 59.958 mm
  Stage 1 (re-ground crankshaft)
    Main bearing shell inside diameter
      Green . . . . 59.721 to 59.755 mm
      Yellow . . . . 59.751 to 60.001 mm
    Crankshaft journal diameter
      Green . . . . 59.689 to 59.698 mm
      Yellow . . . . 59.699 to 59.708 mm
Crankshaft main bearing journal width. . . . . 25.02 to 25.053 mm
Guide bearing shell identification – colour mark on edge of shells
  Stage 0
    Crankshaft journal diameter
      Green . . . . 59.939 to 59.948 mm
      Yellow . . . . 59.949 to 59.958 mm
  Stage 1
    Crankshaft journal diameter
      Green . . . . 59.689 to 59.698 mm
      Yellow . . . . 59.699 to 59.708 mm
Guide bearing oil clearance
  Standard. . . . . 0.020 to 0.066 mm
  Service limit . . . . 0.095 mm
Guide bearing width. . . . . 24.89 to 24.94 mm

Auxiliary shaft

Radial clearance
  Standard front. . . . . 0.025 to 0.075 mm
  Standard rear . . . . 0.020 to 0.062 mm
  Service limit . . . . 0.170 mm

Clutch

Friction plate thickness (service limit). . . . . 4.4 to 4.6 mm
Clutch fluid . . . . Vitamol V10

Transmission

Gear ratios (no. of teeth)
  1st gear
    Standard. . . . . 2.375 to 1 (38/16T)
    Optional GS Adventure. . . . . 2.600 to 1 (39/15T)
  2nd gear . . . . 1.696 to 1 (39/23T)
  3rd gear . . . . 1.296 to 1 (35/27T)
  4th gear . . . . 1.065 to 1 (33/31T)
  5th gear . . . . 0.939 to 1 (31/33T)
  6th gear . . . . 0.848 to 1 (28/33T)

Transmission (continued)

Primary drive ratio .... 1.737 to 1

Final drive ratio
 R1200 GS and GS Adventure................................. 2.91 to 1
 R1200 RT .... 2.62 to 1
 R1200 R .... 2.75 to 1

Input shaft
 Assembled length... 181.85 to 181.90 mm

Intermediate shaft
 Total assembled length.................................... 181.85 to 181.90 mm
 4th gear endplay... 0.10 to 0.50 mm
 5th gear endplay... 0.10 to 0.25 mm

Output shaft
 Front end assembled length.............................. 117.50 to 117.55 mm
 Total assembled length.................................... 184.60 to 184.65 mm
 1st gear endplay... 0.15 to 0.30 mm
 2nd gear endplay.. 0.15 to 0.41 mm
 3rd gear endplay... 0.15 to 0.30 mm
 6th gear endplay... 0.15 to 0.35 mm

Selector forks
 2nd/3rd gear selector fork contact face width................. 4.825 to 4.90 mm
 1st/6th gear selector fork recess width .... 4.050 to 4.125 mm
 4th/5th gear selector fork recess width .... 4.050 to 4.125 mm

Gear shift sliding sleeves
 2nd/3rd gear sliding sleeve selector fork recess width .... 5.00 to 5.10 mm
 1st/6th gear sliding sleeve selector fork web width.............. 3.90 to 4.00 mm
 4th/5th gear sliding sleeve selector fork web width.............. 3.90 to 4.00 mm
 2nd/3rd gear sliding sleeve endplay......................... 0.100 to 0.275 mm
 4th/5th gear selector fork clearance........................ 0.050 to 0.225 mm
 1st/6th gear selector fork clearance........................ 0.050 to 0.225 mm

Selector drum
 Total assembled length.................................... 141.4 to 141.5 mm

Torque settings

ABS modulator mounting bolts .... 8 Nm

Alternator belt cover screws................................. 5 Nm

Alternator belt drive pulley nut
 Initial stage setting.. 40 Nm
 Final setting .... 140 Nm

Auxiliary shaft drive sprocket bolts .... 8 Nm

Auxiliary shaft driven sprocket bolts .... 8 Nm

Auxiliary shaft drive chain tensioner bolts .... 8 Nm

Balancer shaft gear nut .... 75 Nm

Balance weight bolt
 Initial setting .... 10 Nm
 Final setting .... 90°

Camchain guide and tensioner blade 10 mm bolts................. 18 Nm

Camchain guide and tensioner blade 6 mm bolts................. 8 Nm

Camchain tensioner... 32 Nm

Camshaft holder bolts....................................... 10 Nm

Camshaft sprocket bolt .... 65 Nm

Clutch cover plate bolts..................................... 12 Nm

Clutch housing bolts
 Initial setting.. 40 Nm
 Final setting .... angle-tighten 40°

Clutch hose banjo bolts..................................... 18 Nm

Clutch release cylinder mounting bolts .... 8 Nm

Clutch top cover screws..................................... 8 Nm

Connecting rod big-end bolts
 1st stage setting... 5 Nm
 2nd stage setting.. 20 Nm
 Final setting .... 105°

Crankcase bolts
 6 mm bolts.. 8 Nm
 8 mm bolts.. 19 Nm
 10 mm bolts
  Initial setting .... 25 Nm
  Final setting .... angle-tighten 90°

Torque settings (continued)

Crankshaft position sensor screw	8 Nm
Cylinder 6 mm screws	8 Nm
Cylinder head 10 mm nut	
Initial setting	20 Nm
Second stage setting	angle-tighten 75°
Final setting	angle-tighten 75°
Cylinder head 8 mm bolt	20 Nm
Cylinder head 6 mm screw	9 Nm
Engine breather union	8 Nm
Engine mountings	
Front sub-frame	
Front strut-to-engine through-bolt	110 Nm
Rear strut to rear sub-frame/engine bolts	38 Nm
Telelever pivot bolt – all models	
Initial stage setting	45 Nm
Final setting	72 Nm
Rear sub-frame	
Upper mounting bolts	38 Nm
Lower mounting bolts	55 Nm
Rear front strut to rear sub-frame/engine bolts	38 Nm
Frame to gearbox	28 Nm
Gear position sensor bolts	9 Nm
Gearbox cover bolts	9 Nm
Gearchange lever pinch bolt	8 Nm
Gearchange mechanism stopper arm pivot bolt	8 Nm
Intake manifold screws	8 Nm
Knock sensor bolt	19 Nm
Oil cooler feed pipe bolts	8 Nm
Oil cooler return pipe banjo bolt	35 Nm
Oil level indicator bolts	9 Nm
Oil pump mounting bolts	
Initial setting	4 Nm
Final setting	angle-tighten 90°
Oil pressure relief valve	42 Nm
Oil pressure switch	30 Nm
Oil temperature sensor	16 Nm
Oil strainer bolts	8 Nm
Oil thermostat/cooler feed pipe flange bolts	8 Nm
Temperature sensor	10 Nm
Timing chain rail to timing gear carrier	8 Nm
Timing cover screws	9 Nm
Timing gear carrier jump stop	10 Nm
Valve cover bolts	10 Nm
Valve cover guard bolts	10 Nm

1 General information

The engine unit is an air/oil-cooled, horizontally-opposed twin. There are four valves per cylinder, operated by twin overhead camshafts above each cylinder. The camshafts are chain driven off the auxiliary shaft, which in turn is driven by chain off the crankshaft. The auxiliary shaft runs at half crankshaft speed.

The engine incorporates a balancer shaft.

The separate engine and gearbox cases are constructed from aluminium alloy. The engine and gearbox units are bolted together with a dry, single plate diaphragm clutch located between the two. The engine/gearbox unit supports the front and rear suspension systems – there is no motorcycle frame in the conventional sense.

The crankcase is divided vertically and incorporates a wet sump, pressure-fed lubrication system which utilises a dual-rotor oil pump driven by the auxiliary shaft. An oil filter is located externally on the underside of the crankcase. To assist engine cooling, oil is pumped to a cooler mounted at the front of the machine, underneath the headlight.

Power from the crankshaft is routed to the transmission input shaft in the gearbox via the clutch. The input shaft has a sprung damper. The transmission is a six-speed constant-mesh unit, and drive to the rear wheel is by shaft via bevel gears in a final drive unit.

2 Component access

Operations possible with the engine in the frame

The components and assemblies listed below can be removed without having to remove the front or rear sub-frames and suspension systems.

Oil cooler and hoses
Valve covers
Camchain tensioners
Cam follower and camshaft assemblies
Cylinder heads and valves

Cylinders, pistons and piston rings
Connecting rods and bearings
Alternator drive belt and pulley
Alternator
Balancer shaft gears
Auxiliary shaft sprockets and chain
Oil pump, pressure relief valve and oil
  thermostat
Starter motor
Clutch release cylinder

Operations requiring removal of the front or rear sub-frames

It is necessary to remove either the front or rear sub-frames and suspension systems, or both, to gain access to the following components.

Gearbox, gearchange mechanism and
  selector drum/forks
Clutch
Auxiliary shaft
Camchains, tensioner blades and guide
  blades
Crankshaft and bearings
Oil strainers

3 Engine wear assessment

 Warning: Be careful when working on the hot engine – the exhaust pipes, the engine and engine components can cause severe burns.

Cylinder compression test

Special tools: *A compression gauge with an appropriate threaded adapter (see illustration 3.6) and spark plug cap/ignition coil extractor are necessary for this procedure.*

1 Among other things, poor starting and engine performance may be caused by leaking valves, a leaking head gasket or worn pistons, rings and/or cylinder walls. A cylinder compression check will help pinpoint these conditions.

2 Before carrying out the test, check that the valve clearances are correct (see Chapter 1).

3 Run the engine until it reaches normal operating temperature, then turn the ignition OFF. Support the machine on its centre stand or on an auxiliary stand.

4 Follow the procedure in Chapter 1, Section 5,

3.6 Using the cylinder compression gauge and adapter

and disconnect the ignition coils from all four spark plugs, then unscrew the primary spark plugs from both cylinder heads.

5 Reconnect the ignition coil wiring connectors. Fit the primary spark plugs back into their coils and install two spare spark plugs in the secondary coils. Arrange the plugs so that their metal bodies are earthed against the adjacent cylinder.

6 Working on the first cylinder to be tested, thread the adapter into the spark plug hole then install the compression gauge **(see illustration)**.

7 Open the throttle fully and crank the engine over on the starter motor until the gauge reading stabilises – after one or two revolutions the pressure should build up to a maximum figure and then remain stable. Make a note of the pressure reading and then repeat the procedure on the other cylinder. Turn the ignition OFF when the test has been completed.

8 Compare the results with the specifications at the beginning of this Chapter. If they are both within the specified range (normal to good) and relatively equal, the engine is in good condition. If there is a marked difference between the readings, or if the readings are lower than specified, inspection of one or both engine top-ends is required (see Sections 10 to 14).

9 Follow the procedure in Chapter 1, Section 5, and install the spark plugs and coils.

Note: *High compression pressure indicates excessive carbon build-up in the combustion chamber and on the top of the piston. If this is the case, remove the cylinder heads and clean the carbon deposits off. Note that excessive carbon build-up is less likely with the use of modern fuels.*

Engine oil pressure check

Special tools: *An oil pressure gauge with an appropriate threaded adapter is necessary for this procedure.*

Note: *Even if the engine appears to be in good condition and the oil pressure warning light is not coming on, an oil pressure check can provide useful information about the internal condition of the engine.*

10 The oil pressure warning light should come on together with a red general warning light when the ignition switch is first turned ON – this is part of the electronic 'self-checking' system and serves as a check that the warning indicators are working. If the oil pressure light comes on whilst the engine is running, low oil pressure is indicated – stop the engine immediately and carry out an oil level check (see *Pre-ride checks*).

11 If the oil level is correct, test the oil pressure switch (see Chapter 7). If the switch is good, carry out an oil pressure check.

12 To check the oil pressure, a suitable gauge and adapter piece (which screws into the crankcase) will be needed – see the example shown in Section 3 of *Reference* at the end of this manual.

13 Run the engine until it reaches normal

operating temperature then turn the ignition OFF. Support the bike upright on its centre stand.

14 Unscrew the oil pressure switch (see Chapter 7) then quickly screw the adapter into the crankcase threads. Connect the pressure gauge to the adapter.

15 Start the engine and increase the engine speed whilst watching the gauge reading. Make a note of the pressure reading, then stop the engine, unscrew the gauge and adapter from the crankcase and install the oil pressure switch.

16 The oil pressure should be similar to that given in the *Specifications* at the beginning of this Chapter. If the pressure is significantly lower than that specified, either the pressure relief valve is stuck open, the oil strainer(s) or filter is blocked, the oil pump is worn or there is other engine wear or damage.

17 Begin diagnosis by checking the pressure relief valve (see Section 19) and fitting a new oil filter (see Chapter 1). Next inspect the oil pump (see Section 19) and finally the strainer – this last procedure requires engine removal and crankcase separation (see Section 22). If everything is in good condition, it is likely that the crankshaft bearing oil clearances are excessive and the engine needs to be overhauled.

18 If the pressure is too high, either an oil passage is clogged, the relief valve is stuck closed or the wrong grade of oil is being used.

4 Engine removal and installation

Note 1: *The engine is not removed from the bike, rather the rest of the bike is removed from around the engine. For ease of operation, the rear suspension and its sub-frame are removed first, followed by the front suspension and its sub-frame. If required, only one of the sub-frames can be removed independently of the other to gain access to a specific area of the engine/gearbox unit.*

Note 2: *The machines covered in this manual were available from new fitted with a range of optional electrical extras. When working on your machine, take care to ensure that all relevant electrical components are disconnected on disassembly and subsequently reconnected during the rebuild. Always take the precaution of disconnecting the battery negative (-) terminal before disconnecting an electrical wiring connector.*

Removal

1 Support the bike upright on its centre stand or on an auxiliary stand. Prior to removing the rear sub-frame, the engine will have to be supported underneath the crankcase; BMW produces an engine jack and adapter for this purpose (Part Nos. 001571, 001572 and 001575). Provision should be made to secure the engine unit to prevent it toppling over – this can be achieved by securing the cylinders to both sides of the motorcycle ramp with tie-down straps.

2 Remove the seat, the frame side panels

4.6a Bolt secures front sump guard bracket

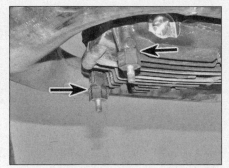

4.6b Fit spanner to upper end of rear sump guard mountings

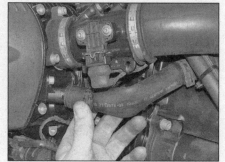

4.11 Remove the engine breather hose

4.18a Cut the cable-ties on the frame . . .

4.18b . . . and the rear mudguard

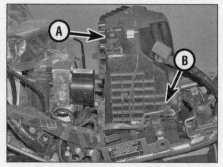

4.20a Intake air temperature sensor (A) and sidestand switch (B) wiring connectors

and the fairing side panels, as appropriate to your model, to gain access to the engine and related components (see Chapter 6). On R1200 GS Adventure models, remove the front crash bar assembly. On R1200 RT models, remove the left and right-hand fairing brackets.

3 Remove the fuel tank panels (see Chapter 6).

4 Remove the battery (see Chapter 7).

5 If the engine is dirty, particularly around its mountings, wash it thoroughly before starting any major dismantling work. This will make work much easier and rule out the possibility of dirt falling into some vital component.

6 Drain the engine oil and remove the oil filter (see Chapter 1). If work is being carried out on the gearbox, drain the gearbox oil (see Chapter 1). If applicable, undo the bolt securing the front sump guard bracket and remove the bracket, and unscrew the rear sump guard mountings **(see illustrations)**.

7 Remove the air intake duct (see Chapter 1, Section 6).

8 Remove the fuel tank (see Chapter 3).

9 Follow the procedure in Chapter 1, Section 5, and remove the primary and secondary ignition coils.

10 Where fitted, remove the crash bars (see Chapter 6).

11 Release the clips securing the engine breather hose to the air filter housing and pull the hose off **(see illustration)**.

12 Follow the procedure in Chapter 3 and remove both throttle bodies from the intake manifolds. Remove the throttle cable splitter.

13 On R1200 RT models, remove the left-hand footrest bracket (see Chapter 4).

14 Remove the exhaust system and exhaust control valve servo motor (see Chapter 3).

15 On R1200 RT models, remove the right-hand footrest bracket (see Chapter 4).

16 Remove the rear carrier and, if applicable the seat cowling (see Chapter 6).

17 Remove the rear light unit (see Chapter 7).

18 Displace any electrical units (such as the RDC tyre pressure control unit and the BMW diagnostic tester connector) located on the top of the rear mudguard (see Chapter 6). Note the location of the cable-ties securing the wiring to the mudguard and rear sub-frame, then cut the ties and secure the wiring well clear of the rear sub-frame **(see illustrations)**.

19 Remove the rear mudguard (see Chapter 6).

20 Disconnect the wiring connectors for the sidestand switch, intake air temperature sensor and rear wheel speed sensor **(see illustrations)**. On machines not fitted with ABS, disconnect the rear brake light switch wiring connector **(see illustration)**. Undo the screws securing the wiring loom guide and lift it off the sub-frame **(see illustration)**.

4.20b Rear wheel speed sensor wiring connector

4.20c Disconnect the rear brake light switch wiring connector

4.20d Undo the screws securing the wiring loom guide

4.22a Remove the rear brake hose guide

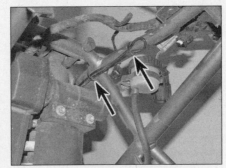

4.22b Ties secure speed sensor wiring

4.24 Remove the swingarm/final drive unit assembly

4.25a Release the clip . . .

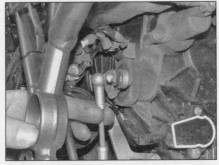

4.25b . . . and disconnect the gearchange rod

4.26a Displace the clutch release cylinder

4.26b Withdraw the clutch pushrod (arrowed) . . .

21 Remove the rear wheel (see Chapter 5).
22 Undo the screws securing the rear brake hose guide and lift the guide off the Paralever arm (see illustration). Trace the wiring from the rear wheel speed sensor – note the location of the cable-ties securing the wiring to the frame (see illustration), then cut the ties and secure the wiring next to the final drive unit, well clear of the rear sub-frame.
23 Displace the rear brake caliper (see Chapter 5), then secure the caliper to the rear sub-frame. Note that it is not necessary to disconnect the brake hose from the caliper.
24 Follow the procedure in Chapter 4 and remove the rear shock absorber, withdraw the drive shaft from the swingarm and remove the swingarm/final drive unit assembly (see illustration).
25 Release the clip securing the gearchange rod to the lever on the selector shaft and disconnect the rod (see illustrations).
26 Note the location of the cable-ties securing the clutch hose to the frame, then cut the ties. Undo the bolts securing the clutch release cylinder to the back of the gearbox and position the cylinder clear of the rear sub-frame (see illustration). Withdraw the clutch pushrod for safekeeping, noting how it fits – note the location of the seal on the pushrod (see illustrations).
27 On machines fitted with ABS, undo the flare nuts securing the rear brake pipes to the ABS modulator (see illustration). Wrap a

4.26c . . . noting the location of the seal

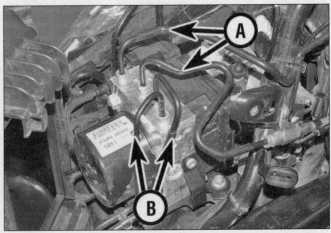

4.27 Front brake pipes (A) and rear brake pipes (B) on ABS modulator

4.29 Ensure that the engine/front suspension assembly is securely supported

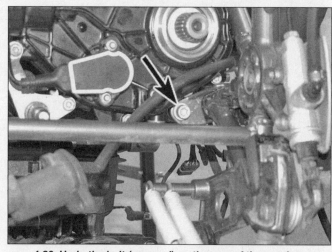

4.30 Undo the bolt (arrowed) on the rear of the gearbox

clean rag around the modulator to catch any spilled brake fluid and be prepared to catch any residual fluid in the pipes. Seal the open pipes with suitable caps and cover the unions on the modulator with duct tape to prevent dirt entering.

28 Check that all the wiring is free from the rear sub-frame.

29 If not already done, place a support underneath the crankcase and secure the engine unit to prevent it toppling over (see illustration).

30 Undo the bolt securing the rear sub-frame to the rear of the gearbox (see illustration).

31 To hold the front sub-frame in position while the rear sub-frame is removed, prepare two studs 25 mm long cut from suitable M10 bolts (see illustration). Cut a screwdriver slot in one end of each stud.

32 Working on both sides of the machine, undo the uppermost frame mounting bolts, then screw in the studs so that they support the rear struts of the front sub-frame only (see illustrations).

33 Loosen the bolts securing the upper and lower struts of the rear sub-frame (see illustrations).

34 Have an assistant support the rear sub-frame, then withdraw the bolts, noting the location of any washers (see illustration).

Note: The engine mounting bolts are micro-encapsulated. New bolts should be fitted on reassembly, or the threads of the old bolts should be cleaned and coated with a suitable non-permanent thread-locking compound. Lubricate the underside of the heads of the bolts that secure the brackets and front sub-frame rear struts with Optimoly TA high temperature assembly grease.

35 Ease the rear sub-frame away carefully

4.31 Cut two studs 25 mm in length

4.32a Undo the uppermost frame mounting bolts . . .

4.32b . . . and screw in the studs

4.33a Bolts (arrowed) secure upper . . .

4.33b . . . and lower rear sub-frame struts

4.34 Note location of any washers on the bolts

4.35 Removing the rear sub-frame

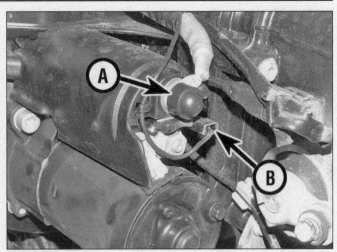

4.36a Battery lead terminal nut (A) and wiring connector (B)

4.36b Undo the bolts (arrowed) . . .

4.36c . . . and lift off the starter motor

from the engine unit, ensuring the wiring is free of the frame members **(see illustration)**.

36 Remove the cover, then undo the terminal nut and disconnect the battery lead from the starter solenoid, then disconnect the wiring connector **(see illustrations)**. If required, undo the bolts securing the starter motor and lift it off, noting how the starter gear engages with the clutch ring gear **(see illustrations)**. Note that if the gearbox is going to be removed, the starter motor must be removed first.

37 Release the clips securing the fuel hoses and the pressure regulator and lift the assembly off **(see illustrations)**.

38 Cut the tie securing the gear position sensor wiring and disconnect the connector **(see illustrations)**.

39 At this point, if required, the gearbox can be separated from the engine, either to gain access to the clutch or to reduce the overall weight of the engine unit if it is to be lifted onto the workbench. If the gearbox is going to be left in place, proceed to Step 44.

40 Undo the bolts securing the clutch top cover and lift the cover off **(see illustrations)**.

41 Undo the upper and lower bolts securing

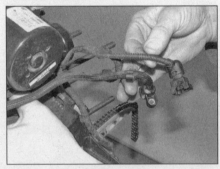

4.37a Unclip the fuel hoses from the fuel injector sub-loom . . .

4.37b . . . and remove the pressure regulator assembly

4.38a Release the gear position sensor wiring . . .

4.38b . . . and disconnect the connector

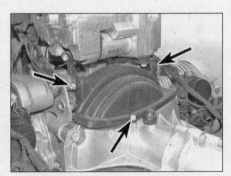

4.40a Undo the bolts (arrowed) . . .

4.40b . . . and lift the clutch top cover off

4.40c The two upper bolts (arrowed) support the ABS modulator, where fitted

4.41a Undo the two upper bolts . . .

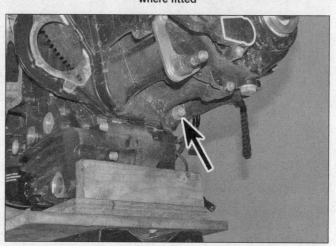

4.41b . . . and the lower bolt securing the gearbox

the gearbox to the engine crankcases, noting where they fit **(see illustrations)**.

42 Draw the gearbox off the back of the engine **(see illustration)**. If the gearbox is stuck, tap around the joint face with a soft-faced mallet and drive a wood wedge behind the prise point on the lower edge of the gearbox case – don't exert too much pressure with the wedge or the case may be damaged. Apply heat in the area of the dowels and,

once the gearbox starts to come free, soak the dowels with penetrating fluid. **Note:** *This procedure is best performed with the aid of an assistant to support the gearbox and ensure it is drawn back level with the engine to avoid damaging the transmission input shaft which locates inside the centre of the clutch.*

43 Lay the gearbox upright on a level surface to prevent oil leakage through the breather.

44 On machines fitted with ABS, undo the

flare nuts securing the front brake pipes to the ABS modulator **(see illustration 4.27)**. Wrap a clean rag around the modulator to catch any spilled brake fluid and be prepared to catch any residual fluid in the pipes. Seal the open pipes with suitable caps and cover the unions on the modulator with duct tape to prevent dirt entering. Undo the screws and cut the tie securing the brake hose and position it clear of the engine unit **(see illustrations)**.

4.42 Draw the gearbox off, keeping it level

4.44a Undo the screws . . .

4.44b . . . and cut the tie securing the brake hose

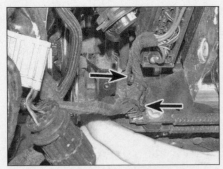

4.45a Cut the cable-ties

4.45b Pull up the catch . . .

4.45c . . . and disconnect the connector

4.45d Modulator front mounting bolt

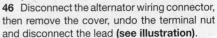

4.45e Lift the modulator off

and lift the modulator off **(see illustrations)**. **Note:** *The modulator to engine bolts are micro-encapsulated. New bolts should be fitted on reassembly, or the threads of the old bolts should be cleaned and coated with a suitable non-permanent thread-locking compound.*

46 Disconnect the alternator wiring connector, then remove the cover, undo the terminal nut and disconnect the lead **(see illustration)**.

47 At this point, if required, the alternator can be removed to reduce the overall weight of the engine unit. If the alternator is going to be left in place, proceed to Step 49.

48 Remove the alternator drive belt (see Chapter 1). Undo the screws securing the top belt cover and remove it **(see illustrations)**. Undo the left and right-hand mounting bolts and lift the alternator out **(see illustrations)**.

45 To remove the ABS modulator, first cut the ties securing the modulator connector wiring loom **(see illustration)**. Pull up the catch on the multi-pin connector and release it from the modulator **(see illustrations)**. If not already done, undo the two bolts securing the rear of the modulator **(see illustration 4.40c)**. Undo the bolt securing the front of the modulator

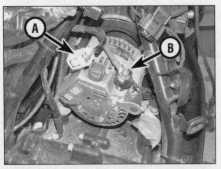

4.46 Alternator wiring connector (A) and terminal nut (B)

4.48a Undo the screws . . .

4.48b . . . and remove the cover

4.48c Undo the left . . .

4.48d . . . and right-hand mounting bolts

4.48e Lift the alternator off

4.49 Disconnect the earth wire

4.50a Disconnect the wiring connectors

49 Undo the screw securing the earth wire to the top of the crankcase (see illustration).
50 Working on the right-hand side of the engine, cut the cable-ties and disconnect the knock sensor, temperature sensor and camshaft sensor wiring connectors (see illustration). Cut the cable-tie securing the wiring to the cylinder (see illustration). Undo the screw securing the earth wire to the cylinder head (see illustration).
51 Disconnect the wiring connector for the oil temperature sensor (see illustration). Where fitted, trace the wiring from the oil

level indicator on the right-hand side of the crankcase and disconnect it at the connector (see illustration).
52 Trace the wiring from the crankshaft position sensor on the top of the timing cover and disconnect it at the connector (see illustration).
53 Working on the left-hand side of the engine, release the cable-tie and disconnect the knock sensor wiring connector (see illustration). Undo the screw securing the earth wire to the cylinder head (see illustration).
54 Disconnect the wiring connector for the oil pressure switch on the left-hand side of the

4.50b Release the wiring from the cylinder

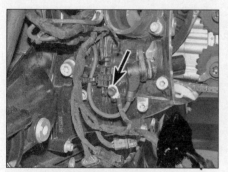

4.50c Disconnect the earth wire

4.51a Oil temperature sensor wiring connector

4.51b Location of the oil level indicator

4.52 Location of the crankshaft position sensor

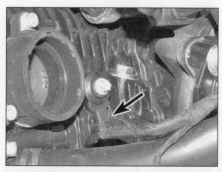

4.53a Knock sensor wiring connector

4.53b Location of the earth wire terminal screw

4.54 Oil pressure switch wiring connector

4.55a Oil cooler return pipe banjo bolt

4.55b Oil cooler feed pipe connection

crankcase **(see illustration)**. **Note:** *On R1200 R models the pressure switch is only used for factory testing during production – no wiring connector is fitted.*

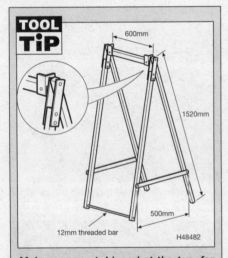

TOOL TiP

600mm

1520mm

500mm

12mm threaded bar

H48482

Make a support, hinged at the top, for the front sub-frame and suspension to the dimensions shown. Use 25 mm square section steel tube for the top cross member and legs, and brace them with 25 mm steel strip. The height of the support can be adjusted using different length cross braces (500 mm shown). Either bolt the support to a bike ramp or strengthen the structure with two lengths of 12 mm threaded bar between the bottom of the legs.

55 On R1200 R models, remove the oil cooler (see Section 6). On all models, have some rag ready to catch any residual oil, then undo the banjo bolt securing the left-hand oil cooler return pipe to the crankcase **(see illustration)**. Disconnect the pipe and remove the screws securing it to the crankcase and support bracket (see Section 6). Undo the bolts securing the right-hand oil cooler feed pipe to the crankcase **(see illustration)**. Lift the pipe and displace it, noting the location of the baffle on top of the oil thermostat, and remove the screw securing the pipe to the support bracket (see Section 6). Wrap clean plastic bags over the ends of the pipes to prevent dirt entering the system.

56 Check that all the wiring, pipes and hoses are free from the engine unit, and that the engine unit is secure. Unless provision is made to hold the front sub-frame and suspension assembly (see ***Tool Tip***) it will be unsupported when the Telelever pivot shaft and engine

mounting through-bolt are removed and must be lifted away immediately.

57 Mask the cylinder fins below the Telelever pivots with duct tape to prevent accidental damage. Prise off the covers on both ends of the Telelever pivot shaft **(see illustration)**.

58 Counter-hold the head of the pivot shaft and undo the bolt on the right-hand side **(see illustrations)**. Position small blocks of wood underneath both sides of the Telelever arm to support it as the pivot shaft is withdrawn, then pull out the shaft **(see illustration)**. The wood blocks will prevent the Telelever arm dropping down over the engine mounting through-bolt.

59 Undo the nut on the left-hand end of the engine mounting through-bolt **(see illustration)**. Note that the nut is thread-locked and BMW advise heating it to 80°C to release it. Have an assistant support the front sub-frame and suspension assembly and withdraw the through-bolt **(see illustration)**.

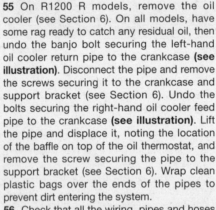

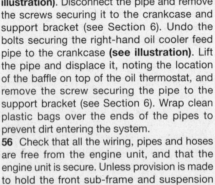

4.57 Prise off the covers

4.58a Undo the bolt on the right-hand side

4.58b Withdraw the Telelever pivot shaft

4.59a Undo the nut on the through-bolt . . .

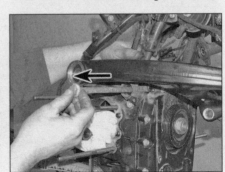

4.59b . . . then withdraw the through-bolt

4.60 Unscrew the studs on both sides

60 Unscrew the studs supporting the rear struts of the sub-frame **(see illustration)**.

61 Support the ends of the Telelever arm and manoeuvre the sub-frame and suspension assembly off **(see illustration)**. Support the sub-frame and suspension assembly in an upright position to avoid brake and clutch fluid leaking from the fluid reservoirs.

 Warning: The engine is very heavy. It is strongly recommended that you have at least one assistant to help lift the engine if it is being moved. Personal injury or damage could occur if the engine falls or is dropped.

Installation

62 Installation is the reverse of removal, noting the following:
● Tighten all bolts to the torque settings specified at the beginning of this Chapter.
● Ensure the engine unit is supported at the right height for the installation of the front and rear sub-frame assemblies, and is held securely **(see illustration)**.
● If the alternator has been removed, it can be installed at this stage, before fitting the front sub-frame and suspension assembly.
● When installing the front sub-frame and suspension assembly, ensure the left-hand oil pipe is located inside the Telelever arm.
● Install the engine mounting though-bolt first

(see illustration 4.59b) and tighten the nut finger-tight. Align the rear struts of the front sub-frame with the crankcase and install the studs **(see illustration 4.32)**. Apply a suitable non-permanent thread-locking compound (BMW recommends Loctite 243) to the threads of the through-bolt nut and tighten it to the torque setting specified at the beginning of this Chapter.
● Lubricate the Telelever pivot shaft with high temperature assembly grease (BMW recommends Optimoly TA). Install the shaft and tighten the bolt to the specified torque setting **(see illustration 4.58b and a)**.
● Fit a new O-ring onto the right-hand oil pipe and don't forget to install the baffle on top of the oil thermostat before installing the pipe (see Section 6).
● Fit new sealing washers to both sides of the left-hand oil pipe banjo union (see Section 6).
● On machines fitted with ABS, the modulator mounting bolts should be thread-locked. It is essential that the brake system is topped-up and bled before the machine is ridden (see Chapter 5).
● If the gearbox has been removed, smear the crankcase-to-gearbox case dowels and the splines on the transmission input shaft with clutch assembly grease (BMW specify Optimoly MP 3) before installing the gearbox. Ensure the gearbox mounting bolts are positioned in their correct locations.
● If the starter motor has been removed, install it before fitting the rear sub-frame (see Step 36).
● Position the fuel pressure regulator and fuel hose assembly before installing the rear sub-frame (see Step 37).
● Ensure no wiring becomes trapped between the engine unit and the rear sub-frame when the sub-frame is installed. Note that the brackets on the upper struts fit outside the front struts (see Step 32). Only tighten the mounting bolts to the specified torque

settings when all the wiring and hoses have been correctly routed and secured.
● Don't forget to install the clutch pushrod before installing the clutch release cylinder to the back of the gearbox
● Follow the procedure in Chapter 4 to install the rear shock absorber and swingarm/ final drive unit assembly.
● Follow the procedure in Chapter 5 to install the rear brake caliper and rear wheel.
● Follow the procedure in Chapter 3 to install the throttle bodies and throttle cables.
● Refill the engine and gearbox with the correct amount of oil (see Chapter 1).
● Check the operation of all electrical systems before taking the bike on the road.

5 Engine overhaul – general information

Disassembly

1 Before disassembling the engine, the external surfaces of the unit should be thoroughly cleaned and degreased. This will prevent contamination of the engine internals, and will also make working a lot easier and cleaner. A high flash-point solvent, such as paraffin (kerosene) can be used, or better still, a proprietary engine degreaser such as Gunk. Use old paintbrushes and toothbrushes to work the solvent into the various recesses of the engine casings. Take care to exclude solvent or water from the electrical components and from the intake and exhaust ports.

 Warning: The use of petrol (gasoline) as a cleaning agent should be avoided because of the risk of fire.

2 When the engine is clean and dry, clear a suitable clear area for working – a workbench is desirable for all operations once a component

4.61 Lift the front sub-frame/suspension assembly off

4.62 Ensure the engine unit is supported and held securely

A useful engine support stand can be made from short lengths of 2 x 4 inch wood screwed together into a rectangle. The stand should be just big enough to accommodate the crankcase within it, so that the bottom of the engine rests on the bench. If necessary, additional blocks of wood can be used to support the cylinders.

has been removed from the machine. Gather a selection of small containers and plastic bags so that parts can be grouped together in an easily identifiable manner. Some paper and a pen should be on hand so that notes can be made and labels attached where necessary. A supply of clean rag is also required. If the engine has been removed from the bike (see

Section 4), have an assistant help you lift it onto the workbench.

3 Before commencing work, read through the appropriate section so that some idea of the necessary procedure can be gained. When removing components it should be noted that great force is seldom required, unless specified. In many cases, a component's reluctance to be removed is indicative of an incorrect approach or removal method – if in any doubt, re-check with the text.

4 When disassembling the engine, keep 'mated' parts together (e.g. valve and camshaft assemblies, cylinders, pistons and connecting rods, that have been in contact with each other during engine operation). These 'mated' parts must be reused or renewed as assemblies.

5 A complete engine stripdown should be done in the following general order with reference to the appropriate Sections.

   Remove the starter motor (if not done when removing the engine)
   Remove the gearbox (if not done when removing the engine)
   Remove the alternator (if not done when removing the engine)
   Remove the valve covers
   Remove the camchain tensioners
   Remove the cam follower and camshaft assemblies
   Remove the cylinder heads

   Remove the cylinders
   Remove the pistons
   Remove the balancer gears and balancer shaft
   Remove the auxiliary shaft drive chain, tensioner and sprockets
   Remove the oil pump
   Separate the crankcase halves
   Remove the crankshaft and connecting rods
   Remove the auxiliary shaft, camchains and tensioner blades

6 Access to the clutch, selector drum/forks and gearshafts can be gained after removing the gearbox.

Reassembly

7 Reassembly is accomplished by reversing the general disassembly sequence.

---

6 Oil cooler and hoses

Special tool: *A pair of hose clip pliers is necessary for this procedure (see illustration 6.9a).*

Oil cooler

Note: *If the engine has been running, allow it to cool before commencing work. If the machine is left to stand, oil will drain down from the cooler into the crankcase, reducing the amount of residual oil in the cooler.*

1 On R1200 GS and GS Adventure models, the oil cooler is located at the front of the machine behind the upper front mudguard **(see illustration)**. On R1200 RT models, the oil cooler is located at the front of the machine behind the headlight panel **(see illustration)**. Remove the bodywork according to your model to gain access (see Chapter 6).

2 On R1200 R models, the oil cooler is located behind a cover at the front of the engine. To remove the cover, undo the two screws on the top edge and disengage it from the lugs on the bottom edge of the oil cooler **(see illustrations)**.

6.1a Location of the oil cooler – R1200 GS shown

6.1b Location of the oil cooler – R1200 RT shown

6.2a Undo the screws . . .

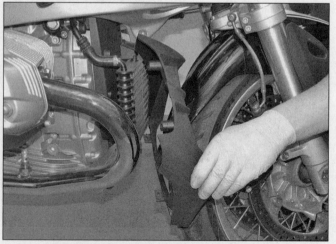

6.2b . . . and remove the cover – R1200 R

6.4a Undo screw on left . . .

6.4b . . . and right-hand side

6.5a Oil cooler mounting bolts

6.5b Release the hose clips . . .

6.5c . . . and disconnect the hoses carefully

6.5d Note the location of the spacers

3 If required, drain the engine oil (see Chapter 1). Alternatively, have a suitable container ready to catch any residual oil from the cooler when the feed and return hoses are disconnected. **Note:** *Once the hoses have been disconnected, secure them in an upright position to avoid leakage and cover the open ends to prevent dirt getting in.*

 Warning: Be careful when disconnecting the oil hoses – hot oil can cause severe burns.

4 Where fitted, undo the screws securing the upper ends of the oil pipes **(see illustrations)**.
5 On R1200 GS, GS Adventure and RT models, loosen the left and right-hand bolts securing the cooler to the fairing bracket, then support the cooler and withdraw the bolts **(see illustration)**. Displace the cooler, release the clips securing the oil hoses, then pull them off carefully **(see illustrations)**. Note the location of the spacers in the mounting grommets **(see illustration)**.
6 On R1200 R models, release the clips securing the oil hoses, then pull them off carefully **(see illustration)**. Remove the two bolts securing the oil cooler to the timing cover, noting the location of the washers, then lower the cooler to disengage its top mounting from the lug on the cover **(see illustrations)**.
7 Check the oil cooler for signs of damage and

6.6a Disconnect the left and right-hand oil hoses

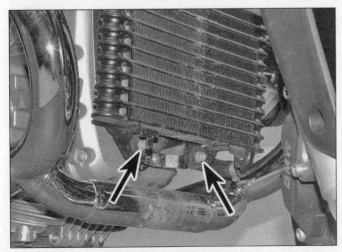

6.6b Undo the mounting bolts . . .

6.6c . . . and disengage cooler from top mounting lug

6.9a Use the correct pliers . . .

6.9b . . . to tighten the oil hose clips securely

6.13a Undo the screw – R1200 GS shown

6.13b Unscrew the banjo bolt and sealing washers

clear any dirt or debris that might obstruct air flow using water or low pressure compressed air directed through the fins from the back. If the fins are bent or distorted, straighten them carefully with a screwdriver. Bent or damaged fins will restrict the air flow and impair the efficiency of the cooler causing the engine to overheat. If there is substantial damage to the oil cooler's surface area, renew it.

8 Check the oil cooler mounting bushes, and renew them if necessary.

9 Installation is the reverse of removal. Secure the hoses with new clips and tighten the clips with the correct type of pliers to avoid damaging them (see illustrations). Tighten the cooler mounting bolts securely.

10 Check the engine oil level and top-up or refill the engine as necessary (see *Pre-ride checks* and Chapter 1)

Oil hoses

11 On R1200 GS, GS Adventure and RT models, remove the fairing side panels, if applicable, then remove the fuel tank panels (see Chapter 6). Remove the intake duct from the air filter housing (see Chapter 1). Remove the fuel tank (see Chapter 3).

12 On R1200 R models, remove the air intake duct (see Chapter 1) and the front cover (see Step 2).

13 Examine the oil hoses and pipes for damage and signs of deterioration, and check the unions on the crankcase for signs of leakage (see illustrations 4.55a and b). If the left-hand (return) pipe union is leaking, first undo the screw securing the lower end of the pipe, where fitted (see illustration). Undo the banjo bolt, being prepared to catch any residual oil and remove the sealing washers (see illustration). Ensure the sealing surfaces of the crankcase, the banjo union and the banjo bolt are clean and smooth. Fit new sealing washers to both sides of the union, then install the bolt and tighten it to the torque setting specified at the beginning of this Chapter. Secure the pipe.

14 To remove the return pipe, first free the upper end from the oil cooler (see Steps 3 to 6). Remove the alternator belt cover for access (see Chapter 1). Undo any mounting screws or clips and the banjo bolt and manoeuvre the pipe off. Installation is the reverse of removal. Check the engine oil level and top-up as necessary (see *Pre-ride checks*).

15 If the right-hand (feed) pipe union is leaking, first undo the screw securing the pipe, where fitted (see illustration 6.4b). Undo the flange bolts securing the pipe to the top of the crankcase (see illustration 4.55b). Lift the pipe out of its socket, being prepared to catch any residual oil, then ease off the O-ring from the end of the pipe (see illustration). Take care not to displace the baffle on top of the oil thermostat (see illustration). Ensure the mating surfaces of the crankcase and the pipe flange are clean and smooth. Fit a new O-ring onto the pipe and lubricate it with a smear of clean engine oil, then press the pipe into its socket and tighten the flange bolts to the torque setting specified at the beginning of this Chapter. Secure the pipe.

16 To remove the feed pipe, first free the upper end from the oil cooler (see Steps 3 to 6). Undo any mounting screws or clips and the flange bolts and manoeuvre the pipe off. Installation is the reverse of removal. Check the engine oil level and top-up as necessary (see *Pre-ride checks*).

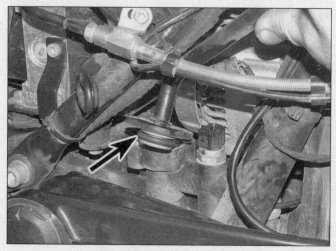

6.15a Note location of the O-ring

6.15b Note location of the baffle

7.3a Undo the valve cover bolts . . .

7.3b . . . and pull the cover off

7.4a Remove the outer . . .

7 Valve covers

Removal

1 Support the bike upright on its centre stand. Working on one side of the engine at a time, follow the procedure in Chapter 1, Section 5, and remove the primary ignition coil.
2 Position a drain tray below the valve cover to catch any residual oil when the cover is removed.
3 Undo the valve cover bolts and pull the cover off the cylinder head **(see illustrations)**. If it is stuck, tap it gently around the sides with a soft-faced mallet or block of wood to dislodge it – do not try to lever it off and risk damaging the sealing surface.
4 Note the location of the outer and inner cover seals and remove them if they are loose **(see illustrations)**.
5 Check the condition of the cover bolt sealing grommets **(see illustration)**. If they are damaged or deteriorated, or if there are signs of oil leakage, fit new bolt and seal assemblies.
6 Note the location of the support block and remove it for safekeeping if it is loose **(see illustration)**. If required, undo the bolt securing the cover support and remove it **(see illustrations)**.
7 The inner and outer cover seals are re-usable; however, if they are damaged or deteriorated, or if there are signs of oil leakage, renew them.

Installation

8 Clean the sealing surfaces of the cylinder head and the valve cover with suitable solvent. Note that the right-hand cover incorporates the oil filler cap.
9 If removed, clean the threads of the cover support bolt and apply a suitable non-permanent thread-locking compound. Install the support and tighten the bolt **(see illustration 7.6c and b)**. Ensure the support block is pressed firmly into position **(see illustration)**.
10 Fit the outer cover seal onto the cylinder

7.4b . . . and inner seals

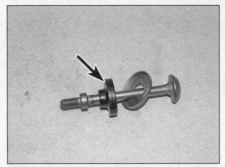

7.5 Location of the bolt sealing grommet

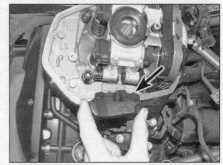

7.6a Remove the support block

7.6b Undo the bolt . . .

7.6c . . . and remove the cover support

7.9 Installed position of the support block

7.10 Note how the locating points on the seal fit against the castings

7.11 Position the open end of the clip as shown

head **(see illustration 7.4a)**. Ensure the half-circles on the seal locate around the castings in the head **(see illustration)**. Press the inner seal onto the spark plug location **(see illustration 7.4b)**.

11 Ensure that the open end of the E-clip securing the upper exhaust cam follower faces the cylinder head **(see illustration)**.

12 Position the cover on the cylinder head, making sure the seals stay in place, then tighten the bolts finger-tight **(see illustration 7.3a)**.

13 Once the cover is correctly seated on the seals, tighten the bolts to the torque setting specified at the beginning of this Chapter.

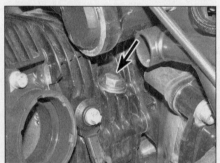

8.1a Location of the left-hand camchain tensioner

8.7 Ensure timing marks are correctly aligned

14 Check the engine oil level and top-up as necessary (see *Pre-ride checks*).

8 Camchain tensioners

Note: *The camchain tensioners can be removed with the engine in the frame, although access to the left-hand cylinder's tensioner is extremely limited. To access the tensioner blades and guide blades the engine must be removed and the crankcases split.*

8.1b Location of the right-hand camchain tensioner

8.8 Insert the TDC locating pin into the hole (arrowed)

Special tool: *A top dead centre (TDC) locating pin is required for this procedure (see Step 8).*

Removal

1 The left-hand tensioner is located on the top of the cylinder immediately below the Telelever pivot **(see illustration)**. The right-hand tensioner is located on the underside of the cylinder **(see illustration)**.

2 Support the bike upright on its centre stand. On R1200 GS, GS Adventure and RT models, remove the fairing side panels as appropriate; on R1200 RT models, remove the frame side panels (see Chapter 6).

3 Remove the primary spark plugs (see Chapter 1).

Left-hand side

4 Follow the procedure in Chapter 3 and displace the left-hand throttle body. Secure the throttle body with a cable-tie to avoid straining the throttle cable.

5 Remove the valve cover (see Section 7).

6 Before removing the tensioner, the left-hand piston must be at top dead centre (TDC) on the compression stroke. To turn the engine to this position, select a high gear and have an assistant turn the rear wheel slowly by hand in the normal direction of rotation (forwards). Alternatively, remove the alternator belt cover (see Chapter 1) and turn the crankshaft clockwise with a spanner on the pulley nut.

Caution: Be sure to turn the engine in its normal direction of rotation only.

7 With the piston at TDC on the compression stroke, all the valves will be closed and the timing marks on the ends of the camshafts should face each other **(see illustration)**.

8 Insert the TDC locating pin into the hole in the right-hand side of the gearbox case **(see illustration)**. The pin should pass through the clutch assembly and locate in a hole in the crankcase. BMW produces a service tool (Part No. 112650) for this purpose. Alternatively, a similar tool can be made (see *Tool Tip*).

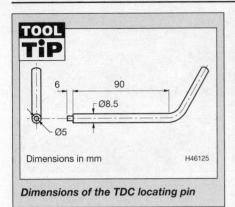

Dimensions in mm   H46125

Dimensions of the TDC locating pin

8.9a Unscrew the left-hand tensioner . . .

8.9b . . . and pull it out

9 Unscrew the tensioner and pull it out – discard the sealing washer as a new one must be used **(see illustrations)**. Remove the spring, piston rod and piston **(see illustration)**.
10 Follow the procedure in Steps 16 to 18 to inspect the tensioner.

Right-hand side

11 Remove the valve cover (see Section 7).
12 Before removing the tensioner, the right-hand piston must be at top dead centre (TDC) on the compression stroke. Follow the procedure in Step 6 to turn the engine to this position.
Caution: Be sure to turn the engine in its normal direction of rotation only.
13 With the piston at TDC on the compression stroke, all the valves will be closed and the timing marks on the ends of the camshafts should face each other **(see illustration 8.7)**.
14 Insert the TDC locating pin into the hole in the right-hand side of the gearbox case (see Step 8).
15 Position a drain tray below the engine to catch any residual oil, then unscrew the tensioner and pull it out – discard the sealing washer as a new one must be used **(see illustration)**. Remove the sleeve and piston assembly.

Inspection

16 Examine the tensioner components for signs of wear, scoring or damage **(see illustrations)**.
17 Check that the plunger moves freely in and out of the tensioner body, and that the spring tension is good.

8.9c Remove the spring, piston rod and piston

18 If the any of the tensioner components are worn or damaged a new tensioner must be fitted.

Installation

Left-hand side

19 Ensure that the piston is at TDC on the compression stroke and the timing marks on the ends of the camshafts face each other **(see illustration 8.7)**.
20 Insert the TDC locating pin into the hole in the right-hand side of the gearbox case **(see illustration 8.8)**.
21 Ensure the piston, piston rod and spring are correctly installed **(see illustration)**. Fit a new sealing washer and tighten the tensioner to the torque setting specified at the beginning of this Chapter.
22 Remove the TDC locating pin.
23 Install the remaining components in the reverse order of removal. Check the engine oil

8.15 Unscrew the right-hand tensioner

level and top-up as necessary (see *Pre-ride checks*).

Right-hand side

24 Ensure that the piston is at TDC on the compression stroke and the timing marks on the ends of the camshafts face each other **(see illustration 8.7)**.
25 Insert the TDC locating pin into the hole in the right-hand side of the gearbox case **(see illustration 8.8)**.
26 Fit the sleeve on the tensioner and fit a new sealing washer, then install the tensioner and tighten it to the torque setting specified at the beginning of this Chapter **(see illustration 8.15)**.
27 Remove the TDC locating pin.
28 Install the remaining components in the reverse order of removal.
29 Check the engine oil level and top-up as necessary (see *Pre-ride checks*).

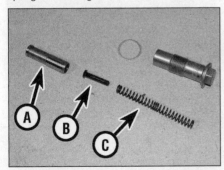

8.16a Left-hand tensioner piston (A), piston rod (B) and spring (C)

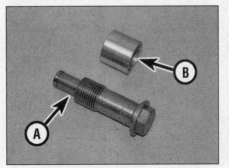

8.16b Right-hand tensioner piston assembly (A) and sleeve (B)

8.21 Install the components carefully

9.2a Undo the bolt . . .

9.2b . . . and remove the engine breather union

9.3 Loosen the camshaft sprocket bolts

9.4a Undo the bolts . . .

9.4b . . . securing the upper guide blade . . .

9.4c . . . and lift it off

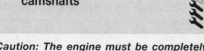

9 Cam followers and camshafts

Caution: The engine must be completely cool before beginning this procedure or the cylinder head(s) may become warped.
Note: The cam followers and camshafts can be removed with the engine in the frame. If the engine has been removed, ignore the steps which do not apply.

Special tools: *A top dead centre (TDC) locating pin (see Section 8), a camshaft locking tool (see Step 45) and a camchain tension adjuster (see Step 46) are required for this procedure.*

Removal

Left-hand side

1 Follow the procedure in Section 8 to remove the camchain tensioner.
2 Undo the bolt securing the engine breather union and remove the union (see illustrations).
3 Counter-hold the front of the appropriate camshaft with a 15 mm spanner and loosen the camshaft sprocket bolts (see illustration).
4 Undo the bolts securing the upper camchain guide blade and remove the blade (see illustrations).
5 Remove the upper camshaft sprocket bolt and washer (see illustration). Remove the sprocket, noting how it fits, then disengage it from the chain (see illustration).

9.5a Remove the sprocket bolt and washer (arrowed)

9.5b Note chamfer on inside edge of sprocket

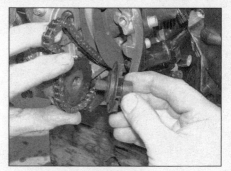

9.6a Remove the bolt and breather impeller

9.6b Note chamfer on inside edge of sprocket

9.7a Undo the pivot bolt . . .

9.7b . . . and remove the upper chain tensioner blade

9.8 Remove the spring plate

9.9 Remove the seal holder

9.10a Undo the bolts . . .

9.10b . . . and remove the camshaft holder

9.10c Note location of lower seal

6 Remove the lower camshaft sprocket bolt and breather impeller **(see illustration)**. Lift the chain off the lower sprocket and remove the sprocket, noting how it fits **(see illustration)**.
7 Undo the pivot bolt securing the upper left-hand chain tensioner blade and remove the blade **(see illustrations)**.
8 Undo the bolts and washers and remove the spring plate **(see illustration)**.
9 Undo the bolts and washers and remove the seal holder **(see illustration)**.
10 Undo the remaining bolts securing the camshaft holder and lift it off, taking care not to dislodge the valve clearance shims **(see illustrations)**. Note the location of the lower holder seal **(see illustration)**. If it is damaged or distorted fit a new one on reassembly.
11 Remove the valve shims **(see illustration)** and store them in a container which is divided into eight compartments (there are four shims in each cylinder head). Label each compartment

with the location of its corresponding valve in the cylinder head. If a container is not available, use labelled plastic bags. **Note:** *It is essential that the cam followers and shims are stored according to their position in the*

9.11 Remove the valve shims

head and fitted back on their original valves otherwise all the clearances will be wrong.
12 Note the location of the dowels in the camshaft holder and remove them for safekeeping if they are loose **(see illustration)**.

9.12 Note location of the dowels

9.13a Undo the bolt . . .

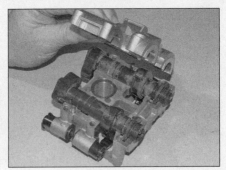

9.13b . . . and remove the upper half of the holder

9.14 Lift out the camshafts

9.15a Remove the inner seal

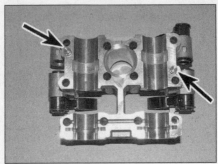

9.15b Note location of the dowels

13 Undo the bolt and washer securing the upper half of the camshaft holder and lift it off (see illustrations).

14 Lift out the camshafts, noting how they fit (see illustration).

15 Remove the camshaft holder inner seal (see illustration). If it is damaged or distorted fit a new one on reassembly. Note the location of the dowels in the lower half of the camshaft holder and remove them for safekeeping if they are loose (see illustration).

16 Using a suitable pair of pliers, pull out the E-clips securing the cam followers and shafts and remove them (see illustrations). Mark each shaft according to its position in the holder and keep matched assemblies together. Discard the E-clips as new ones must be used.

Right-hand side

17 Follow the procedure in Section 8 to remove the camchain tensioner. Note: If the left-hand camshafts have already been removed, support the left-hand camchain when turning the engine to TDC compression on the right-hand cylinder prior to removing the tensioner.

18 Counter-hold the front of the appropriate camshaft with a 15 mm spanner and loosen the camshaft sprocket bolts (see illustration).

19 Undo the bolts securing the upper camchain guide blade and remove the blade (see illustrations).

20 Release the tie securing the camshaft position sensor wiring, then undo the bolt

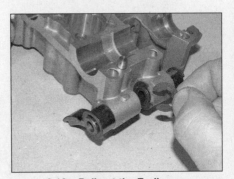

9.16a Pull out the E-clips . . .

9.16b . . . and remove the cam followers and shafts

9.18 Loosen the sprocket bolts

9.19a Remove the bolts (arrowed) . . .

9.19b . . . to free the upper guide blade

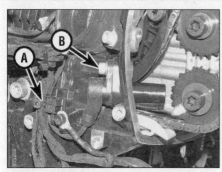

9.20a Wiring tie (A). Undo bolt (B) . . .

9.20b . . . and remove sensor, noting O-ring

9.21 Remove the upper camshaft sprocket

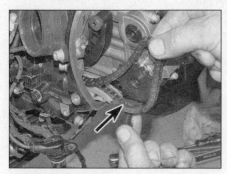

9.22 Note how the tab (arrowed) locates

9.23 Camchain guide blade bolt

9.25 Inspect the cam followers and shafts for wear

securing the sensor and withdraw it from the cylinder head **(see illustrations)**. Note the location of the O-ring and discard it as a new one must be fitted.

21 Remove the upper camshaft sprocket bolt and washer, then draw the sprocket off the camshaft, noting how it fits and disengage it from the chain **(see illustration)**.

22 Remove the lower camshaft sprocket bolt and camshaft position sensor trigger. Note how the tab on the inside face of the trigger locates in the small hole in the sprocket **(see illustration)**. Lift the chain off the lower sprocket and draw the sprocket off the camshaft, noting how it fits.

23 Undo the bolt securing the camchain guide blade **(see illustration)**.

24 Follow the procedure in Steps 8 to 16 to remove the camshaft holder and camshafts.

Inspection

25 Inspect the bearing face of the cam followers for wear, score marks, spalling (a pitted appearance) and cracks **(see illustration)**. Inspect the surface of the follower shafts for wear and pitting. The followers should be a sliding fit on their shafts with no discernable freeplay – if any components are worn or damaged, they must be renewed.

26 Inspect the bearing surfaces of the

camshaft holder and the corresponding journals on the camshaft **(see illustrations)**.

27 Check the camshaft lobes for heat discoloration (blue appearance), score marks, chipped areas, flat spots and spalling. If there is evidence of damage or excessive wear, the camshaft must be replaced with a new one.

28 Check the camshaft sprockets for wear, chipped teeth and other damage **(see illustration)**. If the sprockets are worn, the chain and the drive sprocket on the auxiliary shaft are probably worn as well and should be checked (see Section 25).

29 If available, blow through any oil passages with compressed air.

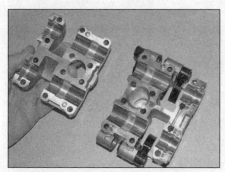

9.26a Inspect the camshaft holder . . .

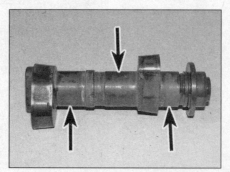

9.26b . . . and the camshaft journals

9.28 Check the camshaft sprockets for wear

9.32 Installed position of the camshafts

9.35 Ensure lower seal is correctly installed

Installation

Note: *If both pairs of camshafts have been removed, refer to the timing marks on the crankshaft and balancer shaft gears to position the appropriate cylinder at TDC compression (see Section 17).*

Left-hand side

30 Lubricate the cam follower shafts with

9.36a Align the camshaft holder . . .

clean engine oil and assemble the followers on the shafts. Install the shaft assemblies into the holder and secure them with new E-clips **(see illustration 9.16b and a)**.

31 Ensure the dowels are in position in the lower half of the camshaft holder **(see illustration 9.15b)**. If required, fit a new camshaft holder seal **(see illustration 9.15a)**.

32 Lubricate the camshaft journals and lay the camshafts in position in the holder **(see illustration)**.

33 Press the upper half of the holder into position firmly and secure it with the bolt and washer **(see illustration 9.13b and a)**. Tighten the bolt to the torque setting specified at the beginning of this Chapter.

34 Lubricate the valve shims and fit them into the appropriate cam followers **(see illustration 9.11)**. **Note:** *It is most important that the shims are returned to their original positions otherwise the valve clearances will be inaccurate.*

35 If required, fit a new lower camshaft holder seal **(see illustration)**.

36 Position the camshafts so that the timing marks face each other, then align the camshaft holder with the cylinder head and tighten the outer mounting bolts finger tight – don't forget to install the washers and spring plate **(see illustrations)**.

37 Install the seal holder, bolts and washers **(see illustrations 9.9)**.

38 Ensure all the components are correctly aligned, then tighten all the camshaft holder bolts evenly in a criss-cross pattern to the specified torque setting.

39 Install the upper chain tensioner blade and tighten the pivot bolt to the specified torque setting **(see illustrations 9.7b and a)**.

40 Fit the camchain around the lower camshaft sprocket and locate the sprocket on the end of the camshaft with the chamfered side facing the camshaft **(see illustration 9.6b)**. Install the breather impeller and sprocket bolt finger-tight **(see illustration 9.6a)**.

41 Fit the chain around the upper sprocket and locate the sprocket on the end of the

9.36b . . . and secure it on the cylinder head

9.36c Don't forget to install the washers and spring plate (arrowed)

9.45a Check camshaft timing mark alignment . . .

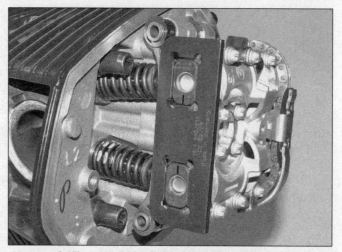

9.45b . . . and install the camshaft locking tool

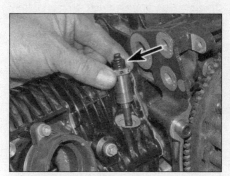

9.46a Set the adjuster as shown

9.46b Install the adapter . . .

9.46c . . . then tighten the adjuster

camshaft with the chamfered side facing the camshaft (see illustration 9.5b). Install the sprocket bolt and washer finger-tight (see illustration 9.5a).

42 Install the upper camchain guide blade and tighten the bolts to the specified torque setting (see illustrations 9.4c, b and a).

43 Make sure that the piston is at TDC on the compression stroke and install the TDC locating pin.

44 Loosen the upper and lower camshaft sprocket bolts so that the sprockets can be rotated without disturbing the camshafts.

45 Ensure the camshaft timing marks are correctly aligned and install the camshaft locking tool (BMW service tool Part No. 111511) (see illustrations).

46 To set the left-hand camchain tension correctly the BMW adjuster (Part No. 111512) and ratchet spanner (Part No. 111514) are required. Adjust the chain tension adjuster so that the outer edge is below the inner edge, then install the adjuster (see illustration). Install the adapter, then using the ratchet spanner, tighten the adjuster until it releases, then click it three more times (see illustrations).

47 Apply a register mark to the upper camshaft sprocket with a dab of paint (see illustration).

48 Withdraw the TDC locating pin and rotate the crankshaft two full revolutions in the normal direction of rotation – the camshaft sprocket should rotate one revolution and return to its original position as indicated by the register mark (see illustration 9.47). Install the TDC locating pin.

49 Tighten the camchain tension adjuster until it releases, then click it once more (see illustration 9.46c).

50 Tighten the camshaft sprocket bolts to the specified torque setting (see illustration).

51 Withdraw the TDC locating pin and remove the camshaft locking tool.

52 Rotate the crankshaft in the opposite direction to normal rotation until the chain tension adjuster is relieved, then remove the adjuster.

53 Install the camchain tensioner assembly with a new sealing washer and tighten it to the specified torque setting (see illustrations 8.9c, b and a).

54 Install the engine breather union. Clean the threads of the mounting bolt and apply a suitable non-permanent thread-locking compound, then tighten the bolt to the specified torque setting (see illustration 9.2b and a).

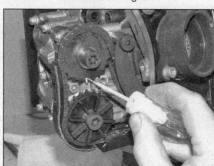

9.47 Mark the position of the upper sprocket

9.50 Tighten both sprocket bolts

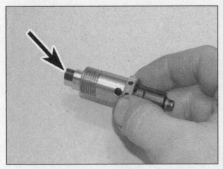

9.64a Set the adjuster as shown

9.64b Install the adjuster and sleeve . . .

9.64c . . . then tighten the adjuster

55 Check the valve clearances (see Chapter 1).
56 Install the remaining components in the reverse order of removal.
57 Before installing the valve cover, ensure that the open end of the E-clip securing the upper exhaust cam follower faces the cylinder head **(see illustration 7.11)**.

Right-hand side

58 Follow the procedure in Steps 30 to 38 to install the camshafts and camshaft holder.
59 Follow the procedure in Steps 40 to 42 to install the camchain, sprockets and upper camchain guide blade. Ensure that the camshaft position sensor trigger is fitted correctly on the outside of the lower camshaft sprocket.
60 Install the camshaft position sensor with a new O-ring **(see illustrations 9.20b and a)**.
61 Install the bolt securing the camchain guide blade and tighten it to the specified torque setting **(see illustration 9.23)**.
62 Make sure that the piston is at TDC on the compression stroke and install the TDC locating pin.
63 Follow the procedure in Steps 44 and 45 to loosen the camshaft sprocket bolts and install the camshaft locking tool.
64 To set the right-hand camchain tension correctly the BMW adjuster (Part No. 111512), adjuster sleeve (Part No. 111513) and ratchet spanner (Part No. 111514) are required. Adjust the chain tension adjuster

so that the centre thread is screwed in as far as possible, then install the adjuster and sleeve **(see illustrations)**. Using the ratchet spanner and adapter, tighten the adjuster until it releases, then click it three more times **(see illustration)**.
65 Apply a register mark to the upper camshaft sprocket with a dab of paint **(see illustration)**.
66 Withdraw the TDC locating pin and rotate the crankshaft two full revolutions in the normal direction of rotation – the camshaft sprocket should rotate one revolution and return to its original position as indicated by the register mark **(see illustration 9.65)**. Install the TDC locating pin.
67 Tighten the camchain tension adjuster until it releases, then click it once more.
68 Tighten the camshaft sprocket bolts to the specified torque setting.
69 Follow the procedure in Steps 51 and 52, then install the camchain tensioner assembly with a new sealing washer and tighten it to the specified torque setting **(see illustration 8.15)**.
70 Check the valve clearances (see Chapter 1).
71 Install the remaining components in the reverse order of removal. Before installing the valve cover, ensure that the open end of the E-clip securing the upper exhaust cam follower faces the cylinder head **(see illustration 7.11)**.

10 Cylinder head removal and installation

Caution: The engine must be completely cool before beginning this procedure or the cylinder head(s) may become warped.
Note: *The cylinder heads can be removed with the engine in the frame. If the engine has been removed, ignore the steps which do not apply.*
Special tool: *A degree disc is required for angle-tightening the cylinder head nuts.*

Removal

1 Disconnect the battery negative (-) terminal (see Chapter 7).
2 Remove the exhaust system (see Chapter 3).
3 Displace the throttle bodies (see Chapter 3).
4 Remove the valve covers (see Section 7).
5 Remove the camchain tensioners (see Section 8).
6 Remove the cam followers and camshafts (see Section 9).
7 Release the clips securing the breather hose on the left-hand side and remove the hose **(see illustration)**. Undo the screw securing the earth wire terminal **(see illustration 4.53b)**.
8 On the right-hand side, trace the wiring from the temperature sensor and disconnect

9.65 Mark the position of the upper sprocket

10.7 Remove the breather hose

10.8a Trace wiring from the temperature sensor . . .

10.8b . . . and disconnect the connector

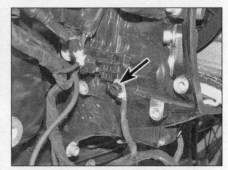

10.8c Undo the earth terminal screw

10.8d Undo the bolt . . .

10.8e . . . noting the sealing washer . . .

10.8f . . . and remove the camchain guide blade

it at the connector (see illustrations). Undo the screw securing the earth wire terminal (see illustration). Undo the bolt securing the camchain guide blade and withdraw the blade (see illustrations). Discard the sealing washer as a new one must be fitted.

9 Release the cable-ties securing the wiring on the underside of both cylinders and remove the brackets (see illustration).

10 Working on one side of the engine at a time, stuff clean rag into the camchain tunnel to prevent anything falling inside, then undo the three 6 mm screws and 8 mm bolt securing the cylinder head (see illustration).

11 Undo the cylinder head nuts evenly and in a criss-cross pattern and remove the washers (see illustrations).

12 Pull the cylinder head up off the studs

(see illustration). If it is stuck, tap around the joint face between the head and the cylinder with a soft-faced mallet to free it. Do not

attempt to free the head by levering with a screwdriver between the head and cylinder – you'll damage the sealing surfaces.

10.9 Remove the lower cover brackets

10.10 6 mm screws (A), 8 mm bolt (B)

10.11a Undo the cylinder head nuts . . .

10.11b . . . noting the location of the washers

10.12 Remove the cylinder head

10.13 Remove the cylinder head gasket

10.14 Location of the dowels

13 Remove the cylinder head gasket **(see illustration)**.

14 Ensure that the dowels are a tight fit in the top of the cylinder and check that the four studs are tight **(see illustration)**.

15 Check the old cylinder head gasket and the sealing surfaces on the cylinder head and cylinder for signs of leakage, which could indicate a warped head. Discard the gasket once it has been inspected as a new one must be used.

16 Clean any traces of old gasket material from the cylinder head and cylinder. If a scraper is used, take care not to scratch or gouge the soft aluminium. Be careful not to let any of the gasket material fall into the crankcase or the oil passages.

17 If required, remove the temperature sensor (see Chapter 3).

18 If required, undo the screws securing the intake manifold and remove the manifold, noting how it fits.

Installation

19 If removed, install the temperature sensor (see Chapter 3). Install the intake manifolds and tighten the screws to the torque setting specified at the beginning of this Chapter.

20 Working on one side at a time, ensure the dowels are in place in the top of the cylinder **(see illustration 10.14)**.

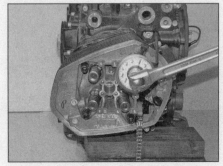

10.25 Angle-tighten the nuts using a degree disc

21 Fit the new head gasket, making sure all the holes are correctly aligned **(see illustration 10.13)**. Never re-use the old gasket.

22 Carefully fit the cylinder head over the studs and onto the cylinder, feeding the camchain and tensioner blade or guide blade, as appropriate, up through the tunnel.

23 Install the cylinder head nuts with their washers, with the collared end of the nuts facing the cylinder head **(see illustration 10.11b)**. Tighten the nuts finger-tight.

24 Install the 8 mm bolt and washer and the three 6 mm screws and tighten them all finger-tight **(see illustration 10.10)**.

25 Tighten the cylinder head nuts evenly, a little at a time and in a criss-cross sequence, to the initial torque setting specified at the beginning of this Chapter. Next, using a degree disc (see *Tools and Workshop Tips*), angle-tighten each nut in the same sequence to the second, and then to the final stage settings **(see illustration)**.

26 Tighten the 8 mm bolt to the specified torque setting, then tighten the three 6 mm screws to the specified torque setting.

27 Install the right-hand camchain guide blade **(see illustration 10.8f)**. Fit a new sealing washer to the bolt and tighten it to the specified torque setting.

28 Follow the procedure in Section 9 to install the cam followers and camshafts.

29 Install the remaining components in the reverse order of removal, noting the following:

● Check the valve clearances and adjust if necessary (see Chapter 1).
● Check the engine oil level and top-up if necessary (see *Pre-ride checks*).

11 Cylinder head and valve overhaul

1 Because of the complex nature of this job and the special tools and equipment required, most owners leave servicing of the valves, valve seats and valve guides to a professional. However,

you can make an initial assessment of whether the valves are seating correctly, and therefore sealing, by pouring a small amount of solvent into the valve ports. If the solvent leaks past the valve into the combustion chamber area the valve is not seating correctly and sealing.

2 With the correct tools (a valve spring compressor is essential – make sure it is suitable for motorcycle work), you can also remove the valves and associated components from the cylinder head, clean them and check them for wear to assess the extent of the work needed. Unless seat cutting or guide replacement is required, the head can then be reassembled.

3 A dealer service department or specialist engineer can renew the guides and re-cut the valve seats.

4 After the valve service has been performed, be sure to clean the head very thoroughly before installation on the engine to remove any metal particles or abrasive grit that may still be present from the valve service operations. Use compressed air, if available, to blow out all the holes and passages.

Disassembly

Special tool: *A valve spring compressor suitable for motorcycle work is absolutely necessary for this procedure.*

5 Before proceeding, arrange to label and store the valves along with their related components in such a way that they can be returned to their original locations without getting mixed up. A good way to do this is to obtain a container which is divided into eight compartments, and to label each compartment with the identity of the valve which will be stored in it (i.e. left or right-hand cylinder, intake top or bottom and exhaust top or bottom valve). Alternatively, labelled plastic bags will do just as well.

6 If required, remove the temperature sensor **(see illustration 10.8a)**. If work is being undertaken on the cylinder head and there is a danger that the sensor may be damaged, remove it for safekeeping.

11.8a Compress the valve spring . . .

11.8b . . . and remove the collets

7 If not already done, clean any traces of old gasket material from the cylinder head. If a scraper is used, take care not to scratch or gouge the soft aluminium.

 Refer to Tools and Workshop Tips for details of gasket removal methods.

8 Using a suitable valve spring compressor, compress the spring on the first valve, making sure the tool is correctly located onto both ends of the valve assembly **(see illustration)**. Do not compress the spring any more than is absolutely necessary, then remove the collets,

using either needle-nose pliers, tweezers, a magnet, or a screwdriver with a dab of grease on it **(see illustration)**.

9 Carefully release the valve spring compressor and remove the spring retainer, noting which way up it fits, and the spring **(see illustrations)**.

10 Push the valve down into the head and withdraw it from the underside **(see illustration)**. If the valve binds in the guide (won't pull through), push it back into the head and deburr the area above the collet groove with a very fine file or whetstone **(see illustration)**.

11 Note the location of the valve spring seat, then pull the valve stem seal off the top of the

valve guide using either a special removing tool or pliers **(see illustrations)**. Discard the old seal as a new one must be fitted. Lift out the spring seat, noting which way up it fits.

12 Repeat the procedure for the remaining valves. Remember to keep the components for each valve assembly together and in order so they can be reinstalled in the same location.

13 Carefully scrape all carbon deposits out of the combustion chamber area. A hand held wire brush or a piece of fine emery cloth can be used once the majority of deposits have been scraped away. Do not use a wire brush mounted in a drill motor as the head

11.9a Remove the spring retainer . . .

11.9b . . . and the valve spring

11.10a Remove the valve

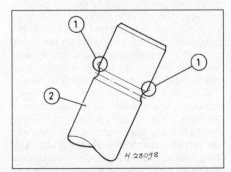

11.10b If necessary, deburr the valve stem (2) above the collet groove (1)

11.11a Note the location of the valve spring seat . . .

11.11b . . . then pull the valve stem seal off

11.17 Inspect the valve seat (arrowed)

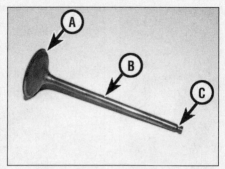

11.18 Valve face (A), stem (B) and collet groove (C)

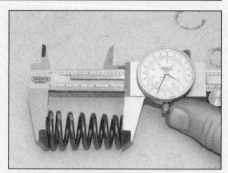

11.20 Measuring valve spring free length

material is soft and may be eroded away. Next, wash the cylinder head with solvent and dry it thoroughly. Compressed air will speed the drying process and ensure that all holes, recessed areas and oil passages are clean.

14 Scrape off any deposits that may have formed on the valves, then use a motorized wire brush to remove deposits from the valve heads and stems. Make sure the valves do not get mixed up.

15 Clean the valve springs, collets, retainers and spring seats with solvent and dry them thoroughly. Clean the parts from one valve at a time so as not to mix them up.

Inspection

16 Inspect the head very carefully for cracks and other damage. If cracks are found, a new head will be required.

17 Examine the valve seats in the combustion chamber (see illustration). If they are pitted,

cracked or burned, the head will require work beyond the scope of the home mechanic. Check that the width of the valve seat-to-valve contact area is the same around the entire circumference of the seat. If the width varies, valve seat overhaul is required.

18 Carefully inspect each valve face for cracks, pits and burned spots, and check the valve stem and the collet groove area for scoring and cracks (see illustration). Rotate the valve and check for any obvious indication that it is bent. Check the end of the stem for pitting and excessive wear. Any of the above conditions indicates the need for new valves.

19 If the necessary measuring equipment is available, install the valves in their guides and check the radial play, then measure the internal diameter of the valve guides. Compare the results with the Specifications at the beginning of this Chapter. If the results indicate that the guides are worn, have the

head inspected by a BMW dealer. Note: Carbon build-up inside the lower ends of the exhaust valve guides indicates worn valve stems and/or valve guides.

20 Check the end of each valve spring for wear and pitting. Compare the lengths of the valve springs – if any have sagged renew them as a set (see illustration). It is good practice to fit new valve springs when an engine is being overhauled.

21 Check the spring retainers and collets for obvious wear and cracks. Any questionable parts should not be reused, as extensive damage will occur in the event of failure during engine operation.

22 If the inspection indicates that no overhaul work is required, the valve components can be reinstalled in the head.

Reassembly

23 Unless a valve service has been performed, before installing the valves in the head they should be ground in (lapped) to ensure a positive seal between the valves and seats. This procedure requires coarse and fine valve grinding compound and a valve grinding tool. If a grinding tool is not available, a piece of rubber or plastic hose can be slipped over the valve stem (after the valve has been installed in the guide) and used to turn the valve.

24 Apply a small amount of coarse grinding compound to the valve face (see illustration). Lubricate the valve stem with engine oil and insert it into the guide. Note: Make sure each valve is installed in its correct guide and be careful not to get any grinding compound on the valve stem.

25 Attach the grinding tool (or hose) to the valve and rotate the tool between the palms of your hands (see illustration). Use a back-and-forth motion (as though rubbing your hands together) rather than a circular motion (i.e. so that the valve rotates alternately clockwise and anti-clockwise rather than in one direction only). Lift the valve off the seat and turn it at regular intervals to distribute the grinding compound properly. Continue the grinding procedure until the valve face and seat contact area is of uniform width and unbroken around the entire circumference of the valve face and seat (see illustrations).

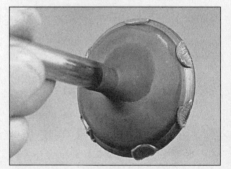

11.24 Apply grinding compound sparingly to the valve face only

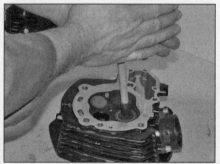

11.25a Rotate the valve grinding tool back and forth between the palms of your hands

11.25b Valve face . . .

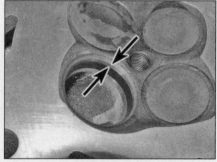

11.25c . . . and valve seat should be of uniform width

11.30 Slide a plastic sleeve over the valve stem

11.31 Press the seal into place

11.36 Tap the end of the valve stem to seat the collets

26 Carefully remove the valve from the guide and wipe off all traces of grinding compound. Use solvent to clean the valve and wipe the seat area thoroughly with a solvent soaked cloth.

27 Repeat the procedure with fine valve grinding compound, then repeat the entire procedure for the remaining valves.

28 Working on each valve in turn, lubricate the stem with engine oil and install the valve into its guide.

29 Install the spring seat with its shouldered side facing up.

30 Slide a suitable plastic sleeve over the upper end of the valve stem, then slide the new valve stem seal down over the sleeve (see illustration). The purpose of the plastic sleeve is to prevent the edges of the collet groove damaging the inside of the stem seal

12.2 Disconnect the knock sensor wiring connector

– electrical heat shrink sleeving is ideal. If a suitable sleeve is not available, take great care when installing the seal.

31 Press the seal over the end of the valve guide with an appropriate size deep socket until it is felt to clip into place (see illustration). Don't twist or cock the seal, or it will not seal properly against the valve stem. Also, don't remove it again or it will be damaged. Remove the plastic sleeve.

32 Install the spring with the wider diameter end facing down (the springs photographed were marked with green paint on their lower ends) (see illustration 11.9b).

33 Install the spring retainer, with its shouldered side facing down so that it fits into the top of the spring (see illustration 11.9a).

34 Apply a small amount of grease to the collets to hold them in place during installation, then compress the spring with the valve spring compressor and install the collets (see illustration 11.8b). Do not compress the spring any more than is absolutely necessary to slip the collets into position. Make certain that the collets are securely located in the collet groove, then release the spring compressor.

35 Repeat the procedure for the remaining valves.

36 Support the cylinder head on blocks so the valves can't contact the workbench top, then gently tap each of the valve stems to seat the collets in their grooves (see illustration).

> **HAYNES HiNT** *Check for proper sealing of the valves by pouring a small amount of solvent into each of the valve ports. If the solvent leaks past any valve into the combustion chamber the valve grinding operation on that valve should be repeated.*

12 Cylinders

Note: *The cylinders can be removed with the engine in the frame.*

Removal

1 Remove the cylinder heads (see Section 10). Ensure that the TDC locating pin is left in place.

2 Disconnect the knock sensor wiring connector (see illustration). If required, undo the mounting bolt and remove the sensor.

3 On the left-hand side, undo the bolt securing the camchain guide blade and withdraw the blade (see illustrations). Discard the sealing washer as a new one must be fitted.

4 Stuff clean rag into the camchain tunnel to prevent anything falling inside, then undo the three 6 mm screws securing the cylinder to the crankcase (see illustration).

5 Ease the cylinder away from the crankcase

12.3a Undo the bolt (arrowed) . . .

12.3b . . . and remove the camchain guide blade

12.4 Undo the 6 mm screws

12.5 Displace the cylinder to access the piston pin (arrowed)

12.6a Remove the circlips . . .

12.6b . . . and withdraw the piston pin

12.7 Draw off the cylinder with the piston inside

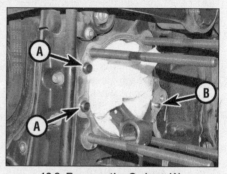

12.8 Remove the O-rings (A). Note dowel (B)

enough to gain access to the piston pin **(see illustration). Note:** *The sealant used between the cylinder and the crankcase can form a strong bond – if the cylinder is stuck, tap around the joint with a soft-faced mallet to free it from the crankcase. Do not attempt to free the cylinder by levering with a screwdriver between the cylinder and the crankcase – you'll damage the sealing surfaces.*

6 Carefully remove the circlip from both ends of the piston pin using circlip pliers **(see illustration).** Discard the circlips as new ones must be used. Push the piston pin out towards the front to free the piston from the connecting rod **(see illustration).** Note which way round the piston pin is fitted.

7 Support the connecting rod and draw

the cylinder, with the piston inside, off the mounting studs **(see illustration).** Once the cylinder has been removed, stuff clean rag around the connecting rod to protect it and to prevent anything falling into the crankcase.

8 Remove the two oil passage O-rings from the crankcase and discard them as new ones must be used **(see illustration). Note:** *The O-rings are very thin and may be embedded in the bead of sealant on the crankcase.* Remove the dowel from the crankcase if it is loose.

9 Slide the piston out of the cylinder carefully to avoid damaging the piston rings. Use a scriber or marker pen to write the cylinder identity (i.e. left or right-hand cylinder) on the piston crown or on the side of the skirt. Note that the valve cut-outs in the piston crown are larger for the

intake valves – these cut-outs face the rear of the engine **(see illustration).** Fit the pin back into the piston to ensure it can be installed the right way round on reassembly.

10 Clean all traces of sealant from the cylinder and crankcase mating surfaces. If a scraper is used, take care not to scratch or gouge the soft aluminium. Be careful not to let any of the old sealant fall into the crankcase or the oil passages. Remove the dowels in the top of the cylinder for safekeeping if they are loose **(see illustration 10.14).**

Inspection

11 The cylinder bores have a wear resistant coating which should last the life of the engine unless damage, caused by a broken piston ring or seizure, has occurred.

12 Working on one cylinder at a time, inspect the cylinder walls carefully for flaking, scratches and score marks. If damage is noted, yet the bore diameter is still within the service limit, seek the advice of a BMW dealer or engine specialist as to the suitability of the cylinder for continued use. The cylinders cannot be rebored.

13 Cylinders and pistons, as fitted at the BMW factory, are designated as either tolerance Group A or Group B. Replacement components (available from a BMW dealer) are designated as tolerance Group A/B. The group letter is stamped into the top of the cylinder, just outside the machined cylinder-to-cylinder head sealing surface **(see illustration).**

12.9 Intake valve cut-outs (B) are larger than exhaust valve cut-outs (A)

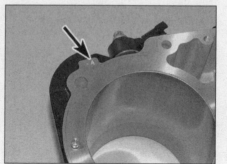

12.13 Location of the cylinder tolerance group letter

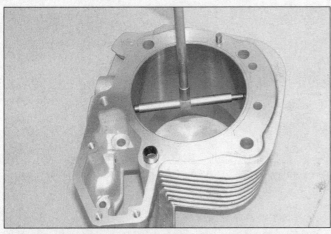

12.14a Measuring the cylinder bore with a telescoping gauge

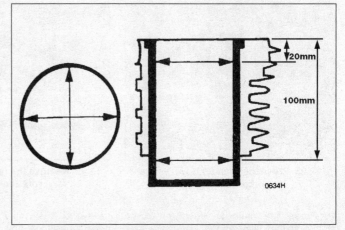

12.14b Take measurements in the directions shown

12.20 Position the piston as shown

12.21a Apply an even bead of sealant . . .

12.21b . . . to the sealing surface of the cylinder

14 Using telescoping gauges and a micrometer (see *Tools and Workshop Tips* in the Reference section), check the dimensions of each cylinder to assess the amount of wear and ovality **(see illustration)**. Take measurements 20 mm and 100 mm from the top of the bore, both parallel with the piston pin and at 90° to it, taking a total of four measurements **(see illustration)**.

15 Compare the results with the specifications at the beginning of this Chapter, then calculate any difference between the measurements to determine ovality in the bore.

16 If the cylinder is worn beyond the service limit, or bore ovality exceeds the service limits, both cylinders (and pistons) must be renewed.

Installation

17 Ensure that the TDC locating pin is in place.

18 Working on one side of the engine at a time, check that the sealing surfaces of the cylinder and crankcase are clean and free from oil and old sealant. Check that the four cylinder studs are tight – to remove and install the studs refer to Section 22.

19 If removed, install the dowel in the crankcase, then fit new oil passage O-rings **(see illustration 12.8)**.

20 Ensure that the piston ring end gaps are correctly staggered and install the piston in the cylinder, noting the importance of positioning the valve cut-outs correctly (see Section 13). Push the piston down inside the cylinder until the piston pin bore is visible below the lower edge of the cylinder bore **(see illustration)**. Don't push the piston too far, otherwise the oil control ring will come out of its groove.

21 Apply an even bead of suitable sealant to the sealing surface of the cylinder **(see illustrations)**.

Caution: Do not apply an excessive amount of sealant as it will ooze out and may obstruct oil passages.

22 Install the cylinder over the studs **(see illustration)**. Check that the piston is positioned the correct way round, with the larger (intake) valve cut-outs facing the rear of the engine and the smaller (exhaust) valve cut-outs facing the front. Remove the rag from around the connecting rod.

23 Slide the cylinder towards the crankcase, ensuring the camchain is positioned so that it enters the tunnel without causing an obstruction. Guide the connecting rod small-end into the piston – it may be necessary to adjust the position of the piston slightly so that the piston pin bore aligns with the small-end, but take care not to pull the piston out from the cylinder.

24 Lubricate the piston pin with clean engine oil and press it into position, then secure the pin with a new circlip at both ends **(see illustration)**.

12.22 Slide the cylinder over the studs

12.24 Fit new circlips on the piston pin

12.25 Press the cylinder down – note camchain

13.3a Remove the rings carefully, using your thumbs . . .

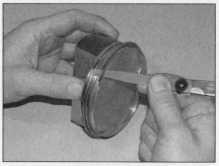

13.3b . . . or a thin blade – a feeler gauge is ideal

25 Press the cylinder down onto the crankcase **(see illustration)**.
26 Secure the cylinder with the 6 mm screws and tighten them to the torque setting specified at the beginning of this Chapter **(see illustration 12.4)**.
27 Install the left-hand camchain guide blade **(see illustration 12.3b)**. Fit a new sealing washer and tighten the bolt to the specified torque setting.
28 If removed, install the knock sensor and tighten the bolt to the specified torque setting – note that the correct torque for the sensor bolt is critical, otherwise the sensor will not function correctly. Connect the sensor wiring connector **(see illustration 12.2)**.
29 If removed, install the dowels in the top of the cylinder, then install the cylinder head (see Section 10).

13 Pistons

Note: *The pistons can be removed with the engine in the frame.*
Special tool: *A piston ring clamp is required for installing the pistons.*

Removal

1 Follow the procedure in Section 12 to remove the piston with the cylinder **(see illustration 12.7)**. New pistons are printed with identification marks on the crown indicating weight class, part number, tolerance group (AB), left or right-hand fitment (L or R) and direction of installation arrow, but these marks are unlikely to be visible once the engine has been run. Ensure the piston is clearly marked to ensure correct installation if you are going to refit the existing pistons. If both pistons have been removed, work on them separately to avoid getting parts mixed up.
2 Before the inspection process can be carried out, remove the piston rings and clean the piston.
3 Using your thumbs or a thin blade, carefully ease the rings off the piston **(see illustrations)**. Do not nick or gouge the piston in the process. Note which way up each ring fits and in which

groove as they must be installed in their original positions if being re-used. The upper surface of each ring is marked 'TOP'. Note that the oil control ring (lowest on the piston) has an expander fitted behind it.
4 Scrape all traces of carbon from the piston crown. A hand-held wire brush or a piece of fine emery cloth can be used once most of the deposits have been scraped away. Do not, under any circumstances, use a wire brush mounted in a drill motor to remove deposits from the piston – the piston material is soft and will be eroded away by the wire brush.
5 Use a piston ring groove cleaning tool to remove any carbon deposits from the ring grooves. If a tool is not available, a piece broken off an old ring will do the job. Be very careful to remove only the carbon deposits. Do not remove any metal and do not nick or gouge the sides of the ring grooves.
6 Once the deposits have been removed, wash the piston with solvent and dry it thoroughly. Make sure the oil return holes in the back of the oil ring groove are clear. If the identification mark made on removal is cleaned off, be sure to re-mark the piston with the correct identity (L or R).

Inspection

7 Inspect the piston for cracks and damage around the skirt, at the pin bosses and at the ring lands **(see illustration)**. Normal wear appears as light, vertical marks on the thrust surfaces of the skirt and slight looseness of the top ring in its groove. If the skirt is scored or

scuffed, the piston and cylinder are probably worn beyond the service limit. Alternatively, the engine may have been suffering from overheating caused by lack of lubrication or abnormal combustion. Check the operation of the oil pump (see Section 19) and, if necessary, have the engine management system checked by a BMW dealer.
8 A hole in the top of the piston (only likely in extreme circumstances) or burned areas around the edge of the piston crown, indicate that pre-ignition or knocking under load have occurred. The knock sensors fitted to the cylinders should ensure correct ignition under all circumstances, but if a sensor fails, or if it is fitted incorrectly, the engine management system will not be able to set the correct ignition timing. If you find evidence of any problems, the causes must be corrected or the damage will occur again.
9 Measure the piston diameter 6 mm up from the bottom of the skirt and at 90° to the piston pin axis **(see illustration)**. Compare the result with the specifications at the beginning of this Chapter. If the piston is worn beyond the service limit new cylinders and pistons will have to be fitted.
10 Subtract the piston diameter from the bore diameter (see Section 12) to obtain the clearance and compare the result with the service limit specified at the beginning of this Chapter. If it is greater than specified, new pistons will have to be fitted (see Step 12).
11 Apply clean engine oil to the piston pin, insert it part way into the piston and check

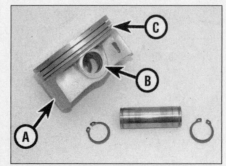

13.7 Inspect the piston skirt (A), pin boss (B) and ring lands (C)

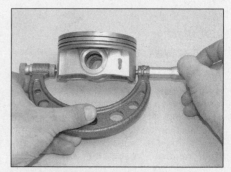

13.9 Measuring piston diameter

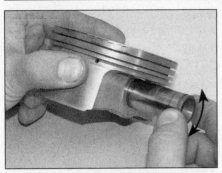

13.11 Check for freeplay between the piston and pin

13.16 Install the piston into the top of the bore

13.17 Ease the piston down the bore carefully . . .

for any freeplay between the two – there should be no discernable freeplay **(see illustration)**.

12 Note that new pistons are supplied as a pair, complete with rings. It is not possible to purchase and fit just one new piston. This is to ensure even weight and balance between the cylinders.

Installation

13 Ensure that the TDC locating pin is in place. Work on one side of the engine at a time.

14 Install the piston rings and ensure that the ring end gaps are correctly staggered (see Section 14).

15 Lubricate the piston, rings and the inside of the ring clamp with clean engine oil. Install the clamp over the rings and tighten it enough to compress the rings into their grooves, but not so tight that it locks onto the piston – as the piston is pressed into the cylinder bore, the clamp must be able to slide off. Once the clamp is in place, don't rotate it as the position of the ring end gaps will alter.

16 Lubricate the appropriate cylinder bore with clean engine oil, then install the lower end of the piston into the top of the bore **(see illustration)** – check that the L marked piston is fitted in the left cylinder and the R marked piston in the right cylinder (see Step 1). Also ensure that the piston is installed the right way round with the larger (intake) valve cut-outs

13.18a . . . and remove the ring clamp

facing the rear of the cylinder and the smaller (exhaust) valve cut-outs and direction arrow to the front – again, don't rotate the piston once it had been pressed all the way into the cylinder as the position of the ring end gaps will alter.

17 Press down on the top of the piston and slowly ease it into the bore **(see illustration)**. If the rings snag on the top lip of the bore, tighten the clamp slightly to compress the rings further into their grooves.

Caution: Do not force the piston down – this will only result in broken rings.

18 The ring clamp will become free once the piston is safely inside the cylinder **(see illustrations)**.

19 Follow the procedure in Section 12 to install the piston and cylinder.

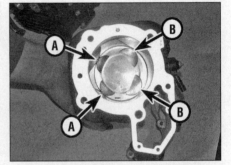

13.18b Check location of the valve cut-outs – exhaust (A) and intake (B)

14 Piston rings

1 It is good practice to fit new piston rings when an engine is being overhauled. Before installing the piston rings, the ring end gaps must be checked with the rings installed in the cylinder.

2 First, check that the cylinder bore is not worn beyond the service limit (see Section 12).

3 Lay out the pistons and the new ring sets so the rings will be matched with the same piston and cylinder during the measurement procedure and engine assembly. The upper surface of each ring is marked 'TOP' **(see illustration)**. Note that the oil control ring (lowest on the piston) has a wire expander fitted behind it.

4 To measure the installed ring end gap, insert each ring into the top of the cylinder and square it up with the cylinder walls by pushing it in with the top of the piston. The ring should be about 20 mm below the top edge of the cylinder. To measure the end gap, slip a feeler gauge between the ends of the ring and compare the measurement to the specifications at the beginning of this Chapter **(see illustration)**. Note that the end gaps for the top and second ring are different from the oil control ring.

5 If the gap is larger or smaller than specified, double check to make sure that you have the

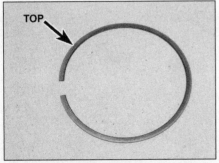

14.3 Upper surface of each piston ring is marked TOP

14.4 Measuring piston ring end gap with a feeler gauge

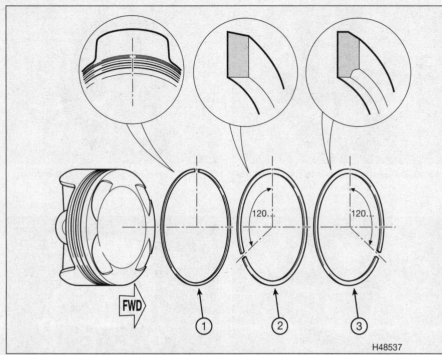

14.11 Piston ring end gap positions and profiles

1 Oil control ring   2 Second ring   3 Top ring

correct rings before proceeding. Excess end gap is not critical unless it exceeds the service limit.

6 The oil control ring (lowest on the piston) is installed first. It is composed of two separate components – the expander and the ring. Pull the ends of the expander apart enough to fit it over the top of the piston and slip it into its groove, then press the ends back together. Ensure that the straight wire is not pulled out of either end of the coiled wire. Now install the oil control ring over the expander. Make sure that the 'TOP' mark is facing up and that the end gap in the ring is on the opposite side of the piston to the end gap in the expander. Do not expand the ring any more than is necessary to slide it into place. To avoid breaking the ring, slide a thin blade around the piston while easing the ring on **(see illustration 13.3b)**.

7 After the oil ring components have been installed, check that the ring can be turned smoothly in the ring groove.

8 Install the second ring next. Fit the ring into the middle groove in the piston and use a thin blade, as with the oil ring, to ease the ring on without breaking it.

9 Finally, install the top ring into the top groove in the piston.

10 Once the rings are correctly installed, check they move freely without snagging.

11 Before fitting the piston into the cylinder, stagger the ring end gaps 120° apart. Viewed as fitted onto the connecting rod, the oil control ring end gap should be facing up, the second ring gap facing back and down, and the top ring gap facing forwards and down **(see illustration)**.

15 Connecting rods

Note 1: The connecting rods can be removed with the engine in the frame, gaining access to the big-end bolts for each rod via the cylinder aperture in the crankcase on the opposite side of the engine. However, accurate assessment of wear to the crankshaft crankpins requires the engine removed from the frame and the crankcase halves separated to gain access to the crankshaft.

Note 2: The big-end bolts are of the stretch type – new bolts must be fitted when the engine is finally reassembled.

Special tool: A degree disc is required for angle-tightening the connecting rod big-end bolts.

15.10a Mark the cylinder identity on the connecting rods . . .

Removal – with engine in the frame

1 Remove the cylinder heads (see Section 10) and the cylinders and pistons (see Section 12).

2 Position the crankshaft to provide the best access to the big-end bolts on the connecting rod being removed.

3 Using paint or a marker pen, mark the cylinder identity (L or R) on the connecting rod and cap **(see illustration 15.10a and b)**. Use the marks to indicate which way round the rod is fitted.

4 Undo the big-end bolts and separate the cap and its bearing shell from the crankpin **(see illustrations 15.11a and b)**.

Caution: Ensure the bearing shells do not fall out of either the cap or the rod and into the crankcase.

5 Withdraw the connecting rod and its bearing shell from the other side of the engine. Keep the rod, cap and the bearing shells together to ensure correct installation.

6 If required, follow the same procedure to remove the other connecting rod from the crankshaft.

Removal – engine out of the frame

7 Separate the crankcase halves (see Section 22).

8 Lift out the crankshaft assembly, taking care not to dislodge the crankshaft main and guide bearing shells (see Section 24).

9 Before removing the rods from the crankshaft, measure the big-end side clearance. Working on one rod at a time, push it to one side on the crankpin and measure the clearance between the big-end and the crankshaft with a feeler gauge. If the clearance is greater than the service limit listed in the *Specifications* at the beginning of this Chapter, the rod must be renewed.

10 Using paint or a marker pen, mark the cylinder identity (L or R) on the connecting rod and cap. Use the marks to indicate which way round the rod is fitted **(see illustrations)**.

11 Undo the big-end bolts and separate the rod and cap from the crankpin **(see**

15.10b . . . and on the big-end caps

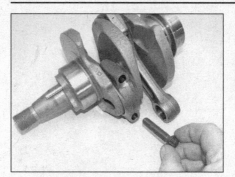

15.11a Undo the big-end bolts . . .

15.11b . . . and separate the rod and cap

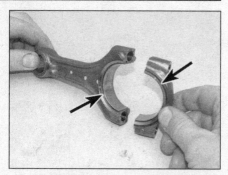

15.11c Keep the rod, cap and the bearing shells (arrowed) together

illustrations). Keep the rod, cap and the bearing shells together to ensure correct installation **(see illustration).**

12 Follow the same procedure to remove the other connecting rod from the crankshaft.

Inspection

13 The connecting rods are fitted as paired sets dependant upon their weight. Weight class identification is represented by lettering on the side of the big-end or by coloured dots (white, blue or yellow) painted on the sides of the rods (see *Specifications* at the beginning of this Chapter for details) **(see illustration).**

14 The joint between the connecting rod and the cap is a fractured joint that can only be assembled one way round **(see illustration).** Take care not to damage the joint surfaces – if the surfaces are not a perfect match, the two halves of the big-end will not come-together

properly and a new connecting rod will have to be fitted.

15 Check the connecting rods for cracks and other obvious damage.

16 To check the rod small-end, lubricate the appropriate piston pin with clean engine oil, then insert it in the rod and measure the radial play between the two. If the play is greater than the specification, measure the pin external diameter and the small-end bore diameter and compare the results with the specifications to see whether it is the pin or the small-end that is worn beyond its service limit **(see illustrations).** Renew the pin or the rod as required. Repeat the check with the other connecting rod. **Note:** *If a new connecting rod is fitted, it must be of the same weight class as the other rod in the engine (see Step 13).*

17 Examine the big-end bearing shells **(see illustration).** If they are scored, badly scuffed or appear to have seized, check

the corresponding crankpin. Damage to the surface of the crankpin on a standard crankshaft can be corrected by re-grinding and fitting oversize (+0.25 mm) bearing shells. If the crankshaft has already been reground, indicated by paint marks on the front crankshaft web, a new crankshaft will have to be fitted. If there is any doubt about the condition of the crankshaft, have it checked by a BMW dealer.

18 If the bearing shells show signs of normal wear they should be renewed – always renew the shells in both big-ends as a set. Note that the shells are colour-coded red or blue according to their position – the colour mark is on the edge of the shell **(see illustration 15.17).** Shells with a red mark are fitted in the rod cap and shells with a blue mark are fitted in the rod. Remove the bearing shells by easing them out to one side with your fingers, noting how they fit **(see illustration).**

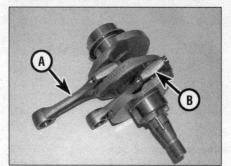

15.13 Look for weight class markings on the rods (A) or big-ends (B)

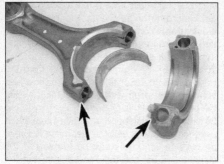

15.14 Note the uneven surface of the fractured joint (arrowed)

15.16a Measuring the piston pin external diameter . . .

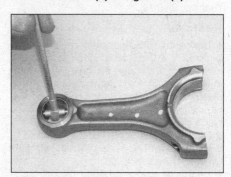

15.16b . . . and the small-end bore diameter

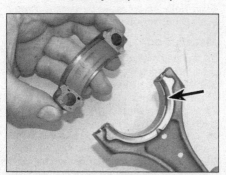

15.17 Examine the bearing shells – note the location of the colour mark (arrowed)

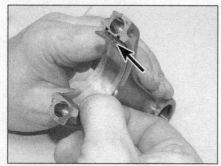

15.18 Ease the shells out carefully – note the locating tab (arrowed)

15.22 Measuring the diameter of the crankpin

15.24 Measuring the big-end bore diameter with shells installed

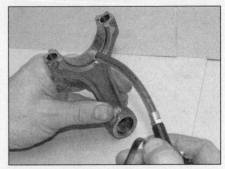

15.27 Lubricate the shells generously with clean engine oil

19 Check the rod big-end for radial wear. Assemble the cap on the rod, ensuring that the two halves of the fractured joint are a perfect fit, then install the bolts and tighten them to the second stage setting (see *Specifications* at the beginning of this Chapter). Use the old bolts for the purpose of the check. Measure the diameter of the big-end bore with a telescoping gauge and micrometer and compare the result with the specification at the beginning of this Chapter. If it is greater than the specified figure, renew the connecting rod (see **Note**, Step 16).

20 If you are in doubt about their straightness, have the rods checked for twist and bending by a BMW dealer. Note that the sintered-metal type connecting rods used in this engine cannot be straightened due to risk of fracture.

Oil clearance check

Note: *This procedure can only be undertaken with any degree of accuracy once the crankshaft has been removed from the engine (see Section 24).*

21 Whether new bearing shells are being fitted or the original ones are being re-used, the connecting rod big-end bearing oil clearance should be checked prior to reassembly. Bearing oil clearance is measured using a micrometer and telescoping gauge.

22 First measure the diameter of the crankpin in two different planes with the micrometer and note the results **(see illustration)**. Wear on the crankpin can be determined by comparing the results with the specifications at the beginning of this Chapter. Note that a re-ground

15.30 Tighten the big-end bolts using a degree disc

(Stage 1) crankshaft is identified by paint marks on the front crankshaft web.

23 Next, working on the corresponding connecting rod, clean the backs of the bearing shells and the shell locations in both the rod and cap with a suitable solvent. Press the shells into their locations, ensuring that the tab on each shell engages the notch in the connecting rod or cap **(see illustration 15.18)**. Make sure the shells are fitted in the correct locations and take care not to touch the bearing surfaces with your fingers.

24 Assemble the cap on the rod, ensuring that the two halves of the fractured joint are a perfect fit. Lubricate the threads and the underside of the heads of the big-end bolts with engine oil, then tighten them to the second stage setting (see *Specifications* at the beginning of this Chapter). Use the old bolts for the purpose of the check. Measure the diameter of the big-end bore with bearing shells with a telescoping gauge and micrometer and note the result **(see illustration)**. With reference to Step 22, note that a re-ground crankshaft will be fitted with appropriately sized Stage 1 shells.

25 Subtract the crankpin diameter from the bore diameter to obtain the clearance and compare the result with the specifications at the beginning of this Chapter.

26 If the original bearing shells have been used for the check and the clearance is within the service limit, they can be re-used. If the clearance is beyond the service limit, but the crankpin journal is good (see Step 22), fit new bearing shells and check the oil clearance once again. **Note:** *Always renew the bearing shells in both connecting rods at the same time.*

Installation

27 Working on one connecting rod at a time, press the bearing shells into their locations (see Step 23). Lubricate the shells and the crankpin with clean engine oil **(see illustration)**.

28 Lubricate a set of new big-end bolts with clean engine oil.

29 Install the connecting rod and cap on the crankpin, ensuring they are the right way round (see Step 10). Ensure that the two halves of the fractured joint are a perfect fit, then install the new bolts and tighten them finger-tight.

30 Tighten the bolts evenly to the second

stage setting (see *Specifications* at the beginning of this Chapter), then use a degree disc (see *Tools and Workshop Tips* in the *Reference* section) to tighten them to the final setting in one continuous movement **(see illustration)**.

31 Check that the connecting rod is free to rotate smoothly and freely on the crankpin. If the rod feels tight, tap on the bottom of the cap with a soft-faced mallet to free it. If there are still signs of roughness or tightness, detach the rod and recheck the assembly. **Note:** *New big-end bolts must be used each time they are disturbed.*

32 Install the other rod in the same way. Ensure that all components have been returned to their original locations using the marks made on disassembly.

33 As appropriate, follow the procedures in Sections 12 and 10 to install the pistons, cylinders and cylinder heads, or Section 24 and install the crankshaft assembly in the crankcase.

16 Alternator drive pulley and engine timing cover

Note: *The alternator drive components and the engine timing cover can be removed with the engine in the frame.*
Special tools: *A top dead centre (TDC) locating pin is required for this procedure (see Tool Tip, Section 8). Seal installation guides are required to fit the crankshaft oil seal (see Tool Tip, Step 18).*

Removal

1 During this procedure the engine should be locked in the TDC position by inserting a locating pin through the hole in the right-hand side of the gearbox case **(see illustration 8.8)**. Remove the body panels as appropriate to your machine to access the hole (see Chapter 6).

2 Drain the engine oil (see Chapter 1, Section 1).

3 Remove the alternator drive belt (see Chapter 1, Section 9).

4 Undo the screws securing the alternator drive belt top cover and remove the cover **(see illustrations 4.48a and b)**.

16.7 Remove the crankshaft position sensor

16.8 Remove the alternator drive pulley

16.10 Note the location of the dowels

5 Remove both primary spark plugs (see Chapter 1, Section 5).

6 Turn the engine clockwise with a spanner on the crankshaft pulley nut until both pistons are at TDC. Insert the TDC locating pin into the hole in the right-hand side of the gearbox case. The pin should pass through the clutch assembly and locate in a hole in the crankcase.

7 Undo the screw securing the crankshaft position sensor and pull the sensor out of its location in the top of the timing cover, noting the location of the sealing O-ring **(see illustration)**.

8 Undo the nut securing the alternator belt drive pulley, remove the washer, then lift off the pulley, noting which way round its fits **(see illustration)**.

9 Undo the screws and washers securing the timing cover to the crankcase and remove the cover. The sealant used between the cover and the crankcase can form a strong bond – if the cover is stuck, tap around the joint with a soft-faced mallet to free it from the crankcase. Do not attempt to free the cover by levering with a screwdriver between the cover and the crankcase – you'll damage the sealing surfaces.

10 Note the location of the dowels in either the cover or the crankcase and remove them if they are loose **(see illustration)**.

11 Clean all traces of sealant from the cover and crankcase mating surfaces. If a scraper is used, take care not to scratch or gouge the soft aluminium. Be careful not to let any of the old sealant fall into the crankcase.

12 Support the cover on the work surface and drive out the old crankshaft oil seal, noting which way round it fits **(see illustration)**. Clean the inside of the seal housing with suitable solvent.

Installation

Note: *Two types of crankshaft seal are supplied by BMW – either spring lipped or Teflon lipped (see Step 17). Check which type of seal has been supplied.*

13 If removed, fit the dowels into the crankcase or cover (see Step 10).

14 Apply an even bead of suitable sealant to the sealing surface of the cover **(see illustration)**.

15 Install the timing cover, then install the cover screws and washers and tighten them evenly to the torque setting specified at the beginning of this Chapter.

16.12 Driving out the old crankshaft seal

16 Install a new O-ring on the crankshaft position sensor **(see illustration 16.7)**. Install the sensor and tighten the screw to the specified torque setting.

17 Before installation, check which type of crankshaft seal is being fitted **(see illustration)**. A spring lipped seal should be lubricated with a smear of engine oil, a Teflon lipped seal should be fitted dry.

18 Care must be taken to avoid damaging the inner lip of the new crankshaft seal when it is installed – a suitable seal guide and sleeve

16.14 Apply an even bead of sealant to the cover

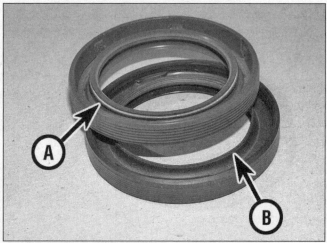

16.17 Spring lipped seal (A), Teflon lipped seal (B)

16.18a Slip the seal over the end of the guide . . .

16.18b . . . then press the seal onto the crankshaft with the sleeve

16.18c Withdraw the guide

16.18d Use threaded sleeve . . .

16.18e . . . to press the seal into the cover

16.18f The installed seal should look like this

must be used (see **Tool Tip**). BMW produces a set of tools for this purpose. Slip the seal, inner side first, over the shaped end of the guide (Part No. 115713) **(see illustration)**. Install the guide on the end of the crankshaft and press the seal into position with the sleeve (Part No. 115711) **(see illustration)**. Withdraw the guide **(see illustration)**. Screw on the threaded sleeve (Part No. 115712) to press the seal fully into the cover **(see illustrations)**. The outer face of the installed seal should be level with the edge of the seal housing **(see illustration)**.

19 Install the alternator belt drive pulley, writing facing out, then install the washer and nut **(see illustration 16.8)**. Ensure that the TDC locating pin is securely in place and tighten the pulley nut to the first stage torque setting, then tighten the nut to the final torque setting specified at the beginning of this Chapter.

20 Install the alternator drive belt top cover and tighten the screws to the specified torque.

21 Follow the procedure in Chapter 1, Section 9, and install the alternator drive belt.

22 Refill the engine with oil to the correct level (see Chapter 1).

23 Install the remaining components in the reverse order of removal.

17 Balancer shaft gears and balancer shaft

Note: *The crankshaft and balancer shaft gears can be removed with the engine in the frame. To remove the balancer shaft, shaft bearing and oil seal, first remove the gearbox (see Section 4).*

Special tools: *A two-legged puller is required to remove the crankshaft gear and a centre bolt puller is required to remove the balancer shaft gear.*

Balancer shaft gears

Removal

1 Remove the alternator drive pulley and engine timing cover (see Section 16).

2 Remove the primary spark plugs (see Chapter 1). Turn the engine in the normal direction of

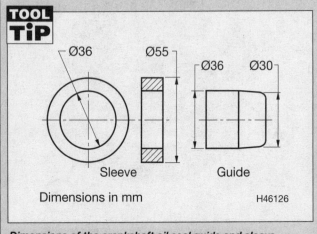

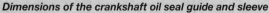

Dimensions of the crankshaft oil seal guide and sleeve

17.2 Align the register marks on the gears

17.3a Unscrew the balancer shaft gear nut

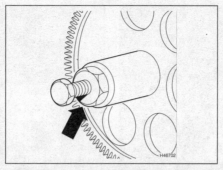

17.3b Use a centre bolt puller to draw off the gear

17.3c Use a two-legged puller to draw off the gear

rotation until the register marks on the crankshaft and balancer shaft gears align **(see illustration)**. In this position the engine is at TDC compression on the right-hand cylinder. Insert the TDC locating pin into the hole in the right-hand side of the gearbox case (see Section 8).

3 Hold the balancer shaft gear **(see illustration 17.11)** and unscrew the nut **(see illustration)**. BMW produces a service tool (Part No. 124600) for holding the gear. If available, use a centre bolt puller that screws onto the threads on the gear to draw the gear off **(see illustration)** – BMW puller (Part No. 112742). Alternatively, protect the end of the balancer shaft with a suitable block of soft metal and use a two-legged puller as shown **(see illustration)**. Note the location of the Woodruff key in the shaft and remove it for safekeeping if it is loose **(see illustration)**.

4 Remove the TDC locating pin.

5 Temporarily screw the alternator pulley nut onto the end of the crankshaft to protect the threads, position a suitable block of soft metal over the nut and assemble a two-legged puller as shown **(see illustration)**. Pretension the puller, then heat the hub of the crankshaft gear to approximately 100°C and draw the gear off the taper on the shaft. Note the position of the gear locating pin **(see illustration)**.

Installation

6 Ensure the crankshaft and the auxiliary shaft are in the TDC (compression, right-hand cylinder) position – the locating pin for the crankshaft gear should be facing up, and the notch on the auxiliary shaft sprocket should also be facing up **(see illustration 18.2)**. Install the TDC locating pin.

17.3d Note location of the Woodruff key

17.5b Note the position of the locating pin (arrowed)

7 Use a suitable solvent to ensure the taper on the crankshaft and the inside of the crankshaft gear are clean and free from oil **(see illustrations)**. Align the hole in the gear with the locating pin and install the gear on

17.5a Set-up for drawing the crankshaft gear off

17.7a Clean the crankshaft taper . . .

the shaft, then temporarily install the alternator pulley, washer and nut **(see illustrations)**.

8 Ensure that the TDC locating pin is securely in place and tighten the pulley nut to the first stage torque setting, then tighten the nut to the

17.7b . . . and the inside of the gear

17.7c Install the crankshaft gear . . .

17.7d . . . alternator pulley, washer and nut

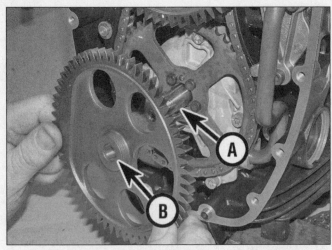

17.10 Align the shaft key (A) with the slot in the gear (B)

17.11 Tighten the balancer shaft nut to the specified torque

final torque setting specified at the beginning of this Chapter. With the gear pressed firmly onto the crankshaft taper, undo the nut and remove the washer and pulley.

9 If removed, install the Woodruff key in the balancer shaft **(see illustration 17.3d)**. If the key is loose it can be secured with a suitable high temperature adhesive (BMW recommends Loctite 648).

10 The register mark on the crankshaft gear should be facing down. Position the balancer shaft gear with its register marks facing up and rotate the balancer shaft so that the key on the shaft aligns with the slot in the centre of the gear **(see illustration)**. Align the teeth of the balancer shaft gear with the crankshaft

gear and press it into position on the shaft. With the gear installed, check the alignment of the register marks **(see illustration 17.2)**. Fit the shaft nut finger-tight.

11 Ensure that the TDC locating pin is securely in place. Hold the balancer shaft gear and tighten the shaft nut to the specified torque setting **(see illustration)**. Remove the TDC locating pin.

12 Install the remaining components in the reverse order of removal.

Balancer shaft, oil seal and bearing

Removal

13 Remove the gearbox (see Section 4).

14 Remove the clutch (see Section 20).

15 Remove the alternator drive belt cover (see Chapter 1).

16 Counter-hold the alternator drive pulley nut and unscrew the balance weight bolt from the rear of the engine, then pull off the balance weight, noting how it fits **(see illustrations)**. Discard the bolt as a new one must be fitted.

17 Prise the shaft oil seal out of the crankcase using a flat-bladed screwdriver **(see illustration)**. Note which way round the seal is fitted.

18 If a new oil seal is to be fitted and no further disassembly is required, go to Step 26.

19 To remove the balancer shaft and bearing, first follow the procedure in Steps 1 to 3 and remove the alternator drive pulley, engine timing cover and balancer shaft gear. Note the position of the Woodruff key on the balancer shaft **(see illustration 17.3d)**. If the key is not laying flat, remove it to avoid damage to the internal auxiliary shaft bearing.

20 Working from the rear of the crankcase, remove the bearing retaining circlip **(see illustration)**. Discard the circlip as a new one must be fitted. Push the balancer shaft, complete with the bearing, out from the front **(see illustration)**. Note that a new bearing must be fitted.

21 Inspect the bearing surface on the inside front end of the auxiliary shaft **(see**

17.16a Unscrew the balance weight bolt . . .

17.16b . . . then pull off the balance weight

17.17 Prise out the shaft oil seal

17.20a Remove the circlip . . .

17.20b . . . then push the shaft and bearing out

17.21 Inspect the bearing surface (arrowed)

17.22a Inspect the lugs on the rear . . .

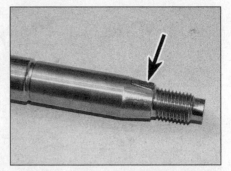

17.22b . . . and the threads on the front end of the shaft. Note position of Woodruff key (arrowed)

illustration). If it is scored, badly scuffed or chipped, a new auxiliary shaft will have to be fitted (see Section 25).

22 Inspect the lugs on the rear end of the balancer shaft **(see illustration)**. Note that the lugs are offset – the balance weight can only be fitted in one position. Inspect the threads on the front end of the shaft **(see illustration)**. If the key has not been removed, ensure it is pressed firmly into its slot.

Installation

23 Lubricate the inside of the auxiliary shaft

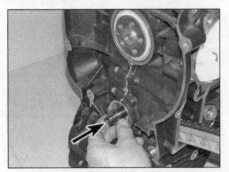

17.23a Install the shaft from the rear

with engine oil, then slide the balancer shaft into position from the rear **(see illustration)**. Press the new bearing into place and drive it all the way into its housing with a bearing driver or suitably sized socket **(see illustrations)**. BMW produces a sleeve and driver for this purpose (Part Nos. 115742 and 115741). With the bearing fully installed, the circlip groove should be visible all the way round. Secure the bearing with a new circlip **(see illustration 17.20a)**.

24 Ensure the engine is at TDC compression on the right-hand cylinder (see Step 6).

25 If removed, install the key in the balancer shaft (see Step 9), then install the balancer shaft gear and tighten the nut to the torque setting specified at the beginning of this Chapter (see Steps 10 and 11).

26 Before fitting a new oil seal to the rear of the casing, clean the inside of the seal housing with suitable solvent. Two types of balancer shaft seal are supplied by BMW – either spring lipped or Teflon lipped. Check which type of seal is being fitted (see Section 16, Step 17). To avoid damaging the inner lip of a Teflon lipped seal when it is installed, a suitable seal guide and sleeve must be used. BMW produces a set of tools for this purpose. Slip the seal over the shaped end of the guide

(Part No. 115742). Install the guide on the end of the balancer shaft and press the seal into position with the sleeve (Part No. 115741). The outer face of the installed seal should be level with the edge of the seal housing.

27 Lightly lubricate the balance weight friction face with engine oil and install it over the lugs on the end of the shaft **(see illustration 17.16b)**. Install the new balance weight bolt and hold the balancer shaft gear **(see illustration 17.11)**. Tighten the bolt to the initial torque setting (see *Specifications* at the beginning of this Chapter), then use a degree disc (see *Tools and Workshop Tips* in the *Reference* section) to tighten it to the final setting in one continuous movement.

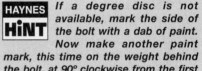

HAYNES HiNT *If a degree disc is not available, mark the side of the bolt with a dab of paint. Now make another paint mark, this time on the weight behind the bolt, at 90° clockwise from the first mark. Tighten the bolt until both marks align.*

28 Install the remaining components in the reverse order of removal.

17.23b Install the new bearing . . .

17.23c . . . and drive it into its housing

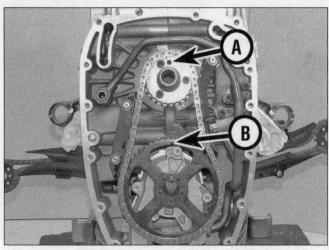

18.2 Locating pin (A) and notch (B) should be facing up

18.3a Undo the banjo bolt . . .

18 Auxiliary shaft drive chain, tensioner and sprockets

Note: *The auxiliary shaft drive chain, tensioner and sprockets can be removed with the engine in the frame.*

Removal

1 Remove the balancer shaft gears (see Section 17).
2 Ensure that the crankshaft is in the TDC compression position for the right-hand cylinder. To confirm this position, the locating pin for the crankshaft sprocket should be facing up, and the notch on the auxiliary shaft sprocket should also be facing up **(see illustration)**.
3 Undo the internal oil pipe banjo bolt and

remove the bolt and sealing washers **(see illustrations)**. Discard the washers as new ones must be used. Note the location of the ball valve inside the banjo bolt and ensure that it is free to move **(see illustration)**. Undo

18.3b . . . and remove the washers

the oil pipe bracket bolts, then ease the lower end of the pipe out from the side of the oil pump and remove it **(see illustrations)**. An O-ring is located inside the pipe socket **(see illustration 19.8)**. Unless the pump is going to

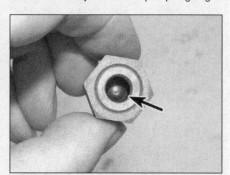

18.3c Note the location of the ball valve (arrowed)

18.3d Undo the bracket bolts . . .

18.3e . . . then ease the end of the pipe out of the oil pump

18.4a Note how blade locates in bracket

18.4b Note location of gasket

18.5a Remove the E-clip . . .

18.5b . . . and washer . . .

18.5c . . . then lift out the blade

18.5d Note second washer

be removed (see Section 19), ease the O-ring out carefully and discard it as a new one must be fitted.

4 Note how the camchain tensioner blade bracket supports the blade, then undo the bolts and lift the bracket off **(see illustration)**. Note the location of the gasket behind the bracket and discard it as a new one must be fitted **(see illustration)**.

5 Remove the E-clip and washer securing the chain tensioner blade, then lift out the blade **(see illustrations)**. Note the location of the

washer fitted behind the tensioner blade **(see illustration)**.

6 Remove the E-clips and washers securing the chain guide blade, then lift out the blade **(see illustration)**.

7 Mark the outside faces of the auxiliary shaft and crankshaft sprockets with a dab of paint to aid reassembly. Hold the auxiliary shaft sprocket to prevent it turning, then undo the bolts securing both sprockets **(see illustrations)**. Note that the locating pin for the auxiliary shaft sprocket is facing up in

18.6 E-clips and washers secure guide blade

18.7a Undo the bolts securing the auxiliary shaft sprocket . . .

18.7b . . . and the bolts securing the crankshaft sprocket

18.7c Note the alignment of the pins (arrowed)

18.7d Lift the sprockets and chain off as an assembly

18.15a Fit a new O-ring into the oil pipe socket

18.15b Ease the pipe into the socket

alignment with the pin on the crankshaft, then lift the sprockets and chain off as an assembly **(see illustrations)**.

Inspection

8 Check the tensioner blade and the guide blade for wear or damage and renew them if necessary.
9 Check the sprockets for worn or damaged teeth and renew the sprockets and chain as a set.

Installation

10 Ensure that the crankshaft is in the TDC compression position for the right-hand cylinder. To confirm this position, the locating

pins for the crankshaft and auxiliary shaft sprockets should be facing up. Ensure that the TDC locating pin is securely in place.
11 Install the two sprockets in the chain so that the holes for the locating pins are in alignment, then install the sprockets onto the shafts and tighten the bolts finger-tight **(see illustrations 18.7d, c, b and a)**. Hold the auxiliary shaft as on removal and tighten the bolts to the torque setting specified at the beginning of this Chapter.
12 Check that the locating pins and the notch in the auxiliary shaft sprocket are all in alignment and facing up **(see illustration 18.2)**.
13 Install the chain guide blade and tensioner blade on their lugs with the washers,

then secure them with new E-clips **(see illustrations 18.6, 5d, c, b and a)**. Check that the tensioner blade pivots freely on its lug.
14 Install the support bracket with a new gasket, making sure the tensioner blade locates correctly on the bracket **(see illustration 18.4b and a)**. Tighten the tensioner mounting bolts to the specified torque setting.
15 Fit a new O-ring into the socket for the oil pipe in the side of the oil pump **(see illustration)**. Lubricate the lower end of the pipe with engine oil, then carefully ease it into the socket **(see illustration)**. Align the banjo union with the oilway in the crankcase, install the banjo bolt using new sealing washers on both sides of the union, then tighten the bolt finger-tight **(see illustration 18.3b and a)**.
16 Install the oil pipe bracket bolts, then tighten the banjo bolt and the bracket bolts to the specified torque settings.
17 Install the balancer shaft gears (see Section 17).

19 Oil pump, pressure relief valve and thermostat

Note 1: *The oil pump can be removed with the engine in the frame.*
Note 2: *New mounting bolts must be used when the oil pump is reassembled.*
Special tool: *A degree disc is required for angle-tightening the oil pump mounting bolts.*

Oil pump

Removal

1 Remove the auxiliary shaft drive chain, tensioner and sprockets (see Section 18).
2 Undo the bolts securing the oil pump, noting which length fits where **(see illustrations)**. Discard the bolts as new ones must be fitted.
3 Lift off the pump cover **(see illustration)**. Note the location of the dowels in the pump housing. Note the register marks on the outside face of the cooling oil rotors, and the

19.2a Location of 40 mm oil pump bolts

19.2b Location of 45 mm oil pump bolts

19.3a Lift off the cover

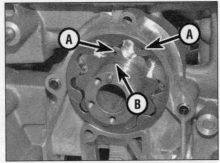

19.3b Note the register marks (A) and the key (B)

19.4a Draw the inner . . .

19.4b . . . and outer cooling oil rotors off

19.5a Remove the oil pump housing

19.5b Note location of the outer lubricating oil rotor

key that locates the inner rotor on the auxiliary shaft **(see illustration)**.

4 Draw the inner and outer cooling oil rotors off **(see illustrations)**.

5 Lift off the oil pump housing **(see illustration)**. Note the location of the outer lubricating oil rotor which may remain inside the housing – note the register mark on the outside face of the rotor **(see illustrations)**. **Note:** *Take care not to mix-up the outer cooling oil and lubricating oil rotors.*

6 The inner lubricating oil rotor is an integral part of the auxiliary shaft. Note the location of the Woodruff key in the shaft and remove it if it is loose; note the location of the dowels in the crankcase **(see illustration)**.

Inspection

7 Clean all the components in a suitable solvent.

8 Ease out the oil pipe O-ring from the socket in the side of the pump housing, noting how it

fits **(see illustration)**. Discard the O-ring as a new one must be fitted.

9 Inspect the pump cover, housing and rotors for scoring and wear. If any damage or wear is evident, renew the components as required.

10 Lay the rotors in the appropriate sides of the housing and use a straight-edge and feeler gauge to measure the clearance **(see illustration)**. Compare the results to the specifications at the beginning of this Chapter. If the clearance is greater than specified, measure the rotor thickness with a micrometer to determine whether the rotors or the housing, or both, are worn, and renew the components as required.

11 If the inner lubricating oil rotor is worn or damaged, refer to Section 25 to access the auxiliary shaft.

Installation

12 During installation, ensure that the pump

19.5c Note the register mark on the rotor

rotors are generously lubricated with clean engine oil. The register marks on the pump rotors must face forward, i.e. towards the front of the machine

13 Lubricate a new O-ring with clean engine

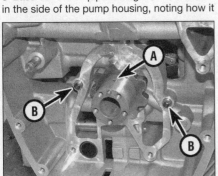

19.6 Note the Woodruff key (A) and the dowels (B)

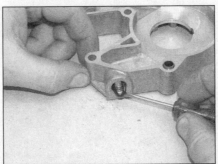

19.8 Ease the O-ring out carefully

19.10 Measuring rotor clearance

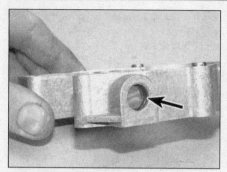

19.13 Ensure that the O-ring is correctly installed

19.20 Location of the oil pressure relief valve

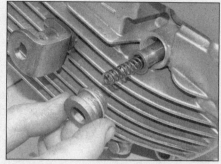

19.21 Remove the cap and withdraw the spring and relief valve

oil and fit it into the groove in the socket in the side of the pump housing **(see illustration)**.

14 If removed, fit the Woodruff key into its slot in the auxiliary shaft **(see illustration 19.6)**.

15 Install the outer lubricating oil rotor on the inner rotor, then fit the housing over the end of the auxiliary shaft and onto the crankcase dowels **(see illustration 19.5b)**.

16 Install the outer cooling oil rotor, then align the slot in the inner rotor with the key on the auxiliary shaft and install the inner rotor **(see illustrations 19.4b, a, and 3b)**. Check that the lobes on the inner and outer rotors are correctly aligned.

17 Install the pump cover, making sure it fits over the dowels in the housing **(see illustration 19.3a)**.

18 Install the new oil pump mounting bolts – ensure the bolts are fitted in their correct positions **(see illustration 19.2a and b)**. Tighten the bolts to the initial torque setting specified at the beginning of this Chapter. Next, using a degree disc (see *Tools and Workshop Tips*), angle-tighten each bolt in a criss-cross sequence to the final stage torque setting. If a degree disc is not available, refer to the **Haynes Hint** in Section 17.

19 Install the auxiliary shaft drive chain, tensioner and sprockets (see Section 18).

Oil pressure relief valve

20 The pressure relief valve cap is located on the right-hand side of the crankcase **(see illustration)**. If the engine oil has not been drained, position a drain tray below the engine

to catch any residual oil when the valve is removed.

21 Unscrew the cap and sealing washer, then withdraw the spring and valve **(see illustration)**.

22 Wash the components in a suitable solvent and examine them for signs of wear, scoring or damage **(see illustration)**.

23 No specifications are available for checking the valve. If any of the valve components are worn or damaged, or if an oil pressure test (see Section 3) suggests the valve is not operating correctly, fit a new valve assembly.

24 Installation is the reverse of removal. Fit a new sealing washer to the cap and tighten it to the torque setting specified at the beginning of this Chapter.

25 Check the engine oil level and top-up as necessary (see *Pre-ride checks*)

Oil thermostat

26 The oil thermostat is located in the top of the crankcase on the right-hand side, below the flange for the oil cooler feed pipe (see Section 6).

27 To gain access to the thermostat, follow the procedure in Section 6 and displace the feed pipe, noting the O-ring on the end of the pipe.

28 Lift out the baffle, then withdraw the thermostat and spring **(see illustrations)**.

29 No specifications are available for checking the thermostat. If the engine oil is not circulating through the oil cooler, resulting in high oil

temperatures, oil thinning and a possible loss in oil pressure, fit a new thermostat assembly.

Note: *Check that the oil cooler itself is not damaged or blocked internally.*

30 Installation is the reverse of removal. Follow the procedure in Section 6 to install the oil cooler feed pipe.

20 Clutch

Note 1: *To gain access to the clutch, it is first necessary to remove the rear shock absorber and swingarm/final drive unit assembly (see Chapter 4), the rear sub-frame and the gearbox (see Section 4).*

Note 2: *New bolts must be used to secure the clutch housing on installation.*

Special tools: *A top dead centre (TDC) locating pin (see **Tool Tip**, Section 8) or suitable substitute (see Step 3) is required for this procedure. A clutch centring tool is required for this procedure (see **Tool Tip**, Step 23). A degree disc is required for angle-tightening the clutch housing bolts. Seal installation guides are required to fit the crankshaft oil seal (see Steps 15 and 16).*

Removal

1 Remove both primary spark plugs (see Chapter 1, Section 5).

19.22 Examine the pressure relief valve components for wear

19.28a Lift out the baffle . . .

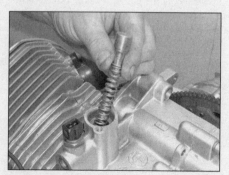

19.28b . . . then withdraw the thermostat and spring

20.3 Clutch locked using a twist drill

20.4a Loosen the bolts (arrowed) in a criss-cross sequence . . .

2 Remove the alternator drive belt cover (see Chapter 1, Section 9).

3 Turn the engine with a spanner on the crankshaft pulley nut until both pistons are at TDC. Insert the TDC locating pin or an 8.5 mm twist drill through the hole in the clutch assembly and locate it in the hole in the crankcase to lock the clutch **(see illustration)**.

4 Undo the cover plate bolts evenly and a little at a time in a criss-cross sequence to

release the spring pressure, then lift off the clutch assembly **(see illustrations)**.

5 The cover, friction plate and pressure plate will come away together, joined by the locating pins between the cover and pressure plate. Carefully lever the cover and pressure plates apart, noting which way round they fit **(see illustration)**. Lift off the friction plate **(see illustration)**.

6 If required, undo the bolts securing the clutch housing to the end of the crankshaft,

noting the location of the reinforcing disc **(see illustrations)**. Remove the housing, noting how the peg on the back locates in the hole in the end of the crankshaft **(see illustration)**. Discard the bolts as new ones must be used.

Inspection

7 After an extended period of service the friction plate will wear resulting in clutch slip. Measure the thickness of the plate in several places and compare the result with the

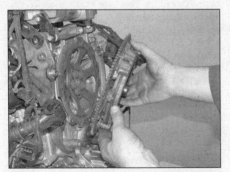

20.4b . . . and lift off the clutch assembly

20.5a Locating pins (arrowed) hold clutch assembly together

20.5b Lift off the friction plate

20.6a Undo the bolts securing the clutch housing . . .

20.6b . . . noting the location of the reinforcing disc

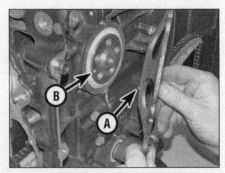

20.6c Note how peg (A) locates in hole (B)

20.7 Measuring the thickness of the clutch friction plate

20.9a Check the surface of the pressure plate (arrowed) . . .

20.9b . . . and the cover plate for wear and damage

specification at the beginning of this Chapter **(see illustration)**. If the plate has worn down to the service limit it must be renewed. If the plate smells burnt, is contaminated with oil or grease or is glazed, it must be replaced with a new one. **Note:** *If there is oil contamination on the clutch plate, check the crankshaft rear oil seal and the gearbox front oil seal for leakage (see Step 13).*

8 Check the friction plate splines and the corresponding splines on the gearbox input shaft for signs of wear and damage. Fit the friction plate on the input shaft splines and check that it is able to move freely on the splines, but without undue freeplay – note that wear between the two components may result in a rattle when the machine is in neutral.

9 Check the surface of the pressure plate and the cover plate for distortion using a straight-edge **(see illustrations)**. If the surface of either plate is distorted, badly scored or blued through overheating, renew the pressure plate, cover plate and friction plate as a set.
10 Inspect the teeth of the starter motor ring gear for wear and damage. The gear is an integral part of the pressure plate assembly – renew the pressure plate if necessary.
11 If the clutch has been slipping and the friction plate thickness is satisfactory, it is likely the diaphragm spring in the pressure plate has lost its tension. Renew the pressure plate.
12 Slide the seal off the clutch pushrod **(see illustration 4.26c)**. Check that the pushrod is

straight by rolling it on a flat surface such as a piece of glass, or setting it up in V-blocks and measuring runout with a dial gauge. If the pushrod is bent, it must be renewed.
13 Check for signs of any oil leakage from either the crankcase or the gearbox. If the gearbox front oil seal on the transmission input shaft has failed, follow the procedure in Section 27 to renew it. If the crankshaft rear oil seal has failed, renew it as follows.
14 Using a 3 mm drill bit, drill two holes on opposite sides of the seal. Take care to only drill through the outer surface of the seal. Next, thread two self-tapping screws part-way into the holes. Position a piece of thick card over the outer surface of the seal housing to protect it, then carefully lever out the seal using a pair of curved, thin-nosed pliers. Work evenly on both sides of the seal **(see illustration 27.17)**.
15 Two types of crankshaft seal are supplied by BMW – either spring lipped or Teflon lipped. Check which type of seal is being fitted (see Section 16, Step 17). Take care to avoid damaging the inner lip of the new seal when it is installed – a suitable seal guide and sleeve must be used. BMW provide a set of tools for this purpose **(see illustration)**. Slip the seal over the end of the guide (BMW Part No. 115702), position the guide on the sleeve (BMW Part No. 115703), then slide the seal onto the sleeve and remove the guide **(see illustrations)**.
16 Locate the sleeve over the end of the

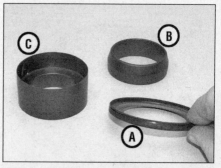

20.15a Crankshaft oil seal (A), seal guide (B) and sleeve (C)

20.15b Position the seal on the guide . . .

20.15c . . . then position the guide on the sleeve

20.15d Slide the seal onto the sleeve . . .

20.15e . . . then remove the guide

20.16a Locate the sleeve over the end of the crankshaft . . .

20.16b . . . then use the driver . . .

20.16c . . . to install the seal

20.16d Remove the sleeve. Note the alignment of the outer edge of the seal

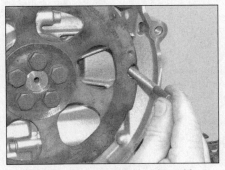

20.19 Lock the clutch housing with a suitable pin

20.20 Tighten the bolts to the final setting with a degree disc

crankshaft and press the seal into position with a suitable driver (BMW Part No. 115705 and Part No. 115701) **(see illustrations)**. When installed, the outer edge of the seal should be level with the outer face of the housing. Withdraw the sleeve **(see illustration)**.

Installation

17 Make sure all the components are clean and dry.
18 Align the peg on the back of the housing with the hole in the end of the crankshaft and install the housing **(see illustration 20.6c)**.

Lightly oil the threads and the underside of the heads of the new housing bolts, then fit the reinforcing disc and install the bolts finger-tight **(see illustration 20.6b and a)**.
19 Align the cut-out on the edge of the housing with the hole in the crankcase and install the locking pin **(see illustration)**.
20 Tighten the bolts evenly and in a criss-cross pattern to the initial torque setting specified at the beginning of this Chapter, then use a degree disc (see *Tools and Workshop Tips* in the *Reference* section) to tighten them to the final setting in one continuous

movement **(see illustration)**. Remove the locking pin.
21 Position the friction plate on the pressure plate, then align the locating pins on the cover plate with the holes in the pressure plate and press the cover plate into position **(see illustrations 20.5b and a)**.
22 Align the clutch assembly with the flywheel and install the cover plate bolts finger-tight **(see illustrations)**.
23 Before the cover plate bolts are tightened, the clutch friction plate, pressure plate and crankshaft centres must be aligned. BMW

20.22a Align the clutch assembly with the flywheel . . .

20.22b . . . and install the cover plate bolts

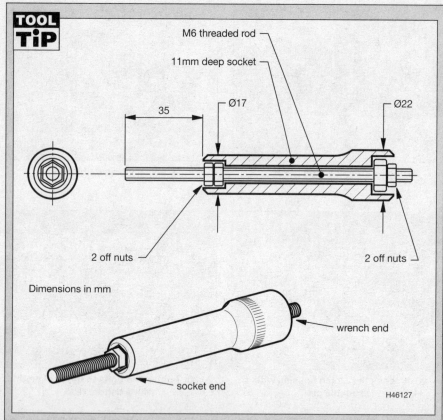

TOOL TiP

M6 threaded rod

11mm deep socket

35   Ø17   Ø22

2 off nuts   2 off nuts

Dimensions in mm

wrench end

socket end

H46127

A clutch centering tool can be made using an 11 mm deep socket, a length of 6 mm diameter threaded rod and a handful of nuts.

20.23 Using the home-made clutch centering tool

20.24 Tighten the cover plate bolts in a criss-cross sequence

provide a service tool for this purpose (Part No. 212673). Alternatively, a similar tool can be made (see *Tool Tip*). Insert the aligning tool into the centre of the clutch, ensuring it goes all the way in – if necessary, slacken the cover plate bolts to aid installation **(see illustration)**.

24 Install the locking pin, then tighten the cover plate bolts evenly and a little at a time in a criss-cross sequence to the specified torque setting **(see illustration)**.

25 Install the remaining components in the reverse order of removal.

21 Clutch release mechanism

1 All the models covered in this manual are fitted with an hydraulic clutch. The clutch system comprises the master cylinder on the handlebars, the hose and the release cylinder at the rear of the gearbox. The system requires no maintenance other than inspection at the specified service interval (see Chapter 1) and a check of the clutch fluid level (see *Pre-ride checks*).

2 If there is evidence of air in the system (spongy feel to the lever, difficulty in engaging gear), bleed the system (see Steps 27 to 36).

3 If clutch fluid is leaking from any part of the system, first check that the hose banjo union bolts are tight. If necessary, renew the sealing washers on both sides of the banjo unions. If either the master cylinder or the release cylinder is leaking, a new component will have to be installed – no rebuild kits are available for the cylinders.

4 If the clutch handlebar lever feels stiff, check the lever and the lever bracket for damage.

5 On R1200 GS and GS Adventure models, remove the hand protector if fitted (see Chapter 6).

6 Turn the lever span adjuster to its lowest setting (see Chapter 1). Undo the lever pivot bolt locknut on the underside of the lever **(see illustration)**. Withdraw the pivot bolt and lift the lever off **(see illustration)**.

7 Clean the contact surfaces of the lever, bracket and pivot bolt. If they are in good condition, lubricate the components with dry film lubricant prior to assembly.

8 If, after cleaning and lubricating the lever, the clutch action is still stiff, the master cylinder will have to be removed from the machine and checked.

Master cylinder

Removal

9 Before starting, make sure you have some new Vitamol V10 clutch fluid, some clean rags and a suitable container for the old clutch fluid.

10 On R1200 GS and GS Adventure models, remove the hand protector if fitted (see

21.6a Undo the locknut (arrowed) . . .

21.6b . . . and withdraw the pivot bolt

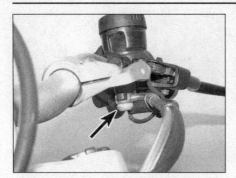

21.12 Undo the clutch hose banjo bolt
(arrowed)

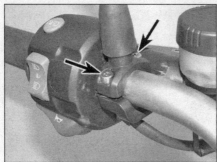

21.13a Undo the clamp screws . . .

21.13b . . . and lift the master cylinder off –
R1200 GS shown

Chapter 6). On GS and R models, remove the left-hand mirror (see Chapter 6).

11 Refer to the procedure in Chapter 7 and displace the clutch switch from the master cylinder.

12 Undo the clutch hose banjo bolt and separate the hose from the master cylinder, noting its alignment **(see illustration)**. Be prepared to catch any residual fluid in the union. Discard the sealing washers as new ones must be used. Wrap a clean plastic bag over the end of the hose to prevent dirt entering the system and secure the hose in an upright position to minimise fluid loss.

Caution: Do not operate the clutch lever while the hose is disconnected.

13 On R1200 GS, GS Adventure and R models, support the master cylinder, then undo the handlebar clamp screws and remove the clamp **(see illustration)**. Note the alignment of the master cylinder with the handlebar, then lift the master cylinder off **(see illustration)**. Press the locking tabs in and unscrew the cap, then remove the locking ring and diaphragm (see *Pre-ride checks*).

14 On R1200 RT models, support the master cylinder, then undo the handlebar clamp screws and remove the clamp **(see illustrations)**. Note the alignment of the master cylinder with the handlebar, then lift the master cylinder off **(see illustration)**. Undo the screws securing the reservoir cover and lift off the cover and diaphragm (see *Pre-ride checks*).

15 Empty the clutch fluid into a suitable container.

16 To check the action of the master cylinder piston, temporarily install the reservoir cover or cap. Wrap some clean rag over the open end of the master cylinder hose union and operate the lever. If the lever sticks, or the action is stiff, there is a fault with the master cylinder piston. No rebuild kit is available for the master cylinder – if it is not working correctly, a new one will have to be fitted. If the lever moves smoothly, it is likely that the release cylinder is faulty (see below).

Caution: Do not, under any circumstances, use a petroleum-based solvent to clean the master cylinder.

Installation

17 Installation is the reverse of removal, noting the following:

● Align the master cylinder as noted on removal and tighten the handlebar clamp screws securely.

● Align the clutch hose with the master cylinder and fit new sealing washers on each side of the banjo union.

● Tighten the banjo bolt to the torque setting specified at the beginning of this Chapter.

● Back-fill and bleed the system with new Vitamol V10 clutch fluid (see Steps 27 to 36).

● Check the operation of the clutch before riding the motorcycle.

21.14a Undo the clamp screws . . .

Release cylinder

18 The release cylinder is located at the back of the gearbox **(see illustration)**.

19 If the clutch action is stiff, and the master cylinder is good, it is likely that the release cylinder is faulty. No rebuild kit is available for the release cylinder – if it is not working correctly, a new one will have to be fitted.

Removal

20 Before starting, make sure you have some new Vitamol V10 clutch fluid, some clean rags and a suitable container for the old clutch fluid.

21 Remove the body panels as applicable to gain access to the release cylinder and to the clutch hose where it is secured to the rear sub-frame (see Chapter 6).

21.14b . . . and lift off the clamp – R1200
RT shown

21.14c Lift the master cylinder off

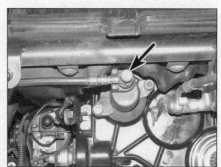

21.18 Location of the clutch release
cylinder. Note bleed valve (arrowed)

21.22 Cut the ties securing the clutch hose

21.23 Lift the release cylinder off

21.32 Fill reservoir to the MAX level line

22 Cut the ties securing the clutch hose to the rear sub-frame **(see illustration)**.

23 Slacken the clutch hose banjo bolt, then tighten it lightly as an aid to removal. Undo the release cylinder mounting bolts and lift the cylinder off **(see illustration)**.

24 Undo the clutch hose banjo bolt and separate the hose from the release cylinder, noting its alignment. Be prepared to catch any residual fluid in the union. Discard the sealing washers as new ones must be used. Wrap a clean plastic bag over the end of the hose to prevent dirt entering the system and secure the hose in an upright position to minimise fluid loss.

Caution: Do not operate the clutch lever while the hose is disconnected.

25 Check that the clutch push rod is free to move inside the transmission input shaft – if necessary, remove the rear shock absorber (see Chapter 4), then withdraw the pushrod and check that it is clean and free from corrosion **(see illustration 4.26b and c)**. Note the location of the seal on the pushrod and renew it if necessary. Lubricate the pushrod with a smear of clutch assembly grease (BMW recommend Optimoly MP 3) before installation.

Installation

26 Installation is the reverse of removal, noting the following:

● Align the release cylinder with the clutch pushrod and tighten the mounting bolts to the torque setting specified at the beginning of this Chapter.
● Align the clutch hose with the release cylinder and fit new sealing washers on each side of the banjo union.
● Tighten the banjo bolt to the specified torque setting.
● Secure the clutch hose to the sub-frame as noted on removal.
● Back-fill and bleed the system with new Vitamol V10 clutch fluid (see Steps 27 to 36).
● Check the operation of the clutch before riding the motorcycle.

Bleeding the clutch release mechanism

27 Bleeding the clutch is simply the process of removing air from the master cylinder, hose and the release cylinder. Bleeding is necessary whenever an hydraulic connection is loosened,

or when a component or hose is renewed. Leaks in the system may also allow air to enter, but leaking clutch fluid will reveal their presence and warn you of the need for repair.

28 To bleed the clutch, you will need some new Vitamol clutch fluid, a length of clear vinyl or plastic tubing, a syringe with a capacity of 100 cc to back-fill the system (BMW produces service tool Part No. 342551), some rags and a spanner to fit the release cylinder bleed valve.

Note: *It is essential that the syringe and hose are not contaminated with any other fluids.*

29 Temporarily displace the master cylinder and empty any old clutch fluid from the master cylinder reservoir (see Steps 13 to 15).

30 Install the master cylinder on the handlebars and tighten the clamp screws securely. Position the handlebars so that the top of the master cylinder reservoir is as level as possible. Do not fit the diaphragm, locking ring or cover.

31 Remove the cap from the bleed valve **(see illustration 21.18)**. If using a ring spanner, fit it over the bleed valve now. Attach one end of the clear tubing to the bleed valve and secure it with a cable-tie. Fill the syringe with new Vitamol V10 clutch fluid and connect it to the other end of the tubing.

32 Open the bleed valve and slowly inject the clutch fluid into the system via the release cylinder until it reaches the upper level in the reservoir **(see illustration)**. Do not overfill. Close the bleed valve.

33 Carefully squeeze the clutch lever to ensure no air is trapped in the upper end of the system, then release the lever slowly.

34 Disconnect the hose from the bleed valve and ensure that the valve is tightened securely. Fit the valve cap. Wipe up any spilled clutch fluid.

35 Check the fluid level in the reservoir (see *Pre-ride checks*), then install the reservoir cover or cap.

36 Check the operation of the clutch before riding the motorcycle.

 If it's not possible to produce the correct feel to the lever the clutch fluid may be aerated. Let the fluid in the system stabilise for a few hours and then check for air trapped in the upper end of the system again.

22 Crankcase

Note: *To separate the crankcase halves, the engine must be removed from the frame (see Section 4).*

Special tools: *A degree disc is required for angle-tightening the 10 mm crankcase bolts.*

Separation

1 To access the crankshaft and its bearings, the auxiliary shaft, camchains, tensioner and guide blades, and the oil strainers, the crankcase must be split into two parts.

2 Before the crankcase halves can be separated, the following components must be removed:

● Gearbox (if not done when removing the engine – see Section 4)
● Alternator (see Chapter 7)
● Cylinder heads (see Section 10)
● Cylinders and pistons (see Section 12)
● Balancer shaft gears and balancer shaft (see Section 17)
● Auxiliary shaft drive chain, tensioner and sprockets (see Section 18)
● Oil pump (see Section 19)
● Clutch and clutch housing (see Section 20)

3 If not already done, wrap clean rag around the connecting rods to prevent them striking the crankcase.

4 Unscrew the cylinder/cylinder head studs from both sides of the crankcase. To do this, lock two nuts together on each stud, then unscrew the stud using a spanner on the lower nut **(see illustration)**.

22.4 Use locked nuts to unscrew the cylinder studs

22.6a Location of the crankcase 6 mm bolts (arrowed) –
right-hand side

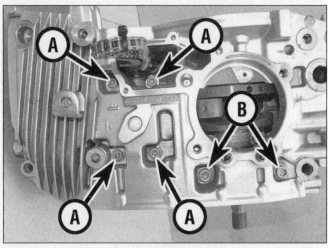

22.6b Location of the crankcase 8 mm (A) and 10 mm (B) bolts –
right-hand side

5 Before separating the crankcase halves, measure the amount of crankshaft end-float using a dial gauge (see *Tools and Workshop Tips* in the *Reference* section). Press the crankshaft into the crankcase, then mount the dial gauge with its pointer sitting against the front end of the crankshaft. Zero the gauge, then pull the crankshaft out of the casing and record the end-float. Compare the result to the specifications at the beginning of this Chapter. If the end-float exceeds the service limit, measure the width of the crankshaft guide bearing, then compare the result with the specification at the beginning of this Chapter to determine whether the bearing or the crankshaft has worn (see Section 24).

> **HAYNES HiNT**
> *Make a cardboard template for both sides of the crankcase and punch a hole for each bolt location. As each bolt is removed, store it in its relative position in the template. This will ensure all bolts are installed correctly on reassembly – this is important, as many bolts differ slightly in length.*

6 Lay the engine onto its left-hand side, making sure it is properly supported using blocks of wood. Unscrew the two 6 mm bolts followed by the four 8 mm bolts, then the two 10 mm bolts **(see illustrations)**. Unscrew the bolts evenly, a little at a time, until they are loose, then remove them and their washers and store them on the cardboard crankcase template for the right-hand side **(see illustration)**. Note that the 8 mm x 60 mm bolt is fitted with a sealing washer – a new sealing washer must be used on reassembly.

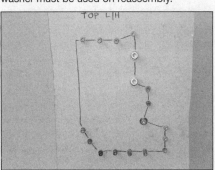

22.6c Store the bolts in a cardboard template

7 Turn the engine over so that it rests on its right-hand side, making sure it is properly supported using blocks of wood.
8 Unscrew the fifteen 6 mm bolts followed by the single 8 mm bolt, then the two 10 mm bolts **(see illustrations)**. Unscrew the bolts evenly, a little at a time, until they are loose, then remove them and their washers store them on the cardboard crankcase template for the left-hand side. Note that the 8 mm bolt is fitted with a sealing washer – a new sealing washer must be used on reassembly.

22.8a Location of the crankcase upper 6 mm bolts – left-hand side

22.8b Location of the crankcase centre rear 6 mm bolts – left-hand side

22.8c Location of the crankcase lower 6 mm bolts – left-hand side

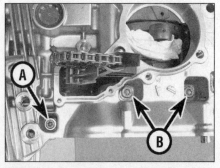

22.8d Location of the crankcase 8 mm (A) and 10 mm (B) bolts – left-hand side

22.9 Lift the left-hand crankcase half off the right-hand half

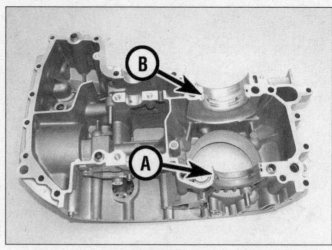

22.10 Location of the crankshaft main bearing (A) and guide bearing (B) shells

9 Carefully lift the left-hand crankcase half off the right-hand half **(see illustration)**. If the halves do not separate easily, first make sure all the bolts have been removed. The sealant used between the crankcase halves can form a strong bond – if the two halves are stuck, tap around the joint with a soft-faced mallet to free them. Do not attempt to lever the cases apart with a screwdriver – you'll damage the sealing surfaces.

10 Note the location of the crankshaft main bearing and guide bearing shells in the left-hand crankcase half and take care not to dislodge them **(see illustration)**.

11 Note the location of the balancer shaft oil seal, bearing and bearing retaining circlip and remove them from the crankcase. All three components can be installed after the crankcases have been reassembled – discard the old oil seal and circlip as new ones must be fitted (see Section 17).

12 Note the location of the four dowels in the left-hand crankcase half and remove them if they are loose **(see illustration)**.

Inspection

13 Before the crankcase halves can be inspected, the following components must be removed:

● Crankshaft and crankshaft bearings (see Section 24)
● Auxiliary shaft and camchains, and camchain tensioner blades (see Section 25)
● Oil pressure relief valve and oil thermostat (see Section 19)
● Oil temperature sensor (see Chapter 3)
● Oil pressure switch and oil level indicator (see Chapter 7)

14 Undo the bolts securing the oil strainers and ease the strainers out from their sockets **(see illustrations)**. The larger strainer is for the lubricating oil and the smaller strainer is for the cooling oil. Carefully ease out the O-rings from the grooves in the sockets, taking care not to damage the soft aluminium – discard the O-rings as new ones must be used **(see illustration)**.

15 Ease the crankcase vent valve out, noting which way round it is fitted **(see illustration)**.

16 Clean the crankcases thoroughly with suitable solvent and dry them with compressed air. Blow out all oil passages with compressed air.

17 Remove all traces of old sealant from the mating surfaces. If a scraper must be used,

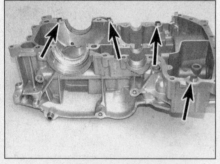

22.12 Location of the dowels in the left-hand crankcase half

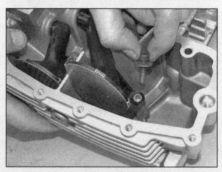

22.14a Undo the bolts . . .

22.14b . . . and ease out the oil strainers

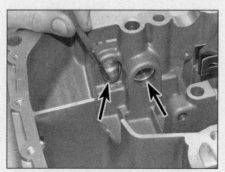

22.14c Remove the O-rings carefully

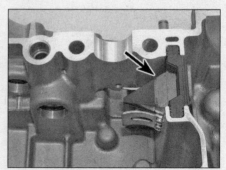

22.15 Location of the crankcase vent valve

be very careful not to nick or gouge the soft aluminium or oil leaks will result.

18 Check the cases for any damage. Small cracks or holes in aluminium castings can be repaired with an epoxy resin adhesive as a temporary measure or a more secure repair can be made with one of the low temperature home welding kits, such as Lumiweld. Argon-arc welding is another solution, but only a specialist in this process is in a position to advise on the economy or practical aspect of such a repair. If any damage is found that can't be repaired, renew the crankcase halves as a set.

19 Damaged threads can be economically reclaimed by using a diamond section wire insert. These are easily fitted after drilling and re-tapping the affected thread.

20 Sheared studs or screws can usually be removed with stud extractors – if you are in any doubt, consult a BMW dealer or a specialist motorcycle engineer.

 HAYNES HINT *Refer to Tools and Workshop Tip in the Reference sections for details of installing a thread insert and using stud extractors.*

Reassembly

21 Clean the threads of all the crankcase bolts.

22 Check the crankcase vent valve for particles of trapped dirt. If necessary, wash the valve with suitable solvent and dry it with compressed air. Do not attempt to scrape dirt off the surface of the valve reeds – they are fragile and easily damaged. The reeds should lay flat against the body of the valve – hold the valve up to the light to check. If the reeds have been sprained, fit a new valve, otherwise oil mist from the lower crankcase will be forced into the top of the engine and cause a smoky exhaust. Ensure that the screws securing the reed stopper plates are secure, then install the vent valve in the right-hand crankcase.

23 Lubricate the new oil strainer O-rings with clean engine oil and install them in the grooves in the strainer sockets **(see illustration 22.14c)**. Note that the lower O-ring is smaller than the upper O-ring.

24 Ensure that the oil strainers are thoroughly clean. Do not attempt to prise the gauze filters off the strainers – they must remain a tight fit. If necessary, wash the strainers with suitable solvent and dry them with compressed air. Install the strainers carefully, taking care not to displace the O-rings, then install the bolts and washers and tighten them to the torque setting specified at the beginning of this Chapter **(see illustration)**.

25 Install the oil temperature sensor (see Chapter 3). Install the oil pressure switch and oil level warning sender (see Chapter 7).

26 Install the oil pressure relief valve and oil thermostat (see Section 19).

27 Make sure the auxiliary shaft and camchains (see Section 25) and the crankshaft and crankshaft bearings (see Section 24) are correctly positioned in the right-hand crankcase half. Ensure the crankcase half is properly supported using blocks of wood. Generously lubricate all the components with clean engine oil, then use a rag soaked in high flash-point solvent to wipe over the mating surfaces of both crankcase halves to remove all traces of oil.

28 Make sure the crankshaft bearings are correctly positioned in the left-hand crankcase half (see Section 24). If removed, install the four locating dowels in the left-hand crankcase half **(see illustration 22.12)**.

29 Apply a thin, even bead of suitable sealant to the mating surface of the right-hand crankcase half **(see illustrations)**. Apply sealant around the clip on the rear end of the left-hand camchain tensioner blade pivot pin to prevent oil leaking into the clutch housing and bed the pin into the right-hand crankcase **(see illustration)**. Note: *The right-hand tensioner blade can be installed once the crankcases have been reassembled (see Section 25).*

Caution: Don't apply an excessive amount of sealant as it will ooze out when the case halves are assembled and may obstruct oil passages. Do not apply the sealant on or too close to any of the bearing shells or surfaces.

30 Carefully lower the left-hand crankcase half down onto the right-hand half – it is worthwhile having an assistant to support the left-hand connecting rod and the camchain and tensioner blade assembly as the left-hand crankcase half as it is fitted. Ensure the crankshaft bearings remain in position in the left-hand crankcase half and make sure the dowels all locate correctly. Check that the crankcase halves are correctly seated all the way round.

22.24 Installed position of the oil strainers

22.29a Apply an even bead of sealant . . .

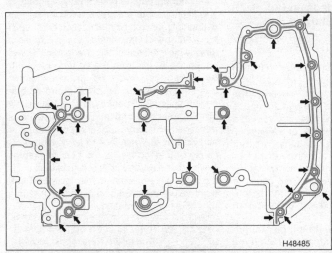

22.29b . . . to the right-hand crankcase half

22.29c Apply sealant to the end of the tensioner blade pivot pin

22.40a Screw the studs into the crankcases . . .

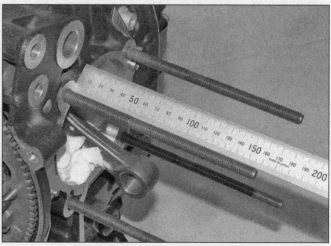

22.40b . . . to the specified installed height

Caution: The crankcase halves should fit together without being forced. If they're not correctly seated, separate them and investigate the problem. DO NOT attempt to pull them together by tightening the crankcase bolts.

31 Install the two 10 mm bolts and their washers, followed by the single 8 mm bolt with a new sealing washer, then the fifteen 6 mm bolts and their washers **(see illustrations 22.8d, c, b and a)**. Secure all the bolts hand-tight.

32 Turn the engine over so that it rests on its left-hand side, making sure it is properly supported using blocks of wood.

33 Install the two 10 mm bolts and their washers, followed by the four 8 mm bolts and their washers, then the two 6 mm bolts and their washers **(see illustrations 22.6b and a)**. Don't forget to fit a new sealing washer on the 8 mm x 60 mm bolt.

34 Tighten the 10 mm bolts to the initial torque setting specified at the beginning of this Chapter, then use a degree disc (see Tools and Workshop Tips in the Reference section) to tighten them to the final setting in one continuous movement.

35 Tighten the 8 mm bolts evenly and a little at a time in a criss-cross sequence to the specified torque setting, then tighten the 6 mm bolts to the specified torque setting.

36 Turn the engine over so that it rests on its right-hand side. Tighten the 10 mm bolts to the initial torque setting specified at the beginning of this Chapter, then use a degree disc to tighten them to the final setting in one continuous movement.

37 Tighten the 8 mm bolt to the specified torque setting, then tighten the 6 mm bolts evenly and a little at a time in a criss-cross sequence to the specified torque setting.

38 With all crankcase fasteners tightened, check that the crankshaft and auxiliary shaft are free to rotate. Support the connecting rods to prevent them striking the crankcase and take care not to dislodge the camchains

from the auxiliary shaft. If there are any signs of undue stiffness or rough spots, or of any other problem, the fault must be rectified before proceeding further.

39 Follow the procedure in Section 20, Steps 15 and 16, and install a new crankshaft oil seal.

40 Prior to installation, clean the threads of the cylinder/cylinder head studs and apply a suitable non-permanent thread-locking compound. Using the two nuts locked together, screw the studs into the crankcases to the specified installed height above the cylinder base mating surface **(see illustrations)**. Ensure the studs are tight, then unlock the nuts without disturbing the studs, and thread the nuts off.

41 Install the remaining components in the reverse order of removal, noting that the auxiliary shaft drive chain and sprockets should be left off until after the cylinder heads and camshafts are installed to enable the timing to be set up correctly.

23 Crankshaft bearings and connecting big-end rod bearings – general information

1 Even though the crankshaft and connecting rod bearings are generally replaced with new ones during the engine overhaul, the old bearings should be retained for close examination as they may reveal valuable information about the condition of the engine.

2 Bearing failure occurs mainly because of lack of lubrication, the presence of dirt or other foreign particles, overloading the engine and/or corrosion. Regardless of the cause of bearing failure, it must be corrected before the engine is reassembled to prevent it from happening again.

3 When examining the bearings, match them with their corresponding journal on the crankshaft to help identify the cause of any problem. Note that the bearing shells are pressed into their locations in the crankcase

halves and connecting rods and caps, and should only be disturbed when required for examination. It is essential to keep the bearing shells in the right order – lay them on a clean sheet of card and mark the locations on the card.

4 Dirt and other foreign particles get into the engine in a variety of ways. They may be left in the engine during assembly or they may pass through filters or breathers, then get into the oil and from there into the bearings. Metal chips from machining operations and normal engine wear are often present. Abrasives are sometimes left in engine components after reconditioning operations, especially when parts are not thoroughly cleaned using the proper cleaning methods. Whatever the source, foreign objects often end up imbedded in the soft bearing material and are easily recognised. Large particles will not imbed in the bearing and will score or gouge the bearing and journal. The best prevention for this type of bearing failure is to clean all parts thoroughly and keep everything spotlessly clean during engine reassembly. Regular oil and filter changes are also essential.

5 Lack of lubrication or lubrication breakdown has a number of interrelated causes. Excessive heat (which thins the oil), overloading (which squeezes the oil from the bearing face) and oil leakage or throw off (from excessive bearing clearances, worn oil pump or high engine speeds) all contribute to a breakdown of the protective lubricating film. Blocked oil passages will starve a bearing of lubrication and destroy it. When lack of lubrication is the cause of bearing failure, the bearing material is wiped or extruded from the steel backing of the bearing. Temperatures may increase to the point where the steel backing and the journal turn blue from overheating.

 HAYNES HINT *Refer to Tools and Workshop Tips in the Reference section for bearing fault finding.*

6 Riding habits can have a definite effect on bearing life. Full throttle, low speed operation, or labouring the engine, puts very high loads on bearings, which tend to squeeze out the oil film. These loads cause the bearings to flex, which produces fine cracks in the bearing face (fatigue failure). Eventually the bearing material will loosen in pieces and tear away from the steel backing. Short trip riding leads to corrosion of bearings, as insufficient engine heat is produced to drive off the condensed water and corrosive gases produced. These products collect in the engine oil, forming acid and sludge. As the oil is carried to the engine bearings, the acid attacks and corrodes the bearing material.

7 Incorrect bearing installation during engine assembly will lead to bearing failure as well. Tight fitting bearings which leave insufficient bearing oil clearances result in oil starvation. Dirt or foreign particles trapped behind a bearing shell result in high spots on the bearing which lead to failure.

8 To avoid bearing problems, clean all parts thoroughly before reassembly, double check all bearing clearance measurements and lubricate the new bearings with clean engine oil during installation.

24 Crankshaft main and guide bearings

Note: *To remove the crankshaft the engine must be removed from the frame (see Section 4).*

Removal

1 Follow the procedure in Section 22 and separate the crankcase halves.

2 Lift the crankshaft assembly out of the right-hand crankcase half, taking care not to dislodge the crankshaft main and guide bearing shells **(see illustrations)**. Note the location of the oil seal on the rear of the crankshaft and discard it as a new one must be fitted after the crankcases have been reassembled.

3 Remove the auxiliary shaft and camchains, and camchain tensioner blades (see Section 25).

4 Follow the procedure in Section 15 and remove the connecting rods from the crankshaft.

24.2a Location of the crankshaft main bearing . . .

Inspection

5 Examine the crankshaft bearing shells in both halves of the crankcase **(see illustrations)**. If there are any signs of wear on the bearing surfaces they should be renewed – always renew the main bearing and guide bearing shells as a set. The shells are colour-coded green or yellow according to their original tolerance fit – the colour mark is on the edge of the shell **(see illustration)**. Always fit new shells of the same colour code.

6 Refer to the general information in Section 23. If the bearing shells are scored, badly scuffed or appear to have seized, check the corresponding crankshaft journal. Damage to the surface of the journal on a standard crankshaft can be corrected by re-grinding and fitting oversize (+0.25 mm) bearing shells. If the crankshaft has already been reground, indicated by paint marks on the front

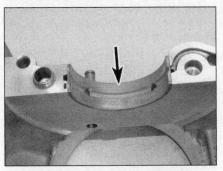
24.5a Examine the crankshaft main bearing shells . . .

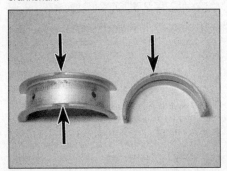
24.5c Location of the colour coding on the bearing shells (arrowed)

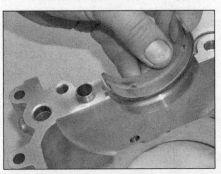
24.7a Remove the main bearing shells by pushing their centres to one side

24.2b . . . and guide bearing shells

crankshaft web, a new crankshaft will have to be fitted. If there is any doubt about the condition of the crankshaft, have it checked by a BMW dealer.

7 Remove the main bearing shells from each crankcase half by pushing their centres to the side, then lifting them out **(see illustration)**. Remove the guide bearing shells by pressing down on one end of the shell so that it slips round in the housing **(see illustration)**. If there are no obvious signs of damage, keep the shells in order so that they can be returned to their original locations for accurate oil clearance measurement prior to reassembly.

8 Clean the crankshaft with suitable solvent and blow dry it with compressed air – also blow through the oil passages to ensure they are clear.

Oil clearance check

9 Whether new bearing shells are being fitted or the original ones are being re-used, the

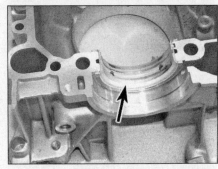
24.5b . . . and the guide bearing shells

24.7b Remove the guide bearing shells by rotating them in the housing

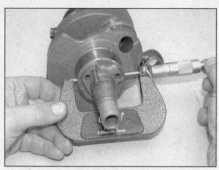

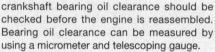

24.10a Measuring the diameter of the crankshaft main bearing journal

24.10b Measuring the diameter of the crankshaft guide bearing journal

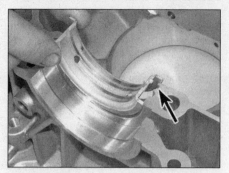

24.11 Make sure the tab (arrowed) engages with the notch in the case

crankshaft bearing oil clearance should be checked before the engine is reassembled. Bearing oil clearance can be measured by using a micrometer and telescoping gauge.

10 First measure the diameter of both crankshaft journals in two different planes with the micrometer and note the results **(see illustrations)**. Wear on the journals can be determined by comparing the results with the specifications at the beginning of this Chapter. **Note:** *A re-ground (Stage 1) crankshaft is identified by paint marks on the front crankshaft web.*

11 Next, clean the backs of the bearing shells and the bearing housings in both crankcase halves with a suitable solvent. Press the shells into their locations, ensuring that the tab on each shell engages in the notch in the crankcase **(see illustration)**. Make sure the shells are fitted in their correct locations and take care not to touch any shell's bearing surface with your fingers.

12 Carefully lower the left-hand crankcase half down onto the right-hand half. Ensure the crankshaft bearings remain in position in the left-hand half and make sure the crankcase dowels all locate correctly. Check that the crankcase halves are correctly seated all the way round.

13 Ensure that the threads of all the crankcase bolts are clean, then follow the procedure in Section 22, Steps 31 to 37, to tighten the crankcase bolts. Note that for the purpose of this check it is not necessary to fit new sealing washers to the 8 mm bolts.

14 Measure the inside diameter of the

crankshaft bearing shells with a telescoping gauge and micrometer and note the results **(see illustration)**. With reference to Step 10, note that a re-ground crankshaft will be fitted with appropriately sized Stage 1 main and guide bearing shells.

15 Subtract each crankshaft journal diameter from the appropriate bearing shells inside diameter to obtain the oil clearances and compare the results with the service limits specified at the beginning of this Chapter.

16 If the original bearing shells have been used for the check and the clearances are within the service limit, they can be re-used. If the clearances are beyond the service limit, but the crankpin journals are good (see Step 10), fit new bearing shells and check the oil clearances once again. Always renew the main bearing and guide bearing shells as a set. The shells are colour-coded green or yellow according to their original tolerance fit – the colour mark is on the edge of the shell **(see illustration 24.5c)**. Always fit new shells of the same colour code.

End-float check

17 To check the crankshaft end-float in the guide bearing, measure the crankshaft guide bearing journal width, then measure the overall width of both guide bearing shells – unless they have worn unevenly, both shells should be the same overall width.

18 To calculate the end-float, subtract the shell width from the journal width, then compare the result with the specifications at the beginning of this Chapter.

19 If the end-float is greater than the service limit, compare your measurements with the

specifications to determine which component is worn and renew it as necessary.

Installation

20 Ensure the backs of the bearing shells and the bearing housings in both crankcase halves are clean. If new shells are being fitted, ensure that all traces of the protective grease are cleaned off using suitable solvent.

21 Press the shells into their locations, ensuring that the tab on each shell engages in the notch in the crankcase **(see illustration 24.11)**. Make sure the shells are fitted in their correct locations and take care not to touch any shell's bearing surface with your fingers.

22 Follow the procedure in Section 15 and install the connecting rods onto the crankshaft.

23 Install the auxiliary shaft and camchains, and camchain tensioner blades (see Section 25).

24 Lubricate the crankshaft bearings with clean engine oil, then install the crankshaft assembly **(see illustrations 24.2a and b)**. **Note:** *The rear crankshaft oil seal is fitted after the crankcase halves have been reassembled (see Section 20).*

25 Reassemble the crankcase halves (see Section 22).

25 Auxiliary shaft, camchains and tensioner/guide blades

Note: *To remove the auxiliary shaft and associated components the engine must be removed from the frame.*

Removal

Note: *The upper left-hand tensioner blade is removed prior to removing the camshaft holder (see Section 9).The right-hand guide blade is removed prior to removing the cylinder head (see Section 10). The left-hand guide blade is removed prior to removing the cylinder (see Section 12).*

1 Follow the procedure in Section 22 and separate the crankcase halves.

2 Follow the procedure in Section 24 and lift the crankshaft assembly out of the right-hand crankcase half.

3 Lift out the left-hand tensioner blade and pivot pin, noting how it fits **(see illustration 22.29c)**.

4 Support the left-hand camchain and lift the auxiliary shaft and right-hand camchain out **(see illustration)**.

24.14 Measuring the inside diameter of the crankshaft bearing shells

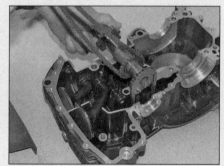

25.4 Lift out the auxiliary shaft and camchains

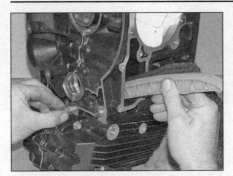

25.5 Remove the right-hand tensioner blade

25.7 Inspect the sprockets on the auxiliary shaft

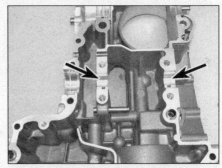

25.8 Auxiliary shaft bearing surfaces in the left-hand crankcase half

5 Working on the right-hand crankcase half, undo the pivot bolt securing the right-hand tensioner blade and withdraw the blade from the crankcase half **(see illustration)**. Note the sealing washer on the bolt and discard it as a new one must be fitted.

Inspection

6 Except in cases of oil starvation, the camchains wear very little. If the chains have stretched, indicated by play between the links, they must be renewed. If the chains have worn, it is likely that the auxiliary shaft sprockets and camshaft sprockets are worn also.

7 Check the auxiliary shaft sprockets for wear and other damage and renew the shaft if necessary **(see illustration)**. Note that if a new shaft is installed, new camchains and camshaft sprockets should also be installed.

8 Inspect the bearing surfaces of the auxiliary shaft and the corresponding surfaces in the crankcase halves **(see illustration)**. If there is any wear, scoring or other damage, renew the components as necessary.

9 Check the tensioner and guide blades and their pivots for signs of wear and damage and renew them if necessary **(see illustration)**. Ensure that the E-clips on the left-hand tensioner blade pivot pin are secure and renew them if necessary. If an E-clip is removed, always fit a new one on installation.

Installation

10 Install the left-hand tensioner blade prior

to assembling the crankcase halves (see Section 22).

11 Once the crankcase halves have been assembled, support the right-hand camchain and align the lower end of the tensioner blade with the pivot bolt hole. Install the bolt with a new sealing washer and tighten it to the torque setting specified at the beginning of this Chapter **(see illustration)**.

12 Refer to the appropriate parts of the procedures in Sections 12, 10 and 9 to install the left-hand guide blade, right-hand guide blade and upper left-hand tensioner blade.

---

26 Gearbox removal and installation

1 The rear suspension and sub-frame must be removed before the gearbox can be detached from the back of the engine.

2 To remove the gearbox, follow the procedure in Section 4, Steps 1 to 43. **Note:** *If work is being carried out on the gearbox, drain its oil prior to removal (see Chapter 1).*

3 Installation is the reverse of removal (see Section 4, Step 62).

---

27 Gearbox oil seals

Special tools: *BMW produces a series of seal installation tools as mentioned in the*

text. *Although extremely useful, they are not essential if care is taken fitting the seals using the alternative methods described.*

1 The gearbox oil seals should be renewed whenever there are signs of oil leakage, or when the gearbox housing or transmission shafts have been removed. If the gearbox is to be disassembled, remove the seals once the appropriate shafts have been removed.

2 Great care should be taken when installing new seals, especially over splined shafts which can damage the inner lip of the seal. BMW provide a number of guides, sleeves and drivers for this purpose.

Transmission input shaft seals

Rear seal

3 To access the rear oil seal, first remove the rear wheel (see Chapter 5) and the rear shock absorber (see Chapter 4). Follow the procedure in Section 21 to displace the clutch release cylinder – note that it is not necessary to disconnect the clutch hose from the cylinder. Withdraw the clutch pushrod from the input shaft.

4 Note the location of the oil seal on the end of the transmission shaft **(see illustration)**.

5 To avoid damaging the seal housing or the surface of the shaft, use a 3 mm drill bit to drill a hole on one side of the seal. Take care to only drill through the outer surface of the seal. Thread a self-tapping screw part-way into the hole and position a piece of thick card over the outer surface of the seal housing to protect it,

---

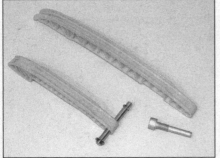

25.9 Inspect the surfaces of the tensioner and guide blades for wear

25.11 Secure the right-hand tensioner blade with the pivot bolt (arrowed)

27.4 Location of the input shaft rear oil seal

27.5 Removing the oil seal as described

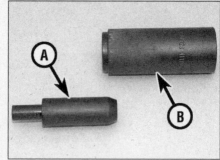

27.6 BMW installation guide (A) and sleeve (B) – input shaft rear oil seal

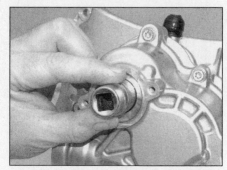

27.8 Installing the seal with a suitably sized socket

then carefully lever out the seal using a pair of curved, thin-nosed pliers **(see illustration)**.

6 If available, use the BMW tools to install the new seal **(see illustration)**. Lubricate the inner lip of the seal with a smear of clean gearbox oil, then slip the seal over the end of the guide (Part No. 234842) and install the smaller diameter end of the guide into the end of the input shaft.

7 Position the sleeve (Part No. 234841) over the end of the guide, and press the seal into position with the sleeve.

8 Alternatively, press the seal into position carefully with a suitably sized socket that locates on the outer edge of the seal only **(see illustration)**.

9 When installed, the outer edge of the seal should be level with the inner face of

the housing and the end of the shaft should protrude through the centre of the seal **(see illustration 27.4)**.

Front seal

10 To access the front oil seal, the gearbox must be removed (see Section 26).

11 If the BMW installation tools are not available, measure the installed depth of the old seal before it is removed **(see illustration)**.

12 Follow the procedure in Step 5 to remove the old seal **(see illustrations)**.

13 If available, use the BMW tools to install the new seal **(see illustration)**. Lubricate the inner lip of the seal with a smear of clean gearbox oil, then slip the seal over the end of the guide (Part No. 234712). Locate the guide

over the end of the shaft, then position the driver (Part No. 234713) over the end of the guide, and press the seal into position with the driver. The end of the driver is shaped to ensure that the seal is pressed fully home inside its housing, clear of the splines on the shaft **(see illustration)**.

14 Alternatively, wrap self-adhesive tape around the splines of the shaft to protect the inner lip of the seal, then install the seal on the shaft and press it into position carefully with a suitably sized driver that locates on the outer edge of the seal only **(see illustrations)**. Check that the seal has been installed evenly and to the depth measured before the old seal was removed, then remove the self-adhesive tape.

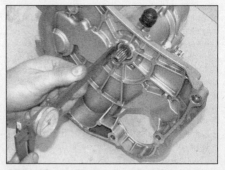

27.11 Measuring the installed depth of the input shaft front oil seal

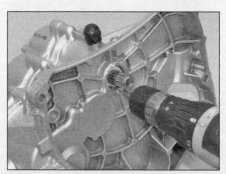

27.12a Drill a small hole in one side of the old seal . . .

27.12b . . . then thread a self-tapping screw into the seal . . .

27.12c . . . and pull the seal out with thin-nosed pliers

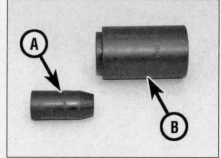

27.13a BMW installation guide (A) and driver (B) – input shaft front oil seal

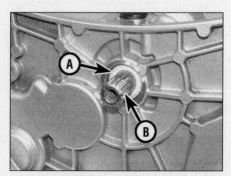

27.13b Installed seal (A) must be clear of the splines (B) on the input shaft

27.14a Cover the shaft splines with tape to protect the oil seal . . .

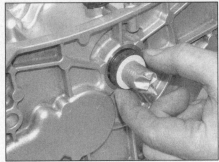

27.14b . . . then install the seal . . .

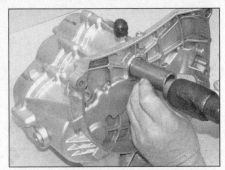

27.14c . . . and press it into place with a suitably sized driver

Transmission output shaft seal

15 To access the output shaft oil seal, first remove the rear shock absorber and swingarm/final drive unit assembly (see Chapter 4).

16 Note the location of the seal in its housing and on the output shaft **(see illustration)**.

17 Follow the procedure in Step 5 to remove the old seal, this time drilling two holes on opposite sides of the old seal to ensure the seal is levered out evenly **(see illustration)**.

18 If available, use the BMW tools to install the new seal **(see illustration)**. Lubricate the inner lip of the seal with a smear of clean gearbox oil, then slip the seal over the end of the guide (Part No. 234733). Locate the guide over the end of the shaft, then position the

driver (Part No. 234731) over the end of the guide, and press the seal into position with the driver. The end of the driver is shaped to ensure that the seal is pressed fully home inside its housing, clear of the splines on the shaft **(see illustration 27.16)**.

19 Alternatively, wrap self-adhesive tape around the shaft to protect the inner lip of the seal, then install the seal on the shaft and press it into position carefully with a suitably sized driver that locates on the outer edge of the seal only.

20 When installed, the outer edge of the seal should be level with the inner face of the housing and the inner lip should be clear of the splines on the shaft. Remove the self-adhesive tape.

Selector drum seal

21 The seal is located behind the gear position sensor at the rear of the gearbox. If not already done, release the sensor wiring from the guide and disconnect the wiring connector **(see illustration)**. Undo the bolts securing the sensor and lift it off **(see illustration)**.

22 To renew the seal, lever it out carefully with a small, flat-bladed screwdriver, taking care not to damage the surface of the housing. Note which way round the seal is fitted.

23 Lubricate the new seal with a smear of clean gearbox oil. If available, use the BMW tool (Part No. 234771) to install the new seal. Alternatively, press the seal in with a suitably sized socket **(see illustration)**.

27.16 Location of the output shaft oil seal (arrowed)

27.17 Levering out the old output shaft oil seal

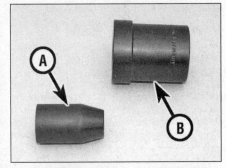

27.18 BMW installation guide (A) and driver (B) – output shaft oil seal

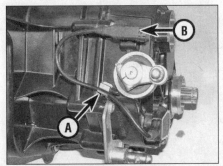

27.21a Sensor wiring guide (A) and connector (B)

27.21b Undo the sensor mounting bolts (arrowed)

27.23 Lubricate the new seal with a smear of gearbox oil

27.24 Locate the sensor over the selector drum shaft

27.27 Mark (arrowed) aligns with slot in lever

27.28a Drill a small hole in one side of the old seal . . .

27.28b . . . then thread in a self-tapping screw . . .

27.28c . . . and pull the old seal out

24 Install the sensor, ensuring it locates correctly over the selector drum shaft **(see illustration)**. Tighten the mounting bolts to the torque setting specified at the beginning of this Chapter.

25 Reconnect the wiring connector and secure the wiring as noted on removal.

Gearchange shaft seal

26 If the gearchange shaft oil seal is leaking, or to inspect the shaft bearings, remove the old seal as follows.

27 If not already done, disconnect the lever from the gearchange shaft – first release the clip securing the gearchange rod to the lever and disconnect the rod (see Section 4, Step 25). Check for a mark on the gearchange shaft that

aligns with the slot in the lever **(see illustration)**. If a mark isn't visible, make your own with a dab of paint, then remove the pinch bolt and pull the lever off the shaft.

28 Using a 3 mm drill bit, drill a hole on one side of the seal **(see illustration)**. Take care to only drill through the outer surface of the seal. Next, thread a self-tapping screw part-way into the hole. Position a small piece of wood over the outer edge of the seal housing to protect it, then carefully lever out the seal using a pair of curved, thin-nosed pliers **(see illustrations)**.

29 Lubricate the new seal with a smear of clean gearbox oil. If available, use the BMW tool (Part No. 234851) to install the new

seal, ensuring it is the right way round **(see illustration)**. Alternatively, press the seal in with a suitably sized socket that bears on the outer edge of the seal only.

30 Install the gearchange lever and tighten the pinch bolt securely.

28 Selector drum and forks

Note: *To remove the selector drum and forks the gearbox must first be removed (see Section 26).*

Special tools: *A stand is required to support the gearbox during this procedure (see **Tool Tip**). A knife-edged bearing puller is required to remove the selector drum bearings.*

Removal

1 Ensure that the transmission is in neutral – the input and output shafts should rotate independently from each other. If not, temporarily install the gearchange lever and select neutral. To avoid damage, undo the bolts securing the gear position sensor and lift the sensor off **(see illustrations 27.21a and b)**.

2 Undo the bolts securing the gearbox end cover to the gearbox housing, then remove the bolts together with the exhaust system bracket **(see illustration)**.

27.29 Ensure the seal is fitted the correct way round

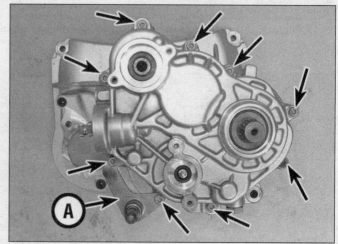

28.2 Location of the gearbox end cover bolts and exhaust bracket (A)

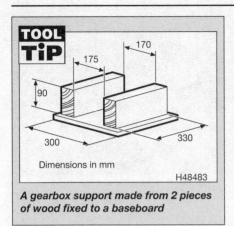

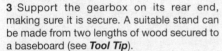

A gearbox support made from 2 pieces of wood fixed to a baseboard

28.4 Wear gloves when handling the heated gearbox housing

28.5a Location of the gearbox internal components

3 Support the gearbox on its rear end, making sure it is secure. A suitable stand can be made from two lengths of wood secured to a baseboard (see **Tool Tip**).

4 Using a hot air gun, heat the gearbox housing around the locations for the internal bearings to release the bearings from the housing, then tap around the joint between the housing and the end cover with a soft-faced mallet to separate them. The sealant used between the casings can form a strong bond, but do not attempt to lever them apart with a screwdriver – you'll damage the sealing

surfaces. If the housing won't lift off, it isn't hot enough – BMW suggest a separation temperature between 50°C to 80°C **(see illustration)**.

⚠ *Warning: Be careful when separating the gearbox casings – when heated, the housing could cause severe burns.*

5 Lift off the gearbox housing – the gearbox internal components will remain in the end cover **(see illustration)**. Note the location of the two dowels in the housing and remove them if they are loose **(see illustration)**.

6 Note the location of the oil deflector blade

and remove it for safekeeping, noting how it fits **(see illustration)**.

7 Lift out the magnet from the lower edge of the gearbox and clean it thoroughly to remove any metal swarf **(see illustration)**.

8 Before removing the selector forks, mark each one according to its location and which way up it fits as an aid to installation **(see illustration)**. Note how the guide pins on the forks locate in the grooves in the selector drum.

9 Lift out the fork shaft supporting the upper 1st/6th and lower 2nd/3rd gear selector forks **(see illustration)**.

10 Note how the 1st/6th gear selector fork

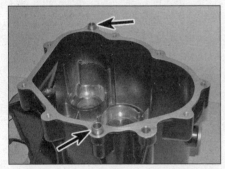

28.5b Note the location of the dowels (arrowed)

28.6 Remove the oil deflector blade

28.7 Location of the magnet

28.8 Gear selector forks – 1st/6th gear (A), 2nd/3rd gear (B), 4th/5th gear (C). Selector drum (D)

28.9 Lift out the selector fork shaft

28.10 Pull the selector fork out of the shift sleeve

28.11a Note the location of the washers (arrowed) . . .

28.11b . . . then lift out the shaft and remove the washers

28.12a Disengage the guide pin (arrowed) from the selector drum

28.12b Withdraw the fork from the shift sleeve on the intermediate shaft

locates in its shift sleeve on the transmission output shaft and lift the selector fork off **(see illustration)**. Slide the fork back onto its shaft the right way round.

11 Note the location of the plain and wave washers between the 4th/5th gear selector fork and the selector arm **(see illustration)**. Carefully lift out the fork shaft and remove the washers **(see illustration)**. Slide the washers onto the fork shaft for safekeeping.

12 Disengage the guide pin on the 4th/5th gear selector fork from the selector drum, then withdraw the fork from the shift sleeve on the transmission intermediate shaft **(see illustrations)**. Slide the fork back onto its shaft the right way round.

13 Note the location of the selector arm – the centralising spring locates on the same pin as the stopper arm return spring, and the selector arm pawls engage with the pins on the lower end of the selector drum **(see illustration)**. Lift the selector arm out **(see illustration)**. Note the position of the peg on the gearchange shaft **(see illustration)**.

14 Manoeuvre the 2nd/3rd gear selector fork to disengage the guide pin from the selector drum, then ease the stopper arm away from the gearchange cam on the lower end of the selector drum and lift the selector drum out **(see illustration)**. Note the location of the shim on the lower end of the selector drum shaft **(see illustration)**.

28.13a Note location of the selector arm . . .

28.13b . . . then lift it out

28.13c Note position of the peg (arrowed)

28.14a Lift out the selector drum . . .

28.14b . . . noting location of the shim

28.15 Lift out the 2nd/3rd gear selector fork

28.16 Stopper arm (A) and selector drum bearing (B)

28.18a Inspect the selector forks for wear . . .

15 Note how the 2nd/3rd gear selector fork locates in its shift sleeve on the transmission output shaft and lift the selector fork out (see illustration). Slide the fork back onto its shaft the right way round.

16 Note the location of the stopper arm and selector drum bearing (see illustration).

Inspection

17 Check closely to see if the forks are bent. If the forks are in any way damaged they must be renewed.

18 Inspect the selector forks for any signs of wear or damage, especially where the forks engage with the sliding sleeves on the transmission shafts (see illustrations). Measure the width of the contact surfaces of the 2nd/3rd gear fork and compare the results with the

specification at the beginning of this Chapter. Measure the width of the recess in the 1st/6th and 4th/5th gear forks and compare the results with the specifications. If any component is worn outside the specification it must be renewed.

19 With the transmission shafts removed (see Section 30), check that each fork fits correctly in its sliding sleeve (see illustration). Measure the width of the recess in the 2nd/3rd gear sliding sleeve and compare the result with the specifications (see illustration). Measure the width of the 1st/6th and 4th/5th gear sleeve webs and compare the results with the specifications (see illustrations). Measure the clearance between the gear sleeve webs and the corresponding fork recesses and compare the results with the specifications. If any component is worn outside the specification

the transmission shaft must be renewed – individual components are not available.

20 Check that the forks fit correctly on their shafts. They should move freely with a light fit but no appreciable freeplay. Replace the forks and/or shaft if excessive wear is noted. Check that the fork shaft holes in the casing and end cover are not worn or damaged.

21 Check that the selector fork shafts are straight by rolling them along a flat surface. A bent shaft will cause difficulty in selecting gears and make the gearchange action heavy, and should be replaced with a new one.

22 Inspect the grooves in the selector drum and guide pins on the selector forks for signs of wear or damage (see illustration). Any components with wear or damage should be renewed.

28.18b . . . especially where they engage with the sliding sleeves

28.19a Each fork must fit correctly in its sleeve

28.19b Fork recess in the 2nd/3rd gear sliding sleeve – output shaft

28.19c Sleeve web on 1st/6th gear – output shaft

28.19d Sleeve web on 4th/5th gear – intermediate shaft

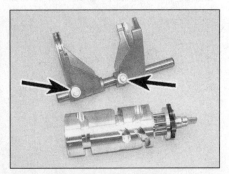

28.22 Inspect the guide pins (arrowed) and the grooves in the drum

28.28a Locate the 2nd/3rd gear selector fork guide pin in the lower groove

28.28b Stopper arm roller should locate in the neutral detent

23 Check that the bearing in the end of the selector drum rotates freely. To renew the bearing, heat the end of the drum with a hot air gun and pull the bearing out with a knife-edged bearing puller (see *Tools and Workshop Tips* in the *Reference* section). Note which way round the bearing is fitted. Drive the new bearing in with a bearing driver or suitably sized socket. Take great care not to damage the components on the lower end of the selector drum shaft when renewing the bearing. Measure the assembled length of the selector drum and compare the result with the specification at the beginning of this Chapter.

24 Check that the selector drum bearing in the gearbox end cover rotates freely **(see illustration 28.16)**. To renew the bearing, first remove the gearchange mechanism and transmission shafts (see Sections 29 and 30). Heat the housing with a hot air gun and pull the bearing out with a knife-edged bearing puller. Note which way round the bearing is fitted. Drive the new bearing in with a bearing driver or suitably sized socket.

Installation

25 Prior to installation, remove all traces of old sealant from the mating surfaces of the gearbox housing and end cover. If a scraper must be used, be very careful not to nick

28.36 Apply sealant to the end cover mating surface

or gouge the soft aluminium or oil leaks will result. Take care not to let any old sealant fall into the end cover.

26 Ensure that the gearbox end cover is securely supported (see Step 3). If removed, install the transmission shafts and gearchange mechanism.

27 Fit the 2nd/3rd gear selector fork in its shift sleeve on the transmission output shaft, making sure it is the right way round **(see illustration 28.15)**.

28 Secure the shim on the lower end of the selector drum shaft with a dab of grease **(see illustration 28.14b)**, then install the selector drum in the gearbox end cover. Locate the guide pin on the 2nd/3rd gear selector fork in the lower groove in the selector drum **(see illustration)**. Ensure that the stopper arm roller is located in the neutral detent on the gearchange cam **(see illustration)**.

29 Ensure the peg on the gearchange shaft is facing up, then install the selector arm **(see illustration 28.13c and b)**. Ensure the selector arm pawls and centralising spring are correctly located **(see illustration 28.13a)**.

30 Install the 4th/5th gear selector fork in the shift sleeve on the transmission intermediate shaft, then locate the guide pin in the middle groove on the selector drum **(see illustrations 28.12b and a)**. Slide the fork shaft through the selector fork, the plain washer (uppermost) and the wave washer **(see illustration 28.11b)**, the selector arm and into its location in the gearbox end cover **(see illustration 28.11a)**. Ensure shaft is pressed fully into place.

31 Install the 1st/6th gear selector fork in its shift sleeve on the transmission output shaft, then locate the guide pin in the upper groove in the selector drum **(see illustration 28.10)**. Slide the fork shaft through the upper and lower selector forks and into its location in the gearbox end cover **(see illustration 28.9)**. Ensure the shaft is pressed fully into place.

32 Check that the selector forks are correctly installed **(see illustration 28.8)**.

33 If removed, fit the dowels into the end cover **(see illustration 28.5b)**.

34 Clean the threads of all the cover bolts.

35 Generously lubricate all the components with clean gearbox oil (see Chapter 1), then use a rag soaked in high flash-point solvent to wipe over the mating surfaces of the casings to remove all traces of oil.

36 Apply a thin, even bead of suitable sealant to the mating surface of the end cover **(see illustration)**.

Caution: Don't apply an excessive amount of sealant as it will ooze out when the gearbox housing and end cover are assembled.

37 Carefully lower the housing over the transmission components – align the input shaft with the bearing in the housing and align the mating surfaces of the housing and end cover. Using a hot air gun, heat the gearbox housing around the locations for the internal bearings, then tap the housing down onto the end cover with a soft-faced mallet. If the housing won't drop into place, either the shafts are not properly aligned with their locations in the housing, or the housing isn't hot enough – BMW suggest an assembly temperature between 50°C to 80°C. Check that the gearbox casings are correctly seated all the way round.

Caution: The gearbox casings should fit together without being forced. If they're not correctly seated, separate them and investigate the problem. DO NOT attempt to pull them together by tightening the cover bolts.

38 Carefully turn the gearbox over, then install the cover bolts and the exhaust system bracket **(see illustration 28.2)**. Tighten the bolts in a criss-cross sequence to the torque setting specified at the beginning of this Chapter.

39 Temporarily install the gearchange lever and check that all the gears can be selected and that the transmission shafts rotate smoothly in every gear.

29.2a Location of the stopper arm . . .

29.2b . . . and stopper arm return spring

29.4a Remove the circlip . . .

40 Install the gear position sensor and tighten the bolts to the specified torque setting **(see illustrations 27.21b and a)**.

41 Before installing the gearbox, renew the transmission input and output shaft oil seals (see Section 27).

29 Gearchange mechanism

Note: *To remove the gearchange mechanism the gearbox must first be removed (see Section 26).*

Special tools: *A stand is required to support the gearbox during this procedure (see **Tool Tip** in Section 28). A knife-edged bearing puller is required to remove the inner gearchange shaft bearing.*

Removal

1 Follow the procedure in Section 28 to remove the selector drum and forks.

2 Note the location of the return spring on the stopper arm **(see illustration)**. Undo the pivot bolt and lift out the stopper arm. Note the location of the return spring and lift it out **(see illustration)**.

3 To inspect the shaft bearings, first remove the oil seal (see Section 27).

4 The gearchange shaft and caged ball bearing are retained by a circlip – remove the circlip and draw the shaft assembly out **(see illustrations)**. The inner end of the shaft is supported by a needle roller bearing **(see illustration)**.

Inspection

5 Inspect the pawls on the selector arm and the pins on the selector drum **(see illustration)**.

Ensure that the centralising spring is a tight fit on the selector arm and note the location of the small spring on the pawl mechanism – the mechanism should move smoothly, but not be loose **(see illustration)**.

6 Inspect the stopper arm return spring, the stopper arm and the roller and the corresponding lobes on the gearchange cam **(see illustration)**.

7 If any of the components are found to be worn or damaged, or the springs fatigued, they must be renewed.

8 Inspect the gearchange shaft for damage to the splines and renew the shaft if necessary **(see illustration)**. Check the peg on the shaft and the corresponding fork on the selector arm for wear. Check the condition of the shaft bearings. The caged ball bearing is secured on the shaft by a circlip – if required, remove the circlip and press the shaft out. Only remove

29.4b . . . and draw out the gearchange shaft assembly

29.4c Note the location of the needle roller bearing (arrowed)

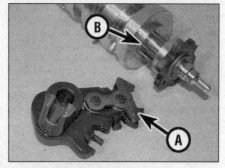

29.5a Inspect the pawls (A) and the pins (B)

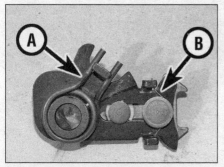

29.5b Inspect the pawl mechanism – note centralising spring (A) and pawl spring (B)

29.6 Inspect the stopper arm return spring, roller and gearchange cam lobes

29.8 Inspect the gearchange shaft splines (arrowed)

30.2 Note the location of the three transmission shafts

30.3 Lift the transmission shafts out as an assembly

the shaft needle roller bearing if it is going to be renewed – draw the old bearing out with a knife-edged bearing puller and press the new bearing in carefully with a suitably sized socket.

Installation

9 If removed, secure the caged ball bearing on the gearchange shaft with the circlip, then install the shaft assembly and secure it with the circlip **(see illustrations 29.4b and a)**. Ensure both circlips are correctly fitted in their grooves – it is good practice to renew the circlips, especially if they are corroded or fatigued. Fit a new gearchange shaft oil seal (see Section 27).

10 Install the return spring and stopper arm and tighten the pivot bolt to the torque setting specified at the beginning of this Chapter **(see illustrations 29.2b and a)**. The ends of the spring should be positioned so that the stopper arm roller is held under tension against the selector drum cam **(see illustration 28.28b)**.

11 Follow the procedure in Section 28 to install the selector drum and forks.

30 Transmission shafts

Note 1: *To remove the transmission shafts the gearbox must first be removed (see Section 26).*
Note 2: *The assembled length of the transmission shafts is critical to ensure that they fit inside the gearbox casings. If new bearings are fitted, be sure to check the assembled length before installation.*
Special tools: *A knife-edged bearing puller with both long and short-reach arms is required for this procedure.*

Removal

1 Follow the procedure in Section 28 to remove the selector drum and forks.
2 Note the relative positions of the three

transmission shafts and how they fit together **(see illustration)**.
3 Using a hot air gun, heat the gearbox end cover around the locations for the internal bearings to release the bearings from the cover, then lift the transmission shafts out as an assembly **(see illustration)**. Don't try to pull the shafts out individually, if the assembly won't lift out, the cover isn't hot enough – BMW suggest a separation temperature between 90°C to 100°C.

 Warning: Be careful when removing the transmission shafts – when heated, the end cover could cause severe burns.

4 Lay the transmission shafts on a clean work surface. Keep the shafts in their correct order **(see illustration)**.

Input shaft
Inspection and bearing renewal

5 Inspect the shaft splines for signs of wear or damage **(see illustration)**. Inspect the lobes of the drive cam and driven gear for wear, and

30.4 Keep the output (A), intermediate (B) and input shafts (C) in their correct order

30.5a Inspect the shaft splines

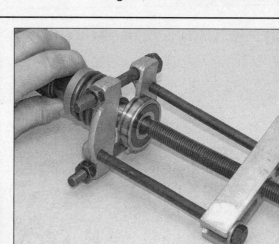

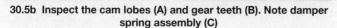

30.5b Inspect the cam lobes (A) and gear teeth (B). Note damper spring assembly (C)

30.9 Set-up for pulling the rear bearing off the input shaft

inspect the gear teeth for chipping, pitting and wear (see illustration). If the driven gear teeth are worn or damaged, check the teeth on the corresponding gear on the intermediate shaft.
6 Ensure there is no freeplay in the damper spring assembly (see illustration 30.5b).
7 If any components are worn or damaged, a new transmission shaft will have to be fitted – individual components are not available.
8 Check the bearings for wear or damage (see Tools and Workshop Tips in the Reference section), replacing them with new ones if necessary.
9 Using a bearing puller, pull the rear bearing off the rear end of the shaft, noting which way round it is fitted (see illustration).
10 Slide off the shim and splined collar for safekeeping (see illustrations). Note the combined width of the old bearing and the shim, and ensure the combined width of the new bearing and shim is the same. If the width is too great, fit a thinner shim to correct it. There are 17 thicknesses of shim available, from 3.0 to 3.4 mm thickness – see a BMW dealer for details.
11 To remove the bearing from the front end of the shaft, assemble the puller as before, with a piece of soft metal (brass is ideal) on the end of the shaft to protect the splines.
12 Install the front bearing with a driver that

locates on the inner race of the bearing only, and drive the bearing all the way on.
13 Slide on the splined collar and the shim (see illustrations 30.10b and a).
14 Press on the rear bearing with a driver that locates on the inner race of the bearing only, and drive the bearing all the way on.
15 Measure the assembled length of the input shaft and compare the result with the specification at the beginning of this Chapter (see illustration). If the length is too great, check that the bearings have been fitted fully onto the shaft.

Intermediate shaft

Inspection and bearing renewal

16 Inspect the gear teeth for wear and damage (see illustration) and check the teeth on the corresponding gears on the output shaft (see illustration 30.4). Check the endplay of the 4th and 5th gear pinions and compare the results with the specifications at the beginning of this Chapter. If any components are worn or damaged, a new transmission shaft will have to be fitted – individual components are not available.
17 Check the bearings for wear or damage and renew them if necessary (see Tools and Workshop Tips in the Reference section). Both

bearings are a press fit on the shaft – note which way round they are fitted, then remove them using a puller (see illustration 30.9).
18 A shim is fitted behind the front bearing – note the combined width of the old bearing and the shim, and ensure the combined width of the new bearing and shim is the same. If the width is too great, fit a thinner shim to correct it. There are 29 thicknesses of shim available, from 1.5 to 2.3 mm thickness – see a BMW dealer for details.
19 Drive the new bearings into place using a suitable socket or bearing driver.
20 Measure the assembled length of the

30.10a Slide off the shim . . .

30.10b . . . and the splined collar

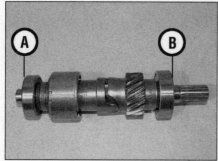

30.15 Assembled input shaft – measure the length between the points A and B

30.16 Inspect the gear teeth – intermediate shaft

30.20 Assembled intermediate shaft – measure the length between the points A and B

30.21a Inspect the shaft splines

30.21b Check the endplay of the 1st (A) and 6th (B) gear . . .

30.21c . . . and 3rd (C) and 2nd (D) gear pinions

intermediate shaft and compare the result with the specification at the beginning of this Chapter **(see illustration)**. If the length is too great, check that the bearings have been fitted fully onto the shaft.

Output shaft

Inspection and bearing renewal

21 Inspect the shaft splines for signs of wear or damage **(see illustration)**. Inspect the gear teeth for wear and damage. Check the endplay of the 1st, 2nd, 3rd and 6th gear pinions and compare the results with the specifications at the beginning of this Chapter **(see illustrations)**. If any components are worn or damaged, a new transmission shaft will have to be fitted – individual components are not available.

22 Check the bearings for wear or damage and renew them if necessary (see *Tools and Workshop Tips* in the *Reference* section). Both

bearings are retained by circlips and are a press fit on the shaft – note which way round they are fitted before removal.

23 Remove the circlip from the front end of the shaft **(see illustration)**. Discard the circlip as a new one must be fitted.

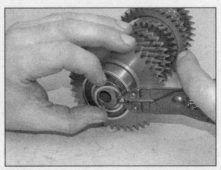

30.23 Remove the circlip from the front end of the shaft

24 Using a bearing puller, pull the front bearing off the shaft, noting which way round it is fitted **(see illustration)**. If a knife-edged puller is not available, position the puller behind the 1st gear pinion to displace the bearing. Remove the shim, noting which way

30.24 Set-up for pulling the front bearing off the output shaft

30.26 Tapered side of shim (arrowed) faces out

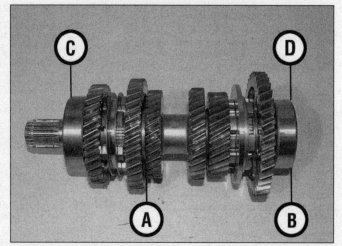

30.27 Assembled output shaft – measure assembled lengths between points shown. Front end A to B. Total length C to D

30.29 Remove the circlip from the rear end of the output shaft

30.30 Set-up for pulling the rear bearing off the output shaft

round it is fitted, and slide the 1st gear pinion back onto the shaft

25 Note the combined width of the old bearing and the shim, and ensure the combined width of the new bearing and shim is the same. If the width is too great, fit a thinner shim to correct

30.32 Tapered side of shim (arrowed) faces out

it. There are 29 thicknesses of shim available, from 1.8 to 2.5 mm thickness – see a BMW dealer for details.

26 Install the shim with its tapered side facing out **(see illustration)**. Press the front bearing onto the end of the shaft with a driver that locates on the inner race of the bearing only.

27 Measure the assembled length of the components on the front end of the output shaft and compare the result with the specification at the beginning of this Chapter **(see illustration)**. If the length is too great, check that the bearing has been fitted fully onto the shaft.

28 Secure the bearing with a new circlip.

29 Remove the circlip from the rear end of the shaft **(see illustration)**. Discard the circlip as a new one must be fitted.

30 Using a bearing puller, pull the rear bearing off the shaft, noting which way round it is fitted **(see illustration)**. If a knife-edged puller is not available, position the puller behind the 3rd gear pinion to displace the bearing. Remove

the shim, noting which way round it is fitted, and slide the 3rd gear pinion back onto the shaft.

31 Note the combined width of the old bearing and the shim, and ensure the combined width of the new bearing and shim is the same. If the width is too great, fit a thinner shim to correct it. There are 29 thicknesses of shim available, from 1.8 to 2.5 mm thickness – see a BMW dealer for details.

32 Install the shim with its tapered side facing out **(see illustration)**. Press the rear bearing onto the end of the shaft.

33 Measure the total assembled length of the output shaft and compare the result with the specification at the beginning of this Chapter **(see illustration 30.27)**. If the length is too great, check that the bearing has been fitted fully onto the shaft.

34 When the total assembled length is correct and the bearing is fully installed, measure the width of the circlip groove on the end of the shaft with a feeler gauge and fit the appropriate

30.34 Measuring the width of the circlip groove

sized new circlip **(see illustration)**. Three thicknesses of circlip are available, from 1.1 to 1.3 mm in thickness – see a BMW dealer for details.

Installation

35 Installation is the reverse of removal, noting the following:

- Ensure that the gearbox end cover is supported securely.
- Lay the assembled shafts in the correct order (see illustration 30.4).
- Heat the gearbox end cover around the locations for the shaft bearings – BMW suggest an installation temperature between 90°C to 100°C.
- Install the transmission shafts as an assembly (see illustration 30.3).

- Check that the relative positions of the three transmission shafts is as noted on removal (see illustration 30.2).
- Generously lubricate all the components with clean gearbox oil (see Chapter 1).
- Install the selector drum and forks (see Section 28).
- Don't forget to renew the transmission input and output shaft oil seals (see Section 27).

31 Running-in procedure

1 Make sure the engine and gearbox oil levels are correct (see *Pre-ride checks* and Chapter 1).
2 Check that the kill switch is in the RUN position and the gearbox is in neutral, then turn the ignition switch ON.
3 Start the engine and allow it to run until it reaches operating temperature.

⚠️ *Warning: If the oil pressure warning light doesn't go off, or it comes on while the engine is running, stop the engine immediately. Note that the warning light is not fitted to R1200 R models.*

4 If a lubrication failure is suspected, stop the engine immediately and try to find the cause. If an engine is run without the oil circulating, even for a short period of time, severe damage will occur.

5 Check carefully for oil leaks and make sure the transmission and controls, especially the brakes, function properly before road testing the machine.
6 Treat the machine gently for the first few miles to make sure oil has circulated throughout the engine and any new parts installed have started to seat.
7 Extra care is necessary if new pistons, rings or bearing shells have been fitted. If this is the case, the bike will have to be run in as when new. This means greater use of the transmission and a restraining hand on the throttle until at least 600 miles (1000 km) have been covered.
8 Upon completion of the road test, and after the engine has cooled down completely, recheck the valve clearances (see Chapter 1) and check the engine and gearbox oil levels (see *Pre-ride checks* and Chapter 1).
9 BMW advise that the engine should not exceed 5500 rpm for the first 125 miles (200 km) of the running-in period. For the next 125 miles the engine speed can be increased to 6500 rpm and for a further 125 miles the speed can be increased to 7500 rpm. The main idea is to keep from labouring the engine and to gradually increase performance, varying the throttle position, up to the 375 miles (600 km) mark. For the final stage of the running-in period, between 375 and 560 miles (600 to 900 km) give the engine short bursts of maximum rpm. Experience is the best guide, since it's easy to tell when an engine is running freely.

Chapter 3
Engine management systems

Contents

Section number

Air filter . . . . see Chapter 1
Catalytic converter and oxygen sensors 10
ECU – removal and installation 15
Engine management system and ECU – fault finding 14
Evaporative emission control system – US models 3
Exhaust system 9
Fuel hoses and pressure regulator 5
Fuel injectors 7
Fuel level sensor . . . . see Chapter 7
Fuel pump and strainer 4
Fuel tank 2

Section number

General information and precautions 1
Ignition coils 12
Ignition switch . . . . see Chapter 7
Ignition system checks 11
Sensors 16
Spark plugs . . . . see Chapter 1
Starter interlock circuit 13
Throttle bodies 6
Throttle cable check and adjustment . . . . see Chapter 1
Throttle cables 8

Degrees of difficulty

Easy, suitable for novice with little experience	**Fairly easy,** suitable for beginner with some experience	**Fairly difficult,** suitable for competent DIY mechanic	**Difficult,** suitable for experienced DIY mechanic	**Very difficult,** suitable for expert DIY or professional

Specifications

Fuel
Grade
  All models . . . . Unleaded, minimum 98 RON (Research Octane Number)
  R1200 GS and GS Adventure (optional) . . . . Unleaded, minimum 91 RON (Research Octane Number)
Tank capacity
  R1200 GS . . . . 20 litres
  R1200 GS Adventure . . . . 33 litres
  R1200 RT . . . . 25 litres
  R1200 R . . . . 18 litres
Quantity remaining when level warning light comes on
  R1200 R . . . . 3 litres
  All other models . . . . 4 litres

Exhaust system
Exhaust flow control valve cable freeplay . . . . 0.8 to 1.2 mm

Throttle bodies
Internal diameter . . . . 50 mm

Torque settings

Exhaust system
    Control valve servo motor mounting bolt . . . .   8 Nm
    Silencer rear mounting bolt . . . .   19 Nm
    Silencer-to-pipe clamp bolt
        R1200 GS, GS Adventure and R1200 R . . . .   28 Nm
        R1200 RT . . . .   55 Nm
    Downpipe assembly mounting clamp bolts . . . .   8 Nm
    Downpipe manifold nuts . . . .   21 Nm
    Oxygen sensors . . . .   45 Nm
Fuel tank mounting bolt
    R1200 GS and GS Adventure . . . .   19 Nm
    R1200 RT . . . .   16 Nm
    R1200 R . . . .   22 Nm
Fuel pump retaining ring . . . .   35 Nm
Fuel injector mounting screws . . . .   5 Nm
Intake manifold bolts . . . .   8 Nm
Sensors
    Camshaft position sensor screw . . . .   8 Nm
    Crankshaft position sensor screw . . . .   8 Nm
    Cylinder head temperature sensor . . . .   10 Nm
    Gear position sensor . . . .   9 Nm
    Knock sensor bolt . . . .   19 Nm
    Engine oil temperature sensor . . . .   30 Nm
    Engine oil pressure switch . . . .   30 Nm

1 General information and precautions

General information

All models covered in this manual are fitted with BMW's own digital engine management system (BMS-K) which monitors, controls and co-ordinates both the fuel and ignition system functions.

The system is operated by the engine control unit, or ECU. A second unit, the central electronics (ZFE) unit, is responsible for monitoring and control of all other electrical systems such as lighting, switches and accessories. The two units are linked for such functions as starting and engine immobilisation.

The ECU uses engine speed and throttle valve position as the basis for determining optimum engine operation. Additional data, supplied by temperature sensors, oil pressure, gear position and knock sensors, and exhaust gas analysers, when combined with control maps and correction values embedded within the ECU, fine tune injection volume and ignition timing to meet the engine's requirements in any given circumstance.

The engine management system has in-built diagnostic functions which record and store all data should a fault occur. If this happens, the engine warning light in the instrument cluster illuminates and, unless the fault is serious, the engine runs in emergency 'limp home' mode. Otherwise, the engine will stop. BMW advise that in 'limp home' mode, full engine power may not be available and the machine should

be ridden with this in mind. Have the machine checked by a BMW dealer – recorded faults can then be analysed using the BMW diagnostic tester and remedial action taken.

Because of their nature, individual system components cannot be repaired. Once the faulty component has been isolated, the only cure is to replace the part with a new one. Keep in mind that most electrical parts, once purchased, cannot be returned. To avoid unnecessary expense, make very sure the faulty component has been positively identified before buying a new part.

Fuel system

The fuel system consists of the fuel tank, fuel pump and strainer, fuel hoses and pressure regulator, throttle bodies, fuel injectors and throttle control cables, and the air intake system. Cruise control is fitted as optional equipment (OE) to R1200 RT models. Details of the set-up are given in Section 8.

The fuel pump, with integral filter on GS, Adv and RT models, is housed inside the tank. The fuel strainer is mounted on the bottom of the pump. R1200 R models have an external in-line filter. On R1200 GS Adventure models, a balance pump is located in the right-hand side of the tank.

There is an injector for each cylinder, housed in the throttle body. Cold starting, warm-up and engine idle speed are controlled by the ECU acting on information sent by the engine and intake air temperature sensors – there is no manual method (i.e. a choke) for assisting cold starting.

Information on fuel level is provided by a level sensor in the tank which is linked to the fuel gauge and low fuel level warning in instrument cluster. The tripmeter will calculate

the range available on the remaining fuel and present this information on the multi-function panel in the instrument cluster.

The exhaust system is a two-into-one design, incorporating a catalytic converter, oxygen sensors and exhaust control valve.

 Warning: Petrol (gasoline) is extremely flammable, so take extra precautions when you work on any part of the fuel system. Don't smoke or allow open flames or bare light bulbs near the work area, and don't work in a garage where a natural gas-type appliance is present. If you spill any fuel on your skin, rinse it off immediately with soap and water. When you perform any kind of work on the fuel system, wear safety glasses and have a fire extinguisher suitable for a class B type fire (flammable liquids) on hand.

Ignition system

The ignition system, due to its lack of mechanical parts, is totally maintenance-free.

On all models, the ignition coil for each spark plug (there are two per cylinder) is incorporated in the spark plug cap. The system incorporates ignition advance controlled by the ECU, which reacts to the information sent to it from the various sensors to provide the sparks at the optimum time – during low speed engine operation, the primary and secondary plugs fire independently of each other to ensure maximum fuel burn efficiency.

Knock sensors located on both cylinders allow the ECU to adjust ignition timing to protect the engine from detonation due to high operating temperatures or poor quality fuel.

The system incorporates a safety interlock

circuit which prevents the engine from being started with the side stand down unless the gearbox is in neutral. The interlock circuit will also cut the ignition if the side stand is put down whilst the engine is running and in gear, or if a gear is selected whilst the engine is running and the side stand is down.

⚠️ *Warning: The very high output of the engine management system means that it can be very dangerous or even fatal to touch live components or terminals of any part of the system while in operation. Take care not to touch any part of the system when the engine is running, or even with it stopped and the ignition ON. Before working on an electrical component, make sure that the ignition switch is OFF, then disconnect the battery negative lead (-ve) and insulate it away from the battery terminal.*

Precautions

Always perform fuel-related procedures in a well-ventilated area to prevent a build-up of fumes.

Never work in a building containing a gas appliance with a pilot light, or any other form of naked flame. Ensure that there are no naked light bulbs or any sources of flame or sparks nearby.

Do not smoke (or allow anyone else to smoke) while in the vicinity of petrol (gasoline) or of components containing it. Remember the possible presence of vapour from these sources and move well clear before smoking.

Check all electrical equipment belonging to

the house, garage or workshop where work is being undertaken (see the Safety first! section of this manual). Remember that certain electrical appliances such as drills, cutters etc. create sparks in the normal course of operation and must not be used near petrol (gasoline) or any component containing it. Again, remember the possible presence of fumes before using electrical equipment.

Always mop up any spilt fuel and safely dispose of the rag used.

Any stored fuel that is drained off during servicing work must be kept in sealed containers that are suitable for holding petrol (gasoline), and clearly marked as such; the containers themselves should be kept in a safe place. Note that this last point applies equally to the fuel tank if it is removed from the machine; also remember to keep its filler cap closed at all times.

Read the Safety first! section of this manual carefully before starting work.

Owners of machines used in the US, particularly California, should note that their machines must comply at all times with Federal or State legislation governing the permissible levels of noise and of pollutants such as unburnt hydrocarbons, carbon monoxide etc. that can be emitted by those machines. All vehicles offered for sale must comply with legislation in force at the date of manufacture and must not subsequently be altered in any way which will affect their emission of noise or of pollutants.

In practice, this means that adjustments may not be made to any part of the fuel,

ignition or exhaust systems by anyone who is not authorised or mechanically qualified to do so, or who does not have the tools, equipment and data necessary to properly carry out the task. Also if any part of these systems is to be replaced it must be replaced with only genuine BMW components or by components which are approved under the relevant legislation. The machine must never be used with any part of these systems removed, modified or damaged.

2 Fuel tank

⚠️ *Warning: Refer to the precautions given in Section 1 before starting work.*

R1200 GS and GS Adventure

Fuel tank

1 Remove the seats (see Chapter 6).
2 Remove the frame side covers and the fuel tank side panels (see Chapter 6).
3 On R1200 GS models, remove the air filter intake duct (see Chapter 1).
4 On R1200 GS Adventure models, remove the air deflectors (see Chapter 6).
5 Remove the screws securing the front edge of the tank top panel on both sides **(see illustration)**.
6 Release the tabs securing the wiring connectors for the fuel pump and fuel level sensor and disconnect the connectors **(see illustration)**.
7 Release the quick-release coupling securing the fuel delivery hose and disconnect the hose from the pump **(see illustration)**. Note the location of the O-ring on the union and fit a new one if it is damaged or distorted.
8 Release the coupling on the fuel return hose union **(see illustration)**. On GS Adventure models the return hose is connected to the balance pump on the right-hand side of the tank **(see illustration)**. Disconnect the hose, being prepared to catch any residual fuel. Note the location of the O-ring on the union and fit a new one if it is damaged or distorted.
9 Trace the drain hose down the left-hand side

2.5 Remove the screws on both sides

2.6 Disconnect the wiring connectors

2.7 Disconnect the fuel delivery hose

2.8a Release the return hose coupling

2.8b Return hose coupling – R1200 GS Adventure

2.9 Disconnect the drain hose

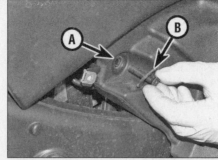

2.10 Note rubber (A) and steel (B) washers

2.11a Disconnect the breather hose

2.11b Location of hose clip – R1200 GS Adventure

2.12a Undo the bolt . . .

2.12b . . . and remove the right-hand bracket

2.12c Undo the bolt . . .

2.12d . . . and remove the left-hand bracket

2.13a Draw the tank back off the mounting bushes . . .

of the tank and disconnect it at the connector **(see illustration)**.

10 On R1200 GS Adventure models, undo the left and right-hand mounting bolts, noting the location of the steel and rubber washers **(see illustration)**. Lift the rear of the tank and remove the air filter intake duct (see Chapter 1).

11 Trace the breather hose down the right-hand side of the tank and disconnect it at the connector **(see illustration)**. On R1200 GS Adventure models, note that the front section of the hose is secured by a clip on the inside edge of the tank **(see illustration)**.

12 On R1200 GS models, undo the bolt

securing the right-hand mounting bracket and remove the bracket **(see illustrations)**. Undo the bolt securing the left-hand mounting bracket and remove the bracket **(see illustrations)**.

13 Make sure the fuel filler cap is secure, then draw the tank back off the front mounting bushes and lift it off **(see illustrations)**.

2.13b . . . and lift it off

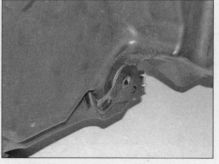

2.13c Note location of right-hand . . .

2.13d . . . and left-hand side panel brackets

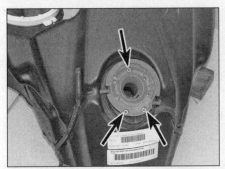

2.18 Undo the filler neck screws

2.19a Lift out the filler neck assembly – R1200 GS shown

2.19b Feed the guide wire through from the fuel pump opening (arrowed)

On R1200 GS Adventure models, note the location of the rear tank side panel brackets and remove them for safekeeping if they are loose **(see illustrations)**.

14 Installation is the reverse of removal, noting the following:

● Check the condition of the front mounting bushes and renew them if they are damaged or deteriorated **(see illustration 2.13a)**.

● Ensure that the fuel delivery and return hoses are correctly routed. Lubricate the hose union O-rings with a smear of silicone grease.

● To connect the fuel hose couplings, hold the clip on the female side open, then insert the male side of the union and release the clip.

● Ensure that the breather and drain hoses are clipped in position.

● Tighten the mounting bolts to the torque setting specified at the beginning of this Chapter.

● Check the hose unions for leaks before installing the bodywork.

Fuel tank filler neck

15 On R1200 GS models, a tip-over cut-off valve for the tank breather is located on the underside of the filler neck. A lever-type fuel level sensor is clipped to the underside of the filler neck. On R1200 GS Adventure models, a tip-over cut-off valve for the tank breather is located on the underside of the filler neck. On machines manufactured prior to August 2010, a film-type fuel level sensor was clipped to the underside of the fuel filler neck. From August 2010, a lever-type sensor integral with the fuel pump is fitted (see Section 4). For access, remove the filler neck as follows.

16 Follow the procedure in Chapter 6 and remove the tank side panels, filler cap and the tank top panel.

17 On R1200 GS models, and early R1200 GS Adventure models, follow the procedure in Section 4 to remove the fuel pump. Attach a length of wire to the fuel level sensor wiring connector to facilitate reassembly.

18 Ease the breather and drain hoses off the unions on the filler neck and undo the screws securing the filler neck **(see illustration)**.

19 Lift the filler neck assembly out from the tank, noting which way round it is fitted. On R1200 GS models, take care not to damage the arm of the fuel level sensor float **(see illustration)**. Feed the wire attached to the level sensor wiring connector through from the fuel pump opening **(see illustration)**. On

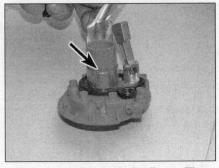

2.19c Note alignment of collar on filler neck

R1200 GS models, note how the collar on the level sensor bracket aligns with the filler neck and draw the sensor assembly off **(see illustration)**. On early R1200 GS Adventure models, unclip the level sensor from the underside of the filler neck. Refer to Chapter 7 to check the operation of the sensor.

20 Note the location of the tip-over valve and ensure that the valve pendulum moves freely to open and close the valve **(see illustration)**. Note the location of the filler neck seal and renew it if it is damaged or deteriorated **(see illustration)**.

21 Installation is the reverse of removal.

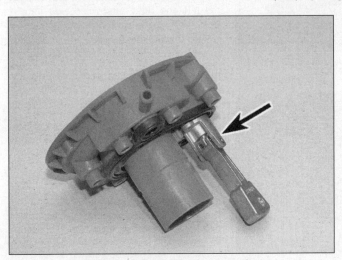

2.20a Location of the tip-over valve

2.20b Location of the filler neck seal

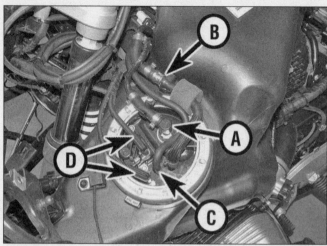

2.24 Fuel delivery hose (A), fuel return hose (B), drain hose (C) and wiring connectors (D)

2.28 Screw on the front top edge of the fuel tank

R1200 RT

Fuel tank

22 Remove the seats (see Chapter 6).

23 Remove the fairing upper side panels, the tank rail and the left and right-hand main side panels (see Chapter 6).

24 Release the quick-release coupling securing the fuel delivery hose and disconnect the hose from the pump **(see illustration)**. Note the location of the O-ring on the union and fit a new one if it is damaged or distorted.

25 Release the coupling on the fuel return hose and disconnect the hose, being prepared to catch any residual fuel **(see illustration 2.24)**. Note the location of the O-ring on the union and fit a new one if it is damaged or distorted.

26 Disconnect the drain hose **(see illustration 2.24)**.

27 Release the tabs securing the wiring connectors for the fuel level sensor and the fuel pump and disconnect the connectors **(see illustration 2.24)**. Undo the screws securing the wiring guides to the fuel tank.

28 Undo the screw on the front top edge of the fuel tank **(see illustration)**.

29 Disconnect the breather hose on the front right-hand side of the fuel tank **(see illustration)**.

30 Undo the left and right-hand mounting bolts, noting the location of the steel and rubber washers **(see illustration)**.

31 Make sure the fuel filler cap is secure, then draw the tank back off the front mounting bushes and lift it off **(see illustration)**.

32 Installation is the reverse of removal, noting the points in Step 14.

Fuel tank filler neck

Note: *Prior to August 2010, R1200 RT models were fitted with a film-type fuel level sensor secured to the underside of the fuel filler neck. From August 2010, a lever-type sensor integral with the fuel pump was fitted and a drain hose was fitted to the underside of the filler neck.*

33 To remove the filler neck, first remove the left and right-hand main side panels, then remove the fuel tank top panel (see Chapter 6).

34 On early models (see **Note** above), follow the procedure in Section 4 to remove the fuel pump. Attach a length of wire to the fuel level sensor wiring connector to facilitate reassembly. Lift the filler neck assembly out from the tank, noting which way round it is fitted. Feed the wire attached to the level sensor wiring connector through from the fuel pump opening. Unclip the level sensor from the underside of the filler neck. Refer to Chapter 7 to check the operation of the sensor.

35 On later models (see **Note** above), lift the filler neck assembly out from the tank, noting which way round it is fitted. Note the location of the drain hose **(see illustration)**. If required, renew the drain hose and secure it with a new clip.

36 Note the location of the filler neck seal

2.29 Disconnect the breather hose

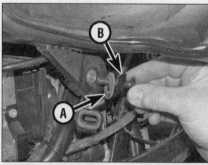

2.30 Note rubber (A) and steel (B) washers

2.31 Draw the tank back off the front mounting bushes

2.35 Note location of the drain hose

2.36 Note location of the filler neck seal

2.39a Undo the screws on both sides . . .

2.39b . . . and remove the trim panel

2.40 Disconnect the breather and drain hoses

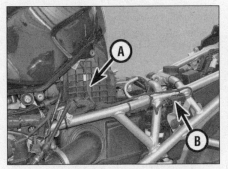

2.41 Trace the wiring (A) to the connector (B)

2.42a Undo the bolt . . .

and renew it if it is damaged or deteriorated **(see illustration)**.

37 Installation is the reverse of removal.

R1200 R

Fuel tank

38 Remove the seat and the sidepanels from both sides (see Chapter 6).

39 Remove the black plastic trim panel from the front inside edge of the tank. It is retained to the tank by two screws on each side **(see illustrations)**.

40 Disconnect the breather hose and the drain hose from the unions on the right inside edge of the tank – they are a push fit **(see**

illustration). Label the hoses to ensure you refit them to the correct union.

41 Trace the fuel pump and level sensor wiring from the rear left-hand side of the tank and disconnect it at the connector **(see illustration)**. Release the wiring from any clips or ties.

42 Remove the bolt and washer from the left side of the tank **(see illustrations)**. Lift the tank at the rear sufficiently to gain access to the fuel hoses and support the tank in this position.

43 Disconnect the quick-release couplings on the fuel delivery and return hoses, being prepared to catch any residual fuel **(see illustrations)**.

2.42b . . . noting location of the washer

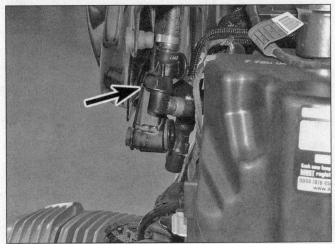

2.43a Disconnect the . . .

2.43b . . . quick-release couplings

2.44a Ease the tank rearwards . . .

2.44b . . . off its front mounting bushes

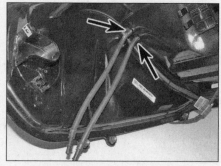

2.44c Location of hose unions

44 Ease the tank rearwards off its front mounting bushes and lift it off **(see illustrations)**. Note the location of the breather and drain hoses and how they are connected to the unions on the underside of the tank **(see illustration)**.

45 Installation is the reverse of removal, noting the points in Step 14.

Fuel tank filler neck

46 A tip-over cut-off valve for the tank breather is located on the underside of the filler neck. A film-type fuel level sensor is clipped to the breather pipe inside the tank. For access, remove the filler neck as follows.

47 Undo the screws securing the filler cap and lift it off **(see illustration)**.

48 Undo the screws securing the filler neck and lift it off **(see illustration)**. Note the location of the tip-over valve and ensure that the valve pendulum moves freely to open and close the valve **(see illustration 2.20a)**. Note the location of the filler neck seal and renew it if it is damaged or deteriorated **(see illustration 2.20b)**.

49 Note the location of the fuel level sensor clipped inside the tank **(see illustration)**.

50 Installation is the reverse of removal.

Fuel tank cleaning and repair – all models

51 All repairs to the fuel tank should be carried out by a professional who has experience in this critical and potentially dangerous work. Even after cleaning and flushing of the fuel system, explosive fumes can remain and

ignite during repair of the tank. If sending the tank for repair, first remove the fuel pump and fuel level sensor from inside the tank.

52 If the fuel tank is removed from the bike, it should not be placed in an area where sparks or open flames could ignite the fumes coming out of the tank. Be especially careful inside garages where a natural gas-type appliance is located, because the pilot light could cause an explosion.

3 Evaporative emission control system – US models

1 When the engine is stopped, fuel vapour from the tank vents into a cylindrical charcoal filter, rather than venting directly into the atmosphere as on other market models. When the engine is running, a regeneration valve, operated by the ECU, directs fuel vapours stored in the filter canister back into the fuel system via the left-hand throttle body. Apart from periodic checks of the hoses, the system is essentially maintenance-free.

_R1200 RT_

2 The filter canister and regeneration valve are mounted on the front sub-frame behind the right-hand fairing side panel. Remove the side panel for access (see Chapter 6).

3 Disconnect the regeneration valve wiring connector. Ease the valve out from its holder and disconnect the two hoses from the valve, noting how they fit.

4 Disconnect the vapour supply and return hoses from the filter canister. Release the cable-ties securing the canister to its mounting bracket and lift it off.

5 Install the components in the reverse order of removal. Secure the canister with new cable-ties and ensure the hoses are connected as noted on removal.

_R1200 R_

6 The filter canister and regeneration valve are mounted on the sub-frame in front of the front suspension shock absorber. Remove the left-hand fuel tank side panel for access (see Chapter 6).

7 Disconnect the regeneration valve wiring connector. Ease the valve out from its holder and disconnect the two hoses from the valve, noting how they fit.

8 Disconnect the vapour supply and return hoses from the filter canister. Release the cable-ties securing the canister to its mounting bracket and lift it off.

9 Install the components in the reverse order of removal. Secure the canister with new cable-ties and ensure the hoses are connected as noted on removal.

R1200 GS and GS Adventure

10 The regeneration valve is located under the fuel tank on the left-hand side of the air filter housing – remove the fuel tank as described in the previous section for access. The filter canister is mounted to the rear sub-frame on the left-hand side and is easily accessible.

2.47 Undo the filler cap screws

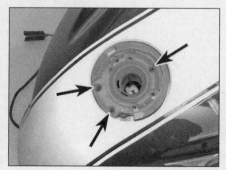

2.48 Undo the filler neck screws

2.49 Location of the fuel level sensor

4.5a Disconnect the fuel delivery hose

4.5b Cable-ties secure fuel filter

4.5c Disconnect the wiring connectors

4.6a Set-up for unscrewing the retaining ring

4.6b Using a commercially available tool . . .

4.6c . . . to unscrew the retaining ring

4 Fuel pump and strainer

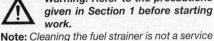

> **Warning: Refer to the precautions given in Section 1 before starting work.**

Note: *Cleaning the fuel strainer is not a service item. However, if fuel delivery problems are suspected, the strainer should be inspected.*

1 The fuel pump is located inside the fuel tank on the left-hand side. On R1200 R models, an external in-line fuel filter is located on the underside of the tank and a strainer is located on the bottom of the pump. On all other models, a filter is incorporated in the body of the pump and a strainer is located on the bottom of the pump.

2 On R1200 GS Adventure models, a balance pump is located in the right-hand side of the tank. The balance pump transfers fuel from the right to the left-hand side of the tank. The pump is activated by vacuum created in the fuel return hose. No strainer is fitted to the balance pump.

3 Before attempting to unscrew the pump from the tank, any fuel should be emptied from the tank using a commercially available pump.

Fuel pump

Removal

4 Follow the procedure in Section 2 and remove the fuel tank.

5 On R1200 R models, release the quick-release coupling securing the fuel delivery hose and disconnect the hose from the pump **(see illustration)**. Release the cable-ties securing the fuel filter, noting how it fits, and remove the filter and fuel hose assembly **(see illustration)**. Disconnect the pump and level sensor wiring connectors **(see illustration)**.

6 Unscrew the pump retaining ring **(see illustration)**. BMW produces a service tool to do this (Part No. 161021). Alternatively, use the set-up shown, taking care not to damage the tabs on the ring. On R1200 R models, due to the restricted space, a commercially available fuel pump retaining ring tool can be used **(see illustrations)**.

7 Ease the pump assembly part-way out from the tank, noting which way round it is fitted **(see illustrations)**.

8 On R1200 GS and early R1200 RT models, disconnect the wiring connector (coloured blue) for the fuel level sensor **(see illustration)**.

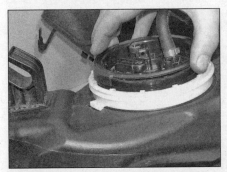

4.7a Ease the pump assembly out . . .

4.7b . . . noting how it fits

4.8 Disconnect the wiring connector

4.9 Lift the pump out of the tank

4.10a Lift the pump out of the tank . . .

4.10b . . . and disconnect the wiring connector – R1200 R

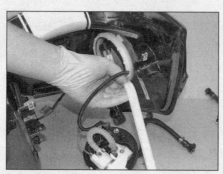

4.10c Manoeuvre the sensor out

seal and discard it as a new one must be fitted.

14 Connect the jumper wires as before to the terminals on the top of the pump assembly. If the pump operates the controller is faulty and a new one must be fitted. Ensure the new seal is correctly located and tighten the screws securely.

15 If the pump does not operate it is faulty and a new one will have to be fitted.

16 If the pump operates when tested, ensure that the terminals in the pump wiring connector are clean, then connect the connector and turn the ignition ON. The pump should operate. If not, inspect the wiring and terminals for physical damage or loose or corroded connections. Turn the ignition OFF when the test is complete.

17 If the pump operates but is thought to be delivering an insufficient amount of fuel, check that the fuel tank breather hose is not obstructed, pinched or trapped.

18 If all appears to be good, have the fuel pump's output pressure, and the operation of the fuel pressure regulator (see Section 5), checked by a BMW dealer.

Installation

19 Installation is the reverse of removal, noting the following:
- Ensure that the sealing ring is correctly seated. Lubricate the ring with tyre fitting gel.
- On R1200 GS, R1200 R and early R1200 RT models, don't forget to connect the fuel level sensor wiring connector.
- Tighten the retaining ring securely. If the BMW service tool is available, tighten the ring to the torque setting specified at the beginning of this Chapter.

Balance pump – R1200 GS Adventure

20 Follow the procedure in Section 2 and remove the fuel tank.

21 Follow the procedure in Step 6 and unscrew the pump retaining ring **(see illustration)**.

9 Lift the pump out of the tank **(see illustration)**. On R1200 GS Adventure later R1200 RT models, take care not to damage the arm of the fuel level sensor float (see Chapter 7). **Note:** *Prior to August 2010, R1200 RT models were fitted with a film-type fuel level sensor secured to the underside of the fuel filler neck. From August 2010, a lever-type sensor integral with the fuel pump was fitted.*

10 On R1200 R models, lift the pump out of the tank and disconnect the fuel level sensor wiring connector **(see illustrations)**. To remove the level sensor from the tank, first remove the tank filler neck and unclip the sensor from the breather pipe **(see illustration 2.49)**. Manoeuvre the sensor out through the opening for the pump **(see illustration)**.

11 Check the pump sealing ring for splits and deterioration and renew it if necessary **(see illustration)**.

Check

12 Pump efficiency will be severely restricted if the strainer is blocked (see Steps 35 and 36). If the strainer is good, test the pump as follows. **Note:** *On R1200 R models, also check the external fuel filter for a blockage.*

13 Using a fully charged 12 volt battery and two insulated jumper wires, connect the positive (+) battery terminal to the positive terminal on the pump controller, and the negative (-) battery terminal to the negative terminal. The pump should operate. If not, undo the screws securing the controller and lift it out. Note the location of the

4.11 Inspect the seal for damage

4.21 Unscrew the pump retaining ring

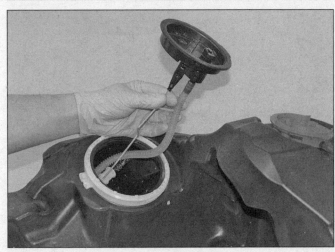

4.22a Ease the assembly out . . .

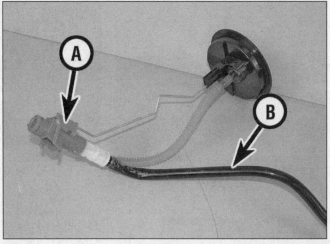

4.22b . . . noting the location of the pump (A) and transfer hose (B)

22 Ease the top panel off and lift the fuel return hose, pump and fuel transfer hose out, noting how the assembly fits **(see illustrations)**. Note the position of the transfer hose inside the tank and ensure it is correctly located on installation.

23 Inspect the assembly for damage and blockages. If necessary fit a new assembly, individual components are not available.

24 Installation is the reverse of removal. Follow the procedure in Step 19 where applicable.

Fuel filter – R1200 R

Note: BMW advise that new fuel hoses should be fitted with a new filter to avoid fuel leakage at the unions. New hose clips must be used.

Special tool: A pair of hose clip pliers is necessary for this procedure **(see illustration 4.31a)**.

25 The external in-line filter is a sealed unit. If it is blocked a new one must be fitted.

26 Follow the procedure in Section 2 and remove the fuel tank to access the filter.

27 Follow the procedure in Step 5 to remove the fuel filter and hose assembly **(see illustrations 4.5a and b)**.

28 Slide the rubber sleeve off the filter body – note the direction of fuel flow arrow on the filter body **(see illustration)**.

29 Release the hose clips and detach the hose unions from the old hoses.

30 Assemble new hose clips on the new hoses and push the hoses fully onto the unions of the new filter, noting the direction of fuel flow arrow **(see illustration 4.28)**.

31 Position the clips 3 mm from the ends of the hoses, then use hose clip pliers to crimp the clips as shown **(see illustrations)**.

32 Fit new hose clips and the male and female quick-release couplings into the appropriate ends of the hoses – male union to fuel pump, female union to fuel delivery hose union **(see illustration 4.28)**. Position the clips and crimp them as before (see Step 31).

33 Slide the rubber sleeve onto the filter body. Secure the filter to the underside of the tank with cable-ties and reconnect the delivery hose to the pump (see Step 5).

Fuel strainer

34 Follow the procedure in Section 2 and remove the fuel tank, then remove the fuel pump (see Steps 4 to 11 of this Section).

35 The strainer is located on the lower end of the pump assembly **(see illustration)**. Allow

the strainer element to dry, they use a soft brush to remove any dirt or sediment. If the strainer is heavily soiled, clean accumulated dirt out of the tank.

36 Inspect the strainer for splits and holes – if any damage is found, a new one should be fitted. **Note:** Although the strainer is available as a separate item, if it is damaged it is likely sediment will have entered the pump body and the internal filter may have become blocked. Under these circumstances, a new pump will have to be fitted.

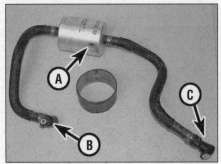

4.28 Direction of fuel flow arrow (A). Note male hose union (B) and female hose union (C)

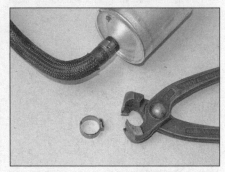

4.31a Use hose clip pliers . . .

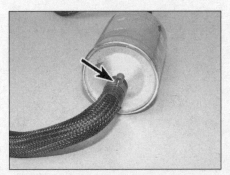

4.31b . . . to close clip eye (arrowed) to 4 mm

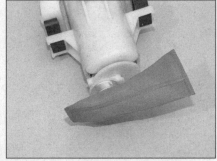

4.35 Location of the fuel strainer

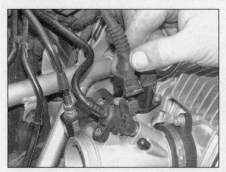

5.5 Disconnect the fuel injector wiring connector

5.6a Undo the screw . . .

5.6b . . . then carefully withdraw the injector

5 Fuel hoses and pressure regulator

⚠ *Warning: Refer to the precautions given in Section 1 before starting work.*

1 The fuel hoses, between the tank unions and the fuel injectors, are part of a one-piece distribution assembly that incorporates the fuel pressure regulator **(see illustration 5.8b)**.

2 The pressure regulator monitors fuel supply from the pump to the injectors and maintains delivery at a constant pressure. At high engine speeds, the regulator opens to allow the injectors to draw more fuel from the system; at low engine speeds, the regulator closes and diverts excess fuel back into the tank via the return hose. This prevents any risk of the pump overloading.

3 BMW provides no test data or procedure for checking the regulator. If a known good regulator is available, substitute that for the suspect one and see if the fault is cured.

4 To remove the fuel distribution assembly, first remove the fuel tank (see Section 2).

5 Working on one side at a time, release the clip securing the fuel injector wiring connector and disconnect the connector **(see illustration)**.

6 Undo the screw securing the fuel hose connector to the throttle body, then carefully withdraw the injector from the throttle body **(see illustrations)**. Note the location of the O-ring on the injector – a new O-ring must be fitted on reassembly (see Section 7). Cover the end of the injector to prevent it getting damaged.

7 Release the clip securing the fuel hose to the fuel injector and disconnect the hose being prepared to catch any residual fuel **(see illustration)**. Note the location of the O-ring on the injector and discard it – a new one must be fitted on reassembly (see Section 7).

8 Note the location of the pressure regulator **(see illustration)**. Release the fuel hoses from any clips or ties and lift the assembly off, noting the routing of the hoses **(see illustration)**. Take care not to bend any of the hoses – if they become kinked this will restrict fuel flow.

9 The quick-release unions on the delivery and return hoses are secured to the main assembly by clips and short sections of flexible hose. Whenever the quick-release unions are disconnected, check the condition of the flexible hose and renew the hose and hose clips if there are signs of deterioration, cracking or fuel leakage (see Section 4, Step 31).

10 The pressure regulator is secured in its holder by a large U-clip **(see illustration)**. Withdraw the clip and pull the regulator off, noting the location of the sealing O-ring. Discard the O-ring as a new one must be used.

11 Installation is the reverse of removal, noting the following:

● Install a new O-ring on the pressure regulator.

● Check that there are no leaks from the pressure regulator and hose union seals before installing the bodywork.

5.7 Release the clip and disconnect the hose

5.8a Location of the pressure regulator

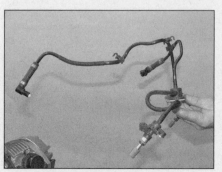

5.8b Fuel pressure regulator assembly

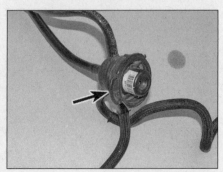

5.10 U-clip secures pressure regulator

6 Throttle bodies

⚠ *Warning: Refer to the precautions given in Section 1 before starting work.*

Removal

1 Remove the frame side panels and the fairing side panels to gain access to the throttle bodies (see Chapter 6).

2 Make sure the ignition is switched OFF.

3 Release the clamps securing the air ducts to the air filter housing and the throttle bodies

6.3a Air ducts are secured by two clamps

6.3b Using long nose pliers to release the clamps

6.3c Note how the air ducts fit

(see illustrations). Take care removing the clamps to avoid damaging them. Pull the air ducts off carefully, noting which way round they fit – the ducts should be marked L (left) and R (right), if not mark them to aid reassembly **(see illustration)**.

4 Working on one throttle body at a time, release the clips securing the fuel injector wiring connector and the idle speed actuator connector and disconnect the connectors **(see illustration)**.

5 On the left-hand throttle body, note the location of the security tab on the throttle position sensor wiring connector **(see illustration)**. Prise out the tab, then release the clip securing the connector and disconnect it **(see illustrations)**.

6 Following the procedure in Section 5, undo the screw securing the fuel hose connector to the throttle body, then withdraw the injector from the throttle body. Cover the end of the injector to prevent it getting damaged.

7 Cut the cable-ties securing the wiring to the underside of the throttle body **(see illustration)**.

8 Release the clamp securing the throttle body to the intake manifold and ease the throttle body off **(see illustration)**. Stuff clean rag into the intake manifold to prevent anything falling inside.

9 If required, the left and right-hand throttle

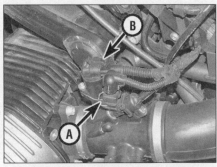

6.4 Fuel injector connector (A) and idle speed actuator connector (B)

6.5a Location of the security tab

6.5b Prise out the tab . . .

6.5c . . . and disconnect the connector

6.7 Wiring is secured by ties

6.8 Ease off the throttle body

6.10a Displace the cover

6.10b Detach the inner cable from the pully

6.16 Tab (arrowed) must align with notch in the manifold

bodies and the cable splitter can be displaced or removed as an assembly (see Section 8).

10 Alternatively, displace the cover from the throttle valve actuating mechanism **(see illustration)**. Rotate the throttle pulley to the fully open position and detach the end of the inner cable from the pulley, then unscrew the cable adjuster from the mechanism backplate **(see illustration)**. Do not disturb the setting of the throttle cam stop screw.

11 If required, undo the screws securing the idle speed actuator and remove the actuator. *Caution: Do not remove the throttle position sensor from the left-hand throttle body as its position is pre-set. If it is disturbed, its position will have to be reset by a BMW dealer using the BMW MOSS diagnostic tester.*

Inspection

12 Inspect the throttle bodies and air ducts for cracks or any other damage which may result in air leakage and renew any components as necessary. The joints between the intake manifolds and the cylinder heads are sealed with O-rings. If the manifolds are removed, fit new O-rings on installation and tighten the manifold bolts to the torque setting specified at the beginning of this Chapter.

13 Check that the throttle butterfly moves smoothly and freely in the body, and make sure that the inside of the body is completely clean.

14 Check that the throttle pulley moves smoothly and freely, taking into account spring pressure. Clean any dirt from around the pulley.

15 Check the condition of the clamps for the air ducts and the throttle bodies – if the clamps were damaged during removal, renew them.

7.6 Note the location of the O-rings

Installation

16 Installation is the reverse of removal, noting the following:

● Install the throttle cable on the pulley and secure the actuating mechanism cover before installing the throttle body.

● Fit the throttle body clamp loosely over the intake manifold, then align the tab on the throttle body with the notch in the manifold and press the throttle body all the way in **(see illustration)**.

● Secure the throttle body clamps with clamp pliers to avoid damage.

● Check the operation of the throttle cables and adjust them if necessary (see Chapter 1).

● Install new O-rings on the injectors (see Section 7).

● Tighten the injector screws to the torque setting specified at the beginning of this Chapter.

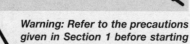

7 Fuel injectors

⚠ *Warning: Refer to the precautions given in Section 1 before starting work.*

Removal

1 Make sure the ignition is switched OFF.

2 Remove the frame side panels and the fairing side panels to gain access to the throttle bodies (see Chapter 6).

3 Release the clip securing the fuel injector wiring connector and disconnect the connector **(see illustration 5.5)**.

8.3 Throttle cable adjuster lock ring (arrowed)

4 Following the procedure in Section 5, undo the screw securing the fuel hose connector to the throttle body, then withdraw the injector from the throttle body **(see illustrations 5.6a and b)**.

5 Release the clip securing the fuel hose connector and disconnect the injector from the connector, being prepared to catch any residual fuel **(see illustration 5.7)**.

6 Note the location of the two O-rings on the injector body, then carefully ease them off – new O-rings must be fitted on reassembly **(see illustration)**.

7 Modern fuels contain detergents which should keep the injectors clean and free of gum or varnish. If either injector is suspected of being blocked, flush it through with injector cleaner.

Installation

8 Installation is the reverse of removal, noting the following:

● Install new O-rings on the injectors.

● Tighten the injector screws to the torque setting specified at the beginning of this Chapter.

● Ensure that the fuel hose connections are secure.

● Check the fuel hose unions for leaks before installing the bodywork.

8 Throttle cables

Note: *For information relating to R1200 RT models fitted with cruise control refer to Steps 13 to 41*

1 Three separate cables are fitted – the cable from the throttle twistgrip goes into a splitter located on the front of the air filter housing, then two cables go from the splitter to the throttle bodies, one on either side. All three cables are available individually.

Removal

2 Remove the fuel tank (see Section 2). Remove the intake duct from the air filter housing (see Chapter 1).

3 Loosen the lock ring on the adjuster at the twistgrip end of the cable and turn the adjuster all the way in to create slack in the cable **(see illustration)**.

8.5 Remove the top half of the twistgrip housing

8.6 Cable elbow is secured by lock ring (arrowed)

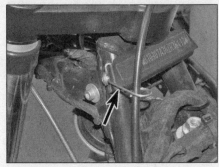

8.7 Note any guides (arrowed) that secure the cable

4 On R1200 RT models, undo the screw on the upper front edge of the twistgrip housing and unclip the upper half of the housing **(see illustrations 8.16a and b)**.

5 On all other models, undo the screw on the lower front edge of the twistgrip housing and unclip the upper half of the housing **(see illustration)**.

6 Disconnect the inner cable end from the throttle pulley. Undo the lock ring securing the cable elbow in the lower half of the housing **(see illustration)**. Draw the cable out of the housing.

7 Feed the cable back to the splitter, noting its routing **(see illustration)**. Release the cable from any clips or ties.

8 Displace the throttle bodies and detach the cables from the cam and backplate (see Section 6).

9 Unclip the top edge of the splitter cover and remove it **(see illustration)**.

10 Mark the outer face of the splitter pulley with a dab of paint so that it can be reassembled correctly. Note the location of the inner cables on the splitter pulley, then displace the pulley and detach the cables **(see illustration)**. Note how the tab inside the pulley housing below the pulley spindle locates in the slot in the lower half of the throttle cable pulley.

8.9 Remove the splitter cover

11 Separate the cables from the splitter housing **(see illustration)**. If required, release the tab on the top of the splitter housing and detach it from the air filter housing.

Installation

12 Installation is the reverse of removal, noting the following:

● Install the cables onto the throttle bodies first.

● Install all three cables onto the splitter pulley **(see illustration)**. Adjust the cables between the splitter and the throttle bodies, then check the operation of the splitter.

8.10 Displace the pulley and detach the cables

● Follow the procedure in Section 6 to install the throttle bodies.

● Ensure that the cable to the handlebar twistgrip is correctly routed and secured with any clips or ties.

● Tighten the lock ring securing the cable elbow securely.

● Adjust the throttle cables (see Chapter 1).

⚠ *Warning: Turn the handlebars all the way through their travel with the engine idling. Idle speed should not change. If it does, the cables may be routed incorrectly. Correct this condition before riding the bike.*

8.11 Splitter housing cables (arrowed)

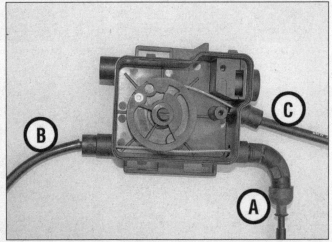

8.12 Main cable to twistgrip (A), cable to right-hand throttle body (B), cable to left-hand throttle body (C)

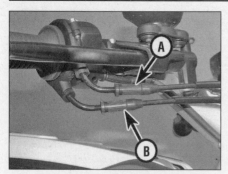

8.15 Opening cable (A) and closing cable (B)

8.16a Undo the screw . . .

8.16b . . . and remove the upper half of the housing

R1200 RT models with cruise control

13 Five separate cables are fitted – two cables from the throttle twistgrip connect to a pulley inside the splitter located on the front of the air filter housing, then two more cables go from the same pulley to the throttle bodies, one on either side. A fifth cable links the cruise control unit to a second pulley inside the splitter housing. All five cables are available individually.

Removal

14 Disconnect the battery negative (-) lead (see Chapter 7). Remove the fuel tank (see Section 2). Remove the intake duct from the air filter housing (see Chapter 1).

15 Loosen the lock rings on the adjusters at the twistgrip ends of the opening and closing cables and turn the adjusters all the way in to

create slack in the cables **(see illustration)**.

16 Undo the screw on the upper front edge of the twistgrip housing and unclip the upper half of the housing **(see illustrations)**.

17 Disconnect the inner cable ends from the throttle pulley **(see illustration)**. Undo the lock rings securing the cable elbows in the lower half of the housing **(see illustration 8.6)**. Draw the cables out of the housing.

18 Feed the cables back to the splitter, noting their routing **(see illustration 8.7)**. Release the cables from any clips or ties.

19 Displace the throttle bodies and detach the cables from the cam and backplate (see Section 6).

20 The cruise control unit is located on the front, right-hand side of the machine behind the oil cooler **(see illustration)**. Remove the headlight panel for access (see Chapter 6).

21 To disconnect the cable from the unit,

first pull back the sleeve on the unit end of the cable, then unclip the connector from the union on the unit. Disconnect the end of the inner cable from the connector on the unit.

22 Unclip the top edge of the splitter cover and remove it **(see illustration)**.

23 The outer pulley for the cruise control cable is secured by the return spring **(see illustration)**. Remove the spring, noting how it fits, then draw out the pulley and disconnect the end of the inner cable. Note how the tab on the back of the cruise control pulley locates in the slot in the upper half of the throttle cable pulley. Withdraw the cable from the splitter housing.

24 Mark the outer face of the splitter pulley with a dab of paint so that it can be reassembled correctly. Note the location of the inner cables on the splitter pulley, then displace the pulley and detach the cables **(see illustration 8.10)**. Note how the tab inside the pulley housing below the pulley spindle locates in the slot in the lower half of the throttle cable pulley.

25 Separate the cables from the splitter housing **(see illustration)**. The throttle closing cable elbow is secured by an E-clip on the inside of the housing. To access the E-clip, first undo the screws securing the cruise control system micro-switch and displace the switch. Note the location of the switch bridge and return spring.

26 If required, release the tab on the top of the splitter housing and detach it from the air filter housing. Trace the wiring from

8.17 Disconnect the inner cable ends (arrowed)

8.20 Location of the cruise control unit

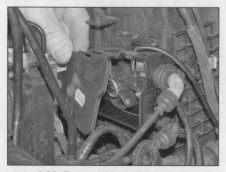

8.22 Remove the splitter cover

8.23 Location of the return spring

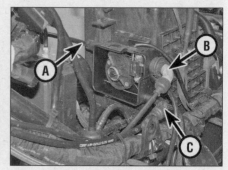

8.25 Cruise control cable (A), closing cable (B) and opening cable (C)

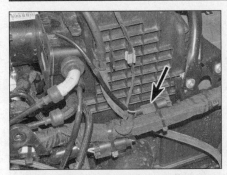

8.26 Micro-switch wiring connector

the micro-switch and disconnect it at the connector **(see illustration)**.

Installation

27 If removed, secure the splitter housing to the air filter housing.

28 Install the micro-switch bridge return spring and bridge, insert the closing cable elbow and secure it in the housing with the E-clip. Install the micro-switch and ensure the wiring connector is secure.

29 Install the cables onto the throttle bodies (see Section 6).

30 Fit the cables onto the splitter pulley – the cables from the throttle bodies locate in the inner face of the pulley and the cables from the twistgrip locate in the outer face. Install the pulley.

31 Adjust the cables between the splitter and the throttle bodies.

32 Follow the procedure in Section 6 to install the throttle bodies.

33 Ensure that the cables to the handlebar twistgrip are correctly routed and secured with

any clips or ties. Connect the cables to the twistgrip and tighten the lock rings securing the cable elbows securely. Adjust the freeplay in the throttle cables (see Chapter 1) and fit the upper half of the twistgrip housing.

34 Check the operation of the splitter pulley.

35 Fit the cruise control cable onto its pulley and install the pulley – ensure the tab on the back of the pulley locates in the slot in the upper half of the throttle cable pulley. Secure the cruise control pulley with the spring **(see illustration 8.23)**.

36 Install the splitter housing cover **(see illustration 8.22)**.

37 Ensure that the cable to the cruise control unit is correctly routed. Connect the inner cable end to the unit then clip the outer cable connector to the unit. Install the cable sleeve.

38 To check the cable adjustment, pull back the boot on the lower end of the cable to access the adjuster. Check for 2 to 3 mm of freeplay between the end of the outer cable and the adjuster. Loosen the adjuster locknut and adjust the cable if necessary. Don't forget to refit the boot.

39 Install the remaining components in the reverse order of removal.

 Warning: Turn the handlebars all the way through their travel with the engine idling. Idle speed should not change. If it does, the cables may be routed incorrectly. Correct this condition before riding the bike.

Cruise control unit

40 If the cruise control is thought to be faulty, first check the throttle cable adjustment (see Chapter 1), then check the cables themselves (see above).

41 If the cables are good, refer to Chapter 7 and check the handlebar switch and the wiring between the switch and the cruise control unit.

9 Exhaust system

 Warning: If the engine has been running the exhaust system will be very hot. Allow the system to cool before carrying out any work.

Silencer

R1200 GS, GS Adventure and R1200 R

1 Loosen the bolt on the clamp securing the silencer to the downpipe assembly **(see illustration)**.

2 Undo the bolt securing the silencer to the rear sub-frame, then support the silencer and withdraw the bolt and washer **(see illustrations)**.

3 Draw the silencer off **(see illustration)**.

4 Note the location of the rubber bush and spacer inside the silencer clamp **(see illustration)**.

5 Note the alignment marks on the two exhaust clamps and the body of the exhaust flow control valve **(see illustration)**.

6 Prior to installation, clean the exhaust clamp and lubricate the inside surface with high-temperature assembly grease. Fit the clamp over the end of the silencer front pipe.

7 Push the silencer over the end of the exhaust flow control valve and secure it to the rear sub-frame with the bolt and washer **(see illustration 9.2a)**. Tighten the bolt to the

9.1 Loosen the silencer clamp bolt

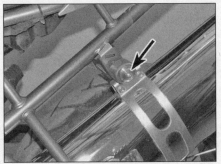

9.2a Undo the bolt . . .

9.2b . . . noting the washer

9.3 Draw the silencer off

9.4 Note location of rubber bush and spacer

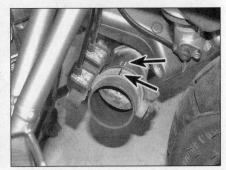

9.5 Note the alignment marks

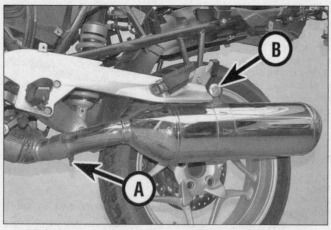

9.10 Location of silencer clamp bolt (A) and support bolt (B)

9.19 Exhaust flow control valve – fully open

torque setting specified at the beginning of this Chapter.

8 Align the appropriate mark on the exhaust clamp with the mark on the exhaust flow control valve and tighten the clamp bolt to the specified torque setting **(see illustration 9.5)**.

9 On R1200 R models, check the gap between the silencer and the rear tyre. BMW specify a minimum of 15 mm. If necessary, loosen the exhaust clamp bolt and the screws on the silencer mounting clamp and adjust the position of the silencer to achieve the correct gap. Don't forget to tighten the fixings on completion.

9.21 Displace the control valve

R1200 RT

10 Loosen the bolt on the clamp securing the silencer to the downpipe assembly **(see illustration)**.

11 Undo the bolt securing the silencer to the rear sub-frame, then support the silencer and withdraw the bolt and washer **(see illustration 9.10)**.

12 Draw the silencer off.

13 Note the alignment marks on the exhaust clamp and the body of the silencer.

14 Prior to installation, clean the exhaust clamp and lubricate the inside surface with high-temperature assembly grease. Fit the clamp over the end of the silencer front pipe.

15 Push the silencer over the end of the downpipe assembly and secure it to the rear sub-frame with the bolt and washer **(see illustration 9.2b)**. Tighten the bolt to the torque setting specified at the beginning of this Chapter.

16 Align the appropriate mark on the exhaust clamp with the mark on the silencer body and tighten the clamp bolt to the specified torque setting **(see illustration 9.5)**.

17 Check the gap between the silencer and the rear tyre. BMW specify a minimum of 15 mm.

If necessary, loosen the exhaust clamp bolt and the screw on the silencer mounting clamp and adjust the position of the silencer to achieve the correct gap. Don't forget to tighten the fixings on completion.

Exhaust flow control valve

Removal

18 Remove the silencer (see above).

19 Note the position of the valve, then turn the ignition ON to actuate the valve – it should return to the fully open position **(see illustration)**. Turn the ignition OFF.

20 Note the alignment marks on the exhaust clamp and the body of the exhaust flow control valve **(see illustration 9.5)**.

21 Loosen the clamp bolt and pull the valve off **(see illustration)**. Note how the tab on the valve body aligns with the cut-out in the edge of the exhaust pipe.

22 If required, the control valve and servo motor can be removed as an assembly. Disconnect the wiring connector, then undo the screw and washer securing the motor and pull it off the rear mounting peg **(see illustration)**. Lift the assembly off **(see illustration)**.

23 To remove the control valve only, undo

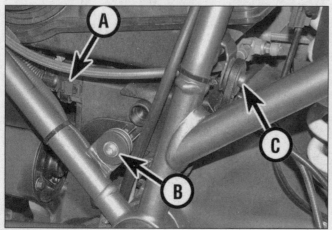

9.22a Wiring connector (A), mounting screw (B) and peg (C)

9.22b Removing control valve and servo motor as an assembly

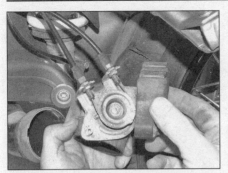

9.23a Remove the valve cover

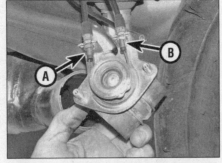

9.23b Opening cable (A) and closing cable (B)

9.34a Remove the lower cylinder head covers

9.34b Cut the wiring ties . . .

9.34c . . . and displace the connectors

9.34d Release the wiring connector catches

the screws and remove the valve cover **(see illustration)**. Loosen the locknuts securing the outer cables and displace the cables, noting how the opening and closing cables fit **(see illustration)**. Disconnect the inner cable ends from the valve pulley.

24 To remove the servo motor, follow the procedure in Steps 22 and 23, then undo the screws securing the motor cover. Pull the ends of the outer cables out from the motor body and disconnect the inner cable ends from the valve pulley, noting how they fit – when the motor is in situ, the upper cable is the actuating cable.

Installation

25 Fit the cables onto the servo motor as noted on removal (see Step 24). Fit the cover and tighten the screws securely. Ensure the motor mounting grommets are in good condition and renew them if necessary. Tighten the mounting bolt to the torque setting specified at the beginning of this Chapter and reconnect the wiring connector.

26 Fit the cables onto the control valve as noted

on removal (see Step 23). There should be a small amount of freeplay in the cables. Turn the ignition ON to actuate the valve – it should return to the fully open position. Turn the ignition OFF.

27 Working on one cable at a time, displace the boot from the top of the adjuster. Loosen the locknut on the underside of the cable stop bracket and turn the adjuster anticlockwise to take up all the freeplay in the cable. Now turn the adjuster back (clockwise) two to three turns and tighten the locknut. There should be approximately 1 mm freeplay in the cables before the pulley moves. Fit the cover and tighten the screws securely.

28 Prior to installation, clean the exhaust clamp and lubricate the inside surface with high-temperature assembly grease. Fit the clamp over the end of the exhaust pipe.

29 Push the control valve into the pipe and check the alignment (see Step 21).

30 Align the appropriate mark on the exhaust clamp with the mark on the control valve and tighten the clamp bolt to the specified torque setting.

Downpipe assembly

Removal

31 On R1200 RT models, remove the fairing side panels (see Chapter 6).

32 On all models, remove the silencer and displace the exhaust flow control valve (see above).

33 If fitted, remove the sump guard (see Chapter 1, Section 1).

34 Undo the screws and remove the lower cylinder head covers **(see illustration)**. Trace the wiring from both oxygen sensors to the wiring connectors – release the wiring from any ties and displace the connectors from their brackets **(see illustrations)**. Release the catches securing the connectors and disconnect them **(see illustration)**.

35 Undo the screws securing the support clamp, noting the location of the spacer, then prise the clamp open and pull it back off the peg on the back of the gearbox **(see illustrations)**. Remove the clamp **(see illustration)**.

36 Undo the nuts securing the downpipes to

9.35a Support clamp screws and spacer

9.35b Prise the clamp open . . .

9.35c . . . and ease it off the mounting peg

9.36a Undo the nuts . . .

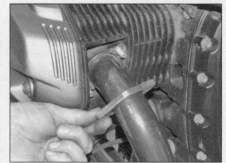

9.36b . . . and draw off the collars

9.37 Manoeuvre the downpipe assembly off

the cylinder heads, then draw the collars off the studs **(see illustrations)**.

37 Carefully manoeuvre the downpipe assembly forwards, then lower it off the bike **(see illustration)**.

38 Remove the old gaskets from the exhaust ports and discard them as new ones must be fitted **(see illustration)**. Clean any corrosion off the cylinder head studs with a wire brush.

39 If required, unscrew the oxygen sensors from the exhaust pipes (see Section 10).

Installation

40 Check the condition of the bush in the support clamp bracket and renew it if it is deformed or deteriorated – the bush should be a firm push fit onto its mounting peg.

41 If removed, install the oxygen sensors (see Section 10).

42 Fit a new gasket into each exhaust port **(see illustration 9.38)**. If required, apply a smear of grease to the gaskets to keep them in place whilst fitting the downpipe. Lubricate the cylinder head studs with a smear of copper-based grease.

43 Manoeuvre the assembly into position, align the front of the downpipes with the exhaust ports and slide the collars onto the studs. Tighten the nuts finger-tight **(see illustrations 9.36b and a)**.

44 Slide the support clamp over the rear end of the pipe and press the bracket onto the peg on the back of the gearbox **(see illustration 9.35b)**. Install the spacer and screws loosely **(see illustration)**.

45 Tighten the nuts on the cylinder head

studs evenly to the torque setting specified at the beginning of this Chapter.

46 Ensure the support clamp bracket is pressed firmly onto the peg, then tighten the clamp screws to the specified torque setting **(see illustration 9.35a)**.

47 Connect the wiring connectors for the left and right-hand oxygen sensors and secure the connectors and wiring as noted on removal. Install the lower cylinder head covers.

48 Install the exhaust flow control valve. Install the silencer.

49 Run the engine and check that there are no air leaks from the joints.

50 Install the remaining components in the reverse order of removal.

---

10 Catalytic converter and oxygen sensors

 Warning: If the engine has been running the exhaust system will be very hot. Allow the system to cool before carrying out any work.

Catalytic converter

1 All models have a three-way catalytic converter located in the rear end of the exhaust downpipe assembly. The purpose of the catalytic converter is to minimise the amount of pollutants which escape into the atmosphere. Hot exhaust gasses pass through the flow channels in the converter which are coated with a precious metal catalyst. The

catalyst reduces nitrous oxides into nitrogen and oxygen, and oxidises unburned harmful hydrocarbons and carbon monoxide into water and carbon dioxide. The efficiency of the catalyst is reduced if the flow channels become clogged or if the precious metal coating becomes covered with carbon, lead or oil.

2 The catalytic converter is simple in operation and requires no maintenance, although the following precautions should be noted.

● Always use unleaded fuel – the use of leaded fuel will destroy the converter.
● Do not use any fuel or oil additives.
● Keep the fuel and ignition systems in good order.
● Handle the downpipe assembly with care when it is off the machine – the catalyst is fragile.

Oxygen sensors

3 The oxygen sensors measure exhaust gas oxygen content and relay this information to the ECU. The ECU compares exhaust gas oxygen content with the oxygen content in the ambient air and, depending on whether the engine is running rich or lean, adjusts the fuel/air mixture accordingly.

4 The sensors are threaded into the left and right-hand exhaust downpipes **(see illustration)**.

5 To remove a sensor, first remove the lower cylinder head cover and disconnect the wiring connector (see Section 9, Step 34).

6 Unscrew the sensor carefully to avoid

9.38 Discard the old exhaust port gaskets

9.44 Fit the clamp loosely around the pipe

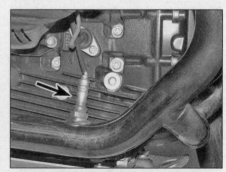

10.4 Location of the right-hand oxygen sensor

damage to its tip. If the sensor threads are corroded, soak them with penetrating oil before proceeding.

7 Deposits on the sensor tip are an indication of poor engine running – light rust coloured deposits indicate lead contamination through the use of the wrong fuel, black or dark brown deposits are a sign that oil is getting into the combustion chamber through worn valve stem seals or piston rings.

8 A contaminated sensor will send an inaccurate signal to the ECU, which should, in turn, illuminate the engine warning light in the instrument cluster. Do not attempt to clean the sensor – if it is contaminated, a new one will have to be fitted.

9 No data is available for checking the oxygen sensors individually – have the overall engine efficiency checked by a BMW dealer using the diagnostic tester.

10 Before installing the oxygen sensor, clean the threads and lubricate them with a smear of high temperature assembly grease. If a suitable tool is available, tighten the sensor to the torque setting specified at the beginning of this Chapter.

11 Ensure that the terminals in the wiring connector are clean and make sure that the connection is secure.

11 Ignition system checks

 Warning: Refer to the Warning given in Section 1 before starting work.

1 As no means of adjustment is available, any failure of the system can be traced to failure of a system component or a simple wiring fault. Of the two possibilities, the latter is by far the most likely. In the event of failure, check the system in a logical fashion, as described below. **Note:** *Before making any tests, check that the battery is in good condition and fully charged.*

2 Ignition faults can be divided into two categories, namely those where the ignition system has failed completely, and those which are due to a partial failure. The likely faults are listed below, starting with the most probable source of failure. Work through the list systematically, referring to the subsequent sections for full details of the necessary checks and tests, where information is available.

● Loose, corroded or damaged wiring connections, broken or shorted wiring between any of the component parts of the ignition system (see Chapter 7).
● Faulty spark plug, dirty, worn or corroded plug electrodes, or incorrect gap between electrodes (see Chapter 1).
● Faulty ignition coil (see Section 12).
● Faulty ignition switch or engine kill switch (see Chapter 7).
● Faulty starter interlock circuit (see Section 13).

● Faulty engine control unit (ECU) (see Section 14).
● Faulty crankshaft position sensor or camshaft position sensor (see Section 16).

3 If the above checks don't reveal the cause of the problem, have the ignition system tested by a BMW on the MOSS diagnostic tester. The diagnostic tester permits full testing of the ignition system components and reads the ECU fault code memory.

12 Ignition coils

 Warning: Refer to the Warning given in Section 1 before starting work.

1 Working on one coil at a time, follow the procedure in Chapter 1, Section 5, disconnect the wiring connector and pull the coil off the spark plug.

2 Ensure that the terminals inside the wiring connector are clean **(see illustration)**, then reconnect the wiring connector. Connect the coil to a new spark plug of the correct type and lay the plug on the engine with the threads contacting the engine. If necessary, hold the plug in position with an insulated tool.

 Warning: Do not remove any of the spark plugs from the engine to perform this check – atomised fuel being pumped out of the open spark plug hole could ignite, causing severe injury!

3 Check that the kill switch is in the RUN position and the transmission is in neutral, then turn the ignition switch ON and turn the engine over on the starter motor. If the system is in good condition a regular, fat blue spark should be evident at the plug electrodes. If the spark appears thin or yellowish, or is non-existent, further investigation is necessary. Turn the ignition OFF. Repeat the check for the other coils.

4 The ignition system must be able to produce a spark which is capable of jumping a particular size gap. BMW provide no specification, but a healthy system should

produce a spark capable of jumping at least 6 mm. A commercially available ignition spark gap tester tool will be required for this check **(see illustration)**.

5 Connect the coil to the protruding electrode on the test tool, and connect the tool to a good earth (ground) on the engine. Check that the kill switch is in the RUN position, turn the ignition switch ON and turn the engine over on the starter motor. If the system is in good condition a regular, fat blue spark should be seen to jump across the gap on the tool. Repeat the test for the other coils. If the test results are good the entire ignition system can be considered good.

6 If the spark at one plug appears thin or yellowish, or is non-existent, substitute the appropriate ignition coil from the other cylinder and test again. If the result is good it is likely the original coil is defective. If there is no improvement the fault lies with the ignition system.

7 Check the coil visually for damage, and measure the primary and secondary coil resistances with a multimeter.

8 To check the coil primary resistance, set the multimeter to the ohms x 1 scale and connect its probes across the two primary wire terminals on the coil, marked 1 and 3. **Note:** *The terminal numbers are very small and are located inside the connector socket on the coil – you may need to view them with a flash-light.* Record the result.

9 To check the coil secondary resistance, set the meter to the K-ohms scale. Connect the positive (+) meter probe to the spark plug terminal inside the coil and the negative (-) meter probe to the No. 2 wire terminal on the coil. Record the result

10 Repeat the test for the remaining ignition coils. Although no specifications are available, if any of the results vary widely from the others it is likely that coil is defective and should be renewed.

11 In order to determine conclusively that an ignition coil is defective, it should be tested by a BMW dealer equipped with the diagnostic tester.

12 Follow the procedure in Chapter 1, Section 5, to install the ignition coil.

12.2 Check the terminals inside the wiring connectors

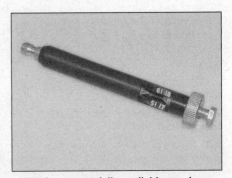

12.4 A commercially available spark gap test tool

14.5a Location of the diagnostic tool plug – R1200 RT shown

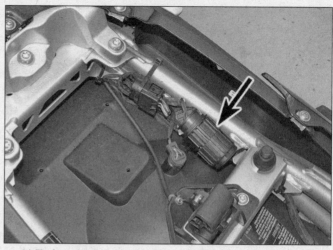

14.5b Location of the diagnostic tool plug – R1200 R shown

13 Starter interlock circuit

1 Check the operation of the starter interlock system as follows:
● Position the bike on its centrestand. Make sure the transmission is in neutral, and the side stand retracted (up), then start the engine. Pull in the clutch lever and select a gear. Extend the side stand – the engine should stop as the side stand is extended.
● Check that when the side stand is extended (down), the engine can only be started if the transmission is in neutral.
● Make sure the engine is in neutral and the side stand is extended (down). Start the engine, pull in the clutch lever and select a gear – the engine should cut out.
● Check that when the side stand is retracted (up) and the transmission is in gear, the engine can only be started if the clutch lever is pulled in.
2 If the circuit does not operate as described, refer to Chapter 7 and check the operation of the side stand switch, gear position switch and clutch switch, and check the wiring between the switches and the engine control unit (ECU).

14 Engine management system and ECU – fault finding

1 For a general description of the system, see Section 1.

Diagnostic tester and fault identification

2 To diagnose the exact cause of a failure in the system, the BMW MOSS diagnostic tester, specifically designed for this system, is essential. Hence if a problem occurs, the motorcycle should be taken to a BMW dealer.

3 The engine management system has in-built diagnostic functions which record and store all data should a fault occur. Recorded faults can then be checked using BMW's diagnostic tester, which analyses the data and identifies the exact fault.
4 Should a fault occur, the engine warning light in the instrument cluster illuminates. If this happens, the management system switches itself into 'limp home' mode, so that in theory you should not be left stranded. Depending on the problem, it is possible that you will notice no difference in the running of the motorcycle. However, BMW advise that in 'limp home' mode, full engine power may not be available and the machine should be ridden with this in mind.
5 In order to diagnose the problem and to turn the warning light off, the diagnostic tester is essential. Take your machine to a BMW dealer and have them check the system. For information, the tester plugs into the main wiring harness at a connection point under the seat (see illustrations).
6 It is possible to perform certain tests and checks to identify a particular fault, but the difficulty is knowing in which part of the system the fault has occurred, and therefore where to start checking. Further details on the location and function of the individual sensors are given in the following Sections.

Fault finding

7 If a fault is indicated, first check the wiring and connectors to and from the ECU and the various sensors and all their related components. It may be that a connector is dirty or corroded or has come loose – a dirty or corroded terminal or connector will affect the resistance in that circuit, which will distort the information transmitted to the ECU, and therefore affect its control of the system. To deter corrosion, spray the wiring loom connector pins lightly with electrical contact cleaner.
8 A wire could be pinched and is shorting out

– a continuity test of all wires from connector to connector will locate this. Albeit a fiddly and laborious task, the only way to determine any wiring faults is to systematically work through the wiring diagrams at the end of Chapter 7 and test each individual wire and connector for continuity – all wires are colour-coded. The wiring diagrams show the terminal number for each wire on the ECU – match these to the terminals on the ECU connectors when making the tests (see illustration 15.8b and c). Refer also to Section 30 of Chapter 7.

15 ECU – removal and installation

⚠ **Warning: Refer to the Warning given in Section 1 before starting work.**

Removal

1 Disconnect the battery negative (-) lead (see Chapter 7).
2 Remove the fuel tank (see Section 2). The ECU is located underneath the central electronics (ZFE) unit mounted on the frame behind the steering head (see illustration). **Note:** On R1200 GS and GS Adventure models, the starter relay is located underneath

15.2 Location of the ZFE unit

15.3 Hinge the ZFE forwards

15.4a Cut the ties securing the wiring loom

15.4b Location of speed sensor wiring connector

the ECU. To access the relay it is only necessary to displace the ZFE unit and ECU, not disconnect them.

3 To displace the ZFE unit in order to access the ECU, release the catches on the left and right-hand sides of the unit holder and hinge the unit forwards **(see illustration)**. Now go to Step 9.

4 To remove the ZFE unit, first cut the cable-ties securing the wiring loom along the top edge of the assembly **(see illustration)**. On machines fitted with ABS, disconnect the front wheel speed sensor wiring connector on the front, right-hand edge of the ECU holder **(see illustration)**.

5 Release the catch on the double multi-pin wiring connector for the ZFE unit and disconnect the connectors **(see illustrations)**. If the catch or connector appears to be stuck, don't force it. Spray around the sides with a suitable electrical connector lubricant such as WD-40, then pull up on the connector as the catch is pulled out.

6 Disconnect the wiring connector on the upper, left-hand side of the ZFE unit **(see illustration)**.

7 Release the catches on the top edge of the ZFE unit holder, hinge the holder back and lift the ZFE unit off **(see illustration)**.

8 Release the catches on the left and right-hand sides of the ZFE unit holder and hinge the holder up **(see illustrations)**.

9 To displace the ECU, lift it out of its holder, taking care not to strain the wiring loom **(see illustration)**.

15.5a Pull out the catch . . .

15.5b . . . and lift up the connectors

15.6 Disconnect the wiring connector

15.7 Lift off the ZFE unit

15.8a Release the catches . . .

15.8b . . . and hinge the holder up

15.9 Lift out the ECU

15.10a Pull out the catches . . .

15.10b . . . disconnect the connectors . . .

15.10c . . . and remove the ECU

10 To remove the ECU, release the catches securing the two multi-pin wiring connectors and disconnect the connectors, then lift the ECU off **(see illustrations)**. If a catch or connector appears to be stuck, follow the procedure in Step 5 to release it.

Installation

11 Installation is the reverse of removal, noting the following:
● Ensure that the terminals in the multi-pin connectors are clean and undamaged.
● Spray the connector pins lightly with electrical contact cleaner.
● Ensure the connectors are locked in position with the catches.

16 Sensors

⚠ **Warning: Refer to the Warning given in Section 1 before starting work.**
Caution Before disconnecting the wiring connector from any sensor, make sure the ignition is switched OFF, then disconnect the battery (see Chapter 7).
1 No data is available for testing the sensors which supply data to the ECU. If a sensor is faulty, the engine warning light in the instrument cluster will illuminate. The machine must then be taken to a BMW dealer who will be able to identify the faulty component using the BMW diagnostic tester. Once the faulty component had been renewed, the fault code can be erased from the engine management system.

Crankshaft position sensor

Function

2 The sensor reads the position of the crankshaft and how fast it is turning; this information is used by the ECU to determine which cylinder is on its ignition stroke and when it should fire. The ECU combines engine speed with information from other sensors to determine fuelling and ignition requirements.

Removal and installation

3 The crankshaft position sensor is located on the front top edge of the timing cover, just below the alternator pulley **(see illustration)**. Follow the procedure in Chapter 1, Section 9, to remove the alternator drive belt cover.
4 Remove the fuel tank (see Section 2).
5 Trace the wiring from the sensor and disconnect it at the connector. Free the wiring from any ties.
6 Undo the screw securing the sensor and pull it out **(see illustration)**. Note the location of the O-ring and discard it as a new one must be fitted **(see illustration)**.
7 The sensor is triggered by the teeth on the crankshaft gear inside the engine timing cover. To inspect the gear teeth, follow the procedure in Chapter 2, Section 16, and remove the cover.
8 Installation is the reverse of removal, noting the following:
● Fit a new O-ring to the sensor and lubricate it with a smear of clean engine oil.
● Tighten the sensor screw to the torque

setting specified at the beginning of this Chapter.
● Ensure the terminals in the wiring connector are clean.
● Ensure the wiring is securely connected and renew any cable-ties.

Camshaft position sensor

Function

9 The sensor reads the position of the camshaft and how fast it is turning. This information is used by the ECU to determine which cylinder is on its ignition stroke and when it should fire.

Removal and installation

10 The camshaft position sensor is located in the rear of the right-hand cylinder head below the throttle body **(see illustration)**. Remove the body panels as appropriate to your machine to access the sensor (see Chapter 6).

16.3 Location of the crankshaft position sensor

16.6a Undo the screw and remove the sensor . . .

16.6b . . . noting the location of the O-ring

16.10 Location of the camshaft position sensor

11 Free the wiring from the ties clipped to the cylinder head and on the underside of the throttle body, then disconnect the sensor wiring connector.

12 Undo the screw securing the sensor and pull it out **(see illustration)**. Note the location of the O-ring and discard it as a new one must be fitted **(see illustration)**.

13 The sensor is activated by a trigger retained by the camshaft sprocket bolt **(see illustration 16.12a)**. To inspect the trigger, follow the procedure in Chapter 2, Section 9. Note that the position of the trigger is determined by a tab which locates in a small hole in the camshaft sprocket.

14 Installation is the reverse of removal, noting the points in Step 8.

Knock sensors

Function

15 The sensors detect the precise frequency vibrations caused by detonation or 'pinking' inside the combustion chambers. When detonation occurs, a signal is sent to the ECU which then retards the ignition timing to avoid engine damage through mechanical stress or over-heating.

Removal and installation

16 The knock sensors are located on the left and right-hand cylinders, inboard of the throttle bodies **(see illustration)**. Remove the throttle bodies to access the sensors (see Section 6).

17 Follow the procedure in Chapter 2, Section 12 to remove the sensors.

18 Installation is the reverse of removal, noting the relevant points in Step 8. Note that the correct torque for the sensor bolt is critical, otherwise the sensor will not function correctly.

Intake air temperature sensor

Function

19 The sensor reads the temperature of the air in the airbox. As changes in temperature affect air density, the ECU uses the information to determine fuelling requirements.

Removal and installation

20 The intake air temperature sensor is located in the left-hand side of the airbox at

16.12a Pull out the sensor. Note location of sensor trigger (arrowed)

16.16 Location of the left-hand knock sensor

the front **(see illustration)**. Remove the body panels as appropriate to your machine to access the sensor (see Chapter 6).

21 Release the clip securing the sensor wiring connector and disconnect the connector.

22 Release the clip securing the sensor in the airbox, then draw the sensor out, noting the location of the O-ring **(see illustrations)**.

23 Check the condition of the sensor O-ring and renew it if it is deformed or deteriorated.

24 Installation is the reverse of removal, noting the relevant points in Step 8.

Engine oil temperature sensor

Function

25 The sensor reads the temperature of the oil in the cooling circuit and the ECU uses the information to determine fuelling and ignition

16.12b Discard the sensor O-ring

16.20 Location of the intake air temperature sensor

requirements, particularly for hot and cold starting.

Removal and installation

Note: *If the engine has been running, allow it to cool before commencing work. If the machine is left to stand, oil will drain down from the cooler into the crankcase, reducing the amount of residual oil in the cooler.*

26 The engine oil temperature sensor is located on the top of the engine on the right-hand side **(see illustration)**. Remove the fuel tank to access the sensor (see Section 2).

27 Release the clip securing the sensor wiring connector and disconnect the connector.

28 Unscrew the sensor and lift it out, being prepared to catch any residual oil (see **Note** above). Note the location of the sealing

16.22a Release the clip . . .

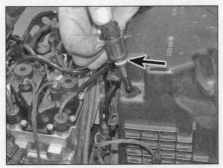

16.22b . . . and pull the sensor out. Note the O-ring (arrowed)

16.26 Location of the oil temperature sensor

16.28 Unscrew the temperature sensor. Note the sealing washer (arrowed)

16.33 Cylinder head temperature sensor

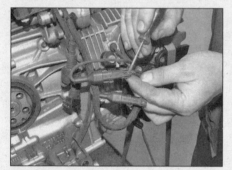

16.34 Release the clip to disconnect the wiring connector

16.38 Location of the oil pressure switch

washer and discard it as a new one must be fitted (see illustration).

29 Installation is the reverse of removal, noting the relevant points in Step 8. Don't forget to fit a new sealing washer and tighten the sensor to the torque setting specified at the beginning of this Chapter.

Oxygen sensors

30 The oxygen sensors measure exhaust gas oxygen content and the ECU uses the information to determine fuelling requirements.

31 Refer to the procedure in Section 10 to remove and install the oxygen sensors.

Cylinder head temperature sensor

Function

32 A temperature sensor is fitted in the right-hand cylinder head. The sensor reads the temperature of the cylinder head and the ECU uses this information to determine fuelling and ignition requirements.

Removal and installation

33 The temperature sensor is located inboard of the throttle body (see illustration). Remove the throttle body to access the sensor (see Section 6).

34 Free the sensor wiring from the tie, then release the clip securing the sensor wiring connector and disconnect the connector (see illustration).

35 Unscrew the sensor and lift it out.

36 Installation is the reverse of removal, noting the relevant points in Step 8.

Engine oil pressure switch

37 While the engine is running under normal circumstances, the switch is held in the OFF position by oil pressure in the lubricating circuit. If the pressure drops, the switch illuminates the oil pressure warning light in the instrument cluster. If this happens, the engine should be stopped immediately and the cause of the loss of pressure investigated.

38 The oil pressure switch is located in the left-hand side of the crankcase below the cylinder (see illustration). Refer to the procedure in Chapter 7 for testing, removal and installation of the oil pressure switch.

Throttle position sensor

Function

39 The sensor monitors the position of the butterfly valve in the left-hand throttle body and the ECU uses the information to determine fuelling and ignition requirements.

Removal and installation

Note: The sensor should not be removed unless it is known to be faulty. When a new sensor is installed its position must be reset using the BMW diagnostic tester.

40 The throttle position sensor is located on the side of the left-hand throttle body (see illustration). Disconnect the sensor wiring connector (see Section 6, Step 5), then undo the screws securing the sensor and lift it off. Note how the valve spindle locates inside the sensor.

Gear position sensor

Function

41 The sensor monitors the position of the selector drum in the gearbox and the ECU uses the information, combined with engine speed, to determine fuelling and ignition requirements.

Removal and installation

42 The gear position sensor is located on the back of the gearbox (see illustration). To gain access, follow the procedure in Section 9 and remove the exhaust silencer and downpipe assembly. Where fitted, remove the exhaust flow control valve and servo motor assembly.

43 Release the cable-tie securing the sensor wiring connector and disconnect the connector (see illustration).

44 Refer to the procedure in Chapter 2, Section 27, for removal and installation of the sensor.

16.40 Location of the throttle position sensor

16.42 Location of the gear position sensor

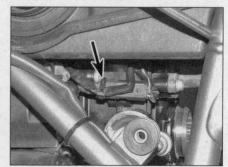

16.43 Cut the cable-tie securing the connector

Chapter 4
Frame, suspension and final drive

Contents

Section number

Final drive unit 12
Footrests, brake pedal and gearchange lever 3
Front suspension 6
General information 1
Handlebars and levers 5
Handlebar switch housings .... see Chapter 7
Rear shock absorber 9
Steering damper.. 8

Section number

Stand lubrication .... see Chapter 1
Stands 4
Steering bearings...................................... 7
Sub-frames... 2
Suspension adjustment 10
Suspension check .... see Chapter 1
Swingarm and driveshaft 11

Degrees of difficulty

Easy, suitable for novice with little experience	**Fairly easy,** suitable for beginner with some experience	**Fairly difficult,** suitable for competent DIY mechanic	**Difficult,** suitable for experienced DIY mechanic	**Very difficult,** suitable for expert DIY or professional

Specifications

Front suspension

Type .... BMW Telelever
Fork oil type .... BMW telescopic fork oil (10W)
Fork oil capacity
   R1200 GS and GS Adventure .... 0.65 litre
   R1200 RT and R1200 R .... 0.64 litre
Fork tube runout limit...................................... 0.1 mm

Rear suspension

Type .... BMW Paralever

Brake pedal

Brake pedal-to-stop clearance............................... 2.0 to 3.0 mm

Torque settings

Brake and clutch lever clamp bolts	5 Nm
Brake and clutch lever pivot bolt	7 Nm
Brake pedal pivot bolt	
R1200 GS, GS Adventure and R1200 R	21 Nm
R1200 RT	38 Nm
Centre stand pivot bolts.	40 Nm
Final drive unit pivot bolt	100 Nm
Footrest bracket mounting bolts	19 Nm
Front suspension	
Top yoke bearing stud nut	130 Nm
Fork tube top stud nut	40 Nm
Fork air bleed screw.	2.3 Nm
Fork bridge clamp bolts	25 Nm
Fork bridge ball joint nut.	130 Nm
Fork bridge ball joint.	230 Nm
Front shock absorber – R1200 RT	
Upper mounting nut	35 Nm
Lower mounting bolt.	40 Nm
Front shock absorber – R1200 GS, GS Adventure and R1200 R	
Upper and lower mounting bolts	34 Nm
Telelever pivot shaft bolt	
Initial setting	45 Nm
Final setting	73 Nm
Steering damper-to-fork bridge nut	19 Nm
Steering damper-to-Telelever bolt	19 Nm
Gearchange lever pinch bolt	8 Nm
Handlebars	
R1200 GS and GS Adventure	
Front handlebar clamp bolts.	36 Nm
Rear handlebar clamp bolts	16 Nm
Handlebar end-weight bolts.	21 Nm
R1200 RT	
Handlebar mounting bolts	19 Nm
Handlebar end-weight bolts.	19 Nm
R1200 R	
Handlebar clamp bolts	24 Nm
Handlebar end-weight bolts	19 Nm
Rear brake master cylinder mounting bolts – R1200 RT	6 Nm
Rear suspension	
Paralever mounting bolts	
Front	42 Nm
Rear	42 Nm
Rear shock absorber	
Upper mounting bolt nut.	50 Nm
Lower mounting bolt.	58 Nm
Adjuster knob mounting screw (R1200 R)	19 Nm
Swingarm left-hand bearing pin	
Initial setting	20 Nm
Final setting	7 Nm
Swingarm left-hand bearing pin locknut	145 Nm
Swingarm right-hand bearing pin screws.	9 Nm
Sidestand pivot bolt.	40 Nm

1 General information

There is no frame in the traditional sense – the front suspension and sub-frame and rear suspension and sub-frame mount directly to the engine/transmission unit.

Front suspension and steering are managed separately by BMW's Telelever system. Telelever uses an arrangement of telescopic fork legs to support the front wheel and provide steering, together with a swingarm and shock absorber to provide suspension control – unlike conventional front forks, the Telelever forks contain neither damping mechanism nor springs, only oil to lubricate the friction surfaces.

At the top of the Telelever system, the fork tubes are held in a yoke, which is mounted to the front sub-frame via the steering head bearing. Midway down the assembly, the fork sliders are linked by a bridge which is attached to the front of the Telelever swingarm via a ball joint. The swingarm pivots around a shaft which passes through the front of the engine crankcases, with the shock absorber located between the swingarm and the front sub-frame.

Rear suspension is provided by a single-sided swingarm and centrally mounted shock absorber. The drive shaft to the rear wheel is housed inside the swingarm. The joint between the swingarm and the final drive unit is pivoted, with a link arm, BMW's Paralever system, controlling movement between the two. The Paralever system counteracts the adverse effect of the shaft drive on suspension movement.

The rear shock absorber is located between the swingarm and the rear sub-frame.

2 Sub-frames

1 The front sub-frame supports the steering and suspension, the fuel tank and a number of electrical components, including the engine control unit and the ZFE central electronics unit. The sub-frame bolts directly to the engine's crankcase.

2 The rear sub-frame supports the swingarm and provides the top mounting for the rear shock absorber. The sub-frame also supports the seat, rear mudguard, air filter housing, battery and electrical components. The sub-frame bolts directly to the engine's crankcase.

3 The sub-frames should not require attention unless accident damage has occurred. In most cases, renewal is the only satisfactory remedy for such damage. A few frame specialists have the jigs and other equipment necessary for straightening the sub-frame assemblies to the required standard of accuracy, but even then there is no simple way of assessing to what extent the frame components may have been over-stressed.

4 Remember that misalignment of the front and rear suspension/sub-frame assemblies will cause handling problems. If misalignment is suspected, first check the wheel alignment (see Chapter 5).

5 To check the sub-frame assemblies it will be necessary to remove the body panels (see Chapter 6) and fuel tank (see Chapter 3).

6 Loose bolts can cause ovaling or fracturing of the sub-frame mountings. On a high mileage bike, the sub-frame assemblies should be examined closely for signs of cracking or splitting at the welded joints. Minor damage can often be repaired by welding, depending on the extent and nature of the damage, but this is a task for an expert. Always remove the battery, ECU (engine control unit), ZFE central electronics unit and instrument cluster before using electric welding equipment.

7 Follow the relevant Steps in Chapter 2, Section 4, to remove the front and rear sub-frames. Note that the wiring loom remains connected to the front sub-frame when it is removed.

3 Footrests, brake pedal and gearchange lever

Footrests

R1200 GS and Adventure

1 To remove the rider's footrests, first remove the E-clip from the bottom of the footrest pivot pin, then withdraw the pivot pin and remove the return spring and the footrest (see illustration). Note how the spring ends locate in the footrest and on the mounting bracket.

2 To remove the passenger's footrests, first remove the E-clip from the bottom of the footrest pivot pin, then withdraw the pivot pin and remove the footrest (see illustration).

R1200 RT

3 The rider's and passenger's footrests are located on mounting brackets. To remove the left-hand bracket, first undo the screws securing the fairing side panel to the top edge of the bracket, then undo the bracket mounting bolts and lift the bracket off (see illustration). Follow the procedure in Steps 1 and 2 to remove the footrests from the bracket.

4 The right-hand bracket also supports the rear brake pedal and master cylinder. Before removing the bracket, release the clip securing the pedal to the master cylinder pushrod and separate the pushrod from the brake pedal (see below), then undo the two bolts securing the master cylinder to the rear of the bracket and displace the master cylinder. **Note**: *BMW advises it may be necessary to heat the bracket in the area of the master cylinder bolts to approximately 100°C to release the thread lock on the bolts*. If applicable, trace the wiring from the rear brake light switch on the back of the panel to the wiring connector and disconnect it. Release the wiring from any ties. Undo the bracket mounting bolts and remove the bracket, footrests and rear brake pedal as an assembly.

R1200 R

5 The rider's footrests are located on mounting brackets. To remove the left-hand bracket, undo the bracket mounting bolts and lift the bracket off (see illustration). Follow the procedure in Step 1 to remove the footrest from the bracket.

3.1 Remove the E-clip (arrowed) from the pivot pin – R1200 GS rider's footrest

3.2 Remove the E-clip (arrowed) from the pivot pin – R1200 GS passenger's footrest

3.3 Footrest bracket mounting bolts (arrowed) – R1200 RT right-hand side shown

3.5 Footrest bracket mounting bolts – R1200 R left-hand side

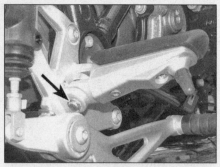

3.6 Remove the E-clip (arrowed) from the pivot pin – R1200 R rider's footrest

3.7a Passenger's footrest bracket mounting bolts – R1200 R left-hand side

3.7b Remove the E-clip (arrowed) from the pivot pin – passenger's footrest

6 The right-hand bracket also supports the rear brake pedal and master cylinder – follow the procedure in Step 1 to remove the footrest only **(see illustration)**. Alternatively, follow the procedure in Chapter 5 and displace the master cylinder. Undo the bracket mounting bolts, then undo the screw securing the rear brake light switch to the back of the panel. Remove the bracket, footrest and rear brake pedal as an assembly.

7 The passenger's footrests are located on mounting brackets. Undo the bracket mounting bolts and lift the bracket off **(see illustration)**. To remove the footrest from the bracket, remove the E-clip from the bottom of the footrest pivot pin, then withdraw the pivot pin and remove the footrest **(see illustration)**.

Installation

8 If they are worn, the footrest rubbers can be released by undoing the screws on the bottom and replacing with new ones.
9 Installation is the reverse of removal. Always use new E-clips to secure the pivot pins. On R1200 RT models, either fit new micro-encapsulated master cylinder bolts or clean all old locking compound from the old bolts, apply fresh thread-locking compound and tighten them to the specified torque setting.

Brake pedal

R1200 GS and Adventure

10 Note the location of the clip securing the brake master cylinder pushrod clevis pin, then ease the clip off the pushrod and withdraw the pin **(see illustrations)**. Separate the pushrod from the brake pedal **(see illustration)**.
11 Note how the ends of the pedal return spring locate on the bracket and the underside of the pedal **(see illustrations)**. Undo the pivot bolt and lift the pedal and spring off.
12 On GS Adventure models, the height of the pedal can be altered by raising or lowering the hinged toe plate. The plate is spring loaded – from the UP position, press it rearwards and fold it down until it locks in position **(see illustrations)**. From the DOWN

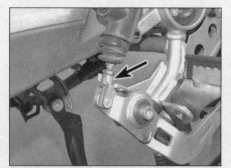

3.10a Release the clip (arrowed) . . .

3.10b . . . and pull out the clevis pin . . .

3.10c . . . then remove the pushrod

3.11a One end of the spring (arrowed) locates on the bracket . . .

3.11b . . . the other end locates underneath the pedal

3.12a Fold the toe plate down . . .

3.12b . . . to raise the pedal height

3.16 Note the location of the pedal return spring (arrowed) – R1200 R

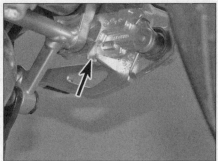

3.18a Location of the brake pedal stop – R1200 R

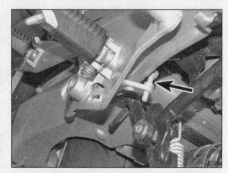

3.18b Brake pedal stop bolt – R1200 RT

position, press it forwards and fold it up until it locks in position.

R1200 RT

13 Separate the pushrod from the brake pedal (see Step 10).

14 Undo the nut on the back of the pedal pivot bolt and remove the washer and return spring – note how the spring locates against the lugs on the back of the mounting bracket. Support the pedal and withdraw the bolt, then lift the pedal off.

R1200 R

15 Separate the pushrod from the brake pedal (see Step 10).

16 Note how the ends of the pedal return spring locate on the bracket and the underside of the pedal (see illustration). Undo the pivot bolt and lift the pedal and spring off.

Installation

17 Installation is the reverse of removal, noting the following:
● Lubricate the pedal pivot with a smear of grease.
● Make sure the spring ends are correctly positioned.
● Tighten the pivot bolt to the torque setting specified at the beginning of this Chapter.
● Renew the clevis pin and clip assembly if the clip is sprained or corroded.

Adjusting the brake pedal freeplay

18 When pressure is applied to the brake pedal there should be a small amount of freeplay between the pedal and the pedal stop on the mounting bracket before the brake pushrod contacts the master cylinder piston (see illustration). On R1200 RT models, a fixed bolt located on the inside edge of the pedal rests against the stop on the bracket (see illustration).

19 Where fitted, remove the plastic cover (see illustration). Apply light pressure to the pedal and measure the clearance using a feeler gauge (see illustration). Compare the

result with the specification at the beginning of this Chapter. If the clearance is outside the specification, loosen the lock nut on the master cylinder pushrod and screw the pushrod in or out of the clevis until the gap is correct (see illustration). Tighten the lock nut.

Gearchange lever

20 To remove the lever, check for the mark on the end of the gearchange linkage shaft that aligns with the slot in the lever, or for a mark on the shaft that aligns with a mark on the lever (see illustration). If the mark isn't visible, make your own with a dab of paint,

3.19a Remove the plastic cover

3.19b Measure the clearance (arrowed)

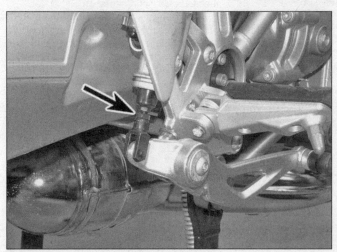

3.19c Loosen the locknut (arrowed) and adjust the pushrod

3.20 Mark on shaft aligns with slot (arrowed) in lever

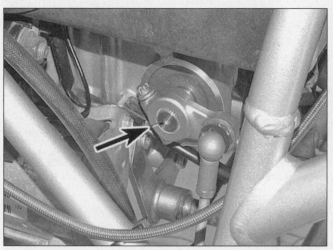

3.22a Mark on shaft aligns with slot (arrowed) in linkage lever

3.22b Removing the gearchange linkage

3.23a Foot pedal pinch bolt – R1200 RT

3.23b Foot pedal pinch bolt – R1200 GS Adventure

3.24 Location of the gearchange linkage rod

then remove the pinch bolt and pull the lever off the shaft.

21 Where fitted, follow the procedure in Chapter 3, Section 9, and displace the exhaust flow control valve servo motor to access the gearchange linkage.

22 To remove the gearchange linkage, check for the mark on the gearchange shaft that aligns with the slot in the lever **(see illustration)**. If the mark isn't visible, make your own with a dab of paint, then remove the pinch bolt and pull the lever off the shaft. Pull the linkage out of the bracket in the frame **(see illustration)**. Note the location of the washer on the shaft. Clean the shaft and lubricate it

with a smear of grease before reassembly.
23 To adjust the position of the gearchange lever on R1200 RT and GS Adventure models, first loosen the pinch bolt securing the foot pedal **(see illustrations)**. Twist the pedal to the desired position, then tighten the pinch bolt.
24 To adjust the position of the gearchange lever on all other models, first loosen the locknuts on both ends of the linkage rod **(see illustration)**. Turn the rod to achieve the desired lever position, then tighten the locknuts. **Note:** *Ensure a minimum of 3 threads are screwed into the connectors on both ends of the rod.*

4 Stands

1 All models covered in this manual are fitted with a centre stand and a sidestand. Lubricating the stand pivots is part of routine maintenance (see Chapter 1).
2 Make sure the stand springs (there are 2 on each stand) are in good condition and capable of holding the stand up when not in use. A broken or weak spring is an obvious safety hazard – always renew a spring that is damaged or has sagged.

Centre stand

3 To remove the stand, first ensure the machine is securely supported with an auxiliary stand
4 Unhook the stand springs from the lug on the frame **(see illustration)**.
5 The centre stand is secured on the left and right-hand sides by bolts which screw into pivot bushes in the rear sub-frame **(see illustration)**. On R1200 GS and GS Adventure models, the bolts are inserted from the outside; on R1200 RT and R1200 R models, the bolts are inserted from the inside. Counter-hold

4.4 Stand springs hook over lug on frame

4.5 Undo centrestand pivot bolts

each bush and undo the bolts, then lift the stand off

6 Inspect the stand, pivot holes and bushes for signs of wear and renew any components as necessary. Note the location of the O-rings on the bushes and renew them if they are damaged.

7 Before installation, ensure that the pivot holes are clean and apply a smear of grease to the bushes.

8 Install the stand and bushes, then tighten the pivot bolts to the torque setting specified at the beginning of this Chapter.

9 Install the stand springs, ensuring the ends are securely located.

10 Check the operation of the stand before riding the motorcycle.

Sidestand

11 Ensure the machine is securely supported on its centre stand or on an auxiliary stand, then unhook the stand springs **(see illustration)**.

12 The sidestand switch is secured by two circlips and a washer. On R1200 GS and GS Adventure models, the fixings are located on the underside of the stand pivot; on R1200 RT and R models, the fixings are located on the top of the pivot **(see illustration)**.

13 Remove the circlips and washer and displace the switch. Discard the circlips as new ones must be fitted. Note how the switch locates against the peg on the stand bracket, and how the pin on the switch locates in the hole in the stand.

14 Unscrew the pivot bolt and remove the stand. Remove the bushes from the bracket if they are loose.

15 On installation, ensure that the pivot hole and bracket are clean and apply a smear of grease to the bushes.

16 Clean the threads of the pivot bolt and apply a suitable non-permanent thread locking compound, then install the stand and tighten the bolt to the torque setting specified at the beginning of this Chapter.

17 Install the stand springs, ensuring the ends are securely located.

18 Install the sidestand switch and secure it with the washer and two new circlips.

19 Check the operation of the starter interlock system (see Chapter 3).

20 Check the operation of the stand before riding the motorcycle.

4.11 Location of the sidestand springs

---

5   Handlebars and levers

Handlebars

Note 1: *The handlebars can be displaced without having to remove the lever or switch assemblies. In all cases, take care to avoid straining the handlebar wiring. Support or tie the handlebar assembly using rags to cushion it and anything it sits against. Also cover the master cylinder(s) with rag in case of leakage.*

Note 2: *The machines covered in this manual were available from new fitted with a range of optional electrical extras. When working on your machine, take care to ensure that all relevant electrical components are disconnected on disassembly and subsequently reconnected during the rebuild. Always take the precaution of disconnecting the battery negative (-) terminal before disconnecting an electrical wiring connector.*

R1200 GS and GS Adventure

1 Disconnect the battery negative lead (see Chapter 7). Remove the mirrors, bar end-weights and hand protectors (see Chapter 6).

2 Follow the procedure in Chapter 2, Section 21, and displace the clutch master cylinder. There is no need to disconnect the clutch hose. Keep the reservoir upright to prevent fluid spillage and make sure no strain in placed on the hose.

3 Follow the procedure in Chapter 7 and remove the left-hand switch housing.

4.12 Sidestand switch fixings – R1200 RT and R1200 R

4 On machines with unheated handlebar grips, if required, pull the left-hand grip off the handlebar. Push a screwdriver between the grip and the bar and use spray lubricant to loosen the grip. If the grip has been bonded in place you may need to cut it free.

5 On machines with heated grips, hold back the flange of the grip to reveal the retaining screw. Remove the screw and slide the grip off the handlebar.

6 Follow the procedure in Chapter 5 and displace the front brake master cylinder. There is no need to disconnect the brake hose. Keep the reservoir upright to prevent fluid spillage and make sure no strain in placed on the hose.

7 Follow the procedure in Chapter 7 and remove the right-hand switch housing.

8 Detach the throttle cable from the twistgrip pulley (see Chapter 3). Temporarily install the top half of the twistgrip housing.

9 Loosen the clamp screw and slide the twistgrip off the handlebar **(see illustration)**.

10 Unclip the throttle cable guard **(see illustration)**.

11 Loosen the bolts securing the handlebar clamps **(see illustration)**. Support the handlebars and remove the clamps, then lift the handlebars off. Note the larger clamp bolts are fitted at the front.

12 Installation is the reverse of removal, noting the following:

● To ensure that the handlebars are central in the clamps align the punch marks on the bars with the inner front edges of the clamp joints.

● Tighten the clamp bolts to the torque

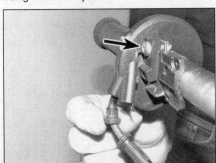

5.9 Twistgrip is secured by clamp screw

5.10 Unclip the throttle cable guard

5.11 Handlebar clamp bolts – R1200 GS

5.12 Align clamp surface with moulding (arrowed)

5.13 Remove the bar end-weights

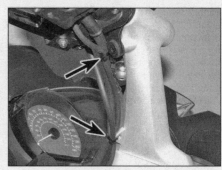

5.14 Cut the cable-ties – left-hand side

settings specified at the beginning of this Chapter – tighten the front bolts first, ensuring there is no gap between the faces of the clamps at the front, then the rear bolts.

● Align the lugs on the switch housings with the marks on the handlebars.

● Fit the front brake and clutch master cylinders so that the rear clamp mating surfaces align with the lugs in the switch assemblies **(see illustration)**.

R1200 RT

Note: *Although not strictly necessary, before removing the handlebars it is recommended that the windshield is removed (see Chapter 6). This will improve access and prevent accidental damage should a tool slip.*

13 Disconnect the battery negative lead (see Chapter 7). Undo the screws and remove the bar end-weights **(see illustration)**.

14 Release the ties securing the wiring to the left-hand handlebar **(see illustration)**.

15 Follow the procedure in Chapter 7 and disconnect the wiring connectors from the left-hand switch housing. Slide the handlebar grip and switch housing off the handlebar.

16 Follow the procedure in Chapter 2, Section 21, and displace the clutch master cylinder. There is no need to disconnect the clutch hose. Keep the reservoir upright to prevent fluid spillage and make sure no strain in placed on the hose.

17 Release the ties securing the wiring to the right-hand handlebar **(see illustration)**.

18 Follow the procedure in Chapter 7 and remove the right-hand switch housing.

19 Undo the screw on the upper edge of the handlebar and slide the complete twistgrip assembly off the handlebar. If there is insufficient slack in the throttle cable(s), disconnect them first (see Chapter 3, Section 8).

20 Follow the procedure in Chapter 5 and displace the front brake master cylinder. There is no need to disconnect the brake hose. Keep the reservoir upright to prevent fluid

spillage and make sure no strain in placed on the hose.

21 Undo the bolts securing the left and right-hand handlebars to the top yoke and lift them off **(see illustration)**. Note the O-rings fitted to the tops of the fork tubes and renew them if necessary on installation.

22 Do not attempt to remove the handlebar from its bracket. Individual components are not available – if the bar or bracket is damaged, fit a new assembly.

23 Installation is the reverse of removal, noting the following:

● Tighten the mounting bolts to the torque setting specified at the beginning of this Chapter.

● Fit the front brake and clutch master cylinders so that the rear clamp mating surfaces align with the punch mark in the handlebar.

R1200 R

24 Disconnect the battery negative lead (see Chapter 7).

25 Undo the screws and remove the bar end-weights **(see illustration 5.13)**.

26 Follow the procedure in Steps 2 to 9 to remove the components from the handlebars.

27 Loosen the bolts securing the handlebar clamp **(see illustration)**. Support the handlebars and remove the clamp **(see illustration)**, then lift the handlebars off.

28 Installation is the reverse of removal, noting the following:

● To ensure that the handlebars are central in the clamps align the + marks on the bars with the inner front edges of the clamp joints **(see illustration)**.

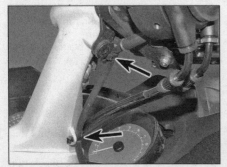

5.17 Cut the cable-ties – right-hand side

5.21 Handlebar mounting bolts – R1200 RT

5.27a Undo the bolts . . .

5.27b . . . and remove the clamp

5.28 Align marks (arrowed) with clamps

- Tighten the clamp bolts to the torque setting specified at the beginning of this Chapter – tighten the front bolts first, ensuring there is no gap between the faces of the clamps at the front, then the rear bolts.
- Align the lugs on the switch housings with the marks on the handlebars.
- Fit the front brake and clutch master cylinders so that the rear clamp mating surfaces align with the lugs in the switch housings **(see illustration 5.12).**

Levers

29 Follow the procedure in Chapter 2, Section 21, to remove and install the clutch lever.

30 Follow the procedure in Chapter 5, Section 5, to remove and install the front brake lever.

31 To adjust the lever span, refer to Chapter 1, Sections 10 and 11.

6 Front suspension

Fork leg

Removal

Note: *Unlike a conventional telescopic fork leg, the fork tube is not secured in the slider by the fork bushes or damper rod. When removing the fork leg, take care not to pull the tube out of the slider accidentally. If the tube and slider are separated, new oil seals must be fitted.*

1 Position the bike on its centre stand or support it securely on an auxiliary stand. Work can be made easier by raising the machine to a suitable working height on an hydraulic ramp or a suitable platform. Make sure the machine is secure and will not topple over.

2 Refer to the procedure in Chapter 6 and remove the fairing panels, according to your model, to gain access to the front suspension.

3 Remove the front wheel (see Chapter 5).

4 Remove the front mudguard (see Chapter 6).

5 On machines fitted with ABS, undo the screw securing the ABS sensor to the

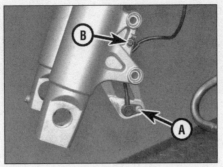
6.5 ABS sensor is secured by screw (A). Wiring is secured by clip at (B)

left-hand fork slider **(see illustration)**. Release the sensor wiring from the clips on the slider and withdraw the sensor, noting how it fits. Secure the sensor clear of the fork legs.

6 On R1200 GS, GS Adventure and R1200 R models, prise out the fork top cap **(see illustration)**.

7 On R1200 RT models, first displace the handlebars (see Section 5). Note that it is not necessary to remove any of the handlebar components. Keep the front brake and clutch master cylinders upright to prevent fluid spillage and make sure no strain in placed on the hoses and wiring.

8 Counter-hold the fork top bolt and undo the nut securing the fork top stud in the top yoke **(see illustration)**.

9 Loosen the clamp bolts in the fork bridge **(see illustration)**. Note the routing of all cables and wiring around the forks, then slide

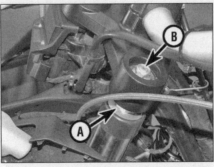
6.8 Counter-hold the fork top bolt (A) and undo the nut (B)

6.9b Slide the fork leg down through the fork bridge

the fork leg down and out through the fork bridge **(see illustration)**.

Overhaul

10 If fitted, lift off the protective sleeve **(see illustration)**.

11 Inspect the area above the dust seal on the fork slider for signs of oil leakage, then carefully lever up the dust seal using a flat-bladed screwdriver and inspect the area above the oil seal **(see illustration)**. If leakage is evident, new seals must be fitted.

12 Check the fork tube for score marks, scratches, flaking of the chrome finish and excessive or abnormal wear. Any damage to the surface of the tube will wear the seals, so the tube must be renewed. Look for dents in the tube and renew both fork tubes if any are found.

13 To separate the tube from the slider, first

6.6 Prise off the fork top cap

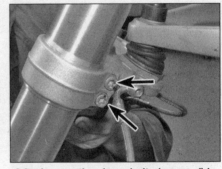
6.9a Loosen the clamp bolts (arrowed) in the fork bridge

6.10 Remove the protective sleeve from the top of the fork tube

6.11 Check for oil leaks underneath the dust seal

6.13a Undo the air bleed screw . . .

6.13b . . . and slide off the dust seal

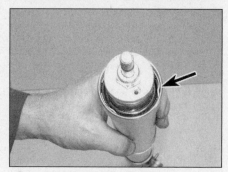

6.15 Remove the retaining clip carefully

undo the air bleed screw, noting the sealing O-ring, then slide off the dust seal **(see illustrations)**.

14 Support the fork leg upright and withdraw the tube from the slider, being prepared to catch any residual oil as the tube and slider are separated. Invert the slider over a suitable container and drain out all the oil. **Note:** *Do not loosen the bolt in the bottom of the slider – it is not a drain plug.*

15 Note the location of the oil seal retaining clip, then prise the clip out carefully **(see illustration)**.

16 Carefully lever out the oil seal using a large flat-bladed screwdriver, taking care not to damage the rim of the slider **(see illustration)**. Note which way up the seal is fitted. Note the location of the washer above the top fork bush.

17 If the fork tube is thought to be bent, check it for runout using V-blocks and a dial gauge **(see illustration)**. If the amount of runout exceeds the service limit specified, the tube should be renewed.

⚠ ***Warning: If either fork tube is bent, it should not be straightened; replace both fork tubes with new ones.***

18 If, when the fork oil was drained, it contained metallic particles, wear has been taking place on the bushes. Slide the tube into the slider and check for play between the two components. If there is any play, either the bushes or the tube itself are worn. The bushes are located inside the slider and require special equipment for removal and installation. Have the fork legs inspected by a BMW dealer.

19 Refill the slider with the specified type and amount of oil **(see illustration)**.

20 Insert the tube fully into the slider and install the washer on top of fork bush.

21 Lubricate the new oil seal with a smear of fork oil and slide it over the tube with the small recess facing up. Tap the seal into place using a suitable piece of tubing or drift **(see illustration)**. Take care not to scratch the fork tube – make sure that the fork tube is pushed fully into the slider so that any accidental scratching is confined to the area above the oil seal.

22 When the seal is correctly seated, the groove for the retaining clip will be visible above the seal. Install the clip, making sure it is correctly located in its groove **(see illustration)**.

23 Lubricate the lips of the new dust seal then slide it down the fork tube and press it into position **(see illustration 6.13b)**.

24 Fit a new O-ring onto the air bleed screw and install the screw loosely **(see illustration 6.13a)**.

25 If fitted, install the protective sleeve **(see illustration 6.10)**.

Installation

26 Slide the fork leg up through the fork bridge, making sure all cables, hoses and wiring are correctly routed. When the slider is correctly seated in the fork bridge, tighten the clamp bolts just enough to hold

6.16 Lever the oil seal out carefully

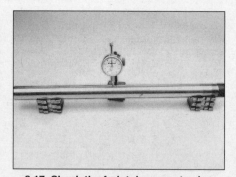

6.17 Check the fork tube runout using V-blocks and a dial gauge

6.19 Refill the slider with the specified type and amount of oil

6.21 Install the new seal carefully to avoid damage

6.22 Install the seal retaining clip

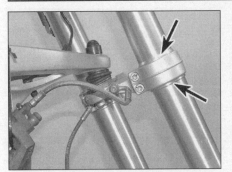

6.26a Ensure that the leg is correctly positioned in the bridge

6.26b Install the axle to ensure fork alignment

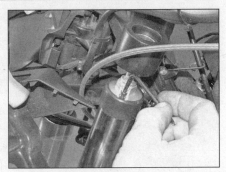

6.27 Tighten the air bleed screw

the slider in position (see illustration). If removed, install the other fork leg, then install the axle to ensure both legs are correctly aligned (see illustration). When the alignment has been checked, tighten the fork bridge clamp bolts to the torque setting specified at the beginning of this Chapter.

27 Push the tube up as far as it will go into the top yoke, then tighten the air bleed screw (see illustration).

28 Apply a suitable non-permanent thread-locking compound to the fork top stud, then install the nut (see illustration). Counter-hold the fork top bolt and tighten the nut to the specified torque setting. Install the fork top cap. Install the remaining components in the reverse order of removal.

Shock absorber

Removal

Note: *On machines equipped with electronic suspension adjustment (ESA), the operation of the ESA should be checked with both shocks in place on the bike (see Section 10).*

29 Position the bike on its centre stand or support it securely on an auxiliary stand. Work can be made easier by raising the machine to a suitable working height on an hydraulic ramp or a suitable platform.

30 If the front wheel is off the ground,

place a block of wood under it to prevent it from dropping when the shock absorber lower bolt is removed. If the weight of the machine is on the front wheel, place a jack or block of wood under the engine to take the weight. It is essential that no loading is placed on the shock absorber. Make sure the motorcycle is secure and will not topple over.

31 Refer to the procedure in Chapter 6 and remove the fairing panels, according to your model, to gain access to the front suspension. Remove the fuel tank (see Chapter 3). On 1200 R models remove the oil cooler shroud (see Chapter 2).

32 On machines equipped with electronic suspension adjustment (ESA), trace the wiring from the shock absorber to the

connector located on the front top edge of the ECU holder and disconnect it. Note that on R1200 GS and GS Adventure models equipped with WP Suspension units, there are two connectors (see illustration). Unclip the connector(s) from the ECU holder and free the wiring from any ties securing it to the front sub-frame and Telelever arm (see illustration).

33 On R1200 GS and GS Adventure models, release the tie securing the wiring to the top edge of the anti-twist bracket (see illustration). Ease the top edge of the bracket up to release the pegs securing the anti-twist bracket between the ends of the bracket on the frame (see illustration).

34 Counter-hold the stud on the top of the

6.28 Install the fork top nut

6.32a ESA wiring connectors – R1200 GS shown

6.32b Free the ESA wiring

6.33a Cut the cable-tie (arrowed)

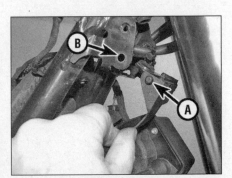

6.33b Release the anti-twist bracket (A) from the frame (B)

6.34a Counter-hold the stud to undo the nut . . .

6.34b . . . then remove the washer

6.35 Bolt secures lower end of front shock absorber

6.36 Withdraw the shock from its upper mounting

6.37 Remove the bushes and spacer (arrowed)

- Tighten the upper and lower mountings to the torque settings specified at the beginning of this Chapter.
- On R1200 GS and GS Adventure models, ensure the anti-twist bracket is correctly secured in the frame bracket.
- On machines equipped with ESA, reconnect the wiring connector(s) and secure the wiring to the sub-frame. Do this with the forks extended to avoid strain on the wiring when the machine is in use.

Telelever arm

Arm removal

Special tool: *A ball joint splitter is necessary for this procedure (see illustration 6.49b).*

Note: *The fork bridge is part of the front brake system, linking the hose from the handlebar master cylinder with the hoses to the brake calipers. During this procedure, the brake hoses are disconnected and the brake system must be topped-up and bled after reassembly (see Chapter 5).*

43 Follow the procedure in Steps 1 to 9 and remove both fork legs.

44 On R1200 R models, remove the steering damper (see Section 8).

45 Follow the procedure in Chapter 5, Section 9, and separate the brake hoses from the fork bridge.

46 Follow the procedure in Steps 31 to 37 and remove the shock absorber.

47 Prise off the covers on both ends of the Telelever pivot shaft, noting the location of the

shock using an Allen key, undo the nut and remove the washer **(see illustrations)**.

35 Undo the bolt securing the lower end of the shock absorber, support the shock and withdraw the bolt **(see illustration)**. Note that the bolt will have been thread-locked in place; use heat if necessary to help break the seal.

36 Withdraw the shock absorber from its upper mounting **(see illustration)**.

37 Remove the upper and lower bushes and the spacer from the upper shock absorber mounting **(see illustration)**.

Inspection

38 Inspect the shock absorber for obvious physical damage. Check the spring for looseness, cracks or signs of fatigue and, where applicable, check that the spring pre-load adjuster is clean and free to turn **(see illustration)**.

39 Inspect the damper rod for signs

of bending, pitting and oil leakage **(see illustration)**.

40 Inspect the pivot hardware at the top and bottom of the shock for wear or damage.

41 Apart from the shock mounting components, individual component parts for the front shock absorber are not available. The entire unit must be renewed if it is worn or damaged although it may be worth first seeking advice from a suspension specialist.

Shock installation

42 Installation is the reverse of removal, noting the following:

- Renew the upper and lower mounting bushes if they are damaged or fatigued.
- Lubricate the shoulder of the lower mounting bolt with a smear of grease.
- Apply a suitable non-permanent thread-locking compound to the upper mounting nut and lower mounting bolt.

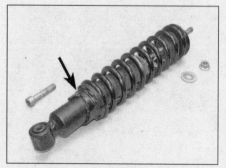

6.38 Ensure that the pre-load adjuster is free to turn

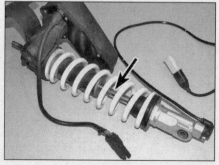

6.39 Inspect the damper rod for damage

6.47a Prise off the covers on both ends of the Telelever pivot shaft

6.47b Counter-hold the head of the pivot shaft . . .

6.47c . . . and undo the bolt

6.48a Withdraw the pivot shaft . . .

O-rings **(see illustration)**. Counter-hold the head of the pivot shaft and undo the bolt on the right-hand side **(see illustrations)**.

48 Support the Telelever arm and withdraw the pivot shaft, then lift the Telelever arm off **(see illustrations)**.

49 Prise the cap off the top of the ball joint on the front of the Telelever arm. Using a hot air gun, heat the ball joint retaining nut to approximately 120°C, then counter-hold the stud on the top of the ball joint using an Allen key and undo the nut **(see illustration)**. Displace the boot on the ball joint and use a ball joint splitter to separate the Telelever arm from the fork bridge **(see illustration)**.

6.48b . . . then lift the Telelever arm off

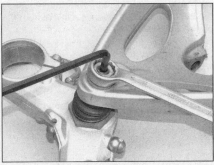

6.49a Counter-hold the stud and undo the ball joint nut

> **HAYNES HiNT**
>
> *Heating the nut softens the threadlock and will make it easier to undo. This will work on the particular threadlock that BMW use on assembly, however if the nut has since been tightened using a different type of threadlock, heat may actually make it more difficult to remove. If this is the case, allow the parts to cool and try again.*

Arm inspection

50 Thoroughly clean all the components, removing all traces of dirt, corrosion and grease. Inspect all components closely, looking for obvious signs of wear such as heavy scoring and cracks or distortion due to accident damage. Any damaged or worn component must be renewed.

51 Slide the pivot shaft through the bearings and check that there is no resistance due to distortion of the Telelever arm. If there is, first ensure that the pivot shaft is straight by checking for runout using V-blocks and a dial gauge **(see illustration 6.17)**. If the shaft is straight, then the arm itself could be bent – have it checked by a BMW dealer.

52 There are two bearings fitted in each side of the arm – the outer bearing is a sealed caged ball bearing and the inner bearing is a needle roller bearing with a sleeve **(see illustrations)**. Press the sleeves out, noting which side they fit, and clean off the old grease. Refer to *Tools and Workshop Tips* in the *Reference* section and inspect the bearings and sleeves for wear or damage. If the bearings do not turn smoothly or if there is excessive freeplay, they must be renewed.

53 Inspect the ball joint on the fork bridge for signs of wear or damage. It should move freely with no signs of roughness or notchiness. There should be no noticeable play in the joint.

54 To renew the ball joint, the fork bridge must be held securely in a vice and heated to approximately 120°C. BMW produces service tools to hold the bridge (Part Nos. 315741, 315742 and 315673). If the tools are not available, great care must be taken to avoid damaging the bridge. Clamp the bridge in a soft-jawed vice and apply heat using a hot air gun, then unscrew the ball joint (see *Haynes Hint*).

55 The threads of the new ball joint will be microencapsulated with locking compound. Ensure that the threads in the fork bridge are clean prior to installation. Install the ball joint and tighten it to the torque setting specified at the beginning of this Chapter.

56 Fit the Telelever arm onto the fork bridge. Apply a suitable non-permanent thread locking

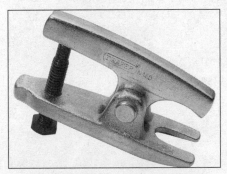

6.49b Separate the arm from the fork bridge using a ball joint splitter

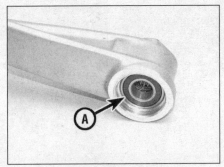

6.52a Outer sealed caged ball bearing (A) . . .

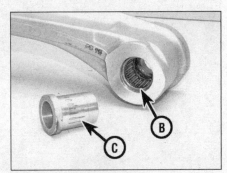

6.52b . . . and inner needle roller bearing (B) and bearing sleeve (C)

compound to the ball joint stud threads and install the nut. Counter-hold the stud using an Allen key and tighten the nut to the specified torque setting **(see illustration 6.49a)**. Press the cap onto the top of the ball joint.

Arm installation

57 Lubricate the bearings with fresh grease and install the bearing sleeves **(see illustration 6.52b)**. Lubricate the pivot shaft with a smear of grease.

58 Fit the Telelever arm onto its engine mountings and install the pivot shaft from the left-hand side **(see illustrations 6.48b and a)**. Install the bolt on the right-hand side, then counter-hold the pivot shaft and tighten the bolt to the initial torque setting specified at the beginning of this Chapter. Now tighten the bolt to the final torque setting specified, again counter-holding the pivot shaft.

59 If necessary, fit new O-rings onto the pivot shaft covers, then press the covers into place **(see illustration 6.47a)**.

60 Install the shock absorber (see Step 42).

61 If applicable, install the steering damper (see Section 8).

62 Follow the procedure in Chapter 5 to reconnect the brake hoses.

63 Install the fork legs (see Steps 26 to 28).

7 Steering bearings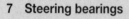

1 The steering turns on a bearing in the top yoke and a ball joint that links the front of the Telelever arm to the fork bridge. These will wear during normal use, and may cause steering wobble – a condition that is potentially dangerous.

Check

2 Position the bike on its centre stand or support it securely on an auxiliary stand. Raise the front wheel off the ground either by having an assistant push down on the rear, or by placing a support under the engine.

7.12a Cover is secured by two screws (arrowed)

3 Point the front wheel straight ahead, then slowly turn the handlebars from side to side. Any roughness in the bearings will be felt and the bars will not move smoothly and freely. If it is thought that the bearings are worn or damaged it will be necessary to partially disassemble the steering and suspension components for further investigation.

4 To check the ball joint on the Telelever arm, first follow the procedure in Section 6 and remove both fork legs. On R1200 R models, detach the steering damper from the fork bridge (see Section 8). The fork bridge should move freely without any sign of roughness or play in the joint. Check that the boot shows no signs of deterioration and is free from cracks and splits. To renew the ball joint, follow the procedure in Section 6, Steps 53 to 55.

5 To check the steering head bearing, position the bike on its centre stand or support it securely on an auxiliary stand. Make sure the machine is secure and will not topple over.

6 Refer to the procedure in Chapter 6 and remove the fairing panels, according to your model, to gain access to the front suspension.

7 Remove the fuel tank (see Chapter 3).

8 Follow the procedure in Section 5 and displace the handlebars. Note that it is not necessary to remove any of the handlebar

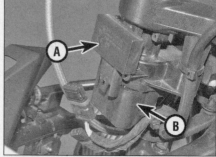

7.12b Disconnect the immobiliser (A) and ignition switch (B) wiring connectors

components. Keep the front brake and clutch master cylinders upright to prevent fluid spillage and make sure no strain in placed on the hoses and wiring.

9 Follow the procedure in Section 6 and release the fork tubes from the top yoke. Pull the tubes down into the sliders until they are clear of the top yoke. Note that it may be necessary to loosen the air bleed screws in the fork top bolts to reduce pressure inside the fork legs **(see illustration 6.27)**.

10 The top yoke should turn freely on its bearing without any sign of roughness or play. To renew the bearing proceed as follows.

Removal and installation

11 If not already done, follow the procedure in Steps 6 to 9 to access the top yoke. On R1200 R models remove the headlamp and its mounting bracket (see Chapter 7).

12 Undo the screws securing the ignition switch wiring connector cover and lift the cover off, then disconnect the switch and ignition immobiliser wiring connectors **(see illustrations)**.

13 Remove the steering head cap **(see illustration)**.

14 Counter-hold the stud in the centre of the steering head bearing using an Allen key and undo the nut on the underside of the steering head **(see illustration)**. Lift the top yoke off.

7.13 Remove the steering head cap

7.14 Location of the nut on the underside of the steering head

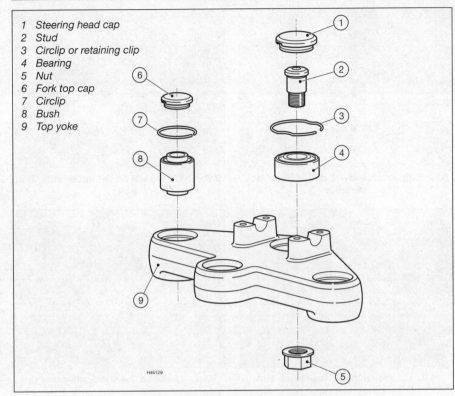

1 Steering head cap
2 Stud
3 Circlip or retaining clip
4 Bearing
5 Nut
6 Fork top cap
7 Circlip
8 Bush
9 Top yoke

H46129

7.16 Fork top yoke components – R1200 GS shown

15 The ignition switch is secured to the yoke by tamper-proof screws which must be drilled-out if the switch is to be removed (see Chapter 7). If left in place, take extreme care to protect the switch when using heat or force on the top yoke.
16 Prise out the circlip securing the top edge of the bearing in the yoke **(see illustration)**.
17 The bearing must be driven out of the top yoke from the underside. Support the yoke on blocks of wood with sufficient clearance to allow the bearing to come out. Use a hot air gun to heat the bearing housing, then drive

the bearing and stud out with a suitably sized socket. Note which way round the bearing is fitted.
18 Press the stud out from the bearing taking care not to damage the stud threads.
19 The fork top studs locate in bushes in the top yoke **(see illustration 7.16)**. If the bearing is being renewed, it is good practice to renew the bushes also. Remove the circlip from the top of each bush, then turn the yoke over and press the bushes out from the underside of the yoke. Install the new bushes from the top using a drawbolt set-up (see *Tools and*

Workshop Tips in the Reference section). Secure the bushes with new circlips.
20 Press the stud into the new steering head bearing.
21 The new bearing must be driven into the top yoke from the top. Support the top yoke on blocks of wood with sufficient clearance to allow the bearing/stud assembly to be fully installed. Use a hot air gun to heat the top yoke bearing housing, then drive the bearing in. Ensure that the socket or driver bears only on the bearing's outer race.
22 Secure the bearing with a new circlip, making sure it seats properly in its groove.
23 If removed, install the ignition switch with new tamper-proof screws (see Chapter 7).
24 Ensure that the threads of the stud are clean, then apply a suitable non-permanent thread-locking compound. Install the yoke onto the steering head and tighten the nut finger-tight. Counter-hold the stud using an Allen key and tighten the nut to the torque setting specified at the beginning of this Chapter. Fit the steering head cap **(see illustration 7.13)**.
25 Connect the ignition switch and immobiliser wiring connectors and install the cover **(see illustrations 7.12b and a)**.
26 Install the remaining components in the reverse order of removal.

8 Steering damper

Check

1 A steering damper is fitted as standard to the R1200 R.
2 Support the bike securely on an auxiliary stand with the front wheel off the ground, then turn the forks from lock-to-lock and check that there is no freeplay between the damper unit and its mountings **(see illustration)**.
3 If any freeplay is evident, check that the rose joint and mounting bolt are tightened securely **(see illustration)**. Note that the nut

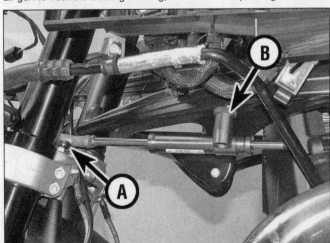

8.2 Steering damper is secured to the fork bridge (A) and the Telelever arm (B)

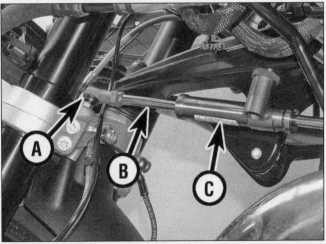

8.3 Steering damper rose joint (A), damper rod (B) and body (C)

9.5 Place a support (arrowed) underneath the swingarm

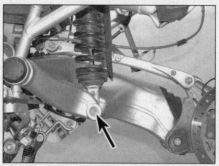

9.6a Bolt secures lower end of the shock absorber

9.6b Undo the nut on the upper mounting bolt . . .

9.6c . . . then support the shock and withdraw the bolt . . .

9.6d . . . and lift the shock absorber out

for the rose joint is on the underside of the fork bridge. If the mountings are tight, then either the rose joint itself is worn, or the bushes in the body mounting are worn. The bushes are available separately, but the rose joint is integral with the damper so a new steering damper will have to be fitted.

4 Check that the damper rod moves smoothly in and out of the damper body with no signs of roughness or binding **(see illustration 8.3)**.

5 Check the rod for pitting and corrosion, and around each end of the damper body for signs of fluid leakage. Renew the damper if any of the above are evident.

Removal and installation

6 Follow the procedure in Chapter 5 to remove the front wheel, then remove the front mudguard (Chapter 6).

7 Counter-hold the hex below the rose joint and undo the nut on the underside of the fork bridge. Separate the damper rod from the fork bridge.

8 Undo the damper mounting bolt on the underside of the Telelever arm and lift the damper off, noting the location of the bushes.

9 Installation is the reverse of removal. If the old damper is being fitted, clean the threads on the rose joint and mounting bolt and apply a suitable non-permanent thread-locking compound. Ensure that the mountings are tightened to the torque setting specified at the beginning of this Chapter.

10 With the front wheel off the ground, check that the forks turn smoothly from lock-to-lock.

---

9 Rear shock absorber

Removal

Note: *On models equipped with electronic suspension adjustment (ESA), the operation of the ESA should be checked with the shock absorber on the bike (see Section 10).*

1 Remove the seat(s) (see Chapter 6).

2 Remove the exhaust silencer (see Chapter 3).

3 Remove the rear wheel (see Chapter 5).

4 On R1200 RT models, remove the seat cowling and the front section of the rear mudguard (see Chapter 6).

5 Position a support (a block of wood or an axle stand is ideal) underneath the final drive unit to prevent the swingarm dropping when the lower shock absorber bolt is removed **(see illustration)**. Do not place the support under the rear brake disc.

6 On R1200 GS and GS Adventure models equipped with a manually adjusted shock, first undo the bolt securing the lower end of the shock absorber to the swingarm **(see illustration)**. Undo the nut on the upper mounting bolt, support the shock and withdraw the bolt, then lift the shock out **(see illustrations)**.

7 On R1200 RT models, equipped with a manually adjusted shock, undo the screw securing the adjuster assembly and displace it **(see illustration)**. Undo the nut on the upper mounting bolt and withdraw the bolt **(see illustrations 9.6b and c)**. Loosen the bolt securing the lower end of the shock absorber to the swingarm **(see illustration 9.6a)**. Raise the swingarm slightly, withdraw the bolt and lift the shock out.

8 On R1200 R models equipped with a manually adjusted shock, first undo the screw securing the adjuster knob, then displace the starter relay from its tab **(see illustration)**. Follow the procedure in Step 6 to undo the lower and upper mountings and remove the shock.

9 On R1200 GS and GS Adventure models equipped with electronic suspension adjustment (ESA), first disconnect the two

9.7 Spring pre-load adjuster knob is secured by screw (arrowed) – R1200 RT

9.8 Spring pre-load adjuster knob (A) and starter relay tab (B) – R1200 R

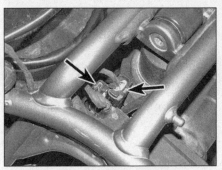

9.9a Disconnect the ESA wiring connectors – R1200 GS

9.9b Undo the lower mounting bolt

9.9c Undo the upper nut and bolt . . .

wiring connectors **(see illustration)**. Undo the bolt securing the lower end of the shock absorber to the swingarm **(see illustration)**. Undo the nut on the upper mounting bolt, support the shock and withdraw the bolt, then lift the shock out **(see illustrations)**.

10 On R1200 RT models equipped with electronic suspension adjustment (ESA), first disconnect the two connectors **(see illustration)**. Release the wiring from any clips or ties and feed it back to the shock, noting the routing. Follow the procedure in Step 7 to undo the upper and lower mountings and remove the shock.

11 On R1200 R models equipped with electronic suspension adjustment (ESA), first disconnect the three wiring connectors and any ties securing the wiring **(see illustration)**. Follow the procedure in Step 7 to undo the upper and lower mountings and remove the shock.

9.9d . . . and lift the shock absorber out

Inspection

12 Inspect the shock absorber for obvious physical damage. Check the spring for looseness, cracks or signs of fatigue **(see illustration)**. Where applicable, check the

9.10 Disconnect the ESA wiring connectors – R1200 RT

operation of the spring pre-load adjuster **(see illustration)**.

13 Inspect the damper rod for signs of bending, pitting and oil leakage **(see illustration)**.

14 Inspect the pivot bushes at the top and bottom of the shock for wear or damage.

15 Individual components for the rear shock absorber are not available. The entire unit must be replaced with a new one if it is worn or damaged.

Installation

16 Installation is the reverse of removal, noting the following.
● Lubricate the shoulders of the mounting bolts with a smear of grease **(see illustration)**.
● Apply a suitable non-permanent thread-locking compound to the mounting bolts.
● Tighten the nuts and bolts to the torque

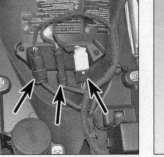

9.11 Disconnect the ESA wiring connectors – R1200 R

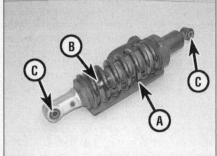

9.12a Inspect the rear shock spring (A), damper rod (B) and mounting bushes (C)

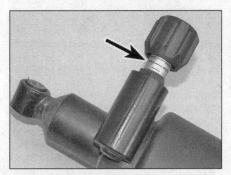

9.12b Spring pre-load adjuster. Note the calibrations (arrowed)

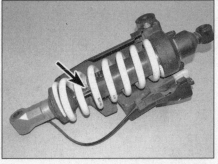

9.13 Inspect the damper rod for damage

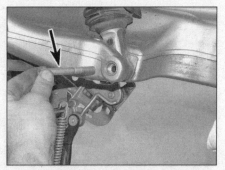

9.16 Apply a smear of grease to the shoulder (arrowed) of each mounting bolt

settings specified at the beginning of this Chapter.
● On ESA-equipped machines, ensure that the wiring connectors are clean and secure. Renew any cable-ties as noted on removal.
● Adjust the suspension as required (see Section 10).

10 Suspension adjustment

Manually adjusted shock absorbers

1 Before adjusting the suspension, position the bike on its centre stand or support it securely upright on an auxiliary stand.

R1200 GS and GS Adventure

Front shock absorber

2 The front shock is adjustable for spring pre-load. Adjustment is made using a suitable C-spanner (one is provided in the toolkit) to turn the spring seat on the base of the shock absorber **(see illustration)**.

3 There are five settings. Position 1 is the softest setting, position 5 is the hardest. Align the setting required with the adjustment stopper. BMW recommends position 2 for road use, position 3 for gravel tracks and with load, and position 5 for off-road riding.

Rear shock absorber

4 The rear shock absorber is adjustable for spring pre-load and damping. Suspension damping must be set-up to suit spring pre-load. An increase in pre-load requires firmer damping, a reduction in pre-load requires softer damping.

5 Spring pre-load adjustment is made by turning the adjuster knob on the shock **(see illustration)**. BMW recommend the following settings. For rider-only use, turn the knob fully anti-clockwise (LOW arrow), then turn it 10 clicks clockwise (HIGH) arrow.

6 If further adjustments are required, turn the knob anti-clockwise (LOW arrow) to reduce pre-load, and clockwise (HIGH arrow) to increase pre-load. The setting can be confirmed by counting the number of grooves

10.2 Adjusting the front shock spring pre-load – R1200 GS

visible on the spindle of the adjuster knob – 5 grooves indicates fully LOW.

7 Damping adjustment is made by turning the adjuster screw on the lower end of the shock **(see illustration)**.

8 For rider-only use, turn the screw fully clockwise (H arrow), then turn it 1½ turns anti-clockwise (S arrow). If further adjustments are required, turn the screw clockwise (H arrow) for harder damping and anti-clockwise (S arrow) for softer damping.

9 For rider use only with optional (OE) lowered suspension, turn the screw fully clockwise (H arrow), then turn it ¾ of a turn anti-clockwise (S arrow).

R1200 RT and R1200 R

Front shock absorber

10 The front shock is not adjustable.

Rear shock absorber

11 The rear shock absorber is adjustable for spring pre-load and damping. Suspension damping must be set-up to suit spring pre-load. An increase in pre-load requires firmer damping, a reduction in pre-load requires softer damping.

12 Follow the procedure in Chapter 6 to remove the passenger's seat (R1200 RT) or the seat (R1200 R) to access the pre-load adjuster **(see illustrations 9.7 and 9.8)**.

13 BMW recommend the following settings. For rider-only use, turn the knob fully anti-clockwise (LOW arrow), then turn it 10 clicks clockwise (HIGH) arrow – this should equate to the STD setting on the adjuster scale.

14 If further adjustments are required, turn

10.5 Rear shock spring pre-load adjuster knob – R1200 GS

the knob anti-clockwise (LOW arrow) to reduce pre-load, and clockwise (HIGH arrow) to increase pre-load.

15 Damping adjustment is made by turning the adjuster screw on the lower end of the shock **(see illustration)**.

16 On R1200 RT models, for rider-only use, turn the screw fully clockwise (H arrow), then turn it ¾ of a turn anti-clockwise (S arrow).

17 On R1200 R models, for rider-only use, turn the screw fully clockwise (H arrow), then turn it 1½ turns anti-clockwise (S arrow).

18 If further adjustments are required on either model, turn the screw clockwise (H arrow) for harder damping and anti-clockwise (S arrow) for softer damping.

Electronic suspension adjustment (ESA)

19 A combination of spring pre-load and damping options can be selected using the ESA button on the left-hand switch assembly. Both shock absorbers are adjustable simultaneously by the ESA system – there is no provision for adjusting the shocks individually or manually. Adjustments are complete when the ESA display stops flashing and disappears from the multi-function panel. In cold weather make adjustments before any passenger boards the machine.

R1200 GS and GS Adventure

20 Turn the ignition ON and press the ESA button briefly to display the current setting. The selected options are displayed at the bottom of the multi-function display panel on the instrument cluster – damping (COMF, NORM, SPORT etc.) on the left and spring pre-load (a helmet icon for road riding and a terrain icon for off-road riding) on the right.

21 To change the damping setting, turn the ignition ON and note the selected pre-load icon, then press the ESA button to scroll through each corresponding damping option in turn. Pre-load set for road riding – COMF (comfortable damping), NORM (normal damping) and SPORT (sports damping). Pre-load set for off-road riding – SOFT, NORM, HARD. Stop pressing the button when the desired setting is displayed and allow a few seconds for the system to adjust.

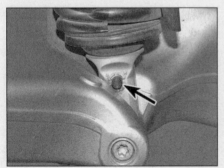

10.7 Suspension damping adjuster screw – R1200 GS

10.15 Suspension damping adjuster screw – R1200 RT and R1200 R

The ESA display will then disappear from the panel.

22 To change the pre-load setting, first start the engine. Press the ESA button briefly to display the current setting, note the selected pre-load icon, then press the ESA button to scroll through each pre-load option in turn. For road riding – helmet icon (rider only), helmet and bag icon (rider with luggage), two helmets icon (rider, passenger and luggage). For off-road riding – small mountains (generally smooth terrain), large mountains (severe, uneven terrain). Stop pressing the button when the desired setting is displayed. Wait until adjustment is complete and the display stops flashing before riding the motorcycle. The ESA display will then disappear from the panel.

R1200 RT and R1200 R

23 The procedure for adjusting the suspension settings on these models is as described above, with the following exceptions:

● On R1200 RT models, turn the ignition ON and start the engine to change both the suspension damping and pre-load settings.

● On R1200 R models, the selected ESA options are displayed in the centre of the multi-function panel.

● On these machines, only road riding pre-load settings are available (see Step 22).

● On these machines, only COMF, NORM and SPORT damping options are available (see Step 21).

ESA operation check

Note: *If the check and measurements do not give the results as described, it is likely the shock is defective and must be renewed, although it is advisable to have this confirmed by a BMW dealer. No individual components are available.*

R1200 GS models

24 Refer to Steps 20 to 22 above to check the damping function.

25 To check the spring pre-load function, sit on the bike with the stands up and start the engine. Press the ESA button, then press and hold it down until the helmet icon appears on the display. Note any change in the pre-load, then select the off-road pre-load setting large mountains icon. You should notice the suspension rise considerably.

26 If there is no real difference in ride height, measure the distance between the top of the spring and the main body of the shock – note that the sleeve inside the top of the spring is part of the adjusting mechanism **(see illustration)**. This distance should be 11 to 13 mm on the front shock and 9 to 10 mm on the rear in the large mountains (severe, uneven terrain) off-road riding pre-load position.

27 The distance can be checked in other pre-load positions (see table).

Icon	Front shock	Rear shock
One helmet	0 mm	0 mm
One helmet and bag	0 mm	4 to 6 mm
Two helmets	0 mm	9 to 10 mm
Small mountains	5 to 7 mm	4 to 6 mm
Large mountains	11 to 13 mm	9 to 10 mm

R1200 RT models

28 To check that the ESA is changing the damping, sit on the bike with the stands up. Turn the ignition ON and start the engine.

29 Use the ESA button to select the COMF (comfortable damping) setting (see Step 21). Turn the ignition OFF.

30 Move your weight forwards in the seat and start a 'rocking' effect in the suspension, then turn the ignition ON – as the ESA re-adjusts, there should be a noticeable increase in the suspension damping for a short while. Turn the ignition OFF.

31 If no change is noted in the damping, have the system checked by a BMW dealer using the BMW MOSS diagnostic tester.

32 The operation of the spring pre-load function can only be checked using the BMW MOSS diagnostic tester.

R1200 R models

33 To check that the ESA is changing the damping, sit on the bike with the stands up. Turn the ignition ON and use the ESA button to select the COMF (comfortable damping) setting (see Step 21). Turn the ignition OFF.

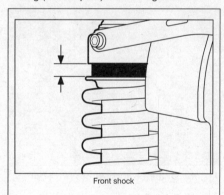
Front shock

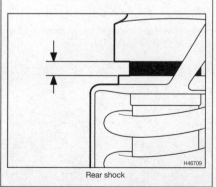
Rear shock

10.26 ESA shock pre-load measurement points

34 Move your weight forwards in the seat and start a 'rocking' effect in the suspension, then turn the ignition ON – as the ESA re-adjusts, there should be a noticeable increase in the suspension damping. Turn the ignition OFF.

35 If no change is noted in the damping, have the system checked by a BMW dealer using the BMW MOSS diagnostic tester.

36 To check that the ESA is changing the spring pre-load, first remove the seat cowling to access the rear shock absorber (see Chapter 6).

37 Sit on the bike with the stands up. Turn the ignition ON and start the engine and use the ESA button to select a new pre-load setting (see Step 22). Turn the ignition OFF. Depending upon whether the ESA has increased or decreased the pre-load, there should have been a noticeable rise or fall at the rear of the machine.

38 If there is no real difference in ride height, measure the distance between the top of the spring and the main body of the rear shock – note that the sleeve inside the top of the spring is part of the adjusting mechanism **(see illustration 10.26)**.

39 With the pre-load on its softest setting (helmet icon – rider only) there should be zero clearance. With the pre-load on its middle setting (helmet and bag icon – rider with luggage) there should be 4 to 6 mm clearance. With the pre-load on its hardest setting (two helmets icon – rider, passenger and luggage) there should be 9 to 10 mm clearance.

11 Swingarm and driveshaft

Removal

Special tool: *A slide-hammer is necessary for this procedure (see illustrations 11.16a and b).*

1 The swingarm, driveshaft and final drive unit can be removed as an assembly. If the final drive unit has already been removed, ignore the steps which do not apply.

2 Position the bike on its centre stand or support it securely on an auxiliary stand.

3 Remove the seat (see Chapter 6).

4 On R1200 RT models, remove the fairing side panels and the lower section of the rear mudguard (see Chapter 6) and the left and right-hand footrest mounting brackets (see Section 3).

5 Remove the exhaust silencer (see Chapter 3).

6 Remove the rear wheel (see Chapter 5).

11.7a Lift out the document tray

11.7b Undo the screws (arrowed) . . .

11.7c . . . and lift off the brake hose guide

11.7d Trace the wiring from the speed sensor . . .

11.7e . . . and disconnect it at the connector

7 Lift out the document tray, where fitted (see illustration). Undo the screws securing the rear brake hose guide and lift the guide off the Paralever arm (see illustrations). Trace the wiring from the rear wheel speed sensor to the wiring connector and disconnect it (see illustrations). Note the location of the cable-ties securing the wiring to the frame, then cut the ties and secure the wiring next to the final drive unit, well clear of the rear sub-frame.

8 Displace the rear brake caliper (see Chapter 5), then secure the caliper to the rear sub-frame. Note that it is not necessary to disconnect the brake hose from the caliper.

9 Remove the rear shock absorber (see Section 9). Place a support (a block of wood or an axle stand is ideal) underneath the final drive unit. Do not place the support under the rear brake disc

10 Counter-hold the bolts and undo the nuts securing the Paralever arm to the swingarm (front) and final drive unit (rear) (see illustration). Withdraw the bolts and lift the Paralever arm off, noting the location of the sealing washers on both sides at the front of the arm (see illustrations).

11 Cut the cable-tie securing the driveshaft boot to the rear of the gearbox (see illustration).

12 Remove the support underneath the final drive unit, then carefully tilt the unit back, displacing the coupling boot, to expose the

11.10a Undo the nuts (arrowed) . . .

11.10b . . . then withdraw the front bolt . . .

11.10c . . . and the rear bolt

11.10d Note the location of the sealing washers

11.11 Cut the cable-tie on the driveshaft boot

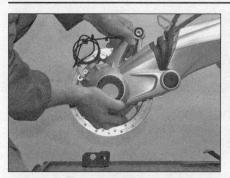

11.12a Remove the support and tilt the drive unit back . . .

11.12b . . . to displace the coupling boot (arrowed) . . .

11.12c . . . and expose the driveshaft coupling

rear driveshaft coupling **(see illustrations)**. Note how the splined end of the bevel gear in the final drive housing locates inside the driveshaft coupling **(see illustration)**.

13 A circlip inside the front driveshaft coupling secures the coupling to the gearbox output shaft. To separate the driveshaft from the gearbox, first pull the driveshaft boot away from the gearbox. Insert a suitable bar or strong screwdriver between the two halves of the front driveshaft coupling so that it bears on the end of the gearbox output shaft, then prise the coupling off the gearbox shaft **(see illustrations)**. Withdraw the driveshaft from the swingarm, noting which way round it fits **(see illustration)**.

14 Undo the screws on the right-hand swingarm bearing pin **(see illustration)**.

15 Prise the cover off the left-hand bearing

11.12d Note how the splined end of the bevel gear (arrowed) locates inside the coupling

pin **(see illustration)**. Loosen the pin locknut, then unscrew the pin **(see illustrations)**.

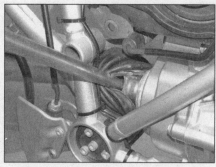

11.13a Lever the front driveshaft coupling off the gearbox output shaft . . .

16 Support the swingarm assembly. Using a slide-hammer or similar tool, threaded into the

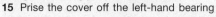

CIRCLIP

H46132

11.13b . . . by releasing the internal circlip from the groove in the output shaft

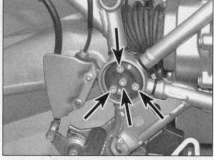

11.13c Withdraw the driveshaft from the swingarm

11.14 Undo the screws on the right-hand swingarm bearing pin

11.15a Prise the cover off the left-hand bearing pin . . .

11.15b . . . then loosen the locknut (arrowed) . . .

11.15c . . . and unscrew the pin

11.16a Using a slide-hammer . . .

11.16b . . . to draw the right-hand bearing pin out

11.17 Lift the swingarm assembly off

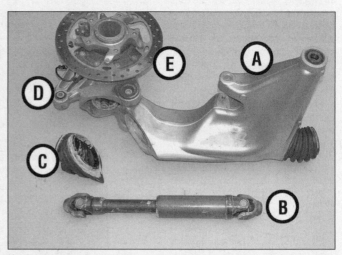

11.18 Swingarm assembly components. Swingarm (A), driveshaft (B), coupling boot (C), final drive unit (D) and rear brake disc (E)

centre hole in the right-hand bearing pin, draw the pin out **(see illustrations)**.

17 Lift the swingarm assembly off **(see illustration)**.

18 If required for inspection, lift off the coupling boot **(see illustration)**.

19 If required, follow the procedure in Section 12 and separate the final drive unit from the swingarm.

Inspection

20 Remove the driveshaft boot from the swingarm, noting the location of the internal coupling **(see illustration)**. Check the condition of the boot and renew it if it is cracked or split.

21 Clean all the components thoroughly, removing all traces of dirt, corrosion and grease.

22 Inspect the components closely for signs of wear or accident damage. Any

damaged or worn components must be renewed.

23 Check the driveshaft coupling universal joints for wear. The joints should move smoothly and freely with no sign of roughness

and there should be no play between the halves of the coupling **(see illustration)**. If wear is evident, a new driveshaft must be fitted – individual components are not available..

24 Inspect the splines for wear **(see**

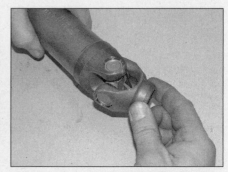

11.20 Driveshaft boot and internal coupling (arrowed)

11.23 Check the universal joints for wear

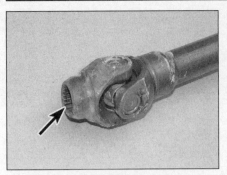

11.24 Inspect the splines inside the driveshaft couplings

11.25a Check the condition of the swingarm bearings . . .

11.25b . . . and the surface of the bearing pins (arrowed)

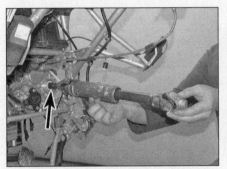

11.27a Align the driveshaft with the gearbox output shaft (arrowed) . . .

11.27b . . . and hammer the front coupling into place . . .

11.27c . . . until it is secured by the internal circlip

illustration). The driveshaft couplings should be a sliding fit on the splined end of the bevel gear and on the gearbox output shaft. If there is excessive clearance at either end of the shaft the worn components must be renewed. To renew the gearbox output shaft, refer to Chapter 2, Section 30.

25 Inspect the swingarm bearings and the surface of the bearing pins **(see illustrations)**. Refer to *Tools and Workshop Tips* in the *Reference* section for details of bearing inspection and renewal.

26 Inspect the bush in the front end of the Paralever arm. If the bush has deteriorated it should be renewed. Use a drawbolt arrangement to press the old bush out and the new bush in (see *Tools and Workshop Tips* in the *Reference* section).

Installation

27 Lubricate the gearbox output shaft splines with molybdenum disulphide grease. Push the driveshaft onto the output shaft, then hammer the front driveshaft coupling into place to ensure the internal circlip is located in its groove in the output shaft **(see illustrations)**. Use a suitable length of wood or soft metal (aluminium or brass) as a drift. Make sure the driveshaft is secure on the output shaft.

28 Lubricate both ends of the driveshaft boot with silicone grease and install the boot on the swingarm **(see illustration 11.20)**.

29 Lubricate the right-hand bearing pin with a smear of grease, then slide the swingarm over the driveshaft and press the pin into place to secure it **(see illustrations)**.

30 Back-off the locknut on the left-hand bearing pin, lubricate the pin and install it finger-tight **(see illustration 11.15c)**. Place a support underneath the swingarm.

31 Tighten the three outer screws and the shorter single centre screw securing the right-hand bearing pin to the torque setting specified at the beginning of this Chapter **(see illustration 11.14)**

32 Tighten the left-hand bearing pin to the specified torque setting (first to the initial setting, then loosen it and retighten to the final setting), then mark the position of the pin with a dab of paint **(see illustration)**. Tighten the locknut to the specified torque setting. Check that the bearing pin is still in the same position and check that the swingarm moves freely up and down.

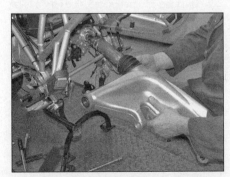

11.29a Slide the swingarm over the driveshaft . . .

11.29b . . . and secure it with the right-hand bearing pin

11.32 Mark the position of the bearing pin

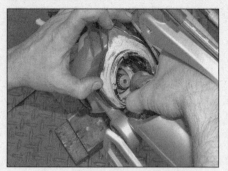

11.37a Engage the splined end of the bevel gear inside the driveshaft coupling

11.37b Locate the lip of the coupling boot inside the swingarm . . .

11.37c . . . and secure the final drive unit to the Paralever arm with the bolt

33 Install the rear shock absorber (see Section 9).
34 Ensure that the driveshaft boot is located fully around the end of the gearbox and secure it with a new cable-tie **(see illustration 11.11)**.
35 If removed, install the final drive unit (see Section 12).
36 Fit the sealing washers onto the front end of the Paralever arm **(see illustration 11.10d)**. Position the arm inside the bracket on the rear sub-frame and secure it with the bolt **(see illustration 11.10b)**.
37 Lubricate the end of the coupling boot with silicone grease, then lift the final drive unit and engage the splined end of the bevel gear inside the driveshaft coupling **(see illustration)**. Ensure that the lip of the boot locates correctly inside the end of the swingarm and secure the

final drive unit to the Paralever arm with the bolt **(see illustrations)**.
38 Apply a suitable non-permanent thread locking compound to the nuts and install the washers and nuts on the bolts securing the Paralever arm **(see illustration 11.10a)**. Counter-hold the bolts and tighten the nuts to the specified torque settings.
39 Install the remaining components in the reverse order of removal.

12 Final drive unit

Note: *This procedure covers removal and installation of the final drive unit. Further dismantling and set-up of the final drive unit*

requires special tools and is beyond the scope of this manual. If the final drive unit is thought to be faulty have it checked by a BMW dealer.

Removal

1 Position the bike on its centre stand or support it securely on an auxiliary stand.
2 Remove the exhaust silencer (see Chapter 3).
3 Remove the rear wheel (see Chapter 5).
4 On R1200 RT models, remove the right-hand footrest mounting bracket (see Section 3).
5 Remove the seat (see Chapter 6), then lift out the document tray, where fitted **(see illustration 11.7a)**. Undo the screws securing the rear brake hose guide and lift the guide off the Paralever arm **(see illustration 11.7b and c)**. Trace the wiring from the rear wheel speed sensor to the wiring connector and disconnect it **(see illustrations 11.7d and e)**. Note the location of the cable-ties securing the wiring to the frame, then cut the ties and secure the wiring next to the final drive unit, well clear of the rear sub-frame.
6 Displace the rear brake caliper (see Chapter 5), then secure the caliper to the rear sub-frame. Note that it is not necessary to disconnect the brake hose from the caliper.
7 Note the location of the breather on the top of the drive housing – if required, pull the breather out and clean it **(see illustrations)**. If it is damaged or deteriorated, fit a new one on installation.
8 Undo the nut and remove the washer on the bolt securing the Paralever arm to the final drive unit **(see illustration)**. Support the drive unit and withdraw the bolt, then carefully tilt the unit back, displacing the coupling boot **(see illustration)**. Support the drive unit on a block of wood. Note how the splined end of the bevel gear in the final drive housing locates inside the driveshaft coupling **(see illustration 11.12d)**. Ease the coupling boot off the drive unit, noting which way round it fits **(see illustration 11.12b)**.
9 Prise the cover off the right-hand pivot sleeve on the drive unit, then counter-hold

12.7a Location of drive housing breather

12.7b Pull the breather out for cleaning

12.8a Undo the nut and washer (arrowed)

12.8b Tilt the unit back and displace the boot

12.9a Prise off the cover . . .

12.9b . . . then counter-hold the pivot sleeve and undo the pivot bolt

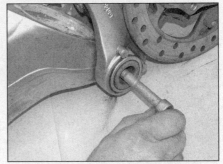

12.10 Withdraw the pivot bolt

the pivot sleeve and undo the pivot bolt **(see illustrations)**.

10 Withdraw the pivot bolt **(see illustration)**.

11 Support the drive unit and pull out the left-hand pivot pin, noting the location of the seal, then use a suitable drift to drive the right-hand pivot sleeve out **(see illustrations)**. Lift the drive unit off, noting the location of the spacer on the inside of the right-hand bearing housing **(see illustration)**.

Inspection

12 Clean the drive unit thoroughly, removing all traces of dirt and corrosion. Check for any evidence of oil leakage, particularly behind the brake disc flange and around the bevel gear shaft **(see illustration)**. Renewal of the drive unit seals must be undertaken by a BMW dealer.

13 Inspect the bearing surfaces of the pivot

sleeve and the pivot pin **(see illustration)**. If they are worn, pitted or scored, renew them. Inspect the corresponding bearings in the drive unit – a needle roller bearing is fitted in

12.11a Pull out the left-hand pivot pin, noting the seal (arrowed)

the left-hand side and a sealed ball bearing is in the right-hand side **(see illustrations)**. Note that the ball bearing is secured by a circlip. Refer to *Tools and Workshop Tips* in

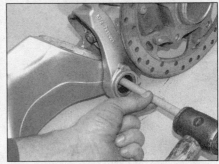

12.11b Use a suitable drift . . .

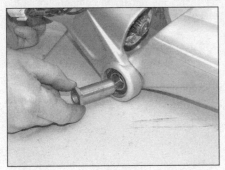

12.11c . . . to drive out the right-hand pivot sleeve

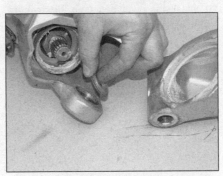

12.11d Note the spacer on the inside of the right-hand bearing housing

12.12 Check for oil leakage around the brake disc flange (arrowed)

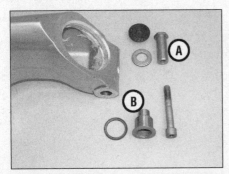

12.13a Inspect the bearing surfaces of the pivot sleeve (A) and the pivot pin (B)

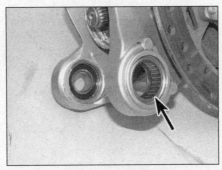

12.13b Left-hand side needle roller bearing (arrowed)

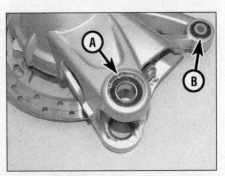

12.13c Sealed ball bearing is secured by circlip (A). Note location of bush (B)

12.18 Lubricate the coupling boot with silicone grease before installation

12.19a Press the pivot sleeve in from the right-hand side . . .

12.19b . . . and the pivot pin in from the left-hand side

12.20 Install the pivot bolt

the *Reference* section for details of bearing inspection and renewal.

14 Inspect the bush in the top of the unit housing **(see illustration 12.13c)**. If the bush has deteriorated it should be renewed. Use a drawbolt arrangement to press the old bush out and the new bush in (see *Tools and Workshop Tips* in the *Reference* section).

Installation

15 Press the spacer into the inside of the right-hand bearing housing **(see illustration 12.11d)**.

16 Lubricate the splined end of the bevel gear with molybdenum disulphide grease.

17 Lubricate the pivot sleeve and the pivot pin with a smear of grease. Fit a new seal to the pivot pin.

18 Lubricate both ends of the coupling boot with silicone grease and install the boot on the drive unit **(see illustration)**.

19 Support the drive unit in position and press the pivot sleeve in from the right-hand side and the pivot pin in from the left-hand side **(see illustrations)**.

20 Install the pivot bolt **(see illustration)**. Counter-hold the pivot sleeve and tighten the pivot bolt to the torque setting specified at the beginning of this Chapter **(see illustration 12.9b)**.

21 Lift the final drive unit and engage the splined end of the bevel gear inside the driveshaft coupling **(see illustration 11.37a)**. Ensure that the lip of the coupling boot locates correctly inside the end of the swingarm and insert the bolt to secure the final drive unit to the Paralever arm **(see illustrations 11.37b and c)**.

22 Apply a suitable non-permanent thread locking compound to the nut and install the washer and nut on the bolt **(see illustration 11.10c)**. Counter-hold the bolt and tighten the nut to the specified torque setting.

23 Install the cover on the right-hand pivot sleeve **(see illustration 12.9a)**.

24 Install the remaining components in the reverse order of removal.

Chapter 5
Brakes, wheels and tyres

Contents

Section number

ABS 17
ASC (Automatic Stability Control) system 18
Brake fluid change and brake bleeding 10
Brake fluid level check . . . . see *Pre-ride checks*
Brake hoses, pipes and unions 9
Brake light switches . . . . see Chapter 7
Brake pad renewal 2
Brake pad wear check . . . . see Chapter 1
Brake system check . . . . see Chapter 1
Front brake calipers 3
Front brake discs 4
Front brake master cylinder 5
Front wheel. 12

Section number

General information 1
RDC (tyre pressure monitoring) system 19
Rear brake caliper 6
Rear brake disc 7
Rear brake master cylinder 8
Rear wheel 13
Spokes – wire spoked wheels 15
Tyres – general information 16
Tyre sizes, pressures and condition . . . . see *Pre-ride checks*
Wheel check. . . . . see Chapter 1
Wheel bearings. 14
Wheel runout and alignment 11

Degrees of difficulty

Easy, suitable for novice with little experience 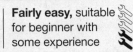	**Fairly easy,** suitable for beginner with some experience	**Fairly difficult,** suitable for competent DIY mechanic	**Difficult,** suitable for experienced DIY mechanic	**Very difficult,** suitable for expert DIY or professional

Specifications

Front brake

Brake fluid type	DOT 4
Brake pad friction material thickness (min)	1.0 mm
Disc thickness	
Standard.	4.5 mm
Service limit	4.0 mm
Disc diameter	
R1200 GS and GS Adventure.	305 mm
R1200 RT and R1200 R	320 mm
Runout (service limit)	0.15 mm

Rear brake

Brake fluid type	DOT 4
Disc thickness	
Standard.	5.0 mm
Service limit	4.5 mm
Disc diameter (all models)	265 mm
Runout (service limit)	0.35 mm

Wheels

Maximum wheel runout (axial and radial)	
Cast wheels (front and rear)	1.5 mm
Spoke wheels (front and rear).	1.7 mm

Tyres

Tyre pressures	see *Pre-ride checks*	
Tyre sizes*	**Front**	**Rear**
R1200 GS and GS Adventure.	110/80 H19	150/70 H17
R1200 RT and R1200 R	120/70 ZR 17	180/55 ZR 17

*Also refer to your owners handbook or the tyre information label under the bike's seat.

Torque settings

Brake hose banjo bolts. . . . . 24 Nm
Brake pipe flare nuts to adapters. . . . . 24 Nm
Brake pipe flare nuts to pressure modulator . . . . 14 Nm
Brake pipe adapters to frame. . . . . 8 Nm
Front axle . . . . 50 Nm
Front axle clamp bolt . . . . 19 Nm
Front brake caliper bleed valve
   R1200 GS, GS Adventure and R1200 RT. 10 Nm
   R1200 R . . . . 8 Nm
Front brake master cylinder bleed valve . . . . 5 Nm
Front brake master cylinder clamp bolts . . . . 8 Nm
Front brake caliper mounting bolts . . . . 30 Nm
Front brake caliper pad pin . . . . 7 Nm
Front brake disc bolts . . . . 19 Nm
Rear brake caliper bleed valve. . . . . 5 Nm
Rear brake caliper mounting bolts. . . . . 24 Nm
Rear brake disc bolts
   Initial setting . . . . 12 Nm
   Final setting . . . . 30 Nm
Rear brake master cylinder mounting bolts
   R1200 GS, GS Adventure and R1200 R. . . . . 8 Nm
   R1200 RT . . . . 6 Nm
Rear wheel bolts. . . . . 60 Nm
Spoke (cross-spoke wheels) – R1200 GS and GS Adventure
   Nipple initial setting . . . . 1 Nm
   Nipple final setting . . . . 4 Nm
   Grub screw. . . . . 1 Nm
Spoke – R1200 R Classic. . . . . 3.5 Nm
Wheel speed sensor screws. . . . . 4 Nm

1 General information

All models covered in this manual are fitted with front and rear hydraulically operated disc brakes. The front brake calipers have four opposed pistons each, and the rear brake has two pistons in a sliding caliper. An ABS (anti-lock braking system) that prevents the wheels from locking-up under hard braking is fitted as standard equipment to R1200 RT models and is available as optional equipment (OE) on all other models.

The cast alloy wheels on R1200 GS, R1200 RT and R1200 R models are designed for tubeless tyres only. R1200 GS Adventure models have wire spoked wheels, but these are of a cross-spoke design; the spokes are attached to the rim outside of the tyre's sealing area, thus permitting the use of tubeless tyres. These wheels are available as optional equipment (OE) on R1200 GS models.

R1200 R Classic models have conventional wire spoked wheels requiring the use of tubed tyres.

Caution: Disc brake components rarely require disassembly. Do not disassemble components unless absolutely necessary. The dust created by the brake system may contain asbestos, which is harmful to your health. Never blow it out with compressed air and don't inhale any of it. An approved filtering mask should be worn when working on the brakes. Do not use solvents for cleaning brake system components. Solvents will cause the seals to swell and distort. Use only clean brake fluid or dedicated brake system cleaner. Use care when working with brake fluid as it can injure your eyes and will damage painted surfaces and plastic parts.

2 Brake pad renewal

⚠ *Warning: The dust created by the brake system may contain asbestos, which is harmful to your health. Never blow it out* with compressed air and don't inhale any of it. An approved filtering mask should be worn when working on the brakes.

Front brake pads

1 On R1200 GS, GS Adventure and R1200 RT models, pull out the spring clip and unscrew the pad pin **(see illustrations)**. Lift off the pad spring, noting how it fits, and withdraw the pads from the caliper **(see illustrations)**.

2 On R1200 R models, remove the two screws to free the pad spring **(see illustration)**. Withdraw the R-clip from the pad pin, then push the pin out from the inner side of the caliper **(see illustration)**.

2.1a Pull out the spring clip . . .

2.1b . . . and unscrew the pad pin

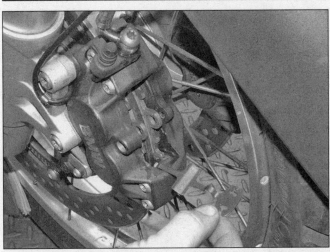
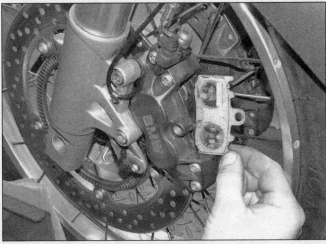

2.1c Lift off the pad spring . . .

2.1d . . . and pull the pads out of the caliper

Remove the pads from the caliper **(see illustration)**.
Caution: Do not operate the front brake lever whilst the pads are out of the caliper.
3 Inspect the surface of each pad for contamination and check that the friction material has not worn down to the wear limits (refer to Chapter 1, Section 11) or the minimum thickness (see Specifications).
4 If any pad is worn, fouled with oil or grease, or heavily scored or damaged, all the pads must be renewed as a set. Note that it is not possible to degrease the friction material – if the pads are contaminated in any way they must be renewed.
5 If the pads are in good condition clean them carefully, using a fine wire brush which is completely free of oil and grease to remove all traces of road dirt and corrosion. Use a pointed instrument to dig out any embedded particles of foreign matter. Ensure that the anti-chatter shims are a firm fit on the back of the pads.
6 Check the condition of the brake disc (see Section 4).
7 Remove all traces of corrosion from the pad pin. Inspect the pin for signs of wear and renew it if necessary. Renew the pin clip if it is corroded or sprained.

8 If you are installing new pads, follow the procedure in Section 3 and displace the caliper, then clean around the exposed section of each piston inside the caliper to remove any dirt or debris that could damage the piston seals **(see illustration)**.
9 Push the pistons back into the caliper to create room for the new pads – BMW produces a service tool to do this (Part Nos. 341531 and 341532). Alternatively, use a commercially available piston spreading tool **(see illustration 2.21)**, use a piece of wood as leverage, or install the old pads and use a

metal bar or a screwdriver inserted between them. Do not lever against the brake disc. Do not push the pistons back further than is necessary to install the pads.
10 If displaced, install the caliper (see Section 3). Smear the backs of the pads and the shank of the pad pin with copper-based grease, making sure that none gets on the front or sides of the pads, then insert the pads into the caliper so that the friction material faces the disc **(see illustration)**.
11 On R1200 GS, GS Adventure and R1200 RT models, install the pad spring, ensuring

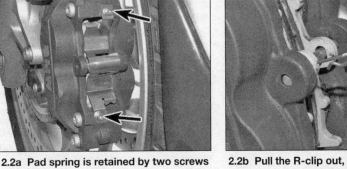

2.2a Pad spring is retained by two screws

2.2b Pull the R-clip out, then push out the pad pin . . .

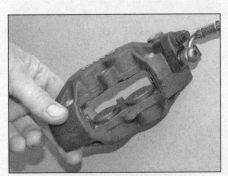

2.2c . . . and lift out the pads

2.8 Clean the inside of the caliper, especially around the pistons

2.10 Ensure the friction material on the pads faces the disc

2.11 Ensure the pad spring (arrowed) is fitted correctly

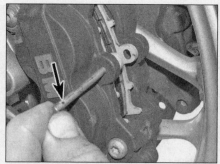

2.12a Position the clip hole (arrowed) correctly when fitting the pad pin

2.12b Pads and pin installed and secured by R-clip (arrowed)

2.16a Pull out the R-clip . . .

2.16b . . . and drive out the pad pin

2.17 Pull out the pads

it is the right way round **(see illustration)**. Insert the pad pin so that it passes through both pads and over the top of the spring, then tighten the pin to the specified torque setting **(see illustration 2.1b)**. Secure the pad pin with the spring clip.

12 On R1200 R models, insert the pad pin from the outside of the caliper, rotated so that its hole is accessible, and pass it through both pads and into the caliper bore on the inner side **(see illustration)**. Insert the R-clip through the hole in the pin **(see illustration)**. Install the pad spring and tighten the screws securely.

13 Operate the brake lever several times to bring the pads back into contact with the discs.

14 Check the operation of the brakes before riding the motorcycle.

Rear brake pads

15 On R1200 GS and GS Adventure models, remove the rear spray guard (see Chapter 6).

16 Pull out the R-clip, then use a suitable punch to drive the pad pin out **(see illustrations)**.

17 Withdraw the pads from the caliper **(see illustration)**.

Caution: Do not operate the rear brake pedal whilst the pads are out of the caliper.

18 Inspect the surface of each pad for contamination and check that the friction material has not worn down to the wear limit hole as described in Chapter 1, Section 11 or the minimum thickness (see Specifications).

19 Follow Steps 4 to 7 to assess the condition of the pads and to check the disc, pad pin and R-clip. Note the spring clip on the pad pin and ensure that it is secure **(see illustration)**.

20 If you are installing new pads, follow the procedure in Section 6 and displace the caliper, then clean around the exposed section of both pistons to remove any dirt or debris that could damage the piston seals. Note the location of the pad spring inside the caliper **(see illustration)**.

21 Push the pistons back into the caliper to create room for the new pads – BMW produces a service tool to do this (Part Nos. 341531 and 341536). Alternatively, use a commercially available piston spreading tool **(see illustration)**, use a piece of wood as leverage, or install the old pads and use a metal bar or a screwdriver inserted between them. Do not lever against the brake disc. Do not push the pistons back further than is necessary to install the pads.

22 Smear the backs of the pads and the

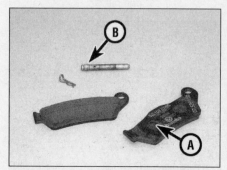

2.19 Location of the wear limit hole (A) in the back of the brake pad. Note spring clip (B) on pad pin

2.20 Location of the pad spring inside the rear brake caliper

2.21 Install the piston spreading tool as shown

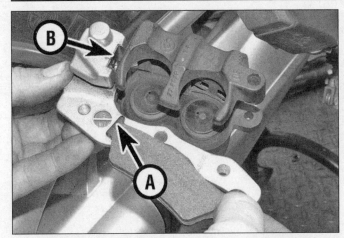

2.23a Locate end (A) of pad against caliper bracket (B)

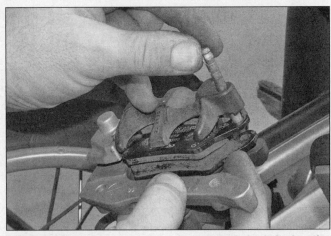

2.23b Ensure the pad pin passes through the holes in both pads

shank of the pad pin with copper-based grease, making sure that none gets on the front or sides of the pads.

23 If the caliper has been displaced, the pads can be installed before fitting the caliper onto the bike. Ensure that the pad spring is in position; the stamped arrow on the spring must point in the forward direction when in situ **(see illustration 2.20)**. Insert the pads so that the flat ends are pressed firmly against the caliper bracket and the friction material on both pads faces the disc **(see illustration)**. Press the pads against the pad spring and insert the pad pin **(see illustration)**. Install the caliper (see Section 6). Now go to Step 25.

24 If the caliper has not been removed, insert the pads into the caliper so that the friction material faces the disc **(see illustration 2.17)**. Ensure that both pads are pressed firmly against the caliper bracket, then align the holes in the pads with the holes in the caliper and insert the pad pin.

25 Use a suitable punch to drive the pad pin in so that the spring clip engages in the caliper **(see illustration)**.

26 Secure the pad pin with the R-clip **(see illustration)**.

27 On R1200 GS and GS Adventure models, install the rear spray guard (see Chapter 6).

28 Operate the brake pedal several times to bring the pads into contact with the disc. Check the operation of the brakes before riding the motorcycle.

2.25 Drive the pad pin in until the spring clip engages

2.26 Note the location of the R-clip (arrowed)

filtering mask should be worn when working on the brakes. Do not use petroleum-based solvents for cleaning brake system components – they will cause the seals to swell and distort. Use only clean brake fluid or dedicated brake system cleaner. Use care when working with brake fluid as it can injure your eyes and will damage painted surfaces and plastic parts

Removal

1 It is only necessary to disconnect the brake hose if the caliper is being removed completely. The brake hose can remain attached if you are just displacing the caliper for wheel removal, pad renewal or cleaning.

2 If poor brake action is the result of a sticking piston, or if a piston seal has failed and brake fluid is leaking from the caliper, the caliper must be overhauled. This procedure must be undertaken by a BMW dealer.

3 Remove the brake pads (see Section 2).

4 Cover the area around the end of the brake hose with clean rag to catch fluid spills. Note the alignment of the brake hose banjo union with the brake caliper, then undo union bolt and separate the hose from the caliper **(see illustration)**. Note the sealing washers fitted to both sides of the banjo union **(see illustration)**.

3 Front brake calipers

⚠ *Warning: If a caliper indicates the need for an overhaul (usually due to leaking fluid or sticky operation), all old brake fluid should be flushed from the system. Also, the dust created by the brake system may contain asbestos, which is harmful to your health. Never blow it out with compressed air and don't inhale any of it. An approved*

3.4a Note the alignment of the union (arrowed) with the caliper

3.4b Sealing washers are fitted to both sides of the banjo union

3.6a Undo the bolts (arrowed) . . .

3.6b . . . and slide the caliper off the disc

4.2 Measuring the thickness of the disc with a micrometer

5 Plug the hose end or wrap a plastic bag tightly around it to minimise fluid loss and prevent dirt entering the system. **Note:** *Do not operate the brake lever while the brake hose is disconnected.* Discard the sealing washers as new ones must be used on installation. Plug the caliper to avoid fluid spillage.

6 Undo the caliper mounting bolts and slide the caliper off the disc **(see illustrations)**.

Installation

7 Ensure that the pistons are pushed back into the caliper to create room for the pads (see Section 2).

8 Slide the caliper onto the brake disc and install the mounting bolts, then tighten the bolts to the torque setting specified at the beginning of this Chapter **(see illustrations 3.6b and a)**.

9 Connect the brake hose to the caliper, using new sealing washers on each side of the banjo union. Align the union as noted on removal **(see illustration 3.4a)**. Tighten the banjo union bolt to the torque setting specified at the beginning of this Chapter.

10 Install the brake pads (see Section 2).

11 Top-up the master cylinder reservoir with DOT 4 brake fluid (see *Pre-ride checks*) and bleed the brake system as described in Section 10.

12 Check for leaks and thoroughly test the operation of the brakes before riding the motorcycle.

4	Front brake discs

Inspection

1 Inspect the surface of the disc for score marks and other damage. Light scratches are normal after use and won't affect brake operation, but deep grooves and heavy score marks will reduce braking efficiency and accelerate pad wear. If a disc is badly grooved it must be machined or renewed.

2 The disc must not be machined or allowed to wear down to a thickness less than the service limit as listed in this Chapter's Specifications and as marked on the disc itself. The thickness of the disc can be checked with a micrometer **(see illustration)**. If the thickness of the disc is less than the service limit, it must be renewed.

3 To check disc runout, support the bike upright so that the front wheel is raised off the ground. Mount a dial gauge to the fork slider, with the plunger on the gauge touching the surface of the disc about 10 mm (1/2 in) from the outer edge **(see illustration)**. Rotate the wheel and watch the gauge needle, then compare the reading with the limit listed in the Specifications at the beginning of this Chapter.

4 If the runout is greater than the service

limit, check the wheel bearings for play (see Chapter 1). If the bearings are worn they must be renewed (see Section 14). If the bearings are good, either the disc is warped, or the rivet and washer assemblies in the disc mountings are damaged or worn **(see illustration 4.9)** – remove the disc to check. In both cases a new disc will have to be fitted – individual components are not available.

Removal

5 Remove the wheel (see Section 12).

Caution: Do not lay the wheel down and allow it to rest on either disc – the disc could become warped. Set the wheel on wood blocks so the disc doesn't support the weight of the wheel.

6 Mark the relationship of the disc to the wheel, so it can be installed in the same position, and mark the disc itself to indicate left-or right-hand side, and which is the outer face. Undo the disc retaining bolts, loosening them a little at a time in a criss-cross pattern to avoid distorting the disc **(see illustration)**.

7 Lift off the disc. On ABS models, if working on the left side disc, note the location of the sensor ring **(see illustration)**.

Installation

8 Before installing the disc, make sure there is no dirt or corrosion where the disc seats. If the disc does not sit flat when it is bolted down,

4.3 Set-up for checking brake disc runout with a dial gauge

4.6 Loosen the disc retaining bolts in a criss-cross pattern to avoid distorting the disc

4.7 Location of the ABS sensor ring

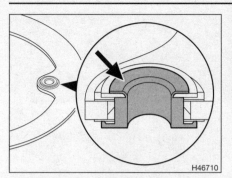

4.9 Disc must be installed with the beaded edge (arrowed) facing outwards

5.2a Undo the locknut . . .

5.2b . . . and remove the pivot bolt

it will appear to be warped when checked or when the brake is used.

9 If applicable, lay the ABS sensor ring in place on the wheel. Lay the disc on the wheel, aligning the previously made matchmarks if installing the original discs. Note that the side with the beaded edge to the rivet centres must face outwards **(see illustration)**.

10 Clean up the threads of the disc mounting bolts and apply a suitable non-permanent thread-locking compound. Note that the bolts are micro-encapsulated with locking compound when new and BMW advises that new bolts are fitted.

11 Tighten the bolts evenly and a little at a time in a criss-cross pattern to the torque setting specified at the beginning of this Chapter.

12 Clean the disc using acetone or brake system cleaner. If a new brake disc has been installed, remove any protective coating from its working surfaces.

13 Install the wheel (see Section 12).

14 Operate the brake lever several times to bring the pads into contact with the disc. Check the operation of the brakes carefully before riding the bike.

5 Front brake master cylinder

Brake lever

1 If the handlebar lever feels stiff, check the lever and the lever bracket for damage. On GS models, remove the hand protector, if fitted (see Chapter 6).

2 Turn the lever span adjuster to its lowest setting (see Chapter 1). Undo the lever pivot bolt locknut on the underside of the lever, then withdraw the pivot bolt and lift the lever and pushrod assembly off **(see illustrations)**. Note how the pushrod on the lever locates on the master cylinder piston. Note the location of the lever return spring.

3 Clean the contact surfaces of the lever, bracket and pivot bolt. If they are in good condition, lubricate the components with dry film lubricant prior to assembly.

4 If, after cleaning and lubricating the lever, the lever action is still stiff, the master cylinder will have to be removed from the machine and checked.

Master cylinder

5 If there is evidence of air in the system (spongy feel to the lever), bleed the system (see Section 10).

6 If brake fluid is leaking from the master cylinder, a new master cylinder must be fitted – seal kits are not available.

Removal

Note 1: *If the master cylinder is just being displaced and not completely removed from the motorcycle it is not necessary to disconnect the brake hose. Secure the master cylinder to the machine with a cable-tie to avoid straining the hose and keep the reservoir upright to prevent air entering the system.*

Note 2: *To prevent damage to the paint from spilled brake fluid, always cover the fuel tank and bodywork when working on the master cylinder.*

7 Prior to removing the brake master cylinder, on R1200 GS models, remove the hand protector, if fitted (see Chapter 6). On R1200 GS, GS Adventure and R1200 R models, remove the right-hand mirror (see Chapter 6).

8 On all models, refer to the procedure in Chapter 7 and displace the brake light switch from the underside of the master cylinder.

9 Undo the brake hose banjo bolt and separate the hose from the master cylinder,

noting its alignment **(see illustration)**. Be prepared to catch any residual fluid in the union. Discard the sealing washers as new ones must be used. Wrap a clean plastic bag over the end of the hose to prevent dirt entering the system and secure the hose in an upright position to minimise fluid loss.

Caution: Do not operate the brake lever while the hose is disconnected.

10 Support the master cylinder, undo the handlebar clamp bolts and remove the clamp **(see illustration)**. Note the alignment of the master cylinder clamp with the handlebar switch unit (see Chapter 4, Section 5).

11 On R1200 RT models, undo the screws securing the reservoir cover and lift off the cover and diaphragm (see *Pre-ride checks*).

12 On all other models, press the locking tabs in and unscrew the cap, then remove the locking ring and diaphragm (see *Pre-ride checks*).

13 Empty the brake fluid into a suitable container.

14 To check the action of the master cylinder piston, temporarily install the reservoir cover or cap. Wrap some clean rag over the open end of the master cylinder hose union and operate the lever. If the lever sticks, or the action is stiff, there is a fault with the master cylinder piston. Seal kits are not available – a new master cylinder will have to be fitted.

Caution: Do not, under any circumstances, use a petroleum-based solvent to clean the master cylinder.

5.9 Location of the brake hose banjo bolt on the master cylinder

5.10 Remove the master cylinder clamp

Installation

15 Installation is the reverse of removal, noting the following:

● Align the master cylinder as noted on removal and tighten the clamp bolts to the torque setting specified at the beginning of this Chapter.

● Align the brake hose with the master cylinder and fit new sealing washers on both sides of the banjo union.

● Tighten the banjo union bolt to the specified torque setting.

● Fill the fluid reservoir with new DOT 4 fluid (see *Pre-ride checks*). Bleed the air from the brake system (see Section 10).

● Check the operation of the brake before riding the motorcycle.

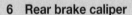

6 Rear brake caliper

⚠ *Warning: If the caliper indicates the need for an overhaul (usually due to leaking fluid or sticky operation), all old brake fluid should be flushed from the system. Also, the dust created by the brake system may contain asbestos, which is harmful to your health. Never blow it out with compressed air and don't inhale any of it. An approved filtering*

6.8a Undo the caliper mounting bolts (arrowed) . . .

mask should be worn when working on the brakes. Do not use petroleum-based solvents for cleaning brake system components – they will cause the seals to swell and distort. Use only clean brake fluid or dedicated brake system cleaner. Use care when working with brake fluid as it can injure your eyes and will damage painted surfaces and plastic parts

Removal

1 On R1200 GS and GS Adventure models, remove the rear spray guard (see Chapter 6).

2 If required, undo the screws securing the rear brake hose guide and lift the guide off the Paralever arm (see Chapter 4, Section 11).

6.2 Unclip the speed sensor wiring from the brake hose

6.8b . . . and slide the caliper off the disc

6.6 Note the alignment of the union (arrowed) with the caliper

Unclip the speed sensor wiring from the brake hose **(see illustration)**.

3 It is only necessary to disconnect the brake hose if the caliper is being removed completely. The brake hose can remain attached if you are just displacing the caliper for wheel removal, pad renewal or cleaning.

4 If poor brake action is the result of a sticking piston, or if a piston seal has failed and brake fluid is leaking from the caliper, the caliper must be overhauled. This procedure must be undertaken by a BMW dealer.

5 Remove the brake pads (see Section 2).

6 Cover the area around the end of the brake hose with clean rag to catch fluid spills. Note the alignment of the brake hose banjo union with the brake caliper, then undo union bolt and separate the hose from the caliper **(see illustration)**. Note the sealing washers fitted to both sides of the banjo union.

7 Plug the hose end or wrap a plastic bag tightly around it to minimise fluid loss and prevent dirt entering the system. **Note:** *Do not operate the brake pedal while the brake hose is disconnected.* Discard the sealing washers as new ones must be used on installation. Plug the caliper to avoid fluid spillage.

8 Undo the caliper mounting bolts and slide the caliper off the disc **(see illustrations)**.

9 Note how the caliper locates on the slider pins on the caliper bracket, then draw the caliper off the bracket **(see illustrations)**.

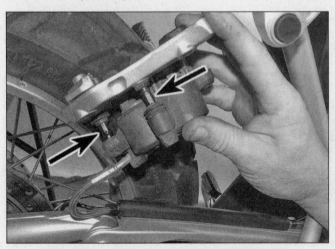

6.9a Rear brake caliper locates on the slider pins

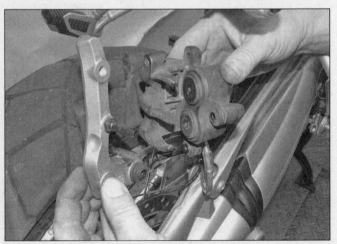

6.9b Draw the caliper off the bracket

6.12 Use long bolt to ensure sprayguard bracket is correctly aligned

Installation

10 Ensure that the slider pins are clean and free from corrosion, then lubricate the pins with a smear of silicone grease. If the brake pads have been removed, check that the pad spring is correctly located inside the caliper **(see illustration 2.20)**. Slide the caliper onto the bracket.

11 If removed, install the brake pads (see Section 2).

12 Slide the caliper onto the brake disc and install the mounting bolts, then tighten the bolts to the torque setting specified at the beginning of this Chapter **(see illustrations 6.8b and a)**. Note: *On GS and GS Adventure models fitted with a sprayguard, use the long guard mounting bolt to align the guard bracket with the bolt hole before tightening the caliper bracket bolts* **(see illustration)**.

13 Connect the brake hose to the caliper, using new sealing washers on each side of the banjo union. Align the union as noted on removal **(see illustration 6.6)**. Tighten the union bolt to the torque setting specified at the beginning of this Chapter.

14 Top-up the master cylinder reservoir with DOT 4 brake fluid (see *Pre-ride checks*) and bleed the brake system as described in Section 10.

15 If applicable, clip the speed sensor wiring from the brake hose. Install the brake hose

guide on the Paralever arm (see Chapter 4, Section 11).

16 On R1200 GS and GS Adventure models, install the rear spray guard (see Chapter 6).

17 Check that there are no leaks and thoroughly test the operation of the brake before riding the motorcycle.

7 Rear brake disc

Inspection

1 Refer to the procedure in Section 4 to check the condition of the disc. When checking disc runout, displace the brake caliper and mount the dial gauge on the final drive unit. If runout is greater than the service limit, either the disc is warped or the final drive unit bearings are worn. If the bearings need attention, have the machine checked a BMW dealer.

Removal

2 Displace the rear brake caliper (see Section 6).

3 Remove the exhaust silencer (see Chapter 3).

4 Remove the rear wheel (see Section 13).

5 The brake disc is mounted on the external flange of the final drive unit **(see illustration)**. Mark the relationship of the disc to the flange, so it can be installed in the same position, and mark the disc itself to indicate which is the outer face.

6 Undo the disc retaining bolts, loosening them a little at a time in a criss-cross pattern to avoid distorting the disc – note that the disc must be rotated each time to make each bolt accessible in turn **(see illustration)**.

7 Lift off the disc, manoeuvring it off the final drive unit flange.

Installation

8 Before installing the disc, make sure there is no dirt or corrosion where the disc seats. If the disc does not sit flat when it is bolted down, it will appear to be warped when checked or when the brake is used.

9 Position the disc on the final drive flange –

if the original disc is being installed, align the previously applied matchmarks.

10 Clean up the threads of the disc mounting bolts and apply a suitable non-permanent thread-locking compound. Note that the bolts are micro-encapsulated with locking compound when new and BMW advises that new bolts are fitted.

11 Tighten the bolts evenly and a little at a time in a criss-cross pattern, to the initial torque setting specified at the beginning of this Chapter, then tighten them to the final torque setting – note that the disc must be rotated each time to make each bolt accessible in turn **(see illustration 7.6)**.

12 Clean the disc using acetone or brake system cleaner. If a new brake disc has been installed, remove any protective coating from its working surfaces.

13 Install the remaining components in the reverse order of removal.

14 Operate the brake pedal several times to bring the pads into contact with the disc. Check the operation of the brakes carefully before riding the bike.

8 Rear brake master cylinder

1 If there is evidence of air in the brake system (spongy feel to the pedal), bleed the system (see Section 10).

2 If brake fluid is leaking from the master cylinder, a new master cylinder must be fitted – seal kits are not available.

Removal

Note 1: *If the master cylinder is just being displaced and not completely removed from the motorcycle it is not necessary to drain the fluid reservoir or disconnect the reservoir hose from the master cylinder. Keep the reservoir upright to prevent air entering the system. However, note that due to the rigid brake pipe connecting the master cylinder to the brake*

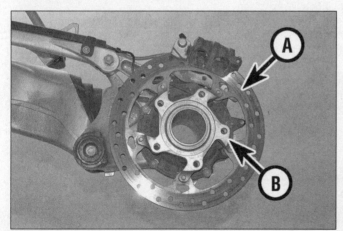

7.5 Brake disc (A) is mounted on the final drive unit flange (B)

7.6 Access to the disc retaining bolts is only available one at a time (arrowed)

8.3a Location of the rear brake fluid reservoir – R1200 GS

8.3b Location of the rear brake fluid reservoir – R1200 RT and R1200 R

8.5a Remove the heel plate . . .

8.5b . . . to access the rear brake master cylinder

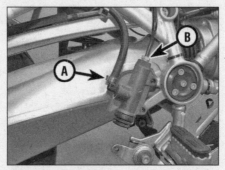

8.5c Reservoir hose is secured by clamp (A), brake pipe is secured by nut (B)

line adapter, movement of the master cylinder is limited – take care not to damage or bend the brake pipe.

Note 2: *To prevent damage to the paint from spilled brake fluid, always cover any painted parts when working on the master cylinder.*

3 On R1200 GS and GS Adventure models, the brake fluid reservoir is located on the right-hand side of the machine **(see illustration)**. On R1200 RT and R1200 R models, the brake fluid reservoir is located underneath the rider's seat **(see illustration)**. Follow the procedure in Chapter 6 to remove the seat.

4 Remove the reservoir cover and diaphragm (see *Pre-ride checks*) and siphon the brake fluid into a suitable container. Temporarily install the diaphragm and reservoir cover.

5 On R1200 GS, GS Adventure and R1200 R

models, undo the screws securing the heel plate and lift it off **(see illustrations)**. Temporarily secure the master cylinder to its mounting bracket. Follow the procedure in Chapter 4, Section 3, and disconnect the master cylinder pushrod from the brake pedal. Undo the hose clamp securing the reservoir hose to the elbow on the master cylinder and disconnect the hose, being prepared to catch any residual brake fluid **(see illustration)**. Discard the hose clamp as a new one must be fitted. Undo the brake pipe flare nut and separate the pipe from the master cylinder, being prepared to catch any residual brake fluid **(see illustration 8.5c)**. Wrap clean plastic bags over the ends of the pipe and hose to prevent dirt entering the system and to minimise fluid spillage.

6 On R1200 RT models, the rear brake master cylinder is mounted on the back of the right-hand footrest bracket. Follow the procedure in Chapter 4, Section 3, to remove the bracket. Follow the procedure in Step 5 to disconnect the reservoir hose and the brake pipe from the master cylinder.

Installation

7 Installation is the reverse of removal, noting the following:

● Tighten the brake pipe flare nut to the torque setting specified at the beginning of this Chapter.

● Tighten the fluid reservoir hose clamp securely.

● Tighten the master cylinder mounting bolts to the specified torque setting. On R1200 RT models, either fit new micro-encapsulated bolts or clean all old locking compound from the old bolts, apply fresh thread-locking compound and tighten them to the specified torque setting.

● Check the brake pedal freeplay (see Chapter 4, Section 3).

● Fill the reservoir with new DOT 4 fluid (see *Pre-ride checks*). Bleed the air from the brake system (see Section 10).

● Check the operation of the brake before riding the motorcycle.

9 Brake hoses, pipes and unions

Inspection

1 The condition of the brake hoses and pipes should be checked regularly as described in Chapter 1.

2 Check the unions on the brake line adapters **(see illustrations)**. Ensure the brake hose banjo bolts and the brake pipe flare nuts are tightened to the torque settings specified at the beginning of this Chapter.

3 On machines equipped with ABS, rigid brake pipes connect the pressure modulator to the flexible brake hoses from the front master cylinder and calipers. Remove the fuel tank (see Chapter 3) to inspect the rigid brake

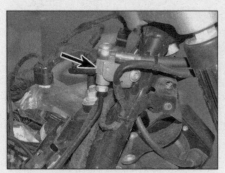

9.2a Check the unions on front . . .

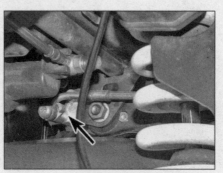

9.2b . . . and rear brake line adapters

9.3 Check the brake pipes and unions

9.5a Brake hose banjo union

pipes and the pipe unions **(see illustration).** Check that there are no signs of corrosion or fluid leakage.

Renewal

Note: *Do not operate the brake lever or pedal while a brake hose is disconnected.*

4 Before loosening a hose or pipe connection, cover the surrounding area with plenty of rags to soak up any spilled brake fluid and prevent damage to painted parts.

5 The brake hoses have banjo unions on both ends and the brake pipes have flare nuts **(see illustrations).**

6 To renew a brake hose, note the alignment of the banjo unions, then undo the union bolts. Note the sealing washers fitted on both sides of the banjo union and discard them as new ones must be used **(see illustration).** Make careful note of the exact routing of the hose and the position of all retaining clips.

7 Position the new hose exactly as noted on removal, making sure it isn't twisted or strained. Fit new sealing washers on both sides of the banjo unions and tighten the union bolts finger-tight. Make sure the hose is routed clear of all moving components, then tighten the banjo bolts to the torque setting

specified at the beginning of this Chapter. Secure the hose with any clips or ties.

8 To renew a brake pipe, undo the flare nuts, then pull the pipe out from its unions. Note that the nuts are retained on the pipe. Make careful note of the exact routing of the pipe and the position of all retaining clips.

9 Position the new pipe exactly as noted on removal and tighten the nuts to the torque setting specified at the beginning of this Chapter.

10 Top-up the appropriate fluid reservoir with new DOT 4 brake fluid and use the brake bleeding procedure to flush the old brake fluid from the system (see Section 10).

11 Check the operation of the brakes before riding the motorcycle.

---

10 Brake fluid change and brake bleeding

Brake fluid change

Note: *Unless alternative equipment is available (see Tool Tip), an assistant will be required for this procedure.*

1 The brake fluid should be changed at the prescribed service interval.

2 To change the brake fluid you will need some new DOT 4 brake fluid, a length of clear vinyl or plastic hose to fit the front and rear brake caliper bleed valves and the front brake master cylinder bleed valve, a suitable tool for siphoning the fluid out of the fluid reservoir, a container partially filled with clean brake fluid and large enough to take all the old fluid when it is flushed out of the system, a brake piston spreading tool (see Section 2), some rags and a spanner to fit the brake caliper bleed valve.

Front brake

3 Cover the fuel tank and other painted components to prevent damage in the event that brake fluid is spilled.

4 Remove the reservoir cap or cover, locking ring (if fitted) and diaphragm (see *Pre-ride checks*). On R1200 GS, GS Adventure and R1200 R models, lift out the reservoir insert and dispose of it as a new one must be fitted **(see illustration)**; note that the insert was not fitted to 2012-on models. Siphon the old brake fluid out of the reservoir.

5 Remove the brake pads from both front brake calipers (see Section 2).

9.5b Brake pipe flare nut

9.6 Note sealing washers fitted on both sides of the banjo union

10.4 Reservoir insert must be renewed (where fitted)

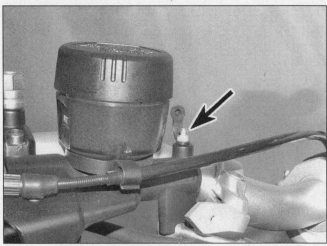

10.7 Front brake master cylinder bleed valve

10.11 Set-up for changing the front brake fluid and bleeding the brakes

6 Using the brake piston spreading tool, force the pistons back into the calipers and secure them in position with suitable blocks of wood. Siphon any remaining fluid out of the reservoir and wipe the inside clean.

7 Pull the dust cap off the master cylinder bleed valve **(see illustration)**. Attach one end of the clear hose to the bleed valve and submerge the other end in the clean brake fluid in the container. **Note:** *To avoid damaging the bleed valve during the procedure, loosen it and then tighten it temporarily with a ring spanner before attaching the hose. With the hose attached, the valve can then be opened and closed with an open-ended spanner.*

8 Position the handlebars so that the top of the reservoir is level and fill it to the MAX level line with new brake fluid.

9 Carefully pump the brake lever three or four times, then hold it in while opening the bleed valve. When the valve is opened, brake fluid will flow out of the master cylinder into the hose, and the lever will move toward the handlebar. Any air trapped in the upper end of the system will be indicated by air bubbles in the fluid leaving the master cylinder. Retighten the bleed valve, then release the brake lever gradually.

10.18 Install the reservoir insert carefully

10 Repeat the procedure until fresh fluid is visible in the clear hose and no air bubbles are present. Tighten the bleed valve to the torque setting specified at the beginning of this Chapter.

> **HAYNES HINT** *Old brake fluid is invariably much darker in colour than new fluid, making it easy to see when all old fluid has been expelled from the system.*

11 Pull the dust cap off the left-hand brake caliper bleed valve, attach one end of the clear hose to the bleed valve and submerge the other end in the clean brake fluid in the container **(see illustration)**. **Note:** *To avoid damaging the bleed valve during the procedure, loosen it and then tighten it temporarily with a ring spanner before attaching the hose. With the hose attached, the valve can then be opened and closed with an open-ended spanner.*

12 Carefully pump the brake lever three or four times and hold it in while opening the caliper bleed valve. When the valve is opened, brake fluid will flow out of the caliper into the hose, and the lever will move toward the handlebar. Air in the system will be indicated by air bubbles in the fluid leaving the caliper. Retighten the bleed valve, then release the brake lever gradually.

13 Keep the reservoir topped-up with new fluid above the MIN level at all times or air may enter the system and greatly increase the length of the task. Repeat the process until fresh fluid is visible in the clear hose and no air bubbles can be seen emerging from the bleed valve. Tighten the bleed valve to the specified torque setting and fit the dust cap.

14 Repeat the procedure for the right-hand brake caliper. Remember to keep the

reservoir topped-up with new brake fluid.

15 Finally, repeat the procedure in Steps 7 and 9 to bleed any remaining air from the upper end of the system. Tighten the bleed valve to the specified torque setting and fit the dust cap.

16 Remove the blocks from the brake calipers and install the brake pads (see Section 2). Operate the brake lever several times to bring the pads back into contact with the discs.

17 Check the fluid level in the reservoir and top-up as necessary (see *Pre-ride checks*).

18 On 2010 and 2011 R1200 GS, GS Adventure and R1200 R models, install a new reservoir insert, pressing it down gently **(see illustration)**. Install the locking ring and reservoir cap (see *Pre-ride checks*).

19 On R1200 RT models, install the diaphragm and reservoir cover (see *Pre-ride checks*).

20 Check that there are no fluid leaks and test the operation of the brakes thoroughly before riding the motorcycle.

Rear brake

21 Cover the final drive housing and the area around the reservoir to prevent damage in the event that brake fluid is spilled.

22 Remove the reservoir cap and diaphragm (see *Pre-ride checks*) and siphon the old brake fluid out of the reservoir.

23 Remove the brake pads (see Section 2). Follow the procedure in Section 6 to displace the brake caliper, then draw the caliper off the caliper bracket

24 Using the brake piston spreading tool, force the pistons back into the caliper. Siphon any remaining fluid out of the reservoir and wipe the inside clean.

25 Pull the dust cap off the caliper bleed valve, attach one end of the clear hose to the bleed valve and submerge the other end in the clean brake fluid in the container **(see**

10.25 Set-up for changing the rear brake fluid and bleeding the brakes

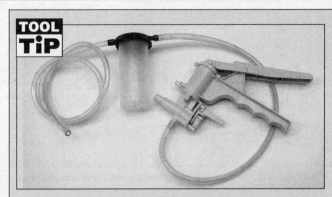

In its simplest form, the brake bleeding equipment described in Step 2 will be required. A quicker alternative would be a 'one-person' brake bleeding kit consisting of a non-return valve in the hose which prevents air being drawn back into the caliper. If, however, either set-up fails to bleed the brake effectively, use a vacuum-type brake bleeding tool as shown here.

illustration). **Note:** *To avoid damaging the bleed valve during the procedure, loosen it and then tighten it temporarily with a ring spanner before attaching the hose. With the hose attached, the valve can then be opened and closed with an open-ended spanner.*

26 Fill the reservoir to the MAX level line with new brake fluid.

27 Carefully pump the brake pedal three or four times and hold it down while opening the caliper bleed valve. When the valve is opened, brake fluid will flow out of the caliper into the hose, and the pedal will move down. Air in the system will be indicated by air bubbles in the fluid leaving the caliper. Retighten the bleed valve, then release the brake pedal gradually.

28 Keep the reservoir topped-up with new fluid above the MIN level at all times or air may enter the system and greatly increase the length of the task. Repeat the process until fresh fluid is visible in the clear hose and no air bubbles can be seen emerging from the bleed valve. Tighten the bleed valve to the specified torque setting and fit the dust cap.

29 Remove the piston spreading tool and install the brake pads (see Section 2). Install the brake caliper (see Section 6). Operate the brake pedal several times to bring the pads back into contact with the disc.

30 Check the fluid level in the reservoir and top-up as necessary (see *Pre-ride checks*). Install the diaphragm and cap.

Brake bleeding

31 Bleeding the brakes is simply the process of removing all the air bubbles from the brake system – the hoses, calipers and master cylinders. Bleeding is necessary whenever a brake system connection is loosened, when a component or hose is renewed. Leaks in the system may also allow air to enter, but leaking brake fluid will reveal their presence and warn you of the need for repair.

32 To bleed the brakes, you will need some new DOT 4 brake fluid and the equipment described in Step 2.

33 BMW advise that bleeding the brakes is more effective if the pads are removed, and the pistons pushed back into the calipers and held in this position, thus reducing the fluid volume in the system. This procedure is described in Steps 6 and 24, but note that some brake fluid should be siphoned from the appropriate reservoir first to avoid fluid displaced by the pistons over-filling the reservoir.

34 On R1200 GS, GS Adventure and R1200 R models, lift out the reservoir insert and dispose of it as a new one must be fitted **(see illustration 10.4)**; note that the insert was not fitted to 2012-on models.

35 Follow the procedure in Steps 7 to 20 to bleed the front brakes and 25 to 30 to bleed the rear brake.

> **HAYNES HiNT** *If it is not possible to produce a firm feel to the lever or pedal, the brake fluid may be aerated. Let the new fluid in the system stabilise for a few hours and then repeat the procedure to ensure any tiny air bubbles have settled out.*

11 Wheel runout and alignment

Wheel runout

1 In order to carry out a proper inspection of the wheels, it is necessary to support the bike upright so that the wheel being inspected is raised off the ground. Position the motorcycle on its centre stand or an auxiliary stand.

2 Clean the wheels thoroughly to remove mud and dirt that may interfere with the inspection procedure or mask defects. Make a general check of the wheels (see Chapter 1, Section 13) and tyres (see *Pre-ride checks*).

3 Attach a dial gauge to the fork or the swingarm and position its tip against the side

of the rim. Spin the wheel slowly and check the axial (side-to-side) runout of the rim **(see illustration)**.

4 In order to accurately check radial (out-of-round) runout with the dial gauge, the wheel will have to be removed from the machine, and the tyre from the wheel. With the axle clamped in a vice and the dial gauge positioned on the top of the rim, the wheel can be rotated to check the runout **(see illustration 11.3)**.

5 An easier, though slightly less accurate, method is to attach a stiff wire pointer to the fork or the swingarm and position the end a fraction of an inch from the wheel (where the wheel and tyre join). If the wheel is true, the distance from the pointer to the rim will be constant as the wheel is rotated. **Note:** *If wheel*

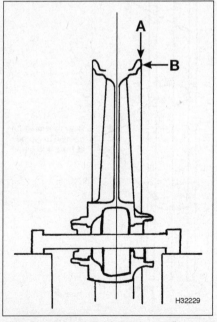

11.3 Check for radial (out-of-round) runout at point A, and axial (side-to-side) runout at point B

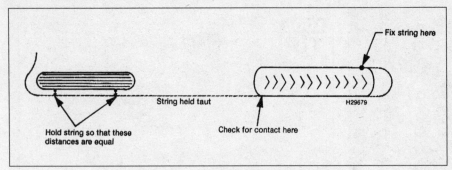

11.10 Checking the wheel alignment with string

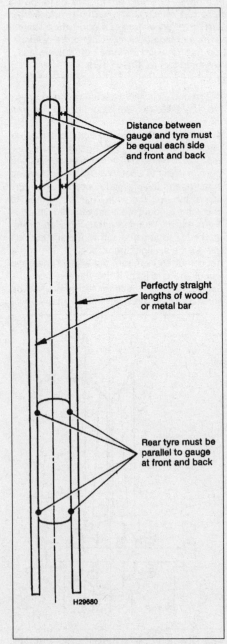

Distance between gauge and tyre must be equal each side and front and back

Perfectly straight lengths of wood or metal bar

Rear tyre must be parallel to gauge at front and back

11.13 Checking the wheel alignment with a straight-edge

runout is excessive, check the wheel bearings (front wheel) or final drive unit bearings (rear wheel) very carefully before renewing the wheel.

Wheel alignment

6 Misalignment of the wheels can cause serious handling problems. Due to the BMW's solid engine and running gear construction, the normal problem areas for wheel misalignment (distorted frame or cocked rear wheel) do not apply. If the wheels are out of alignment, this could be due to worn or damaged Telelever components at the front, or worn swingarm bearings at the rear. If accident damage has occurred, the machine should be taken to a BMW dealer for a thorough check of the structural components.

7 To check wheel alignment you will need an assistant, a length of string or a perfectly straight length of wood or metal bar, and a ruler. A plumb bob or spirit level will also be required.

8 Support the bike in an upright position, either on its centre stand or on an auxiliary stand. Measure the width of both tyres at their widest points. Subtract the smaller measurement from the larger measurement, then divide the difference by two. The result is the amount of offset that should exist between the front and rear tyres on both sides.

9 If a string is used, have your assistant hold one end of it about halfway between the floor and the rear axle, touching the rear sidewall of the rear tyre.

12.4 Location of the axle clamp bolt (arrowed)

10 Run the other end of the string forward and pull it tight so that it is roughly parallel to the floor. Slowly bring the string into contact with the front sidewall of the rear tyre, then turn the front wheel until it is parallel with the string **(see illustration)**. Measure the distance from the front tyre sidewall to the string.

11 Repeat the procedure on the other side of the motorcycle.

12 The distance from the front tyre sidewall to the string should be the same on both sides of the bike and equal to the tyre width offset. If the measurement differs, the wheels are out of alignment by this amount.

13 As previously mentioned, a perfectly straight length of wood or metal bar may be substituted for the string **(see illustration)**. The procedure is the same.

14 If the wheels are out of alignment, and the fault cannot be traced to the Telelever or swingarm assemblies, the bike should be taken to a BMW dealer for verification of your findings using a track alignment gauge.

15 If the front-to-back alignment is correct, the wheels still may be out of alignment vertically.

16 Using a plumb bob or spirit level, check the rear wheel to make sure it is vertical. To do this with the plumb bob, hold the string against the tyre upper sidewall and allow the weight to settle just off the floor. When the string touches both the upper and lower tyre sidewalls and is perfectly straight, the wheel is vertical. If necessary, place thin spacers under one leg of the stand until the wheel is vertical. Using a spirit level, the level should be held against the upper and lower tyre sidewalls.

17 Once the rear wheel is vertical, check the front wheel in the same manner. If the front wheel is not perfectly vertical, the frame and/or major suspension components are bent.

12 Front wheel

Removal

1 Position the bike on its centre stand or support it securely on an auxiliary stand so that the front wheel is off the ground. Always make sure the motorcycle is properly supported.

2 On R1200 RT models, remove the front section of the front mudguard (see Chapter 6).

3 Displace the front brake calipers (see Section 3). There is no need to disconnect the hoses from the calipers. Support the calipers with a piece of wire or cable-tie so that no strain is placed on the brake hoses. **Note:** *Do not operate the front brake lever with the calipers displaced.*

4 Loosen the axle clamp bolt on the bottom of the right-hand fork slider **(see illustration)**.

5 Locate a suitable hex drive tool in the head of the axle and unscrew the axle from the

12.5a Use a hex-head tool to loosen the axle . . .

12.5b . . . then pull the axle out

12.6a Note the location of the spacer . . .

left-hand fork slider, then support the wheel and withdraw the axle (see illustrations).

6 Note the location of the spacer on the left-hand side of the wheel, then withdraw the wheel and remove the spacer for safekeeping (see illustrations). On ABS equipped machines, take care not to damage the ABS sensor located on the left-hand fork slider (see illustration).

Caution: Don't lay the wheel down and allow it to rest on either brake disc – the disc could become warped. Set the wheel on wood blocks so the tyre supports the weight of the wheel.

7 Check the axle for straightness by rolling it on a flat surface such as a piece of plate glass (first wipe off all old grease and remove any corrosion using wire wool). If the equipment is available, check the axle runout using V-blocks and a dial gauge.

8 Check the condition of the wheel bearings (see Section 14).

12.6b . . . and remove it for safekeeping

Installation

9 Lubricate the axle and the inside of the left-hand hub seal with a smear of grease, then install the spacer into the seal (see illustration 12.6b).

10 Manoeuvre the wheel into position, then

12.6c Take care not to damage the ABS sensor

insert the axle from the right-hand side, making sure that the spacer remains in place. Screw the axle into the left-hand fork slider finger-tight. On ABS equipped machines, take care not to damage the ABS sensor located on the left-hand fork slider (see illustration 12.6c).

11 Temporarily take the bike off its stand and compress the front suspension several times to align the wheel and fork legs.

12 Tighten the axle to the torque setting specified at the beginning of this Chapter, then tighten the axle clamp bolt to the specified torque.

13 Install the front brake calipers (see Section 3).

14 On R1200 RT models, install the front section of the front mudguard (see Chapter 6).

15 Check for correct operation of the front brake before riding the motorcycle.

13 Rear wheel

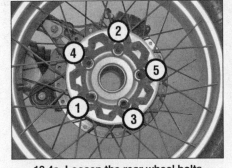

13.4a Loosen the rear wheel bolts evenly . . .

13.4b . . . then withdraw the bolts – R1200 GS Adventure shown

Removal

1 Position the bike on its centre stand or support it securely on an auxiliary stand so that the rear wheel is off the ground. Always make sure the motorcycle is properly supported.

2 On R1200 GS and GS Adventure models, remove the rear spray guard (see Chapter 6).

3 On R1200 RT and R1200 R models, remove the exhaust silencer (see Chapter 3).

4 Loosen the bolts securing the wheel to the flange on the final drive unit evenly in a criss-cross pattern, then support the wheel and withdraw the bolts (see illustrations).

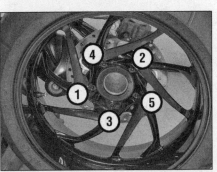

13.4c Loosen the rear wheel bolts evenly . . .

13.4d . . . then withdraw the bolts – R1200 R shown

5 Lift the wheel off the flange **(see illustrations)**.

Installation

6 Make sure the contact faces between the wheel hub and the final drive flange are clean.
7 Clean the threads of the wheel bolts and the bolt holes in the flange.
8 Lift the wheel onto the flange, making sure it engages correctly, and install the bolts finger-tight.
9 Tighten the bolts evenly in a criss-cross pattern to the torque setting specified at the beginning of this Chapter **(see illustrations 13.4a and c)**.
10 On R1200 RT and R1200 R models, install the exhaust silencer (see Chapter 3).
11 On R1200 GS and GS Adventure models, install the rear spray guard (see Chapter 6).

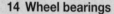

14 Wheel bearings

Front wheel bearings

Note: *Always renew the wheel bearings in pairs, never individually. Avoid using a high pressure cleaner on the wheel bearing area.*

Check and removal

1 Remove the wheel (see Section 12).
2 Set the wheel on wood blocks so the tyre supports the weight of the wheel.

13.5a Lift the wheel off the flange – R1200 GS Adventure shown

3 Prise out the seals on both sides of the wheel hub using a flat-bladed screwdriver – use a piece of wood or thick card to protect the edge of the bearing housing **(see illustration)**. Discard the seals as new ones must be used.
4 Refer to *Tools and Workshop Tips* in the *Reference* section and inspect the bearings for wear or damage. If the bearings do not turn smoothly or if there is freeplay between the races, they must be renewed **(see illustration)**.
5 To remove the bearings, support the wheel with the right-hand side uppermost. Heat the hub around the bearing housing to 100°C and use a knife-edged bearing puller and slide-hammer arrangement to draw the right-hand bearing out (see *Tools and Workshop Tips* in the Reference section). Lift out the bearing spacer, then heat the hub around the left-hand bearing housing and

13.5b Lift the wheel off the flange – R1200 R shown

drive the bearing out from the right-hand side with a metal rod inserted through the centre of the hub (preferably a brass drift). Note which way round the bearings are fitted.
6 Alternatively, heat the hub, then use a metal rod (preferably a brass drift) inserted through the centre of the upper bearing to tap evenly around the inner race of the lower bearing to drive it from the hub **(see illustrations)**. The bearing spacer will also come out. Turn the wheel over so that the remaining bearing faces down. Drive the bearing out using the same technique as above, heating the hub again if necessary. Note which way round the bearings are fitted.

Installation

7 Thoroughly clean the hub and bearing housings. Use a drawbolt arrangement to install the new bearings one at a time (see *Tools and Workshop Tips* in the *Reference* section). Install the bearings with the marked or sealed side facing outwards. Ensure the drawbolt only bears on the outer race of the bearing.
8 Alternatively, use the old bearing, a bearing driver or a socket large enough to contact the outer race of the bearings to drive them in until they are completely seated **(see illustration)**. After installing the first bearing, turn the wheel over and install the bearing spacer, then drive the second bearing into place.
9 Lubricate the new seals with a smear of

14.3 Prise the old seals out carefully

14.4 Check the bearings as described

14.6a Driving out the wheel bearings

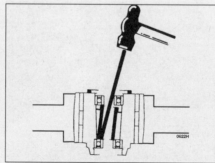

14.6b Locate the drift against the inner edge of the lower bearing

14.8 Driving a bearing in using a suitably-sized socket

grease, then press them into the hub **(see illustration)**. Ensure that the seals are level with the edge of the hub by tapping them with a flat piece of wood **(see illustration)**.

10 Clean any grease off the brake discs using acetone or brake system cleaner, then install the wheel (see Section 12).

Rear wheel bearings

11 The rear wheel bearings are part of the final drive unit. If the unit is thought to be faulty have it checked by a BMW dealer – dismantling and set-up of the final drive requires special tools and is beyond the scope of this manual. To remove the final drive unit follow the procedure in Chapter 4.

15 Spokes –
wire spoked wheels

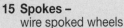

Caution: If a machine is ridden off-road, BMW recommend that the spoke tension should be checked on a daily basis.

1 Support the machine on its centre stand so that the wheels are free to rotate. Check each spoke for looseness by tapping it gently with a small spanner or screwdriver and listening to the sound **(see illustration)**. The 'tone' of each spoke should sound the same.

2 If a spoke sounds dull or rattles, try to pull it backwards and forwards to confirm that it is loose.

3 A loose spoke can be tightened with the correct size Torx socket or a spoke key (see Steps 7 to 9 as appropriate).

4 If several spokes are loose it is likely that the wheel will be out of true – follow the procedure in Section 11 to check the radial and axial runout. If necessary, take the wheel to a wheel building expert for correction.

5 If a spoke is bent it must be replaced with a new one. First check the wheel runout (see Section 11). If the wheel is true, the damaged spoke can be replaced, but if the wheel is out of true, it must be taken to a wheel building expert for correction. To replace a spoke on the R1200 R Classic, remove the tyre and unscrew the spoke nipple; remove the

14.9a Install the seals carefully . . .

14.9b . . . and ensure they are level with the edge of the hub

damaged spoke, noting its alignment with adjacent spokes, then insert the new spoke and tighten it to the specified torque setting. On the cross-spoke design of wheel fitted to GS and GS Adventure models, unscrew the grub screw and nipple, then withdraw the spoke from the rim end; refer to Step 7 for installation.

6 If a spoke is damaged, inspect the wheel rim for damage and flat spots also.

R1200 GS and GS Adventure

Special tool: A Torx socket is necessary for this procedure (see illustration 15.7b).

7 To tighten a loose spoke, first loosen the grub screw securing the spoke nipple using a 2 mm Allen key **(see illustration)**. Tighten the spoke carefully to the initial, then final, torque settings specified at the beginning of

this Chapter with a Torx socket and a torque wrench **(see illustration)**. Tighten the grub screw to the specified torque setting on completion.

R1200 R Classic

Special tool: A spoke key is necessary for this procedure (see illustration 15.8b).

8 R1200 R Classic models are fitted with conventional wire spoked wheels **(see illustration)**. A loose spoke can be tightened with a spoke key **(see illustration)**. Tighten the spoke gradually until the 'tone' is the same as the others.

9 If a new spoke is being fitted, make sure it doesn't protrude into the well of the wheel rim to cause a puncture. Always ensure that a rim tape is fitted to protect the inner tube from chaffing on the spoke ends.

15.1 Check each spoke by tapping with a small screwdriver

15.7a Loosen the grub screw (arrowed) inside the spoke nipple

15.7b Tighten the spokes carefully to the specified torque

15.8a Conventional wire spoked wheels – R1200 R Classic

15.8b Spokes can be tightened with a spoke key

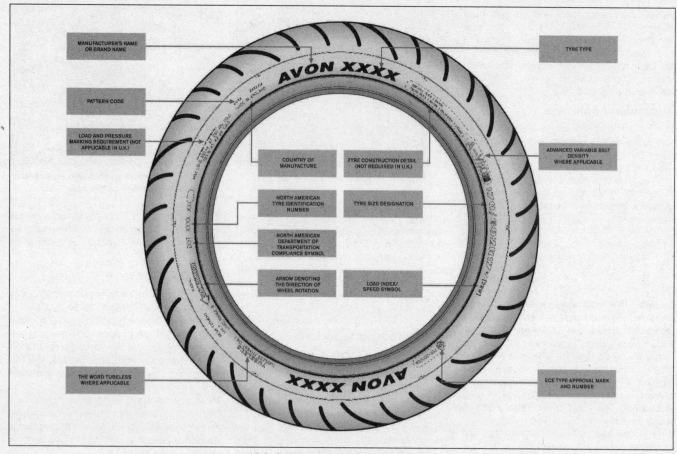

MANUFACTURER'S NAME OR BRAND NAME

PATTERN CODE

LOAD AND PRESSURE MARKING REQUIREMENT (NOT APPLICABLE IN U.K.)

TYRE TYPE

COUNTRY OF MANUFACTURE

TYRE CONSTRUCTION DETAIL (NOT REQUIRED IN U.K.)

ADVANCED VARIABLE BELT DENSITY WHERE APPLICABLE

NORTH AMERICAN TYRE IDENTIFICATION NUMBER

TYRE SIZE DESIGNATION

NORTH AMERICAN DEPARTMENT OF TRANSPORTATION COMPLIANCE SYMBOL

ARROW DENOTING THE DIRECTION OF WHEEL ROTATION

LOAD INDEX/ SPEED SYMBOL

THE WORD TUBELESS WHERE APPLICABLE

ECE TYPE APPROVAL MARK AND NUMBER

16.3 Common tyre sidewall markings

16 Tyres – general information

General information

1 The conventional spoked wheels fitted to the R1200 R Classic are designed to take tubed tyres only. The wheels on all other models, including cross-spoke design, use tubeless tyres.
2 Refer to the *Pre-ride checks* for details of tyre maintenance.

Fitting new tyres

Note: *On machines equipped with the RDC tyre pressure control system (see Section 19) special care should be taken to avoid damaging the wheel sensors.*
3 When selecting new tyres, refer to the tyre sizes given at the beginning of this chapter, the tyre options listed in rider's handbook and the tyre information label under the bike's seat. Ensure that the front and rear tyre types are compatible, and that they are of the correct size and speed rating **(see illustration)**. If necessary, seek advice from a BMW dealer or tyre fitting specialist.
4 It is recommended that tyres are fitted by a motorcycle tyre specialist rather than

attempted in the home workshop. The force required to break the seal between the wheel rim and tyre bead is substantial, and is usually beyond the capabilities of an individual working with normal tyre levers. Additionally, the specialist will be able to balance the wheels after tyre fitting.
5 Note that punctured tubeless tyres can in some cases be repaired. BMW recommend that such repairs are assessed and carried out professionally.

17 ABS

System type

1 All R1200 RT models are equipped with BMW's Integral ABS II system. This system is available as optional equipment (OE) on R1200 GS, GS Adventure and R models.
2 The system features partially integral brakes – operation of the front brake lever applies both front brakes and the rear brake, whereas operation of the rear brake pedal applies only the rear brake.
3 The ABS features an adaptive brake force distribution system that changes the

proportions of front to rear brake power according to load on the wheels, thus ensuring good stability.
4 The system also takes into account the additional loading of luggage and/or passenger.
5 The ABS prevents the wheels from locking-up under hard braking or on uneven road surfaces. A sensor on each wheel transmits wheel speed information to the ABS control unit. If the control unit senses that a wheel is about to lock, the pressure modulator releases brake pressure momentarily to that wheel, preventing a skid.

 Warning: If there is a fault with the ABS, extreme care must be taken when riding the motorcycle, and it should be taken immediately to a BMW dealer for analysis.

System operation

6 The ABS is self-checking. A self-diagnosis test is performed every time the ignition is switched ON and is only completed when the machine moves forwards a few metres and the speed sensors have been checked. During the test the ABS symbol on the instrument cluster will flash. Once the test is completed satisfactorily the ABS symbol will extinguish.
7 If the symbol continues to flash the self-

17.10a Location of the ABS diagnostic tester plug – R1200 RT

17.10b Location of the ABS diagnostic tester plug – R1200 GS

17.17 Note clips securing the sensor wire

diagnosis test has not been completed and the ABS function will not be available, resulting in a reduced braking efficiency. Stop the machine and switch the engine OFF. Carry out the starting procedure once again.

8 If there is a fault with the ABS, the warning symbol will come on and stay illuminated. The machine may be ridden, but the ABS function will not be available and braking efficiency will be reduced.

9 Certain operating conditions can trigger the ABS warning. Running the engine with the machine on its centre stand so that the rear wheel is free to rotate, or engaging a gear with the engine running and the machine on its centre stand. Allowing engine braking to lock the rear wheel while descending a slope with a loose or slippery surface. Under these circumstances, the ABS can be reactivated if the ignition is switched OFF and the starting procedure is carried out again.

10 The ABS control unit stores faults in its memory which can be read and cleared using the BMW MOSS diagnostic tester. The tester connects into a diagnostic plug on the machine (see illustrations). Interrogation of the ABS must be carried out by a BMW dealer who can then rectify the faults and clear the fault codes from the control unit memory.

11 If using an ABS equipped R1200 GS or GS Adventure model off-road, it may be desirable to ride without the ABS functioning. To deactivate the system, stop the machine, or if already at a standstill, switch the ignition ON. Press the ASC/ABS button until the ABS symbol is displayed (the warning will alternate between the ASC symbol and ABS symbol). Release the button. The ABS symbol stays on as a reminder to the rider that ABS is turned off.

12 Initially, the ABS will be deactivated on the front wheel only. To deactivate the ABS on the rear wheel, press down on the brake pedal.

13 To reactivate ABS, again press the ASC/ABS button until the ABS symbol is displayed, then press and hold the button until the light goes out.

14 If the light continues to flash, carry-out the starting procedure (see Step 6).

15 If the light remains on, a fault is registered by the ABS system (see Steps 8 to 10).

Wheel speed sensors – all models

Front wheel

16 The front wheel sensor is located on the left-hand fork slider and the sensor ring is on the left-hand side of the wheel hub (see illustrations 12.6c and 4.7). The air gap between the tip of the sensor and the ring is critical for the ABS to function correctly. Check that the sensor is fitted securely and that the sensor ring is not damaged, then check that the front wheel is fitted correctly and check the wheel bearings for wear (see Chapter 1).

17 Ensure that the sensor and sensor ring are clean and free from obstructions. If the sensor ring is damaged, follow the procedure in Section 4 to remove the left-hand brake disc and renew the ring. To renew the sensor, refer to Chapter 4, Section 6, to remove the sensor from the left-hand front fork slider, noting how the sensor wire is clipped to the brake hose (see illustration). Remove the fuel tank (see Chapter 3) and disconnect the wire at the connector clipped to the front, right-hand edge of the ECU holder (see Chapter 3, Section 15).

18 Installation is the reverse of removal. Don't forget that any fault code arising from the sensor/sensor ring damage will have to be cleared from the control unit memory using the BMW MOSS diagnostic tester.

Rear wheel

19 The rear wheel sensor is located on the inside edge of the final drive unit, behind the drive flange (see Chapter 4, Section 12). The sensor ring is an integral part of the gear assembly inside the housing.

20 To renew the sensor, first remove the rear wheel (see Section 13).

21 Refer to the procedure in Chapter 4, Section 11, and remove the rear brake hose guide from the Paralever arm. Disconnect the sensor wiring connector, cut the ties securing the wiring to the frame and feed the wiring back to the sensor (see illustration). Models from March 2011 onward have an additional wiring clip, near the sensor itself.

22 Undo the screw securing the sensor and draw the sensor out from the housing, noting the location of the sealing O-ring and centring ring (see illustrations). Release the wire from any clips.

23 Installation is the reverse of removal.

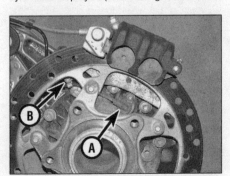

17.21 Location of the rear wheel speed sensor (A) and additional clip (B)

17.22a Screw secures speed sensor

17.22b Note location of O-ring and centring ring

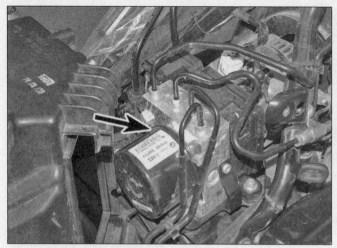

17.24 Location of the ABS control unit and modulator

17.25 Ensure the wiring connector (arrowed) is secure

17.26 Check that the flare nuts are tight

19.1a RDC sensors are either integral with . . .

Ensure that a new O-ring is fitted to the sensor. Don't forget that any fault code arising from a sensor fault will have to be cleared from the control unit memory using the BMW MOSS diagnostic tester.

ABS control unit and pressure modulator

24 The integral control unit and modulator is located under the fuel tank **(see illustration)**. Remove the fuel tank (see Chapter 3) and air intake duct (see Chapter 1, Section 6) for access.

25 The unit is not a service item – if a problem is indicated, all that can be done is to check that the multi-pin wiring connector to the unit is secure, and that the connector contacts are clean and undamaged **(see illustration)**. Disconnect the battery (see Chapter 7) before disconnecting the modulator wiring connector.

26 Ensure that the flare nuts securing the brake pipes to the modulator are tightened securely **(see illustration)**.

27 To remove the modulator, follow the appropriate Steps in Chapter 2, Section 4.

18 ASC (Automatic Stability Control) system

1 ASC is a traction control system which compares the speed of both wheels and via calculation determines the amount of rear wheel slip. If the parameters are exceeded, engine torque is reduced via the engine management unit. The system is entirely automatic in operation, but can be deactivated by the rider if required.

2 An ASC button on the left handlebar switch unit enables the system to be deactivated when the motorcycle is in motion; the ASC warning symbol on the instrument panel will remain on to show that ASC is turned off. To reactivate the system, press the ASC button and release it within 2 seconds – the warning symbol should go out to indicate that ASC is turned on. Alternatively the system will reactivate when the ignition is next turned off and then on again. Note that on R1200 GS and GS Adventure models, the ABS and ASC button is

combined; press the button until the S symbol warning light appears, then press the button and release within 2 seconds to deactivate ASC – the warning light should remain on.

3 In normal use the ASC warning light will be off. Slow flashing of the warning light indicates that the system's self-diagnosis cycle has not yet completed. Quick flashing of the light occurs if ASC is in use, i.e. if the system has detected a traction problem and is reducing rear wheel torque to compensate. If the warning light comes on, and the system hasn't been deactivated by the rider, a fault is indicated in the ASC system and ASC is not working – is this instance the fault must be investigated by a BMW dealer.

19 RDC (tyre pressure monitoring) system

1 Sensors in the wheels, either integral with, or adjacent to, the valves relay tyre pressure values to the instrument display via a wireless link to the RDC receiver unit **(see illustrations)**.

19.1b . . . or adjacent to the valves

19.3a Disconnect the wiring connector . . .

19.3b . . . and remove the unit

19.8 Sticker marks the position of the sensor

2 The system is activated by scrolling down through the display functions using the INFO button on the left handlebar switch unit. RDC denotes the tyre pressure settings, with that for the front tyre on the left and rear tyre on the right – pressures are in Bars. Note that the pressure information is only transmitted once the machine has reached a road speed above 19 mph (30 kph). Tyre pressure information is available for 15 minutes after the machine has come to a halt.

3 The RDC receiver unit is located inside the rear bodywork. To remove the unit, if required, disconnect the wiring connector and undo the screws securing it to the rear mudguard (see illustrations).

4 If the pressure in any tyre is close to the edge of the permitted range the tyre pressure symbol will appear on the multi-function display panel and the appropriate tyre pressure on the display will flash.

5 If the tyre pressure becomes critical the general warning triangle will illuminate yellow.

6 If the pressure falls outside of the permitted range the warning triangle flashes red.

7 Note that the sensors transmit tyre temperature as well as pressure to the receiver unit. The pressure settings are based on a reference temperature of 20°C and the receiver unit ensures that the pressure displayed is 'temperature compensated' to take into account tyre temperature outside of this figure.

8 A sticker on the wheel rim marks the position of the sensor (see illustration). Be sure to advise the dealer or tyre fitter that pressure sensors are fitted as damage could be caused to the sensor if care is not taken in this area.

9 Fitting a new sensor requires the sensor to be registered with the receiver unit using the BMW MOSS diagnostic tester

Chapter 6
Bodywork

Contents

Section number

General information 1
R1200 GS and GS Adventure models 2

Section number

R1200 R models 4
R1200 RT models 3

Degrees of difficulty

Easy, suitable for novice with little experience	**Fairly easy,** suitable for beginner with some experience	**Fairly difficult,** suitable for competent DIY mechanic	**Difficult,** suitable for experienced DIY mechanic	**Very difficult,** suitable for expert DIY or professional

Specifications

Torque settings

Crash bar centre section bolts	19 Nm
Crash bar to crankcase bolts	25 Nm
Crash bar assembly and frame screws	9 Nm
Fuel tank guard to crash bar bolts	19 Nm
Handlebar end-weight bolts	21 Nm
Headlight bracket bolts	19 Nm
Luggage rack	
R1200 GS and GS Adventure	
Centre bolt	10 Nm
Side mounting bolts	10 Nm
Side mounting nuts and bolts	8 Nm
R1200 RT	
Mounting bolts	8 Nm
Mirror adapter	25 Nm
Mirror stem locknut	22 Nm
Pannier bracket screws – R1200 R	10 Nm
Passenger grab handle bolts	19 Nm
Rear brake caliper/spray guard bracket mounting bolt	24 Nm
Seat cowling – R1200 GS and GS Adventure	8 Nm
Side case support brackets – R1200 GS Adventure	
Centre mounting bolts	10 Nm
Clamp bolts	20 Nm
Cross-member screws	10 Nm
Spray guard mounting bolts	8 Nm
Windshield screws	2.4 Nm

1 General information

This Chapter covers the procedures necessary to remove and install the bodywork. Since many service and repair operations on these motorcycles require the removal of the body parts, the procedures are grouped here and referred to from other Chapters.

In the case of damage to the body parts, it is usually necessary to remove the broken component and replace it with a new (or used) one. There are however some shops that specialise in 'plastic welding', so it may be worthwhile seeking the advice of one of these specialists before consigning an expensive component to the bin. Alternatively some of the DIY bodywork repair kits are ideal for small repairs.

When attempting to remove any body panel, first study it closely, noting any fasteners and associated fittings, to be sure of returning everything to its correct place on installation. In some cases the aid of an assistant will be required when removing panels, to help avoid the risk of damage to paintwork. Once the evident fasteners have been removed, try to withdraw the panel as described but DO NOT FORCE IT – if it will not release, check that all fasteners have been removed and try again. Where a panel engages another by means of tabs, be careful not to break the tab or its mating slot or to damage the paintwork. Remember that a few moments of patience at this stage will save you a lot of money in replacing broken fairing panels!

When installing a body panel, first study it closely, noting any fasteners and associated fittings removed with it, to be sure of returning everything to its correct place. Check that all fasteners are in good condition, including all trim nuts or clips and damping/rubber mounts; any of these must be replaced if faulty before the panel is reassembled. Check also that all mounting brackets are straight and repair or replace them if necessary before attempting to install the panel. Where assistance was required to remove a panel, make sure your assistant is on hand to install it.

Tighten the fasteners securely, but be careful not to overtighten any of them or the panel may break (not always immediately) due to the uneven stress.

2 R1200 GS and GS Adventure models

Seats

Removal

1 Insert the ignition key into the seat lock located on the left-hand side. Turn the key clockwise while pressing down on the front of the passenger's seat to unlock it, then lift the front of the seat **(see illustration)**. Note how the hooks on the underside of the seat engage in the top of the seat cowling **(see illustration)**.

2 To remove the rider's seat, turn the key anti-clockwise while pressing down on the rear of the rider's seat to unlock it, then lift the rear of the seat **(see illustration)**. Draw the seat back to release the tabs on the front, inside edges, from the rear of the tank side panels and lift it off **(see illustration)**. Note how the two bars on the underside of the seat rest in the supports on the frame **(see illustration)**.

Height adjustment

3 Note how the two bars on the underside of the rider's seat locate in the support brackets **(see illustration)**. There are two positions for the bars. Ensure that both bars are located in either the HIGH or LOW positions, otherwise the seat will not be held securely on the bike.

Installation

4 Check the operation of the seat catch mechanism **(see illustration)**.

2.1a Lift the passenger's seat from the front

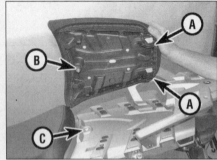

2.1b Note how the hooks (A) locate, and how the lock pin (B) locates in the catch (C)

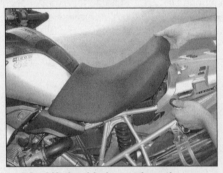

2.2a Lift the rider's seat from the rear

2.2b Seat tabs locate on rear of tank (arrowed)

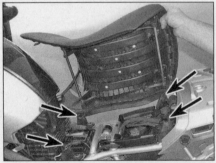

2.2c Note how the bars on the underside of the seat rest in the supports on the frame (arrowed)

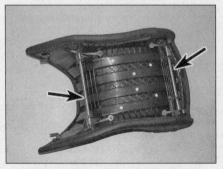

2.3 Note location of height adjustment bars

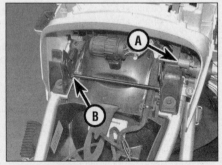

2.4 Check the operation of the seat lock (A) and catch mechanism (B)

5 Install the seats in the reverse order of removal. Ensure the tabs on the front of the rider's seat are correctly located, then press it down until the catch is heard to click. Engage the hooks on the underside of the passenger's seat with the seat cowling and press the seat down until the catch is heard to click.

Luggage rack, side-case support brackets and seat cowling

6 Remove the seats (see above).

R1200 GS

7 Undo the bolts securing the luggage rack and lift it off, noting the arrangement of washers and spacers on the centre rear bolt **(see illustrations)**.

8 Lift off the spacers – note there are spacers on the inside and outside of the side mounting brackets **(see illustrations)**.

9 If fitted, the side-case support brackets must be taken off before the seat cowling can be removed. First, loosen the locknut and

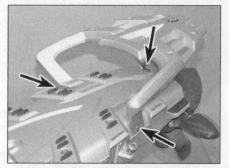

2.7a Luggage rack mounting bolts (arrowed)

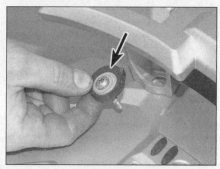

2.7b Note the arrangement of the washers and spacers

unscrew the rear bobbin **(see illustration)**. Counter-hold the nuts on the front mounting bolts, undo the bolts and lift off the rear bracket **(see illustrations)**. Unscrew the rear mounting bolt and remove the support bracket **(see illustration)**. Installation is the reverse of removal.

10 To remove the seat cowling, undo the bolts and washers securing the top of the cowling, and the screws on the inside front edge, and lift it off **(see illustrations)**. Installation is the reverse of removal. Clean the threads of the cowling bolts and apply a suitable non-permanent thread locking compound.

2.8a Remove the spacer at the rear . . .

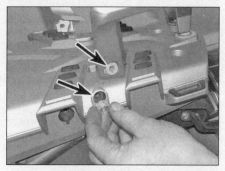

2.8b . . . and the two (arrowed) from the left and right-hand sides

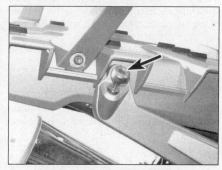

2.9a Unscrew the bobbin

2.9b Undo the bolts (arrowed) . . .

2.9c . . . and remove the rear bracket

2.9d Unscrew rear mounting bolt

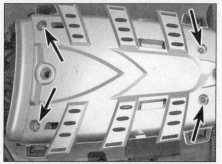

2.10a Undo the bolts . . .

2.10b . . . and the screws on both sides

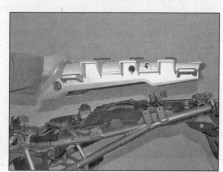

2.10c Lift off the seat cowling

2.12 Undo the bolts (arrowed) on both sides

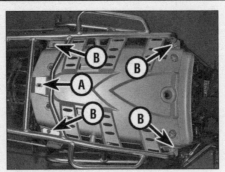

2.13 Undo the centre bolt (A). Note side mounting bolts (B)

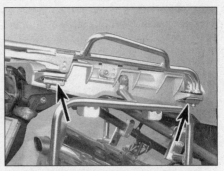

2.14a Note location of mounting plates

Fit the long bolts at the front. Tighten the bolts to the torque setting specified at the beginning of this Chapter. Tighten the screws securely.

11 Don't forget to fit the spacers before installing the luggage rack **(see illustrations 2.8a and b)**. Clean the threads of the luggage rack bolts and apply a suitable non-permanent thread locking compound. Tighten the bolts to the specified torque setting.

R1200 GS Adventure

12 To remove the luggage rack, first undo the left and right-hand mounting bolts and washers **(see illustration)**.

13 Undo the centre bolt and washer **(see illustration)**.
14 Undo the nuts and bolts securing the rack on both sides **(see illustration 2.13)**. Note the location of the mounting plates on the underside of the seat cowling – the plates are marked with their positions **(see illustrations)**.
15 Lift off the rack, the spacers and the mounting inserts **(see illustrations)**.
16 To install the rack, fit the mounting inserts and spacers **(see illustrations 2.15d, c and b)** and secure the rack loosely in position with the centre bolt **(see illustration 2.13)**.
17 Install the mounting plates and tighten the nuts and bolts finger-tight **(see**

illustration 2.14a)**. The front left-hand plate is marked VL; rear left-hand plate HL; front right-hand plate VR; rear right-hand plate HR **(see illustration 2.14b)**.
18 Install the left and right-hand mounting bolts and washers finger-tight **(see illustration 2.12)**.
19 Ensure the rack is correctly aligned, then tighten the left and right-hand bolts to the torque setting specified at the beginning of this Chapter. Tighten the nuts and bolts, then tighten the centre bolt to the specified torque settings.
20 If fitted, the side-case support brackets must be taken off before the seat cowling can be removed **(see illustration)**.

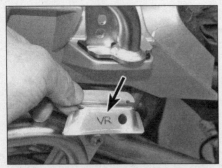

2.14b Plates are marked according to position

2.15a Lift off the rack . . .

2.15b . . . the side spacers . . .

2.15c . . . the top spacer . . .

2.15d . . . and the inserts

2.20 Location of the side-case support brackets

2.21a Note how the bracket halves inter-lock

2.21b Remove the bracket halves

2.22a Undo the bolts . . .

21 Working on one side at a time, note how the two halves of the lower T-bracket inter-lock, then undo the screws and remove the bracket **(see illustrations)**.

22 Undo the clamp bolts and remove the back half of the clamp **(see illustrations)**.

23 Undo the screw securing the cross-member and undo the upper mounting screw **(see illustration)**. If the cross-member is removed completely, note that the longer end is fitted on the left-hand side.

24 Support the bracket and undo the centre mounting bolt **(see illustration)**. Lift off the bracket noting the location of the spacers for the upper mounting screw and centre mounting bolt **(see illustration)**.

25 Install the side-case support brackets in the reverse order of removal with the fixings finger-tight.

26 Ensure the brackets are correctly aligned, then tighten the centre mounting bolts to the torque setting specified at the beginning of this Chapter **(see illustration 2.24a)**. Tighten the upper mounting screws securely.

27 Tighten the upper clamp bolts, then tighten the lower clamp bolts to the specified torque setting **(see illustration 2.22a)**.

28 Tighten the T-bracket screws securely, then tighten the cross-member screws to the specified torque setting.

29 Undo the bolts, screws and washers securing the seat cowling and lift it off (see Step 10). Installation is the reverse of removal.

Spray guard

30 Undo the bolts securing the spray guard and lift it off **(see illustration)**. Note the location of the washer and spacer on the long mounting bolt.

31 Note the location of the mounting bracket which is retained by one of the rear brake caliper mounting bolts. If required, undo the caliper mounting bolt and remove the bracket **(see illustration)**.

32 Installation is the reverse of removal. If the mounting bracket has been removed, use the long mounting bolt to align the bracket with the bolt hole before tightening the caliper bracket bolts (see Chapter 5, Section 6).

2.22b . . . and remove the back half of the clamp

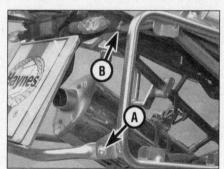

2.23 Undo screws (A) and (B)

2.24a Undo centre mounting bolt

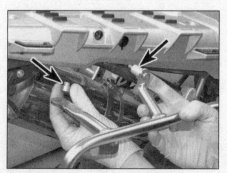

2.24b Note location of the spacers

2.30 Spray guard is secured by three bolts

2.31 Undo the caliper mounting bolt to remove bracket

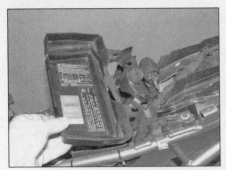

2.35 Lift out the document tray

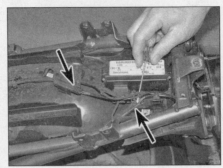

2.36a Disconnect the turn signal wiring connectors (arrowed)

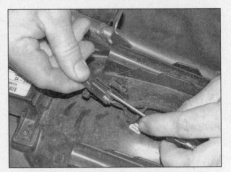

2.36b Release the wiring from any clips or ties

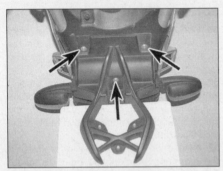

2.37a Tail light/number plate assembly is secured by screws (arrowed)

33 Clean the threads of the spray guard bolts and apply a suitable non-permanent thread locking compound. Tighten the bolts to the torque setting specified at the beginning of this Chapter.

Rear mudguard

34 Remove the seats, luggage rack and seat cowling (see above).
35 Lift out the document tray (see illustration).
36 Trace the wiring from the left and right-hand turn signals and disconnect it at the connectors (see illustration). Release the wiring from any ties and unclip the connectors from the mudguard (see illustration).
37 Undo the screws securing the tail light/number plate bracket assembly and displace the assembly (see illustration). Disconnect the light unit wiring connector and lift the tail light/number plate bracket off (see illustrations).
38 On machines equipped with RDC tyre pressure monitoring, disconnect the wiring connector and unclip the RDC receiver from the mudguard (see Chapter 5, Section 19).
39 Unclip the connector for the BMW diagnostic tool from its holder (see illustration).
40 Release the wiring connector from the back of the accessory socket connector (see illustration).
41 Ensure the wiring loom is free from the mudguard. Undo the screws securing the underside of the mudguard, then lower the mudguard and lift it off (see illustrations).
42 Installation is the reverse of removal. Don't forget to secure the wiring as noted on removal and ensure the connectors are tight. Check the operation of the lights and turn signals before riding the motorcycle.

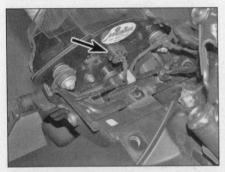

2.37b Disconnect the wiring connector . . .

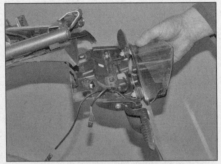

2.37c . . . and lift the assembly off

2.39 Displace the diagnostic tool connector

2.40 Disconnect the accessory socket

2.41a Undo the screws on the underside . . .

2.41b . . . and lift the mudguard off

2.43a Pull the side cover off . . .

2.43b . . . noting location of the grommets

2.46a Side panel rear fixing screws . . .

Side covers and fuel tank panels

Side covers

43 Ease the side cover off, noting how the two pegs on the back of the cover locate in grommets **(see illustrations)**.

44 To ease installation, apply a small amount of dry film lubricant to the grommets before pressing the cover on.

Fuel tank panels

45 The main tank side panel comprises two separate panels that can be removed either as an assembly or individually as required.

46 To remove the side panel assembly, first undo the screws at the rear, then undo the screw on the front edge **(see illustrations)**.

47 Pull the panel back carefully to release the peg on the inside edge from the grommet on the oil cooler bracket **(see illustration)**. Note

how the top edge of the side panel locates on tabs on the adjacent panels **(see illustration)**.

48 To remove the panels individually, first undo the screws securing the front section and lift it off **(see illustrations)**.

49 Undo the screws at the rear **(see illustration 2.46a)**, then pull the panel back carefully to release the peg on the inside edge **(see illustration 2.47a)**.

50 Installation is the reverse of removal. Check the condition of the U-clips securing the screws and renew them if they are sprained. Ensure that the rear and top edges of the panel are correctly located before pressing the peg into the grommet.

51 To remove the rear tank side panels, first remove the seats, the side covers and the main tank side panels (see above).

52 Undo the screws securing the side panel

2.46b . . . and front fixing screw

to the tank, then draw the panel down to release the tab on the top edge and lift it off **(see illustrations)**. Installation is the reverse of removal.

2.47a Release peg from grommet (arrowed)

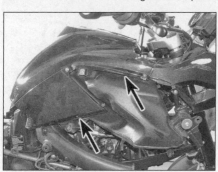

2.47b Note locating tabs

2.48a Undo the screws . . .

2.48b . . . and lift the front section off

2.52a Undo the screws . . .

2.52b . . . and lower the panel off

2.54 Undo the screw (arrowed) on the left and right-hand side

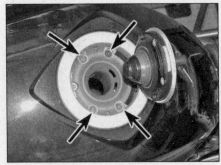

2.55a Undo the screws . . .

2.55b . . . and remove the filler cap assembly

2.56 Lift off the fuel tank top panel

53 To remove the top panel, first remove the seats and all the tank side panels.

54 Undo the screws securing the left and right-hand front edges of the top panel **(see illustration)**.

55 Undo the screws securing the fuel tank filler cap assembly and lift it off **(see illustrations)**.

56 Lift off the top panel **(see illustration)**. Temporarily install the filler cap assembly.

57 Installation is the reverse of removal. Tighten the filler cap assembly screws evenly.

Front mudguards

Upper mudguard

58 Remove both main fuel tank side panels (see above).

59 Undo the screws securing the air deflectors and lift them off **(see illustration)**. Note the location of the grommets in the mounting holes, the top-hat spacers that fit in the grommets and the plastic washers that fit on top of the mudguard **(see illustration)**.

60 Undo the screws securing the top rear edges of the mudguard to the front edges of the fuel tank top panel **(see illustration 2.54)**. Note how the rear edges of the mudguard fit underneath the front edges of the top panel. Note the location of the U-clips **(see illustration)**.

61 Undo the screws on both sides securing the mudguard to the oil cooler bracket **(see illustration)**. On R1200 GS Adventure models, the front screws secure the mudguard trim panel **(see illustrations)**.

2.59a Air deflectors are secured by screws (arrowed)

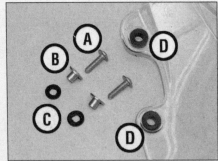

2.59b Air deflector fixings – screws (A), top hat spacers (B), plastic washers (C) and grommets (D)

2.60 Location of U-clip

2.61a Undo screws on both sides

2.61b Front screws on both sides . . .

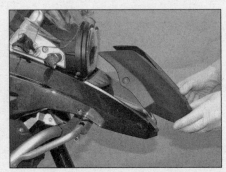

2.61c . . . secure the mudguard trim panel

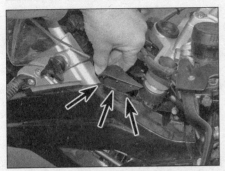

2.62a Unclip the trim panel tabs . . .

2.62b . . . draw the mudguard off the peg on both sides . . .

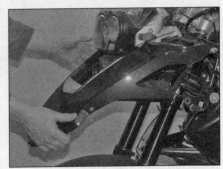

2.62c . . . then lift the mudguard off

62 Unclip the cockpit trim panel from both sides of the mudguard **(see illustration)**, then draw the mudguard forward to free it from the pegs on the headlight brackets and lift the mudguard off **(see illustrations)**.

63 Installation is the reverse of removal. Ensure that the mudguard is correctly aligned and that the trim panel is clipped in position before installing the fixing screws.

Lower mudguard

64 Remove the front wheel (see Chapter 5).

65 Undo the screws on the underside of the mudguard securing it to the front fork bridge, then draw the mudguard forwards and off the bike. **(see illustrations)**.

66 Installation is the reverse of removal.

Cockpit trim panel

67 Remove the upper front mudguard (see above).

68 Release the trim clip securing the centre of the panel then lift it out **(see illustrations)**.

Windshield

69 Undo the screws securing the windshield to the front bracket, taking care to secure the nuts on the inside of the windshield **(see illustrations)**.

70 Counter-hold the locknut on the end of the adjuster knob thread and unscrew the adjuster, then unscrew the adjuster out from the threaded sleeve **(see illustration)** – take care to remove the locknut and inner and

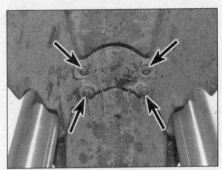

2.65a Mudguard is secured to fork bridge by screws (arrowed)

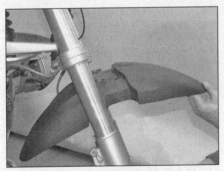

2.65b Draw the mudguard forwards to remove it

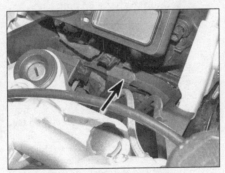

2.68a Release the trim clip . . .

2.68b . . . and lift the panel out

2.69a Undo the screws

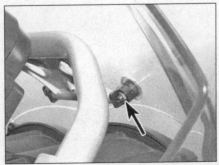

2.69b Take care not to lose the nuts

2.70a Unscrew the adjuster knob

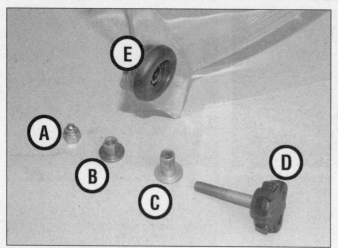

2.70b Components of the windshield adjuster – locknut (A), threaded sleeve (B), outer sleeve (C), knob (D) and latching plates (E)

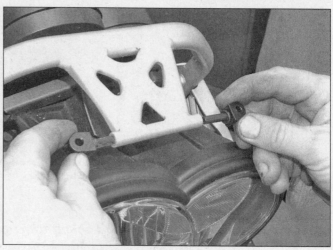

2.71a Note the location of the mounting stubs

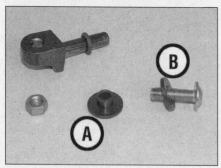

2.71b Note the plastic sleeve (A) and washer (B) on both mounting screws

2.73 Undo the bolts on both sides

outer sleeves with the adjuster knob **(see illustration)**.

71 Lift the windshield off. Note the position of the angled mounting stubs which locate in the ends of the support bracket and remove them for safekeeping **(see illustration)**. Remove the plastic sleeves from the windshield and note the location of the washers on the windshield screws **(see illustration)**.

72 Unless they are damaged, the two-piece latching plates that fit through from either side of the windshield and clip together should be left in position **(see illustration 2.70b)** – trying to prise them apart may result in damage.

73 To remove the windshield support bracket, first remove the headlight unit/instrument cluster assembly (see Chapter 7, Section 7). Trace the wiring from the front turn signal units and disconnect it at the connectors. Free the wiring from any clips or ties. Undo the bolts securing the support bracket and lift it off **(see illustration)**.

74 Installation is the reverse of removal. Ensure that the stubs are installed the correct way round in the support bracket, angled upwards with the recess for the nuts at the back **(see illustration 2.71a)**. Don't forget to fit the plastic sleeves and washers onto

the mounting screws, and apply a suitable non-permanent thread locking compound to the screws. Take care not to over-tighten the screws.

Mirrors

75 The mirror stems are screwed into adapters in the top halves of the clutch and front brake lever brackets. To remove the mirror, first peel back the boot covering the stem locknut, then counter-hold the adapter and loosen the locknut **(see illustration)**. **Note:** *The locknuts and mirror stems are left-hand threaded – turn clockwise to unscrew.* Unscrew the mirror stem from the adapter **(see illustration)**. If required, unscrew the adapter from the lever bracket. The adapters are right-hand threaded – turn anti-clockwise to unscrew.

76 Installation is the reverse of removal. Hold the mirror in the desired position, tighten the locknut and refit the boot. Final adjustment can be made by tilting the mirror head **(see illustration)**.

Hand protectors

77 If required, the upper half of the hand protector can be removed as follows. Undo the screw taking care to remove the nut on

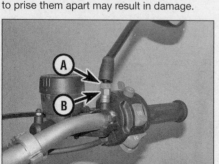

2.75a Counter-hold the adapter (B) and loosen the locknut (A)

2.75b Unscrew the mirror stem

2.76 Make final adjustments by tilting the mirror head

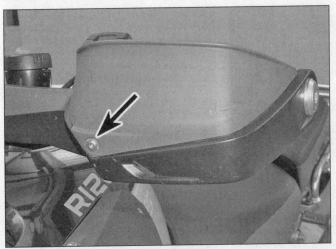

2.77a Undo the screw . . .

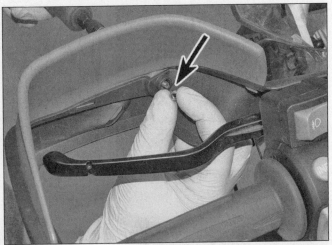

2.77b . . . and remove the nut

2.77c Separate the two halves

2.78 Undo the screw (arrowed)

2.79 End-weight bolt and collar

the inside of the protector **(see illustrations)**. Release the tabs on the lower edge of the upper half from the slots in the lower half **(see illustration)**.

78 To remove the complete hand protector, first undo the screw securing the hand protector to the handlebar bracket **(see illustration)**.

79 Unscrew the handlebar end-weight bolt and withdraw the bolt and collar **(see illustration)**.

80 Lift off the hand protector and pull the end-weight out from the handlebar **(see illustrations)**.

81 If required, undo the handlebar bracket clamp screw and lift the bracket off **(see illustration)**.

82 Installation is the reverse of removal. Ensure that the cables, hoses and wiring are correctly routed inside the hand protector, as appropriate. Apply a suitable non-permanent thread locking compound to the end-weight bolt and tighten it to the specified torque setting.

Crash bar

83 The front crash bar is a four-piece assembly. Working on one side at a time, remove the lower left and right-hand sections first.

84 Undo the screw securing the upper end of the side section **(see illustration)**.

2.80a Lift off the hand protector . . .

2.80b . . . and pull out the end-weight

2.81 Handlebar bracket clamp screw

2.84 Undo the screw

2.85a Undo the bolt (arrowed) . . .

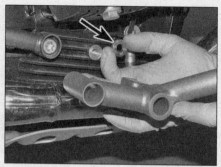

2.85b . . . noting location of the spacer

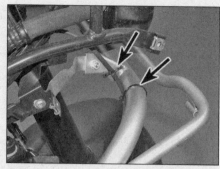

2.86 Ties secure auxiliary headlight wiring

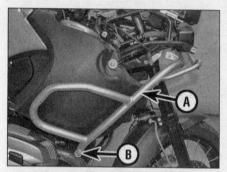

2.87 Crash bar upper section (A). Undo the bolts (B) on both sides

2.88a Undo the screws on both sides . . .

2.88b . . . and manoeuvre the upper section off

85 Undo the bolt securing the lower end of the side section to the crankcase, noting the location of the spacer between the crash bar bracket and the crankcase (see illustrations). Lift the side section off.
86 Follow the procedure in Chapter 7 and remove the auxiliary headlights. Release the ties securing the headlight wiring to the crash bar (see illustration).
87 Undo the left and right-hand bolts securing the upper section of the crash bar to the centre section (see illustration).
88 Support the crash bar. Undo the left and right-hand screws securing the upper section to the upper support brackets (see illustration). Ease the lower ends of the upper section off the ends of the centre section (see illustration).

89 Undo the left and right-hand screws securing the centre section to the crankcases (see illustration).
90 Installation is the reverse of removal. Tighten all the bolts finger-tight and ensure that the crash bar is correctly aligned, then tighten the screws and bolts to the torque settings specified at the beginning of this Chapter.

Sump guard

91 The sump guard must be removed to access the engine oil drain plug and oil filter (see Chapter 1, Section 1).
92 If required, unscrew the rear mountings from the bottom of the crankcase and undo the through bolt securing the front mounting bracket (see Chapter 2, Section 4).
93 Installation is the reverse of removal.

3   R1200 RT models

Seats

Removal

1 Insert the ignition key into the seat lock located below the tail light. Turn the key anticlockwise while pressing down on the rear of the passenger's seat to unlock it. Lift the rear of the seat (see illustration). On models with heated seats, disconnect the seat wiring connector (see illustration). Pull the seat backwards and off.

2.89 Undo the screws on both sides

3.1a Unlock the passenger's seat and lift it from the rear

3.1b Disconnect the seat wiring connector

3.2 Lift the rider's seat from the rear

3.3a Position the front mounting bar (arrowed) in the appropriate holder

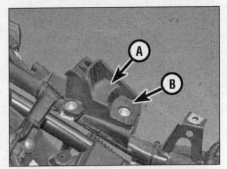

3.3b HIGH (A) and LOW (B) positions on the frame brackets

3.4 Check the operation of the seat catch mechanism

3.8 Location of the rear luggage rack bolts (arrowed)

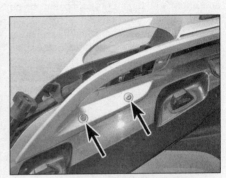

3.9 Undo the bolts on both sides

2 To remove the rider's seat, first remove the passenger's seat. Lift the rear of the seat and pull it backwards (see illustration). On models with heated seats, disconnect the seat wiring connector. Remove the seat.

Height adjustment

3 The height of the rider's seat is adjustable. To adjust the height, position the front mounting bar in the appropriate holder (see illustration). With the bar in the LOW position, the supports on the rear underside of the seat

should locate in the forward mounting position on the frame brackets (see illustration).

Installation

4 Check the operation of the seat catch mechanism (see illustration).
5 Install the seats in the reverse order of removal. Ensure the rider's seat is fully located on the frame brackets, then push the passenger's seat into position and press it down until the catch is heard to click.

Luggage rack

6 Remove the passenger's seat (see above).

7 Displace the tail light unit (see Chapter 7).
8 Undo the bolts securing the rear underside of the luggage rack to the rear sub-frame – note that the bolts are located up inside the frame (see illustration).
9 Undo the bolts securing both sides of the luggage rack to the rear sub-frame (see illustration).
10 Undo the bolts securing the top of the luggage rack and lift the rack off (see illustrations).
11 Installation is the reverse of removal. Clean the threads of the luggage rack bolts

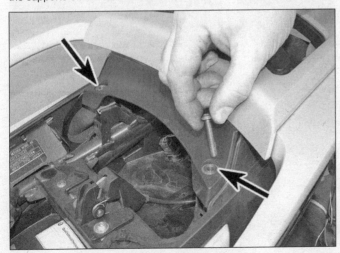

3.10a Undo the bolts (arrowed) . . .

3.10b . . . and lift the luggage rack off

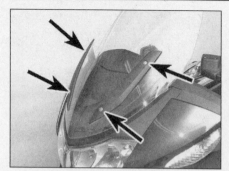

3.12a Undo the screws . . .

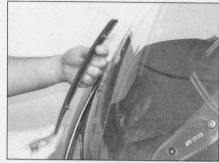

3.12b . . . and lift the windshield trim panels off

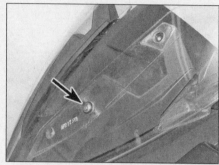

3.13a Undo the screws and washers on both sides

and apply a suitable non-permanent thread locking compound. Tighten the bolts to the torque setting specified at the beginning of this Chapter. Check the operation of the lights before riding the motorcycle.

3.13b Lift off the inner panel

Windshield

12 Undo the screws securing the windshield trim panels and lift the panels off **(see illustrations)**.

13 Undo the screws and washers securing the windshield and lift it off **(see illustration)**. Lift the inner panel off the windshield brackets **(see illustration)**.

14 To remove the windshield brackets, carefully prise the E-clips off the pivot pins **(see illustration)**. Press the pins out, noting how they are fitted, and lift the brackets off **(see illustrations)**.

15 To gain access to the motor that raises and lowers the windshield, follow the 'Headlight panel removal' procedure below and remove the fairing headlight panel.

16 Installation is the reverse of removal. Ensure that the brackets are fitted the right

way round, then press the upper pivot pins in from the outside and the lower pins in from the inside **(see illustrations 3.14c and b)**. If the E-clips are strained or corroded replace them with new ones. Ensure the washers are fitted on the windshield screws and take care not to over-tighten the screws. Check the operation of the windshield motor.

Mirrors

17 The mirrors are secured in their housings by a set screw, accessible through a hole on the underside of the housing. To remove a mirror, first push the lower edge into the housing, then loosen the screw with a suitable Torx key just enough to be able to pull the mirror out **(see illustrations)**.

18 If required, undo the screws securing the backplate and lift it out **(see illustrations)**. Note how the backplate locates on the

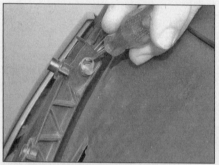

3.14a Prise off the E-clips . . .

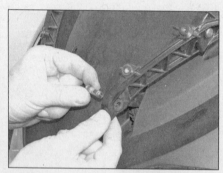

3.14b . . . then press out the pins . . .

3.14c . . . and lift the brackets off

3.17a Loosen the set screw . . .

3.17b . . . and pull the mirror out

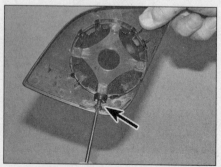

3.17c Location of the screw on the back of the mirror

3.18a Undo the screws . . .

3.18b . . . and remove the backplate

3.18c Note locating peg on headlight panel

peg on the rear of the headlight panel **(see illustration)**.

19 Installation is the reverse of removal.

Fairing panels

Note: *The machines covered in this manual were available from new fitted with a range of optional electrical extras. When working on your machine, take care to ensure that all relevant electrical components are disconnected on disassembly and subsequently reconnected* during the rebuild. *Always take the precaution of disconnecting the battery negative (-) terminal before disconnecting an electrical wiring connector.*
Model specific extras are included in the Wiring Diagrams at the end of Chapter 7.

Upper side panels

20 Undo the screws on the inside front edge of the panel, the screw below the cockpit trim panel and the upper screw on the rear edge of the panel **(see illustrations)**. Ease the panel off carefully. When removing the left-hand panel, disconnect the wiring connector for the accessory socket **(see illustration)**.

21 Installation is the reverse of removal. Ensure that the U-clips are secure on the mounting points **(see illustration)**. Don't forget to connect the wiring connector before installing the panel.

Main side panels

22 Remove the seats (see above).

3.20a Undo the screws on the inside front edge . . .

3.20b . . . the screw next to the steering head . . .

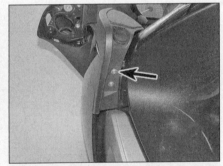

3.20c . . . and the upper screw on the rear edge of the panel

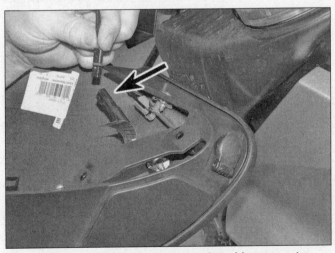

3.20d Disconnect the accessory socket wiring connector

3.21 Check that the U-clips are secure

3.24a Undo the screws at the front . . .

3.24b . . . and at the rear . . .

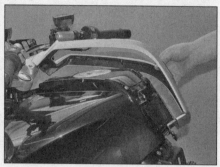

3.24c . . . then lift the tank rail off

3.25a Undo the screws at the front . . .

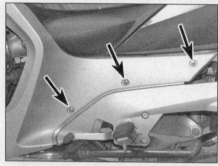

3.25b . . . and at the rear of the fairing panel

3.26a Undo the screws on the front . . .

3.26b . . . and back of the fuel tank

3.27a Undo the screw on the top rear edge . . .

undo the screws located above and below the exhaust header pipe and the screws securing the panel to the footrest bracket **(see illustrations)**.

26 Undo the screws on the front and back of the fuel tank, noting how the edge of the side panel locates over the tabs on the edge of the tank centre panel **(see illustrations)**.

27 Undo the screw on the top rear edge of the side panel, noting how the tab locates above the tab on the seat cowling **(see illustrations)**.

28 Support the panel and undo the quick-release catch, then lift the panel off **(see illustration)**.

29 To remove the fairing right-hand panel, first undo the screws securing the storage compartment lid and lift the lid off **(see illustration)**. Undo the screws securing the

23 Remove the upper side panels as required (see above).

24 Undo the screws securing the front and

rear of the fuel tank rail and lift the rail off **(see illustrations)**.

25 To remove the fairing left-hand panel,

3.27b . . . noting location of side panel and seat cowling (arrowed) tabs

3.28 Undo the quick-release catch

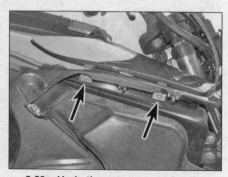

3.29a Undo the screws securing the storage compartment lid

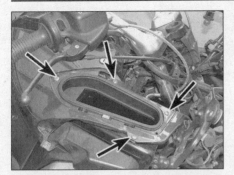

3.29b Panel is secured to the storage compartment by screws (arrowed)

3.30 Displace the air temperature sensor

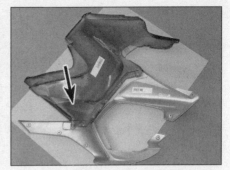

3.32 Location of the trim panel

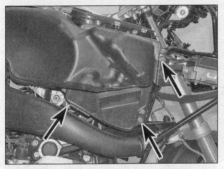

3.33 Screws secure storage compartment

3.34a Left-hand side panel support bracket

3.34b Right-hand side panel support bracket

top of the panel to the storage compartment **(see illustration)**.

30 Unclip the air temperature sensor and wiring from the front edge of the panel **(see illustration)**.

31 Now follow Steps 25 to 28 and lift the panel off.

32 The main side panels are constructed from two sections with a small trim panel **(see illustration)**. If required, undo the screws securing the sections together and separate them carefully.

33 If required, undo the screws securing the storage compartment **(see illustration)** and lift it out

34 Note the location of the left and right-hand side panel support brackets **(see illustrations)**. If required, undo the bolts securing the brackets and remove them. Note that the headlight panel must be removed (see

below) to access the upper mounting bolt on the right-hand bracket **(see illustration)**.

35 Installation is the reverse of removal. Ensure that the U-clips are secure on the mounting points **(see illustration)**. Don't forget to connect the wiring for equipment housed in the panel before installing the panel. Ensure the panel is correctly aligned with its mounting points and adjacent panels before tightening the mounting screws. When installing the right-hand panel, check the operation of the storage compartment lid catch before installing the upper side panel. Renew the quick-release catch if it is too worn to grip in its location **(see illustration 3.28)**.

Headlight panel

36 Remove the windshield and windshield brackets, mirrors and mirror backplates, and fairing upper side panels (see above).

3.34c Right-hand upper mounting bolt

37 Undo the screws securing the front turn signal units and disconnect the wiring connectors from the bulbholders **(see illustrations)**.

3.35 Check that the U-clips are secure

3.37a Undo the screw securing the turn signal unit . . .

3.37b . . . and disconnect the wiring connector

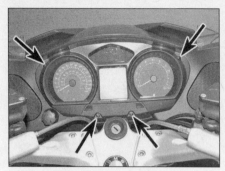

3.38a Undo the screws . . .

3.38b . . . and lift off the cover

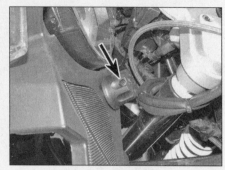

3.39a Undo the screw . . .

3.39b . . . and pull off the knob

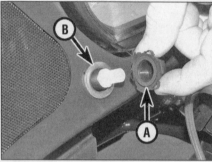

3.39c Note rubber washer (A) and plain washer (B)

3.40a Undo the screws on both sides

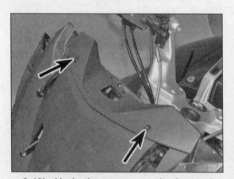

3.40b Undo the screws on the forward edge . . .

3.40c . . . then lift the trim panel off

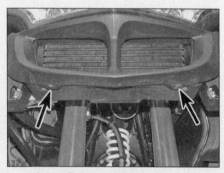

3.41a Release the trim clips . . .

3.41b . . . noting how they fit

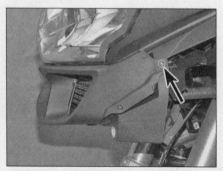

3.41c Undo the screw on both sides . . .

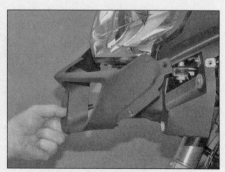

3.41d . . . and remove the cover

3.42 Disconnect the wiring connector

3.43a Undo the screws at the front . . .

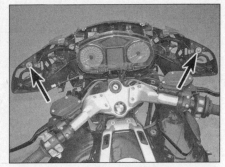

3.43b . . . and at the rear of the headlight panel . . .

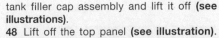

38 Undo the screws securing the instrument cluster cover and remove the cover **(see illustrations)**.

39 Undo the screw securing the headlight heavy load adjuster knob and pull off the knob **(see illustrations)**. Unscrew the nut and remove the rubber washer and plain washer **(see illustration)**.

40 Undo the screws on the left and right-hand side of the cockpit trim panel **(see illustration)**. Undo the screws on the upper forward edge of the trim panel, then lift the panel off **(see illustrations)**.

41 Release the trim clips securing the oil cooler cover **(see illustrations)**. Undo the left and right-hand screws securing the cover and lift it off **(see illustration)**.

42 Disconnect the headlight unit wiring connector **(see illustration)**.

43 Undo the screws on the left and right-hand sides, securing front and rear of the headlight panel, noting the location of the washers and mounting bushes in the support bracket **(see illustrations)**.

44 Draw the headlight panel forwards, noting how the windshield pivot arms locate through the slots in the panel, and then lift the panel off **(see illustration)**. Inspect the bushes on the fairing bracket and renew them if they are damaged or deteriorated.

45 Installation is the reverse of removal. Align the windshield pivot arms correctly. Ensure that the headlight wiring connector is secure and check the operation of the lights before riding the motorcycle. Don't forget to install the headlight heavy load adjuster – see Chapter 7, Section 7 for set-up details.

Fuel tank top panel

46 Remove the left and right-hand main side panels (see above).

47 Undo the screws securing the fuel tank filler cap assembly and lift it off **(see illustrations)**.

48 Lift off the top panel **(see illustration)**. Temporarily install the filler cap assembly.

49 Installation is the reverse of removal. Tighten the filler cap assembly screws evenly.

Seat cowling

50 The left and right-hand cowling panels are remove separately. First, remove both seats and the luggage rack (see above).

51 To remove the right-hand cowling panel, first undo the screw securing the main side panel below the exhaust header pipe and the screws securing the side panel to the footrest bracket **(see illustrations 3.25a and b)**. Ease the rear section of the main side panel back to access the screw on the lower edge of the cowling panel and undo the screw **(see illustration)**. Alternatively, remove the main side panel to access the cowling panel screw (see above).

3.43c . . . noting the location of the washers and bushes

3.44 Lift the headlight panel off

3.47a Undo the screws . . .

3.47b . . . and remove the filler cap assembly

3.48 Lift off the top panel

3.51 Screw on lower edge of cowling panel

3.53 Undo the screws on the upper and lower edges

3.54a Undo the screw on the inside . . .

3.54b . . . and lift the panel off

3.55a Disconnect the accessory socket wiring connector

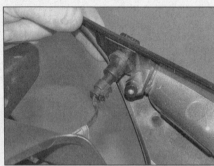

3.55b Note location of the accessory socket

52 Undo the screw securing the front top edge of the cowling, noting how the tab locates underneath the tab on the main side panel **(see illustrations 3.27a and b)**.

53 Undo the screws securing the upper and lower edges of the cowling **(see illustration)**.

54 Undo the screw on the rear inside of the cowling, then lift the cowling over the mounting for the side case **(see illustrations)**.

55 To remove the left-hand cowling panel, first disconnect the wiring connector for the accessory socket **(see illustration)**. Follow the procedure in Steps 51 to 54 to remove the panel. Note the location of the accessory socket **(see illustration)**.

56 If required, undo the screws securing the side case mounting brackets and remove them **(see illustration)**.

57 Installation is the reverse of removal.

Tail light and number plate bracket

58 Remove both seat cowling panels (see above).

59 Undo the screws securing the bracket to the rear sub-frame **(see illustrations)**. Ease the bracket rearwards, taking care to feed the tail light and turn signal bulbholders through the bracket, then lift the bracket off **(see illustrations)**.

60 Installation is the reverse of removal.

Rear mudguard

61 The front section of the rear mudguard must be removed to access the rear shock

3.56 Screws secure side case mounting bracket

3.59a Bracket is secured by screw on both sides . . .

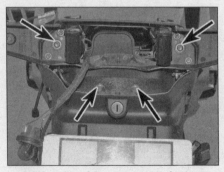

3.59b . . . and four screws at the rear

3.59c Feed the tail light and turn signal bulbholders through the bracket . . .

3.59d . . . and lift the bracket off

3.62 Unclip the ESA wiring

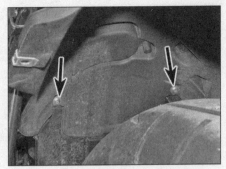

3.63 Screws secure front section of mudguard

3.65a Heated seat connectors

3.65b ESA wiring connectors

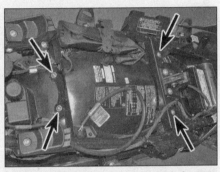

3.66 Undo the screws on the sub-frame cross-members

3.68a Undo the screws on both sides . . .

absorber. To remove the front section, first remove the exhaust silencer (see Chapter 3).

62 Unclip the ESA wiring from the right-hand side of the mudguard **(see illustration)**.

63 Undo the screws securing the front section of the mudguard **(see illustration)** and separate it from the main mudguard.

64 To remove the main mudguard, first remove both seat cowling panels and the tail light and number plate bracket (see above). Remove the front section of the mudguard.

65 A number of electrical components are mounted on the top of the mudguard, including the starter relay and BMW diagnostic tester plug unit, and where applicable, the anti-theft alarm and RDC tyre pressure monitoring receiver. Also note that the connectors for the heated seats and electronic suspension adjustment (ESA) are clipped to the mudguard **(see illustrations)**. Check that all the components, connectors and wiring are free from the mudguard before proceeding.

66 Undo the screws securing the mudguard

to the upper rear sub-frame cross-members and lift the mudguard off **(see illustration)**.

67 Installation is the reverse of removal. Check that all the wiring connectors are secure before installing the seat cowling panels.

Front mudguard

68 To remove the front section of the mudguard, undo the screws on both sides, then draw the front section forwards and unclip it from the main mudguard **(see illustrations)**.

69 Installation is the reverse of removal.

3.68b . . . then draw the front section forwards

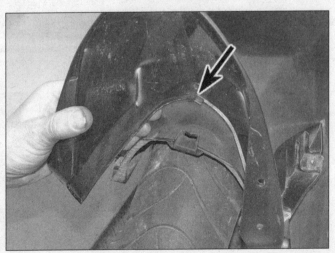

3.68c Note the location of the clip (arrowed)

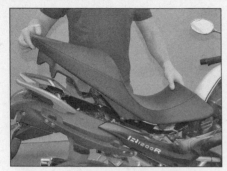

4.1a Unlock the seat and lift it from the rear

4.1b Note how the latch engages in the underside of the base

Ensure that the clip in the centre of the mudguard is correctly located before installing the screws.

70 To remove the main section of the mudguard, first remove the front section, then remove the front wheel (see Chapter 5).

71 Undo the screws on the underside of the mudguard securing it to the front fork bridge, then undo the screws securing the mudguard to the front fork sliders and draw the mudguard forwards and off the bike.

72 Installation is the reverse of removal.

4 R1200 R models

Seat

1 Insert the ignition key into the seat lock located under the tail light. Turn the key clockwise in the lock, lift up the rear of the seat and pull it backwards and off **(see illustration)**. Note how the seat latch engages in the underside of the seat base **(see illustration)**.

2 Install the seat in the reverse order of removal. Ensure that the two hooks on the frame either side of the battery engage the holes in the seat base **(see illustration)**.

3 Firmly press down on the seat at the rear until you hear it click into place and check that the seat is secure.

Side panels and rear bodywork

4 Remove the seat (see above).

5 The small black side covers must be removed before the main side panels can be detached. Working on one side at a time, remove the two screws and pull the side cover downwards to disengage its peg from the side panel **(see illustrations)**.

6 Undo the screws securing the side panels, noting the longer screws fit at the front, and lift off the panels **(see illustration)**. Note the location of the wellnuts in the mountings on the lower edge of the fuel tank **(see illustration)**. Prior to installation, lubricate the screw threads with a smear of grease.

7 Undo the screws securing the centre rear panel and lift it off **(see illustrations)**.

4.2 Mounting holes in seat engage the hooks (arrowed)

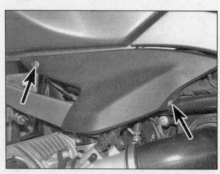

4.5a Side cover is retained by two screws (arrowed) . . .

4.5b . . . and a peg

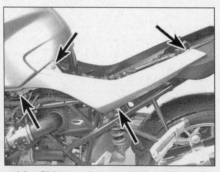

4.6a Side panel screws (arrowed) – left side shown

4.6b Note location of wellnuts

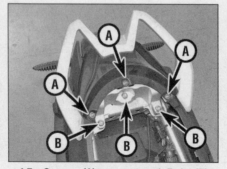

4.7a Screws (A) secure panel. Bolts (B) secure grab handle

4.7b Remove the centre rear panel

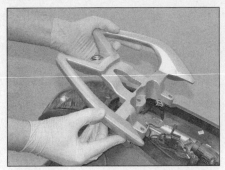

4.8 Remove the passenger grab handle

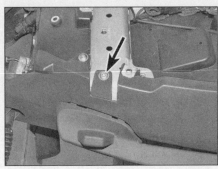

4.13a Pannier bracket upper mounting screw

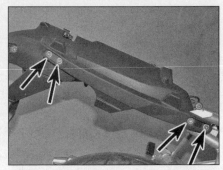

4.13b Undo the front and rear mounting screws . . .

4.13c . . . and lift the bracket off

4.14 Push out access cover from inside

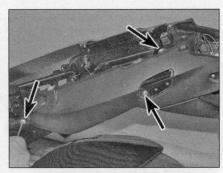

4.15 Location of seat cowling screws

8 Undo the bolts securing the passenger grab handle (see illustration 4.7a) and lift the handle off (see illustration).

9 Installation is the reverse of removal. Clean the threads of the grab handle mounting bolts and apply a suitable non-permanent thread-locking compound. Tighten the bolts to the torque setting specified at the beginning of this Chapter.

Seat cowling

10 Remove the seat, side panels and rear bodywork (see above).

11 Remove the tail light unit (see Chapter 7).

12 The left and right-hand cowling panels are removed separately. First, remove the rear turn signal assembly (see Chapter 7).

13 If fitted, undo the upper mounting screw for the pannier bracket (see illustration). Undo the front and rear mounting screws for the bracket and lift it off (see illustration).

14 Alternatively, push out the plastic cover to gain access to the hidden cowling screw (see illustration).

15 Undo the screws securing the seat cowling and lift it off (see illustration).

16 Installation is the reverse of removal. Where fitted, clean the threads of the pannier bracket screws and apply a suitable non-permanent thread-locking compound.

Check the operation of the lights before riding the motorcycle.

Number plate bracket

17 Remove both seat cowling panels (see above).

18 Release the E-clip securing the end of the outer seat cable, then free the end of the inner cable from the latch (see illustration). Check the condition of the E-clip and fit a new one if it is damaged of distorted.

19 Release the cable-ties securing the rear light wiring, then remove the screws securing the bracket and lift it off (see illustrations).

20 Installation is the reverse of removal.

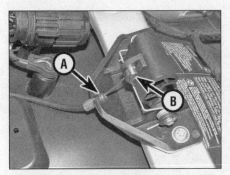

4.18 Release the outer (A) and inner (B) ends of the cable

4.19a Undo the screws . . .

4.19b . . . securing the number plate bracket

4.22a Displace the starter relay . . .

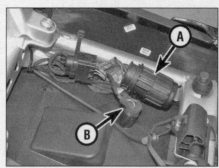

4.22b . . . diagnostic tester plug (A) and bulbholder (B)

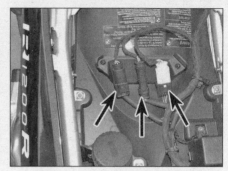

4.22c Location of the ESA wiring connectors

Check the operation of the seat lock before installing the seat.

Rear mudguard

21 Remove the seat, side panels, rear bodywork and number plate bracket (see above).
22 A number of electrical components are mounted on the top of the mudguard, including the starter relay, BMW diagnostic tester plug unit and bulbholder **(see illustrations)**. Where applicable, displace the anti-theft alarm and RDC tyre pressure monitoring unit. Also note that the connectors for the electronic suspension adjustment (ESA) are clipped to the mudguard **(see illustration)**. Check that all the components, connectors and wiring are free from the mudguard before proceeding.
23 Free the rear brake fluid reservoir from its cut-out in the mudguard **(see illustration)**.
24 Remove the screws located on the underside of the mudguard **(see illustrations)**. Ease the mudguard downwards to remove it from the rear frame
25 Installation is the reverse of removal.

Check that all the wiring is correctly secured before installing the bodywork panels.

Front mudguard

26 Undo the screws securing the air deflector on both sides and remove the deflectors, noting how the slot in the lower edge locates on the tab on the bottom edge of the mudguard **(see illustrations)**. Note the location of the wellnuts in the upper screw mountings **(see illustration)**. Prior to installation, lubricate the screw threads with a smear of grease.
27 Remove the front wheel (see Chapter 5).
28 Undo the two screws on the underside of

4.23 Displace the rear brake fluid reservoir

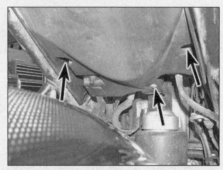

4.24a Location of mounting screws at the front . . .

4.24b . . . and rear of the mudguard

4.26a Air deflector mounting screws

4.26b Note locating slot (arrowed)

4.26c Note location of wellnut

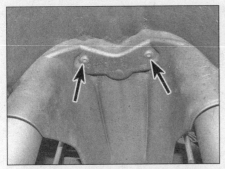

4.28 Screws secure mudguard to fork bridge

4.29 Removing the front mudguard

4.31a Mirror stems are left-hand threaded

4.31b Adapters are right-hand threaded

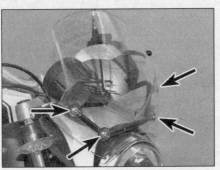

4.32 Windshield mounting screws

4.34a Undo the screws . . .

the mudguard securing it to the fork bridge **(see illustration)**.

29 Draw the mudguard forwards and off the bike **(see illustration)**.

30 Installation is the reverse of removal. Ensure the air deflectors are correctly installed. **Note:** *The air deflectors are designed to assist engine cooling and the machine should not be ridden without them fitted.*

Mirrors

31 To remove and install the mirrors, follow the procedure in Section 2, Steps 75 and 76 **(see illustrations)**.

Windshield

32 The windshield is secured to its support bracket by four screws **(see illustration)**. Undo the screws and plastic washers and lift

the windshield off, noting the location of the spacers and grommets in the mounting holes.

33 To remove the windshield and support bracket assembly, first remove the headlight unit (see Chapter 7, Section 7).

34 Undo the screws on the underside of the headlight bracket and the bolts at the top edge of the bracket and lift the assembly off **(see illustrations)**.

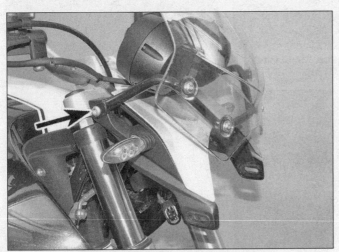

4.34b . . . and the bolts on both sides . . .

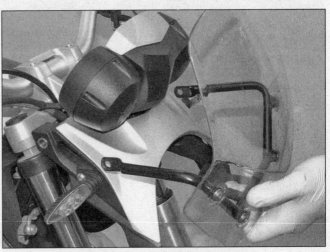

4.34c . . . and lift the assembly off

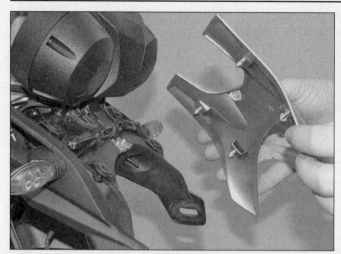

4.38a Ease off the trim panel . . .

4.38b . . . noting the grommets

35 Installation is the reverse of removal. Note that the bolts at the top edge of the bracket also secure the headlight bracket (see Step 43). Take care not to over-tighten the windshield screws.

Headlight bracket

36 The headlight bracket supports the headlight unit, instrument cluster and front turn signals. It also houses the ambient air temperature sensor.

37 To remove the bracket, first remove the headlight unit (see Chapter 7) and, if fitted, the windshield and support bracket assembly (see Step 34).

38 Ease off the headlight trim panel, noting how the pegs on the underside of the panel locate in the grommets **(see illustrations)**.

39 Remove the instrument cluster (see Chapter 7).

40 Release the wiring secured to the headlight bracket from any clips or ties. If required, remove the front turn signals (see Chapter 7).

41 Undo the bolts securing the bracket to the top yoke and draw the bracket forwards **(see illustrations)**. Disconnect the ambient air temperature sensor wiring connector **(see illustration)**.

42 Note the location of the spacers inside the bracket mountings and remove them for safekeeping if they are loose.

43 Installation is the reverse of removal. Clean the threads of the mounting bolts and apply a suitable non-permanent thread-locking compound. Tighten the bolts to the torque setting specified at the beginning of this Chapter.

4.41a Undo the bolts on both sides . . .

4.41b . . . and displace the bracket

4.41c Location of the ambient air temperature sensor

Chapter 7
Electrical system

Contents

Section number

Alternator 29
Ambient air temperature sensor. 19
Auxiliary headlights 4
Battery 3
Brake light switches 11
Brake/tail light bulb(s) 8
Charging system check 28
Clock 13
Clutch switch 21
Cruise control 15
Electrical system fault finding. 2
Fuel level sensor. 20
Fuel pump . . . . see Chapter 3
Gear position sensor . . . . see Chapter 3
General information 1
Handlebar switches 24
Headlight and sidelight bulbs. 6

Section number

Headlight unit 7
Horn 25
Ignition switch 23
Instrument cluster. 12
Lighting system check 5
Oil level indicator 18
Oil pressure switch. 17
Oil temperature sensor. . . . . see Chapter 3
Side stand switch. 22
Speed sensor 16
Starter motor and solenoid. 27
Starter relay 26
Tail light unit 9
Turn signals 10
Windshield motor 14
Wiring diagrams 30

Degrees of difficulty

Easy, suitable for novice with little experience	**Fairly easy,** suitable for beginner with some experience	**Fairly difficult,** suitable for competent DIY mechanic	**Difficult,** suitable for experienced DIY mechanic	**Very difficult,** suitable for expert DIY or professional

Specifications

Alternator
Type . . . . Three-phase AC with integral regulator/rectifier
Maximum output 720W

Battery
R1200 GS, GS Adventure and R1200 R. . . . . 12 V, 14 Ah
R1200 RT . . . . 12 V, 19 Ah

Bulbs
Headlight high and low beam
  R1200 GS, GS Adventure and R1200 RT. . . . . 55W H7 halogen
  R1200 R . . . . 55W H11 halogen
Side light 5W
Brake/tail light
  R1200 GS and GS Adventure. . . . . LED
  R1200 RT 21W
  R1200 R 21/5W
Turn signal lights
  R1200 GS and GS Adventure. . . . . 10W amber RY (LEDs as OE)
  R1200 RT . . . . 21W amber RY
  R1200 R . . . . 10W amber RY (LEDs as OE)
Instrument lighting and warning lights . . . . LED
Auxiliary headlight
  R1200 GS Adventure . . . . 55W H11 halogen

Fuse

Auxiliary headlight – R1200 GS Adventure. 7.5A

On-board accessory socket

Current rating
   R1200 RT . . . . 10 A
   R1200 GS, GS Adventure and R1200 R. . . . . 5 A

Torque settings

Alternator mounting bolts. . . . . 18 Nm
Ignition switch and steering lock bolts. . . . . 20 Nm
Engine oil level indicator bolts . . . . 9 Nm
Engine oil pressure switch . . . . 30 Nm
Engine oil temperature sensor . . . . 30 Nm
Headlight mounting bolts – R1200 R . . . . 8 Nm
Starter motor terminal nut . . . . 10 Nm
Starter motor mounting bolts. . . . . 19 Nm

1 General information

General information

All models covered in this manual have a 12-volt electrical system charged by a three-phase alternator. The alternator has integral regulator and rectifier units.

The regulator maintains the charging system output within the specified range to prevent overcharging, and the rectifier converts the ac (alternating current) output of the alternator to dc (direct current) to power the lights and other components and to charge the battery. The alternator is mounted centrally on top of the engine unit and is driven by belt off a pulley on the front end of the crankshaft.

The starter motor is mounted on the lower left-hand side of the engine. The starting system includes the starter motor, solenoid, starter relay and switches. If the engine kill switch is in the RUN position and the ignition switch is ON, the starter relay allows the starter motor to operate only if the transmission is in neutral or, if the transmission is in gear, with the clutch lever pulled into the handlebar and the side stand up.

CAN-bus technology

All models covered in this manual utilise Controlled Area Network (CAN)-bus technology to create an electronic information network between the control units, sensors and power-consuming components. This allows rapid and reliable data transfer around the network. It also allows comprehensive diagnosis of the entire system from one central point.

To reduce the amount of wiring in the network, all the components are designed to communicate via one or two wires. These wires are known as a 'data bus'. Each control unit (engine control unit, ZFE central electronics unit, instruments cluster and, where fitted, ABS control unit and anti-theft system control unit) has an integral transceiver which sends and receives data 'packets' along the bus. As the data packets travel between the units, each one examines the information and either acts upon it or ignores it, depending upon its relevance.

No fuses are fitted in the network – in the event of a short-circuit or component fault, the affected part of the network is isolated and switched off, leaving the rest of the network intact.

Note: *Keep in mind that electrical parts, once purchased, cannot be returned. To avoid unnecessary expense, make very sure the faulty component has been positively identified before buying a replacement part.*

2 Electrical system fault finding

⚠ *Warning: Make sure that the ignition switch is OFF and that the battery is disconnected before any electrical components are disconnected. Failure to do so will result in fault codes being recorded in the associated system and the need to have these erased using the BMW MOSS diagnostic tester. Depending upon the system concerned, the bike's performance may be affected.*

Fault finding

1 In the absence of test data, traditional probing with a multimeter should be avoided unless a specific result, as detailed in the text, is sought. The ZFE and ECU are extremely sensitive to interference, and for the most part system checks should be confined to continuity tests of relevant sections of the wiring loom with the ignition switch OFF.

2 When testing for power supply to a component, always ensure that the multimeter is securely connected to the relevant wiring terminals before turning the ignition switch ON. It should be noted that in some cases, a test with the power ON may result in a fault being recorded by the ECU.

3 If at all possible, have the machine checked by a BMW dealer – recorded faults can then be analysed using the BMW MOSS diagnostic tester and remedial action taken. Fault codes should be erased from the ECU when the repair has been completed.

4 Note that once a new component has been installed it will be necessary to re-instate the system programme using the diagnostic tester.

Simple wiring checks

5 Electrical problems often stem from simple causes, such as loose or corroded connections. Study the appropriate wiring diagram at the end of this Chapter to get a complete picture of what makes up that individual circuit.

6 Faults can often be tracked down by noting if other components related to that circuit are operating properly or not. If several components or circuits fail at one time, it may be that the fault lies in the earth (ground) connection, as several circuits are routed through the same earth connection.

7 Always check the condition of the wires and connections in the problem circuit. Intermittent failures can be especially frustrating, since you can't always duplicate the failure when it's convenient to test. In such situations, a good practice is to clean all connections in the affected circuit, whether or not they appear to be good. All of the connections and wires should also be wiggled to check for looseness which can cause intermittent failure.

Continuity checks

8 Continuity checks can be made with a continuity tester or a multimeter **(see**

2.8a A digital multimeter can be used for all electrical tests

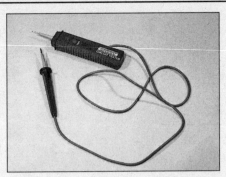

2.8b A battery powered continuity tester

14 Voltage checks are made with the ignition ON. Connect the meter's red lead to the power supply wire and the negative lead to a good earth or directly to the battery's negative terminal **(see illustration)**.

Earth (ground) checks

15 Earth (ground) connections are made either directly to the engine or by a separate wire into the brown wired earth circuit of the wire harness; internal earth circuit connections are represented by DIN symbols 31I, 31II and 31III on the *Wiring Diagrams*.

16 Corrosion is often the cause of a poor earth connection. If total electrical failure is experienced, check the security of the main earth lead from the negative (-) terminal of the battery and also the earth lead connections on the cylinders and crankcase (see Chapter 2, Section 4). If corroded, dismantle the connection and clean all surfaces back to bare metal.

17 To check the earth on a component, use an insulated jumper wire **(see illustration)** to temporarily bypass its earth connection. Connect one end of the jumper wire between the earth terminal or metal body of the component and the other end to the motorcycle's engine or sub-frame.

18 If the circuit works with the jumper wire installed, the original earth circuit is faulty. Check the wiring for open-circuits or poor connections.

illustrations). These testers are self-powered by a battery, therefore the checks are made with the ignition OFF. As a safety precaution, disconnect the battery negative (-) lead before making continuity checks, particularly if the ignition switch is being checked.

9 If using a multimeter, select the appropriate ohms scale and check that the meter reads infinity (∞). Touch the meter probes together and check that the meter reads zero; where necessary adjust the meter so that it reads zero. Make the test across the terminals described **(see illustrations)**. After using the meter always switch if off to conserve its battery.

10 Reconnect the machine's battery, noting the procedure in Section 3.

Voltage checks

Note the possible results of making voltage checks in Step 2.

11 A voltage check can determine whether current is reaching a component. Tests can be made with a multimeter set to the dc volts scale or a test light **(see illustration)**.

12 Check that the multimeter leads are inserted in the correct terminals on the meter, red to positive (+) and black to negative (-). Incorrect connections could damage the meter.

13 The meter (set the dc volts scale) should always be connected in parallel (across the load). Connecting it in series will not harm the meter, but the result will not be meaningful.

3 Battery

Caution: Be extremely careful when handling or working around the battery. The electrolyte is very caustic and an explosive gas (hydrogen) is given off when the battery is charging.

Removal and installation

Note: *Disconnecting the battery leads deletes all memorised settings (e.g. throttle position sensor). Loss of this information could temporarily upset the running of the engine. Make sure the procedure in Step 8 is carried out before starting the engine.*

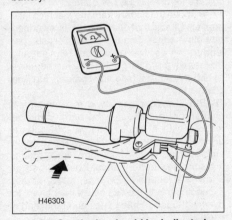

2.9a Continuity should be indicated across switch terminals when the lever is operated

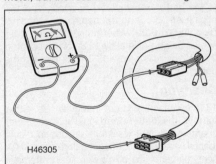

2.9b Wiring continuity check. Connect the meter probes across each end of the same wire

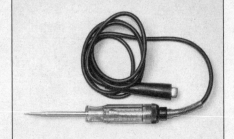

2.11 A simple test light is useful for voltage tests

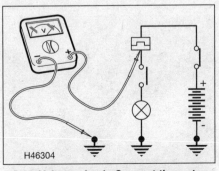

2.14 Voltage check. Connect the meter positive probe to the component and the negative probe to earth

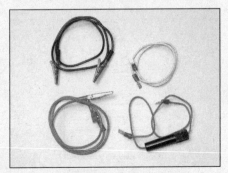

2.17 A selection of insulated jumper wires

3.2 Disconnect the battery negative (-ve) lead first

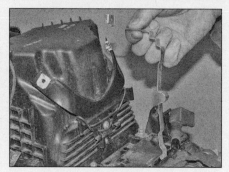

3.3 Remove the battery strap

3.4 Note which way round the battery is fitted

1 Ensure that the ignition is OFF. Remove the seat(s) (see Chapter 6). If fitted, disconnect the anti-theft alarm.
2 Unscrew the negative (-) terminal bolt and disconnect the lead from the battery **(see illustration)**. Next displace the cover from the positive battery terminal and unscrew the positive (+) terminal bolt and disconnect the lead.
3 Undo the screw securing the battery strap, then unhook the lower end of the strap and lift it out **(see illustration)**.
4 Lift out the battery, noting which way round it is installed **(see illustration)**.
5 On installation, ensure that the battery terminals and lead ends are clean. Install the battery so that the positive (+) and negative (-) terminals align with the appropriate leads.
6 Reconnect the leads, connecting the positive (+) terminal first. Don't forget to install the cover over the positive (+) terminal. Secure the battery with its strap.

> **HAYNES HiNT**
> *Battery corrosion can be kept to a minimum by applying a layer of petroleum jelly or battery terminal grease to the terminals after the leads have been connected.*

7 Install the remaining components in the reverse order of removal.
8 Turn the ignition ON. Fully open and close the throttle a couple of times to register the throttle valve positions with the ECU via the throttle position sensor.
9 Reset the clock (see Section 13).
10 If the battery has been disconnected for a prolonged period of time have the date of the service-due indicator reset by a BMW dealer.

Inspection

11 All models are fitted with a sealed MF (maintenance free) battery. All that should be done is to check that the terminals are clean and tight and that the casing is neither damaged nor leaking. **Note:** *Do not attempt to open the battery – the resulting damage will render the battery unserviceable.*
12 Check the condition of the battery by measuring the voltage at the terminals. Connect the voltmeter positive (+) probe to the battery positive (+) terminal, and the negative (-) probe to the negative (-) terminal **(see illustration)**. When fully-charged there should be approximately 12.8 volts present. If the voltage falls below 12.3 volts remove the battery and recharge it.

Charging

13 If the machine is not in regular use, either remove the battery and give it a refresher charge every four weeks as described below (bench charging), or connect a dedicated BMW float charger to the bike's electrical system via the on-board accessory socket to keep the battery charged in situ **(see illustration)**. Do not connect a battery charger to the battery terminals while the battery is on the bike.

Float charging

14 BMW produces two battery chargers for this purpose (220 volts Part No. 71607688864, 110 volts Part No. 71607688865). Using unsuitable chargers can damage the machine's electrics. The charger switches on and off automatically as required.
15 If the battery voltage drops below 9 V, attempting to recharge it via the accessory socket will damage the electrics. Remove the battery and bench charge it.

Bench charging

16 Whatever charger is used, ensure that it is suitable for charging a 12V battery.
17 Remove the battery from the machine (see above). Check that the charger is switched off before connecting the positive (+) charger lead to the positive (+) battery terminal and the negative (-) charger lead to the negative (-) battery terminal **(see illustration)**. Turn the charger on.
18 BMW do not specify a recommended charging rate, although the battery will be marked with a regular charge rate, plus a quick charge rate which can be used in emergencies for a short time. As a guide, a discharged battery should be charged at a low rate (approx. 1.5 amps) for 10 hours. Exceeding this figure can cause the battery to overheat, buckling the plates and rendering it useless.
19 Few owners will have access to an expensive current controlled charger, so if a normal domestic charger is used check that

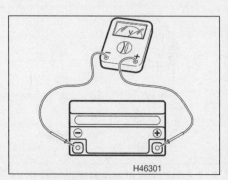

3.12 Checking the battery voltage

3.13 The BMW float charger connected to the on-board accessory socket

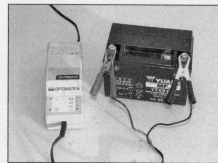

3.17 Battery connected to a bench charger

after a possible initial peak, the charge rate falls to a safe level. If the battery becomes hot during charging **STOP**. Further charging will cause damage. One of the dedicated motorcycle battery chargers is recommended; these charge at a safe rate to prevent overcharging and give an indication of battery condition and state of charge.

20 Let the battery settle for 30 minutes after charging, then measure the voltage across its terminals with a multimeter set to the dc volts scale – meter positive (+) prove to battery positive (+) terminal and meter negative (-) prove to battery negative (-) terminal. The battery should indicate 12.8 volts or more when fully charged.

21 If the recharged battery discharges rapidly if left disconnected it is likely that an internal short caused by physical damage or sulphation has occurred. A new battery will be required. A good battery will tend to lose its charge at about 1% per day. If the battery discharges while the machine is in regular use, either the battery is faulty or the charging system is defective. Refer to Section 28 for details of the charging system output test.

4 Auxiliary headlights

Note: *To prevent over-heating, the auxiliary headlight system will temporarily reduce the brightness of the lights and, in extreme circumstances, turn the lights off completely. The lights should return to full brightness once they have cooled sufficiently.*

1 Auxiliary headlights are fitted as optional equipment (OE) on R1200 GS Adventure models and optional accessories (OA) on R1200 GS models. The headlights are mounted on the underside of the front crash bar. The headlights are illuminated either by LED or halogen bulb.

4.2 Location of the auxiliary headlight switch unit

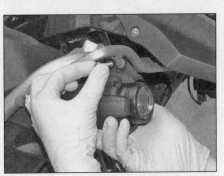

4.4b Undo the mounting bolt

4.4a Disconnect the wiring connector (arrowed)

4.5a Undo the screws . . .

2 The headlight switch is located in the upper section of the left-hand handlebar switch assembly **(see illustration)**. Fuses for the headlights are located on the lower left-hand side of the air filter housing **(see illustration 4.14)**. Wiring connectors for the headlight sub loom are clipped to the central electronics (ZFE) unit holder. A relay for the system is located underneath the ECU.

3 If an auxiliary headlight fails to work, first follow the procedure in Section 5 and check the bulb (if applicable), then check the fuses (see Steps 14 to 20) and the wiring connectors.

4 To access the bulb, disconnect the light

wiring connector, then undo the nut and bolt securing the light unit **(see illustrations)**.

5 Undo the screws securing the back of the light unit and remove it, then turn the bulb assembly anti-clockwise to remove it **(see illustrations)**.

> **HAYNES HINT** *Do not touch the bulb glass as skin acids will shorten the bulb's service life. If the bulb is accidentally touched, it should be wiped carefully when cold with a rag soaked in methylated spirit and dried before fitting.*

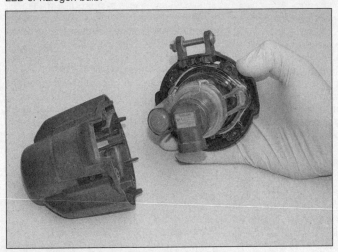

4.5b . . . and remove the back of the light unit

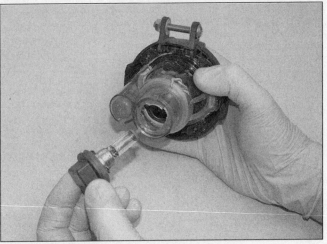

4.5c Remove the bulb assembly

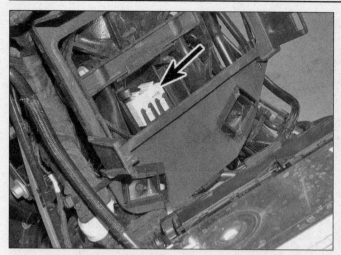

4.9 Location of the auxiliary headlight relay

4.14 Location of the auxiliary headlight fuse holder

6 If an LED auxiliary headlight is found to be faulty, a new unit will have to be fitted – individual components are not available.

7 Installation is the reverse of removal. Check the operation of the auxiliary headlight.

8 Remove the fuel tank (see Chapter 3), then check the operation of the switch (see Section 24) and the sub-loom wiring connectors.

Relay check and renewal

9 To access the relay, follow the procedure in Chapter 3 and displace the ZFE unit and the ECU. The relay is located in its holder on the right of the starter relay **(see illustration)**. Pull the relay out from the holder, noting how it fits.

10 Test the relay as follows. Set a multimeter to the ohms x 1 scale, or use a continuity tester, and connect it across Nos. 3 and 5 terminals on the relay. There should be no continuity (infinite resistance).

11 Using a fully-charged 12 volt battery and two insulated jumper wires, connect the positive (+) battery terminal to the No. 2 terminal of the relay and the negative (-) battery terminal to the No. 1 terminal. The multimeter should now read zero ohms (continuity).

12 If the test results are not as described, the relay is faulty and must be renewed.

13 Installation is the reverse of removal. Ensure that the terminals inside the holder are clean and that the relay is a secure fit.

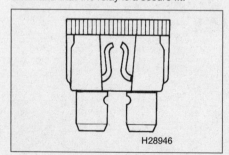

4.17 A blown fuse is easily identified by a break in the element

Fuse check and renewal

14 The fuses are located in a holder on the left-hand side of the machine **(see illustration)** – remove the side cover for access (see Chapter 6, Section 2).

15 Release the tabs securing the fuse holder cover and remove it.

16 The fuses can be checked visually. Use a pair of needle-nose pliers to pull them out.

17 A blown fuse is easily identified by a break in the element **(see illustration)**. Each fuse is clearly marked with its rating and must only be replaced by a fuse of the same rating (see *Specifications* at the beginning of this Chapter).

⚠ **Warning: Never put in a fuse of a higher rating or bridge the terminals with any other substitute, however temporary it may be. Serious damage may be done to the circuit, or a fire may start.**

18 If a fuse blows, be sure to check the wiring circuit very carefully for evidence of a short-circuit. Look for bare wires and chafed, melted or burned insulation. If the fuse is replaced before the cause is located, the new fuse will blow immediately.

19 Occasionally a fuse will blow or cause an open-circuit for no obvious reason. Corrosion of the fuse and fuse holder terminals may occur and cause poor fuse contact. If this happens, remove the corrosion with a small knife or emery paper, then spray the terminals with electrical contact cleaner.

20 Installation is the reverse of removal.

5 Lighting system check

Note 1: *All models will display a warning on the instrument cluster in the event of a bulb failure. For details see Steps 22 to 29.*
Note 2: *If the ignition is switched ON for any checks, remember to switch it OFF again*

before proceeding further or removing any electrical component from the system.

1 The battery provides power for operation of the headlight, tail light, brake light, turn signals and instrument cluster lights. If none of the lights operate, always check battery condition before proceeding (see Section 3).

2 When checking for a blown filament in a bulb, it is advisable to back up a visual check with a continuity test of the filament as it is not always apparent that the filament is broken. When checking continuity, remember that on tail light and turn signal bulbs it is often the metal body of the bulb that is the earth (ground).

Headlight

3 If the headlight fails to work, check the bulb and bulb terminals first (see Section 6). Next disconnect the headlight wiring connector and check for battery voltage on the supply side of the wiring connector with a test light or multimeter as follows. Refer to *Wiring Diagrams* at the end of this Chapter, then connect the negative probe of the multimeter to earth (ground) and the positive probe to either the high or low beam connector terminal as appropriate. Turn the ignition switch ON and select either high or low beam at the handlebar switch while conducting this test.

4 If no voltage is indicated, check the wiring between the connector and the ZFE central electronics unit. Also check the wiring for the dimmer switch and the ignition switch, then check the switches themselves (see Sections 23 and 24).

5 If voltage is indicated, check for continuity between the brown wire connector terminal and earth (ground). If there is no continuity, check the earth (ground) circuit for an open or poor connection.

Sidelight

6 If the sidelight fails to work, check the bulb and the bulb terminals first (see Section 6). Next disconnect the sidelight wiring connector and check for battery voltage on the supply side of the wiring connector with a test light or multimeter as follows. Refer to *Wiring Diagrams* at the end of this Chapter, then connect the negative probe of the multimeter to earth (ground) and the positive probe to the sidelight connector terminal. Turn the ignition switch ON.

7 If no voltage is indicated, check the wiring between the connector and the ZFE central electronics unit. Also check the wiring for the ignition switch, then check the switch itself (see Section 23).

8 If voltage is indicated, check for continuity between the brown wire connector terminal and earth (ground). If there is no continuity, check the earth (ground) circuit for an open or poor connection.

Tail light

Note: *On R1200 R models, if the tail light bulb filament fails, the brake light filament is illuminated at reduced power to compensate. However, the bulb failure warning will remain on in the instrument cluster multifunction display until a new bulb has been fitted (see Steps 22 to 29).*

9 If the tail light fails to work on R1200 RT and R models, check the bulb and the bulb terminals first (see Section 8). Next disconnect the brake/tail light wiring connector and check for battery voltage on the tail light supply side of the connector with a test light or multimeter as follows. Refer to *Wiring Diagrams* at the end of this Chapter, then connect the negative probe of the multimeter to earth (ground) and the positive probe to the tail light connector terminal. Turn the ignition switch ON.

10 If no voltage is indicated, check the wiring between the connector and the ZFE central electronics unit. Also check the wiring for the ignition switch, then check the switch itself (see Section 23).

11 If voltage is indicated, check for continuity between the brown wire connector terminal and earth (ground). If there is no continuity, check the earth (ground) circuit for an open or poor connection.

12 On R1200 GS and GS Adventure models, the tail light consists of a number of LEDs in a sealed unit. When a single LED fails it cannot be renewed, however the failure of one LED will not affect the function of the others. If the tail light fails to work completely, follow Steps 9 to 11 to check for battery voltage and the wiring. When sufficient LEDs have failed so as to impair the safe operation of the motorcycle, renew the tail light unit (see Section 9).

Brake light

Note: *On R1200 R models, if the brake light bulb filament fails, the tail light filament is illuminated at increased power to compensate. However, the bulb failure warning will remain on in the instrument cluster multifunction display until a new bulb has been fitted (see Steps 22 to 29).*

13 If the brake light fails to work on R1200 RT and R models, check the bulb and the bulb terminals first (see Section 8). Next disconnect the brake/tail light wiring connector and check for battery voltage on the brake light supply side of the connector with a test light or multimeter as follows. Refer to *Wiring Diagrams* at the end of this Chapter, then connect the negative probe of the multimeter to earth (ground) and the positive probe to the brake light connector terminal. Turn the ignition switch ON and apply the brake lever or pedal.

14 If no voltage is indicated, check the wiring between the brake light and the ZFE central electronics unit, and check the brake light switches (see Section 11).

15 If voltage is indicated, check for continuity between the brown wire connector terminal and earth (ground). If there is no continuity, check the earth (ground) circuit for an open or poor connection.

16 On R1200 GS and GS Adventure models, the brake light consists of a number of LEDs in a sealed unit. When a single LED fails it cannot be renewed, however the failure of one LED will not affect the function of the others. If the brake light fails to work completely, follow Steps 13 to 15 to check for battery voltage and the wiring. When sufficient LEDs have failed so as to impair the safe operation of the motorcycle, renew the tail light unit (see Section 9).

Turn signal lights

17 If one light fails to work, check the bulb and the bulb terminals (see Section 10). Next disconnect the turn signal wiring connector and check for battery voltage on the supply side of the connector with a test light or multimeter as follows. Refer to *Wiring Diagrams* at the end of this Chapter, then connect the negative probe of the multimeter to earth (ground) and the positive probe to the signal connector terminal. Turn the ignition switch ON and select the appropriate signal (left or right) with the turn signal switch.

18 If no voltage is indicated, check the wiring between the turn signal and the ZFE central electronics unit, and check the turn signal switch (see Section 24).

19 If voltage is indicated, check for continuity between the brown wire connector terminal and earth (ground). If there is no continuity, check the earth (ground) circuit for an open or poor connection.

20 On R1200 GS, GS Adventure and R1200 R models, optional extra (OE) turn signals are available illuminated by LEDs in a sealed unit. When a single LED fails it cannot be renewed, however the failure of one LED will not affect the function of the others. If the turn signal fails to work completely, follow Steps 17 to 19 to check for battery voltage and the wiring. When sufficient LEDs have failed so as to impair the safe operation of the motorcycle, renew the turn signal unit (see Section 10).

Instrument and warning lights

21 The instrument cluster is a sealed unit. In the event of a light failure, have the instrument cluster checked by a BMW dealer.

Defective bulb warnings

22 In the event of a bulb failure, a warning appears on the instrument cluster multifunction display (see details for individual models below). Once the fault has been corrected, the warning will be cancelled, but a fault code will be stored in ZFE central electronics unit which should be erased by a BMW dealer.

R1200 GS and GS Adventure

23 If a headlight, sidelight or front turn signal bulb fails, the general warning light illuminates yellow and the LAMPF warning appears on the multifunction display.

24 If a tail light, brake light or rear turn signal bulb fails, the general warning light illuminates yellow and the LAMPR warning appears on the multifunction display.

25 If a combination of the above faults occurs, the general warning light illuminates yellow and the LAMPS warning appears on the multifunction display.

R1200 RT

26 If a headlight, sidelight or front turn signal bulb fails, the general warning light illuminates yellow and the defective bulb symbol with an arrow pointing forwards appears on the multifunction display.

27 If a tail light, brake light or rear turn signal bulb fails, the general warning light illuminates yellow and the defective bulb symbol with an arrow pointing rearwards appears on the multifunction display.

28 If a combination of the above faults occurs, the general warning light illuminates yellow and the defective bulb symbol with an arrow pointing forwards and rearwards appears on the multifunction display.

R1200 R

29 If any bulb fails, the general warning light illuminates yellow and the LAMP warning appears on the multifunction display.

---

6 Headlight and sidelight bulbs

Note: *The headlight bulb is of the quartz-halogen type. Do not touch the bulb glass as skin acids will shorten the bulb's service life. If the bulb is accidentally touched, it should be wiped carefully when cold with a rag soaked in methylated spirit and dried before fitting.*

R1200 GS and GS Adventure

Headlight

1 To access the headlight unit bulbs, first remove the upper front mudguard and cockpit trim panel (see Chapter 6, Section 2).

6.3a Unscrew the bulb cover . . .

6.3b . . . and pull off the wiring connector

6.4a Release the bulb retaining clip . . .

6.4b . . . and withdraw the bulb

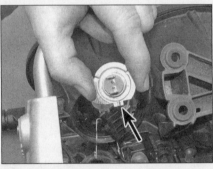

6.4c Tab (arrowed) on high beam bulb should face down

2 The high beam bulb is located on the left-hand side of the unit and the low beam bulb is on the right-hand side.
3 To remove a bulb, turn the bulb cover anti-clockwise, then pull off the wiring connector **(see illustrations)**.
4 Release the bulb retaining clip, noting how it fits, and withdraw the bulb, noting the location of the tab **(see illustrations)**. Note that the position of the tab may differ between the high and low beam bulbs.
5 Install the new bulb, bearing in mind the **Note** at the beginning of this Section, and secure it with the clip.
6 Reconnect the wiring connector.
7 Install the bulb cover, turning it clockwise, so that the TOP lettering is uppermost **(see illustration 6.3a)**.

8 Check the operation of the headlight.

Sidelight

9 The sidelight bulbholder is located on the lower left-hand side of the headlight unit. Follow the procedure in Step 1 for access.
10 Pull the bulbholder out **(see illustration)**. The bulb is of the capless type – pull it out of the bulbholder carefully **(see illustration 6.21c)**.
11 Fit the new bulb and check the operation of the sidelight, then install the bulbholder in the back of the headlight unit.

R1200 RT

Headlight

12 To access the headlight unit bulbs, first

remove the left or right-hand fairing upper side panels as appropriate (see Chapter 6, Section 3).
13 The high beam bulb is located in the centre of the unit, the low beam bulbs are on the left and right-hand sides.
14 To remove a bulb, turn the bulb cover anti-clockwise, then pull off the wiring connector **(see illustrations)**.
15 Release the bulb retaining clip, noting how it fits, and withdraw the bulb, noting the location of the tab **(see illustrations 6.4a, b and c)**. Note that the position of the tab may differ between the high and low beam bulbs.
16 Install the new bulb, bearing in mind the **Note** at the beginning of this Section, and secure it with the clip.
17 Reconnect the wiring connector.
18 Install the bulb cover, turning it clockwise, so that the TOP lettering is uppermost **(see illustration 6.3a)**.
19 Check the operation of the headlight.

Sidelight

20 To access the sidelight bulbs, first remove the left or right-hand mirror, mirror backplate and front turn signal assembly as appropriate (see Chapter 6, Section 3). The sidelight bulbholder is accessible through the opening behind the turn signal assembly.
21 Turn the bulbholder anti-clockwise and withdraw it from the headlight unit, then

6.10 Pull the sidelight bulbholder (arrowed) out from the back of the unit

6.14a Unscrew the bulb cover . . .

6.14b . . . and pull off the wiring connector

6.21a Turn the sidelight bulbholder anti-clockwise . . .

6.21b . . . and withdraw it from the headlight unit . . .

6.21c . . . then carefully pull the capless bulb out

6.23a Remove the screw . . .

6.23b . . . and ease the rim off its locating lugs

6.23c Remove the screw . . .

carefully pull the bulb out of the bulbholder **(see illustrations)**. The bulb is of the capless type.

22 Fit the new bulb and check the operation of the sidelight, then install the bulbholder in the back of the headlight unit.

R1200 R

Headlight and sidelight

23 Remove the screw from the base of the headlight shell and ease the rim off its locating lugs at the top **(see illustrations)**. Now remove the screw from the top of the shell

and withdraw the reflector unit from the shell **(see illustrations)**.

24 The low beam headlight bulb is located in the centre of the reflector, the high beam bulb is below it **(see illustration)**. To remove a headlight bulb, disconnect the wiring connector, then turn the bulb assembly anticlockwise to release it from the reflector **(see illustrations)**.

25 Install the new bulb in the reverse order of removal, bearing in mind the **Note** at the beginning of this Section.

26 The sidelight bulbholder is a push fit in the reflector unit. Pull the bulbholder out, then pull

6.23d . . . and withdraw the reflector unit

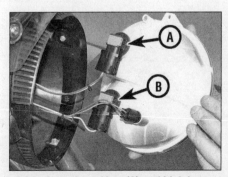

6.24a Location of low (A) and high beam (B) bulbs

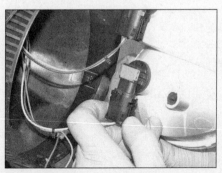

6.24b Disconnect the wiring connector . . .

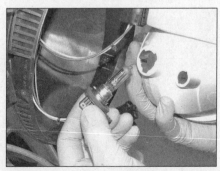

6.24c . . . and turn the bulb assembly anti-clockwise

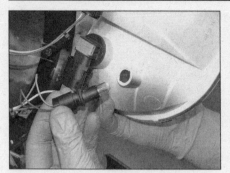

6.26a Pull the bulbholder out . . .

6.26b . . . then pull the bulb out carefully

6.29 Ensure the lugs (arrowed) are correctly located

the bulb out carefully **(see illustrations)**. The bulb is of the capless type.

27 Fit the new bulb and check the operation of the sidelight, then install the bulbholder in the back of the headlight unit.

28 Fit the reflector unit into the headlight shell and secure it with the screw at the top **(see illustration 6.23c)**.

29 Refit the rim, noting that the lugs at the top of the rim must engage the cut-outs in the shell **(see illustration)**. Tighten the lower screw securely **(see illustrations 6.23a)**.

30 Check the operation of the headlight.

7 Headlight unit

Note: *An improperly adjusted headlight may cause problems for oncoming traffic or provide*

poor, unsafe illumination of the road ahead. Before adjusting the headlight aim, be sure to consult with local traffic laws and regulations – for UK models refer to MOT Test Checks in the Reference section.

R1200 GS and GS Adventure

Removal

1 Remove the windshield (see Chapter 6, Section 2).

2 Undo the left and right-hand bolts securing the headlight unit/instrument cluster assembly to the mounting bracket **(see illustration)**.

3 Lift the headlight unit off the pegs on the mounting bracket, then disconnect the wiring connectors for the instrument cluster and headlight unit **(see illustrations)**.

4 Pull the sidelight bulbholder out from the back of the unit **(see illustration 6.10)**.

5 Lift the headlight unit/instrument cluster

assembly off. If required, pull off the clips securing the instrument cluster and separate the instruments from the headlight unit **(see illustrations)**.

Installation

6 Installation is the reverse of removal. Make sure all the wiring is correctly connected and secured. Check the operation of the headlight and sidelight.

7 Check the headlight aim as follows.

Adjustment

8 The headlight beam can be adjusted both horizontally and vertically. Before making any adjustment, check that the tyre pressures are correct and the suspension is adjusted as required. Make any adjustments to the headlight aim with the machine on level ground, with the fuel tank half full and with

7.2 Headlight unit is secured by a bolt (arrowed) on both sides

7.3a Lift the headlight unit off the pegs (arrowed) . . .

7.3b . . . then disconnect the wiring for the instrument cluster . . .

7.3c . . . and for the headlight unit (arrowed)

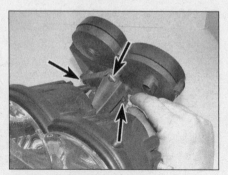

7.5a Pull off the clips securing the instrument cluster . . .

7.5b . . . and separate the instruments from the headlight unit

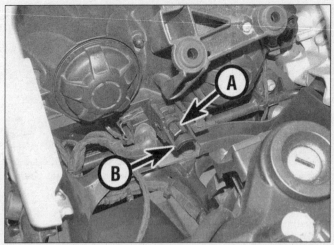

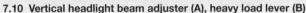

7.10 Vertical headlight beam adjuster (A), heavy load lever (B)

7.12 Horizontal headlight beam adjuster (arrowed)

an assistant sitting on the seat. If the bike is usually ridden with a passenger on the back, have a second assistant to do this. See **Note** at the beginning of this Section.

9 First remove the upper front mudguard and cockpit trim panel (see Chapter 6, Section 2). Start the engine.

10 Vertical adjustment is made by turning the adjuster on the back of the headlight unit between the two lights **(see illustration)**. Ensure that the heavy load lever is in the normal position (straight out), then turn the adjuster to achieve the desired setting.

11 If a heavy load is being carried, the headlight beam can be temporarily lowered without altering the standard setting by pressing the heavy load lever into the 'down' position. Don't forget to reset the lever for normal riding.

12 Horizontal adjustment is made by turning the adjuster on the top right-hand corner of the headlight unit **(see illustration)**.

R1200 RT

Removal

13 Follow the procedure in Chapter 6, Section 3, to remove the fairing headlight panel.

14 Undo the screws securing the headlight unit in the fairing panel and lift the unit out **(see illustration)**. Note the location of the heavy load adjuster cable.

Installation

15 Installation is the reverse of removal. Make sure all the wiring is correctly connected and secured. Check the operation of the headlight and sidelight.

16 Check the headlight aim as follows.

Adjustment

Note: *The adjuster knob on the cockpit trim panel is intended for temporary adjustment of the headlight beam when the machine is heavily loaded.*

17 The headlight beam can be adjusted

both horizontally and vertically. Before making any adjustment, check that the tyre pressures are correct and the suspension is adjusted as required. Make any adjustments to the headlight aim with the machine on level ground, with the fuel tank half full and with an assistant sitting on the seat. If the bike is usually ridden with a passenger on the back, have a second assistant to do this. See **Note** at the beginning of this Section.

18 First remove the left and right-hand fairing upper side panels (see Chapter 6, Section 3).

19 Turn the heavy load adjuster knob fully anti-clockwise – UP direction. Start the engine.

20 Vertical adjustment is made by turning the adjuster on the back of the headlight unit at the point of connection of the heavy load adjuster cable **(see illustration)**. Turn the adjuster to achieve the desired setting.

21 Horizontal adjustment is made by turning the adjuster on the lower right-hand side of the headlight unit **(see illustration 7.20)**.

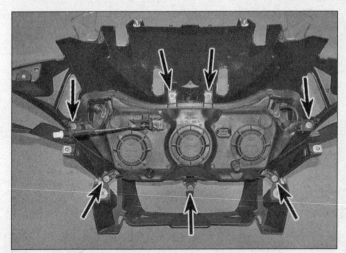

7.14 Screws (arrowed) secure the headlight unit

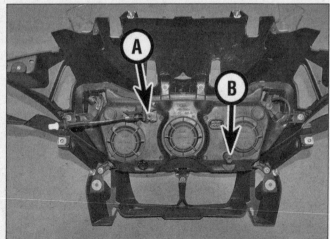

7.20 Location of vertical adjuster (A) and horizontal adjuster (B)

7.22 Location of the serrated washer

7.23 Disconnect the wiring connector

7.27 Slotted mounting facilitates beam adjustment

R1200 R

Removal

22 Undo the mounting bolt from each side of the headlight unit, noting the location of the serrated washers between the headlight shell and the mounting brackets. **(see illustration)**.
23 Lift out the headlight and disconnect the wiring connector from the back of the shell **(see illustration)**.

Installation

24 Installation is the reverse of removal. Make sure the wiring is securely connected. Check the operation of the headlight and sidelight.
25 Before tightening the mounting bolts fully, check the headlight aim as follows.

Adjustment

26 The headlight beam can be adjusted horizontally and vertically. Before making any adjustment, check that the tyre pressures

are correct and the suspension is adjusted as required. Make any adjustments to the headlight aim with the machine on level ground, with the fuel tank half full and with an assistant sitting on the seat. If the bike is usually ridden with a passenger on the back, have a second assistant to do this. See **Note** at the beginning of this Section.
27 Loosen the headlight mounting bolts so that the position of the unit can be moved inside the brackets **(see illustration)**. Start the engine.
28 Vertical adjustment is made by tilting the headlight unit up or down.
29 Horizontal adjustment is made by pivoting the headlight unit in the slotted holes in the mounting brackets.
30 Tighten the mounting bolts to the torque setting specified at the beginning of this Chapter, taking care not to disturb the position of the headlight.

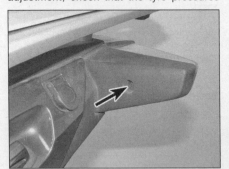

8.1a Undo the screw (arrowed) on both sides . . .

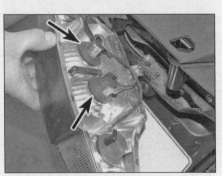

8.2 Twist the bulbholders (arrowed) anti-clockwise to release them

8.1b . . . and displace the tail light assembly

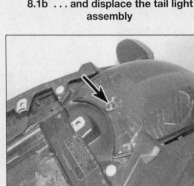

8.8 Screw (arrowed) secures tail light unit

8 Brake/tail light bulb(s)

R1200 RT

1 Undo the screws securing the tail light/turn signal assembly and displace the assembly **(see illustrations)**.
2 Turn the bulbholder anti-clockwise and withdraw it from the assembly **(see illustration)**. Gently push the bulb into the holder and twist it anti-clockwise to remove it.
3 Check the socket terminals for corrosion and clean them if necessary.
4 Line up the pins of the new bulb with the slots in the socket, then push the bulb in and turn it clockwise until it locks into place. **Note:** *It is a good idea to use a paper towel or dry cloth when handling the new bulb to prevent injury if the bulb should break and to increase bulb life.*
5 Fit the bulbholder into the tail light/turn signal assembly.
6 Install the assembly and tighten the screws securely. Check the operation of the brake/tail light.

R1200 R

7 Remove the seat and the centre rear body panel (see Chapter 6, Section 4).
8 Undo the single screw from the top of the tail light unit **(see illustration)**. Pull the unit gently rearwards to ease the guide pins from their mounting holes.
9 Twist the bulbholder anti-clockwise to free it from the unit **(see illustration)**. Push the bulb

8.9 Twist the bulbholder anti-clockwise to release it

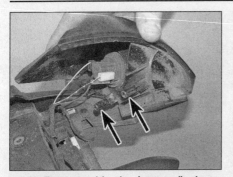

8.12 Engage guide pins (arrowed) when installing the tail light

10.2a Undo the screw (arrowed) at the back of the unit . . .

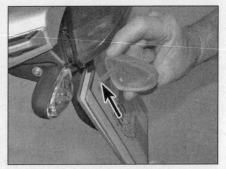

10.2b . . . and lift off the lens. Note how the tab (arrowed) locates

into the holder and twist it anticlockwise to remove it.

10 Check the socket terminals and install the new bulb as described in Steps 3 and 4.

11 Fit the bulbholder into the tail light unit.

12 Install the unit, ensuring the guide pins are correctly located **(see illustration)** and tighten the screw securely. Check the operation of the brake/tail light.

13 Install the remaining components in the reverse order of removal.

R1200 GS and GS Adventure

14 The tail light consists of a number of LEDs in a sealed unit. When a single LED fails it cannot be renewed, however the failure of one LED will not affect the function of the others. If the tail light fails to work completely, refer to Section 5 to check the circuit. When sufficient LEDs have failed so as to impair the safe operation of the motorcycle, renew the tail light unit (see Section 9).

9 Tail light unit

R1200 GS and GS Adventure

1 Follow the procedure in Chapter 6, Section 2, and remove the tail light/number plate bracket.

2 Undo the nuts securing the tail light unit and remove it. Note the arrangement of the washers and grommets on the number plate bracket.

3 Installation is the reverse of removal. Check the operation of the brake/tail light.

R1200 RT

4 Follow the procedure in Section 8 and displace the tail light/turn signal assembly **(see illustrations 8.1a and b)**.

5 Turn the tail light and turn signal bulbholders anti-clockwise and withdraw them from the assembly **(see illustration 8.2)**.

6 To remove the tail light/number plate bracket, refer to Chapter 6, Section 3.

7 Installation is the reverse of removal. Check the operation of the brake/tail lights and turn signals.

R1200 R

8 Follow the procedure in Section 8 to remove and install the tail light unit.

10 Turn signals

1 Most turn signal problems are the result of a burned out bulb or corroded socket. This is especially true when the turn signals function properly in one direction, but fail to flash in the other direction. Check the bulbs and the sockets as follows.

HAYNES HiNT *If the socket contacts are dirty or corroded, scrape them clean and spray with electrical contact cleaner before a new bulb is installed.*

R1200 GS and GS Adventure

Note: *Optional extra (OE) turn signals are available illuminated by LEDs in a sealed unit (see Section 5).*

2 To remove a turn signal bulb, undo the screw securing the turn signal lens and remove the lens, noting how the tab locates **(see illustrations)**.

3 Push the bulb into the holder and twist it anti-clockwise to remove it **(see illustration)**.

4 Check the socket and terminal for corrosion and clean them if necessary. Line up the pins of the new bulb with the slots in the

10.3 Push the bulb in and twist it anti-clockwise to remove it

socket (noting that on amber bulbs the pins are offset), then push the bulb in and turn it clockwise until it locks into place.

5 Locate the tab on the lens on the inner side of the signal body and tighten the screw, taking care not to overtighten it and damage the lens.

6 Check the operation of the turn signals.

Removal and installation

7 To remove a front turn signal unit, first remove the headlight unit/instrument cluster assembly (see Section 7).

8 Trace the wiring from the turn signal and disconnect it at the connector. Free the wiring from any clips or ties.

9 Undo the screw securing the turn signal unit and feed the wiring through the windshield support bracket **(see illustration)**.

10 Installation is the reverse of removal. Check the operation of the turn signals.

11 To remove a rear turn signal unit, first remove the rear tail light/number plate bracket (see Chapter 6, Section 2).

12 Undo the screw securing the turn signal unit and feed the wiring through the bracket.

13 Installation is the reverse of removal. Check the operation of the turn signals.

R1200 RT

Front

14 To remove a turn signal bulb, first remove the appropriate mirror and mirror backplate (see Chapter 6, Section 3).

15 Turn the bulbholder anti-clockwise and withdraw it from the back of the turn signal

10.9 Screw (arrowed) secures turn signal unit

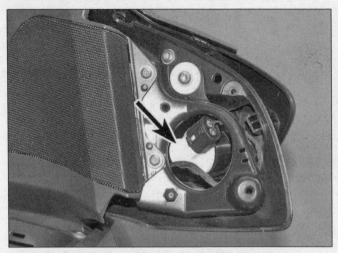

10.15a Turn the bulbholder (arrowed) anti-clockwise

10.15b Push the bulb in and twist it anti-clockwise to remove it

unit, then gently push the bulb into the holder and twist it anti-clockwise to remove it **(see illustrations)**.

16 Check the socket and terminal and install the new bulb as described in Step 4.

17 Installation is the reverse of removal. Check the operation of the turn signals.

18 To remove the turn signal unit, first remove the mirror and mirror backplate, then undo the screw securing the unit and disconnect the wiring connector from the bulbholder (see Chapter 6, Section 3). If required, undo the screws securing the unit in the back of the panel surround **(see illustration)**.

19 Installation is the reverse of removal. Check the operation of the turn signals.

Rear

20 Undo the screws securing the tail light/turn signal assembly and displace the assembly **(see illustrations 8.1a and b)**.

21 Turn the bulbholder anti-clockwise and withdraw it from the assembly **(see illustration)**, then gently push the bulb into the holder and twist it anti-clockwise to remove it.

22 Check the socket and terminal and install the new bulb as described in Step 4.

23 Installation is the reverse of removal. Check the operation of the turn signals.

R1200 R

Note: *Optional extra (OE) turn signals are available illuminated by LEDs in a sealed unit (see Section 5).*

24 To remove and install a turn signal bulb, follow the procedure in Steps 2 to 5. On completion, check the operation of the turn signals.

Removal and installation

25 To remove a front turn signal unit, first remove the windshield and support bracket assembly, if fitted, then ease off the headlight trim panel (see Chapter 6). Release the wiring from any clips or ties and disconnect the appropriate wiring connector **(see illustration)**.

26 To remove a rear turn signal unit, first remove the tail light unit (see Section 8). Release the wiring from any clips or ties and disconnect the appropriate wiring connector **(see illustration)**.

27 Undo the screw securing the turn signal unit and lift it off **(see illustration)**. Feed the wiring through the headlight bracket or seat cowling panel.

28 Installation is the reverse of removal. Check the operation of the turn signals.

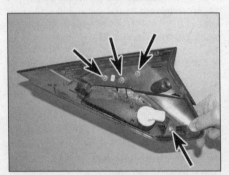

10.18 Screws (arrowed) secure turn signal unit

10.21 Turn the bulbholder anti-clockwise to remove

10.25 Location of the turn signal wiring connectors

10.26 Rear left-hand turn signal wiring connector (arrowed)

10.27 Screw (arrowed) secures turn signal unit

11 Brake light switches

Circuit check

Note: *On machines equipped with ABS, the brake light switches are integral with the ABS control unit (see Chapter 5).*

1 Before checking any electrical circuit, check the bulb (see Section 8) on R1200 RT and R1200 R models, or LED circuit on R1200 GS and GS Adventure models (see Section 5).

2 The front brake light switch is located on the underside of the handlebar lever **(see illustration)**. The rear brake light switch is located adjacent to the rear brake pedal **(see illustration)**.

3 Disconnect the wiring connector from the switch or trace the wiring from the switch and disconnect it at the connector. Using a multimeter or test light connected to a good earth (ground), check for voltage on the supply side of the brake light switch wiring connector with the ignition switch ON. If no voltage is indicated, check the wire between the switch and the ZFE central electronics unit (see *Wiring Diagrams* at the end of this Chapter).

4 If voltage is indicated, check for continuity between the terminals on the switch side of the wiring connector – first with the lever or pedal at rest, then with the lever or pedal applied. There should be continuity with the lever pulled in or pedal depressed. If the switch doesn't behave as described, displace

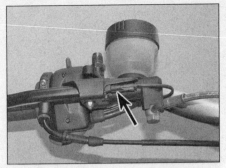

11.2a Location of the front brake light switch (arrowed)

it and check its operation as described below.

Renewal

Front brake lever switch

5 On R1200 GS and GS Adventure models, first remove the right-hand hand protector (see Chapter 6, Section 2).

6 Disconnect the wiring connector from the switch, then loosen the screw securing the switch to the underside of the handlebar lever and pull the switch out **(see illustrations)**.

7 Check that the switch contact is free to move – if it is stuck or dirty, clean it carefully with suitable solvent and lubricate the switch with electrical contact cleaner. Check the operation of the switch as described in Step 4. If the switch is faulty, renew it.

8 Installation is the reverse of removal. Check the operation of the brake light as follows.

11.2b Location of the rear brake light switch (arrowed)

There should be approximately 5 mm of movement in the brake lever before the brake light illuminates. To adjust the setting, loosen the screw securing the switch and move it in or out of the handlebar bracket until the desired setting is achieved. Tighten the screw.

Rear brake pedal switch

9 Trace the wiring from the switch and disconnect it at the connector. Release the wiring from any clips or ties.

10 Pull off the switch cover, then undo the screw securing the switch to its bracket and lift the switch off **(see illustrations)**.

11 Check that the switch contact plate is free to move – if it is stuck or dirty, clean it carefully with suitable solvent and lubricate the switch with electrical contact cleaner. Check the operation of the switch as described in Step 4. If the switch is faulty, renew it.

12 Installation is the reverse of removal. Check the operation of the brake light and ensure that the brake pedal freeplay is adjusted correctly (see Chapter 4, Section 3).

12 Instrument cluster

Note 1: *On no account should the instrument wiring be disconnected without first turning the ignition OFF and disconnecting the battery.*
Note 2: *The instrument cluster is a sealed unit. In the event of an instrument failure, have the instrument cluster checked by a BMW dealer.*

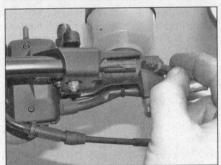

11.6a Disconnect the wiring connector . . .

11.6b . . . then loosen the screw securing the switch . . .

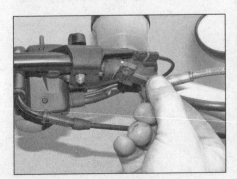

11.6c . . . and pull the switch out

11.10a Pull off the switch cover . . .

11.10b . . . then undo the screw (arrowed) securing the switch

12.5a Pull off the upper clips (arrowed) . . .

12.5b . . . and lower clip (arrowed)

12.5c Disconnect the wiring connector (arrowed)

Note 3: *If a new instrument cluster is being fitted, the BMW MOSS diagnostic tester must be used to register the new unit with the central electronics (ZFE) unit and transfer the mileage and service data.*

R1200 GS and GS Adventure

1 Follow the procedure in Section 7 and remove the headlight unit/instrument cluster assembly, then separate the instrument cluster from the headlight unit **(see illustrations 7.5a and b)**.
2 Note the location of the grommets on the mounting bracket and renew them if they are damaged of deteriorated.
3 Installation is the reverse of removal. Make sure the wiring is correctly connected and secured. Check the operation of the instrument cluster.

R1200 RT

4 Follow the procedure in Chapter 6, Section 3, and remove the fairing headlight panel.
5 Pull off the clips securing the instrument cluster, then disconnect the instruments wiring connector and lift the cluster off **(see illustrations)**.
6 Note the location of the grommets on the mounting bracket and renew them if they are damaged of deteriorated.
7 Installation is the reverse of removal. Make sure the wiring is correctly connected and secured. Check the operation of the instrument cluster.

R1200 R

8 First remove the windshield and support bracket assembly, if fitted, then ease off the headlight trim panel (see Chapter 6).

9 Undo the screws securing the lower cover to the instrument cluster and remove it **(see illustrations)**.
10 Disconnect the wiring connector, then ease off the clips securing the instrument cluster to its mounting bracket and lift it off **(see illustrations)**. Renew any clips that are corroded or damaged.
11 Note the location of the grommets on the mounting bracket and renew them if they are damaged or deteriorated.
12 Installation is the reverse of removal. Ensure the wiring connector is secure and take care not to over-tighten the lower cover screws. Check the operation of the instrument cluster.

13 Clock

1 Whenever the battery or the instrument cluster has been disconnected, the clock will require resetting as follows.

R1200 GS and GS Adventure

2 Turn the ignition ON.
3 On machines not fitted with optional equipment (OE) on-board computer or tyre pressure monitoring, repeatedly press either the clock reset button on the instrument cluster, or the INFO button on the left-hand handlebar switch unit, until the time display appears on the multi-function display panel.
4 On machines fitted with optional equipment (OE) on-board computer or tyre pressure

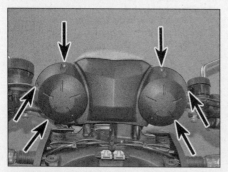

12.9a Undo the screws (arrowed) . . .

12.9b . . . and remove the lower cover

12.10a Disconnect the wiring connector (arrowed)

12.10b Ease off the securing clips

12.10c Lift off the instrument cluster

14.3 Disconnect the motor wiring connector

14.4 Screws (arrowed) secure support bracket

monitoring, repeatedly press the INFO button on the left-hand handlebar switch unit until the time display appears on the multi-function display panel.

5 Press and hold down the button until the hours number flashes. Repeatedly press the button until the hours number is correct.

6 Press and hold down the button until the minutes number flashes. Repeatedly press the button until the minutes number is correct.

7 Press and hold down the button until the minutes number stops flashing.

R1200 RT and R

8 The clock reset button is on the right-hand side of the instrument cluster below the tachometer.

9 Turn the ignition ON.

10 Press and hold down the button until the hours number flashes. Repeatedly press the button until the hours number is correct.

11 Press and hold down the button until the minutes number flashes. Repeatedly press the button until the minutes number is correct.

12 Press and hold down the button until the minutes number stops flashing.

14 Windshield motor

1 R1200 RT models are equipped with an electric motor for windshield height adjustment. The motor is controlled by a switch on the left-hand handlebar.

2 To access the windshield motor, first follow the procedure in Chapter 6, Section 3, and remove the fairing headlight panel.

3 Disconnect the motor wiring connector **(see illustration)**.

4 Undo the screws securing the windshield support bracket and lift the bracket off **(see illustration)**.

5 Undo the screws securing the motor to the underside of the support bracket and lift the motor off, noting the location of the drive shaft.

6 If required, remove the clips securing the raising arms to both ends of the actuator shaft and pull the arms off **(see illustration)**. Remove the clips securing the upper slave arms and pull the arms off, noting the location of the return springs. Renew the clips prior to installation if they are damaged.

7 The windshield motor is a sealed unit. If it appears to be faulty, refer to *Wiring Diagrams* at the end of this Chapter and check the wiring between the connector and the ZFE central electronics unit. Also check the wiring between the handlebar switch and the ZFE central electronics unit. If the wiring is good, the motor is probably faulty – have it tested by a BMW dealer.

8 Installation is the reverse of removal. Make sure all the wiring is correctly connected and secured. Check the operation of the windshield motor.

15 Cruise control

Check

1 Cruise control is fitted as optional equipment (OE) to R1200 RT models.

2 If the system is thought to be faulty, first

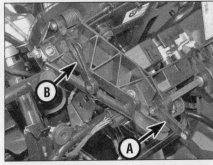

14.6 Raising arms (A) and slave arms (B)

check the adjustment and operation of the cruise control cables (see Chapter 1, Section 3 and Chapter 3, Section 8).

3 If the cables are good, refer to Section 24 and check the handlebar switch.

4 The cruise control unit is located on the front, right-hand side of the machine behind the oil cooler **(see illustration)**. Remove the headlight panel for access (see Chapter 6).

5 If not already done, remove the fuel tank (see Chapter 3).

6 Trace the wiring from the handlebar switch unit to the connector located on the central electronics (ZFE) unit holder **(see illustration)**. Check the connector, then test for continuity

15.4 Location of the cruise control unit

15.6 Location of the cruise control wiring connector

in the wiring between the connector and the cruise control unit.

7 If no faults have been found it is likely the cruise control unit is faulty – have it checked by a BMW dealer.

Renewal

8 If not already done, remove the headlight panel (see Chapter 6) and the fuel tank (see Chapter 3).

9 Release the tabs securing the cruise control unit wiring connector and disconnect the connector.

10 Disconnect the control cable from the cruise control unit (see Chapter 3, Section 8).

11 Undo the bolts on the underside of the unit and lift it off.

12 Installation is the reverse of removal. Make sure all the wiring is correctly connected and secured.

16 Speed sensor

1 The speedometer is activated by a speed sensor located on the inside edge of the final drive unit, behind the drive flange **(see illustration)**. The sensor ring is an integral part of the gear assembly inside the housing. Note that on ABS models, this sensor also supplies rear wheel speed information to the ABS control unit.

2 To access and renew the sensor, follow the procedure in Chapter 5, Section 17.

17 Oil pressure switch

Check

Note: *On R1200 R models the pressure switch is only used for factory testing during production and is not a part of the engine electronics.*

1 Where fitted, the oil pressure warning light should come on together with a general warning light when the ignition switch is first turned ON – this is part of the electronic 'self-checking' system and serves as a check that the warning indicators are working. If the oil pressure light comes on whilst the engine is running, low oil pressure is indicated – stop the engine immediately and check the engine oil level (see *Pre-ride checks*).

2 If the oil level is correct, check the switch wiring connector and the wiring for damage between the switch and the engine control unit (see *Wiring Diagrams* at the end of this Chapter). The switch is located in the left-hand side of the crankcase below the cylinder **(see illustration)**. On R1200 RT models, refer to Chapter 6 to remove the main fairing side panels. Remove the lower cylinder head covers (see Chapter 1, Section 5). Remove the fuel tank to access the ECU (see Chapter 3).

3 If the wiring is good, carry out an oil pressure check (see Chapter 2, Section 3). **Note:** *Some machines are fitted with an oil level warning sender. If an engine oil warning cannot be traced to a faulty pressure switch or low oil pressure, check the operation of the oil level indicator (see Section 18).*

4 If the oil pressure warning light does not come on when the ignition is turned on, check the switch as follows.

5 Disconnect the wiring connector. Use an insulated jumper wire to connect the terminal inside the connector to earth (ground) on the crankcase. Switch the ignition ON and check that the warning light comes on. If the light comes on, the switch is defective and must be renewed.

6 If the light still does not come on, check for voltage at the wire terminal. If there is no voltage, check for a break the wire between the switch and the ECU.

Renewal

7 On R1200 RT models, if not already done, remove the fairing left-hand side panel (see Chapter 6).

8 Detach the wiring connector and unscrew the oil pressure switch from the crankcase. Be prepared to catch any residual oil from the switch location.

9 Before installing the new switch, apply a suitable sealant to the upper portion of the switch threads, leaving the lower 3 to 4 mm of thread clean. Wipe the threads in the crankcase clean, then install the switch and tighten it to the torque setting specified at the beginning of this Chapter. Ensure that the wiring connector is secure.

10 Run the engine and check that the switch operates correctly.

11 Install the remaining components in the reverse order of removal.

18 Oil level indicator

1 The oil level indicator is part of the on-board computer circuit, where fitted. Using the INFO button on the left-hand handlebar switch unit, the oil level status can be displayed on the instrument cluster multi-function panel. To ensure accuracy, the engine should be at normal operating temperature. The machine must be held upright and the engine should be at idle. Confirmation of the oil level status can be made by checking the oil level visually (see *Pre-ride checks*).

2 Where fitted, the oil level indicator is located in the right-hand side of the crankcase below the cylinder **(see illustration)**.

3 If the level indicator is thought to be faulty, remove the lower cylinder head covers (see Chapter 1, Section 5). On R1200 RT models, refer to Chapter 6 to remove the main fairing side panels. Remove the fuel tank to access the ECU (see Chapter 3).

4 Trace the wiring to the connector and free it from any clips or ties. Check for damage between the level indicator and the engine control unit (see *Wiring Diagrams* at the end of this Chapter).

5 If the wiring is good, check the operation of the level indicator as follows. **Note:** *No specifications are available. If, after testing, the level indicator is thought to be faulty, have its condition confirmed by a BMW dealer.*

6 Disconnect the wiring connector. Undo the bolts securing the level indicator in the crankcase and withdraw it carefully to avoid

16.1 Location of the rear wheel speed sensor

17.2 Location of the oil pressure switch

18.2 Location of the oil level indicator

damaging the float assembly. Note the location of the sealing O-ring **(see illustration)**.

7 Check that the float is free to move up and down **(see illustration)**. If required, prise off the E-clip and remove the float, noting which way round it is fitted, then clean the components in suitable solvent. Install the float and secure it with a new E-clip.

8 Using a multimeter set to the ohms x 100 scale, test for resistance between the terminals on the level indicator side of the wiring connector with the float in both the high and low positions. If there is no difference in the results (from high to low positions) it is likely that the level indicator is faulty and a new one must be fitted.

9 Installation is the reverse of removal. Fit a new O-ring and tighten the screws to the torque setting specified at the beginning of this Chapter. Ensure that the wiring connector is secure.

10 Install the remaining components in the reverse order of removal.

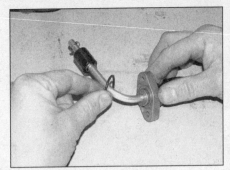

18.6 Note location of O-ring

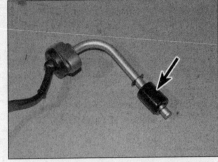

18.7 Ensure float (arrowed) moves freely

19 Ambient air temperature sensor

1 The ambient air temperature sensor is part of the on-board computer circuit, where fitted. Using the INFO button on the left-hand handlebar switch unit, the air temperature can be displayed on the instrument cluster multi-function panel. Note that with the machine at a standstill, engine heat can distort the reading. In these circumstances, the numerals of the temperature display are temporarily replaced by two horizontal dashes (– –).

2 If the air temperature drops below 3°C a snowflake icon appears on the multi-function display panel as a warning of the risk of black ice.

3 Where fitted, the ambient air temperature sensor is located inside the bodywork at the front of the machine **(see illustrations)**. On R1200 R models, the sensor is located inside the headlight bracket (see Chapter 6).

4 If the sensor is thought to be faulty, refer to Chapter 6 to remove the appropriate fuel tank or fairing side panels for access. On R1200 R models, the sensor is located inside the

headlight bracket. Remove the fuel tank to access the ECU (see Chapter 3).

5 No specifications are available for testing the sensor. However, before condemning it, inspect the wiring connector and wiring between the sensor and the engine control unit for damage (see *Wiring Diagrams* at the end of this Chapter).

6 On completion, ensure the sensor is fixed securely in position. Secure the wiring as noted on removal.

7 Install the remaining components in the reverse order of removal.

20 Fuel level sensor

⚠ *Warning: Petrol (gasoline) is extremely flammable, so take extra precautions when you work on any part of the fuel system. Don't smoke or allow open flames or bare light bulbs near the work area, and don't work in a garage where a natural gas-type appliance is present. If you spill any fuel on your skin, rinse it off immediately with soap and water. When you perform any kind of work on the fuel system, wear safety glasses and have a fire extinguisher suitable for a class B type fire (flammable liquids) on hand.*

1 Information on fuel level shown on the instrument cluster multi-function display panel is provided by a level sensor in the tank. When

the fuel level drops to the reserve capacity the yellow general warning light illuminates and either the word FUEL or the fuel pump icon flash on the multi-function display.

2 Two types of fuel level sensor are fitted to the machines covered in this manual. All R1200 GS models have a lever-type sensor located on the underside of the fuel tank filler neck. Prior to August 2010, R1200 GS Adventure and R1200 RT models were fitted with a film-type sensor secured to the underside of the fuel filler neck; from August 2010, a lever-type sensor integral with the fuel pump was fitted. All R1200 R models have a film-type sensor located inside the fuel tank.

3 Follow the appropriate procedure in Chapter 3, Section 2 or 4, to remove the sensor or pump/sensor assembly. Separate the sensor from the fuel filler neck if required **(see illustration)**.

4 No specifications are available for testing the level sensors. However, if the sensor is thought to be faulty, a general check of its function can be made as follows.

Lever-type sensor

5 If the sensor is integral with the pump, refer to the appropriate wiring diagram at the end of this Chapter to identify the sensor wire terminals in the connector on the top of the pump assembly. Otherwise, the sensor wire terminals are in the sensor connector **(see illustration 20.3)**.

6 Connect the probes of a multimeter set to the ohms x 100 scale to the sensor terminals

19.3a Location of the air temperature sensor – R1200 GS shown

19.3b Location of the air temperature sensor – R1200 RT shown

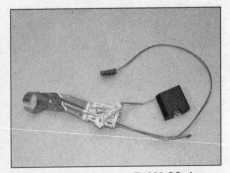

20.3 Fuel level sensor – R1200 GS shown

20.6 Fuel level sensor float in the tank full position

20.7 Fuel level sensor float in the tank empty position

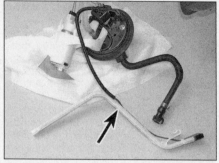

20.10 Film-type fuel level sensor (arrowed)

and measure the resistance with the float in the tank full (up) position **(see illustration)**.

7 Now move the float slowly to the tank empty (down) position **(see illustration)**. If the sensor is working correctly, the meter should show a progressive change in the resistance.

8 If there is no difference in the results it is likely that the level sensor is faulty and a new one must be fitted. If the sensor is integral with the pump, disconnect the sensor wiring connector, then unclip the sensor from the pump assembly. Installation is the reverse of removal.

9 If the level sensor is good, check the wiring between the fuel tank and the ZFE central electronics unit (see *Wiring Diagrams* at the end of the Chapter).

Film-type sensor

Note: *A suitable deep container filled with chilled water is required for this check. It is*

important that the temperature of the water is lower than the ambient air temperature.

10 Separate the sensor from the pump or filler neck **(see illustration)**. If not already done, disconnect the sensor wiring connector.

11 Connect the probes of a multimeter set to the ohms x 100 scale to the sensor terminals and measure the resistance.

12 Now lower the sensor slowly into the water. If the sensor is working correctly, the meter should show a progressive change in the resistance.

13 If there is no difference in the results it is likely that the level sensor is faulty and a new one must be fitted. Installation is the reverse of removal.

14 If the level sensor is good, check the wiring between the fuel tank and the ZFE central electronics unit (see *Wiring Diagrams* at the end of the Chapter).

21 Clutch switch

Check

1 The clutch switch is mounted inside the handlebar lever **(see illustration)**. The switch is part of the safety circuit which allows the starter motor to operate only if the transmission is in neutral or, if the transmission is in gear, with the clutch lever pulled into the handlebar and the side stand up. To check the safety circuit, follow the procedure in Steps 8 to 12. **Note:** *To start the engine with the transmission in gear, switch the ignition ON before pulling the clutch lever in, otherwise the starting system will not be enabled.*

2 Disconnect the switch wiring connector **(see illustration)**.

3 Using a multimeter or test light, check for continuity between the terminals on the switch side of the wiring connector – first with the lever at rest, then with the lever pulled in. There should be continuity with the lever in one position only. If the switch doesn't behave as described, displace it and check its operation as described below.

Renewal

4 On R1200 GS and GS Adventure models, first remove the left-hand hand protector (see Chapter 6, Section 2).

5 On R1200 RT models, displace the clutch master cylinder (see Chapter 2, Section 21). Note it is not necessary to disconnect the clutch hose or empty the clutch fluid reservoir. Undo the screw securing the switch and displace the switch **(see illustration)**. Check that the switch contact is free to move – if it is stuck or dirty, clean it carefully with suitable solvent and lubricate the switch electrical contact cleaner. Check the switch for continuity as described in Step 3. If the switch is proved to be faulty, renew it. Trace the wiring back to the connector and release it from any clips or ties. Installation is the reverse of removal.

6 On all other models, disconnect the wiring connector from the switch, then undo the screw securing the switch to the underside of the handlebar lever and lift the switch off **(see illustration)**. Check that the switch contact

21.1 Location of the clutch switch

21.2 Disconnect the wiring connector

21.5 Screw (arrowed) secures clutch switch – R1200 RT shown

21.6 Screw (arrowed) secures clutch switch – R1200 R shown

is free to move – if it is stuck or dirty, clean it carefully with suitable solvent and lubricate the switch electric contact cleaner. Check the operation of the switch as described in Step 3. If the switch is proved to be faulty, renew it.

7 Installation is the reverse of removal. Check the operation of the clutch switch as follows. There should be between 5 and 9 mm of movement in the clutch lever before the switching point is reached and pressure builds up in the lever. To adjust the setting, loosen the screw securing the switch and move the switch in or out of the handlebar bracket until the desired setting is achieved. Tighten the screw.

Safety circuit check

8 Ensure that the kill switch is OFF, the side stand is UP and the transmission is in neutral. Turn the ignition ON – neutral light N should illuminate on the instrument cluster multifunction display.

9 Select a gear – neutral light should go OFF.

10 Press the starter button – starter should not operate.

11 Extend the side stand DOWN, pull in the clutch lever and press the starter button – starter should not operate.

12 Retract the side stand UP and, with the clutch lever still pulled in, press the starter button – starter should operate.

22 Side stand switch

1 The side stand switch is mounted on the side stand pivot **(see illustration)**. The switch is part of the safety circuit which allows the starter motor to operate only if the transmission is in neutral or, if the transmission is in gear, with the clutch lever pulled into the handlebar and the side stand up.

2 To check the operation of the switch, support the machine on its centre stand or on an auxiliary stand. Trace the wiring back from the switch to its connector and disconnect it **(see illustration)**. Refer to Chapter 6 to remove any bodywork as necessary.

3 Referring to the appropriate wiring diagram at the end of this Chapter, use a multimeter or continuity tester to check for continuity between the wire terminals on the switch side of the connector, first with the stand up and then with the stand down.

4 If the switch does not perform as illustrated in the wiring diagram a new one must be fitted. Follow the procedure in Chapter 4, Section 4, to install a new switch.

5 If the switch is good, check the wiring between the connector and the ECU.

6 If required, follow the procedure in Section 21, Steps 8 to 12, to check the operation of the safety circuit.

22.1 Location of the side stand switch

23 Ignition switch

General

1 Two ignition keys are supplied with each new machine. The keys are security coded and contain an integral transponder. When a key is inserted into the ignition switch the security code is transmitted to the immobiliser and the immobiliser is deactivated. Only the keys supplied with the machine will deactivate the immobiliser.

2 The keys should not be kept together – apart from the obvious risk of losing both keys, the spare key may interfere with the enabling signal for starting and the EWS immobiliser warning will appear on the instrument cluster multi-function display.

3 If a key is lost, or if a key loses its security code, a replacement can only be obtained from a BMW dealer. For security, the new key and the remaining original key can only be re-coded by the dealer.

Switch check

4 Disconnect the battery negative (-) lead (see Section 3).

5 Remove the fuel tank (see Chapter 3) and any fairing panels as necessary to access the front of the steering head (see Chapter 6).

6 Undo the screws securing the ignition switch wiring connector cover and lift the cover off, then disconnect the connector from the base of the ignition switch **(see illustrations)**.

23.6a Screws (arrowed) secure the ignition switch cover

22.2 Location of the side stand switch wiring connector

7 Using an ohmmeter or a continuity tester, check the continuity of the connector terminal pairs according to the ignition switch table – see the relevant wiring diagram at the end of this Chapter. Continuity should exist when the switch connections are joined by a bar in the table.

8 If the switch fails any of the tests, renew it. **Note:** *If a new switch is being fitted, the BMW MOSS diagnostic tester must be used to register the new unit with the ZFE central electronics unit.*

Removal

9 Follow the procedure in Chapter 4, Section 7, and remove the fork top yoke.

10 Special security bolts are used to mount the ignition switch/steering lock assembly on the underside of the top yoke. Drill the heads off the bolts and draw the assembly off. Use a stud extractor to unscrew the remains of the security bolts (see *Tools and Workshop Tips* in the *Reference* section).

Installation

11 Install the switch/lock assembly onto the fork bridge and secure it with new security bolts. Note that these bolts are micro-encapsulated and require a service tool (Part No. 510531) to engage their heads; tighten the bolts to the torque setting specified at the beginning of this Chapter.

12 Follow the procedure in Chapter 4, Section 7, and install the fork top yoke. Make sure wiring for the ignition switch and the immobiliser is securely connected and check the operation of the ignition switch.

23.6b Location of the ignition switch

24 Handlebar switches

1 Generally speaking, the switches are reliable and trouble-free. Most problems, when they do occur, are caused by dirty or corroded contacts, but wear and breakage of internal parts is a possibility that should not be overlooked. If breakage does occur, the entire switch assembly will have to be renewed, since individual parts are not available.
2 The switches can be checked for continuity using an ohmmeter or a continuity test light (see Section 2).

R1200 GS, GS Adventure and R1200 R models

Check

3 On R1200 GS and GS Adventure models, first remove the hand protectors (see Chapter 6).
4 If an additional switch for optional (OA) electrical equipment is fitted to the left-hand handlebar assembly, first undo the screws securing it and lift it off (see Section 4).
5 To access the left-hand switch wiring connectors, undo the screws securing the front half of the housing and ease it off (see illustration). Unclip the wiring connectors from the switch body and disconnect them (see illustration).
6 To access the right-hand switch wiring connectors, undo the screws securing the front half of the housing and ease it off (see illustrations). Undo the screw securing the wiring connector (see illustration). Disconnect the wiring connectors (see illustration).
7 Referring to the appropriate wiring diagram at the end of this Chapter, check for continuity between the terminals on the switch side of the connectors with the switch in various positions e.g. switch OFF – no continuity, switch ON – continuity.
8 The switch housings are sealed – if the continuity check indicates a problem exists a new assembly will have to be fitted.

Removal and installation

9 Follow the procedure in Steps 3 to 6 to disconnect the switch wiring connectors.

24.5a Remove the front half of the housing

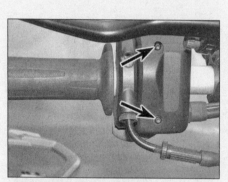

24.6a Undo the screws (arrowed) on the right-hand switch unit . . .

24.6c Screw (arrowed) secures wiring connector

10 To remove the left-hand switch housing, undo the screws securing it to the mounting bracket (see illustration) and lift the housing off.

24.5b Disconnect the switch wiring connectors

24.6b . . . and ease the front half off

24.6d Disconnect the wiring connectors

11 To remove the right-hand switch housing, undo the screws securing it to the mounting bracket and lift the housing off (see illustrations).

24.10 Undo the screws (arrowed) – left-hand side

24.11a Undo the screws (arrowed) – right-hand side . . .

24.11b . . . and remove the housing

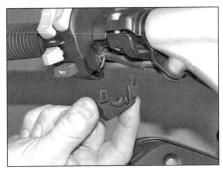

24.15 Remove the lower cover

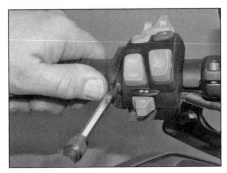

24.16a Hold back the flange . . .

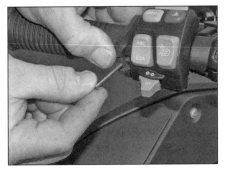

24.16b . . . and undo the screw

24.17a Rotate the grip/switch assembly forwards . . .

24.17b . . . and disconnect the connectors

24.18 Undo the screw at the rear . . .

12 Installation is the reverse of removal. Ensure that the wiring connectors are secure. Check the operation of the switches.

R1200 RT

Check

13 If an additional switch unit for optional (OA) electrical equipment is fitted to the left-hand handlebar unit, first undo the screw securing the switch and unclip it from its mounting, then undo the screws on the underside securing the mounting and lift it off.

14 To access the left-hand switch wiring connectors, first release the ties securing the wiring to the left-hand handlebar (see Chapter 4).

15 Release the clips securing the lower cover and remove it **(see illustration)**.

16 Hold back the flange of the handlebar grip to reveal the retaining screw and undo the screw **(see illustrations)**.

17 Rotate the grip/switch housing assembly forwards to access the wiring connectors and disconnect them **(see illustrations)**.

18 To access the right-hand switch wiring connectors, undo the screw on the rear of the housing **(see illustration)**.

19 Lower the cover at the back, then push it forwards to unclip the front edge **(see illustrations)**. Disconnect the wiring connectors **(see illustration)**.

20 Referring to the appropriate wiring diagram

at the end of this Chapter, check for continuity between the terminals on the switch side of the connectors with the switch in various positions e.g. switch OFF – no continuity, switch ON – continuity.

21 The switch housings are sealed – if the continuity check indicates a problem exists a new assembly will have to be fitted.

Removal and installation

22 Follow the procedure in Steps 13 to 19 to disconnect the switch wiring connectors.

23 To remove the left-hand switch housing, remove the bar end-weight (see Chapter 4), then draw the grip and switch assembly off the handlebar.

24 To remove the right-hand switch assembly,

24.19a . . . and lower the cover (arrowed)

24.19b Unclip the front edge (arrowed)

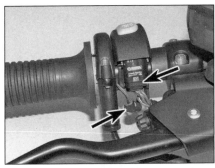

24.19c Disconnect the wiring connectors (arrowed)

24.24 Screw (arrowed) secures right-hand switch assembly

25.1 Horn located on front sub frame – R1200 GS shown

25.2 Location of the horn wiring connector (arrowed)

25.5 Bolt (arrowed) secures horn bracket

26.2 Location of starter relay – R1200 GS models

undo the screw securing the assembly and lift it off **(see illustration)**.

25 Installation is the reverse of removal. Ensure that the fixing screws are tightened securely. Ensure that the wiring connectors are secure and that the wiring is correctly routed and secured by any clips or ties. Check the operation of the switches.

25 Horn

1 The horn is located at the front of the machine on the front sub-frame below the steering head **(see illustration)**. Refer to Chapter 6 to remove any bodywork as necessary to access the horn.
2 Unplug the wiring connector from the horn **(see illustration)**. Using a fully charged 12 volt battery and two insulated jumper wires, apply voltage directly to the terminals on the horn.
3 If the horn sounds, check the switch (see Section 24) and the wiring between the switch, the ZFE central electronics unit and the horn (see *Wring Diagrams* at the end of this Chapter).
4 If the horn doesn't sound, renew it.
5 If not already done, unplug the wiring connector from the horn, then unscrew the bolt securing the horn bracket and remove it from the bike **(see illustration)**.

6 Installation is the reverse of removal. Check the operation of the horn.

26 Starter relay

1 If the starter circuit is faulty, first check that the battery is fully charged. Check that the engine kill switch is in the RUN position, that the side stand is up and that the transmission is in neutral. **Note:** *On R1200 GS, GS Adventure and R1200 R models, the kill switch should be in the middle position. On R1200 RT models, the kill switch should be pressed down at the rear.* If the starter motor still fails to operate, turn the ignition OFF and disconnect the battery negative (-) lead (see Section 3).
2 On R1200 GS and GS Adventure models, the starter relay is located underneath the ECU. Follow the procedure in Chapter 3 and displace the ZFE unit and the ECU. Pull the relay out from the holder, noting how it fits **(see illustration)**.
3 On R1200 RT models, the starter relay is located under the rider's seat inside a cover next to the plug for the BMW diagnostic tool. Undo the screws securing the cover, then draw the relay out and unclip it from its socket **(see illustrations)**.

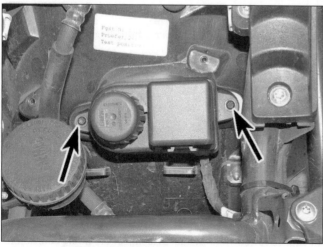

26.3a Undo the screws (arrowed) . . .

26.3b . . . to access the starter relay – R1200 RT

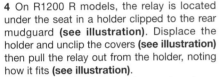

26.4a Location of the starter relay holder – R1200 R

26.4b Unclip the cover . . .

26.4c . . . and unplug the relay from the holder

4 On R1200 R models, the relay is located under the seat in a holder clipped to the rear mudguard **(see illustration)**. Displace the holder and unclip the covers **(see illustration)** then pull the relay out from the holder, noting how it fits **(see illustration)**.

5 Set a multimeter to the ohms x 1 scale, or use a continuity tester, and connect it across the relay's No. 3 and No. 5 terminals. There should be no continuity (infinite resistance).

6 Using a fully-charged 12 volt battery and two insulated jumper wires, connect the positive (+) battery terminal to the relay No. 2 terminal and the negative (-) battery terminal to the relay No. 1 terminal. The multimeter should now read zero ohms (continuity).

7 If the test results are not as described, the relay is faulty and must be renewed.

8 Before installing the relay, refer to the appropriate wiring diagram at the end of this Chapter and check the holder wiring and wiring connections.

9 If the relay and its wiring are good, check the other components in the starter circuit (clutch switch, side stand switch, starter switch and kill switch) as described in the relevant sections of this Chapter. If all components are good, check the wiring between the various components in the starter circuit (see *Wiring Diagrams* at the end of this Chapter).

10 Check the wiring and wiring connector

for the gear position sensor (see Chapter 3, Section 16).

11 If all components in the starter circuit are proved good, the fault could be due to a sticking or damaged starter motor solenoid (see Section 27).

27 Starter motor and solenoid

Removal

1 The starter motor is located on the lower left-hand side of the gearbox.

2 On R1200 RT models, remove the fairing left-hand main side panel (see Chapter 6) and the left-hand footrest bracket (see Chapter 4) to access the starter motor.

3 On all models, disconnect the battery negative (-) lead (see Section 3).

4 Follow the procedure in Chapter 2, Section 4, to remove the starter motor **(see illustration)**.

5 Inspect the starter gear and the clutch ring gear for worn or damaged teeth. If the starter gear is worn a new starter motor will have to be fitted – no individual components are available for the starter motor or solenoid **(see illustration)**. If the clutch ring gear is worn or

damaged, refer to Chapter 2, Section 20, to remove the clutch.

6 If necessary, have the operation of the starter motor and solenoid checked by a BMW dealer.

Installation

7 Installation is the reverse of removal. Tighten the mounting bolts and the starter motor terminal nut to the torque settings specified at the beginning of this Chapter. Ensure that solenoid wiring connector is secure.

8 Check the operation of the starter motor.

28 Charging system check

1 Accurate assessment of alternator output should be undertaken by a BMW dealer. However, a charging voltage output test can be undertaken as follows.

2 Make sure that the battery is fully charged (see Section 3).

3 Start the engine and run it at a fast idle. Using a multimeter set to the 0 to 20 volts DC scale, connect the positive (+) meter lead to the battery positive (+) terminal and the negative (-) lead to the negative (-) terminal. The meter should indicate 13 to 15 volts.

27.4 Removing the starter motor

27.5 Inspect the starter gear teeth (arrowed)

29.7 Lift the alternator out at the front

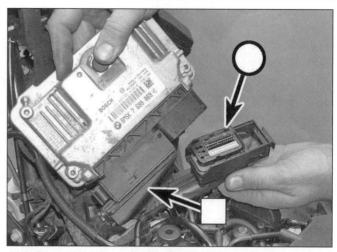

30.2 Terminal numbers are shown in circles or squares to identify the appropriate connector

4 Now select high beam – the voltage may drop momentarily, but should then return to the original indicated 13 to 15 volts.

5 If the output test indicates a voltage either lower or higher than the suggested range, it is likely that the alternator or its inbuilt voltage regulator is faulty – have the charging system checked by a BMW dealer.

6 Refer to Section 29 for details of alternator removal and installation.

29 Alternator

1 Refer to Section 28 to check the alternator output. If the alternator is faulty, a new one must be fitted – no replacement parts are available.

Removal

2 The alternator is located on the top of the crankcase between the left and right-hand struts of the front sub-frame.

3 Disconnect the battery negative (-) lead (see Section 3).

4 Remove the left and right-hand fairing side panels (see Chapter 6) and the fuel tank (see Chapter 3).

5 Remove the front suspension shock absorber (see Chapter 4, Section 6).

6 Remove the alternator drive belt (see Chapter 1, Section 9).

7 Referring to Chapter 2, Section 4, remove the alternator drive belt top cover, then disconnect the wiring connector and terminal lead from the alternator. Undo the mounting bolts and manoeuvre the alternator off towards the front of the machine **(see illustration)**.

Installation

8 Installation is the reverse of removal. Tighten the mounting bolts to the torque setting specified at the beginning of this Chapter. Install the lead and tighten the terminal nut securely, then fit the cover. Ensure that the wiring connector is secure.

9 Follow the procedure in Chapter 1, Section 9, to install the drive belt and cover.

10 Install the remaining components in the reverse order of removal.

30 Wiring diagrams

1 The wiring diagrams for each model are presented as separate circuits e.g. *Starting and charging system, Lighting system* etc.

2 Connector plug terminal number details are given to aid testing and terminal identification. For the engine control unit (ECU) and central electronics (ZFE) unit the terminal numbers are represented in squares or circles to differentiate between the two connectors on the unit **(see illustration)**. Study the wiring diagram and the connectors on the unit to determine the identity of the connector.

3 The control units are drawn with a solid black outline where the unit connections are complete within that circuit. Where a hatched outline is used, their connections are shown on different circuits and thus the unit is not shown complete in any one circuit.

4 Wires can be identified by their colour and wire thickness details, expressed in millimetres.

5 Internal connections within the wiring harness are represented by full points with a DIN symbol alongside, e.g. 31 denoting the earth (ground) circuit.

6 Engine cylinders are referred to as *Cyl 1* for the left-hand cylinder and *Cyl 2* for the right-hand cylinder.

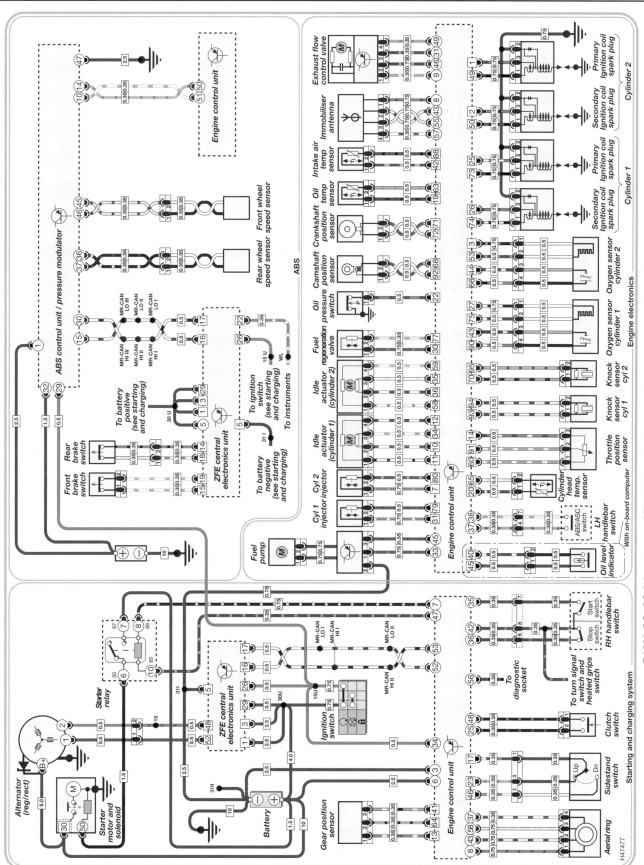

R1200 GS, GS Adventure and R1200 R - starting and charging, engine electronics and ABS

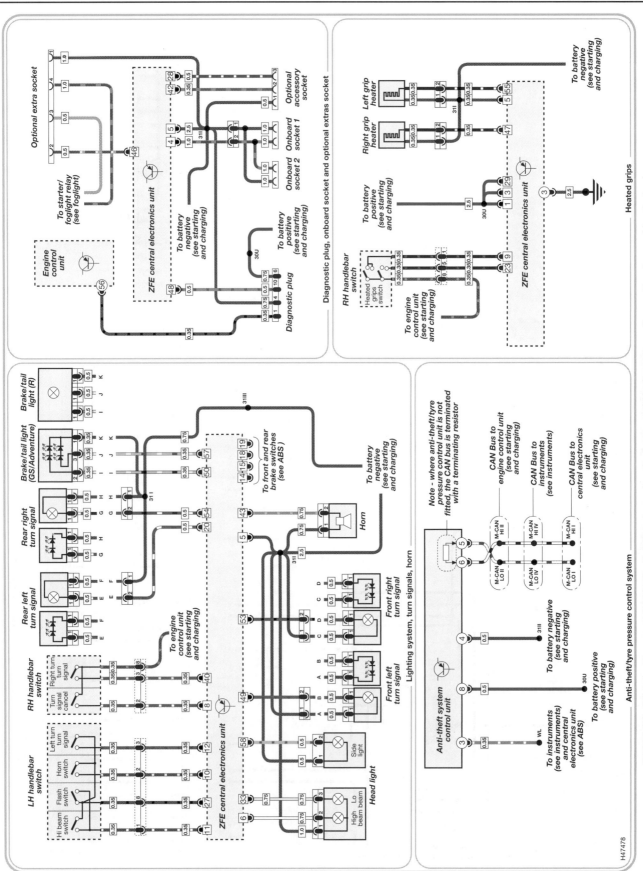

Diagnostic plug, onboard socket and optional extras socket

Heated grips

Lighting system, turn signals, horn

Anti-theft/tyre pressure control system

R1200 GS, GS Adventure and R1200 R – lighting, turn signals, horn, anti-theft system, diagnostic plug and heated grips

H47478

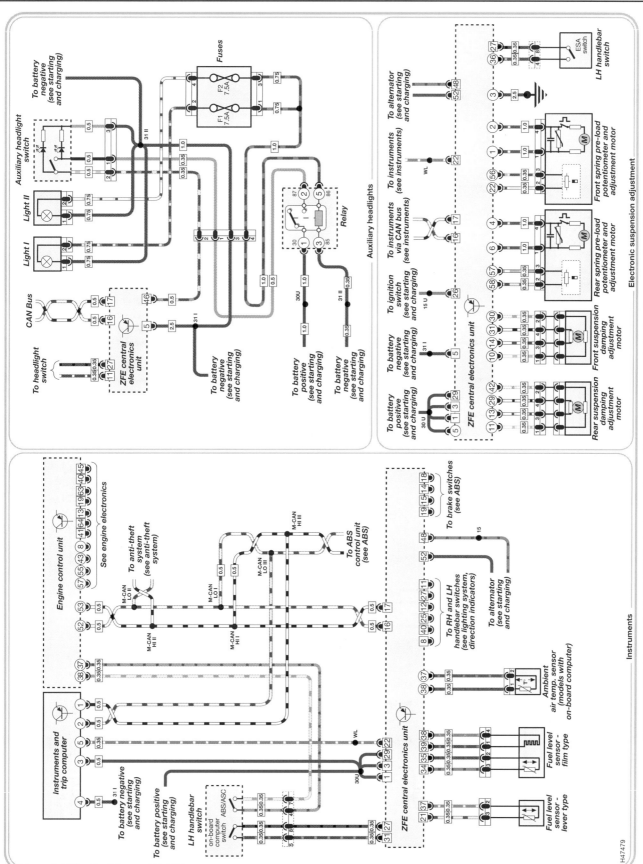

R1200 GS, GS Adventure and R1200 R - instruments, auxiliary headlights and electronic suspension adjustment

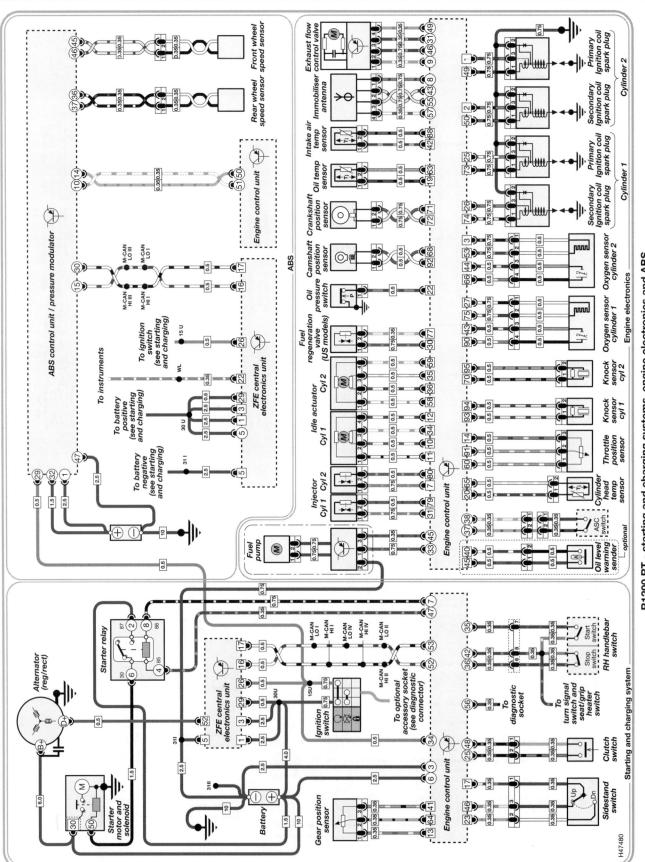

R1200 RT - starting and charging systems, engine electronics and ABS

H47480

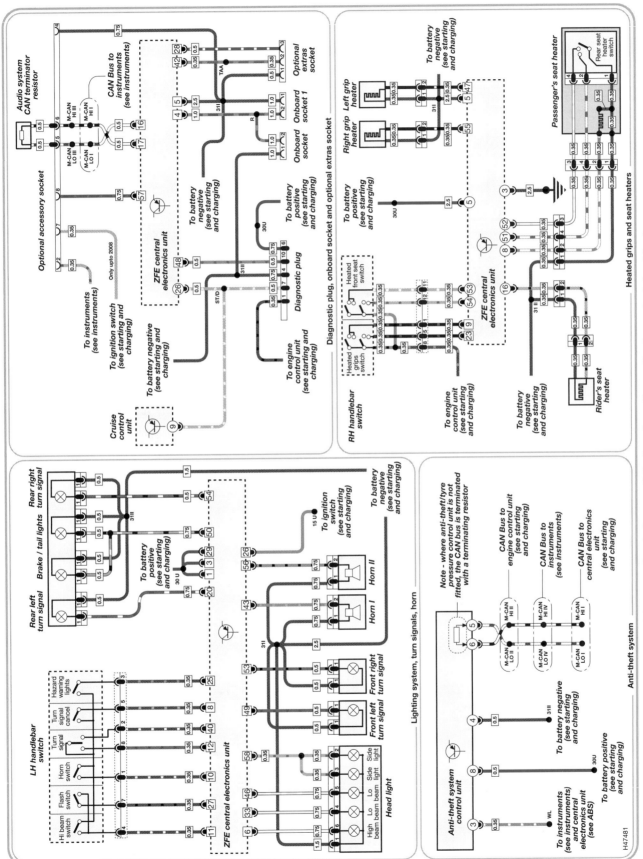

R1200 RT - lighting, turn signals, horn, anti-theft system, diagnostic plug and grip/seat heaters

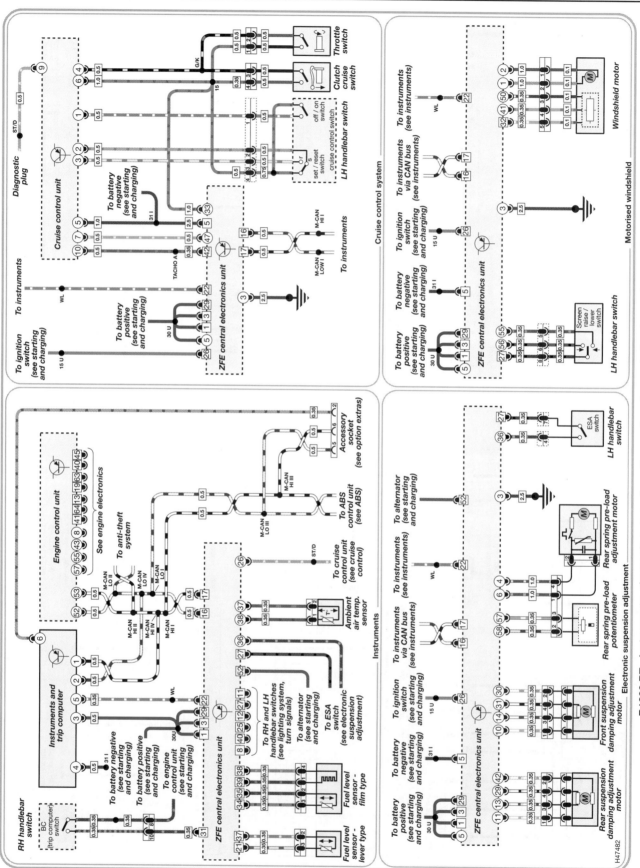

R1200 RT - instruments, electronic suspension adjustment, cruise control and motorised windshield

H47482

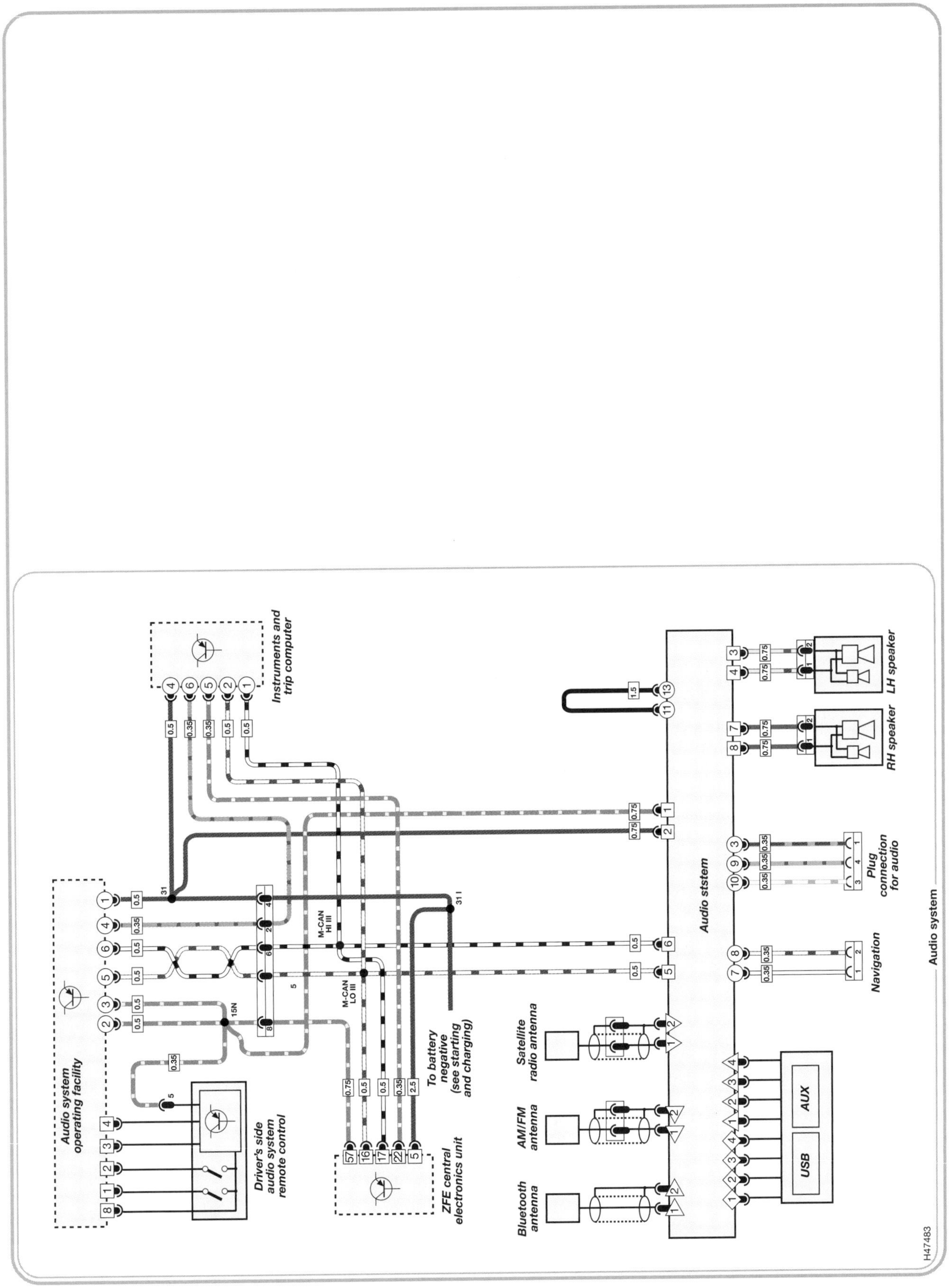

Instruments and trip computer

Audio system operating facility

Driver's side audio system remote control

ZFE central electronics unit

M-CAN HI III

M-CAN LO III

To battery negative (see starting and charging)

Bluetooth antenna

AM/FM antenna

Satellite radio antenna

USB

AUX

Navigation

Plug connection for audio

Audio ststem

RH speaker

LH speaker

Audio system

R1200 RT - audio system

H47483

Notes

Reference

Tools and Workshop Tips REF•2

● Building up a tool kit and equipping your workshop ● Using tools ● Understanding bearing, seal, fastener and chain sizes and markings ● Repair techniques

Security REF•20

● Locks and chains ● U-locks ● Disc locks ● Alarms and immobilisers ● Security marking systems ● Tips on how to prevent bike theft

Lubricants and fluids REF•23

● Engine oils ● Transmission (gear) oils ● Coolant/anti-freeze ● Fork oils and suspension fluids ● Brake/clutch fluids ● Spray lubes, degreasers and solvents

Conversion Factors REF•26

$$34 \ Nm \times 0.738$$
$$= 25 \ lbf \ ft$$

● Formulae for conversion of the metric (SI) units used throughout the manual into Imperial measures

MOT Test Checks REF•27

● A guide to the UK MOT test ● Which items are tested ● How to prepare your motorcycle for the test and perform a pre-test check

Storage REF•32

● How to prepare your motorcycle for going into storage and protect essential systems ● How to get the motorcycle back on the road

Fault Finding REF•35

● Common faults and their likely causes ● How to check engine cylinder compression ● How to make electrical tests and use test meters

Technical Terms Explained REF•43

● Component names, technical terms and common abbreviations explained

Index REF•47

Buying tools

A toolkit is a fundamental requirement for servicing and repairing a motorcycle. Although there will be an initial expense in building up enough tools for servicing, this will soon be offset by the savings made by doing the job yourself. As experience and confidence grow, additional tools can be added to enable the repair and overhaul of the motorcycle. Many of the specialist tools are expensive and not often used so it may be preferable to hire them, or for a group of friends or motorcycle club to join in the purchase.

As a rule, it is better to buy more expensive, good quality tools. Cheaper tools are likely to wear out faster and need to be renewed more often, nullifying the original saving.

Warning: To avoid the risk of a poor quality tool breaking in use, causing injury or damage to the component being worked on, always aim to purchase tools which meet the relevant national safety standards.

The following lists of tools do not represent the manufacturer's service tools, but serve as a guide to help the owner decide which tools are needed for this level of work. In addition, items such as an electric drill, hacksaw, files, soldering iron and a workbench equipped with a vice, may be needed. Although not classed as tools, a selection of bolts, screws, nuts, washers and pieces of tubing always come in useful.

For more information about tools, refer to the Haynes *Motorcycle Workshop Practice Techbook* (Bk. No. 3470).

Manufacturer's service tools

Inevitably certain tasks require the use of a service tool. Where possible an alternative tool or method of approach is recommended, but sometimes there is no option if personal injury or damage to the component is to be avoided. Where required, service tools are referred to in the relevant procedure.

Service tools can usually only be purchased from a motorcycle dealer and are identified by a part number. Some of the commonly-used tools, such as rotor pullers, are available in aftermarket form from mail-order motorcycle tool and accessory suppliers.

Maintenance and minor repair tools

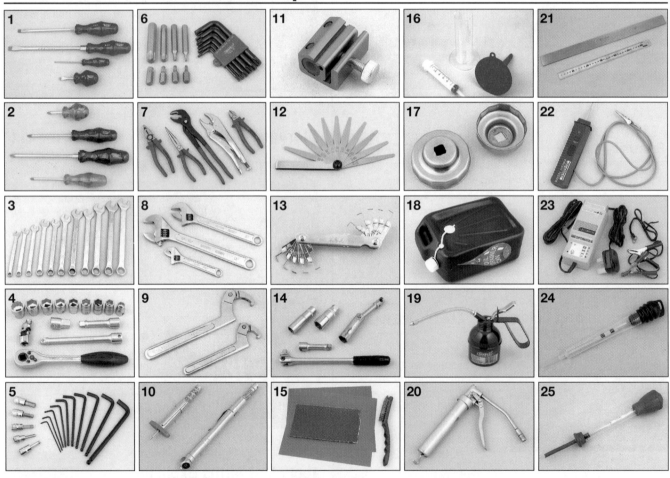

1 Set of flat-bladed screwdrivers
2 Set of Phillips head screwdrivers
3 Combination open-end and ring spanners
4 Socket set (3/8 inch or 1/2 inch drive)
5 Set of Allen keys or bits

6 Set of Torx keys or bits
7 Pliers, cutters and self-locking grips (Mole grips)
8 Adjustable spanners
9 C-spanners
10 Tread depth gauge and tyre pressure gauge

11 Cable oiler clamp
12 Feeler gauges
13 Spark plug gap measuring tool
14 Spark plug spanner or deep plug sockets
15 Wire brush and emery paper

16 Calibrated syringe, measuring vessel and funnel
17 Oil filter adapters
18 Oil drainer can or tray
19 Pump type oil can
20 Grease gun

21 Straight-edge and steel rule
22 Continuity tester
23 Battery charger
24 Hydrometer (for battery specific gravity check)
25 Anti-freeze tester (for liquid-cooled engines)

Repair and overhaul tools

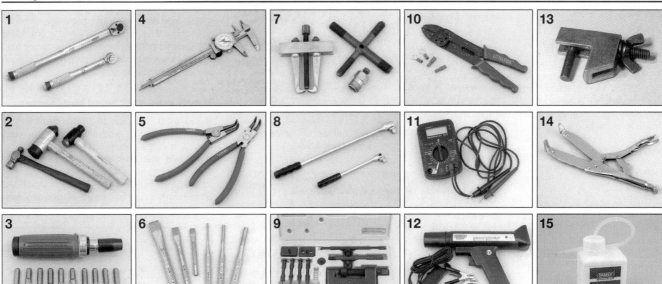

1 Torque wrench
   (small and mid-ranges)
2 Conventional, plastic or
   soft-faced hammers
3 Impact driver set

4 Vernier gauge
5 Circlip pliers (internal and
   external, or combination)
6 Set of cold chisels
   and punches

7 Selection of pullers
8 Breaker bars
9 Chain breaking/
   riveting tool set

10 Wire stripper and
    crimper tool
11 Multimeter (measures
    amps, volts and ohms)
12 Stroboscope (for
    dynamic timing checks)

13 Hose clamp
    (wingnut type shown)
14 Clutch holding tool
15 One-man brake/clutch
    bleeder kit

Specialist tools

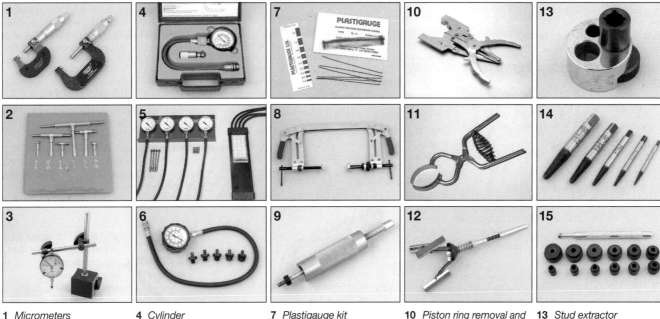

1 Micrometers
   (external type)
2 Telescoping gauges
3 Dial gauge

4 Cylinder
   compression gauge
5 Vacuum gauges (left) or
   manometer (right)
6 Oil pressure gauge

7 Plastigauge kit
8 Valve spring compressor
   (4-stroke engines)
9 Piston pin drawbolt tool

10 Piston ring removal and
    installation tool
11 Piston ring clamp
12 Cylinder bore hone
    (stone type shown)

13 Stud extractor
14 Screw extractor set
15 Bearing driver set

1 Workshop equipment and facilities

The workbench

● Work is made much easier by raising the bike up on a ramp - components are much more accessible if raised to waist level. The hydraulic or pneumatic types seen in the dealer's workshop are a sound investment if you undertake a lot of repairs or overhauls **(see illustration 1.1)**.

1.1 Hydraulic motorcycle ramp

● If raised off ground level, the bike must be supported on the ramp to avoid it falling. Most ramps incorporate a front wheel locating clamp which can be adjusted to suit different diameter wheels. When tightening the clamp, take care not to mark the wheel rim or damage the tyre - use wood blocks on each side to prevent this.
● Secure the bike to the ramp using tie-downs **(see illustration 1.2)**. If the bike has only a sidestand, and hence leans at a dangerous angle when raised, support the bike on an auxiliary stand.

1.2 Tie-downs are used around the passenger footrests to secure the bike

● Auxiliary (paddock) stands are widely available from mail order companies or motorcycle dealers and attach either to the wheel axle or swingarm pivot **(see illustration 1.3)**. If the motorcycle has a centrestand, you can support it under the crankcase to prevent it toppling whilst either wheel is removed **(see illustration 1.4)**.

1.3 This auxiliary stand attaches to the swingarm pivot

1.4 Always use a block of wood between the engine and jack head when supporting the engine in this way

Fumes and fire

● Refer to the Safety first! page at the beginning of the manual for full details. Make sure your workshop is equipped with a fire extinguisher suitable for fuel-related fires (Class B fire - flammable liquids) - it is not sufficient to have a water-filled extinguisher.
● Always ensure adequate ventilation is available. Unless an exhaust gas extraction system is available for use, ensure that the engine is run outside of the workshop.
● If working on the fuel system, make sure the workshop is ventilated to avoid a build-up of fumes. This applies equally to fume build-up when charging a battery. Do not smoke or allow anyone else to smoke in the workshop.

Fluids

● If you need to drain fuel from the tank, store it in an approved container marked as suitable for the storage of petrol (gasoline) **(see illustration 1.5)**. Do not store fuel in glass jars or bottles.

1.5 Use an approved can only for storing petrol (gasoline)

● Use proprietary engine degreasers or solvents which have a high flash-point, such as paraffin (kerosene), for cleaning off oil, grease and dirt - never use petrol (gasoline) for cleaning. Wear rubber gloves when handling solvent and engine degreaser. The fumes from certain solvents can be dangerous - always work in a well-ventilated area.

Dust, eye and hand protection

● Protect your lungs from inhalation of dust particles by wearing a filtering mask over the nose and mouth. Many frictional materials still contain asbestos which is dangerous to your health. Protect your eyes from spouts of liquid and sprung components by wearing a pair of protective goggles **(see illustration 1.6)**.

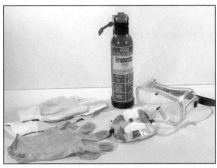

1.6 A fire extinguisher, goggles, mask and protective gloves should be at hand in the workshop

● Protect your hands from contact with solvents, fuel and oils by wearing rubber gloves. Alternatively apply a barrier cream to your hands before starting work. If handling hot components or fluids, wear suitable gloves to protect your hands from scalding and burns.

What to do with old fluids

● Old cleaning solvent, fuel, coolant and oils should not be poured down domestic drains or onto the ground. Package the fluid up in old oil containers, label it accordingly, and take it to a garage or disposal facility. Contact your local authority for location of such sites or ring the oil care hotline.

Note: It is antisocial and illegal to dump oil down the drain. To find the location of your local oil recycling bank in the UK, call 08708 506 506 or visit www.oilbankline.org.uk

In the USA, note that any oil supplier must accept used oil for recycling.

2 Fasteners - screws, bolts and nuts

Fastener types and applications

Bolts and screws

● Fastener head types are either of hexagonal, Torx or splined design, with internal and external versions of each type **(see illustrations 2.1 and 2.2)**; splined head fasteners are not in common use on motorcycles. The conventional slotted or Phillips head design is used for certain screws. Bolt or screw length is always measured from the underside of the head to the end of the item **(see illustration 2.11)**.

2.1 Internal hexagon/Allen (A), Torx (B) and splined (C) fasteners, with corresponding bits

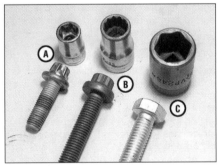

2.2 External Torx (A), splined (B) and hexagon (C) fasteners, with corresponding sockets

● Certain fasteners on the motorcycle have a tensile marking on their heads, the higher the marking the stronger the fastener. High tensile fasteners generally carry a 10 or higher marking. Never replace a high tensile fastener with one of a lower tensile strength.

Washers (see illustration 2.3)

● Plain washers are used between a fastener head and a component to prevent damage to the component or to spread the load when torque is applied. Plain washers can also be used as spacers or shims in certain assemblies. Copper or aluminium plain washers are often used as sealing washers on drain plugs.

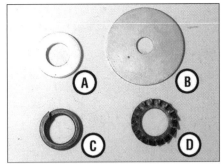

2.3 Plain washer (A), penny washer (B), spring washer (C) and serrated washer (D)

● The split-ring spring washer works by applying axial tension between the fastener head and component. If flattened, it is fatigued and must be renewed. If a plain (flat) washer is used on the fastener, position the spring washer between the fastener and the plain washer.

● Serrated star type washers dig into the fastener and component faces, preventing loosening. They are often used on electrical earth (ground) connections to the frame.

● Cone type washers (sometimes called Belleville) are conical and when tightened apply axial tension between the fastener head and component. They must be installed with the dished side against the component and often carry an OUTSIDE marking on their outer face. If flattened, they are fatigued and must be renewed.

● Tab washers are used to lock plain nuts or bolts on a shaft. A portion of the tab washer is bent up hard against one flat of the nut or bolt to prevent it loosening. Due to the tab washer being deformed in use, a new tab washer should be used every time it is disturbed.

● Wave washers are used to take up endfloat on a shaft. They provide light springing and prevent excessive side-to-side play of a component. Can be found on rocker arm shafts.

Nuts and split pins

● Conventional plain nuts are usually six-sided **(see illustration 2.4)**. They are sized by thread diameter and pitch. High tensile nuts carry a number on one end to denote their tensile strength.

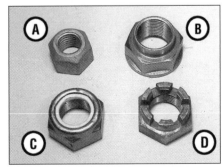

2.4 Plain nut (A), shouldered locknut (B), nylon insert nut (C) and castellated nut (D)

● Self-locking nuts either have a nylon insert, or two spring metal tabs, or a shoulder which is staked into a groove in the shaft - their advantage over conventional plain nuts is a resistance to loosening due to vibration. The nylon insert type can be used a number of times, but must be renewed when the friction of the nylon insert is reduced, ie when the nut spins freely on the shaft. The spring tab type can be reused unless the tabs are damaged. The shouldered type must be renewed every time it is disturbed.

● Split pins (cotter pins) are used to lock a castellated nut to a shaft or to prevent slackening of a plain nut. Common applications are wheel axles and brake torque arms. Because the split pin arms are deformed to lock around the nut a new split pin must always be used on installation - always fit the correct size split pin which will fit snugly in the shaft hole. Make sure the split pin arms are correctly located around the nut **(see illustrations 2.5 and 2.6)**.

2.5 Bend split pin (cotter pin) arms as shown (arrows) to secure a castellated nut

2.6 Bend split pin (cotter pin) arms as shown to secure a plain nut

Caution: If the castellated nut slots do not align with the shaft hole after tightening to the torque setting, tighten the nut until the next slot aligns with the hole - never slacken the nut to align its slot.

● R-pins (shaped like the letter R), or slip pins as they are sometimes called, are sprung and can be reused if they are otherwise in good condition. Always install R-pins with their closed end facing forwards **(see illustration 2.7)**.

**2.7 Correct fitting of R-pin.
Arrow indicates forward direction**

Circlips (see illustration 2.8)

● Circlips (sometimes called snap-rings) are used to retain components on a shaft or in a housing and have corresponding external or internal ears to permit removal. Parallel-sided (machined) circlips can be installed either way round in their groove, whereas stamped circlips (which have a chamfered edge on one face) must be installed with the chamfer facing away from the direction of thrust load **(see illustration 2.9)**.

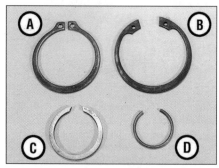

2.8 External stamped circlip (A), internal stamped circlip (B), machined circlip (C) and wire circlip (D)

● Always use circlip pliers to remove and install circlips; expand or compress them just enough to remove them. After installation, rotate the circlip in its groove to ensure it is securely seated. If installing a circlip on a splined shaft, always align its opening with a shaft channel to ensure the circlip ends are well supported and unlikely to catch **(see illustration 2.10)**.

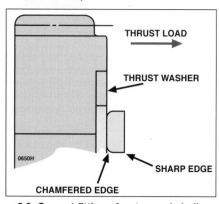

2.9 Correct fitting of a stamped circlip

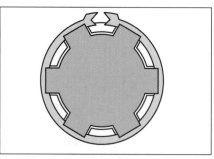

**2.10 Align circlip opening
with shaft channel**

● Circlips can wear due to the thrust of components and become loose in their grooves, with the subsequent danger of becoming dislodged in operation. For this reason, renewal is advised every time a circlip is disturbed.

● Wire circlips are commonly used as piston pin retaining clips. If a removal tang is provided, long-nosed pliers can be used to dislodge them, otherwise careful use of a small flat-bladed screwdriver is necessary. Wire circlips should be renewed every time they are disturbed.

Thread diameter and pitch

● Diameter of a male thread (screw, bolt or stud) is the outside diameter of the threaded portion **(see illustration 2.11)**. Most motorcycle manufacturers use the ISO (International Standards Organisation) metric system expressed in millimetres, eg M6 refers to a 6 mm diameter thread. Sizing is the same for nuts, except that the thread diameter is measured across the valleys of the nut.

● Pitch is the distance between the peaks of the thread **(see illustration 2.11)**. It is expressed in millimetres, thus a common bolt size may be expressed as 6.0 x 1.0 mm (6 mm thread diameter and 1 mm pitch). Generally pitch increases in proportion to thread diameter, although there are always exceptions.

● Thread diameter and pitch are related for conventional fastener applications and the accompanying table can be used as a guide. Additionally, the AF (Across Flats), spanner or socket size dimension of the bolt or nut **(see illustration 2.11)** is linked to thread and pitch specification. Thread pitch can be measured with a thread gauge **(see illustration 2.12)**.

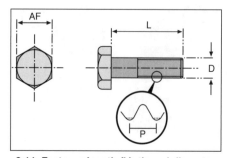

2.11 Fastener length (L), thread diameter (D), thread pitch (P) and head size (AF)

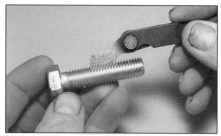

**2.12 Using a thread gauge
to measure pitch**

AF size	Thread diameter x pitch (mm)
8 mm	M5 x 0.8
8 mm	M6 x 1.0
10 mm	M6 x 1.0
12 mm	M8 x 1.25
14 mm	M10 x 1.25
17 mm	M12 x 1.25

● The threads of most fasteners are of the right-hand type, ie they are turned clockwise to tighten and anti-clockwise to loosen. The reverse situation applies to left-hand thread fasteners, which are turned anti-clockwise to tighten and clockwise to loosen. Left-hand threads are used where rotation of a component might loosen a conventional right-hand thread fastener.

Seized fasteners

● Corrosion of external fasteners due to water or reaction between two dissimilar metals can occur over a period of time. It will build up sooner in wet conditions or in countries where salt is used on the roads during the winter. If a fastener is severely corroded it is likely that normal methods of removal will fail and result in its head being ruined. When you attempt removal, the fastener thread should be heard to crack free and unscrew easily - if it doesn't, stop there before damaging something.

● A smart tap on the head of the fastener will often succeed in breaking free corrosion which has occurred in the threads **(see illustration 2.13)**.

● An aerosol penetrating fluid (such as WD-40) applied the night beforehand may work its way down into the thread and ease removal. Depending on the location, you may be able to make up a Plasticine well around the fastener head and fill it with penetrating fluid.

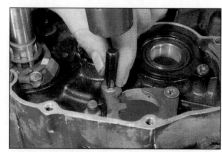

2.13 A sharp tap on the head of a fastener will often break free a corroded thread

● If you are working on an engine internal component, corrosion will most likely not be a problem due to the well lubricated environment. However, components can be very tight and an impact driver is a useful tool in freeing them **(see illustration 2.14)**.

2.14 Using an impact driver to free a fastener

● Where corrosion has occurred between dissimilar metals (eg steel and aluminium alloy), the application of heat to the fastener head will create a disproportionate expansion rate between the two metals and break the seizure caused by the corrosion. Whether heat can be applied depends on the location of the fastener - any surrounding components likely to be damaged must first be removed **(see illustration 2.15)**. Heat can be applied using a paint stripper heat gun or clothes iron, or by immersing the component in boiling water - wear protective gloves to prevent scalding or burns to the hands.

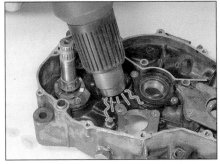

2.15 Using heat to free a seized fastener

● As a last resort, it is possible to use a hammer and cold chisel to work the fastener head unscrewed **(see illustration 2.16)**. This will damage the fastener, but more importantly extreme care must be taken not to damage the surrounding component.

Caution: Remember that the component being secured is generally of more value than the bolt, nut or screw - when the fastener is freed, do not unscrew it with force, instead work the fastener back and forth when resistance is felt to prevent thread damage.

2.16 Using a hammer and chisel to free a seized fastener

Broken fasteners and damaged heads

● If the shank of a broken bolt or screw is accessible you can grip it with self-locking grips. The knurled wheel type stud extractor tool or self-gripping stud puller tool is particularly useful for removing the long studs which screw into the cylinder mouth surface of the crankcase or bolts and screws from which the head has broken off **(see illustration 2.17)**. Studs can also be removed by locking two nuts together on the threaded end of the stud and using a spanner on the lower nut **(see illustration 2.18)**.

2.17 Using a stud extractor tool to remove a broken crankcase stud

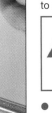

2.18 Two nuts can be locked together to unscrew a stud from a component

● A bolt or screw which has broken off below or level with the casing must be extracted using a screw extractor set. Centre punch the fastener to centralise the drill bit, then drill a hole in the fastener **(see illustration 2.19)**. Select a drill bit which is approximately half to three-quarters the diameter of the fastener

2.19 When using a screw extractor, first drill a hole in the fastener . . .

and drill to a depth which will accommodate the extractor. Use the largest size extractor possible, but avoid leaving too small a wall thickness otherwise the extractor will merely force the fastener walls outwards wedging it in the casing thread.

● If a spiral type extractor is used, thread it anti-clockwise into the fastener. As it is screwed in, it will grip the fastener and unscrew it from the casing **(see illustration 2.20)**.

2.20 . . . then thread the extractor anti-clockwise into the fastener

● If a taper type extractor is used, tap it into the fastener so that it is firmly wedged in place. Unscrew the extractor (anti-clockwise) to draw the fastener out.

> ⚠ *Warning: Stud extractors are very hard and may break off in the fastener if care is not taken - ask an engineer about spark erosion if this happens.*

● Alternatively, the broken bolt/screw can be drilled out and the hole retapped for an oversize bolt/screw or a diamond-section thread insert. It is essential that the drilling is carried out squarely and to the correct depth, otherwise the casing may be ruined - if in doubt, entrust the work to an engineer.

● Bolts and nuts with rounded corners cause the correct size spanner or socket to slip when force is applied. Of the types of spanner/socket available always use a six-point type rather than an eight or twelve-point type - better grip

2.21 Comparison of surface drive ring spanner (left) with 12-point type (right)

is obtained. Surface drive spanners grip the middle of the hex flats, rather than the corners, and are thus good in cases of damaged heads **(see illustration 2.21)**.

● Slotted-head or Phillips-head screws are often damaged by the use of the wrong size screwdriver. Allen-head and Torx-head screws are much less likely to sustain damage. If enough of the screw head is exposed you can use a hacksaw to cut a slot in its head and then use a conventional flat-bladed screwdriver to remove it. Alternatively use a hammer and cold chisel to tap the head of the fastener around to slacken it. Always replace damaged fasteners with new ones, preferably Torx or Allen-head type.

HAYNES HINT

A dab of valve grinding compound between the screw head and screwdriver tip will often give a good grip.

Thread repair

● Threads (particularly those in aluminium alloy components) can be damaged by overtightening, being assembled with dirt in the threads, or from a component working loose and vibrating. Eventually the thread will fail completely, and it will be impossible to tighten the fastener.

● If a thread is damaged or clogged with old locking compound it can be renovated with a thread repair tool (thread chaser) **(see illustrations 2.22 and 2.23)**; special thread

2.22 A thread repair tool being used to correct an internal thread

2.23 A thread repair tool being used to correct an external thread

chasers are available for spark plug hole threads. The tool will not cut a new thread, but clean and true the original thread. Make sure that you use the correct diameter and pitch tool. Similarly, external threads can be cleaned up with a die or a thread restorer file **(see illustration 2.24)**.

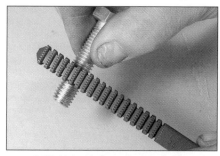

2.24 Using a thread restorer file

● It is possible to drill out the old thread and retap the component to the next thread size. This will work where there is enough surrounding material and a new bolt or screw can be obtained. Sometimes, however, this is not possible - such as where the bolt/screw passes through another component which must also be suitably modified, also in cases where a spark plug or oil drain plug cannot be obtained in a larger diameter thread size.

● The diamond-section thread insert (often known by its popular trade name of Heli-Coil) is a simple and effective method of renewing the thread and retaining the original size. A kit can be purchased which contains the tap, insert and installing tool **(see illustration 2.25)**. Drill out the damaged thread with the size drill specified **(see illustration 2.26)**. Carefully retap the thread **(see illustration 2.27)**. Install the

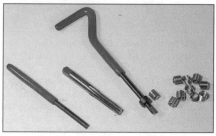

2.25 Obtain a thread insert kit to suit the thread diameter and pitch required

2.26 To install a thread insert, first drill out the original thread . . .

2.27 . . . tap a new thread . . .

2.28 . . . fit insert on the installing tool . . .

2.29 . . . and thread into the component . . .

2.30 . . . break off the tang when complete

insert on the installing tool and thread it slowly into place using a light downward pressure **(see illustrations 2.28 and 2.29)**. When positioned between a 1/4 and 1/2 turn below the surface withdraw the installing tool and use the break-off tool to press down on the tang, breaking it off **(see illustration 2.30)**.

● There are epoxy thread repair kits on the market which can rebuild stripped internal threads, although this repair should not be used on high load-bearing components.

Thread locking and sealing compounds

● Locking compounds are used in locations where the fastener is prone to loosening due to vibration or on important safety-related items which might cause loss of control of the motorcycle if they fail. It is also used where important fasteners cannot be secured by other means such as lockwashers or split pins.

● Before applying locking compound, make sure that the threads (internal and external) are clean and dry with all old compound removed. Select a compound to suit the component being secured - a non-permanent general locking and sealing type is suitable for most applications, but a high strength type is needed for permanent fixing of studs in castings. Apply a drop or two of the compound to the first few threads of the fastener, then thread it into place and tighten to the specified torque. Do not apply excessive thread locking compound otherwise the thread may be damaged on subsequent removal.

● Certain fasteners are impregnated with a dry film type coating of locking compound on their threads. Always renew this type of fastener if disturbed.

● Anti-seize compounds, such as copper-based greases, can be applied to protect threads from seizure due to extreme heat and corrosion. A common instance is spark plug threads and exhaust system fasteners.

---

3 Measuring tools and gauges

Feeler gauges

● Feeler gauges (or blades) are used for measuring small gaps and clearances (see illustration 3.1). They can also be used to measure endfloat (sideplay) of a component on a shaft where access is not possible with a dial gauge.

● Feeler gauge sets should be treated with care and not bent or damaged. They are etched with their size on one face. Keep them clean and very lightly oiled to prevent corrosion build-up.

3.1 Feeler gauges are used for measuring small gaps and clearances - thickness is marked on one face of gauge

---

● When measuring a clearance, select a gauge which is a light sliding fit between the two components. You may need to use two gauges together to measure the clearance accurately.

Micrometers

● A micrometer is a precision tool capable of measuring to 0.01 or 0.001 of a millimetre. It should always be stored in its case and not in the general toolbox. It must be kept clean and never dropped, otherwise its frame or measuring anvils could be distorted resulting in inaccurate readings.

● External micrometers are used for measuring outside diameters of components and have many more applications than internal micrometers. Micrometers are available in different size ranges, eg 0 to 25 mm, 25 to 50 mm, and upwards in 25 mm steps; some large micrometers have interchangeable anvils to allow a range of measurements to be taken. Generally the largest precision measurement you are likely to take on a motorcycle is the piston diameter.

● Internal micrometers (or bore micrometers) are used for measuring inside diameters, such as valve guides and cylinder bores. Telescoping gauges and small hole gauges are used in conjunction with an external micrometer, whereas the more expensive internal micrometers have their own measuring device.

External micrometer

Note: *The conventional analogue type instrument is described. Although much easier to read, digital micrometers are considerably more expensive.*

● Always check the calibration of the micrometer before use. With the anvils closed (0 to 25 mm type) or set over a test gauge

---

3.2 Check micrometer calibration before use

(for the larger types) the scale should read zero (see illustration 3.2); make sure that the anvils (and test piece) are clean first. Any discrepancy can be adjusted by referring to the instructions supplied with the tool. Remember that the micrometer is a precision measuring tool - don't force the anvils closed, use the ratchet (4) on the end of the micrometer to close it. In this way, a measured force is always applied.

● To use, first make sure that the item being measured is clean. Place the anvil of the micrometer (1) against the item and use the thimble (2) to bring the spindle (3) lightly into contact with the other side of the item (see illustration 3.3). Don't tighten the thimble down because this will damage the micrometer - instead use the ratchet (4) on the end of the micrometer. The ratchet mechanism applies a measured force preventing damage to the instrument.

● The micrometer is read by referring to the linear scale on the sleeve and the annular scale on the thimble. Read off the sleeve first to obtain the base measurement, then add the fine measurement from the thimble to obtain the overall reading. The linear scale on the sleeve represents the measuring range of the micrometer (eg 0 to 25 mm). The annular scale

---

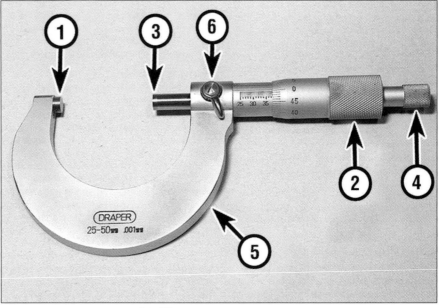

3.3 Micrometer component parts

1 Anvil	3 Spindle	5 Frame
2 Thimble	4 Ratchet	6 Locking lever

on the thimble will be in graduations of 0.01 mm (or as marked on the frame) - one full revolution of the thimble will move 0.5 mm on the linear scale. Take the reading where the datum line on the sleeve intersects the thimble's scale. Always position the eye directly above the scale otherwise an inaccurate reading will result.

In the example shown the item measures 2.95 mm **(see illustration 3.4)**:

Linear scale	2.00 mm
Linear scale	0.50 mm
Annular scale	0.45 mm
Total figure	2.95 mm

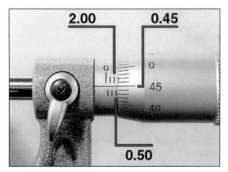

3.4 Micrometer reading of 2.95 mm

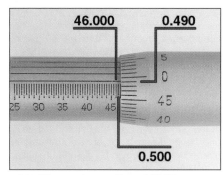

3.5 Micrometer reading of 46.99 mm on linear and annular scales . . .

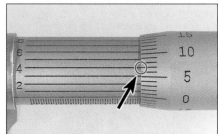

3.6 . . . and 0.004 mm on vernier scale

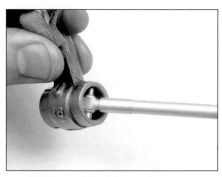

3.7 Expand the telescoping gauge in the bore, lock its position . . .

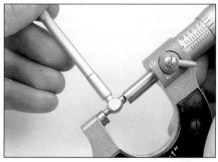

3.8 . . . then measure the gauge with a micrometer

Most micrometers have a locking lever (6) on the frame to hold the setting in place, allowing the item to be removed from the micrometer.
● Some micrometers have a vernier scale on their sleeve, providing an even finer measurement to be taken, in 0.001 increments of a millimetre. Take the sleeve and thimble measurement as described above, then check which graduation on the vernier scale aligns with that of the annular scale on the thimble **Note:** *The eye must be perpendicular to the scale when taking the vernier reading - if necessary rotate the body of the micrometer to ensure this.* Multiply the vernier scale figure by 0.001 and add it to the base and fine measurement figures.

In the example shown the item measures 46.994 mm **(see illustrations 3.5 and 3.6)**:

Linear scale (base)	46.000 mm
Linear scale (base)	00.500 mm
Annular scale (fine)	00.490 mm
Vernier scale	00.004 mm
Total figure	46.994 mm

Internal micrometer

● Internal micrometers are available for measuring bore diameters, but are expensive and unlikely to be available for home use. It is suggested that a set of telescoping gauges and small hole gauges, both of which must be used with an external micrometer, will suffice for taking internal measurements on a motorcycle.
● Telescoping gauges can be used to measure internal diameters of components. Select a gauge with the correct size range, make sure its ends are clean and insert it into the bore. Expand the gauge, then lock its position and withdraw it from the bore **(see illustration 3.7)**. Measure across the gauge ends with a micrometer **(see illustration 3.8)**.
● Very small diameter bores (such as valve guides) are measured with a small hole gauge. Once adjusted to a slip-fit inside the component, its position is locked and the gauge withdrawn for measurement with a micrometer **(see illustrations 3.9 and 3.10)**.

Vernier caliper

Note: *The conventional linear and dial gauge type instruments are described. Digital types are easier to read, but are far more expensive.*
● The vernier caliper does not provide the precision of a micrometer, but is versatile in being able to measure internal and external diameters. Some types also incorporate a depth gauge. It is ideal for measuring clutch plate friction material and spring free lengths.
● To use the conventional linear scale vernier, slacken off the vernier clamp screws (1) and set its jaws over (2), or inside (3), the item to be measured **(see illustration 3.11)**. Slide the jaw into contact, using the thumb-wheel (4) for fine movement of the sliding scale (5) then tighten the clamp screws (1). Read off the main scale (6) where the zero on the sliding scale (5) intersects it, taking the whole number to the left of the zero; this provides the base measurement. View along the sliding scale and select the division which

3.9 Expand the small hole gauge in the bore, lock its position . . .

3.10 . . . then measure the gauge with a micrometer

lines up exactly with any of the divisions on the main scale, noting that the divisions usually represents 0.02 of a millimetre. Add this fine measurement to the base measurement to obtain the total reading.

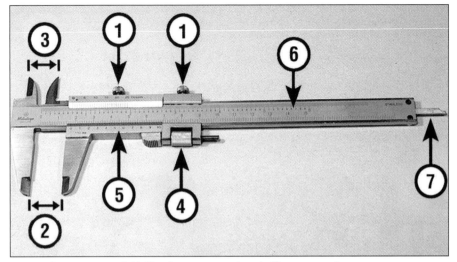

3.11 Vernier component parts (linear gauge)

1 Clamp screws	3 Internal jaws
2 External jaws	4 Thumbwheel

5 Sliding scale	7 Depth gauge
6 Main scale	

In the example shown the item measures 55.92 mm **(see illustration 3.12)**:

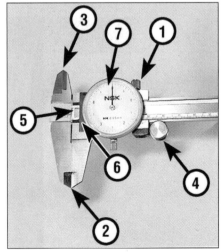

3.12 Vernier gauge reading of 55.92 mm

Base measurement	55.00 mm
Fine measurement	00.92 mm
Total figure	55.92 mm

● Some vernier calipers are equipped with a dial gauge for fine measurement. Before use, check that the jaws are clean, then close them fully and check that the dial gauge reads zero. If necessary adjust the gauge ring accordingly. Slacken the vernier clamp screw (1) and set its jaws over (2), or inside (3), the item to be measured **(see illustration 3.13)**. Slide the jaws into contact, using the thumbwheel (4) for fine movement. Read off the main scale (5) where the edge of the sliding scale (6) intersects it, taking the whole number to the left of the zero; this provides the base measurement. Read off the needle position on the dial gauge (7) scale to provide the fine measurement; each division represents 0.05 of a millimetre. Add this fine measurement to the base measurement to obtain the total reading.

In the example shown the item measures 55.95 mm **(see illustration 3.14)**:

Base measurement	55.00 mm
Fine measurement	00.95 mm
Total figure	55.95 mm

3.13 Vernier component parts (dial gauge)

1 Clamp screw	5 Main scale
2 External jaws	6 Sliding scale
3 Internal jaws	7 Dial gauge
4 Thumbwheel	

3.14 Vernier gauge reading of 55.95 mm

Plastigauge

● Plastigauge is a plastic material which can be compressed between two surfaces to measure the oil clearance between them. The width of the compressed Plastigauge is measured against a calibrated scale to determine the clearance.

● Common uses of Plastigauge are for measuring the clearance between crankshaft journal and main bearing inserts, between crankshaft journal and big-end bearing inserts, and between camshaft and bearing surfaces. The following example describes big-end oil clearance measurement.

● Handle the Plastigauge material carefully to prevent distortion. Using a sharp knife, cut a length which corresponds with the width of the bearing being measured and place it carefully across the journal so that it is parallel with the shaft **(see illustration 3.15)**. Carefully install both bearing shells and the connecting rod. Without rotating the rod on the journal tighten its bolts or nuts (as applicable) to the specified torque. The connecting rod and bearings are then disassembled and the crushed Plastigauge examined.

3.15 Plastigauge placed across shaft journal

● Using the scale provided in the Plastigauge kit, measure the width of the material to determine the oil clearance **(see illustration 3.16)**. Always remove all traces of Plastigauge after use using your fingernails.

Caution: Arriving at the correct clearance demands that the assembly is torqued correctly, according to the settings and sequence (where applicable) provided by the motorcycle manufacturer.

3.16 Measuring the width of the crushed Plastigauge

Dial gauge or DTI (Dial Test Indicator)

● A dial gauge can be used to accurately measure small amounts of movement. Typical uses are measuring shaft runout or shaft endfloat (sideplay) and setting piston position for ignition timing on two-strokes. A dial gauge set usually comes with a range of different probes and adapters and mounting equipment.

● The gauge needle must point to zero when at rest. Rotate the ring around its periphery to zero the gauge.

● Check that the gauge is capable of reading the extent of movement in the work. Most gauges have a small dial set in the face which records whole millimetres of movement as well as the fine scale around the face periphery which is calibrated in 0.01 mm divisions. Read off the small dial first to obtain the base measurement, then add the measurement from the fine scale to obtain the total reading.

In the example shown the gauge reads 1.48 mm (see illustration 3.17):

Base measurement	1.00 mm
Fine measurement	0.48 mm
Total figure	1.48 mm

3.17 Dial gauge reading of 1.48 mm

● If measuring shaft runout, the shaft must be supported in vee-blocks and the gauge mounted on a stand perpendicular to the shaft. Rest the tip of the gauge against the centre of the shaft and rotate the shaft slowly whilst watching the gauge reading (see illustration 3.18). Take several measurements along the length of the shaft and record the

3.18 Using a dial gauge to measure shaft runout

maximum gauge reading as the amount of runout in the shaft. **Note:** *The reading obtained will be total runout at that point - some manufacturers specify that the runout figure is halved to compare with their specified runout limit.*

● Endfloat (sideplay) measurement requires that the gauge is mounted securely to the surrounding component with its probe touching the end of the shaft. Using hand pressure, push and pull on the shaft noting the maximum endfloat recorded on the gauge (see illustration 3.19).

3.19 Using a dial gauge to measure shaft endfloat

● A dial gauge with suitable adapters can be used to determine piston position BTDC on two-stroke engines for the purposes of ignition timing. The gauge, adapter and suitable length probe are installed in the place of the spark plug and the gauge zeroed at TDC. If the piston position is specified as 1.14 mm BTDC, rotate the engine back to 2.00 mm BTDC, then slowly forwards to 1.14 mm BTDC.

Cylinder compression gauges

● A compression gauge is used for measuring cylinder compression. Either the rubber-cone type or the threaded adapter type can be used. The latter is preferred to ensure a perfect seal against the cylinder head. A 0 to 300 psi (0 to 20 Bar) type gauge (for petrol/gasoline engines) will be suitable for motorcycles.

● The spark plug is removed and the gauge either held hard against the cylinder head (cone type) or the gauge adapter screwed into the cylinder head (threaded type) (see illustration 3.20). Cylinder compression is measured with the engine turning over, but not running. The

3.20 Using a rubber-cone type cylinder compression gauge

gauge will hold the reading until manually released.

Oil pressure gauge

● An oil pressure gauge is used for measuring engine oil pressure. Most gauges come with a set of adapters to fit the thread of the take-off point (see illustration 3.21). If the take-off point specified by the motorcycle manufacturer is an external oil pipe union, make sure that the specified replacement union is used to prevent oil starvation.

3.21 Oil pressure gauge and take-off point adapter (arrow)

● Oil pressure is measured with the engine running (at a specific rpm) and often the manufacturer will specify pressure limits for a cold and hot engine.

Straight-edge and surface plate

● If checking the gasket face of a component for warpage, place a steel rule or precision straight-edge across the gasket face and measure any gap between the straight-edge and component with feeler gauges (see illustration 3.22). Check diagonally across the component and between mounting holes (see illustration 3.23).

3.22 Use a straight-edge and feeler gauges to check for warpage

3.23 Check for warpage in these directions

● Checking individual components for warpage, such as clutch plain (metal) plates, requires a perfectly flat plate or piece or plate glass and feeler gauges.

4 Torque and leverage

What is torque?

● Torque describes the twisting force about a shaft. The amount of torque applied is determined by the distance from the centre of the shaft to the end of the lever and the amount of force being applied to the end of the lever; distance multiplied by force equals torque.

● The manufacturer applies a measured torque to a bolt or nut to ensure that it will not slacken in use and to hold two components securely together without movement in the joint. The actual torque setting depends on the thread size, bolt or nut material and the composition of the components being held.

● Too little torque may cause the fastener to loosen due to vibration, whereas too much torque will distort the joint faces of the component or cause the fastener to shear off. Always stick to the specified torque setting.

Using a torque wrench

● Check the calibration of the torque wrench and make sure it has a suitable range for the job. Torque wrenches are available in Nm (Newton-metres), kgf m (kilograms-force metre), lbf ft (pounds-feet), lbf in (inch-pounds). Do not confuse lbf ft with lbf in.

● Adjust the tool to the desired torque on the scale (see illustration 4.1). If your torque wrench is not calibrated in the units specified, carefully convert the figure (see Conversion Factors). A manufacturer sometimes gives a torque setting as a range (8 to 10 Nm) rather than a single figure - in this case set the tool midway between the two settings. The same torque may be expressed as 9 Nm ± 1 Nm. Some torque wrenches have a method of locking the setting so that it isn't inadvertently altered during use.

4.1 Set the torque wrench index mark to the setting required, in this case 12 Nm

● Install the bolts/nuts in their correct location and secure them lightly. Their threads must be clean and free of any old locking compound. Unless specified the threads and flange should be dry - oiled threads are necessary in certain circumstances and the manufacturer will take this into account in the specified torque figure. Similarly, the manufacturer may also specify the application of thread-locking compound.

● Tighten the fasteners in the specified sequence until the torque wrench clicks, indicating that the torque setting has been reached. Apply the torque again to double-check the setting. Where different thread diameter fasteners secure the component, as a rule tighten the larger diameter ones first.

● When the torque wrench has been finished with, release the lock (where applicable) and fully back off its setting to zero - do not leave the torque wrench tensioned. Also, do not use a torque wrench for slackening a fastener.

Angle-tightening

● Manufacturers often specify a figure in degrees for final tightening of a fastener. This usually follows tightening to a specific torque setting.

● A degree disc can be set and attached to the socket (see illustration 4.2) or a protractor can be used to mark the angle of movement on the bolt/nut head and the surrounding casting (see illustration 4.3).

4.2 Angle tightening can be accomplished with a torque-angle gauge ...

4.3 ... or by marking the angle on the surrounding component

Loosening sequences

● Where more than one bolt/nut secures a component, loosen each fastener evenly a little at a time. In this way, not all the stress of the joint is held by one fastener and the components are not likely to distort.

● If a tightening sequence is provided, work in the REVERSE of this, but if not, work from the outside in, in a criss-cross sequence (see illustration 4.4).

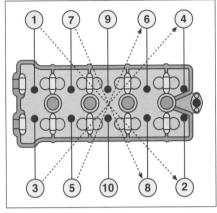

4.4 When slackening, work from the outside inwards

Tightening sequences

● If a component is held by more than one fastener it is important that the retaining bolts/nuts are tightened evenly to prevent uneven stress build-up and distortion of sealing faces. This is especially important on high-compression joints such as the cylinder head.

● A sequence is usually provided by the manufacturer, either in a diagram or actually marked in the casting. If not, always start in the centre and work outwards in a criss-cross pattern (see illustration 4.5). Start off by securing all bolts/nuts finger-tight, then set the torque wrench and tighten each fastener by a small amount in sequence until the final torque is reached. By following this practice, the joint

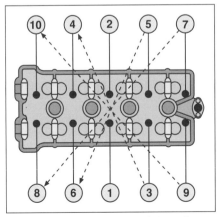

4.5 When tightening, work from the inside outwards

will be held evenly and will not be distorted. Important joints, such as the cylinder head and big-end fasteners often have two- or three-stage torque settings.

Applying leverage

● Use tools at the correct angle. Position a socket wrench or spanner on the bolt/nut so that you pull it towards you when loosening. If this can't be done, push the spanner without curling your fingers around it **(see illustration 4.6)** - the spanner may slip or the fastener loosen suddenly, resulting in your fingers being crushed against a component.

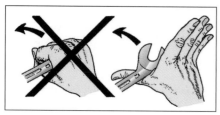

4.6 If you can't pull on the spanner to loosen a fastener, push with your hand open

● Additional leverage is gained by extending the length of the lever. The best way to do this is to use a breaker bar instead of the regular length tool, or to slip a length of tubing over the end of the spanner or socket wrench.
● If additional leverage will not work, the fastener head is either damaged or firmly corroded in place (see Fasteners).

5 Bearings

Bearing removal and installation

Drivers and sockets

● Before removing a bearing, always inspect the casing to see which way it must be driven out - some casings will have retaining plates or a cast step. Also check for any identifying markings on the bearing and if installed to a certain depth, measure this at this stage. Some roller bearings are sealed on one side - take note of the original fitted position.
● Bearings can be driven out of a casing using a bearing driver tool (with the correct size head) or a socket of the correct diameter. Select the driver head or socket so that it contacts the outer race of the bearing, not the balls/rollers or inner race. Always support the casing around the bearing housing with wood blocks, otherwise there is a risk of fracture. The bearing is driven out with a few blows on the driver or socket from a heavy mallet. Unless access is severely restricted (as with wheel bearings), a pin-punch is not recommended unless it is moved around the bearing to keep it square in its housing.

● The same equipment can be used to install bearings. Make sure the bearing housing is supported on wood blocks and line up the bearing in its housing. Fit the bearing as noted on removal - generally they are installed with their marked side facing outwards. Tap the bearing squarely into its housing using a driver or socket which bears only on the bearing's outer race - contact with the bearing balls/rollers or inner race will destroy it **(see illustrations 5.1 and 5.2)**.
● Check that the bearing inner race and balls/rollers rotate freely.

5.1 Using a bearing driver against the bearing's outer race

5.2 Using a large socket against the bearing's outer race

Pullers and slide-hammers

● Where a bearing is pressed on a shaft a puller will be required to extract it **(see illustration 5.3)**. Make sure that the puller clamp or legs fit securely behind the bearing and are unlikely to slip out. If pulling a bearing

5.3 This bearing puller clamps behind the bearing and pressure is applied to the shaft end to draw the bearing off

off a gear shaft for example, you may have to locate the puller behind a gear pinion if there is no access to the race and draw the gear pinion off the shaft as well **(see illustration 5.4)**.

> **Caution: Ensure that the puller's centre bolt locates securely against the end of the shaft and will not slip when pressure is applied. Also ensure that puller does not damage the shaft end.**

5.4 Where no access is available to the rear of the bearing, it is sometimes possible to draw off the adjacent component

● Operate the puller so that its centre bolt exerts pressure on the shaft end and draws the bearing off the shaft.
● When installing the bearing on the shaft, tap only on the bearing's inner race - contact with the balls/rollers or outer race with destroy the bearing. Use a socket or length of tubing as a drift which fits over the shaft end **(see illustration 5.5)**.

5.5 When installing a bearing on a shaft use a piece of tubing which bears only on the bearing's inner race

● Where a bearing locates in a blind hole in a casing, it cannot be driven or pulled out as described above. A slide-hammer with knife-edged bearing puller attachment will be required. The puller attachment passes through the bearing and when tightened expands to fit firmly behind the bearing **(see illustration 5.6)**. By operating the slide-hammer part of the tool the bearing is jarred out of its housing **(see illustration 5.7)**.
● It is possible, if the bearing is of reasonable weight, for it to drop out of its housing if the casing is heated as described opposite.

5.6 Expand the bearing puller so that it locks behind the bearing . . .

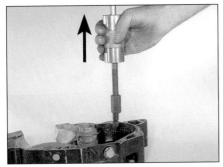

5.7 . . . attach the slide hammer to the bearing puller

If this method is attempted, first prepare a work surface which will enable the casing to be tapped face down to help dislodge the bearing - a wood surface is ideal since it will not damage the casing's gasket surface. Wearing protective gloves, tap the heated casing several times against the work surface to dislodge the bearing under its own weight **(see illustration 5.8)**.

5.8 Tapping a casing face down on wood blocks can often dislodge a bearing

● Bearings can be installed in blind holes using the driver or socket method described above.

Drawbolts

● Where a bearing or bush is set in the eye of a component, such as a suspension linkage arm or connecting rod small-end, removal by drift may damage the component. Furthermore, a rubber bushing in a shock absorber eye cannot successfully be driven out of position. If access is available to a engineering press, the task is straightforward. If not, a drawbolt can be fabricated to extract the bearing or bush.

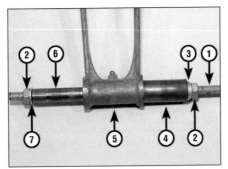

5.9 Drawbolt component parts assembled on a suspension arm

1 Bolt or length of threaded bar
2 Nuts
3 Washer (external diameter greater than tubing internal diameter)
4 Tubing (internal diameter sufficient to accommodate bearing)
5 Suspension arm with bearing
6 Tubing (external diameter slightly smaller than bearing)
7 Washer (external diameter slightly smaller than bearing)

5.10 Drawing the bearing out of the suspension arm

● To extract the bearing/bush you will need a long bolt with nut (or piece of threaded bar with two nuts), a piece of tubing which has an internal diameter larger than the bearing/bush, another piece of tubing which has an external diameter slightly smaller than the bearing/bush, and a selection of washers **(see illustrations 5.9 and 5.10)**. Note that the pieces of tubing must be of the same length, or longer, than the bearing/bush.

● The same kit (without the pieces of tubing) can be used to draw the new bearing/bush back into place **(see illustration 5.11)**.

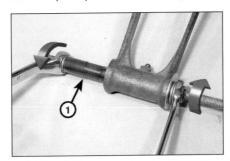

5.11 Installing a new bearing (1) in the suspension arm

Temperature change

● If the bearing's outer race is a tight fit in the casing, the aluminium casing can be heated to release its grip on the bearing. Aluminium will expand at a greater rate than the steel bearing outer race. There are several ways to do this, but avoid any localised extreme heat (such as a blow torch) - aluminium alloy has a low melting point.

● Approved methods of heating a casing are using a domestic oven (heated to 100°C) or immersing the casing in boiling water **(see illustration 5.12)**. Low temperature range localised heat sources such as a paint stripper heat gun or clothes iron can also be used **(see illustration 5.13)**. Alternatively, soak a rag in boiling water, wring it out and wrap it around the bearing housing.

> ⚠ **Warning: All of these methods require care in use to prevent scalding and burns to the hands. Wear protective gloves when handling hot components.**

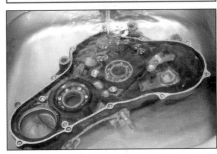

5.12 A casing can be immersed in a sink of boiling water to aid bearing removal

5.13 Using a localised heat source to aid bearing removal

● If heating the whole casing note that plastic components, such as the neutral switch, may suffer - remove them beforehand.

● After heating, remove the bearing as described above. You may find that the expansion is sufficient for the bearing to fall out of the casing under its own weight or with a light tap on the driver or socket.

● If necessary, the casing can be heated to aid bearing installation, and this is sometimes the recommended procedure if the motorcycle manufacturer has designed the housing and bearing fit with this intention.

● Installation of bearings can be eased by placing them in a freezer the night before installation. The steel bearing will contract slightly, allowing easy insertion in its housing. This is often useful when installing steering head outer races in the frame.

Bearing types and markings

● Plain shell bearings, ball bearings, needle roller bearings and tapered roller bearings will all be found on motorcycles (see illustrations 5.14 and 5.15). The ball and roller types are usually caged between an inner and outer race, but uncaged variations may be found.

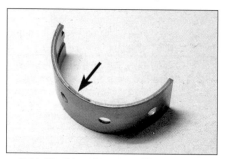

5.14 Shell bearings are either plain or grooved. They are usually identified by colour code (arrow)

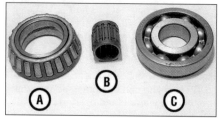

5.15 Tapered roller bearing (A), needle roller bearing (B) and ball journal bearing (C)

● Shell bearings (often called inserts) are usually found at the crankshaft main and connecting rod big-end where they are good at coping with high loads. They are made of a phosphor-bronze material and are impregnated with self-lubricating properties.

● Ball bearings and needle roller bearings consist of a steel inner and outer race with the balls or rollers between the races. They require constant lubrication by oil or grease and are good at coping with axial loads. Taper roller bearings consist of rollers set in a tapered cage set on the inner race; the outer race is separate. They are good at coping with axial loads and prevent movement along the shaft - a typical application is in the steering head.

● Bearing manufacturers produce bearings to ISO size standards and stamp one face of the bearing to indicate its internal and external diameter, load capacity and type (see illustration 5.16).

● Metal bushes are usually of phosphor-bronze material. Rubber bushes are used in suspension mounting eyes. Fibre bushes have also been used in suspension pivots.

5.16 Typical bearing marking

Bearing fault finding

● If a bearing outer race has spun in its housing, the housing material will be damaged. You can use a bearing locking compound to bond the outer race in place if damage is not too severe.

● Shell bearings will fail due to damage of their working surface, as a result of lack of lubrication, corrosion or abrasive particles in the oil (see illustration 5.17). Small particles of dirt in the oil may embed in the bearing material whereas larger particles will score the bearing and shaft journal. If a number of short journeys are made, insufficient heat will be generated to drive off condensation which has built up on the bearings.

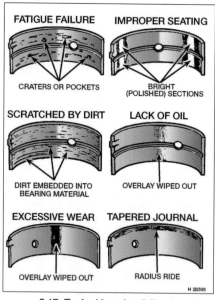

5.17 Typical bearing failures

● Ball and roller bearings will fail due to lack of lubrication or damage to the balls or rollers. Tapered-roller bearings can be damaged by overloading them. Unless the bearing is sealed on both sides, wash it in paraffin (kerosene) to remove all old grease then allow it to dry. Make a visual inspection looking to dented balls or rollers, damaged cages and worn or pitted races (see illustration 5.18).

● A ball bearing can be checked for wear by listening to it when spun. Apply a film of light oil to the bearing and hold it close to the ear - hold the outer race with one hand and spin the

5.18 Example of ball journal bearing with damaged balls and cages

5.19 Hold outer race and listen to inner race when spun

inner race with the other hand (see illustration 5.19). The bearing should be almost silent when spun; if it grates or rattles it is worn.

6 Oil seals

Oil seal removal and installation

● Oil seals should be renewed every time a component is dismantled. This is because the seal lips will become set to the sealing surface and will not necessarily reseal.

● Oil seals can be prised out of position using a large flat-bladed screwdriver (see illustration 6.1). In the case of crankcase seals, check first that the seal is not lipped on the inside, preventing its removal with the crankcases joined.

6.1 Prise out oil seals with a large flat-bladed screwdriver

● New seals are usually installed with their marked face (containing the seal reference code) outwards and the spring side towards the fluid being retained. In certain cases, such as a two-stroke engine crankshaft seal, a double lipped seal may be used due to there being fluid or gas on each side of the joint.

● Use a bearing driver or socket which bears only on the outer hard edge of the seal to install it in the casing - tapping on the inner edge will damage the sealing lip.

Oil seal types and markings

● Oil seals are usually of the single-lipped type. Double-lipped seals are found where a liquid or gas is on both sides of the joint.
● Oil seals can harden and lose their sealing ability if the motorcycle has been in storage for a long period - renewal is the only solution.
● Oil seal manufacturers also conform to the ISO markings for seal size - these are moulded into the outer face of the seal **(see illustration 6.2)**.

6.2 These oil seal markings indicate inside diameter, outside diameter and seal thickness

7 Gaskets and sealants

Types of gasket and sealant

● Gaskets are used to seal the mating surfaces between components and keep lubricants, fluids, vacuum or pressure contained within the assembly. Aluminium gaskets are sometimes found at the cylinder joints, but most gaskets are paper-based. If the mating surfaces of the components being joined are undamaged the gasket can be installed dry, although a dab of sealant or grease will be useful to hold it in place during assembly.
● RTV (Room Temperature Vulcanising) silicone rubber sealants cure when exposed to moisture in the atmosphere. These sealants are good at filling pits or irregular gasket faces, but will tend to be forced out of the joint under very high torque. They can be used to replace a paper gasket, but first make sure that the width of the paper gasket is not essential to the shimming of internal components. RTV sealants should not be used on components containing petrol (gasoline).
● Non-hardening, semi-hardening and hard setting liquid gasket compounds can be used with a gasket or between a metal-to-metal joint. Select the sealant to suit the application: universal non-hardening sealant can be used on virtually all joints; semi-hardening on joint faces which are rough or damaged; hard setting sealant on joints which require a permanent bond and are subjected to high temperature and pressure. **Note:** *Check first if the paper gasket has a bead of sealant*

impregnated in its surface before applying additional sealant.
● When choosing a sealant, make sure it is suitable for the application, particularly if being applied in a high-temperature area or in the vicinity of fuel. Certain manufacturers produce sealants in either clear, silver or black colours to match the finish of the engine. This has a particular application on motorcycles where much of the engine is exposed.
● Do not over-apply sealant. That which is squeezed out on the outside of the joint can be wiped off, whereas an excess of sealant on the inside can break off and clog oilways.

Breaking a sealed joint

● Age, heat, pressure and the use of hard setting sealant can cause two components to stick together so tightly that they are difficult to separate using finger pressure alone. Do not resort to using levers unless there is a pry point provided for this purpose **(see illustration 7.1)** or else the gasket surfaces will be damaged.
● Use a soft-faced hammer **(see illustration 7.2)** or a wood block and conventional hammer to strike the component near the mating surface. Avoid hammering against cast extremities since they may break off. If this method fails, try using a wood wedge between the two components.

> **Caution: If the joint will not separate, double-check that you have removed all the fasteners.**

7.1 If a pry point is provided, apply gently pressure with a flat-bladed screwdriver

7.2 Tap around the joint with a soft-faced mallet if necessary - don't strike cooling fins

Removal of old gasket and sealant

● Paper gaskets will most likely come away complete, leaving only a few traces stuck

Most components have one or two hollow locating dowels between the two gasket faces. If a dowel cannot be removed, do not resort to gripping it with pliers - it will almost certainly be distorted. Install a close-fitting socket or Phillips screwdriver into the dowel and then grip the outer edge of the dowel to free it.

on the sealing faces of the components. It is imperative that all traces are removed to ensure correct sealing of the new gasket.
● Very carefully scrape all traces of gasket away making sure that the sealing surfaces are not gouged or scored by the scraper **(see illustrations 7.3, 7.4 and 7.5)**. Stubborn deposits can be removed by spraying with an aerosol gasket remover. Final preparation of

7.3 Paper gaskets can be scraped off with a gasket scraper tool . . .

7.4 . . . a knife blade . . .

7.5 . . . or a household scraper

7.6 Fine abrasive paper is wrapped around a flat file to clean up the gasket face

7.7 A kitchen scourer can be used on stubborn deposits

the gasket surface can be made with very fine abrasive paper or a plastic kitchen scourer **(see illustrations 7.6 and 7.7)**.

● Old sealant can be scraped or peeled off components, depending on the type originally used. Note that gasket removal compounds are available to avoid scraping the components clean; make sure the gasket remover suits the type of sealant used.

8 Chains

Breaking and joining final drive chains

● Drive chains for all but small bikes are continuous and do not have a clip-type connecting link. The chain must be broken using a chain breaker tool and the new chain securely riveted together using a new soft rivet-type link. Never use a clip-type connecting link instead of a rivet-type link, except in an emergency. Various chain breaking and riveting tools are available, either as separate tools or combined as illustrated in the accompanying photographs - read the instructions supplied with the tool carefully.

> ⚠ **Warning: The need to rivet the new link pins correctly cannot be overstressed - loss of control of the motorcycle is very likely to result if the chain breaks in use.**

● Rotate the chain and look for the soft link. The soft link pins look like they have been

8.1 Tighten the chain breaker to push the pin out of the link . . .

8.2 . . . withdraw the pin, remove the tool . . .

8.3 . . . and separate the chain link

deeply centre-punched instead of peened over like all the other pins **(see illustration 8.9)** and its sideplate may be a different colour. Position the soft link midway between the sprockets and assemble the chain breaker tool over one of the soft link pins **(see illustration 8.1)**. Operate the tool to push the pin out through the chain **(see illustration 8.2)**. On an O-ring chain, remove the O-rings **(see illustration 8.3)**. Carry out the same procedure on the other soft link pin.

> *Caution: Certain soft link pins (particularly on the larger chains) may require their ends to be filed or ground off before they can be pressed out using the tool.*

● Check that you have the correct size and strength (standard or heavy duty) new soft link - do not reuse the old link. Look for the size marking on the chain sideplates **(see illustration 8.10)**.

● Position the chain ends so that they are engaged over the rear sprocket. On an O-ring

8.4 Insert the new soft link, with O-rings, through the chain ends . . .

8.5 . . . install the O-rings over the pin ends . . .

8.6 . . . followed by the sideplate

chain, install a new O-ring over each pin of the link and insert the link through the two chain ends **(see illustration 8.4)**. Install a new O-ring over the end of each pin, followed by the sideplate (with the chain manufacturer's marking facing outwards) **(see illustrations 8.5 and 8.6)**. On an unsealed chain, insert the link through the two chain ends, then install the sideplate with the chain manufacturer's marking facing outwards.

● Note that it may not be possible to install the sideplate using finger pressure alone. If using a joining tool, assemble it so that the plates of the tool clamp the link and press the sideplate over the pins **(see illustration 8.7)**. Otherwise, use two small sockets placed over

8.7 Push the sideplate into position using a clamp

8.8 Assemble the chain riveting tool over one pin at a time and tighten it fully

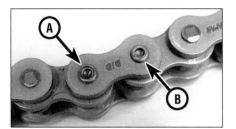

8.9 Pin end correctly riveted (A), pin end unriveted (B)

the rivet ends and two pieces of the wood between a G-clamp. Operate the clamp to press the sideplate over the pins.

● Assemble the joining tool over one pin (following the maker's instructions) and tighten the tool down to spread the pin end securely **(see illustrations 8.8 and 8.9)**. Do the same on the other pin.

> ⚠️ **Warning: Check that the pin ends are secure and that there is no danger of the sideplate coming loose. If the pin ends are cracked the soft link must be renewed.**

Final drive chain sizing

● Chains are sized using a three digit number, followed by a suffix to denote the chain type **(see illustration 8.10)**. Chain type is either standard or heavy duty (thicker sideplates), and also unsealed or O-ring/X-ring type.

● The first digit of the number relates to the pitch of the chain, ie the distance from the centre of one pin to the centre of the next pin **(see illustration 8.11)**. Pitch is expressed in eighths of an inch, as follows:

8.10 Typical chain size and type marking

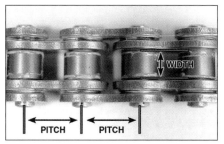

8.11 Chain dimensions

Sizes commencing with a 4 (eg 428) have a pitch of 1/2 inch (12.7 mm)
Sizes commencing with a 5 (eg 520) have a pitch of 5/8 inch (15.9 mm)
Sizes commencing with a 6 (eg 630) have a pitch of 3/4 inch (19.1 mm)

● The second and third digits of the chain size relate to the width of the rollers, again in imperial units, eg the 525 shown has 5/16 inch (7.94 mm) rollers **(see illustration 8.11)**.

9 Hoses

Clamping to prevent flow

● Small-bore flexible hoses can be clamped to prevent fluid flow whilst a component is worked on. Whichever method is used, ensure that the hose material is not permanently distorted or damaged by the clamp.

a) A brake hose clamp available from auto accessory shops **(see illustration 9.1)**.
b) A wingnut type hose clamp **(see illustration 9.2)**.

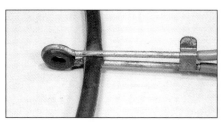

9.1 Hoses can be clamped with an automotive brake hose clamp . . .

9.2 . . . a wingnut type hose clamp . . .

c) Two sockets placed each side of the hose and held with straight-jawed self-locking grips **(see illustration 9.3)**.
d) Thick card each side of the hose held between straight-jawed self-locking grips **(see illustration 9.4)**.

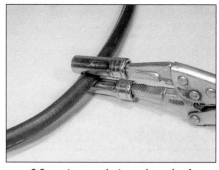

9.3 . . . two sockets and a pair of self-locking grips . . .

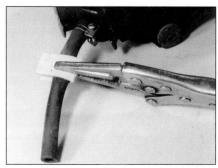

9.4 . . . or thick card and self-locking grips

Freeing and fitting hoses

● Always make sure the hose clamp is moved well clear of the hose end. Grip the hose with your hand and rotate it whilst pulling it off the union. If the hose has hardened due to age and will not move, slit it with a sharp knife and peel its ends off the union **(see illustration 9.5)**.

● Resist the temptation to use grease or soap on the unions to aid installation; although it helps the hose slip over the union it will equally aid the escape of fluid from the joint. It is preferable to soften the hose ends in hot water and wet the inside surface of the hose with water or a fluid which will evaporate.

9.5 Cutting a coolant hose free with a sharp knife

Introduction

In less time than it takes to read this introduction, a thief could steal your motorcycle. Returning only to find your bike has gone is one of the worst feelings in the world. Even if the motorcycle is insured against theft, once you've got over the initial shock, you will have the inconvenience of dealing with the police and your insurance company.

The motorcycle is an easy target for the professional thief and the joyrider alike and the official figures on motorcycle theft make for depressing reading; on average a motor-cycle is stolen every 16 minutes in the UK!

Motorcycle thefts fall into two categories, those stolen 'to order' and those taken by opportunists. The thief stealing to order will be on the look out for a specific make and model and will go to extraordinary lengths to obtain that motorcycle. The opportunist thief on the other hand will look for easy targets which can be stolen with the minimum of effort and risk.

Whilst it is never going to be possible to make your machine 100% secure, it is estimated that around half of all stolen motorcycles are taken by opportunist thieves. Remember that the opportunist thief is always on the look out for the easy option: if there are two similar motorcycles parked side-by-side, they will target the one with the lowest level of security. By taking a few precautions, you can reduce the chances of your motorcycle being stolen.

Security equipment

There are many specialised motorcycle security devices available and the following text summarises their applications and their good and bad points.

Once you have decided on the type of security equipment which best suits your needs, we recommended that you read one of the many equipment tests regularly carried out by the motorcycle press. These tests

Ensure the lock and chain you buy is of good quality and long enough to shackle your bike to a solid object

compare the products from all the major manufacturers and give impartial ratings on their effectiveness, value-for-money and ease of use.

No one item of security equipment can provide complete protection. It is highly recommended that two or more of the items described below are combined to increase the security of your motorcycle (a lock and chain plus an alarm system is just about ideal). The more security measures fitted to the bike, the less likely it is to be stolen.

Lock and chain

Pros: *Very flexible to use; can be used to secure the motorcycle to almost any immovable object. On some locks and chains, the lock can be used on its own as a disc lock (see below).*

Cons: *Can be very heavy and awkward to carry on the motorcycle, although some types* *will be supplied with a carry bag which can be strapped to the pillion seat.*

● Heavy-duty chains and locks are an excellent security measure **(see illustration 1).** Whenever the motorcycle is parked, use the lock and chain to secure the machine to a solid, immovable object such as a post or railings. This will prevent the machine from being ridden away or being lifted into the back of a van.

● When fitting the chain, always ensure the chain is routed around the motorcycle frame or swingarm **(see illustrations 2 and 3).** Never merely pass the chain around one of the wheel rims; a thief may unbolt the wheel and lift the rest of the machine into a van, leaving you with just the wheel! Try to avoid having excess chain free, thus making it difficult to use cutting tools, and keep the chain and lock off the ground to prevent thieves attacking it with a cold chisel. Position the lock so that its lock barrel is facing downwards; this will make it harder for the thief to attack the lock mechanism.

Pass the chain through the bike's frame, rather than just through a wheel . . .

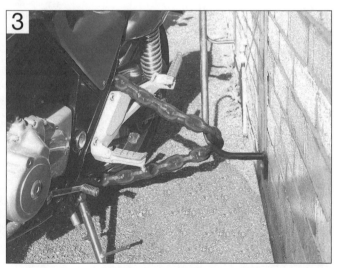

. . . and loop it around a solid object

U-locks

Pros: *Highly effective deterrent which can be used to secure the bike to a post or railings. Most U-locks come with a carrier which allows the lock to be easily carried on the bike.*

Cons: *Not as flexible to use as a lock and chain.*

● These are solid locks which are similar in use to a lock and chain. U-locks are lighter than a lock and chain but not so flexible to use. The length and shape of the lock shackle limit the objects to which the bike can be secured **(see illustration 4)**.

Disc locks

Pros: *Small, light and very easy to carry; most can be stored underneath the seat.*

Cons: *Does not prevent the motorcycle being lifted into a van. Can be very embarrassing if*

U-locks can be used to secure the bike to a solid object – ensure you purchase one which is long enough

you forget to remove the lock before attempting to ride off!

● Disc locks are designed to be attached to the front brake disc. The lock passes through one of the holes in the disc and prevents the wheel rotating by jamming against the fork/brake caliper **(see illustration 5)**. Some are equipped with an alarm siren which sounds if the disc lock is moved; this not only acts as a theft deterrent but also as a handy reminder if you try to move the bike with the lock still fitted.

● Combining the disc lock with a length of cable which can be looped around a post or railings provides an additional measure of security **(see illustration 6)**.

Alarms and immobilisers

Pros: *Once installed it is completely hassle-free to use. If the system is 'Thatcham' or 'Sold Secure-approved', insurance companies may give you a discount.*

Cons: *Can be expensive to buy and complex to install. No system will prevent the motorcycle from being lifted into a van and taken away.*

● Electronic alarms and immobilisers are available to suit a variety of budgets. There are three different types of system available: pure alarms, pure immobilisers, and the more expensive systems which are combined alarm/immobilisers **(see illustration 7)**.

● An alarm system is designed to emit an audible warning if the motorcycle is being tampered with.

● An immobiliser prevents the motorcycle being started and ridden away by disabling its electrical systems.

● When purchasing an alarm/immobiliser system, check the cost of installing the system unless you are able to do it yourself. If the motorcycle is not used regularly, another consideration is the current drain of the system. All alarm/immobiliser systems are powered by the motorcycle's battery; purchasing a system with a very low current drain could prevent the battery losing its charge whilst the motorcycle is not being used.

A typical disc lock attached through one of the holes in the disc

A disc lock combined with a security cable provides additional protection

A typical alarm/immobiliser system

Indelible markings can be applied to most areas of the bike – always apply the manufacturer's sticker to warn off thieves

Chemically-etched code numbers can be applied to main body panels . . .

. . . again, always ensure that the kit manufacturer's sticker is applied in a prominent position

Security marking kits

Pros: *Very cheap and effective deterrent. Many insurance companies will give you a discount on your insurance premium if a recognised security marking kit is used on your motorcycle.*

Cons: *Does not prevent the motorcycle being stolen by joyriders.*

● There are many different types of security marking kits available. The idea is to mark as many parts of the motorcycle as possible with a unique security number **(see illustrations 8, 9 and 10)**. A form will be included with the kit to register your personal details and those of the motorcycle with the kit manufacturer. This register is made available to the police to help them trace the rightful owner of any motorcycle or components which they recover should all other forms of identification have been removed. Always apply the warning stickers provided with the kit to deter thieves.

Ground anchors, wheel clamps and security posts

Pros: *An excellent form of security which will deter all but the most determined of thieves.*

Cons: *Awkward to install and can be expensive.*

● Whilst the motorcycle is at home, it is a good idea to attach it securely to the floor or a solid wall, even if it is kept in a securely locked garage. Various types of ground anchors, security posts and wheel clamps are available for this purpose **(see illustration 11)**. These security devices are either bolted to a solid concrete or brick structure or can be cemented into the ground.

Permanent ground anchors provide an excellent level of security when the bike is at home

Security at home

A high percentage of motorcycle thefts are from the owner's home. Here are some things to consider whenever your motorcycle is at home:
● Where possible, always keep the motorcycle in a securely locked garage. Never rely solely on the standard lock on the garage door, these are usual hopelessly inadequate. Fit an additional locking mechanism to the door and consider having the garage alarmed. A security light, activated by a movement sensor, is also a good investment.

● Always secure the motorcycle to the ground or a wall, even if it is inside a securely locked garage.
● Do not regularly leave the motorcycle outside your home, try to keep it out of sight wherever possible. If a garage is not available, fit a motorcycle cover over the bike to disguise its true identity.
● It is not uncommon for thieves to follow a motorcyclist home to find out where the bike is kept. They will then return at a later date. Be aware of this whenever you are returning

home on your motorcycle. If you suspect you are being followed, do not return home, instead ride to a garage or shop and stop as a precaution.
● When selling a motorcycle, do not provide your home address or the location where the bike is normally kept. Arrange to meet the buyer at a location away from your home. Thieves have been known to pose as potential buyers to find out where motorcycles are kept and then return later to steal them.

Security away from the home

As well as fitting security equipment to your motorcycle here are a few general rules to follow whenever you park your motorcycle.
● Park in a busy, public place.
● Use car parks which incorporate security features, such as CCTV.

● At night, park in a well-lit area, preferably directly underneath a street light.
● Engage the steering lock.
● Secure the motorcycle to a solid, immovable object such as a post or railings with an additional lock. If this is not possible,

secure the bike to a friend's motorcycle. Some public parking places provide security loops for motorcycles.
● Never leave your helmet or luggage attached to the motorcycle. Take them with you at all times.

Lubricants and fluids

A wide range of lubricants, fluids and cleaning agents is available for motor-cycles. This is a guide as to what is available, its applications and properties.

Four-stroke engine oil

● Engine oil is without doubt the most important component of any four-stroke engine. Modern motorcycle engines place a lot of demands on their oil and choosing the right type is essential. Using an unsuitable oil will lead to an increased rate of engine wear and could result in serious engine damage. Before purchasing oil, always check the recommended oil specification given by the manufacturer. The manufacturer will state a recommended 'type or classification' and also a specific 'viscosity' range for engine oil.

● The oil 'type or classification' is identified by its API (American Petroleum Institute) rating. The API rating will be in the form of two letters, e.g. SG. The S identifies the oil as being suitable for use in a petrol (gasoline) engine (S stands for spark ignition) and the second letter, ranging from A to J, identifies the oil's performance rating. The later this letter, the higher the specification of the oil; for example API SG oil exceeds the requirements of API SF oil. **Note:** *On some oils there may also be a second rating consisting of another two letters, the first letter being C, e.g. API SF/CD. This rating indicates the oil is also suitable for use in a diesel engines (the C stands for compression ignition) and is thus of no relevance for motorcycle use.*

● The 'viscosity' of the oil is identified by its SAE (Society of Automotive Engineers) rating. All modern engines require multigrade oils and the SAE rating will consist of two numbers, the first followed by a W, e.g. 10W/40. The first number indicates the viscosity rating of the oil at low temperatures (W stands for winter – tested at –20ºC) and the second number represents the viscosity of the oil at high temperatures (tested at 100ºC). The lower the number, the thinner the oil. For example an oil with an SAE 10W/40 rating will give better cold starting and running than an SAE 15W/40 oil.

● As well as ensuring the 'type' and 'viscosity' of the oil match the recommendations, another consideration to make when buying engine oil is whether to purchase a standard mineral-based oil, a semi-synthetic oil (also known as a synthetic blend or synthetic-based oil) or a fully-synthetic oil. Although all oils will have a similar rating and viscosity, their cost will vary considerably; mineral-based oils are the cheapest, the fully-synthetic oils the most expensive with the semi-synthetic oils falling somewhere in-between. This decision is very much up to the owner, but it should be noted that modern synthetic oils have far better lubricating and cleaning qualities than traditional mineral-based oils and tend to retain these properties for far longer. Bearing in mind the operating conditions inside a modern, high-revving motorcycle engine it is highly recommended that a fully synthetic oil is used. The extra expense at each service could save you money in the long term by preventing premature engine wear.

● As a final note always ensure that the oil is specifically designed for use in motorcycle engines. Engine oils designed primarily for use in car engines sometimes contain additives or friction modifiers which could cause clutch slip on a motorcycle fitted with a wet-clutch.

Two-stroke engine oil

● Modern two-stroke engines, with their high power outputs, place high demands on their oil. If engine seizure is to be avoided it is essential that a high-quality oil is used. Two-stroke oils differ hugely from four-stroke oils. The oil lubricates only the crankshaft and piston(s) (the transmission has its own lubricating oil) and is used on a total-loss basis where it is burnt completely during the combustion process.

● The Japanese have recently introduced a classification system for two-stroke oils, the JASO rating. This rating is in the form of two letters, either FA, FB or FC – FA is the lowest classification and FC the highest. Ensure the oil being used meets or exceeds the recommended rating specified by the manufacturer.

● As well as ensuring the oil rating matches the recommendation, another consideration to make when buying engine oil is whether to purchase a standard mineral-based oil, a semi-synthetic oil (also known as a synthetic blend or synthetic-based oil) or a fully-synthetic oil. The cost of each type of oil varies considerably; mineral-based oils are the cheapest, the fully-synthetic oils the most expensive with the semi-synthetic oils falling somewhere in-between. This decision is very much up to the owner, but it should be noted that modern synthetic oils have far better lubricating properties and burn cleaner than traditional mineral-based oils. It is therefore recommended that a fully synthetic oil is used. The extra expense could save you money in the long term by preventing premature engine wear, engine performance will be improved, carbon deposits and exhaust smoke will be reduced.

● Always ensure that the oil is specifically designed for use in an injector system. Many high quality two-stroke oils are designed for competition use and need to be pre-mixed with fuel. These oils are of a much higher viscosity and are not designed to flow through the injector pumps used on road-going two-stroke motorcycles.

Transmission (gear) oil

● On a two-stroke engine, the transmission and clutch are lubricated by their own separate oil bath which must be changed in accordance with the Maintenance Schedule.
● Although the engine and transmission units of most four-strokes use a common lubrication supply, there are some exceptions where the engine and gearbox have separate oil reservoirs and a dry clutch is used.
● Motorcycle manufacturers will either recommend a monograde transmission oil or a four-stroke multigrade engine oil to lubricate the transmission.
● Transmission oils, or gear oils as they are often called, are designed specifically for use in transmission systems. The viscosity of these oils is represented by an SAE number, but the scale of measurement applied is different to that used to grade engine oils. As a rough guide a SAE90 gear oil will be of the same viscosity as an SAE50 engine oil.

Shaft drive oil

● On models equipped with shaft final drive, the shaft drive gears are will have their own oil supply. The manufacturer will state a recommended 'type or classification' and also a specific 'viscosity' range in the same manner as for four-stroke engine oil.
● Gear oil classification is given by the number which follows the API GL (GL standing for gear lubricant) rating, the higher the number, the higher the specification of the oil, e.g. API GL5 oil is a higher specification than API GL4 oil. Ensure the oil meets or

exceeds the classification specified and is of the correct viscosity. The viscosity of gear oils is also represented by an SAE number but the scale of measurement used is different to that used to grade engine oils. As a rough guide an SAE90 gear oil will be of the same viscosity as an SAE50 engine oil.
● If the use of an EP (Extreme Pressure) gear oil is specified, ensure the oil purchased is suitable.

Fork oil and suspension fluid

● Conventional telescopic front forks are hydraulic and require fork oil to work. To ensure the forks function correctly, the fork oil must be changed in accordance with the Maintenance Schedule.
● Fork oil is available in a variety of viscosities, identified by their SAE rating; fork oil ratings vary from light (SAE 5) to heavy (SAE 30). When purchasing fork oil, ensure the viscosity rating matches that specified by the manufacturer.
● Some lubricant manufacturers also produce a range of high-quality suspension fluids which are very similar to fork oil but are designed mainly for competition use. These fluids may have a different viscosity rating system which is not to be confused with the SAE rating of normal fork oil. Refer to the manufacturer's instructions if in any doubt.

Brake and clutch fluid

● All disc brake systems and some clutch systems are hydraulically operated. To ensure correct operation, the hydraulic fluid must be changed in accordance with the Maintenance Schedule.
● Brake and clutch fluid is classified by its DOT rating with most motorcycle manufacturers specifying DOT 3 or 4 fluid. Both fluid types are glycol-based and can be mixed together without adverse effect; DOT 4 fluid exceeds

the requirements of DOT 3 fluid. Although it is safe to use DOT 4 fluid in a system designed for use with DOT 3 fluid, never use DOT 3 fluid in a system which specifies the use of DOT 4 as this will adversely affect the system's performance. The type required for the system will be marked on the fluid reservoir cap.
● Some manufacturers also produce a DOT 5 hydraulic fluid. DOT 5 hydraulic fluid is silicone-based and is not compatible with the glycol-based DOT 3 and 4 fluids. Never mix DOT 5 fluid with DOT 3 or 4 fluid as this will seriously affect the performance of the hydraulic system.

Coolant/antifreeze

● When purchasing coolant/antifreeze, always ensure it is suitable for use in an aluminium engine and contains corrosion inhibitors to prevent possible blockages of the internal coolant passages of the system. As a general rule, most coolants are designed to be used neat and should not be diluted whereas antifreeze can be mixed with distilled water to provide a coolant solution of the required strength. Refer to the manufacturer's instructions on the bottle.
● Ensure the coolant is changed in accordance with the Maintenance Schedule.

Chain lube

● Chain lube is an aerosol-type spray lubricant specifically designed for use on motorcycle final drive chains. Chain lube has two functions, to minimise friction between the final drive chain and sprockets and to prevent corrosion of the chain. Regular use of a good-quality chain lube will extend the life of the drive chain and sprockets and thus maximise the power being transmitted from the transmission to the rear wheel.
● When using chain lube, always allow some time for the solvents in the lube to evaporate before riding the motorcycle. This will minimise the amount of lube which will 'fling' off from the chain when the motorcycle is used. If the motorcycle is

equipped with an 'O-ring' chain, ensure the chain lube is labelled as being suitable for use on 'O-ring' chains.

Degreasers and solvents
● There are many different types of solvents and degreasers available to remove the grime

and grease which accumulate around the motorcycle during normal use. Degreasers and solvents are usually available as an aerosol-type spray or as a liquid which you apply with a brush. Always closely follow the manufacturer's instructions and wear eye protection during use. Be aware that many solvents are flammable and may give off noxious fumes; take adequate precautions when using them (see Safety First!).

● For general cleaning, use one of the many solvents or degreasers available from most motorcycle accessory shops. These solvents are usually applied then left for a certain time before being washed off with water.

Brake cleaner is a solvent specifically designed to remove all traces of oil, grease and dust from braking system components. Brake cleaner is designed to evaporate quickly and leaves behind no residue.

Carburettor cleaner is an aerosol-type solvent specifically designed to clear carburettor blockages and break down the hard deposits and gum often found inside carburettors during overhaul.

Contact cleaner is an aerosol-type solvent designed for cleaning electrical components. The cleaner will remove all traces of oil and dirt from components such as switch contacts or fouled spark plugs and then dry, leaving behind no residue.

Gasket remover is an aerosol-type solvent designed for removing stubborn gaskets from engine components during overhaul. Gasket remover will minimise the amount of scraping required to remove the gasket and therefore reduce the risk of damage to the mating surface.

Spray lubricants
● Aerosol-based spray lubricants are widely available and are excellent for lubricating lever pivots and exposed cables and switches. Try to use a lubricant which is of the dry-film type as the fluid evaporates, leaving behind a dry-film of lubricant. Lubricants which leave behind an oily residue will attract dust and dirt which will increase the rate of wear of the cable/lever.

● Most lubricants also act as a moisture dispersant and a penetrating fluid. This means they can also be used to 'dry out' electrical components such as wiring connectors or switches as well as helping to free seized fasteners.

Greases

● Grease is used to lubricate many of the pivot-points. A good-quality multi-purpose grease is suitable for most applications but some manufacturers will specify the use of specialist greases for use on components such as swingarm and suspension linkage bushes. These specialist greases can be purchased from most motorcycle (or car) accessory shops; commonly specified types include molybdenum disulphide grease, lithium-based grease, graphite-based grease, silicone-based grease and high-temperature copper-based grease.

Gasket sealing compounds
● Gasket sealing compounds can be used in conjunction with gaskets, to improve their sealing capabilities, or on their own to seal metal-to-metal joints. Depending on their type, sealing compounds either set hard or stay relatively soft and pliable.

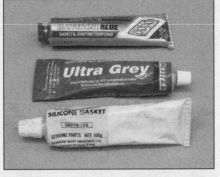

● When purchasing a gasket sealing compound, ensure that it is designed specifically for use on an internal combustion engine. General multi-purpose sealants available from DIY stores may appear visibly similar but they are not designed to withstand the extreme heat or contact with fuel and oil encountered when used on an engine (see 'Tools and Workshop Tips' for further information).

Thread locking compound
● Thread locking compounds are used to secure certain threaded fasteners in position to prevent them from loosening due to vibration. Thread locking compounds can be purchased from most motorcycle (and car) accessory shops. Ensure the threads of the both components are completely clean and dry before sparingly applying the locking compound (see 'Tools and Workshop Tips' for further information).

Fuel additives
● Fuel additives which protect and clean the fuel system components are widely available. These additives are designed to remove all traces of deposits that build up on the carburettors/injectors and prevent wear, helping the fuel system to operate more efficiently. If a fuel additive is being used, check that it is suitable for use with your motorcycle, especially if your motorcycle is equipped with a catalytic converter.

● Octane boosters are also available. These additives are designed to improve the performance of highly-tuned engines being run on normal pump-fuel and are of no real use on standard motorcycles.

Conversion factors

Length (distance)

Inches (in)	x 25.4	= Millimetres (mm)	x 0.0394 =	Inches (in)
Feet (ft)	x 0.305	= Metres (m)	x 3.281 =	Feet (ft)
Miles	x 1.609	= Kilometres (km)	x 0.621 =	Miles

Volume (capacity)

Cubic inches (cu in; in^3)	x 16.387	= Cubic centimetres (cc; cm^3)	x 0.061 =	Cubic inches (cu in; in^3)
Imperial pints (Imp pt)	x 0.568	= Litres (l)	x 1.76 =	Imperial pints (Imp pt)
Imperial quarts (Imp qt)	x 1.137	= Litres (l)	x 0.88 =	Imperial quarts (Imp qt)
Imperial quarts (Imp qt)	x 1.201	= US quarts (US qt)	x 0.833 =	Imperial quarts (Imp qt)
US quarts (US qt)	x 0.946	= Litres (l)	x 1.057 =	US quarts (US qt)
Imperial gallons (Imp gal)	x 4.546	= Litres (l)	x 0.22 =	Imperial gallons (Imp gal)
Imperial gallons (Imp gal)	x 1.201	= US gallons (US gal)	x 0.833 =	Imperial gallons (Imp gal)
US gallons (US gal)	x 3.785	= Litres (l)	x 0.264 =	US gallons (US gal)

Mass (weight)

Ounces (oz)	x 28.35	= Grams (g)	x 0.035 =	Ounces (oz)
Pounds (lb)	x 0.454	= Kilograms (kg)	x 2.205 =	Pounds (lb)

Force

Ounces-force (ozf; oz)	x 0.278	= Newtons (N)	x 3.6 =	Ounces-force (ozf; oz)
Pounds-force (lbf; lb)	x 4.448	= Newtons (N)	x 0.225 =	Pounds-force (lbf; lb)
Newtons (N)	x 0.1	= Kilograms-force (kgf; kg)	x 9.81 =	Newtons (N)

Pressure

Pounds-force per square inch (psi; lbf/in^2; lb/in^2)	x 0.070	= Kilograms-force per square centimetre (kgf/cm^2; kg/cm^2)	x 14.223 =	Pounds-force per square inch (psi; lbf/in^2; lb/in^2)
Pounds-force per square inch (psi; lbf/in^2; lb/in^2)	x 0.068	= Atmospheres (atm)	x 14.696 =	Pounds-force per square inch (psi; lbf/in^2; lb/in^2)
Pounds-force per square inch (psi; lbf/in^2; lb/in^2)	x 0.069	= Bars	x 14.5 =	Pounds-force per square inch (psi; lbf/in^2; lb/in^2)
Pounds-force per square inch (psi; lbf/in^2; lb/in^2)	x 6.895	= Kilopascals (kPa)	x 0.145 =	Pounds-force per square inch (psi; lbf/in^2; lb/in^2)
Kilopascals (kPa)	x 0.01	= Kilograms-force per square centimetre (kgf/cm^2; kg/cm^2)	x 98.1 =	Kilopascals (kPa)
Millibar (mbar)	x 100	= Pascals (Pa)	x 0.01 =	Millibar (mbar)
Millibar (mbar)	x 0.0145	= Pounds-force per square inch (psi; lbf/in^2; lb/in^2)	x 68.947 =	Millibar (mbar)
Millibar (mbar)	x 0.75	= Millimetres of mercury (mmHg)	x 1.333 =	Millibar (mbar)
Millibar (mbar)	x 0.401	= Inches of water (inH$_2$O)	x 2.491 =	Millibar (mbar)
Millimetres of mercury (mmHg)	x 0.535	= Inches of water (inH$_2$O)	x 1.868 =	Millimetres of mercury (mmHg)
Inches of water (inH$_2$O)	x 0.036	= Pounds-force per square inch (psi; lbf/in^2; lb/in^2)	x 27.68 =	Inches of water (inH$_2$O)

Torque (moment of force)

Pounds-force inches (lbf in; lb in)	x 1.152	= Kilograms-force centimetre (kgf cm; kg cm)	x 0.868 =	Pounds-force inches (lbf in; lb in)
Pounds-force inches (lbf in; lb in)	x 0.113	= Newton metres (Nm)	x 8.85 =	Pounds-force inches (lbf in; lb in)
Pounds-force inches (lbf in; lb in)	x 0.083	= Pounds-force feet (lbf ft; lb ft)	x 12 =	Pounds-force inches (lbf in; lb in)
Pounds-force feet (lbf ft; lb ft)	x 0.138	= Kilograms-force metres (kgf m; kg m)	x 7.233 =	Pounds-force feet (lbf ft; lb ft)
Pounds-force feet (lbf ft; lb ft)	x 1.356	= Newton metres (Nm)	x 0.738 =	Pounds-force feet (lbf ft; lb ft)
Newton metres (Nm)	x 0.102	= Kilograms-force metres (kgf m; kg m)	x 9.804 =	Newton metres (Nm)

Power

Horsepower (hp)	x 745.7	= Watts (W)	x 0.0013 =	Horsepower (hp)

Velocity (speed)

Miles per hour (miles/hr; mph)	x 1.609	= Kilometres per hour (km/hr; kph)	x 0.621 =	Miles per hour (miles/hr; mph)

Fuel consumption*

Miles per gallon, Imperial (mpg)	x 0.354	= Kilometres per litre (km/l)	x 2.825 =	Miles per gallon, Imperial (mpg)
Miles per gallon, US (mpg)	x 0.425	= Kilometres per litre (km/l)	x 2.352 =	Miles per gallon, US (mpg)

Temperature

Degrees Fahrenheit = (°C x 1.8) + 32   Degrees Celsius (Degrees Centigrade; °C) = (°F - 32) x 0.56

It is common practice to convert from miles per gallon (mpg) to litres/100 kilometres (l/100km), where mpg x l/100 km = 282

About the MOT Test

In the UK, all vehicles more than three years old are subject to an annual test to ensure that they meet minimum safety requirements. A current test certificate must be issued before a machine can be used on public roads, and is required before a road fund licence can be issued. Riding without a current test certificate will also invalidate your insurance.

For most owners, the MOT test is an annual cause for anxiety, and this is largely due to owners not being sure what needs to be checked prior to submitting the motorcycle for testing. The simple answer is that a fully roadworthy motorcycle will have no difficulty in passing the test.

This is a guide to getting your motorcycle through the MOT test. Obviously it will not be possible to examine the motorcycle to the same standard as the professional MOT tester, particularly in view of the equipment required for some of the checks. However, working through the following procedures will enable you to identify any problem areas before submitting the motorcycle for the test.

It has only been possible to summarise the test requirements here, based on the regulations in force at the time of printing. Test standards are becoming increasingly stringent, although there are some exemptions for older vehicles. More information about the MOT test can be obtained from the TSO publications, *How Safe is your Motorcycle* and *The MOT Inspection Manual for Motorcycle Testing*.

Many of the checks require that one of the wheels is raised off the ground. If the motorcycle doesn't have a centre stand, note that an auxiliary stand will be required. Additionally, the help of an assistant may prove useful.

Certain exceptions apply to machines under 50 cc, machines without a lighting system, and Classic bikes - if in doubt about any of the requirements listed below seek confirmation from an MOT tester prior to submitting the motorcycle for the test.

Check that the frame number is clearly visible.

Electrical System

Lights, turn signals, horn and reflector

● With the ignition on, check the operation of the following electrical components. **Note:** *The electrical components on certain small-capacity machines are powered by the generator, requiring that the engine is run for this check.*

a) *Headlight and tail light. Check that both illuminate in the low and high beam switch positions.*
b) *Position lights. Check that the front position (or sidelight) and tail light illuminate in this switch position.*
c) *Turn signals. Check that all flash at the correct rate, and that the warning light(s) function correctly. Check that the turn signal switch works correctly.*
d) *Hazard warning system (where fitted). Check that all four turn signals flash in this switch position.*
e) *Brake stop light. Check that the light comes on when the front and rear brakes are independently applied. Models first used on or after 1st April 1986 must have a brake light switch on each brake.*
f) *Horn. Check that the sound is continuous and of reasonable volume.*

● Check that there is a red reflector on the rear of the machine, either mounted separately or as part of the tail light lens.
● Check the condition of the headlight, tail light and turn signal lenses.

Headlight beam height

● The MOT tester will perform a headlight beam height check using specialised beam setting equipment **(see illustration 1)**. This equipment will not be available to the home mechanic, but if you suspect that the headlight is incorrectly set or may have been maladjusted in the past, you can perform a rough test as follows.
● Position the bike in a straight line facing a brick wall. The bike must be off its stand, upright and with a rider seated. Measure the height from the ground to the centre of the headlight and mark a horizontal line on the wall at this height. Position the motorcycle 3.8 metres from the wall and draw a vertical

Headlight beam height checking equipment

line up the wall central to the centreline of the motorcycle. Switch to dipped beam and check that the beam pattern falls slightly lower than the horizontal line and to the left of the vertical line **(see illustration 2)**.

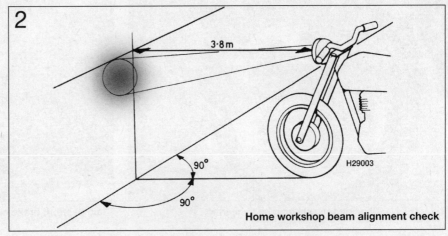

3·8 m

90°

90°

H29003

Home workshop beam alignment check

Exhaust System and Final Drive

Exhaust

● Check that the exhaust mountings are secure and that the system does not foul any of the rear suspension components.

● Start the motorcycle. When the revs are increased, check that the exhaust is neither holed nor leaking from any of its joints. On a linked system, check that the collector box is not leaking due to corrosion.

● Note that the exhaust decibel level ("loudness" of the exhaust) is assessed at the discretion of the tester. If the motorcycle was first used on or after 1st January 1985 the silencer must carry the BSAU 193 stamp, or a marking relating to its make and model, or be of OE (original equipment) manufacture. If the silencer is marked NOT FOR ROAD USE, RACING USE ONLY or similar, it will fail the MOT.

Final drive

● On chain or belt drive machines, check that the chain/belt is in good condition and does not have excessive slack. Also check that the sprocket is securely mounted on the rear wheel hub. Check that the chain/belt guard is in place.

● On shaft drive bikes, check for oil leaking from the drive unit and fouling the rear tyre.

Steering and Suspension

Steering

● With the front wheel raised off the ground, rotate the steering from lock to lock. The handlebar or switches must not contact the fuel tank or be close enough to trap the rider's hand. Problems can be caused by damaged lock stops on the lower yoke and frame, or by the fitting of non-standard handlebars.

● When performing the lock to lock check, also ensure that the steering moves freely without drag or notchiness. Steering movement can be impaired by poorly routed cables, or by overtight head bearings or worn bvearings. The tester will perform a check of the steering head bearing lower race by mounting the front wheel on a surface plate, then performing a lock to lock check with the weight of the machine on the lower bearing **(see illustration 3)**.

● Grasp the fork sliders (lower legs) and attempt to push and pull on the forks

Front wheel mounted on a surface plate for steering head bearing lower race check

(see illustration 4). Any play in the steering head bearings will be felt. Note that in extreme cases, wear of the front fork bushes can be misinterpreted for head bearing play.

● Check that the handlebars are securely mounted.

● Check that the handlebar grip rubbers are secure. They should by bonded to the bar left end and to the throttle cable pulley on the right end.

Front suspension

● With the motorcycle off the stand, hold the front brake on and pump the front forks up and down **(see illustration 5)**. Check that they are adequately damped.

Checking the steering head bearings for freeplay

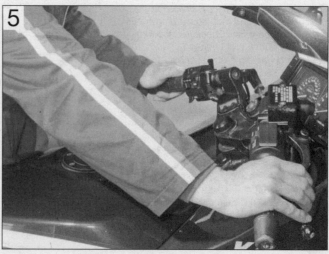

Hold the front brake on and pump the front forks up and down to check operation

Inspect the area around the fork dust seal for oil leakage (arrow)

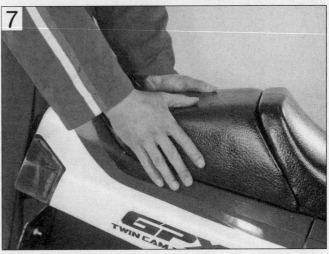

Bounce the rear of the motorcycle to check rear suspension operation

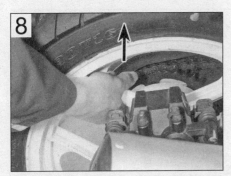

Checking for rear suspension linkage play

● Inspect the area above and around the front fork oil seals **(see illustration 6)**. There should be no sign of oil on the fork tube (stanchion) nor leaking down the slider (lower leg). On models so equipped, check that there is no oil leaking from the anti-dive units.
● On models with swingarm front suspension, check that there is no freeplay in the linkage when moved from side to side.

Rear suspension

● With the motorcycle off the stand and an assistant supporting the motorcycle by its handlebars, bounce the rear suspension **(see illustration 7)**. Check that the suspension components do not foul on any of the cycle parts and check that the shock absorber(s) provide adequate damping.
● Visually inspect the shock absorber(s) and check that there is no sign of oil leakage from its damper. This is somewhat restricted on certain single shock models due to the location of the shock absorber.
● With the rear wheel raised off the ground, grasp the wheel at the highest point and attempt to pull it up **(see illustration 8)**. Any play in the swingarm pivot or suspension linkage bearings will be felt as movement. **Note:** *Do not confuse play with actual suspension movement.* Failure to lubricate suspension linkage bearings can lead to bearing failure **(see illustration 9)**.
● With the rear wheel raised off the ground, grasp the swingarm ends and attempt to move the swingarm from side to side and forwards and backwards - any play indicates wear of the swingarm pivot bearings **(see illustration 10)**.

Worn suspension linkage pivots (arrows) are usually the cause of play in the rear suspension

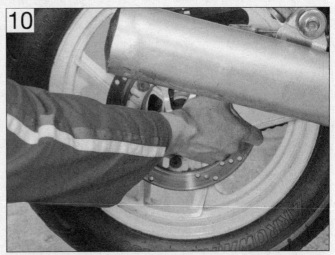

Grasp the swingarm at the ends to check for play in its pivot bearings

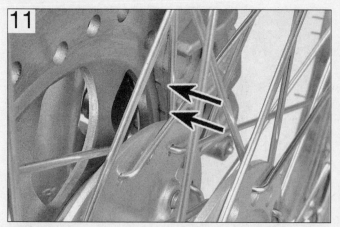

Brake pad wear can usually be viewed without removing the caliper. Most pads have wear indicator grooves (arrowed) and some also have indicator tangs or cut-outs.

On drum brakes, check the angle of the operating lever with the brake fully applied. Most drum brakes have a wear indicator pointer or scale.

Brakes, Wheels and Tyres

Brakes

● With the wheel raised off the ground, apply the brake then free it off, and check that the wheel is about to revolve freely without brake drag.
● On disc brakes, examine the disc itself. Check that it is securely mounted and not cracked.
● On disc brakes, view the pad material through the caliper mouth and check that the pads are not worn down beyond the limit (see illustration 11).
● On drum brakes, check that when the brake is applied the angle between the operating lever and cable or rod is not too great (see illustration 12). Check also that the operating lever doesn't foul any other components.

● On disc brakes, examine the flexible hoses from top to bottom. Have an assistant hold the brake on so that the fluid in the hose is under pressure, and check that there is no sign of fluid leakage, bulges or cracking. If there are any metal brake pipes or unions, check that these are free from corrosion and damage. Where a brake-linked anti-dive system is fitted, check the hoses to the anti-dive in a similar manner.
● Check that the rear brake torque arm is secure and that its fasteners are secured by self-locking nuts or castellated nuts with split-pins or R-pins (see illustration 13).
● On models with ABS, check that the self-check warning light in the instrument panel works.
● The MOT tester will perform a test of the motorcycle's braking efficiency based on a calculation of rider and motorcycle weight. Although this cannot be carried out at home, you can at least ensure that the braking systems are properly maintained. For

hydraulic disc brakes, check the fluid level, lever/pedal feel (bleed of air if its spongy) and pad material. For drum brakes, check adjustment, cable or rod operation and shoe lining thickness.

Wheels and tyres

● Check the wheel condition. Cast wheels should be free from cracks and if of the built-up design, all fasteners should be secure. Spoked wheels should be checked for broken, corroded, loose or bent spokes.
● With the wheel raised off the ground, spin the wheel and visually check that the tyre and wheel run true. Check that the tyre does not foul the suspension or mudguards.
● With the wheel raised off the ground, grasp the wheel and attempt to move it about the axle (spindle) (see illustration 14). Any play felt here indicates wheel bearing failure.

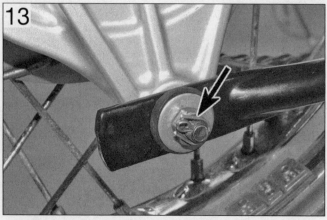

Brake torque arm must be properly secured at both ends

Check for wheel bearing play by trying to move the wheel about the axle (spindle)

Checking the tyre tread depth

Tyre direction of rotation arrow can be found on tyre sidewall

Castellated type wheel axle (spindle) nut must be secured by a split pin or R-pin

Two straightedges are used to check wheel alignment

● Check the tyre tread depth, tread condition and sidewall condition **(see illustration 15)**.
● Check the tyre type. Front and rear tyre types must be compatible and be suitable for road use. Tyres marked NOT FOR ROAD USE, COMPETITION USE ONLY or similar, will fail the MOT.
● If the tyre sidewall carries a direction of rotation arrow, this must be pointing in the direction of normal wheel rotation **(see illustration 16)**.
● Check that the wheel axle (spindle) nuts (where applicable) are properly secured. A self-locking nut or castellated nut with a split-pin or R-pin can be used **(see illustration 17)**.
● Wheel alignment is checked with the motorcycle off the stand and a rider seated. With the front wheel pointing straight ahead, two perfectly straight lengths of metal or wood and placed against the sidewalls of both tyres **(see illustration 18)**. The gap each side of the front tyre must be equidistant on both sides. Incorrect wheel alignment may be due to a cocked rear wheel (often as the result of poor chain adjustment) or in extreme cases, a bent frame.

General checks and condition

● Check the security of all major fasteners, bodypanels, seat, fairings (where fitted) and mudguards.

● Check that the rider and pillion footrests, handlebar levers and brake pedal are securely mounted.

● Check for corrosion on the frame or any load-bearing components. If severe, this may affect the structure, particularly under stress.

Sidecars

A motorcycle fitted with a sidecar requires additional checks relating to the stability of the machine and security of attachment and swivel joints, plus specific wheel alignment (toe-in) requirements. Additionally, tyre and lighting requirements differ from conventional motorcycle use. Owners are advised to check MOT test requirements with an official test centre.

Preparing for storage

Before you start

If repairs or an overhaul is needed, see that this is carried out now rather than left until you want to ride the bike again.

Give the bike a good wash and scrub all dirt from its underside. Make sure the bike dries completely before preparing for storage.

Engine

● Remove the spark plug(s) and lubricate the cylinder bores with approximately a teaspoon of motor oil using a spout-type oil can **(see illustration 1)**. Reinstall the spark plug(s). Crank the engine over a couple of times to coat the piston rings and bores with oil. If the bike has a kickstart, use this to turn the engine over. If not, flick the kill switch to the OFF position and crank the engine over on the starter **(see illustration 2)**. If the nature on the ignition system prevents the starter operating with the kill switch in the OFF position, remove

the spark plugs and fit them back in their caps; ensure that the plugs are earthed (grounded) against the cylinder head when the starter is operated **(see illustration 3)**.

⚠️ **Warning: It is important that the plugs are earthed (grounded) away from the spark plug holes otherwise there is a risk of atomised fuel from the cylinders igniting.**

> **HAYNES HiNT** *On a single cylinder four-stroke engine, you can seal the combustion chamber completely by positioning the piston at TDC on the compression stroke.*

● Drain the carburettor(s) otherwise there is a risk of jets becoming blocked by gum deposits from the fuel **(see illustration 4)**.

● If the bike is going into long-term storage, consider adding a fuel stabiliser to the fuel in the tank. If the tank is drained completely, corrosion of its internal surfaces may occur if left unprotected for a long period. The tank can be treated with a rust preventative especially for this purpose. Alternatively, remove the tank and pour half a litre of motor oil into it, install the filler cap and shake the tank to coat its internals with oil before draining off the excess. The same effect can also be achieved by spraying WD40 or a similar water-dispersant around the inside of the tank via its flexible nozzle.

● Make sure the cooling system contains the correct mix of antifreeze. Antifreeze also contains important corrosion inhibitors.

● The air intakes and exhaust can be sealed off by covering or plugging the openings. Ensure that you do not seal in any condensation; run the engine until it is

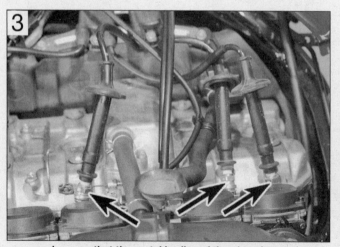

. . . and ensure that the metal bodies of the plugs (arrows) are earthed against the cylinder head

Connect a hose to the carburettor float chamber drain stub (arrow) and unscrew the drain screw

Squirt a drop of motor oil into each cylinder

Flick the kill switch to OFF . . .

Exhausts can be sealed off with a plastic bag

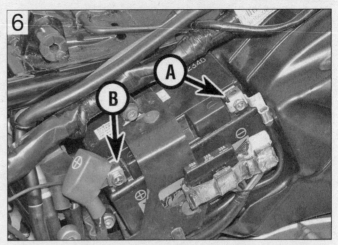

Disconnect the negative lead (A) first, followed by the positive lead (B)

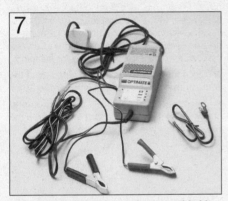

Use a suitable battery charger - this kit also assess battery condition

● Check the electrolyte level and top up if necessary (conventional refillable batteries). Clean the terminals.
● Store the battery off the motorcycle and away from any sources of fire. Position a wooden block under the battery if it is to sit on the ground.
● Give the battery a trickle charge for a few hours every month **(see illustration 7)**.

Tyres

● Place the bike on its centrestand or an auxiliary stand which will support the motorcycle in an upright position. Position wood blocks under the tyres to keep them off the ground and to provide insulation from damp. If the bike is being put into long-term storage, ideally both tyres should be off the ground; not only will this protect the tyres, but will also ensure that no load is placed on the steering head or wheel bearings.
● Deflate each tyre by 5 to 10 psi, no more or the beads may unseat from the rim, making subsequent inflation difficult on tubeless tyres.

Pivots and controls

● Lubricate all lever, pedal, stand and footrest

pivot points. If grease nipples are fitted to the rear suspension components, apply lubricant to the pivots.
● Lubricate all control cables.

Cycle components

● Apply a wax protectant to all painted and plastic components. Wipe off any excess, but don't polish to a shine. Where fitted, clean the screen with soap and water.
● Coat metal parts with Vaseline (petroleum jelly). When applying this to the fork tubes, do not compress the forks otherwise the seals will rot from contact with the Vaseline.
● Apply a vinyl cleaner to the seat.

Storage conditions

● Aim to store the bike in a shed or garage which does not leak and is free from damp.
● Drape an old blanket or bedspread over the bike to protect it from dust and direct contact with sunlight (which will fade paint). This also hides the bike from prying eyes. Beware of tight-fitting plastic covers which may allow condensation to form and settle on the bike.

hot, then switch off and allow to cool. Tape a piece of thick plastic over the silencer end(s) **(see illustration 5)**. Note that some advocate pouring a tablespoon of motor oil into the silencer(s) before sealing them off.

Battery

● Remove it from the bike - in extreme cases of cold the battery may freeze and crack its case **(see illustration 6)**.

Getting back on the road

Engine and transmission

● Change the oil and replace the oil filter. If this was done prior to storage, check that the oil hasn't emulsified - a thick whitish substance which occurs through condensation.
● Remove the spark plugs. Using a spout-type oil can, squirt a few drops of oil into the cylinder(s). This will provide initial lubrication as the piston rings and bores comes back into contact. Service the spark plugs, or fit new ones, and install them in the engine.

● Check that the clutch isn't stuck on. The plates can stick together if left standing for some time, preventing clutch operation. Engage a gear and try rocking the bike back and forth with the clutch lever held against the handlebar. If this doesn't work on cable-operated clutches, hold the clutch lever back against the handlebar with a strong elastic band or cable tie for a couple of hours **(see illustration 8)**.
● If the air intakes or silencer end(s) were blocked off, remove the bung or cover used. preventative, oil or a stabiliser added to the

Hold clutch lever back against the handlebar with elastic bands or a cable tie

fuel, drain and flush the tank and dispose of the fuel sensibly. If no action was taken with the fuel tank prior to storage, it is advised that the old fuel is disposed of since it will go off over a period of time. Refill the fuel tank with fresh fuel.

Frame and running gear

● Oil all pivot points and cables.
● Check the tyre pressures. They will definitely need inflating if pressures were reduced for storage.
● Lubricate the final drive chain (where applicable).
● Remove any protective coating applied to the fork tubes (stanchions) since this may well destroy the fork seals. If the fork tubes weren't protected and have picked up rust spots, remove them with very fine abrasive paper and refinish with metal polish.
● Check that both brakes operate correctly. Apply each brake hard and check that it's not possible to move the motorcycle forwards, then check that the brake frees off again once released. Brake caliper pistons can stick due to corrosion around the piston head, or on the sliding caliper types, due to corrosion of the slider pins. If the brake doesn't free after repeated operation, take the caliper off for examination. Similarly drum brakes can stick due to a seized operating cam, cable or rod linkage.
● If the motorcycle has been in long-term storage, renew the brake fluid and clutch fluid (where applicable).
● Depending on where the bike has been stored, the wiring, cables and hoses may have been nibbled by rodents. Make a visual check and investigate disturbed wiring loom tape.

Battery

● If the battery has been previously removal and given top up charges it can simply be reconnected. Remember to connect the positive cable first and the negative cable last.
● On conventional refillable batteries, if the battery has not received any attention, remove it from the motorcycle and check its electrolyte level. Top up if necessary then charge the battery. If the battery fails to hold a charge and a visual checks show heavy white sulphation of the plates, the battery is probably defective and must be renewed. This is particularly likely if the battery is old. Confirm battery condition with a specific gravity check.
● On sealed (MF) batteries, if the battery has not received any attention, remove it from the motorcycle and charge it according to the information on the battery case - if the battery fails to hold a charge it must be renewed.

Starting procedure

● If a kickstart is fitted, turn the engine over a couple of times with the ignition OFF to distribute oil around the engine. If no kickstart is fitted, flick the engine kill switch OFF and the ignition ON and crank the engine over a couple of times to work oil around the upper cylinder components. If the nature of the ignition system is such that the starter won't work with the kill switch OFF, remove the spark plugs, fit them back into their caps and earth (ground) their bodies on the cylinder head. Reinstall the spark plugs afterwards.
● Switch the kill switch to RUN, operate the choke and start the engine. If the engine won't start don't continue cranking the engine - not only will this flatten the battery, but the starter motor will overheat. Switch the ignition off and try again later. If the engine refuses to start, go through the fault finding procedures in this manual. **Note:** *If the bike has been in storage for a long time, old fuel or a carburettor blockage may be the problem. Gum deposits in carburettors can block jets - if a carburettor cleaner doesn't prove successful the carburettors must be dismantled for cleaning.*
● Once the engine has started, check that the lights, turn signals and horn work properly.
● Treat the bike gently for the first ride and check all fluid levels on completion. Settle the bike back into the maintenance schedule.

This Section provides an easy reference-guide to the more common faults that are likely to afflict your machine. Obviously, the opportunities are almost limitless for faults to occur as a result of obscure failures, and to try and cover all eventualities would require a separate book. Indeed, a number have been written on the subject.

Successful fault finding is not a mysterious 'black art' but the application of a bit of knowledge combined with a systematic and logical approach to the problem. Begin by first accurately identifying the symptom and then checking through the list of possible causes, starting with the simplest or most obvious and progressing in stages to the most complex.

Take nothing for granted, but above all apply liberal quantities of common sense.

The main symptom of a fault is given in the text as a major heading below which are listed the various systems or areas which may contain the fault. Details of each possible cause for a fault and the remedial action to be taken are given, in brief, in the paragraphs below each heading. Further information should be sought in the relevant Chapter.

1 Engine doesn't start or is difficult to start

- [ ] Starter motor doesn't rotate
- [ ] Starter motor rotates but engine does not turn over
- [ ] Starter works but engine won't turn over (seized)
- [ ] No fuel flow
- [ ] Engine flooded
- [ ] No spark or weak spark
- [ ] Compression low
- [ ] Stalls after starting
- [ ] Rough idle

2 Poor running at low speed

- [ ] Spark weak
- [ ] Fuel/air mixture incorrect
- [ ] Compression low
- [ ] Poor acceleration

3 Poor running or no power at high speed

- [ ] Firing incorrect
- [ ] Fuel/air mixture incorrect
- [ ] Compression low
- [ ] Knocking or pinking
- [ ] Miscellaneous causes

4 Overheating

- [ ] Engine overheats
- [ ] Firing incorrect
- [ ] Fuel/air mixture incorrect
- [ ] Compression too high
- [ ] Engine load excessive
- [ ] Lubrication inadequate
- [ ] Miscellaneous causes

5 Clutch problems

- [ ] Clutch slipping
- [ ] Clutch not disengaging completely

6 Gearchange problems

- [ ] Doesn't go into gear, or lever doesn't return
- [ ] Jumps out of gear
- [ ] Overshifts

7 Abnormal engine noise

- [ ] Knocking or pinking
- [ ] Piston slap or rattling
- [ ] Valve noise
- [ ] Other noise

8 Abnormal driveline noise

- [ ] Clutch noise
- [ ] Transmission noise
- [ ] Final drive noise

9 Abnormal frame and suspension noise

- [ ] Front end noise
- [ ] Shock absorber noise
- [ ] Brake noise

10 Oil pressure warning light comes on – GS and RT models

- [ ] Engine lubrication system
- [ ] Electrical system

11 Excessive exhaust smoke

- [ ] White smoke
- [ ] Black smoke
- [ ] Brown smoke

12 Poor handling or stability

- [ ] Handlebar hard to turn
- [ ] Handlebar shakes or vibrates excessively
- [ ] Handlebar pulls to one side
- [ ] Poor shock absorbing qualities

13 Braking problems

- [ ] Brakes are spongy, don't hold
- [ ] Brake lever or pedal pulsates
- [ ] Brakes drag

14 Electrical problems

- [ ] Battery dead or weak
- [ ] Battery overcharged

1 Engine doesn't start or is difficult to start

Starter motor doesn't rotate

- ☐ Engine kill switch OFF.
- ☐ Engine kill switch defective. Check for wet, dirty or corroded contacts. Clean or renew the switch as necessary (Chapter 7).
- ☐ Faulty gear position, side stand or clutch switch. Check starter interlock circuit (Chapter 3). Check the operation of each switch according to the procedures in Chapter 7.
- ☐ Battery voltage low. Check and recharge battery (Chapter 7).
- ☐ Starter relay faulty. Check it according to the procedure in Chapter 7.
- ☐ Starter motor defective. Make sure the wiring to the starter is secure. Make sure the starter relay clicks when the start button is pushed. If the relay clicks, then the fault is in the wiring or motor.
- ☐ Starter switch not contacting. The contacts could be wet, corroded or dirty. Disassemble and clean the switch (Chapter 7).
- ☐ Wiring open or shorted. Check all wiring connections and harnesses to make sure that they are dry, tight and not corroded. Also check for broken or frayed wires that can cause a short to earth (see Wiring Diagrams, Chapter 7).
- ☐ Ignition switch defective. Check the switch according to the procedure in Chapter 7. Renew the switch if it is defective.

Starter motor rotates but engine does not turn over

- ☐ Starter motor solenoid or lever arm defective. Inspect and renew (Chapter 7).
- ☐ Damaged starter pinion or flywheel. Inspect and renew the damaged parts (Chapters 2 and 7).

Starter works but engine won't turn over (seized)

- ☐ Seized engine caused by one or more internally damaged components. Failure due to wear, abuse or lack of lubrication. Damage can include seized valves, camshafts, pistons, crankshaft, connecting rod bearings, or transmission gears or bearings. Refer to Chapter 2 for engine disassembly.

No fuel flow

- ☐ No fuel in tank.
- ☐ Fuel pump failure or filter/strainer blocked (Chapter 3).
- ☐ Fuel tank breather hose obstructed.
- ☐ Injector clogged. For the injectors to be clogged, either a very bad batch of fuel with an unusual additive has been used, or some other foreign material has entered the system. Sometimes, after a machine has been stored for many months without running, the fuel turns to a varnish-like liquid and forms deposits in the injectors.

Engine flooded

- ☐ Starting technique incorrect. Under normal circumstances the machine should start with no throttle. When the ambient temperature is very low, and the engine is cold, open the throttle slightly and pull the clutch lever in after switching the ignition ON. If the engine floods i.e. fuel is injected but not ignited by the spark plugs, check the ignition system (Chapter 3).

No spark or weak spark

- ☐ Engine kill switch OFF.
- ☐ Battery voltage low. Check and recharge the battery (Chapter 7).
- ☐ Spark plugs dirty, defective or worn out (Chapter 1). Locate reason for fouled plugs using spark plug condition chart at the end of this manual.
- ☐ Ignition coils not making good contact. Make sure that the coils fit snugly over the plug ends. Check the coil wiring (Chapter 3).
- ☐ Ignition HT coils defective. Check the coils (Chapter 3).
- ☐ Engine control unit (ECU) or ignition system component faulty (Chapter 3). Refer to a BMW dealer equipped with the MOSS diagnostic tester.
- ☐ Ignition or kill switch shorted. This is usually caused by water, corrosion, damage or excessive wear. Check the operation of the switches and renew if necessary (Chapter 7).
- ☐ Wiring shorted or broken between:
  a) Ignition switch and engine kill switch
  b) ECU and engine kill switch
  c) ECU and ignition HT coils
  d) Ignition system sensors
  Make sure that all wiring connections are clean, dry and tight. Look for chafed and broken wires (Chapters 3 and 7).

Compression low

- ☐ Spark plugs loose. Remove the plugs and inspect their threads. Reinstall and tighten to the specified torque (Chapter 1).
- ☐ Cylinder head not sufficiently tightened down. If the cylinder head is suspected of being loose, then there's a chance that the gasket or head is damaged if the problem has persisted for any length of time. The head nuts should be tightened to the specified torque in the correct sequence (Chapter 2).
- ☐ Improper valve clearance. This means that the valve is not closing completely and compression pressure is leaking past the valve. Check and adjust the valve clearances (Chapter 1).
- ☐ Cylinder and/or piston worn. Excessive wear will cause compression pressure to leak past the rings. This is usually accompanied by worn rings as well. A top-end overhaul is necessary (Chapter 2).
- ☐ Piston rings worn, weak, broken, or sticking. Broken or sticking piston rings usually indicate a lubrication or fuel problem that causes excess carbon deposits to form on the pistons and rings. Top-end overhaul is necessary (Chapter 2).
- ☐ Piston ring-to-groove clearance excessive. This is caused by excessive wear of the piston ring lands. Piston renewal is necessary (Chapter 2).
- ☐ Cylinder head gasket damaged. If the head is allowed to become loose, or if excessive carbon build-up on the piston crown and combustion chamber causes extremely high compression, the head gasket may leak. A new gasket is necessary (Chapter 2).
- ☐ Cylinder head warped. This is caused by overheating or improperly tightened head nuts. Machine shop resurfacing or head renewal is necessary (Chapter 2).
- ☐ Valve spring broken or weak. Caused by component failure or wear, the springs must be renewed (Chapter 2).
- ☐ Valve not seating properly. This is caused by a bent valve (from over-revving or improper valve adjustment), burned valve or seat or an accumulation of carbon deposits on the seat. The valves must be cleaned and/or renewed and the seats serviced (Chapter 2).

Stalls after starting

- ☐ Ignition malfunction (Chapter 3).
- ☐ Injector malfunction (Chapter 3).
- ☐ Fuel pump failure or filter/strainer blocked (Chapter 3).
- ☐ Fuel contaminated. The fuel can be contaminated with either dirt or water, or can change chemically if the machine has been stored for many months without running. Drain the tank and fuel hoses (Chapter 3).
- ☐ Intake air leak. Check for loose throttle body-to-intake manifold and air duct connections (Chapter 3), loose or missing Synchro tester union caps (Chapter 1, Section 3), or loose injectors.

1 Engine doesn't start or is difficult to start (continued)

Rough idle

- [ ] Ignition malfunction (Chapter 3).
- [ ] Throttles not synchronised – have throttle synchronisation checked by a BMW dealer.
- [ ] Injector malfunction (Chapter 3).
- [ ] Fuel contaminated. The fuel can be contaminated with either dirt or water, or can change chemically if the machine has been stored for many months without running. Drain the tank and fuel hoses (Chapter 3).
- [ ] Intake air leak. Check for loose throttle body-to-intake manifold and air duct connections (Chapter 3), loose or missing Synchro tester union caps (Chapter 1, Section 3), or loose injectors.
- [ ] Air filter clogged – renew the filter element (Chapter 1).

2 Poor running at low speeds

Spark weak

- [ ] Battery voltage low – check and recharge battery (Chapter 7).
- [ ] Spark plugs dirty, defective or worn out (Chapter 1). Locate reason for fouled plugs using spark plug condition chart at the end of this manual.
- [ ] Incorrect spark plugs. Wrong type or heat range. Check and install correct plugs (Chapter 1).
- [ ] HT coil not making good contact over spark plug.
- [ ] HT coil or HT wiring defective (Chapter 3).
- [ ] Engine control unit (ECU) or ignition system component faulty (Chapter 3). Refer to a BMW dealer equipped with the MOSS diagnostic tester.

Fuel/air mixture incorrect

- [ ] Air filter clogged, poorly sealed or missing (Chapter 1).
- [ ] Air intake duct blocked or disconnected (Chapter 1).
- [ ] Intake air leak. Check for loose throttle body-to-intake manifold and air duct connections (Chapter 3), loose or missing Synchro tester union caps (Chapter 1, Section 3), or loose injectors.
- [ ] Fuel pump failure or filter/strainer blocked (Chapter 3).
- [ ] Fuel tank breather hose obstructed.
- [ ] Injector clogged. Dirt, water or other contaminants can clog the injectors. Clean the injectors (Chapter 3).

Compression low

- [ ] Spark plugs loose. Remove the plugs and inspect their threads. Reinstall and tighten to the specified torque (Chapter 1).
- [ ] Cylinder head not sufficiently tightened down. If the cylinder head is suspected of being loose, then there's a chance that the gasket and head are damaged if the problem has persisted for any length of time. The head nuts should be tightened to the specified torque in the correct sequence (Chapter 2).
- [ ] Improper valve clearance. This means that the valve is not closing completely and compression pressure is leaking past the valve. Check and adjust the valve clearances (Chapter 1).
- [ ] Cylinder and/or piston worn. Excessive wear will cause compression pressure to leak past the rings. This is usually accompanied by worn rings as well. A top-end overhaul is necessary (Chapter 2).
- [ ] Piston rings worn, weak, broken, or sticking. Broken or sticking piston rings usually indicate a lubrication or mixture problem that causes excess carbon deposits or seizures to form on the pistons and rings. Top-end overhaul is necessary (Chapter 2).
- [ ] Piston ring-to-groove clearance excessive. This is caused by excessive wear of the piston ring lands. Piston renewal is necessary (Chapter 2).
- [ ] Cylinder head gasket damaged. If the head is allowed to become loose, or if excessive carbon build-up on the piston crown and combustion chamber causes extremely high compression, the head gasket may leak. A new gasket is necessary (Chapter 2).
- [ ] Cylinder head warped. This is caused by overheating or improperly tightened head nuts. Machine shop resurfacing or head renewal is necessary (Chapter 2).
- [ ] Valve spring broken or weak. Caused by component failure or wear, the springs must be renewed (Chapter 2).
- [ ] Valve not seating properly. This is caused by a bent valve (from over-revving or improper valve adjustment), burned valve or seat or an accumulation of carbon deposits on the seat. The valves must be cleaned and/or renewed and the seats serviced (Chapter 2).

Poor acceleration

- [ ] Timing not advancing. Refer to a BMW dealer equipped with the MOSS diagnostic tester.
- [ ] Throttles not synchronised – have throttle synchronisation checked by a BMW dealer.
- [ ] Engine oil viscosity too high. Using a heavier oil than that recommended in *Pre-ride checks* can damage the oil pump or lubrication system and cause drag on the engine.
- [ ] Brakes dragging. Usually caused by debris which has entered the brake piston seals, or from a warped disc or bent axle (Chapter 5).

3 Poor running or no power at high speed

Firing incorrect

☐ Air filter clogged – renew the filter element (Chapter 1).
☐ Spark plugs dirty, defective or worn out (Chapter 1). Locate reason for fouled plugs using spark plug condition chart at the end of this manual.
☐ Incorrect spark plugs. Wrong type or heat range. Check and install correct plugs (Chapter 1).
☐ HT coil not in good contact over spark plug.
☐ HT coil or HT wiring defective (Chapter 3).
☐ Engine control unit (ECU) or ignition system component faulty (Chapter 3). Refer to a BMW dealer equipped with the MOSS diagnostic tester.

Fuel/air mixture incorrect

☐ Air filter clogged, poorly sealed or missing (Chapter 1).
☐ Air intake duct blocked or disconnected (Chapter 1).
☐ Intake air leak. Check for loose throttle body-to-intake manifold and air duct connections (Chapter 3), loose or missing Synchro tester union caps (Chapter 1, Section 3), or loose injectors.
☐ Fuel pump failure or filter/strainer blocked (Chapter 3).
☐ Fuel tank breather hose obstructed.
☐ Injector clogged. Dirt, water or other contaminants can clog the injectors. Clean the injectors (Chapter 3).

Compression low

☐ Spark plugs loose. Remove the plugs and inspect their threads. Reinstall and tighten to the specified torque (Chapter 1).
☐ Cylinder head not sufficiently tightened down. If the cylinder head is suspected of being loose, then there's a chance that the gasket and head are damaged if the problem has persisted for any length of time. The head nuts should be tightened to the specified torque in the correct sequence (Chapter 2).
☐ Improper valve clearance. This means that the valve is not closing completely and compression pressure is leaking past the valve. Check and adjust the valve clearances (Chapter 1).
☐ Cylinder and/or piston worn. Excessive wear will cause compression pressure to leak past the rings. This is usually accompanied by worn rings as well. A top-end overhaul is necessary (Chapter 2).
☐ Piston rings worn, weak, broken, or sticking. Broken or sticking piston rings usually indicate a lubrication or mixture problem that causes excess carbon deposits or seizures to form on the pistons and rings. Top-end overhaul is necessary (Chapter 2).
☐ Piston ring-to-groove clearance excessive. This is caused by excessive wear of the piston ring lands. Piston renewal is necessary (Chapter 2).
☐ Cylinder head gasket damaged. If the head is allowed to become loose, or if excessive carbon build-up on the piston crown and combustion chamber causes extremely high compression, the head gasket may leak. A new gasket is necessary (Chapter 2).
☐ Cylinder head warped. This is caused by overheating or improperly tightened head nuts. Machine shop resurfacing or head renewal is necessary (Chapter 2).
☐ Valve spring broken or weak. Caused by component failure or wear, the springs must be renewed (Chapter 2).
☐ Valve not seating properly. This is caused by a bent valve (from over-revving or improper valve adjustment), burned valve or seat or an accumulation of carbon deposits on the seat. The valves must be cleaned and/or renewed and the seats serviced (Chapter 2).

Knocking or pinking

☐ Incorrect or poor quality fuel. Old or improper grades of fuel can cause detonation. This causes the piston to rattle, thus the knocking or pinking sound. Drain old fuel and refill with the recommended fuel grade.
☐ Knock sensors incorrectly fitted or defective (Chapter 3).
☐ Carbon build-up in combustion chamber. Use of a fuel additive that will dissolve the adhesive bonding the carbon particles to the crown and chamber is the easiest way to remove the build-up. Otherwise, the cylinder heads will have to be removed and decarbonised (Chapter 2).
☐ Spark plug heat range incorrect. Uncontrolled detonation indicates the plug heat range is too hot. The plug in effect becomes a glow plug, raising cylinder temperatures. Install the specified plugs (Chapter 1).
☐ Improper air/fuel mixture. This will cause the cylinder to run hot, which leads to detonation. Refer to a BMW dealer equipped with the MOSS diagnostic tester.

Miscellaneous causes

☐ Faulty or incorrectly installed side stand switch causing the safety interlock circuit to cut ignition. Check the installation and function of the switch, and its wiring and connectors (see Chapter 7).
☐ Throttle body valve doesn't open fully. Adjust the throttle cable freeplay (Chapter 1). Have the throttle synchronisation checked by a BMW dealer.
☐ Clutch slipping. May be caused by loose or worn clutch components. Refer to Chapter 2 for clutch overhaul procedures.
☐ Timing not advancing – refer to a BMW dealer equipped with the MOSS diagnostic tester.
☐ Engine oil viscosity too high. Using a heavier oil than the one recommended in Pre-ride checks can damage the oil pump or lubrication system and cause drag on the engine.
☐ Brakes dragging. Usually caused by debris which has entered the brake piston seals, or from a warped disc or bent axle (Chapter 5).

4 Overheating

Engine overheats

☐ Oil cooling circuit defective. Check the oil cooler, hoses, thermostat and the oil pump (see Chapter 2).

Firing incorrect

☐ Spark plugs dirty, defective or worn out (Chapter 1). Locate reason for fouled plugs using spark plug condition chart at the end of this manual.

☐ Incorrect spark plugs. Wrong type or heat range. Check and install correct plugs (Chapter 1).

☐ Engine control unit (ECU) or ignition system component faulty (Chapter 3). Refer to a BMW dealer equipped with the MOSS diagnostic tester.

☐ Ignition HT coils defective (Chapter 3).

Fuel/air mixture incorrect

☐ Air filter clogged, poorly sealed or missing (Chapter 1).
☐ Air intake duct blocked or disconnected (Chapter 1).
☐ Intake air leak. Check for loose throttle body-to-intake manifold and air duct connections (Chapter 3), loose or missing Synchro tester union caps (Chapter 1, Section 3), or loose injectors.
☐ Fuel pump failure or filter/strainer blocked (Chapter 3).
☐ Fuel tank breather hose obstructed.
☐ Injector clogged. Dirt, water or other contaminants can clog the injectors. Clean the injectors (Chapter 3).

Compression too high

☐ Carbon build-up in combustion chamber. Use of a fuel additive that will dissolve the adhesive bonding the carbon particles to the piston crown and chamber is the easiest way to remove the build-up. Otherwise, the cylinder heads will have to be removed and decarbonised (Chapter 2).

☐ Improperly machined head surface or installation of incorrect gasket during engine assembly.

Engine load excessive

☐ Clutch slipping. Can be caused by damaged, loose or worn clutch components. Refer to Chapter 2 for overhaul procedures.

☐ Engine oil level too high. The addition of too much oil will cause pressurisation of the crankcase and inefficient engine operation. Drain to proper level (Chapter 1 and Pre-ride checks).

☐ Engine oil viscosity too high. Using a heavier oil than the one recommended in Pre-ride checks can damage the oil pump or lubrication system as well as cause drag on the engine.

☐ Brakes dragging. Usually caused by debris which has entered the brake piston seals, or from a warped disc or bent axle (Chapter 5).

Lubrication inadequate

☐ Engine oil level too low. Friction caused by intermittent lack of lubrication or from oil that is overworked can cause overheating. The oil provides a definite cooling function in the engine. Check the oil level (Pre-ride checks).

☐ Poor quality engine oil or incorrect viscosity or type. Oil is rated not only according to viscosity but also according to type. Some oils are not rated high enough for use in this engine. Check the Specifications (Pre-ride checks) and drain and refill with the correct oil if necessary (Chapter 1).

Miscellaneous causes

☐ Modification to exhaust system. Most aftermarket exhaust systems cause the engine to run leaner, which make them run hotter.

5 Clutch problems

Clutch slipping

☐ Clutch friction plate worn (Chapter 2).
☐ Clutch diaphragm spring broken or weak (Chapter 2).
☐ Clutch release mechanism faulty (Chapter 2).
☐ Clutch contaminated with oil. Renew the crankshaft and gearbox input shaft oil seals (see Chapter 2).

Clutch not disengaging completely (drag)

☐ Clutch release mechanism faulty (Chapter 2). This will cause clutch drag, which in turn will cause the machine to creep.
☐ Clutch pressure plate warped or damaged (Chapter 2).
☐ Clutch diaphragm spring broken or weak (Chapter 2).

6 Gearchange problems

Doesn't go into gear or lever doesn't return

☐ Clutch not disengaging – check the clutch release mechanism (Chapter 2).

☐ Selector fork(s) bent or seized - overhaul the gearchange mechanism (Chapter 2).

☐ Gear(s) stuck on shaft. Most often caused by a lack of lubrication or excessive wear in transmission bearings. Overhaul the gearbox (Chapter 2).

☐ Selector drum binding. Caused by lubrication failure or excessive wear. Renew the drum and bearing (Chapter 2).

☐ Gearchange lever return spring weak or broken (Chapter 2).

☐ Gearchange lever broken. Splines stripped out of lever or shaft, caused by allowing the lever to get loose. Renew necessary parts (Chapter 2).

☐ Stopper arm broken or worn. Poor gear engagement and rotary movement of selector drum results. Renew the arm (Chapter 2).

☐ Stopper arm spring broken. Allows arm to float, causing sporadic shift operation. Renew spring (Chapter 2).

Jumps out of gear

☐ Selector fork(s) worn – overhaul the transmission (Chapter 2).

☐ Gear groove(s) worn – overhaul the transmission (Chapter 2).

☐ Gear dogs or dog slots worn or damaged. The gears should be inspected and renewed. No attempt should be made to service the worn parts.

Overshifts

☐ Stopper arm spring weak or broken (Chapter 2).

☐ Gearchange shaft return spring post broken or distorted (Chapter 2).

7 Abnormal engine noise

Knocking or pinking

☐ Incorrect or poor quality fuel. Old or improper grades of fuel can cause detonation. This causes the piston to rattle, thus the knocking or pinking sound. Drain old fuel and refill with the recommended fuel grade.

☐ Knock sensors incorrectly fitted or defective (Chapter 2, Section 12).

☐ Carbon build-up in combustion chamber. Use of a fuel additive that will dissolve the adhesive bonding the carbon particles to the crown and chamber is the easiest way to remove the build-up. Otherwise, the cylinder heads will have to be removed and decarbonised (Chapter 2).

☐ Spark plug heat range incorrect. Uncontrolled detonation indicates the plug heat range is too hot. The plug in effect becomes a glow plug, raising cylinder temperatures. Install the specified plugs (Chapter 1).

☐ Improper air/fuel mixture. This will cause the cylinder to run hot, which leads to detonation. Refer to a BMW dealer equipped with the MOSS diagnostic tester.

Piston slap or rattling

☐ Cylinder-to-piston clearance excessive, caused by wear or improper assembly (Chapter 2).

☐ Connecting rod bent. Caused by over-revving, trying to start a badly flooded engine or from ingesting a foreign object into the combustion chamber (Chapter 2).

☐ Piston pin or piston pin bore worn or seized from wear or lack of lubrication (Chapter 2).

☐ Piston rings worn, broken or sticking in their grooves (Chapter 2).

☐ Piston seizure damage. Usually from lack of lubrication or overheating. Renew the pistons and cylinders, as a pair (Chapter 2).

☐ Connecting rod small-end or big-end bearing clearance excessive. Caused by excessive wear or lack of lubrication (Chapter 2).

Valve noise

☐ Incorrect valve clearances (Chapter 1).

☐ Valve spring broken or weak (Chapter 2).

☐ Camshafts or auxiliary shaft worn, or their bearing surfaces worn (Chapter 2).

Other noise

☐ Cylinder head gasket leaking (Chapter 2).

☐ Exhaust pipe leaking at cylinder head connection. Caused by improper fit of pipe(s) or loose exhaust flange. All exhaust fasteners should be tightened evenly and carefully (Chapter 3).

☐ Crankshaft runout excessive. Caused by a bent crankshaft (from over-revving) or damage from an upper cylinder component failure (Chapter 2).

☐ Crankshaft main bearings worn (Chapter 2).

☐ Cam chain tensioner defective (Chapter 2).

☐ Cam chain, sprockets or guides worn (Chapter 2).

8 Abnormal driveline noise

Clutch noise

☐ Loose or damaged clutch components (Chapter 2).

Gearbox noise

☐ Bearings worn. Also includes the possibility that the shafts are worn (Chapter 2).

☐ Gears worn or chipped (Chapter 2).

☐ Metal chips jammed in gear teeth. Probably pieces from a broken gear or selector mechanism that were picked up by the gears. This will cause early bearing failure (Chapter 2).

☐ Gearbox oil level too low. Causes a howl from gearbox (Chapter 1).

Final drive noise

☐ Final drive oil level too low (Chapter 1).

☐ Worn or damaged gears or final drive bearings. Refer to a BMW dealer.

☐ Driveshaft splines or universal joint worn (Chapter 4).

9 Abnormal frame and suspension noise

Front end noise

☐ Telelever ball joint loose or worn (Chapter 4).
☐ Telelever mountings loose or bearings worn (Chapter 4).
☐ Worn fork slider bushes (Chapter 4).
☐ Steering head bearing worn or damaged – clicks when braking (Chapter 4).
☐ Fork bridge or top yoke loose – ensure that all bolts are tight (Chapter 4).
☐ Fork tube bent – possibility if machine has crashed. Renew both fork tubes (Chapter 4).
☐ Front axle or axle clamp bolt loose. Tighten to the specified torque settings (Chapter 5).
☐ Loose or worn wheel bearings (Chapter 5).
☐ Shock absorber faulty (see below).

Rear end noise

☐ Swingarm mountings loose or bearings worn (Chapter 4).
☐ Final drive unit mountings loose or bearings worn (Chapter 4).

☐ Paralever arm mountings loose (Chapter 4).
☐ Shock absorber faulty (see below).

Shock absorber noise

☐ Loose or worn mounting bolts, or worn bushes (Chapter 4).
☐ Fluid level low due to leak caused by defective seal (Chapter 4).
☐ Defective shock absorber with internal damage (Chapter 4).
☐ Bent damper rod or damaged shock body (Chapter 4).

Brake noise

☐ Squeal caused by dust on brake pads – usually found in combination with glazed pads (Chapter 5).
☐ Contamination of brake pads – oil or brake fluid causing brake to chatter or squeal (Chapter 5).
☐ Pads glazed caused by excessive heat from prolonged use or from contamination (Chapter 5).
☐ Disc warped – can cause a chattering, clicking or intermittent squeal, usually accompanied by a pulsating lever and uneven braking (Chapter 5).

10 Oil pressure warning light comes on – GS and RT models

Engine lubrication system

☐ Engine oil level low. Inspect for leak or other problem causing low oil level and top-up with recommended oil (*Pre-ride checks*).
☐ Engine oil viscosity too low. Very old, thin oil or an improper weight of oil used in the engine. Drain and refill with specified oil (Chapter 1).
☐ Engine oil pump defective, blocked oil strainer gauze or failed relief valve. Carry out an oil pressure check (Chapter 2).

☐ Camshafts, auxiliary shaft or crankshaft bearings worn, causing drop in oil pressure (Chapter 2).

Electrical system

☐ Oil pressure switch defective – check the switch (Chapter 7).
☐ Oil pressure warning light circuit defective. Check for pinched, shorted, disconnected or damaged wiring (Chapter 7).

11 Excessive exhaust smoke

White smoke

☐ Piston oil ring worn or broken, causing oil from the crankcase to be pulled past the piston into the combustion chamber. Renew the rings (Chapter 2).
☐ Cylinders worn or scored, caused by overheating or oil starvation. Measure cylinder diameter and renew if necessary (Chapter 2).
☐ Valve oil seals damaged or worn – renew oil seals (Chapter 2).
☐ Valve guides worn – complete valve job required (Chapter 2).
☐ Engine oil level too high, which causes the oil to be forced past the rings. Drain oil to the proper level (Chapter 1 and *Pre-ride checks*).
☐ Head gasket broken between oil return and cylinder. Causes oil to be pulled into the combustion chamber. Renew the head gasket and check the head for warpage (Chapter 2).
☐ Abnormal crankcase pressurisation, which forces oil past the rings. Damaged or dirty vent valve or clogged breather hose is usually the cause (Chapter 2).

Black smoke

☐ Air filter clogged – renew the filter element (Chapter 1).
☐ Engine control unit (ECU) defective. Refer to a BMW dealer equipped with the MOSS diagnostic tester.

Brown smoke

☐ Fuel filter or strainer clogged (Chapter 3).
☐ Fuel flow insufficient. Have a BMW dealer perform a fuel pressure check.
☐ Intake air leak. Check for loose throttle body-to-intake manifold and air duct connections (Chapter 3), loose or missing Synchro tester union caps (Chapter 1, Section 3), or loose injectors.
☐ Air filter poorly sealed or not installed (Chapter 1).

12 Poor handling or stability

Handlebars hard to turn

☐ Steering head bearing defective (Chapter 4).
☐ Front tyre air pressure too low (*Pre-ride checks*).

Handlebar shakes or vibrates excessively

☐ Tyres worn or out of balance. Inspect for wear (*Pre-ride checks*). Have a tyre specialist balance the wheels.
☐ Swingarm or Telelever bearings worn (Chapter 4).
☐ Wheel rim(s) warped or damaged – check wheel runout (Chapter 5).
☐ Wheel bearings worn (Chapter 1).
☐ Handlebar mounting bolts loose (Chapter 4).
☐ Fork bridge or top yoke bolts loose (Chapter 4).

Handlebar pulls to one side

☐ Wheels out of alignment (Chapter 5).
☐ Front or rear suspension components worn or damaged caused by accident. Have the machine checked thoroughly by a BMW dealer or frame specialist.
☐ Fork tube bent – renew both fork tubes (Chapter 4).

Poor shock absorbing qualities

☐ Incorrect adjustment of suspension (Chapter 4).
☐ Tyre pressures incorrect (*Pre-ride checks*).
☐ Front or rear shock absorber damage (Chapter 4).

13 Braking problems

Brakes are spongy, don't hold

☐ Air in brake line. Caused by inattention to master cylinder fluid level or by leakage. Locate problem and bleed brakes (Chapter 5).
☐ Brake fluid leak.
☐ Brake fluid deteriorated through age or contaminated. Change brake fluid (Chapter 5).
☐ Master cylinder internal parts worn or damaged causing fluid to bypass. Fit a new master cylinder (Chapter 5).
☐ Pads or disc worn (Chapter 5).
☐ Brake pads contaminated with oil, grease or brake fluid. Renew pads and clean disc thoroughly with brake cleaner (Chapter 5).
☐ Disc warped (Chapter 5).
☐ ABS system faulty (Chapter 5).

Brake lever or pedal pulsates

☐ Disc warped (Chapter 5).
☐ Axle bent (Chapter 5).

☐ Brake caliper mounting bolts loose (Chapter 5).
☐ Rear brake caliper sliders damaged or sticking, causing caliper to bind. Clean and lubricate the sliders (Chapter 5).
☐ Wheel warped or otherwise damaged (Chapter 5).
☐ Wheel bearings worn (Chapter 1).
☐ ABS system faulty (Chapter 5).

Brakes drag

☐ Master cylinder piston seized (Chapter 5).
☐ Lever balky or stuck (Chapter 1).
☐ Rear brake caliper binds – caused by inadequate lubrication or damage to caliper slider pins (Chapter 5).
☐ Brake caliper piston seized in bore (Chapter 5).
☐ Brake pad damaged. Pad material separated from backing plate, usually caused by faulty manufacturing process or from contact with chemicals. Renew pads (Chapter 5).
☐ Pads improperly installed (Chapter 5).

14 Electrical problems

Battery dead or weak

☐ Battery faulty due to lack of maintenance or internal damage (Chapter 7).
☐ Battery leads making poor contact (Chapter 7).
☐ Load excessive. Caused by addition of high wattage lights or other electrical accessories.
☐ Ignition switch defective. Switch either earths (grounds) internally or fails to shut off system (Chapter 7).
☐ Charging system defective (Chapter 7).
☐ Wiring faulty. Wiring earthed (grounded) or connections loose in ignition, charging or lighting circuits (Chapter 7).

Battery overcharged

☐ Alternator defective. Overcharging is noticed when battery gets excessively warm (Chapter 7).
☐ Battery has internal fault (Chapter 7).
☐ Battery amperage too low, wrong type or size. Install manufacturer's specified amp-hour battery to handle charging load (Chapter 7).

A

ABS (Anti-lock braking system) A system, usually electronically controlled, that senses incipient wheel lockup during braking and relieves hydraulic pressure at wheel which is about to skid.

Aftermarket Components suitable for the motorcycle, but not produced by the motorcycle manufacturer.

Allen key A hexagonal wrench which fits into a recessed hexagonal hole.

Alternating current (ac) Current produced by an alternator. Requires converting to direct current by a rectifier for charging purposes.

Alternator Converts mechanical energy from the engine into electrical energy to charge the battery and power the electrical system.

Ampere (amp) A unit of measurement for the flow of electrical current. Current = Volts ÷ Ohms.

Ampere-hour (Ah) Measure of battery capacity.

Angle-tightening A torque expressed in degrees. Often follows a conventional tightening torque for cylinder head or main bearing fasteners **(see illustration)**.

Angle-tightening con-rod bolts

Antifreeze A substance (usually ethylene glycol) mixed with water, and added to the cooling system, to prevent freezing of the coolant in winter. Antifreeze also contains chemicals to inhibit corrosion and the formation of rust and other deposits that would tend to clog the radiator and coolant passages and reduce cooling efficiency.

Anti-dive System attached to the fork lower leg (slider) to prevent fork dive when braking hard.

Anti-seize compound A coating that reduces the risk of seizing on fasteners that are subjected to high temperatures, such as exhaust clamp bolts and nuts.

API American Petroleum Institute. A quality standard for 4-stroke motor oils.

Asbestos A natural fibrous mineral with great heat resistance, commonly used in the composition of brake friction materials. Asbestos is a health hazard and the dust created by brake systems should never be inhaled or ingested.

ATF Automatic Transmission Fluid. Often used in front forks.

ATU Automatic Timing Unit. Mechanical device for advancing the ignition timing on early engines.

ATV All Terrain Vehicle. Often called a Quad.

Axial play Side-to-side movement.

Axle A shaft on which a wheel revolves. Also known as a spindle.

B

Backlash The amount of movement between meshed components when one component is held still. Usually applies to gear teeth.

Ball bearing A bearing consisting of a hardened inner and outer race with hardened steel balls between the two races.

Bearings Used between two working surfaces to prevent wear of the components and a build-up of heat. Four types of bearing are commonly used on motorcycles: plain shell bearings, ball bearings, tapered roller bearings and needle roller bearings.

Bevel gears Used to turn the drive through 90°. Typical applications are shaft final drive and camshaft drive **(see illustration)**.

Bevel gears are used to turn the drive through 90°

BHP Brake Horsepower. The British measurement for engine power output. Power output is now usually expressed in kilowatts (kW).

Bias-belted tyre Similar construction to radial tyre, but with outer belt running at an angle to the wheel rim.

Big-end bearing The bearing in the end of the connecting rod that's attached to the crankshaft.

Bleeding The process of removing air from an hydraulic system via a bleed nipple or bleed screw.

Bottom-end A description of an engine's crankcase components and all components contained there-in.

BTDC Before Top Dead Centre in terms of piston position. Ignition timing is often expressed in terms of degrees or millimetres BTDC.

Bush A cylindrical metal or rubber component used between two moving parts.

Burr Rough edge left on a component after machining or as a result of excessive wear.

C

Cam chain The chain which takes drive from the crankshaft to the camshaft(s).

Canister The main component in an evaporative emission control system (California market only); contains activated charcoal granules to trap vapours from the fuel system rather than allowing them to vent to the atmosphere.

Castellated Resembling the parapets along the top of a castle wall. For example, a castellated wheel axle or spindle nut.

Catalytic converter A device in the exhaust system of some machines which converts certain pollutants in the exhaust gases into less harmful substances.

Charging system Description of the components which charge the battery, ie the alternator, rectifer and regulator.

Circlip A ring-shaped clip used to prevent endwise movement of cylindrical parts and shafts. An internal circlip is installed in a groove in a housing; an external circlip fits into a groove on the outside of a cylindrical piece such as a shaft. Also known as a snap-ring.

Clearance The amount of space between two parts. For example, between a piston and a cylinder, between a bearing and a journal, etc.

Coil spring A spiral of elastic steel found in various sizes throughout a vehicle, for example as a springing medium in the suspension and in the valve train.

Compression Reduction in volume, and increase in pressure and temperature, of a gas, caused by squeezing it into a smaller space.

Compression damping Controls the speed the suspension compresses when hitting a bump.

Compression ratio The relationship between cylinder volume when the piston is at top dead centre and cylinder volume when the piston is at bottom dead centre.

Continuity The uninterrupted path in the flow of electricity. Little or no measurable resistance.

Continuity tester Self-powered bleeper or test light which indicates continuity.

Cp Candlepower. Bulb rating commonly found on US motorcycles.

Crossply tyre Tyre plies arranged in a criss-cross pattern. Usually four or six plies used, hence 4PR or 6PR in tyre size codes.

Cush drive Rubber damper segments fitted between the rear wheel and final drive sprocket to absorb transmission shocks **(see illustration)**.

Cush drive rubbers dampen out transmission shocks

D

Decarbonisation The process of removing carbon deposits - typically from the combustion chamber, valves and exhaust port/system.

Degree disc Calibrated disc for measuring piston position. Expressed in degrees.

Detonation Destructive and damaging explosion of fuel/air mixture in combustion chamber instead of controlled burning.

Dial gauge Clock-type gauge with adapters for measuring runout and piston position. Expressed in mm or inches.

Diaphragm The rubber membrane in a master cylinder or carburettor which seals the upper chamber.

Diaphragm spring A single sprung plate often used in clutches.

Direct current (dc) Current produced by a dc generator.

Diode An electrical valve which only allows current to flow in one direction. Commonly used in rectifiers and starter interlock systems.

Disc valve (or rotary valve) A induction system used on some two-stroke engines.

Double-overhead camshaft (DOHC) An engine that uses two overhead camshafts, one for the intake valves and one for the exhaust valves.

Drivebelt A toothed belt used to transmit drive to the rear wheel on some motorcycles. A drivebelt has also been used to drive the camshafts. Drivebelts are usually made of Kevlar.

Driveshaft Any shaft used to transmit motion. Commonly used when referring to the final driveshaft on shaft drive motorcycles.

E

Earth return The return path of an electrical circuit, utilising the motorcycle's frame.

ECU (Electronic Control Unit) A computer which controls (for instance) an ignition system, or an anti-lock braking system.

EGO Exhaust Gas Oxygen sensor. Sometimes called a Lambda sensor.

Electrolyte The fluid in a lead-acid battery.

EMS (Engine Management System) A computer controlled system which manages the fuel injection and the ignition systems in an integrated fashion.

Endfloat The amount of lengthways movement between two parts. As applied to a crankshaft, the distance that the crankshaft can move side-to-side in the crankcase.

Endless chain A chain having no joining link. Common use for cam chains and final drive chains.

EP (Extreme Pressure) Oil type used in locations where high loads are applied, such as between gear teeth.

Evaporative emission control system Describes a charcoal filled canister which stores fuel vapours from the tank rather than allowing them to vent to the atmosphere. Usually only fitted to California models and referred to as an EVAP system.

Expansion chamber Section of two-stroke engine exhaust system so designed to improve engine efficiency and boost power.

F

Feeler blade or gauge A thin strip or blade of hardened steel, ground to an exact thickness, used to check or measure clearances between parts.

Final drive Description of the drive from the transmission to the rear wheel. Usually by chain or shaft, but sometimes by belt.

Firing order The order in which the engine cylinders fire, or deliver their power strokes, beginning with the number one cylinder.

Flooding Term used to describe a high fuel level in the carburettor float chambers, leading to fuel overflow. Also refers to excess fuel in the combustion chamber due to incorrect starting technique.

Free length The no-load state of a component when measured. Clutch, valve and fork spring lengths are measured at rest, without any preload.

Freeplay The amount of travel before any action takes place. The looseness in a linkage, or an assembly of parts, between the initial application of force and actual movement. For example, the distance the rear brake pedal moves before the rear brake is actuated.

Fuel injection The fuel/air mixture is metered electronically and directed into the engine intake ports (indirect injection) or into the cylinders (direct injection). Sensors supply information on engine speed and conditions.

Fuel/air mixture The charge of fuel and air going into the engine. See Stoichiometric ratio.

Fuse An electrical device which protects a circuit against accidental overload. The typical fuse contains a soft piece of metal which is calibrated to melt at a predetermined current flow (expressed as amps) and break the circuit.

G

Gap The distance the spark must travel in jumping from the centre electrode to the side electrode in a spark plug. Also refers to the distance between the ignition rotor and the pickup coil in an electronic ignition system.

Gasket Any thin, soft material - usually cork, cardboard, asbestos or soft metal - installed between two metal surfaces to ensure a good seal. For instance, the cylinder head gasket seals the joint between the block and the cylinder head.

Gauge An instrument panel display used to monitor engine conditions. A gauge with a movable pointer on a dial or a fixed scale is an analogue gauge. A gauge with a numerical readout is called a digital gauge.

Gear ratios The drive ratio of a pair of gears in a gearbox, calculated on their number of teeth.

Glaze-busting see **Honing**

Grinding Process for renovating the valve face and valve seat contact area in the cylinder head.

Gudgeon pin The shaft which connects the connecting rod small-end with the piston. Often called a piston pin or wrist pin.

H

Helical gears Gear teeth are slightly curved and produce less gear noise that straight-cut gears.

Installing a Helicoil thread insert

Often used for primary drives.

Helicoil A thread insert repair system. Commonly used as a repair for stripped spark plug threads **(see illustration)**.

Honing A process used to break down the glaze on a cylinder bore (also called glaze-busting). Can also be carried out to roughen a rebored cylinder to aid ring bedding-in.

HT (High Tension) Description of the electrical circuit from the secondary winding of the ignition coil to the spark plug.

Hydraulic A liquid filled system used to transmit pressure from one component to another. Common uses on motorcycles are brakes and clutches.

Hydrometer An instrument for measuring the specific gravity of a lead-acid battery.

Hygroscopic Water absorbing. In motorcycle applications, braking efficiency will be reduced if DOT 3 or 4 hydraulic fluid absorbs water from the air - care must be taken to keep new brake fluid in tightly sealed containers.

I

lbf ft Pounds-force feet. An imperial unit of torque. Sometimes written as ft-lbs.

lbf in Pound-force inch. An imperial unit of torque, applied to components where a very low torque is required. Sometimes written as in-lbs.

IC Abbreviation for Integrated Circuit.

Ignition advance Means of increasing the timing of the spark at higher engine speeds. Done by mechanical means (ATU) on early engines or electronically by the ignition control unit on later engines.

Ignition timing The moment at which the spark plug fires, expressed in the number of crankshaft degrees before the piston reaches the top of its stroke, or in the number of millimetres before the piston reaches the top of its stroke.

Infinity (∞) Description of an open-circuit electrical state, where no continuity exists.

Inverted forks (upside down forks) The sliders or lower legs are held in the yokes and the fork tubes or stanchions are connected to the wheel axle (spindle). Less unsprung weight and stiffer construction than conventional forks.

J

JASO Quality standard for 2-stroke oils.

Joule The unit of electrical energy.

Journal The bearing surface of a shaft.

K

Kickstart Mechanical means of turning the engine over for starting purposes. Only usually fitted to mopeds, small capacity motorcycles and off-road motorcycles.

Kill switch Handebar-mounted switch for emergency ignition cut-out. Cuts the ignition circuit on all models, and additionally prevent starter motor operation on others.

km Symbol for kilometre.

kmh Abbreviation for kilometres per hour.

L

Lambda (λ) sensor A sensor fitted in the exhaust

system to measure the exhaust gas oxygen content (excess air factor).

Lapping see Grinding.

LCD Abbreviation for Liquid Crystal Display.

LED Abbreviation for Light Emitting Diode.

Liner A steel cylinder liner inserted in a aluminium alloy cylinder block.

Locknut A nut used to lock an adjustment nut, or other threaded component, in place.

Lockstops The lugs on the lower triple clamp (yoke) which abut those on the frame, preventing handlebar-to-fuel tank contact.

Lockwasher A form of washer designed to prevent an attaching nut from working loose.

LT Low Tension Description of the electrical circuit from the power supply to the primary winding of the ignition coil.

M

Main bearings The bearings between the crankshaft and crankcase.

Maintenance-free (MF) battery A sealed battery which cannot be topped up.

Manometer Mercury-filled calibrated tubes used to measure intake tract vacuum. Used to synchronise carburettors on multi-cylinder engines.

Tappet shims are measured with a micrometer

Micrometer A precision measuring instrument that measures component outside diameters **(see illustration)**.

MON (Motor Octane Number) A measure of a fuel's resistance to knock.

Monograde oil An oil with a single viscosity, eg SAE80W.

Monoshock A single suspension unit linking the swingarm or suspension linkage to the frame.

mph Abbreviation for miles per hour.

Multigrade oil Having a wide viscosity range (eg 10W40). The W stands for Winter, thus the viscosity ranges from SAE10 when cold to SAE40 when hot.

Multimeter An electrical test instrument with the capability to measure voltage, current and resistance. Some meters also incorporate a continuity tester and buzzer.

N

Needle roller bearing Inner race of caged needle rollers and hardened outer race. Examples of uncaged needle rollers can be found on some engines. Commonly used in rear suspension applications and in two-stroke engines.

Nm Newton metres.

NOx Oxides of Nitrogen. A common toxic pollutant emitted by petrol engines at higher temperatures.

O

Octane The measure of a fuel's resistance to knock.

OE (Original Equipment) Relates to components fitted to a motorcycle as standard or replacement parts supplied by the motorcycle manufacturer.

Ohm The unit of electrical resistance. Ohms = Volts ÷ Current.

Ohmmeter An instrument for measuring electrical resistance.

Oil cooler System for diverting engine oil outside of the engine to a radiator for cooling purposes.

Oil injection A system of two-stroke engine lubrication where oil is pump-fed to the engine in accordance with throttle position.

Open-circuit An electrical condition where there is a break in the flow of electricity - no continuity (high resistance).

O-ring A type of sealing ring made of a special rubber-like material; in use, the O-ring is compressed into a groove to provide the sealing action.

Oversize (OS) Term used for piston and ring size options fitted to a rebored cylinder.

Overhead cam (sohc) engine An engine with single camshaft located on top of the cylinder head.

Overhead valve (ohv) engine An engine with the valves located in the cylinder head, but with the camshaft located in the engine block or crankcase.

Oxygen sensor A device installed in the exhaust system which senses the oxygen content in the exhaust and converts this information into an electric current. Also called a Lambda sensor.

P

Plastigauge A thin strip of plastic thread, available in different sizes, used for measuring clearances. For example, a strip of Plastigauge is laid across a bearing journal. The parts are assembled and dismantled; the width of the crushed strip indicates the clearance between journal and bearing.

Polarity Either negative or positive earth (ground), determined by which battery lead is connected to the frame (earth return). Modern motorcycles are usually negative earth.

Pre-ignition A situation where the fuel/air mixture ignites before the spark plug fires. Often due to a hot spot in the combustion chamber caused by carbon build-up. Engine has a tendency to 'run-on'.

Pre-load (suspension) The amount a spring is compressed when in the unloaded state. Preload can be applied by gas, spacer or mechanical adjuster.

Premix The method of engine lubrication on older two-stroke engines. Engine oil is mixed with the petrol in the fuel tank in a specific ratio. The fuel/oil mix is sometimes referred to as "petroil".

Primary drive Description of the drive from the crankshaft to the clutch. Usually by gear or chain.

PS Pfedestärke - a German interpretation of BHP.

PSI Pounds-force per square inch. Imperial measurement of tyre pressure and cylinder pressure measurement.

PTFE Polytetrafluroethylene. A low friction substance.

Pulse secondary air injection system A process of promoting the burning of excess fuel present in the

exhaust gases by routing fresh air into the exhaust ports.

Q

Quartz halogen bulb Tungsten filament surrounded

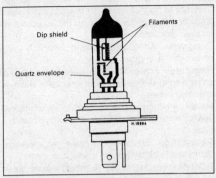

Quartz halogen headlight bulb construction

by a halogen gas. Typically used for the headlight **(see illustration)**.

R

Rack-and-pinion A pinion gear on the end of a shaft that mates with a rack (think of a geared wheel opened up and laid flat). Sometimes used in clutch operating systems.

Radial play Up and down movement about a shaft.

Radial ply tyres Tyre plies run across the tyre (from bead to bead) and around the circumference of the tyre. Less resistant to tread distortion than other tyre types.

Radiator A liquid-to-air heat transfer device designed to reduce the temperature of the coolant in a liquid cooled engine.

Rake A feature of steering geometry - the angle of the steering head in relation to the vertical **(see illustration)**.

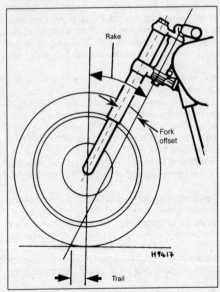

Steering geometry

Rebore Providing a new working surface to the cylinder bore by boring out the old surface. Necessitates the use of oversize piston and rings.

Rebound damping A means of controlling the oscillation of a suspension unit spring after it has been compressed. Resists the spring's natural tendency to bounce back after being compressed.

Rectifier Device for converting the ac output of an alternator into dc for battery charging.

Reed valve An induction system commonly used on two-stroke engines.

Regulator Device for maintaining the charging voltage from the generator or alternator within a specified range.

Relay A electrical device used to switch heavy current on and off by using a low current auxiliary circuit.

Resistance Measured in ohms. An electrical component's ability to pass electrical current.

RON (Research Octane Number) A measure of a fuel's resistance to knock.

rpm revolutions per minute.

Runout The amount of wobble (in-and-out movement) of a wheel or shaft as it's rotated. The amount a shaft rotates `out-of-true'. The out-of-round condition of a rotating part.

S

SAE (Society of Automotive Engineers) A standard for the viscosity of a fluid.

Sealant A liquid or paste used to prevent leakage at a joint. Sometimes used in conjunction with a gasket.

Service limit Term for the point where a component is no longer useable and must be renewed.

Shaft drive A method of transmitting drive from the transmission to the rear wheel.

Shell bearings Plain bearings consisting of two shell halves. Most often used as big-end and main bearings in a four-stroke engine. Often called bearing inserts.

Shim Thin spacer, commonly used to adjust the clearance or relative positions between two parts. For example, shims inserted into or under tappets or followers to control valve clearances. Clearance is adjusted by changing the thickness of the shim.

Short-circuit An electrical condition where current shorts to earth (ground) bypassing the circuit components.

Skimming Process to correct warpage or repair a damaged surface, eg on brake discs or drums.

Slide-hammer A special puller that screws into or hooks onto a component such as a shaft or bearing; a heavy sliding handle on the shaft bottoms against the end of the shaft to knock the component free.

Small-end bearing The bearing in the upper end of the connecting rod at its joint with the gudgeon pin.

Spalling Damage to camshaft lobes or bearing journals shown as pitting of the working surface.

Specific gravity (SG) The state of charge of the electrolyte in a lead-acid battery. A measure of the electrolyte's density compared with water.

Straight-cut gears Common type gear used on gearbox shafts and for oil pump and water pump drives.

Stanchion The inner sliding part of the front forks, held by the yokes. Often called a fork tube.

Stoichiometric ratio The optimum chemical air/ fuel ratio for a petrol engine, said to be 14.7 parts of air to 1 part of fuel.

Sulphuric acid The liquid (electrolyte) used in a lead-acid battery. Poisonous and extremely corrosive.

Surface grinding (lapping) Process to correct a warped gasket face, commonly used on cylinder heads.

T

Tapered-roller bearing Tapered inner race of caged needle rollers and separate tapered outer race. Examples of taper roller bearings can be found on steering heads.

Tappet A cylindrical component which transmits motion from the cam to the valve stem, either directly or via a pushrod and rocker arm. Also called a cam follower.

TCS Traction Control System. An electronically-controlled system which senses wheel spin and reduces engine speed accordingly.

TDC Top Dead Centre denotes that the piston is at its highest point in the cylinder.

Thread-locking compound Solution applied to fastener threads to prevent slackening. Select type to suit application.

Thrust washer A washer positioned between two moving components on a shaft. For example, between gear pinions on gearshaft.

Timing chain See **Cam Chain**.

Timing light Stroboscopic lamp for carrying out ignition timing checks with the engine running.

Top-end A description of an engine's cylinder block, head and valve gear components.

Torque Turning or twisting force about a shaft.

Torque setting A prescribed tightness specified by the motorcycle manufacturer to ensure that the bolt or nut is secured correctly. Undertightening can result in the bolt or nut coming loose or a surface not being sealed. Overtightening can result in stripped threads, distortion or damage to the component being retained.

Torx key A six-point wrench.

Tracer A stripe of a second colour applied to a wire insulator to distinguish that wire from another one with the same colour insulator. For example, Br/W is often used to denote a brown insulator with a white tracer.

Trail A feature of steering geometry. Distance from the steering head axis to the tyre's central contact point.

Triple clamps The cast components which extend from the steering head and support the fork stanchions or tubes. Often called fork yokes.

Turbocharger A centrifugal device, driven by exhaust gases, that pressurises the intake air. Normally used to increase the power output from a given engine displacement.

TWI Abbreviation for Tyre Wear Indicator. Indicates the location of the tread depth indicator bars on tyres.

U

Universal joint or U-joint (UJ) A double-pivoted connection for transmitting power from a driving to a driven shaft through an angle. Typically found in shaft drive assemblies.

Unsprung weight Anything not supported by the bike's suspension (ie the wheel, tyres, brakes, final drive and bottom (moving) part of the suspension).

V

Vacuum gauges Clock-type gauges for measuring intake tract vacuum. Used for carburettor synchronisation on multi-cylinder engines.

Valve A device through which the flow of liquid, gas or vacuum may be stopped, started or regulated by a moveable part that opens, shuts or partially obstructs one or more ports or passageways. The intake and exhaust valves in the cylinder head are of the poppet type.

Valve clearance The clearance between the valve tip (the end of the valve stem) and the rocker arm or tappet/follower. The valve clearance is measured when the valve is closed. The correct clearance is important - if too small the valve won't close fully and will burn out, whereas if too large noisy operation will result.

Valve lift The amount a valve is lifted off its seat by the camshaft lobe.

Valve timing The exact setting for the opening and closing of the valves in relation to piston position.

Vernier caliper A precision measuring instrument that measures inside and outside dimensions. Not quite as accurate as a micrometer, but more convenient.

Wet liner arrangement

VIN Vehicle Identification Number. Term for the bike's engine and frame numbers.

Viscosity The thickness of a liquid or its resistance to flow.

Volt A unit for expressing electrical "pressure" in a circuit. Volts = current x ohms.

W

Water pump A mechanically-driven device for moving coolant around the engine.

Watt A unit for expressing electrical power. Watts = volts x current.

Wear limit see **Service limit**

Wet liner A liquid-cooled engine design where the pistons run in liners which are directly surrounded by coolant **(see illustration)**.

Wheelbase Distance from the centre of the front wheel to the centre of the rear wheel.

Wiring harness or loom Describes the electrical wires running the length of the motorcycle and enclosed in tape or plastic sheathing. Wiring coming off the main harness is usually referred to as a sub harness.

Woodruff key A key of semi-circular or square section used to locate a gear to a shaft. Often used to locate the alternator rotor on the crankshaft.

Wrist pin Another name for gudgeon or piston pin.

Note: *References throughout this index are in the form - "Chapter number" • "Page number"*

A

ABS – 5•18
Air filter – 1•16
Alternator – 7•1, 7•26
Alternator drive belt – 1•18
Alternator drive pulley – 2•40
Ambient air temperature sensor – 7•19
Automatic Stability Control (ASC) – 5•20
Auxiliary headlights – 7•5
Auxiliary shaft – 2•3, 2•62
Auxiliary shaft drive chain, tensioner and
  sprockets – 2•46

B

Balancer shaft and gears – 2•42
Battery – 7•1, 7•3
Bleeding
  brake – 5•13
  clutch – 2•56
Bodywork – 6•1 *et seq*
  R1200 GS and GS Adventure – 6•2
  R1200 R – 6•22
  R1200 RT – 6•12
Brake
  ABS – 5•18
  calipers – 5•5, 5•8
  discs – 5•6, 5•9
  fault finding – REF•42
  fluid – 1•2
  fluid air bleeding – 5•13
  fluid change – 1•3, 1•21, 5•11
  fluid level check and top-up – 0•12
  hoses, pipes and unions – 5•10
  maintenance – 1•20
  master cylinders – 5•7, 5•9
  pad renewal – 5•2
  pad thickness – 1•2
  pad wear check – 1•20
  specifications – 5•1
Brake lever (front) – 5•7
  span adjuster – 1•20
Brake light
  bulb – 7•12
  check – 1•20, 7•7
  switches – 7•15
Brake pedal (rear)
  check – 1•20
  freeplay – 4•5
  removal and installation – 4•4
Bulb
  brake/tail light – 7•12
  defective bulb warning system – 7•7
  headlight – 7•7
  turn signal – 7•13
  wattages – 7•1

C

Cable (throttle) – 1•11, 3•14
Caliper
  front brake – 5•5
  rear brake – 5•8
Cam followers – 2•22
Camchain tensioners – 2•20
Camchains and tensioner/guide
  blades – 2•62
Camshaft position sensor – 3•24
Camshafts – 2•22
CAN-bus technology – 7•2
Catalytic converter – 3•20
Centre stand – 4•6
Charging system check – 7•25
Clock – 7•16
Clutch
  fault finding – REF•39
  fluid – 1•2
  fluid air bleeding – 2•56
  fluid level check and top-up – 0•14
  maintenance – 1•19
  master cylinder – 2•54
  release cylinder – 2•55
  removal, inspection and
    installation – 2•50
  specifications – 2•3
Clutch lever – 2•54
  span adjuster – 1•19
Clutch switch – 7•20
Cockpit trim panel (R1200 GS/Adv) – 6•9
Coil (ignition) – 1•13, 3•22
Connecting rods – 2•2, 2•38
Conversion factors – REF•26
Crankcases – 2•56
Crankshaft – 2•3, 2•61
Crankshaft position sensor – 3•24
Crashbar – 6•11
Cruise control – 7•17
  cables – 3•16
Cylinder compression test – 2•6
Cylinder head temperature
  sensor – 3•26
Cylinder heads – 2•28, 2•30
Cylinders – 2•2, 2•33

D

Dimensions – 0•16
Disc (brake)
  front – 5•6
  maintenance – 1•21
  rear – 5•9
  specifications – 5•1
Driveshaft – 4•19

E

ECU (engine control unit) – 3•22
Electrical system – 8•1 *et seq*
  alternator – 7•26
  battery – 7•3
  bulbs and LEDs – 7•7 to 7•14
  checks and fault finding – 7•2
  fault finding – REF•42
  horn – 7•24
  lighting system check – 7•6
  specifications – 7•1
  switches and sensors – 7•15 to 7•24
  wiring diagrams – 7•27
Engine – 2•1 *et seq*
  alternator drive belt – 1•18
  alternator drive pulley – 2•40
  auxiliary shaft – 2•62
  auxiliary shaft drive chain, tensioner and
    sprockets – 2•46
  balancer shaft and gears – 2•42
  bearings – 2•60
  cam followers and camshafts – 2•22
  camchain tensioners – 2•20
  camchains and tensioner/guide
    blades – 2•62
  connecting rods – 2•38
  crankcases – 2•56
  crankshaft – 2•61
  cylinder compression test – 2•6
  cylinder heads – 2•28, 2•30
  cylinders – 2•33
  fault finding – REF•36
  oil – 0•11, 1•2
  oil and filter change – 1•7
  oil cooler and hoses – 2•16
  oil level check and top-up – 0•11
  oil pressure switch – 3•26
  oil pressure test – 2•6
  oil pump, pressure relief valve and
    thermostat – 2•48
  overhaul information – 2•15
  piston rings – 2•37
  pistons – 2•36
  removal and installation – 2•6
  running-in – 2•76
  timing cover – 2•40
  valve clearances – 1•2, 1•8
  valve covers – 2•19
  valves – 2•30
Engine management system – 3•1 *et seq*
  ECU and fault finding – 3•22
  sensors – 3•24
  specifications – 3•1
Engine oil temperature sensor – 3•25
Engine number – 0•9
Electronic Suspension Adjustment
  (ESA) – 4•18

Note: *References throughout this index are in the form - "Chapter number" • "Page number"*

Evaporative Emission Control System (US) – 3•8
Exhaust flow control valve – 3•1, 3•18
Exhaust system – 3•17

F

Fairing panels (R1200 RT) – 6•15
Fault finding – REF•35
  electrical system – 7•2
  engine management system – 3•22
Filter
  air – 1•16
  engine oil – 1•7
  fuel – 3•11
Final drive
  driveshaft – 4•19
  oil – 1•2
  oil change – 1•16
  pre-ride check – 0•14
  unit – 4•24
Footrests – 4•3
Frame number – 0•9
Front fork legs – 4•9
Front mudguard
  R1200 GS and GS Adventure – 6•8
  R1200 R – 6•24
  R1200 RT – 6•21
Front shock
  adjustment – 4•18
  removal and installation – 4•11
Front wheel – 5•14
Fuel grades and tank capacity – 3•1
Fuel level sensor – 3•5, 3•6, 3•8, 7•19
Fuel system – 3•2
  filter/strainer – 3•11
  hoses – 3•12
  injectors – 3•14
  pressure regulator – 3•12
  pump – 3•9
  tank – 3•3
  tank panels (R1200 GS/Adv) – 6•7
  tank top panel (R1200 RT) – 6•19
  throttle bodies – 3•12
Fuse (auxiliary headlight) – 7•2, 7•6

G

Gear position sensor – 3•26
Gearbox
  fault finding – REF•40
  number – 0•9
  oil – 1•2
  oil change – 1•17
  oil seals – 2•63
  pre-ride check – 0•14
  removal and installation – 2•63
  shafts – 2•72
  specifications – 2•3
Gearchange lever – 4•4
Gearchange mechanism – 2•71
  selector drum and forks – 2•66

H

Hand protectors – 6•10
Handlebar switches – 7•22
Handlebars – 4•7
Headlight – 7•10
  bulb – 7•7
  check – 7•6
Headlight bracket (R1200 R) – 6•26
Headlight panel (R1200 RT) – 6•17
Horn – 7•24

I

Ignition switch – 7•21
Ignition system – 3•2
  checks – 3•21
  coils – 1•13, 3•21
  ECU (engine control unit) – 3•22
  spark plugs – 1•2, 1•13
Injectors – 3•14
Intake air temperature sensor – 3•25
Instruments – 7•15

K

Knock sensors – 3•25

L

Lighting system check – 7•6
Luggage rack (R1200 RT) – 6•13
Luggage rack and side case support brackets (R1200 GS/Adv) – 6•3

M

Main bearings – 2•61
Maintenance – 1•1 *et seq*
Master cylinder
  clutch – 2•54
  front brake – 5•7
  rear brake – 5•9
Mirrors
  R1200 GS and GS Adventure – 6•10
  R1200 R – 6•25
  R1200 RT – 6•14
Model development – 0•17
MOT test checks – REF•27

N

Neutral (gear position) sensor – 3•26
Number plate bracket (R1200 R) – 6•23
Number plate light bracket (R1200 RT) – 6•20

O

Oil
  engine – 0•11, 1•7
  final drive – 1•16
  front forks – 4•1, 4•9
  gearbox – 1•17
  general information – REF•23
  recommendations – 1•2
Oil cooler and hoses – 2•16
Oil level indicator – 7•18
Oil pressure switch – 3•26, 7•18
Oil pressure test – 2•6
Oil pump, pressure relief valve and thermostat – 2•3, 2•48
Oil temperature sensor – 3•25
Oil thermostat – 2•50
Oxygen sensors – 3•20

P

Pads (brake) – 1•2, 1•20, 5•2
Piston rings – 2•2, 2•37
Pistons – 2•2, 2•36
Pre-ride checks – 0•11 *et seq*
Pressure regulator (fuel) – 3•12
Pressure relief valve – 2•50
Pump
  fuel – 3•9
  oil – 2•48

R

RDC (tyre pressure monitoring) system – 5•20
Rear mudguard
  R1200 GS and GS Adventure – 6•6
  R1200 R – 6•24
  R1200 RT – 6•20
Rear shock
  adjustment – 4•18
  removal and installation – 4•16
Rear wheel – 5•15
Relay
  auxiliary headlight – 7•6
  starter – 7•24
Release cylinder (clutch) – 2•55
Routine Maintenance – 1•1 *et seq*

S

Safety information – 0•10, 0•15, 3•3
Screen (windshield)
  R1200 GS and GS Adventure – 6•9
  R1200 R – 6•25
  R1200 RT – 6•14
Seat
  R1200 GS and GS Adventure – 6•2
  R1200 R – 6•22
  R1200 RT – 6•12

Note: *References throughout this index are in the form - "Chapter number" • "Page number"*

Seat cowling
  R1200 GS and GS Adventure – 6•3
  R1200 R – 6•23
  R1200 RT – 6•19
Security – REF•20
Service schedule – 1•3
Servicing – 1•1 *et seq*
Shock absorber
  adjustment – 4•18
  front – 4•11
  rear – 4•16
Side covers (R1200 GS/Adv) – 6•7
**Side panels and rear bodywork
  (R1200 R)** – 6•22
Side stand – 4•7
Side stand switch – 7•21
Sidelight (front)
  bulb – 7•7
  check – 7•6
Spark plug
  gap – 1•2
  removal and installation – 1•13
Specifications
  brakes – 5•1
  clutch – 2•3
  dimensions and weights – 0•16
  electrical – 7•1
  engine – 2•1
  engine management – 3•1
  general spec – 0•17
  lubricants and fluids – 1•2
  maintenance – 1•2
  suspension – 4•1
  transmission – 2•3
  tyres – 0•15, 5•1
  wheels – 5•1
Speed sensor – 7•18
Spokes – 5•17
Spray guard – 6•5
Stand
  centre stand – 4•6
  pivot maintenance – 1•13
  sidestand – 4•7

Starter interlock circuit – 3•22
Starter motor and solenoid – 7•25
Starter relay – 7•24
Steering
  bearings – 4•14
  damper – 4•15
  fault finding – REF•42
  pre-ride checks – 0•14
Storage advice – REF•32
Strainer (fuel) – 3•11
Sub-frames – 4•3
Sump guard – 6•12
Suspension
  adjustment – 4•18
  front – 4•9
  maintenance – 1•23
  pre-ride checks – 0•14
  rear – 4•16
  specifications – 4•1
Swingarm – 4•19

T

Tail light – 7•13
  bulb – 7•12
  check – 7•6
Tail light bracket (R1200 RT) – 6•20
Tank (fuel) – 3•1, 3•3
Telelever arm – 4•12
Throttle bodies – 3•12
Throttle cables
  adjustment – 1•11
  check and lubrication – 1•13
  removal and installation – 3•14
Throttle position sensor – 3•26
Timing cover – 2•40
Tip-over cut-off valve – 3•5, 3•8
Tools and Workshop Tips – REF•2
Torque settings – 1•2, 2•4, 3•2, 4•2, 5•2,
  6•1, 7•2

Transmission (gearbox)
  number – 0•9
  oil – 1•2
  oil change – 1•17
  oil seals – 2•63
  pre-ride check – 0•14
  removal and installation – 2•63
  shafts – 2•72
  specifications – 2•3
Turn signals – 7•13
  check – 7•7
Tyres – 5•18
  pressures and checks – 0•15
  RDC system – 5•20
  sizes – 5•1

V

Valve clearances – 1•2, 1•8
Valve covers – 2•19
Valves – 2•1, 2•30
VIN (Vehicle Identification Number) – 0•9

W

Weights – 0•16
Wheel
  alignment – 5•14
  front – 5•14
  maintenance – 1•22
  rear – 5•15
  runout check – 5•13
  spokes – 5•17
Wheel/final drive bearings – 5•16
  check – 1•22
Windshield
  GS and GS Adventure – 6•9
  R – 6•25
  RT – 6•14
Windshield motor – 7•17
Wiring diagrams – 7•27

Preserving Our Motoring Heritage

< The Model J Duesenberg Derham Tourster. Only eight of these magnificent cars were ever built – this is the only example to be found outside the United States of America

Almost every car you've ever loved, loathed or desired is gathered under one roof at the Haynes Motor Museum. Over 300 immaculately presented cars and motorbikes represent every aspect of our motoring heritage, from elegant reminders of bygone days, such as the superb Model J Duesenberg to curiosities like the bug-eyed BMW Isetta. There are also many old friends and flames. Perhaps you remember the 1959 Ford Popular that you did your courting in? The magnificent 'Red Collection' is a spectacle of classic sports cars including AC, Alfa Romeo, Austin Healey, Ferrari, Lamborghini, Maserati, MG, Riley, Porsche and Triumph.

A Perfect Day Out

Each and every vehicle at the Haynes Motor Museum has played its part in the history and culture of Motoring. Today, they make a wonderful spectacle and a great day out for all the family. Bring the kids, bring Mum and Dad, but above all bring your camera to capture those golden memories for ever. You will also find an impressive array of motoring memorabilia, a comfortable 70 seat video cinema and one of the most extensive transport book shops in Britain. The Pit Stop Cafe serves everything from a cup of tea to wholesome, home-made meals or, if you prefer, you can enjoy the large picnic area nestled in the beautiful rural surroundings of Somerset.

> John Haynes O.B.E., Founder and Chairman of the museum at the wheel of a Haynes Light 12.

< The 1936 490cc sohc-engined International Norton – well known for its racing success

The Museum is situated on the A359 Yeovil to Frome road at Sparkford, just off the A303 in Somerset. It is about 40 miles south of Bristol, and 25 minutes drive from the M5 intersection at Taunton.

Open 9.30am - 5.30pm (10.00am - 4.00pm Winter) 7 days a week, *except Christmas Day, Boxing Day and New Years Day*

Special rates available for schools, coach parties and outings Charitable Trust No. 292048